QuickBASIC
Using Subprograms

James S. Quasney
John Maniotes
Misty Vermaat
Purdue University Calumet

boyd & fraser publishing company

DEDICATION

To the past and present students, faculty, and staff of
Purdue University Calumet.

Credits:

Acquisitions Editor: James H. Edwards
Production Editor: Barbara Worth
Director of Production: Becky Herrington
Manufacturing Coordinator: Karen Truman
Interior Design: Becky Herrington
Cover Design: Hannus Design Associates
Cover Photography: Chris Harvey, Tony Stone WorldWide
Typesetting and Composition: Huntington & Black Typography

© 1993 by boyd & fraser publishing company
A Division of South-Western Publishing Company
One Corporate Place • Ferncroft Village
Danvers, Massachusetts

Manufactured in the United States of America

Library of Congress Cataloging-in-Publication Data

```
Quasney, James S.
    QuickBASIC using subprograms / James S. Quasney, John Maniotes,
  Misty Vermaat.
       p.   cm.
    Includes index.
    ISBN 0-87709-010-6
    1. BASIC (Computer program language)  2. Microsoft QuickBASIC.
  I. Maniotes, John.  II. Vermaat, Misty.  III. Title.
  Qa76.73.B3Q3754   1993
  005.26'2--dc20                                      92-30589
                                                         CIP
```

ISBN 0-87709-010-6

2 3 4 5 6 7 8 9 DH 5 4 3

Contents

Preface

OBJECTIVES OF THIS BOOK

This book was developed specifically for an introductory computer programming course that utilizes MS-DOS QBASIC or the commercial version of Microsoft QuickBASIC on an IBM PC, IBM PS/1, IBM PS/2, or compatible system. The objectives of this book are as follows:

- To acquaint the reader with the proper and correct way to design and write high-quality programs using independent subprograms. The top-down approach, structured programming, and modern programming practices are emphasized early and are consistently used throughout the book.
- To teach the fundamentals of the QuickBASIC programming language.
- To teach good problem-solving techniques that can be used in advanced computing and information-processing courses.
- To emphasize interactive applications and menu-driven programs, the most popular type of programming in today's world.
- To develop an exercise-oriented approach that allows the reader to learn by example.
- To use practical problems to illustrate the applications of computers.
- To encourage independent study, and help those who are working alone on their own personal computer systems.

WHY USE QuickBASIC RATHER THAN BASICA?

QuickBASIC (or MS-DOS QBasic) offers a superb environment in which to learn programming. It has several important advantages over BASICA that make it indispensable for instructors who want to teach their students the correct, structured programming practices right from the start. The major advantages of QuickBASIC over BASICA are as follows:

- QuickBASIC offers subprograms and functions as an alternative to subroutines for modularizing programs.
- The block IF statement allows for multiple lines of code in the THEN and ELSE clauses.
- The SELECT CASE statement can be used to implement the Case structure without the use of the ON GOSUB statement or complex, nested IF statements.
- The DO WHILE...LOOP and DO...LOOP UNTIL statements allow students to implement cleanly the Do-While and Do-Until structures.
- The QuickBASIC editor is powerful, and yet easy to use. The operating environment, which includes windows, pull-down command menus, and the use of a mouse, helps simplify the tasks of entering, modifying, and executing programs. The QuickBASIC interpreter checks each line entered for correct syntax, formats the line, and changes the line to executable form if the syntax is correct.
- The full-screen editor allows the user to insert lines, delete lines, and change lines at the desired location on the screen, thus eliminating the need for line numbers.
- Complete mouse capabilities allow the student to easily navigate through the QuickBASIC operating environment without having to remember keystroke sequences.
- QuickBASIC uses dialog boxes with buttons whenever it needs additional information from the programmer. These dialog boxes make it easier for students to respond to requests made by QuickBASIC.
- Improved on-line debugging tools, that go far beyond the TRON and TROFF statements, are available to the student confronted with baffling logic errors.
- The QB Advisor offers a complete on-line help facility. The QB Advisor is a context-sensitive, electronic help system with instant cross-referencing that answers students' questions as fast as they can click the mouse or press the F1 key. The QB Advisor also provides programming examples that can be copied into the current program.

LEVEL OF INSTRUCTION

No previous experience with a computer is assumed, and no mathematics beyond the high school freshman level is required. The book is written specifically for the student with average ability, for whom continuity, simplicity, and practicality are characteristics we consider essential. Numerous insights, based on the authors' sixty cumulative years of experience in teaching and consulting in the field of computer information systems, are implicit throughout the book. For the past twenty years, one of us has taught introductory programming courses using a dialect of BASIC, the latest being QuickBASIC.

FUNDAMENTAL TOPICS ARE PRESENTED IN DETAIL

Besides introducing students to the correct way to design and write programs by means of structured and top-down techniques, the book presents fundamental topics concerning computers and programming which should be covered in any introductory programming class. These include the stored program concept; getting acquainted with the computer; editing programs; input/output operations; variables and constants; simple and complex computations; the use of functions and subprograms; decision making; the use of counters and running totals; rounding and truncation; looping and end-of-file tests; counter-controlled loops; the use of relational and logical operators; string manipulation; and graphics and sound. Other essential topics include data validation; control breaks; paging reports; table processing; sequence checking; selection; searching; matching; merging; sorting; file processing; and the differences between batch and interactive applications. Every one of these topics is covered in detail in this book.

DISTINGUISHING FEATURES

The distinguishing features of this book include the following:

A Proven Book

This book has evolved over the past twenty years and is based on the authors' seven prior books on BASIC programming. Many instructors and students who have used our books have shared with us their comments and suggestions for improvement as new programming techniques have been developed. They have done much to shape the contents of this book, which reflects modern programming practices using independent subprograms.

Early Presentation of the Top-Down (Modular) Approach and the Structured Programming Approach

Students are introduced to the top-down approach early, before they learn about looping and decision making. By the time they get to the larger and more complex programs, they are solving problems top-down by habit.

To implement the top-down approach, this book consistently uses independent subprograms. That is, the CALL and SUB statements are used rather than the GOSUB and RETURN statements. In Chapter 4, the student is also introduced to important design concepts, including high-level design, detailed design, and the use of stubs. These design concepts are then used throughout the book. Hence, the student is introduced early to the proper and correct way to design and code a program top down.

Particular attention is given to designing proper programs by means of the three logic structures of structured programming: Sequence; Selection (If-Then-Else and Case); and Repetition (Do-While and Do-Until). A disciplined method for implementing the structured design is adhered to throughout the book.

Early and Complete Coverage of File Processing

Complete coverage of sequential, random, and simulated-indexed files provides the reader with knowledge that is central to a real programming environment. Topics include creating all three types of files; file maintenance (matching and merging operations); and an information retrieval system that features simulated-indexed files. Sequential file processing is covered immediately following the presentation of the top-down approach and structured programming.

Student Diskette

The *Student Diskette* that accompanies this book includes all the executable programs and data files presented in the text. Students can use the program and data files on this diskette for the following:

- To step through the **PC Hands-On Exercises** at the end of each chapter
- To select a program similar to their solution for a programming assignment (this will save keying time)
- To experiment on their own with developing alternative solutions to the programming case studies presented in the text
- To access data files required in the programming assignments
- To store their solutions to programming assignments

Program names on the diskette are in the form of PRGc-n, where c represents the chapter number and n represents the program number. For example, PRG2-8 refers to the eighth program presented in Chapter 2. Data file names correspond to the names used in the text.

BASIC Programming Problems with Sample Input and Output

Over 60 challenging, field-tested BASIC Programming Problems are included at the end of the chapters. Each of the problems includes a statement of purpose, a problem statement, sample input data, and the corresponding output results. Solutions to these problems are given in the *Instructor's Manual and Answer Book* and on the *Instructor Diskette*.

Interactive Applications (Menu-Driven Programs)

Although examples of batch processing are presented, the primary emphasis is on interactive processing. The reader is introduced to the INPUT, PRINT, and CLS (Clear Screen) statements early in Chapter 2. The LOCATE statement is presented in Chapter 5 and thereafter is used extensively to build screens. Several menu-driven programs are illustrated to familiarize the reader with the type of programming that is proliferating today.

Emphasis on the Program Development Life Cycle

The program development life cycle is presented early in Chapter 1 and is used throughout the book. Good design habits are reinforced, and special attention is given to testing the design before attempting to implement the logic in a program.

Emphasis on Fundamentals and Style

Heavy emphasis is placed on the fundamentals of producing well-written and readable programs. A disciplined style is consistently used in all program examples. Thorough documentation and indention standards illuminate the implementation of the Selection and Repetition logic structures. The programming and style tips recommended throughout the book are summarized in Appendix C.

Summary of the QuickBASIC Language on a Reference Card

A summary of the statements, functions, special keys, operators, and reserved words can be found on a reference card at the back of the book. This summary is invaluable to the beginning student as a quick reference piece.

Presentation of Programming Case Studies

This book contains 25 completely solved and annotated case studies, illuminating the use of QuickBASIC and computer programming in the real world. Emphasis is placed on problem analysis, program design, and an in-depth discussion of the program solution. The program solutions to these programming case studies, as well as all other programs found throughout the book, are on the accompanying *Student Diskette*.

Program Design Aids

The authors recognize top-down charts and flowcharting as excellent pedagogical aids and as the tools of an analyst or programmer. Hence, many of the programming case studies include both top-down charts and program flowcharts to demonstrate programming style, design, and documentation.

Debugging Techniques and Programming Tips

A characteristic of a good programmer is that he or she has confidence that a program will work the first time it is executed. This confidence implies that careful attention has been given to the design and that the design has been fully tested. Still, errors do occur; and when they do, they must be corrected. Throughout this book, especially in Appendix C, efficient methods for locating and correcting errors are introduced using the QuickBASIC debugger. Tracing, as well as other debugging techniques, is discussed in detail. The sections in Appendix C which deal with programming tips and style tips serve as excellent references, facilitating the writing of efficient, readable code.

Applications-Oriented Approach

More than 150 QuickBASIC programs, illustrating a wide range of practical applications, along with many partial programs, are used to introduce specific statements and the proper and correct way to write programs.

Emphasis on Data Validation

The reliability of a thoroughly tested program cannot be guaranteed once it is turned over to a user. Most abnormal terminations in a production environment are due to user errors rather than programmer errors. This is especially true for programs that interact with the user or are executed on personal computers. Good programmers will attempt to trap as many user errors as possible. This book pays particular attention to the illustration of various data validation methods for ensuring that incoming data is reasonable or within limits.

What You Should Know

Each chapter contains a succinct, list-formatted review entitled What You Should Know, which reinforces key concepts and computer information system terminology.

Test Your BASIC Skills

A set of short-answer exercises identified as Test Your BASIC Skills appears at the end of each chapter. More than 200 problems, many of which are complete programs, are included for practice. Through the use of these exercises, the student can master the concepts presented, and instructors are afforded a valuable diagnostic tool. Answers for the even-numbered Test Your BASIC Skills exercises are available to the students in Appendix E. Answers to the odd-numbered exercises can be found in the *Instructor's Manual and Answer Book*.

Graphics and Sound

Chapter 11 covers all the graphics statements and functions in QuickBASIC that are central to understanding what can be done with graphics on the PC. The topics provide the student with knowledge of how to create, change, display, and store graphic designs and animation sequences. Furthermore, the necessary sound and music statements are discussed and are applied to various applications.

Additional PC Information

Besides a general introduction to personal computers in Chapter 1, Appendix D includes diskette formatting and operating instructions for the PC, and a list of popular magazines, newspapers, and manuals to help keep the student abreast of the new developments in the computer field.

ANCILLARY MATERIALS

A comprehensive instructor's support package accompanies *QuickBASIC Using Subprograms*. These ancillaries are available upon request from the publisher.

Instructor's Manual and Answer Book

The *Instructor's Manual and Answer Book* includes the following:

- Lecture outlines for each chapter
- Transparency masters from each chapter of the text
- Chapter-by-chapter objectives, teaching suggestions, and vocabulary lists
- Answers to the odd-numbered Test Your BASIC Skills exercises
- Program solutions to the more than 60 programming assignments in the book
- Test bank, including true/false, short-answer, fill-in, and multiple-choice questions for quizzes and tests

An *Instructor's Resource Diskette* is also available that includes the solutions to the more than 60 programming assignments found at the end of Chapters 2 through 11.

MicroSWAT III

MicroSWAT III, a computerized test-generating system, is available free to adopters of this textbook. It includes all of the questions from the *Instructor's Manual and Answer Book*. MicroSWAT III is an easy-to-use, menu-driven package that provides instructors with testing flexibility and allows customizing of testing documents. For example, a user of MicroSWAT III can enter his or her own questions and can generate review sheets and answer keys. MicroSWAT III will run on any IBM PC, IBM PS/1, IBM PS/2, or IBM-compatible system with a diskette drive, or a diskette drive and a hard disk.

ACKNOWLEDGMENTS

We would like to thank and express our appreciation to the many fine and talented individuals who have contributed to the success of this book. We were fortunate to have a group of reviewers whose critical evaluations of our first seven BASIC books, *Standard BASIC Programming*, *BASIC Fundamentals and Style*, *Complete BASIC for the Short Course*, *Applesoft BASIC Fundamentals and Style*, *Structured BASIC Fundamentals and Style for the IBM PC and Compatibles*, *Structured Microsoft BASIC: Essentials for Business*, and *QuickBASIC Fundamentals and Style*, were of great value during the preparation of these books. Special thanks again go to the following:

Dory Lyn Anderson, Saint Cloud Community College
William Bailey, Casper College
Chester Bogosta, Saint Leo College
David Bradbard, Auburn University
John J. Couture, San Diego City College
Louise Darcey, Texas A&M University
I. Englander, Bentley College
George Fowler, Texas A&M University
John T. Gorgone, Bentley College
James N. Haag, University of San Francisco
Linda Kosteba, Purdue University Calumet
Riki Kucheck, Orange Coast College
Jerry Lameiro, Colorado State University
Diane Larson, Purdue University Calumet
James Larson, Homewood Flossmoor High School
Marilyn Markowitz, Purdue University Calumet
John Monroe, Roberts Wesleyan College
Donald L. Muench, St. John Fisher College
Leroy Robbins, Bee County College
John Ross, Indiana University at Kokomo
R. Waldo Roth, Taylor University
Al Schroeder, Richland College
Syed Shahabuddin, Central Michigan University
Sumit Sircar, University of Texas at Arlington
Dave Talsky, University of Wisconsin–Milwaukee
Michael Walton, Miami–Dade Community College North
Mick Watterson, Drake University
Charles M. Williams, Georgia State University

The instructional staff of the Information Systems and Computer Programming Department of Purdue University Calumet provided many helpful comments and suggestions, and to them we extend our sincere thanks. Special thanks to Sam A. Maniotes for his contributions to the problem statements and their solutions of Basic Programming Problems 11.6 to 11.9 and Exercises 11.15 to 11.19 involving graphics, animation, and music. Special thanks also goes to Debbie Fansler for testing all the programs on the student diskette and instructor diskette to ensure their correctness.

No book is possible without the motivation and support of an editorial staff. Therefore, our final acknowledgment and greatest appreciation are reserved for the following at boyd & fraser: Thomas K. Walker, publisher and valued friend, for his unfaltering support; James H. Edwards, acquisitions editor, for the opportunity to write this book; Donna Walker, a prized friend, for her constant encouragement; Barbara Worth, production editor, for her assistance; Rosanne Coit, editorial assistant, for her commitment to the project; Becky Herrington, director of production, whose creative talents show up throughout the book; and finally, special praise for Ginny Harvey, for her outstanding copy-edit work.

Hammond, Indiana
January 1993

James S. Quasney
John Maniotes
Misty Vermaat

Notes to the Student

A few things to help you get going:

1. The first occurrence of a computer or programming term in this book is printed in **bold**. Its definition can be found in the same or next sentence.

2. The line numbers that appear to the left of program lines throughout this book are not part of the programs. QuickBASIC does not require line numbers. Their appearance is strictly for reference purposes during the discussion of the program. Beginning in Chapter 5, these line numbers also appear near symbols in top-down charts and program flowcharts in order to show their relationship to the corresponding program.

3. Each chapter ends with an important, useful review section called What You Should Know.

4. The answers to all the even-numbered Test Your BASIC Skills questions are in Appendix E.

5. A convenient, fully detailed language reference for QuickBASIC is never farther away than your F1 key or right Mouse button. Use these context-sensitive help keys whenever you have a question or want to learn more about the item nearest your cursor. This works for BASIC keywords, menu commands, error messages, dialog boxes, and just about anything else you can point to.

6. All the executable programs in the text are on the *Student Diskette* that accompanies this book. The programs on the *Student Diskette* which correspond to those in the text begin with the prefix PRG, followed by the chapter and program numbers. For example, PRG2-8 refers to the eighth executable program in Chapter 2.

   Each chapter-ending Test Your BASIC Skills section includes several PC Hands-On Exercises that utilize the programs on the *Student Diskette*. Follow the directions and load, modify, and execute the programs. These short exercises will help you understand the significance of various QuickBASIC statements and how slight modifications to a program can affect the results.

   You will also find the programs on the *Student Diskette* helpful when you are solving assigned programming problems. These programs can be retrieved from the diskette, and statements can be added, modified, or deleted to arrive at a solution. Most of the programming exercises in this book suggest which program should be loaded from the *Student Diskette* and modified to develop a solution.

7. An easy-to-use reference card at the back of this book contains a summary of the QuickBASIC statements, functions, special keys, operators, limits, and reserved words.

List of Programming Case Studies

Computers and Problem Solving: An Introduction

1.1 WHAT IS A COMPUTER?

A **computer** is a machine that can accept data, process the data at high speeds, and give the results of these processes in an acceptable form. A more formal definition of a computer is given by the American National Standards Institute (ANSI) which defines a computer as a device that can perform substantial computations, including numerous arithmetic and logic operations, without intervention by a human operator.

Computers can handle tedious and time-consuming work and large amounts of data without ever tiring, which makes them indispensable for most businesses. In fact, computers have been among the most important forces in the modernization of business, industry, schools, and society since World War II. Keep in mind, however, that with all their capabilities, computers are merely tools and are not built to think or reason. They extend our intellect, but they do not replace thinking.

Advantages of a Computer

The major advantages of a computer are its speed and accuracy, as well as its capability to store and have ready for immediate recall vast amounts of data. Today's computers can also accept data from anywhere via telephone line or satellite communications. They can generate usable output, such as reports, paychecks, and invoices, at several thousand lines per minute.

Disadvantages of a Computer

Some of the disadvantages of a computer concern obsolescence and ongoing costs for training and maintenance. Currently, computer models become technologically obsolete in a matter of a few years. Furthermore, in order for an organization's staff to derive its maximum benefits from a computer, the organization must continually invest in training and maintenance.

1.2   COMPUTER HARDWARE

Computer hardware is the physical equipment of a computer system. The equipment may consist of mechanical, magnetic, optical, electrical or electronic devices. Although many computers have been built in different sizes, speeds, and costs, and with different internal operations, most of them have the same basic five subsystems, as shown in Figures 1.1 and 1.2.

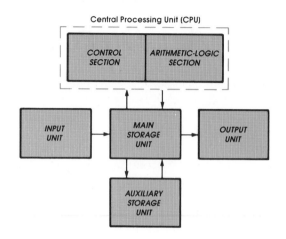

FIGURE 1.1

Basic structure of a digital computer, where the arrows represent the flow of data.

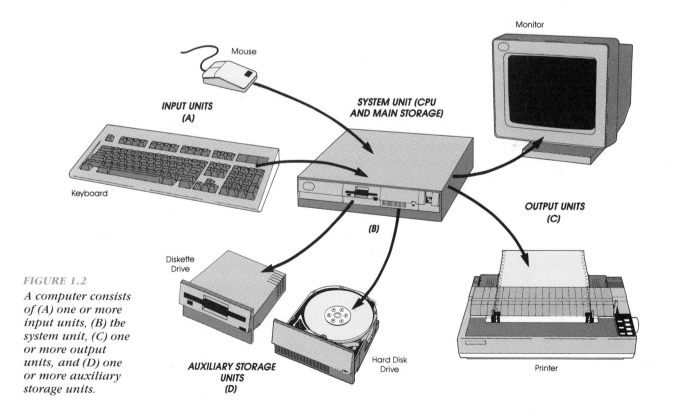

FIGURE 1.2

A computer consists of (A) one or more input units, (B) the system unit, (C) one or more output units, and (D) one or more auxiliary storage units.

Input

An **input unit** is a device that allows **programs**, instructions to the computer, and **data**, such as rate of pay, hours worked and number of dependents, to enter the computer system. This device converts the incoming data into electrical impulses, which are sent to the other units of the computer. A computer system usually has a **keyboard** and **mouse** for input (Figures 1.2, 1.3, and 1.4). The disk drives, which are labelled as auxiliary storage in Figure 1.2, can also serve as an input device.

Main Storage

After the instructions and data have entered the computer through an input unit, they are stored in the computer's **main storage unit**. Because computers can process vast amounts of data in a short time and perform millions of calculations in just one second, the storage unit must be able to retain large amounts of data and make any single item rapidly available for processing.

Main storage in a computer is divided into locations, called **bytes**, each having a unique **address**. Each byte can store a character, such as the letter A or digit 9 or special character $. When instructions and data are entered, they are stored in various locations of main storage. The computer leaves data in a storage location until it is instructed to replace it with new data. While a data item is in storage, the computer can *look it up* as often as it is needed without altering that data item. Thus, when data is retrieved from a storage location, the stored contents remain unaltered. When you instruct the computer to put new data in that location, the old data is replaced.

Central Processing Unit (CPU)

The **CPU** controls and supervises the entire computer system and performs the actual arithmetic and logic operations on data, as specified by the written program. The CPU is divided into the arithmetic-logic section and the control section, as shown in Figure 1.1.

The **arithmetic-logic section** performs such operations as addition, subtraction, multiplication, and division. Depending on the cost and storage capacity of the computer, the speed of the arithmetic unit will range from several million to many billions of operations per second.

The arithmetic-logic section also carries out the decision-making operations required to change the sequence of instruction execution. These operations include testing various conditions, for example, comparing two characters for equality. The result of these tests causes the computer to take one of two or more alternate paths through the program.

The **control section** directs and coordinates the entire computer system according to the program developed by the programmer and placed in main storage. The control section's primary function is to analyze and initiate the execution of instructions. This means that the control section has control over all other subsystems in the computer system.

Auxiliary Storage

The function of the **auxiliary storage unit** is to store data and programs that are to be used over and over again. Common auxiliary storage devices are the magnetic tape drives, hard disk drives and diskette drives. The latter two are shown in Figures 1.2 and 1.3.

These auxiliary storage devices can be used to store programs and data for as long as desired. A new program entering the system overwrites the previous program and data in main storage, but the previous program and data may be permanently stored on an auxiliary storage device for recall by the computer.

Output

When instructed by a program, the computer can communicate the results of a program to output units. A computer usually has a **monitor** for output. Other common output devices include a **printer**, a **plotter**, and a **disk unit**.

The monitor, also called a **video display device** or **screen**, can be used to display the output results in the form of words, numbers, graphs, or drawings. The monitor is shown in Figures 1.2 and 1.3.

1.3   THE PC AND PS FAMILY

In 1981, IBM introduced the IBM Personal Computer (PC), a fully assembled, easy-to-use computer, which has become the personal computer standard throughout the world.

Since that time, the original PC has undergone many enhancements, and additional models have been produced. Some of the popular models include the following:

- IBM PC XT
- IBM PC AT
- IBM Personal System/1(PS/1) Home Computer
- IBM Personal System/2(PS/2) (Figure 1.3)

FIGURE 1.3

The IBM Personal System/2 (PS/2) (Courtesy IBM Corp.).

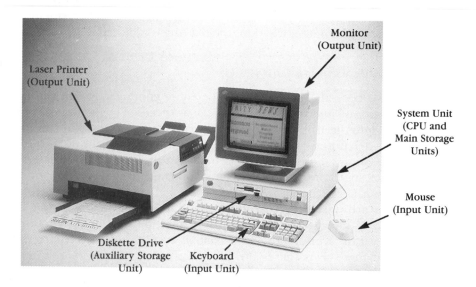

Since 1981, more than 50 million IBM PCs and compatibles have been manufactured. Currently, there are more than 100 manufacturers worldwide who provide PC compatible systems and peripherals. Some of these manufacturers include such well-known names as AT&T, Compaq, Epson, Packard Bell, Tandy, and Zenith.

Many accessories and peripheral devices can be connected to the IBM PC and compatibles. This is possible because when IBM introduced the PC, it incorporated expansion slots so that users would be able to add enhancements at will (Figure 1.6). This "open architecture" has permitted many vendors to manufacture devices that enhance the performance of the PC.

Currently, two new computer architectures have been introduced for PC systems. The proprietary Micro Channel Adapter (MCA) architecture, introduced by IBM, is used for most of the PS/2 systems. The open architecture called Extended Industry Standard Architecture (EISA), introduced by an industry-led consortium of computer manufacturers, is used for many PC compatible systems.

The Keyboard

Figure 1.4 shows the enhanced IBM PS/2 keyboard consisting of 101 keys. The keyboard is similar to that of an ordinary typewriter keyboard, which is also referred to as the Qwerty keyboard. A **keyboard** is an input device used to enter programs and data into the main storage unit. Numeric, alphabetic, and special characters appear in the standard typewriter format on the keyboard.

FIGURE 1.4

The enhanced IBM PS/2 keyboard.

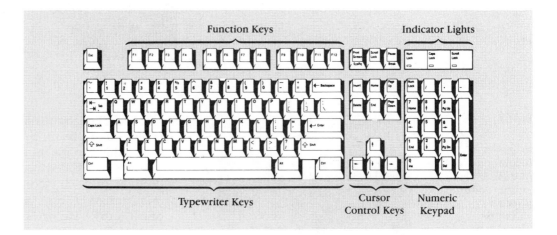

Note the layout of the function keys, the typewriter keys, and the numeric keypad. These keys will be explained in Chapter 2.

Monitor

There are two basic types of monitors — monochrome and color. Monochrome monitors come in black and white, green, or amber. Color monitors can display many different colors. Either device can display 40 or 80 characters per horizontal line. Most monitors have 25 lines on the screen, although some allow for more than twice as many. (Figures 1.2 and 1.3 show examples of monitors.)

Currently, there are five popular graphic standards used with monitors. The Hercules monochrome standard is the least expensive and has only one color.

The Color Graphics Adapter (CGA) was IBM's first attempt at color, and CGA can show up to four colors. The Enhanced Graphics Adapter (EGA) was IBM's second attempt at color, and EGA can show 16 colors on a monitor. Video Graphics Array (VGA) was IBM's third attempt, and it can show 256 colors on a monitor. Extended Graphics Array (XGA) is IBM's latest attempt to show high-resolution graphics on a monitor. Chapter 11 covers these and other various color and graphics standards in greater detail.

CPU and Main Storage Unit

All IBM PCs and IBM compatibles use the Intel 80x86 series or Intel compatible microprocessors (CPUs), such as the 8088/8086, 80286, 80386, 80386 SX, 80486, and the new 80586.

The original IBM PC and its compatibles contain a 16-bit Intel 8088 CPU, called a **microprocessor**, which is miniaturized on a **silicon chip** typically a fraction of an inch long (Figure 1.5). The IBM PC AT and compatibles contain an Intel 80286 CPU, and the advanced models of the IBM PS/2 and compatibles contain an Intel 80386, 80386 SX, 80486, or 80586 CPU. The 80486 CPU is shown in Figure 1.5 on the next page. Each higher numbered chip executes programs several times faster than the previous.

FIGURE 1.5

The Intel 80486 is the world's first 1,000,000 transistor microprocessor. It crams 1.2 million transistors on a sliver of silicon that measures 0.4 inch by 0.6 inch and can execute four times as fast as its predecessor, the 80386.

FIGURE 1.6

A top view of the mother board of an IBM PS/2. The mother board is located within the system unit.

expansion slots

Intel or compatible microprocessor

read-only memory (ROM) chip

random-access memory (RAM) chip

The CPU and main storage unit are contained on the **mother board** (Figure 1.6) within the system unit. Main storage is sometimes called read/write memory, or **RAM** (Random-Access Memory). The original IBM PC can contain a maximum of 640K (659,456 bytes) of main storage, or RAM. The PC AT and PS/2 can contain up to 16MB (16,777,216 bytes). The letter **K** (kilo) represents 1,024 bytes and the letters **MB** (megabyte) represents 1,048,576 bytes.

Read-Only Memory (**ROM**) is another form of storage. It is used to store the disk loader, patterns for graphics characters, and other essential instructions and data.

The term **megahertz** (**MHz**)–million cycles per second–is used as the most common measurement of a CPU's performance. Today's PCs range from 16 to 100 MHz in their CPU performance.

Auxiliary Storage

The IBM PC and compatibles use a 2 inch, 3 1/2 inch or 5 1/4 inch diskette for storing and retrieving information (Figure 1.7).

FIGURE 1.7

Diskettes come in 2 (right), 3 1/2 (left) and 5 1/4 inch (center) sizes. One advantage of the 2 and 3 1/2 inch diskettes is that they come in a rigid housing, which helps prevent damage to the diskette.

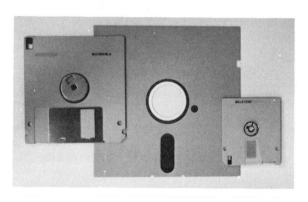

Diskettes are classified as low density, high density, and very high density. Very high-density diskettes can store twice as much data as high-density diskettes. High-density diskettes can store twice as much data as low-density diskettes. To store data in very high density, you need a very high-density diskette unit on your PC, as well as a very high-density diskette. Table 1.1 summarizes the storage capacity of the three sizes of diskettes.

TABLE 1.1   A Comparison of 2, 3 1/2, and 5 1/4 Inch Diskettes

DISKETTE	DENSITY	CAPACITY IN BYTES	NUMBER OF DOUBLE-SPACED TYPEWRITTEN 8-1/2 BY 11 INCH PAGES
2 inch	Low	360K	125
3 1/2 inch	Low	720K	250
3 1/2 inch	High	1.44M	500
3 1/2 inch	Very high	2.88M	1,000
5 1/4 inch	Low	360K	125
5 1/4 inch	High	1.2M	375

A **diskette** is a thin, circular media coated with a magnetic substance and comes in a permanent, protective jacket. With the 5 1/4 inch diskette, the read/write head in the disk unit comes into magnetic contact with the recording surface through the slot hole in the diskette's protective jacket (Figure 1.7). The 2 inch and 3 1/2 inch diskettes each have a shutter that automatically opens and exposes the recording surface when the diskette is placed in the diskette unit (Figure 1.8). Once inside the diskette unit, the diskette is made to spin inside its protective jacket.

FIGURE 1.8
The parts of a 3 1/2 inch diskette (Courtesy Sony Corp.).

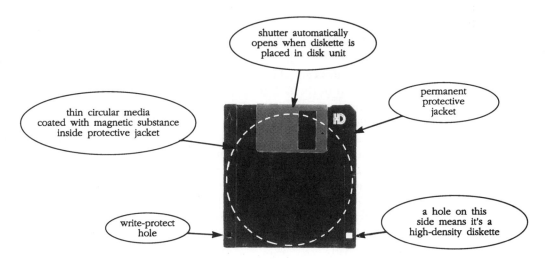

Diskettes are delicate and should be handled and stored with care. Do not place diskettes near heat, cold, or magnetic field sources such as magnets. Do not bend or fold diskettes. Never touch the exposed recording surface; always hold the diskette by the protective jacket. Use a felt-type pen to write on the temporary label before applying the label to the protective jacket of the diskette.

For additional auxiliary storage, a hard disk, containing anywhere from 10MB (million bytes) to 500MB of storage, can be used with a PC. A 10MB hard disk can store the equivalent of 5,500 double-spaced typewritten pages. A 500MB hard disk can store up to 275,000 double-spaced typewritten pages.

Network System

Many schools and businesses have opted to install a **network**, also called a **local area network (LAN)**. A network allows a printer, hard disk drive, other peripheral devices, software packages, and databases to be used by many interconnected personal computers. As shown in Figure 1.9, PCs in a network do not require their own individual printers.

With a network, many students operating PCs can be connected to an instructor-controlled PC. A network also allows students to access their programs and data files from the instructor's disk drives and use the printer. All processing of programs is done by the students on their assigned PC. When the students finish their work, they can store their updated programs and data files on their own diskette drives or on the instructor's hard disk drives.

Some of the leading manufacturers of LAN hardware and software systems are IBM, DEC, Novell, 3 Com, and Banyan.

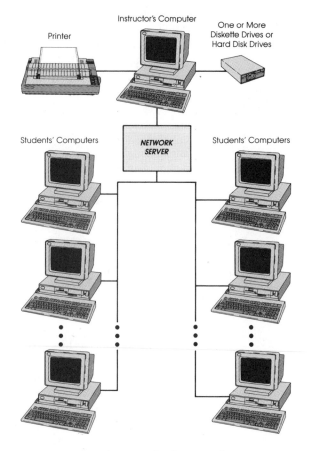

FIGURE 1.9   A network of personal computers.

1.4   THE STORED PROGRAM CONCEPT

Before a computer can take action and produce a desired result, it must have a step-by-step description of the task to be accomplished. The step-by-step description is a series of precise instructions called a **program**. When these instructions are placed into the main storage unit of a computer, they are called the **stored program**. Main storage stores data along with the instructions which tell the computer what to do with the data. The stored program gives computers a great deal of flexibility. Without it, the computer's capability to handle tasks would be reduced to that of a desk calculator.

Once the program is stored, the first instruction is located and sent to the control section, where it is interpreted and executed. Then the next instruction is located, sent to the control section, interpreted and executed. This process continues automatically, instruction by instruction, until the program is completed or until the computer is instructed to halt.

For the computer to perform still another job, a new program must be stored in main storage. Hence, a computer can be easily used to process a large number of different jobs.

1.5   COMPUTER SOFTWARE

Computer software is a set of programming languages and programs concerned with the operation of a computer system. Some essential computer software comes with the purchase of a computer system. Additional software is either purchased or written by the user in a programming language the computer understands. Table 1.2 lists some popular software packages and their functions for business and schools. These packages do not require that you know how to program. They may be purchased at any computer store selling personal computer systems.

TABLE 1.2 Popular Software Packages and Their Functions

SOFTWARE PACKAGE	FUNCTION
WordPerfect™ or Microsoft Word™	A **word processing program** used to write, revise, and edit letters, reports, and manuscripts with efficiency and economy.
Lotus 1-2-3™ or Quattro Pro or Excel	An **electronic spreadsheet program** used to organize data that can be defined in terms of rows and columns. Formulas can be applied to current rows or columns to create new rows and columns of information. Graphic images can be produced on the basis of the data in the spreadsheet. The 1-2-3 refers to the spreadsheet, database, and graphics features of this package.
dBASE III PLUS™ or dBASE IV™ or Paradox™	A **database system** used to organize data on an auxiliary storage device. It also allows for the generation of reports and for easy access to the data.
Harvard Presentation Graphics™	A **graphics program** used to create line graphs, bar graphs, pie charts, and 3-D graphic images.
Ventura™ or PageMaker™	A **desktop publishing system** used to integrate words and pictures and generate typeset quality documents quickly and economically.

Programming languages are classified as **low-level languages**, such as machine language and assembly language, and **high-level languages**, such as BASIC, C, Pascal, COBOL, and FORTRAN. Early generation computers required programmers to program in machine language, and this language was different for each computer manufacturer's system.

Currently, most applications for the PC are programmed in one of the many, popular high-level languages listed in Table 1.3. A high-level language is generally machine or computer independent: this means that programs written in a high-level language like BASIC can easily be transferred from one computer system to another, with little or no change in the programs. The languages listed in Table 1.3 are available for personal computers. However, the most widely used language with personal computers is BASIC.

TABLE 1.3 Popular High-Level Languages and Their Appropriate Area of Usefulness

LANGUAGE	AREA OF USEFULNESS
BASIC	**B**eginner's **A**ll-purpose **S**ymbolic **I**nstruction **C**ode is a very simple problem-solving language that is used with personal computers or with terminals in a time-sharing environment. BASIC is used for both business and scientific applications.
C	This high-level language provides easy access to many assembly language capabilities. C is useful for writing applications packages and systems software, like operating systems.
COBOL	The **CO**mmon **B**usiness **O**riented **L**anguage is an English-like language that is suitable for business data processing applications. It is especially useful for file and table handling and extensive input and output operations. COBOL is a very widely used programming language.
FORTRAN	**FOR**mula **TRAN**slation is a problem-solving language designed primarily for scientific data processing, engineering, and process-control applications.
Pascal	Pascal, named in honor of the French mathematician Blaise Pascal, is a programming language that allows for the formulations of solutions and data in a form that clearly exhibits their natural structure. It is used primarily for scientific applications and systems programming and to some extent for business data processing.

There are many dialects of the BASIC language. **QuickBASIC** is one of the most popular and leading BASIC languages in the marketplace.

The QuickBASIC system for the PC was designed and developed by Microsoft Corporation, one of the largest microcomputer software companies in the world. The QuickBASIC system includes the QuickBASIC language and a fully integrated editor (Chapter 2 and Appendix B), debugger (Appendix C), pull-down menus, and compiler and/or interpreter.

The QuickBASIC system that we cover in this book is called MS-DOS QBasic. This version comes with the operating system (DOS 5.0 and higher). MS-DOS QBasic *looks* and *feels* like the commercial version of QuickBASIC. For example, the repertoire of powerful BASIC statements, the on-line help facility, and the operating environment are identical in both versions. MS-DOS QBasic, however, does not include a compiler (see page 11).

Bulletin Board Systems

Thousands of programs and software packages have been written for the PC. Many of these are available, free of charge or for a minimal charge, through electronic bulletin board systems. A **bulletin board system**, also called **BBS**, is a computer system that provides a service for special interest groups, clubs, and hobbyists. To communicate with a BBS, you need a telephone, modem, communications software, phone number, and PC. Properly equipped, you can communicate with bulletin board systems all over the world. The magazines and newspapers listed in Appendix D are good sources to find out more about bulletin board systems, software packages, and programming languages available for the PC.

The Operating System (MS-DOS and OS/2)

The operating system for the PC was also designed and developed by Microsoft Corporation. The operating system is called **PC-DOS** for the IBM PC and **MS-DOS** for the PC compatibles. MS-DOS stands for Microsoft Disk Operating System. PC-DOS and MS-DOS are essentially the same.

This operating system, through a series of enhancements and new versions, has become the standard operating program for all IBM and IBM compatible personal computer systems. MS-DOS is stored on a diskette, which comes with every PC.

MS-DOS helps to act as an internal ''traffic cop'' in the PC by directing the flow of data into and out of the computer and the peripheral devices (Figure 1.1).

PS/2 personal computers can also use the OS/2 operating system, which was developed jointly by IBM and Microsoft. The **OS/2** operating system is designed to take advantage of the increased main storage and computing power of the 80386, 80486, and 80586 microprocessors. While MS-DOS is a single-user, single-task operating system, OS/2 is a single-user, multitask operating system. **Multitask** means that the computer can run multiple programs concurrently, but not simultaneously, because there is only one CPU.

The Graphical User Interface (Windows)

A Graphical User Interface (GUI and sometimes pronounced as gooey) is the program interface between a user and the PC. A GUI is designed to increase the productivity of the user. An important design consideration for a GUI is that a user does not have to memorize or type commands into a PC but can point the cursor and select the function he or she needs to perform.

There are two popular GUI products with the IBM PCs and IBM compatibles — Microsoft Windows and IBM OS/2 Presentation Manager. Each of these GUIs use windows, icons, and a mouse. Each GUI is easy to use, is graphically oriented and icon driven, allows for the direct manipulation of objects on the screen, and has a consistent user interface across applications.

Furthermore, a GUI provides on the the screen a visual *desktop* where a user can view the **icons** (small graphical figures) representing documents, programs, and files. For example, to activate an application program, such as Lotus 1-2-3 or WordPerfect, a user points to its icon on the screen using a hand-held pointing device called a mouse.

Chapter 2 explains the QuickBASIC environment. Although QuickBASIC is not GUI, it does use various windows, menu bars, scroll bars, dialog boxes, and many other features commonly found in a GUI environment.

| Programming Case Study 1 | Computing an Average

Program 1.1 illustrates a program written in QuickBASIC. It instructs the computer to compute the average of three numbers, 17, 23 and 50.

PROGRAM 1.1

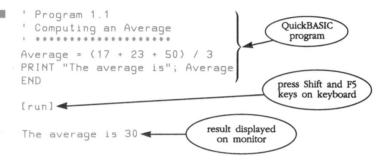

```
' Program 1.1
' Computing an Average
' ********************
Average = (17 + 23 + 50) / 3
PRINT "The average is"; Average
END

[run]

The average is 30
```

The displayed answer, found below [run], is 30. Although we are deferring detailed explanations about this program until the next chapter, Program 1.1 gives you some indication of instructing a computer to calculate a desired result using QuickBASIC.

The Compiler and the Interpreter

Computers cannot directly execute programs, such as Program 1.1, written in a high-level language like QuickBASIC. Computers must first translate the QuickBASIC statements into equivalent machine language instructions that are understood by the computer.

Compilers and interpreters are two types of software programs that perform this translation. The following paragraphs explain some of the differences between these two translation processes.

Figure 1.10 illustrates the use of a compiler to translate programs written in Quick-BASIC. The QuickBASIC **compiler** is a program which, when executed by the PC, will cause an entire QuickBASIC program to be translated into machine language *before* the actual execution of the program begins.

FIGURE 1.10

Compilation procedure for a program written in QuickBASIC.

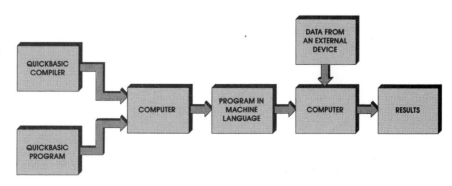

The compiler examines the entire QuickBASIC program, and if it is error free, the compiler generates the machine language instructions. Some PC systems can compile programs at speeds of more than 10,000 QuickBASIC statements per minute.

To produce results or answers, the machine language instructions, together with data from external sources, are then processed by the computer as shown in Figure 1.10.

Figure 1.11 illustrates the use of an interpreter to translate programs written in QuickBASIC. An **interpreter** is a program, which when executed by a computer, will analyze each QuickBASIC statement, translate it into equivalent machine language, and execute the machine langauge instructions to produce results, or answers, without the production of an intermediate machine language program.

FIGURE 1.11

Interpretation procedure for a program written in QuickBASIC.

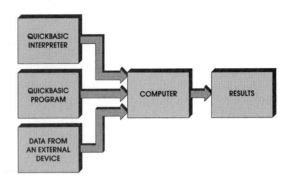

Depending on the content of a QuickBASIC program, compiled QuickBASIC programs execute five to 10 times faster than interpreted QuickBASIC programs. MS-DOS QBasic includes the interpreter, but not the compiler. The compiler is available with the commercial version of QuickBASIC.

1.6   PROBLEM SOLVING AND PROGRAM DEVELOPMENT

Every action the PC is expected to make toward solving a problem must be spelled out in detail in the program. The step-by-step procedures listed in Table 1.4 will help you set up problems for the computer to solve. These procedures make up what is called the **program development life cycle**.

TABLE 1.4   The Program Development Life Cycle

STEP	PROCEDURE	DESCRIPTION
1	**Problem Analysis**	Define the problem to be solved precisely, including the form of the input, the form of the output, and a description of the transformation of input to output.
2	**Program Design**	Devise an **algorithm**, or a method of solution, for the computer to use. This method must be a complete procedure for solving the specified problem in a finite number of steps. There must be no ambiguity (no chance that something can be interpreted in more than one way). Develop a detailed logic plan or logic diagram, using **flowcharts**, **pseudocode**, or some other logic tool to describe each step that the PC must perform to arrive at the solution. As far as possible, the flowcharts or pseudocode must describe *what* job is to be done and *how* the job is to be done. Develop good **test data**. As best you can, select data that will test for erroneous input.
3	**Test the Design**	Step by step, go through the logic diagram, using the test data as if you were the PC. If the logic diagram does not work, repeat steps 1 through 3.
4	**Code the Program**	Code the program in a computer language, like QuickBASIC (see Table 1.3), according to the logic specified in the logic diagram. Include program documentation, like comments and explanations, within the program.
5	**Review the Code**	Carefully review the code. Put yourself in the position of the PC and step through the entire program.
6	**Enter the Program**	Submit the program to the PC via a keyboard or other input device.
7	**Test the Program**	Test the program until it is error free and until it contains enough safeguards to ensure the desired result.
8	**Formalize the Solution**	Run the program, using the input data to generate the results. Review, and, if necessary, modify the documentation for the program.
9	**Maintain the Program**	Correct errors or add enhancements to the program. This step is usually initiated by users that have been running the program. Once errors or enhancements are identified, the Program Development Life Cycle begins again at Step 1.

Flowcharts

A **program flowchart** is a popular logic tool used for showing an algorithm in graphic form. By depicting a procedure for arriving at a solution, a program flowchart also shows how the application or job is to be accomplished.

A programmer prepares a flowchart *before* he or she begins coding it in QuickBASIC. Eight basic symbols are used in program flowcharting. They are given in Table 1.5 on the next page with their respective names, meanings, and some of the QuickBASIC statements that are represented by them.

TABLE 1.5 Flowchart Symbols and Their Meanings

SYMBOL	NAME	MEANING
□	Process Symbol	Represents the process of executing a defined operation or group of operations which results in a change in value, form, or location of information. Examples: LET, DIM, RESTORE, DEF, and other processing statements. Also functions as the default symbol when no other symbol is available.
▱	Input/Output (I/O) Symbol	Represents an I/O function, which makes data available for processing (input) or for displaying (output) of processed information. Examples: READ, INPUT, and PRINT.
Left to Right / Right to Left / Top to Bottom / Bottom to Top	Flowline Symbol	Represents the sequence of available information and executable operations. The lines connect other symbols, and the arrowheads are mandatory only for right-to-left and bottom-to-top flow.
⊐	Annotation Symbol	Represents the addition of descriptive information, comments, or explanatory notes as clarification. The vertical line and the broken line may be placed on the left, as shown, or on the right. Example: REM or
◇	Decision Symbol	Represents a decision that determines which of a number of alternative paths is to be followed. Examples: IF and SELECT CASE statements.
⬭	Terminal Symbol	Represents the beginning, the end, or a point of interruption or delay in a program. Examples: STOP, RETURN, and END statements.
○	Connector Symbol	Represents any entry from, or exit to, another part of the flowchart. Also serves as an off-page connector.
⊏⊐	Predefined Process Symbol	Represents a named process consisting of one or more operations or program steps that are specified elsewhere. Example: CALL.

One rule that is basic to all flowcharts concerns direction. In constructing a flowchart, start at the top (or left-hand corner) of a page. The flow should be top to bottom and left to right. If the flow takes any other course, arrowheads must be used. A plastic template may be obtained from a majority of computer stores or bookstores. This template can be used to help you draw the flowchart symbols.

Figure 1.12 shows a flowchart that illustrates the computations that are required to compute the average commission paid to a company's sales personnel and determine the number of male and female sales personnel. (For an in-depth discussion on flowcharts see Appendix A — especially, for this chapter, Section A.1 through A.6.)

FIGURE 1.12
Flowchart of the sales personnel computations.

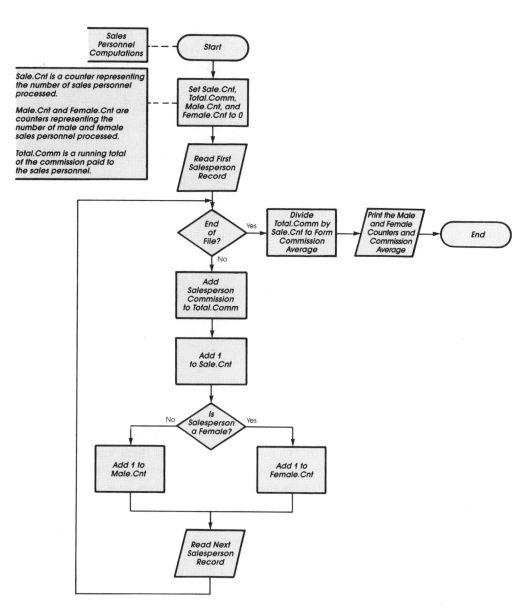

Pseudocode

Pseudocode is an alternative to program flowcharts that uses natural English and resembles QuickBASIC code. It allows for the logic of a program to be formulated without diagrams or charts. Figure 1.13 shows examples of specific operations in pseudocode.

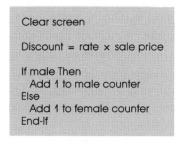

FIGURE 1.13
Examples of operations in pseudocode.

Figure 1.14 shows a pseudocode version of the flowchart solution presented in Figure 1.12. Although psuedocode has few formal rules, we have listed some commonly accepted rules, as well as several examples, in Section A.7 of Appendix A.

FIGURE 1.14

Pseudocode version of the sales personnel computations.

```
Program: Sales Personnel Computations
Set salesperson counter to 0
Set total commission to 0
Set male counter to 0
Set female counter to 0
Read first salesperson record
Do While not end-of-file
    Add salesperson commission to total commission
    Add 1 to salesperson counter
    If female Then
        Add 1 to female counter
    Else
        Add 1 to male counter
    End-If
    Read next salesperson record
End Do
Commission average = total commission / salesperson counter
Display male and female counters and commission average
End: Sales Personnel Computations
```

Appendix A also includes a discussion of Nassi-Schneiderman charts and Warnier-Orr diagrams. Nassi-Schneiderman charts and Warnier-Orr diagrams are alternative logic tools to flowcharts and pseudocode. Also, Chapter 4 presents top-down charts.

Each logic tool has its strengths and weaknesses. As you solve problems in the later chapters of this book, we suggest you try all of them, and then choose the tool that best suits you. Of course, your instructor may have something to say about the logic tool you use for the required assignments.

1.7   ADDITIONAL INFORMATION ON PERSONAL COMPUTERS

We encourage you to seek additional information on personal computers. To assist you in that search Appendix D includes:

- A list of magazines and newspapers oriented to the PC (both provide current information on what is taking place with personal computers)
- A list of QuickBASIC manuals

1.8   WHAT YOU SHOULD KNOW

To help you study this chapter, a summary of the topics covered in it is listed below. These statements apply to all computers, including the PC. This is not a test that includes true and false statements; all of the statements in this list are true.

1. A computer is a device that can perform substantial computations, including numerous arithmetic and logic operations, without intervention by a human operator.
2. The major advantages of a computer are its speed, accuracy and capability to store and have ready for immediate recall vast amounts of data.
3. The major disadvantages of a computer are rapid obsolescence and the ongoing cost of training and maintenance.

4. However fast, computers are not built to think or reason. They extend our intellect, but they do not replace thinking.

5. Computer hardware is the physical equipment of a computer system.

6. A computer has five subsystems — input, output, main storage, auxiliary storage, and the central processing unit (CPU).

7. An input unit allows programs and data to enter the computer system.

8. Main storage is the computer's storage unit, where instructions and data are stored for processing purposes.

9. The central processing unit (CPU) controls and supervises the entire computer system and performs the actual arithmetic and logic operations on data, as specified by the written program. The CPU is made up of two sections — the arithmetic-logic section and the control section.

10. The arithmetic-logic section performs the arithmetic operations and carries out the decision-making operations required by a program.

11. The control section directs and coordinates the entire computer system.

12. The auxiliary storage unit stores data and programs that are to be used over and over again.

13. An output unit is used by the computer to communicate the results of a program.

14. A network is a group of interconnected personal computers that can share software programs and hardware, such as a printer, disk drive, and other peripheral devices. Networks are also called LANs (local-area networks).

15. A computer program is a series of instructions required to complete a procedure or task. When the program is loaded into the main storage unit of a computer, it becomes a stored program.

16. Computer software is a program or a set of programs written for a computer.

17. Software packages that do not require a person to know how to program are available for word processing, electronic spreadsheets, database management, desktop publishing, and graphics.

18. Programming languages are classified as low-level languages, such as machine language and assembly language, and high-level languages, such as BASIC, C, Pascal, COBOL, and FORTRAN.

19. A compiler and interpreter are two types of software programs that are part of the QuickBASIC system. They are used to translate the QuickBASIC statements into equivalent machine language instructions that are understood by the computer.

20. The program development life cycle is a set of step-by-step procedures for solving a problem.

21. In problem analysis, defining the problem is the first step in solving it.

22. Program design is made up of three steps — devising a method of solution, drawing logic diagrams, and selecting good test data.

23. A QuickBASIC program should be coded only after the design is complete and has been carefully reviewed and tested.

24. A program flowchart is a popular logic tool used for showing an algorithm in graphic form.

25. Pseudocode is an alternative to program flowcharts and allows for the logic of a program to be formulated without diagrams or charts.

1.9   TEST YOUR BASIC SKILLS (Even-numbered answers are in Appendix E)

1. State three major advantages that computers have over the manual computation of problems.

2. What are the basic subsystems of a computer system? Briefly describe the function of each subsystem.

3. Name the components of the CPU.
4. Name two devices that serve as both input and output devices.
5. Name five personal computer models.
6. What is meant by the term hardware? Software?
7. What do the following acronyms represent: ALU, CPU, K, MB, MHz, RAM, ROM, VGA?
8. List the different sized diskettes described in the text and their storage capacities.
9. Draw one flowchart which enables the Mechanical Man to accomplish efficiently the objectives in both phase 1 and 2, as illustrated in Figure 1.15.

FIGURE 1.15

The two phases of the Mechanical Man.

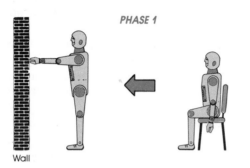

PHASE 1

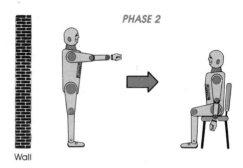

PHASE 2

Wall

The Mechanical Man is seated at an unknown integer number (0,1,2,...) of steps from the wall. He will stand up and walk forward until he touches the wall with his fingertips. When he is in a seated position with arms raised, his fingertips are aligned with the tips of his shoes.

Wall

After touching the wall, the Mechanical Man will return to his chair. Since the chair is too low for him to sense by touch, he can get to it only by going back exactly as rnany steps as he came forward.

The Mechanical Man possesses the following properties:

- He is restricted to carrying out a limited repertoire of instructions.
- He does *nothing* unless given a specific instruction.
- He must carry out any instructions he is given *one at a time*.
- He understands the following instructions:

  a. Physical Movement:
     1. Stand up (into an erect position without moving feet).
     2. Sit down (into a sitting position without moving feet).
     3. Take one step (forward only, can only be done if he is standing, length of steps is always the same).
     4. Raise arms (into one fixed position, straight ahead).
     5. Lower arms (into one fixed position, straight down at his sides).
     6. Turn right (in place without taking a step, can be done only if he is standing, all right turns are 90-degree turns).
  b. Arithmetic:
     1. Add one (to a total that is being developed).
     2. Subtract one (from a total that is being developed).
     3. Record total (any number of totals can be remembered in this way).
  c. Logic: The Mechanical Man can decide what instruction he will carry out next on the basis of answers to the following questions:
     1. Arithmetic results
        a) Is the result positive?
        b) Is the result negative?
        c) Is the result zero?
        d) Is the result equal to a predetermined amount?
     2. Physical status
        a) Are the raised arms touching anything?

10. After reviewing the following three files with their specified records, answer the questions below:

Record Number	Salesperson Number	Salesperson Sex	Salesperson Commission
1	246	Male	$ 400
2	501	Female	1,100
3	876	Female	600
1	123	Male	$ 300

File 1 → records 1, 2, 3
File 2 → record 1
File 3 → This file is empty, that is, there are no records.

   a. According to Figure 1.12, what is the value of Male.Cnt, Female.Cnt, Sale.Cnt, and Commission Average after File 1 is processed and the program terminates?
   b. Same as (a), but refer to File 2.
   c. Same as (a), but refer to File 3.

11. Same as question 9, but use pseudocode to develop the logic that enables the Mechanical Man to accomplish efficiently the objectives shown in Figure 1.15.

12. Explain the function of each of the following applications: word processing, spreadsheets, database, graphics, desktop publishing, and windows. Identify a major software package for each application.

13. Payroll Problem I: Weekly Payroll

Problem: Construct the flowchart to calculate a weekly payroll using the following rules:
   a. Time and a half is paid for hours worked in excess of 40.
   b. $38.46 is allowed as nontaxable income for each dependent claimed.
   c. The withholding tax is 20 percent of the taxable income.
   d. Assume that end-of-file is defined as the condition in which the value for the number of hours worked is negative.

Input: Each employee record includes the following data:
   a. Name
   b. Hourly rate of pay
   c. Number of hours worked
   d. Number of dependents

Output: Display the following for each employee:
   a. Name
   b. Gross pay
   c. Net pay
   d. Income tax withheld

14. Identify the manufacturer, model number, and MHz of the computer system you will use to process QuickBASIC programs. Does the system include both a QuickBASIC compiler and interpreter?

1.10   PC HANDS-ON EXERCISES

The following exercises are designed to acquaint you with your personal computer system. Consult with your instructor before running these exercises on your PC. Also consult Appendix D, which contains some of the operating instructions for the PC.

1. Identification of Keys on the Keyboard

Find the important keys on your keyboard listed in Table 1.6. Make a check in the third column as you find each key.

TABLE 1.6   Special Keys on Keyboard

KEY	SYMBOL	CHECK	KEY	SYMBOL	CHECK	KEY	SYMBOL	CHECK
Enter	↵		Print Screen	Print Screen		Home	Home	
Escape	Esc		Capital Lock	Caps Lock		End	End	
Tab	↹		Numeral Lock	Num Lock		Insert Key	Insert	
Control	Ctrl		Scroll Lock	Scroll Lock		Function Key 1	F1	
Shift	⇧		Alternate	Alt		Delete	Delete	
Backspace	←							

2. Formatting a Diskette

When you purchase a diskette, it is blank (that is, it has nothing recorded on the surface). For programs or data to be placed on a diskette, it must first be formatted.

Obtain a blank diskette following the recommendation of your instructor and format it carefully following the instructions in Section D.2 of Appendix D.

DO NOT FORMAT THE STUDENT DISKETTE THAT ACCOMPANIES THIS BOOK.

QuickBASIC: An Introduction

2.1 CREATING A QuickBASIC PROGRAM

In this chapter we will concentrate on "simple" program illustrations, input/output operations, and the QuickBASIC (QB) operating environment. The **QB operating environment** allows you to create, maintain, and execute QuickBASIC programs on your PC. Upon successful completion of this chapter, you should be able to develop some elementary programs written in QuickBASIC and submit them to your PC for execution.

General Characteristics of a QuickBASIC Program

A QuickBASIC program is composed of a sequence of lines. Each line may contain one or more statements, up to a maximum of 255 characters. Statements instruct the PC to carry out an action, such as assigning the value of an expression to a variable or displaying the value of a variable. In general, programmers enter one statement per line followed immediately by the Enter key. The statements are placed in the program in the order they are to be executed (Figure 2.1).

Programming Case Study 2 illustrates the composition of a QuickBASIC program.

FIGURE 2.1
The general form of a QuickBASIC program.

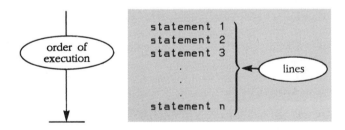

Programming Case Study 2 | Determining a Salesperson's Commission

Most salespeople work on a commission basis. Their earned commissions are often determined by multiplying their assigned commission rate by the amount of dollar sales. The dollar sales amount is computed by deducting any returned sales from the sum of their weekly sales. Given a biweekly period, the earned commission can be determined from the following formula:

Earned Commission = Rate × (Week 1 Sales + Week 2 Sales − Returns)

Let's assume that for the biweekly period, a salesperson's assigned commission rate is 15% and sales are $1,200 the first week, $1,500 the second week. The returned sales are $75.

Program 2.1 instructs the PC to compute the earned amount and display it on the screen. The earned commission of 393.75 is just below [run]. When you see [run] in this book, it signals you to press Shift + F5 (hold down one of the Shift keys and press the function key F5, and then release both keys) to execute the program. (See Figure 1.4 in Chapter 1 for the location of the Shift keys and function key F5 on your keyboard.)

PROGRAM 2.1

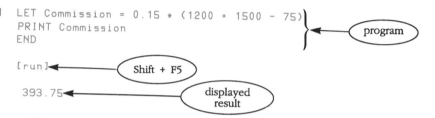

```
LET Commission = 0.15 * (1200 + 1500 - 75)
PRINT Commission
END

[run]

393.75
```

Keywords

There are three lines in this program. The first line contains a LET statement. The LET statement consists of the keyword LET, a variable name Commission, an equal sign, four **constants** (0.15, 1200, 1500 and 75), and three **arithmetic operators** (*, +, and −).

A **keyword** is a predefined word that has special meaning to QuickBASIC. It indicates the type of action to be performed. In Program 2.1, there are three keywords: LET, PRINT and END. Keywords are also called **reserved words**. (See the inside back cover of this book for a complete list of the QuickBASIC keywords.)

If a statement does not begin with a keyword and contains an equal sign, then QuickBASIC assumes it is a LET statement. For example, the first statement in Program 2.1 may be written in the following form:

```
Commission = 0.15 * (1200 + 1500 - 75)
```

Although the statement does not contain the keyword LET, it is still called a LET statement. It may also be referred to as an **assignment statement**. Except for Program 2.1, in this book all LET statements will be written without the keyword LET.

Variable Names and Constants

In programming, a **variable** is a location in main storage whose value can change as the program is executed. In Program 2.1, the variable name Commission references the storage location assigned to it by QuickBASIC. The first statement instructs the PC to complete the arithmetic operations and assign the resulting value of 393.75 to the storage location assigned to Commission. A **variable name** begins with a letter and may be followed by up to 39 letters, digits and decimal points. Keywords, such as LET, PRINT and END that have special meaning to QuickBASIC may not be used as a variable name.

The equal sign in any LET statement means that the value of the variable to the left of the equal sign is to be replaced by the final value of the expression to the right of the equal sign.

Constants, such as 0.15, 1200, 1500 and 75, represent ordinary numbers that do not change during the execution of a program. Both constants and variables are covered in detail in Chapter 3.

Arithmetic Operators

The **plus sign** (+) in the LET statement in line 1 of Program 2.1 signifies addition between the two constants that represent the weekly sales. The **minus sign** (–) indicates subtraction of the returned sales from the sum of the weekly sales. The **asterisk** (*) indicates multiplication between the rate and the actual sales. The seven QuickBASIC arithmetic operators are given in Table 2.1. As is the case in mathematics, the set of parentheses is used to override the normal sequence of arithmetic operations.

TABLE 2.1 The Seven Arithmetic Operators			
ARITHMETIC OPERATOR	**MEANING**	**EXAMPLES OF USAGE**	**MEANING OF THE EXAMPLES**
^	Exponentiation	2 ^ 3	Raise 2 to the third power, which in this example is 8.
*	Multiplication	6.1 * A1	Multiply the value of A1 by 6.1.
/	Division	H / 10	Divide the value of H by 10.
\	Integer Division	5 \ 3	The integer quotient of 5 divided by 3, which in this example is 1. (Operands are rounded to whole numbers.)
MOD	Modulo	5 MOD 3	The integer remainder of 5 divided by 3, which in this example is 2.
+	Addition	3.14 + 2.9	Add 3.14 and 2.9.
–	Subtraction	T - 35.4	Subtract 35.4 from the value of T.

The PRINT Statement

The second statement in Program 2.1 is called a PRINT statement. PRINT statements instruct the PC to bring a result out from main storage and display it on an output device. The statement causes the PC to display 393.75, the value of Commission. The PRINT statement is covered in detail in Chapter 3.

The END Statement

The last line of Program 2.1 includes the END statement. When executed, the END statement instructs the PC to stop executing the program. While the END statement is not required, it is recommended that you always include one.

Some Relationships Between Statements

The PRINT statement in Program 2.1 would display a result of zero if earlier in the program we had failed to instruct the PC to assign a value to the variable Commission. That is, the PC cannot correctly display the value of Commission before it determines this value. Therefore, if Program 2.1 were incorrectly written, as below, the PC would not display the correct results, unless by chance the earned commission was zero.

```
PRINT Commission
Commission = 0.15 * (1200 + 1500 - 75)          invalid
END

[run]

0
```

The following program is incorrect for the same reason:

```
Pay = 0.15 * (1200 + 1500 - 75)
PRINT Commission
END
```
}← invalid

```
[run]

  0
```

When this program is executed, the PC calculates a value of 393.75 for the variable Pay, but displays a result of zero. It displays zero because QuickBASIC assigns all numeric variables a value of zero before executing the first statement in the program, and the value of Commission is not assigned any value in the program itself.

The correct program can be written as Program 2.1 or as Program 2.2.

PROGRAM 2.2

```
Pay = 0.15 * (1200 + 1500 - 75)
PRINT Pay
END

[run]

393.75
```

Using the variable name Pay is no different from using the variable name Commission, as long as the same name is used consistently. The relationship between output statements, such as the PRINT statement, and other statements in a program can now be stated as follows:

OUTPUT RULE 1   *Every variable appearing in an output statement must have been previously defined in the program.*

Although the flexibility of the QuickBASIC language permits certain statements to be placed anywhere in a program, logic, common sense, and style dictate where these statements are placed. Style is nothing more than disciplined, consistent programming. Discipline and consistency help programmers construct readable, reliable, and maintainable programs.

2.2 THE INPUT STATEMENT

One of the major tasks of any computer program is to integrate the data to be processed into the program. In Programming Case Study 2, the data includes a rate of 15%, week 1 sales of $1,200, week 2 sales of $1,500, and return sales of $75. In Program 2.1, the data was included directly in the LET statement as constants. This technique has its limitations. For example, the LET statement must be modified each time a new salesperson is processed. An alternative method of integrating the data into the program is shown in Program 2.3.

PROGRAM 2.3

```
Rate = 0.15
Week1 = 1200           data as
Week2 = 1500          constants
Returns = 75
Commission = Rate * (Week1 + Week2 - Returns)
PRINT Commission
END

[run]

393.75
```

In this new program, data in the form of constants is assigned to the variables Rate, Week1, Week2 and Returns in the first four LET statements. The fifth LET statement, which calculates the earned commission, contains the variables that have been assigned the data. When it executes Program 2.3, the PC must be informed of the numeric values for Rate, Week1, Week2 and Returns before it can calculate a value for Commission. This can be generalized as follows:

ARITHMETIC RULE 1 *Every variable appearing to the right of the equal sign in a LET statement must be previously defined in the program.*

This second method of integrating the data into the program has the same limitations as Program 2.1. That is, the first four lines would have to be modified in order to process a new salesperson. The only advantage to Program 2.3 is that the LET statement that computes the commission in line 5 will work for any salesperson.

A third way to integrate data into the program is through the use of the INPUT statement. The INPUT statement provides for assignment of data to variables from a source outside the program during execution. The data is supplied during execution of the program.

Through the use of the INPUT statement, the solution to Programming Case Study 2 can be made more general for calculating the earned commission for any salesperson, no matter what his or her commission rate, weekly sales or returned sales. One version of the rewritten program is shown as Program 2.4.

PROGRAM 2.4

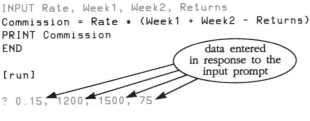

```
INPUT Rate, Week1, Week2, Returns
Commission = Rate * (Week1 + Week2 - Returns)
PRINT Commission
END

[run]

? 0.15, 1200, 1500, 75

393.75
```

data entered in response to the input prompt

The function of the INPUT statement in line 1 is to display an **input prompt** and suspend execution of the program until data has been supplied. QuickBASIC displays a **question mark** (?) for the input prompt. It is then up to the user to supply the data. It is necessary that the user press the Enter key following entry of the data.

Once the necessary data is supplied, the LET statement in line 2 determines the earned commission; line 3 prints the earned commission; and finally, line 4 terminates the program.

This third way of integrating data into a program, by means of the INPUT statement, is far more efficient than the other two ways, because we can process other sales personnel without modifying statements within the program. For example, to determine the earned commission for three salespeople, we can run the program three times, each time entering different data in response to the INPUT statements.

It is important that the variable names in the INPUT statement and the data supplied in response to the input prompt be separated by commas. A comma is used to establish a **list**, which is a set of distinct elements, each separated from the next by a comma. The comma must be used so that the PC can distinguish how many variables or data elements occur in each list. The order of the list of variables in the INPUT statement is also important. The INPUT statement in Program 2.4 INPUT Rate, Week1, Week2, Returns may have been written as

```
INPUT Returns, Week2, Week1, Rate
```

If so, however, the data supplied for Salesperson 1 must be entered as

```
? 75, 1500, 1200, 0.15
```

It is also important that the user respond with numeric data. For example, if the value 6AB were entered as the last item, rather than 75, then the PC would respond with the following message:

```
Redo from start
```

The same message will appear if too few data items are entered in response to the INPUT statement.

Input Prompt Message

To ensure that the data is entered in the proper sequence, QuickBASIC allows for an **input prompt message** to be placed in the INPUT statement. When the PC executes an INPUT statement containing an input prompt message, the message, rather than the question mark, is displayed on the screen. Execution is then suspended until the data is supplied. The following program requests one entry per INPUT statement:

PROGRAM 2.5

```
INPUT "Commission rate =====> ", Rate
INPUT "Week 1 sales ========> ", Week1
INPUT "Week 2 sales ========> ", Week2
INPUT "Return sales ========> ", Returns
Commission = Rate * (Week1 + Week2 - Returns)
PRINT Commission
END

[run]

Commission rate =====> 0.15
Week 1 sales ========> 1200
Week 2 sales ========> 1500
Return sales ========> 75
 393.75
```

When line 1 is executed in Program 2.5, the PC displays the input prompt message:

```
Commission rate =====>
```

After displaying the message requesting the commission rate, the PC suspends execution of the program until a response is entered.

If an acceptable response is entered, the PC displays the next input prompt message and suspends execution again. This process continues until the last INPUT statement has been executed.

After the last data item is entered for the INPUT statement in line 4, line 5 determines the earned commission. Then the PRINT statement in line 6 displays the earned commission, and finally, the END statement terminates the program.

The quotation marks (") surrounding the input prompt message and the comma (,) separating the message from the variable in the first four lines of Program 2.5 are required punctuation. If a semicolon (;) is used to separate the message from the variable, then a question mark (?) displays immediately after the input prompt message. For example, the following INPUT statement

```
INPUT "What is the commission rate"; Rate
```

displays the message followed by the question mark as shown here:

```
What is the commission rate?
```

Table 2.2 gives the general form of the INPUT statement. The INPUT statement consists of the keyword INPUT followed by an optional input prompt message, followed by a list of variables separated by mandatory commas. Here is the rule for determining the placement of the INPUT statement in a program:

INPUT RULE 1   *Every variable appearing in the program whose value is directly obtained through the keyboard must be listed in an INPUT statement before it is used elsewhere in the program.*

TABLE 2.2   The INPUT Statement

General Form: INPUT variable, . . ., variable

or

INPUT "input prompt message", variable, . . ., variable

Purpose: Provides for the assignment of values to variables from an external device, like the keyboard.

Examples:

INPUT Statements	Data from the keyboard
INPUT A	23.5
INPUT X, Y, Z	2, 4, 6
INPUT A$, B	Gross, -2.73
INPUT "Please enter the sales tax: ", T	0.05
INPUT "What is your name"; N$	John
INPUT "Part number ====> ", P	1289

Note: In the second general form, a question mark is displayed immediately after the input prompt message if a semicolon, rather than a comma, follows the message within quotation marks.

The INPUT statement allows the user complete interaction with the computer while the program executes. The main use of the INPUT statement is found in applications that involve the following:

1. Small amounts of data to be entered into a program
2. Data input that is dependent on the output or conditions of previous parts of a program
3. The processing of data as it occurs

This section on the INPUT statement has introduced you to one method of assigning values to variables in a program. Later, we will discuss two other methods that are used to process data, the READ and DATA statements (Chapter 5) and the use of data files (Chapters 7 and 10).

2.3   THE PRINT AND CLS STATEMENTS

One of the functions of the PRINT statement is to display the values of variables defined earlier in a program. You should understand by now that the following

```
X = 99
PRINT X
```

displays 99, the *value* of X, and not the letter X. The PRINT statement can also be used to display messages that identify a program result. This is shown by line 8 in Program 2.6 on the next page. Line numbers have been added to the left of Program 2.6 so that you can easily follow the program discussion.

PROGRAM 2.6

```
1    CLS
2    INPUT "Commission rate =====> ", Rate
3    INPUT "Week 1 sales ========> ", Week1
4    INPUT "Week 2 sales ========> ", Week2
5    INPUT "Return sales ========> ", Returns
6    Commission = Rate * (Week1 + Week2 - Returns)
7    PRINT
8    PRINT "Earned commission ===>"; Commission
9    END

     [run]

     Commission rate =====> 0.15
     Week 1 sales ========> 1200
     Week 2 sales ========> 1500
     Return sales ========> 75

     Earned commission ===> 393.75
```

As with the INPUT statement, it is necessary in a PRINT statement to begin and end a message with quotation marks. The quotation marks in a PRINT statement inform Quick-BASIC that the item to be displayed is a message rather than a variable.

The semicolon following the message in line 8 instructs the PC to keep the cursor exactly where it is on the screen following the display of the message in quotation marks. The **cursor** is a movable, blinking marker on the screen that indicates where the next point of character entry, change or display will be. This means that the value of Commission will display immediately after the message.

QuickBASIC displays a numeric value which consists of a sign, the decimal representation and a **trailing space**. Appearing immediately before the number, the sign is a **leading space** if the number is positive or zero and a **leading minus sign** if the number is negative. The space following the message displayed by line 8 in Program 2.6 represents the sign of the variable Commission as shown below:

Clearing the Screen — The CLS Statement

One of the responsibilities of the programmer is to ensure that the prompt messages and results are meaningful and easy to read. A cluttered screen on a monitor can make it difficult for you to locate necessary information. QuickBASIC includes the CLS statement, which erases the information on the output screen and places the cursor in the upper left corner. The **output screen** is the one that shows the results due to the execution of the current program. We will talk more about the output screen later in this chapter. The CLS statement is usually one of the first statements to be executed in a program. The general form of the CLS statement is found in Table 2.3.

TABLE 2.3 The CLS Statement	
General Form:	CLS
Purpose:	Erases the information on the output screen.
Example:	CLS

Consider again Program 2.6. When the program is executed, the PC clears the output screen due to the CLS statement in line 1. Next, it displays the input prompt message

```
Commission rate =====>
```

as the first line of output. After obtaining a response through the keyboard, the PC displays the next input prompt message, and the rest of the program is executed. Line 7 in Program 2.6, which contains a PRINT statement without a list, shows how to instruct the PC to display a blank line in order to separate the input prompt messages from the results. A **null list** or **empty list** like this causes the PRINT statement to display a blank line.

2.4 CODING AND DOCUMENTING

In the preceding programs, only one statement is written on each line, and the first letter in each statement is always written under the first letter of the statement above it. A program written in such a form is usually easier to read and debug, which is the process of removing errors from a program. As you will discover now, however, this is only an optional practice.

Coding Techniques

A QuickBASIC program can be written on an ordinary sheet of paper. However, it is sometimes more convenient to write it on a specially printed sheet of paper called a **coding form**. Figure 2.2 shows Program 2.7 written on a coding form.

FIGURE 2.2

Program 2.7 written on a coding form.

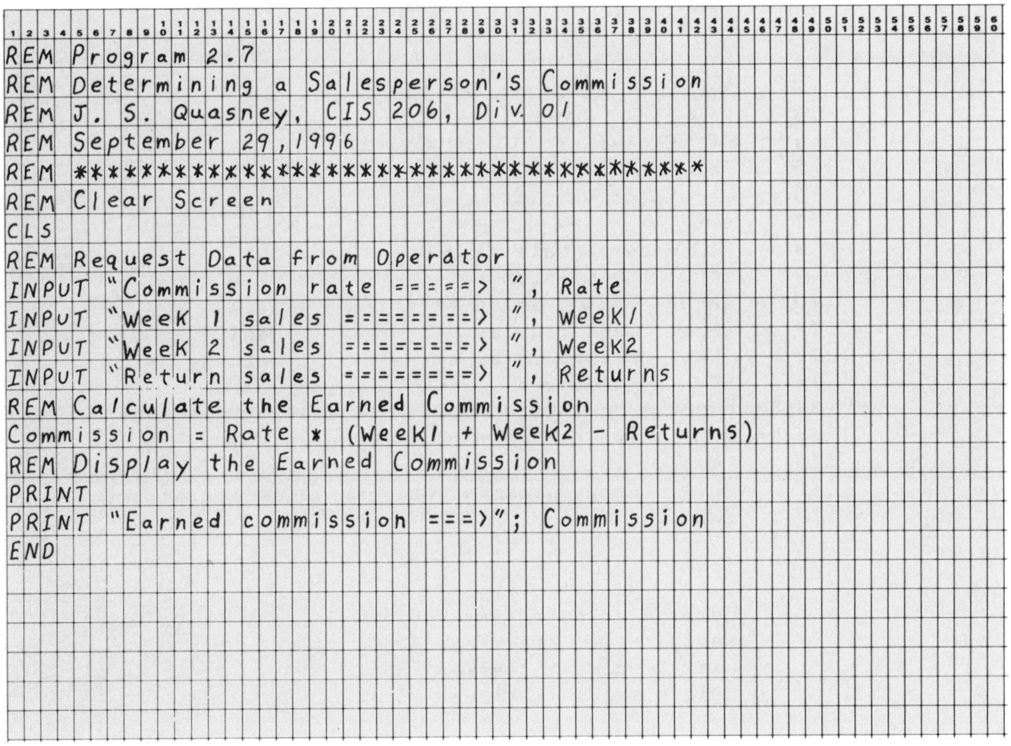

```
REM Program 2.7
REM Determining a Salesperson's Commission
REM J. S. Quasney, CIS 206, Div. 01
REM September 29, 1996
REM ******************************************
REM Clear Screen
CLS
REM Request Data from Operator
INPUT "Commission rate =====> ", Rate
INPUT "Week 1 sales ========> ", Week1
INPUT "Week 2 sales ========> ", Week2
INPUT "Return sales ========> ", Returns
REM Calculate the Earned Commission
Commission = Rate * (Week1 + Week2 - Returns)
REM Display the Earned Commission
PRINT
PRINT "Earned commission ===>"; Commission
END
```

The coding form is divided into columns identified by the numbers near the top of the form. When constructing a QuickBASIC statement, place the first letter in each statement, such as the P in PRINT, in column one.

The **space**, or **blank**, is also a character. It is obtained on a keyboard by pressing the Spacebar once for each blank character desired. The blank character may be used freely to improve the appearance of the program. A useful rule of thumb for blank characters is this: Leave spaces in a statement in the same places that you would leave spaces in an English sentence. If you don't, QuickBASIC will automatically insert spaces around the equal sign, around any arithmetic operator, and after the comma and semicolon in a list. QuickBASIC will also insert a semicolon followed by a space if no punctuation mark is placed between two items in a PRINT statement.

Capitalize the first letter of all variable names. Follow the first letter with lowercase letters. For example, use Commission, rather than COMMISSION or commission. All three of these variable names refer to the same storage location, but it is good practice to be consistent in the way you capitalize variable names.

Keywords are always capitalized. However, you may enter the keyword in lowercase. QuickBASIC will immediately capitalize all the letters in the keyword when the Enter key is pressed. Finally, for purposes of readability, QuickBASIC allows you to enter blank lines in a program. (For additional programming style tips, see Section C.5 in Appendix C.)

Documenting a Program — The REM Statement

Documentation is the readable description of what a program or procedure within a program is supposed to do. More often than not, programmers are asked to support the programs they write by means of internal comments. Documentation is used to identify programs and clarify parts of a program that would otherwise be difficult for others to understand.

The REM statements in Program 2.7, lines 1 through 6, 8, 13, and 15, are called **remark lines** or **comment lines**. The remark line consists of the keyword REM followed by a comment, or explanation, intended solely for programmers. A REM statement can be located anywhere in a program.

PROGRAM 2.7

```
1     REM Program 2.7
2     REM Determining a Salesperson's Commission
3     REM J. S. Quasney, CIS 206, Div. 01
4     REM September 29, 1996
5     REM **************************************
6     REM Clear Screen
7     CLS
8     REM Request Data from Operator
9     INPUT "Commission rate =====> ", Rate
10    INPUT "Week 1 sales ========> ", Week1
11    INPUT "Week 2 sales ========> ", Week2
12    INPUT "Return sales ========> ", Returns
13    REM Calculate the Earned Commission
14    Commission = Rate * (Week1 + Week2 - Returns)
15    REM Display the Earned Commission
16    PRINT
17    PRINT "Earned commission ===>"; Commission
18    END

[run]

Commission rate =====> 0.15
Week 1 sales ========> 1200
Week 2 sales ========> 1500
Return sales ========> 75

Earned commission ===> 393.75
```

REM statements are nonexecutable, which means they have no effect on the results of a QuickBASIC program. Program 2.7, which includes REM statements, and Program 2.6, which does not, both produce the same results. However, REM statements do take up space in main storage.

QuickBASIC permits you to use an apostrophe (') as an abbreviation for the keyword REM. QuickBASIC also permits the placement of a remark or comment on the right-hand side of a statement by requiring the insertion of an apostrophe before the comment. The following two lines are valid:

```
' Initialization Routine
CLS          ' Clear Screen
```

The general form for the REM statement is found in Table 2.4.

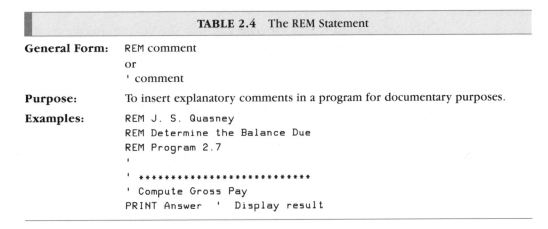

TABLE 2.4   The REM Statement

General Form:	REM comment
	or
	' comment
Purpose:	To insert explanatory comments in a program for documentary purposes.
Examples:	REM J. S. Quasney
	REM Determine the Balance Due
	REM Program 2.7
	'
	' **************************
	' Compute Gross Pay
	PRINT Answer ' Display result

Here are a few basic suggestions for including explanatory remarks in a program.

1. Write and include your remarks as you code the program.
2. Write a prologue, including the program name, date, author and any other desirable remarks, at the beginning of each program. (See Section 2.13.)
3. Remark lines should come before any major procedure in a program.
4. Variable names should be defined when it is not apparent what they represent.
5. Use remark lines only where the code is not self-explanatory. Do not insert remarks for their own sake. Insert them to make your program readable.

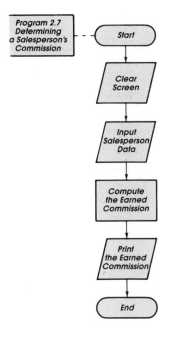

FIGURE 2.3

A general flowchart for Program 2.7.

Program Flowcharts

A general flowchart that corresponds to Program 2.7 is shown in Figure 2.3. A flowchart does not have to include a symbol for each statement in the program. For example, the four INPUT statements in Program 2.7 are represented by the single input/output (I/O) symbol "Input Salesperson Data," which follows the "Clear Screen" symbol in the flowchart in Figure 2.3. Furthermore, it is not necessary to include an annotation symbol in the flowchart for every REM statement.

Multiple Statements Per Line

QuickBASIC allows you to write multiple statements per line, up to a maximum of 255 characters. For example, Program 2.2 can be rewritten as the following:

```
' Program 2.2
Pay = 0.15 * (1200 + 1500 - 75) : PRINT Pay : END
```

The statements in the second line are separated by colons. The purpose of the colon is to inform QuickBASIC that a statement has ended and that a new statement follows on the same line.

Do not precede any statement with a REM statement when using multiple statements per line. QuickBASIC considers all characters following the keyword REM or the apostrophe (') to be a comment, including the colon. For the purpose of readability, it is recommended that you use multiple statements per line sparingly.

2.5   GETTING ACQUAINTED WITH THE QB OPERATING ENVIRONMENT

To enter a program, like Program 2.7, into the PC and execute it, you must familiarize yourself with the QB operating environment.

Starting a QuickBASIC Session

Boot the PC following the steps outlined by your instructor, or those found in the PC's Operations manual. Once the PC is operational, you start QuickBASIC by loading it into main storage. If you are using MS-DOS QBASIC (the version that comes with DOS 5.0 or later), follow the steps in Table 2.5 if you are using the DOS Shell. Use Table 2.6 if you are starting QuickBASIC from the DOS prompt.

If you are using the commercial version of QuickBASIC, change to the subdirectory containing the QuickBASIC program and type QB followed by the Enter key.

Several seconds will elapse while the QuickBASIC program is loaded from the disk into main storage. The status light on the disk drive turns on during this loading process. After the QuickBASIC program is loaded into main storage, it is automatically executed.

TABLE 2.5   Loading MS-DOS QBASIC from the DOS Shell

1.   Place your data disk in one of the disk drives.

2.   With the DOS Shell Window on the screen, use the Tab key to move the highlight down to the Program-list area titled Main.

3.   Use the Up and Down arrow keys to highlight MS-DOS QBASIC and press the Enter key.

TABLE 2.6   Loading MS-DOS QBASIC from the DOS Prompt

1.   Place your data disk in one of the disk drives.

2.   At the DOS prompt, type QBASIC and press the Enter key.

The first screen displayed by QuickBASIC includes a Welcome message. In the Welcome message, QuickBASIC directs you to press the Esc key to display the QB screen (Figure 2.4) to begin entering a program or press the Enter key to obtain help from the QB Advisor. The **QB Advisor** is an on-line help system that answers your questions about QuickBASIC as fast as you can click the mouse or press the F1 key. The QB Advisor is discussed in more detail later in Section 2.9.

The QB Screen

There are four parts to the QB screen — the view window, menu bar, immediate window, and the status line as shown in Figure 2.4.

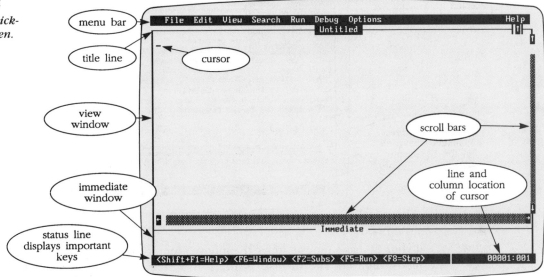

FIGURE 2.4

The QB (Quick-BASIC) screen.

View Window. The **view window** is the largest part of the screen, and the one that contains the cursor (Figure 2.4). In the view window, you can enter, modify, and display programs. When the QuickBASIC program first executes, the view window is active. That is, if you start typing characters, they will appear on the first line of the view window. At the top of the view window is the title line. The **title line** displays the name of the current program. The program title is highlighted when the view window is active. The program is called "Untitled" until it is given a name. Program names will be discussed shortly.

Along the bottom and the right side of the view window are the scroll bars. If you have a mouse, you can move the pointer along the scroll bars and move the window in any direction to see code that does not appear in the view window. (See Appendix B for additional information on moving the window in any direction.)

Menu Bar. The **menu bar**, the line at the very top of the QB screen (Figure 2.4), displays a list of menu names. Each menu name has a corresponding menu of commands. These commands are useful when entering and modifying programs. In this chapter, we will discuss the most often used commands. (See Appendix B for a complete listing and description of all the QuickBASIC commands.)

To activate the menu bar, press the **Alt key**. Next, type the first letter of the name of the menu you want to open. You can also select a menu by using the Right Arrow and Left Arrow keys to highlight the menu name. With the menu name highlighted, press the Enter key. QuickBASIC immediately displays a *pull-down menu* that lists a series of commands. Figure 2.5 on the next page shows the File menu which is superimposed over the display of Program 2.7. To deactivate the menu bar or any menu and activate the view window, press the Esc key.

FIGURE 2.5

The File menu.

file menu is "pulled down" when File is selected from menu bar

status line describes highlighted command in the File menu

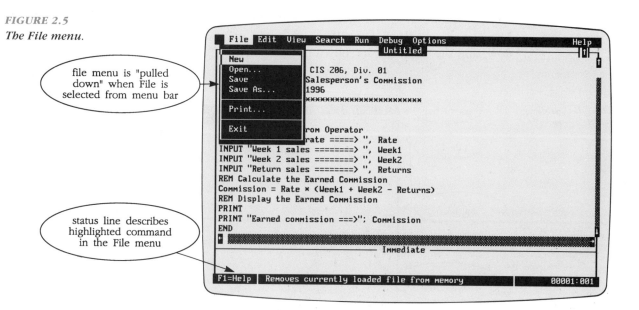

If your PC has a mouse, move the mouse pointer to the desired menu name and click the mouse button. The **mouse pointer** is a character-sized, rectangular box on the screen. The **mouse button** is the left button on the mouse. To deactivate the menu bar and reactivate the view window, move the mouse pointer to any part of the view window and click the mouse button.

Immediate Window. The narrow window below the view window is called the **immediate window**. The immediate window is used to execute statements as soon as they are entered. Statements entered in the immediate window are not part of the current program.

At any time, you can activate the immediate window by pressing the function key F6. This moves the cursor from the view window to the immediate window. Quick-BASIC highlights the word Immediate. The function key F6 is like a **toggle switch**. Press it once, and the cursor moves from the view window to the immediate window. Press it again, and the cursor moves back to the view window. Use of the immediate window as a calculator and debugging tool is discussed in Chapter 3 and in Appendix C.

If you have a mouse, move the pointer to the inactive window and click the mouse button.

Status Line. The line at the very bottom of the QB screen is the status line. This line contains a list of the most often used function keys and the line and column location of the cursor on the screen. Keyboard indicators, such as C for Caps Lock and N for Num Lock, display immediately to the left of the cursor line and column location counter when these keys are engaged.

If the menu bar is active and one of the menus is selected, then the status line displays the function of the highlighted command in the menu (Figure 2.5).

Dialog Boxes

QuickBASIC uses **dialog boxes** to display messages and request information from you. For example, if you use a keyword for a variable name, such as PRINT LET instead of PRINT Bet, QuickBASIC displays a dialog box when you move the cursor off the line containing the invalid variable name LET. You move the cursor off the line by pressing the Enter key or the Up or Down Arrow key.

The dialog box, shown in Figure 2.6, displays if you attempt to end the QuickBASIC session and return control to DOS without saving the latest changes made to the program in the view window. Dialog boxes list acceptable user responses in buttons and text boxes. **Buttons** are labelled to indicate what they represent. **Text boxes** are used to enter information, such as a file name.

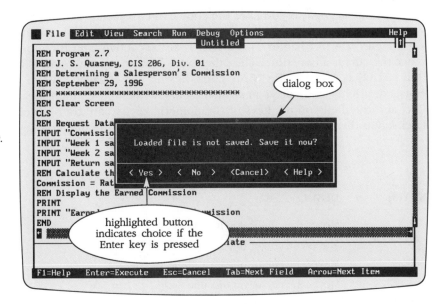

FIGURE 2.6

QuickBASIC displays a dialog box in the middle of the screen when it requires a response from the user before it can continue.

In response to the message in the dialog box in Figure 2.6, you can use the Tab key or mouse pointer to select one of four buttons — Yes, No, Cancel or Help. When you press the Enter key, the highlighted button, the one with the cursor, is selected. Table 2.7 summarizes the important keys for responding to a dialog box.

If your PC has a mouse, move the mouse pointer to the desired button or text box and click the mouse button.

TABLE 2.7 Important Keys for Responding to a Dialog Box*

KEY(S)	RESULT
Alt	Highlights letters in all boxes and buttons. Type the letter while the Alt key is pressed to activate the box or select the button.
Esc	Causes the dialog box to disappear and activates the view window.
Enter	Selects the highlighted button.
Shift + Tab	Moves the cursor to the previous button or text box.
Tab	Moves the cursor to the next button or text box.
Y, N, or H	Selects the corresponding button without requiring that you press the Enter key.
Mouse	Clicks on the desired box or button.

* The plus sign between the two keys means hold down the first key and press the second key, and then release both keys.

Cursor Movement Keys

Several keys on the keyboard are used to move the cursor on the screen. These keys are called the **cursor movement keys**. The arrow keys are used to move the cursor in the windows, menu bar, or menu, one position at a time. Other keys, such as the **Home** and **End keys**, are used to move the cursor more than one position at a time. The cursor movement keys are summarized in Table 2.8.

On some keyboards you have the choice of two sets of cursor movement keys. Both sets carry out the same functions. One set is immediately to the right of the typewriter keys (Figure 1.4 in Chapter 1). This set is always active, and therefore, may be used to move the cursor at any time. The other set is located on the numeric keypad. This set is only active as long as the **Num Lock key** is not engaged. When the Num Lock is engaged, a letter N displays next to the cursor line and column location on the status line, and the digits on the keys of the numeric keypad are transmitted. When the Num Lock key is disengaged, the cursor movement keys on the numeric keypad are active.

TABLE 2.8 Cursor Movement Keys*

KEY(S)	RESULT
↓	Moves the cursor down one line.
←	Moves the cursor one position to the left.
→	Moves the cursor one position to the right.
↑	Moves the cursor up one line.
Home	Moves the cursor left to the beginning position on the same line.
End	Moves the cursor right to the last position on the same line.
Ctrl + →	Moves the cursor one word to the right.
Ctrl + ←	Moves the cursor one word to the left.
Ctrl + Q, E	Moves the cursor to the top of the screen.
Ctrl + Q, X	Moves the cursor to the bottom of the screen.
Page Down	Moves the view window down one full screen (page) of lines.
Page Up	Moves the view window up one full screen (page) of lines.
Ctrl + Home	Moves the cursor to the first character in the first line of the program.
Ctrl + End	Moves the cursor to the last character in the last line of the program.
Mouse Device	Moves the mouse pointer to any character position on the screen. Click the mouse button, and the cursor moves to the location of the mouse pointer.

* The plus sign between two keys means hold down the first key and press the second key, and then release both keys. A comma between two keys means press and release the first key, and then press and release the second key.

Function Keys

IBM-type keyboards include a set of ten or twelve **function keys**, also called **PF keys**, which are located to the far left side of the keyboard or along the top of the typewriter keys (Figure 1.4 in Chapter 1). The function keys are labelled F1 through F10 or F12. Pressing these keys instructs QuickBASIC to carry out various tasks. For example, if you press function key F1 with the cursor in a keyword, QuickBASIC displays a help screen. If you press Shift + F5, then QuickBASIC executes the current program in the view window. Table 2.9 summarizes the often used function keys and their associated tasks. (For a complete list, see the reference card in the back of this book.)

FUNCTION KEY	RESULT
	TABLE 2.9 Often Used Function Keys in QuickBASIC
F1	Displays a help screen regarding the keyword or symbol that the cursor is on.
Shift + F1	Activates the QB Advisor on-line help facility system.
F4	Displays the output screen.
Shift + F5	Executes the current program.
F6	Activates the next window on the screen.
F8	Executes the current program, one line at a time.

Terminating a QuickBASIC Session

To terminate your QuickBASIC session, press the Alt key to activate the menu bar. With the cursor on the word File, type the letter F or press the Enter key to display the File menu (Figure 2.5). Next, type the letter X for Exit or use the arrow keys to move the cursor to the word Exit and press the Enter key. Thus, the sequence of keystrokes Alt, F, X instructs the PC to return control to DOS. To quit QuickBASIC using a mouse, click on File in the menu bar and click on Exit in the File menu. The term *click on* means move the mouse pointer to the specified word and click the mouse button.

If you did not save the latest version of the current program, then the dialog box shown earlier in Figure 2.6 appears. QuickBASIC requests that you select one of the buttons before continuing. An alternative to selecting a button is to press the Esc key, which cancels the command and returns control to the view window.

When the DOS prompt appears, remove your diskettes from the disk drives. Turn the PC's power switch to Off. Turn the monitor power switch to Off. Finally, if using a printer, turn the power switch to Off.

2.6   EDITING QUICKBASIC PROGRAMS

QuickBASIC programs are entered one line at a time into the view window. The Enter key signals QuickBASIC that a line is complete. During the process of entering a program, it is easy to make keyboard errors and grammatical errors because of your inexperience with the QuickBASIC language and your unfamiliarity with the keyboard. Logical errors can also occur in a program if you have not considered all the details associated with the problem.

Some of the errors can be eliminated if you use coding forms and logic tools and if you carefully review your design and program before you enter it into the view window. Any remaining errors are resolved by editing the program. **Editing** is the process of entering and altering a program.

The remainder of this section describes the most common types of editing. You will find the editing features of QuickBASIC to be both powerful and easy to use. (For additional editing features, see Appendix B.)

Deleting Previously Typed Characters.   Use the arrow keys or mouse to position the cursor. Press the **Delete key** to delete the character under the cursor and the **Backspace key** to delete the character to the left of the cursor.

To delete a series of adjacent characters in a line, position the cursor on the leftmost character to be deleted. Hold down one of the Shift keys and press the Right Arrow key until the characters to delete are highlighted. Press the Delete key.

If you have a mouse, select the adjacent characters to delete by moving the pointer from the first character to the last while holding down the mouse button.

Changing or Replacing Previously Typed Lines.   Move the cursor to the character position where you want to make a change. Begin typing the new characters. QuickBASIC is by default in the insert mode. In the **insert mode**, the cursor is a blinking underline, and the character under the cursor and those to the right are *pushed* to the right as you enter new characters in the line. In the **overtype mode**, the cursor is a blinking box, and the character under the cursor is replaced by the one you type. Use the **Insert key** to toggle between the insert and overtype modes. As you enter new characters in these modes, they replace the old characters.

Adding New Lines.   Press the Enter key to add a new or blank line. To add a new line above the current line, move the cursor to the first character in the line and press the Enter key. To add a new line below the current line, move the cursor immediately to the right of the last character and press the Enter key.

The Enter key should only be pressed with the cursor at the beginning or end of a line. If you press the Enter key in the middle of a line, it is split. To join the split lines, press the Backspace key with the cursor on the first character of the second line.

Deleting a Series of Lines.   Position the cursor at the beginning or end of the series of lines to delete. Hold down one of the Shift keys and press the Up Arrow or Down Arrow key to highlight the series of lines. Press the Delete key.

If you have a mouse, highlight the lines to delete by holding down the mouse button and moving the pointer from the first character to the last in the series of lines. With the lines highlighted, press the Delete key.

Moving Text.   Moving text from one location to another in a program is called **cut and paste**. To cut and paste text, do the following:

1. Use the arrow keys or mouse to move the cursor to the beginning of the text you want to move.

2. Hold down one of the Shift keys and use the arrow keys to select the text. If you are using a mouse, click the mouse button and move the pointer to select the text.
3. Hold down one of the Shift keys and press the Delete key to *cut* the text. The deleted text is placed in the clipboard. The **clipboard** is a temporary storage area that contains the last text deleted through the use of the Shift and Delete keys.
4. Move the cursor to the new location using the arrow keys or the mouse. Hold down one of the Shift keys and press the Insert key to *paste* the text.

Copying Lines.   Copying text from one location to another in a program is called **pasting**. To paste text, do the following:

1. Use the arrow keys or mouse to move the cursor to the beginning of the text you want to paste.

2. Hold down one of the Shift keys and use the arrow keys to select the text. If you are using a mouse, hold down the mouse button and move the pointer to select the text.
3. Hold down the Ctrl key and press the Insert key to copy the text into the clipboard.
4. Move the cursor to the new location using the arrow keys or the mouse. Hold down one of the Shift keys and press the Insert key to *paste* the text.

Table 2.10 summarizes the primary keys used to edit a program. Some of these keys are called **shortcut keys** because they execute a command found in one of the command menus.

TABLE 2.10 Primary Keys Used to Edit a Program*	
KEY(S)	**RESULT**
Backspace	Deletes the character to the left of the cursor.
Delete	Deletes the character under the cursor or the highlighted text.
Enter	Inserts a new or blank line.
Insert	Switches QuickBASIC between insert and overtype modes.
Ctrl + Insert	Copies highlighted text to the clipboard.
Shift + any arrow key	Highlights (selects) text.
Shift + Delete	Cuts (deletes) highlighted text and places it into the clipboard.
Shift + Insert	Pastes (inserts) at the location of the cursor text from the clipboard.

* The plus sign between two keys means hold down the first key, press the second key, and then release both keys.

2.7 EXECUTING PROGRAMS AND HARD-COPY OUTPUT

The menu bar at the top of the screen contains eight menu names (Figure 2.4). Each menu name has a menu of commands. As indicated earlier, to activate the menu bar, press the Alt key. Next, open a menu in one of two ways: (1) type the first letter in the menu name; or (2) use the Left or Right Arrow keys to move the cursor to the menu name and press the Enter key.

If you have a mouse, you can activate the menu bar and select the menu name by moving the pointer to the desired menu name and clicking the mouse button.

Perhaps the two most important menu names are Run and File. The Run menu is primarily used to execute the current program. The File menu contains several important commands. One in particular, the Print command, is used to print all or part of the current program.

Executing the Current Program

You execute, or run, the current program by selecting the Start command in the Run menu (Figure 2.7). The Start command can be selected in three different ways as described in Table 2.11 on the next page.

FIGURE 2.7
The Run menu.

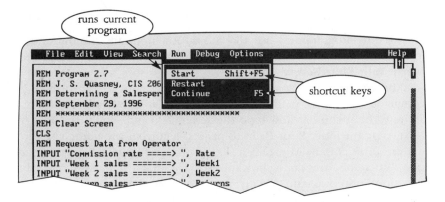

TABLE 2.11	Executing the Current Program
METHOD	**DESCRIPTION**
Menu	Press the Alt key to activate the menu bar. Type the letter R to select the **R**un menu. Type the letter S for **S**tart or press the Enter key since Start is highlighted.
Shortcut keys	Press Shift + F5
Mouse	Click on Run in the menu bar and click on Start in the Run menu.

When the program first executes, QuickBASIC replaces the QB screen with the output screen. The **output screen** shows the results due to the execution of the current program. Figure 2.8 shows the output screen for Program 2.7. After reading the output results, you can redisplay the QB screen by pressing any key on the keyboard. This is indicated at the bottom of the output screen. To redisplay the output results, press the function key F4.

The remaining commands in the Run menu are described in Appendix B.

FIGURE 2.8

The output screen.

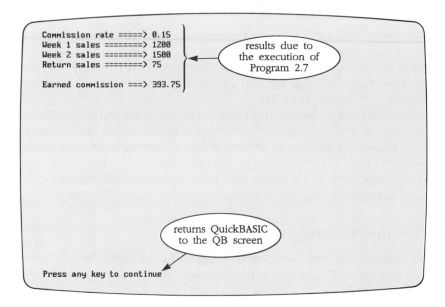

Listing Program Lines to the Printer

Most BASIC programmers use a keyboard for input and a monitor for output. In many instances, it is desirable to list the program and the results on a printer. A listing of this type is called **hard-copy output**.

You can list all or part of the current program to the printer by using the Print command in the File menu. With the printer in the Ready mode, press the Alt key to activate the menu bar and type the letter F to pull down the **F**ile menu (Figure 2.9). Next, type the letter P for **P**rint to print the current program. The three periods following the Print command means a dialog box will appear requesting additional information. When the Print dialog box appears (Figure 2.10), make sure the bullet is next to the selection Entire Program. Finally, press the Enter key.

If you have a mouse, click on File, click on Print, and click on OK when the Print dialog box appears.

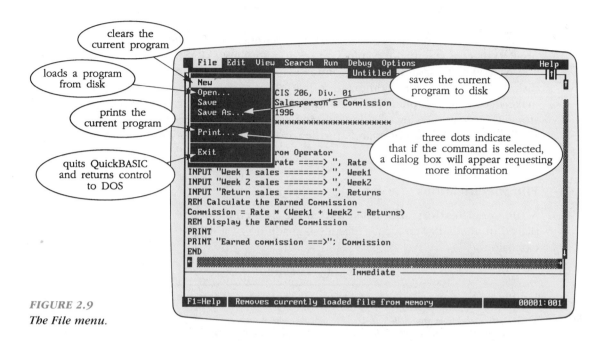

FIGURE 2.9
The File menu.

Listing a Portion of the Program to the Printer

To print a portion of the current program, use the Shift key and arrow keys (or the mouse) to highlight the lines in the program you want to print. Next, follow the steps outlined in the previous paragraphs for printing the program. When the Print dialog box appears on the screen, the bullet should be in front of Selected Text (Figure 2.10). QuickBASIC automatically assigns the bullet to Selected Text when a series of lines is selected prior to issuing the Print command.

FIGURE 2.10
Dialog box for the Print command.

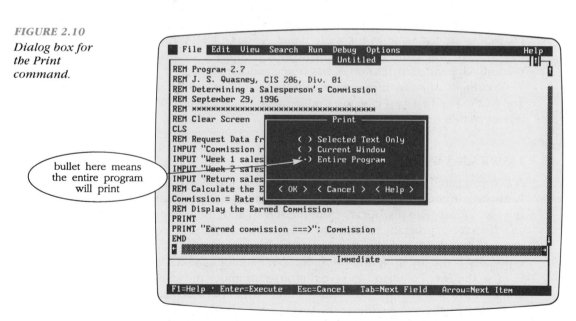

Printing the Results on the Output Screen

To print a copy of the output screen, press Print Screen (Shift + PrtSc on older keyboards) while the output screen displays on the monitor. Later in Chapter 3, we will discuss the LPRINT statement as an alternative means to generating hard-copy output.

2.8   SAVING, LOADING, AND ERASING PROGRAMS

Besides the Print command, there are four additional commands in the File menu (Figure 2.9) that are essential for your first session with QuickBASIC — Save, Save As, Open, and New. The Save and Save As commands allow you to store the current program to disk. Later, use the Open command to load the program from disk into main storage to make it the current one. The New command erases the current program from main storage. It clears the view window and indicates the beginning of a new program. Before we discuss these four commands further, it is important that you understand the concept of a file specification.

File Specifications

A **file specification**, also called a **filespec**, is used to identify programs and data files placed in auxiliary storage. A filespec is made up of a device name, file name, and an extension.

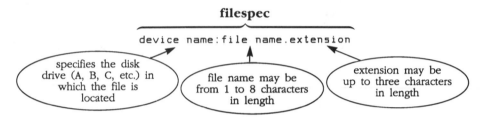

The device name refers to the disk drive. If no device is specified, then the filespec refers to the default drive of the PC. If a device name is included in the filespec, then it must be followed by a colon.

File names may be anywhere from 1 to 8 characters in length. Valid characters are uppercase or lowercase A–Z, 0–9, and certain special characters ($ & # @ ! % " ( ) – { } _ / \). If an extension is used, then the file name must be followed by a period.

An extension that is up to 3 characters in length may be used to classify a file. Valid characters are the same as for a file name. With QuickBASIC, the default extension is bas. That is, when you use a command that requires a filespec, QuickBASIC will automatically append an extension of bas if one is not included.

Examples of valid filespecs include b:payroll, b:LAB2-1, PAYROLL.BAS, Accounts and S123. The first two examples reference files on drive B. The latter three examples reference files on the default drive.

Saving the Current Program to Disk

When you enter a program through the keyboard, it is stored in main storage (RAM), and it displays in the view window. When you quit QuickBASIC or turn the computer off, the current program disappears from the screen and, more importantly, from main storage. To save a program to disk for later use, use the Save command or the Save As command in the File menu. (See Appendix B for additional information on saving files, especially if you are using the commercial version of QuickBASIC.)

Use the Save command to save the program under the same name. Use the Save As command to save the program under a new name. Because this is the first time we are saving the program, we will use the Save As command.

To select the Save As command, press the Alt key to activate the menu bar. Type the letter F to pull down the **F**ile menu (Figure 2.9). Type the letter A for Save **A**s. Here again, the three periods following the Save As command mean QuickBASIC requires additional information. In this case it needs to know the filespec.

When the Save As dialog box appears (Figure 2.11), enter the file name and press the Enter key. In Figure 2.11, we entered the file name prg2-7. QuickBASIC stores the current program using the filespec a:prg2-7.bas. Note in Figure 2.11 that the default drive (A:\) is specified below the file name box.

FIGURE 2.11

Dialog box for the Save As command.

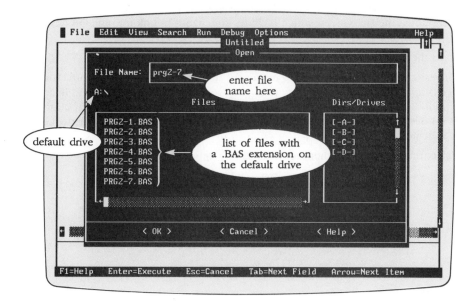

The **dirs/drives box** in the lower portion of the Save As dialog box includes a list of the disk drives and any subdirectories that are part of the current default drive. You may use the Tab key or mouse to activate this box and select a different default drive.

If you loaded the current program from disk or saved the program earlier, the file name will be in the file name box when you issue the Save As command. To save the program under the old file name, press the Enter key. To change the file name, just begin typing. What you type replaces the old name. In this case, the old file remains in its present form, and a new file is created on disk.

To save the current program using a mouse, click on File and click on Save As. Enter the name in the file name box and click on the OK button.

FIGURE 2.12

Dialog box for the Open Program command.

Loading a Program from Disk

To load a program stored on disk into main storage, use the Open command in the File menu (Figure 2.9). This command causes the dialog box shown in Figure 2.12 to display.

In the middle of the dialog box, QuickBASIC displays the files box. The **files box** lists the file names on the default drive that have an extension of bas. The current default drive displays just above the files box. To display any other directory on your PC, enter the disk drive, or path, in the file name box or select one from the dirs/ drive box and press the Enter key.

In the file name box, enter the name of the program you want to load from auxiliary storage into main storage. In Figure 2.12 we entered the file name prg2-7. Enter the file name by typing it on the keyboard, or use the Tab key and arrow keys to select the file name from the file name box. Each time you press an arrow key, the name of the program under the cursor displays in the file name box. To complete the command, press the Enter key.

If you did not save the current program before attempting to load a new one, Quick-BASIC will give you the opportunity to save it before it loads the new program into main storage.

To load a program from disk using the mouse, click on File and click on Open. Double click on the name of the program in the files box.

Starting a New Program

The New command in the File menu (Figure 2.9) instructs QuickBASIC to erase the current program from main storage. This also clears the view window. Use this command when you are finished with the current program and wish to start a new one from scratch. Note that it is not necessary to clear the current program if you are loading a program from disk. The Open command clears main storage before it loads the new program.

2.9   THE QB ADVISOR ON-LINE HELP SYSTEM

The QB Advisor is a fully integrated on-line help system with instant access to any QuickBASIC question. You can request immediate help when you first enter QuickBASIC by pressing the Enter key rather than the Esc key. Thereafter, at any time while you are using QuickBASIC, you can interact with the QB Advisor and display help screens on any QuickBASIC topic using the keys described in Table 2.12. The QB Advisor is literally a complete reference manual at your fingertips.

	TABLE 2.12 QB Advisor Help Keys
KEY(S)	**RESULT**
Alt + H	Pulls down the Help menu which includes commands to link into the QB Advisor (Figure 2.15).
Esc	Exits the QB Advisor and activates the view window.
F1	Displays **context-sensitive help** menus for the topic the cursor is within. For example, position the cursor within a keyword, menu name, command in a pull-down menu, or any symbol and press the F1 key or click the **right button** on the mouse. Figure 2.14 shows the context-sensitive help screen for the LET statement.
Right Button on mouse	
Help Button	Select the Help button whenever a dialog box appears on the screen.
Shift + F1	Displays the general help screen shown in Figure 2.13.

FIGURE 2.13

The initial Help screen when you press Shift + F1.

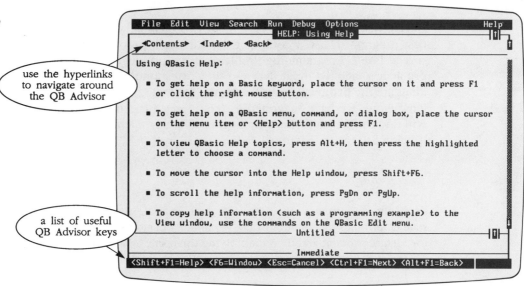

The best way to familiarize yourself with the QB Advisor is to use it. Question 14 in the Test Your BASIC Skills section of this chapter asks that you display and print several help screens.

FIGURE 2.14

The Help screen for the keyword LET.

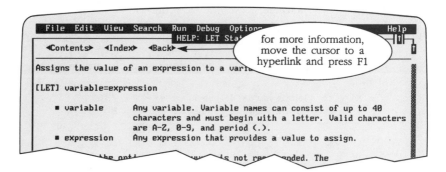

FIGURE 2.15

The Help menu.

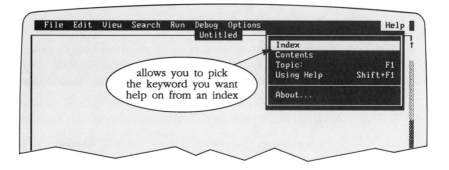

2.10   A GUIDE TO WRITING YOUR FIRST PROGRAM

Having read the first nine sections of this chapter, you should be ready to write your first program to use a computer for solving a problem. At the end of Chapter 2 are several BASIC Programming Problems. Each problem includes a short statement of the problem, suggested input data and the corresponding output results. Collectively, these items are the **program specifications**. Following the sample BASIC Programming Problem below, we have suggested a step-by-step procedure for solving the problem. You will find this helpful when you begin solving problems on your own. You will also find it helpful to review Section 1.6 on page 12.

Sample BASIC Programming Problem: Computation of State Tax

Problem: Construct a program that will compute the state tax owed by a taxpayer. The state determines the amount of tax by taking a person's yearly income, subtracting $500.00 for each dependent and then multiplying the result by 2% to determine the tax due. Use the following formula:

Tax = 0.02 * (Income – 500 * Dependents)

Code the program so that it will request that the taxpayer's income and the number of dependents be entered through the keyboard.

Input Data: Use the following sample input data:

Taxpayer's income: $73,000.00

Number of dependents: 8

Output Results: The following results are displayed:

```
Taxpayer's income ========> 73000
Number of dependents ======> 8

State Tax Due ============> 1380
```

The following systematic approach to solving this exercise, as well as the other BASIC Programming Problems in this textbook, is recommended. In essence, this list is the same as the program development life cycle in Section 1.6.

Step 1: Problem Analysis

Review the program specifications until you thoroughly understand the problem to be solved. Ascertain the form of input, the form of output and the type of processing that must be performed. For this problem, you should have determined the following:

Input: The program must allow for the user to supply the data through the use of INPUT statements. There are two data items: taxpayer's income and number of dependents.

Processing: The formula Tax = 0.02 * (Income – 500 * Dependents) will determine the state tax.

Output: The required results include the input prompt messages and the state tax due.

Step 2: Program Design

Develop a method of solution the PC will use. One way to do this is to list the program tasks sequentially. For this exercise, the **program tasks** are as follows.

FIGURE 2.16

A general flow-chart for Sample BASIC Programming Problem.

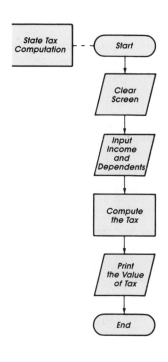

1. Clear the screen.
2. Prompt the user for the necessary data.
3. Calculate the state tax.
4. Display the state tax.

Once the program tasks have been determined, select the variable names you plan to use in the program solution. There are three variable names required. We will use the following:

1. Income for Taxpayer's income
2. Dependents for Number of dependents
3. Tax for State Tax

Next, draw a program flowchart or write pseudocode that shows how the program will accomplish the program tasks. The flowchart for the sample programming exercise is shown in Figure 2.16.

Step 3: Test the Design

Carefully review the design by stepping through the program flowchart or pseudocode to ensure that it is logically correct.

Step 4: Code the Program

Code the program, as shown in Figure 2.17, according to the program design.

FIGURE 2.17

Program solution for Sample BASIC Programming Problem on coding form.

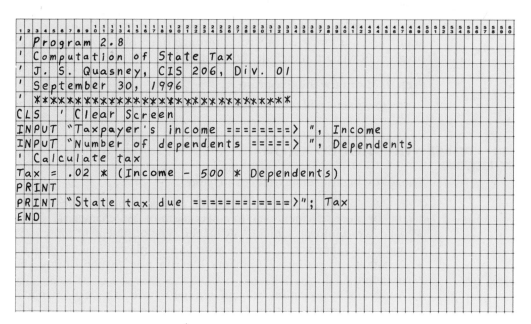

```
' Program 2.8
' Computation of State Tax
' J. S. Quasney, CIS 206, Div. 01
' September 30, 1996
' *************************
CLS     ' Clear Screen
INPUT "Taxpayer's income ========> ", Income
INPUT "Number of dependents ======> ", Dependents
' Calculate tax
Tax = .02 * (Income - 500 * Dependents)
PRINT
PRINT "State tax due ============>"; Tax
END
```

Step 5: Review the Code

Carefully review the code. Put yourself in the position of the PC and step through the program. This is sometimes referred to as desk checking your code. Be sure the syntax of each instruction is correct. Check to be sure that the sequence of the instructions is logically correct so that the program will work the first time it is executed.

Step 6: Enter the Program

Enter the program into the PC, as shown in the upper screen in Figure 2.18. Before starting this step, you should be familiar with "booting the PC," loading the Quick-BASIC program, and the commands discussed in the previous sections.

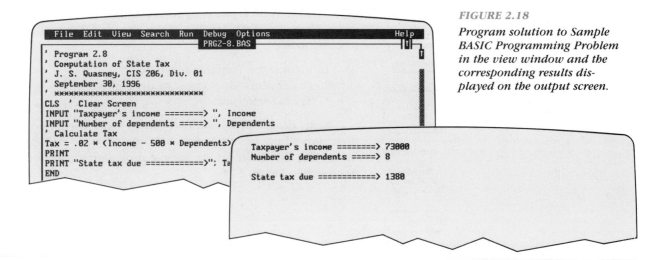

FIGURE 2.18

Program solution to Sample BASIC Programming Problem in the view window and the corresponding results displayed on the output screen.

Step 7: Test the Program

Test the program by executing it. Hold down the Shift key and press the function key F5. The output results are shown in the lower screen in Figure 2.18. If the input data does not produce the expected results, the program must be reviewed and corrected. (See Appendix C for debugging techniques.)

Step 8: Formalize the Solution

Obtain a hard copy, a listing, of the source program and the output results. If the program logic was modified in Steps 4 through 6, revise the documentation and redraw the program flowchart to include the changes.

Step 9: Maintain the Program

Correct errors or add enhancements to the program as per your instructor's request.

2.11 WHAT YOU SHOULD KNOW

The following list summarizes this chapter:

1. A QuickBASIC program is composed of a sequence of lines. Each line may contain one or more statements, up to a maximum of 255 characters.
2. A keyword informs QuickBASIC of the type of statement to be executed. LET, PRINT and END are keywords. The keyword LET is optional in a LET statement.
3. Constants are ordinary numbers that do not change during the execution of a program.
4. A variable is a location in main storage whose value can change as the program is executed. Variables are referenced by their names.
5. A variable name begins with a letter and may be followed by up to 39 letters, digits and decimal points. It is invalid to use a keyword as a variable name.
6. The equal sign in a LET statement means that the value of the variable to the left of the equal sign is to be replaced by the final value to the right of the equal sign.
7. Constants represent ordinary numbers that do not change during the execution of a program.
8. The PRINT statement instructs the PC to bring a result out from its main storage area and display it on the screen.

9. The line containing the END statement terminates the execution of the program.

10. Each program should contain an END statement.

11. Every variable appearing in an output statement should appear at least once earlier in the program in such a way that its value can be determined.

12. Although most QuickBASIC statements can be placed anywhere in a given program, logic, common sense and style dictate where these statements are placed.

13. Every variable appearing to the right of the equal sign in a LET statement should appear at least once earlier in the same program in such a way that its value can be determined.

14. The function of the INPUT statement is to display an input prompt and to suspend execution of the program until data has been supplied from a source outside the program, such as the keyboard. The input prompt must be followed by a comma or a semicolon separator. If a semicolon follows the input prompt, then a question mark is displayed following the input prompt when the INPUT statement is executed.

15. A comma is used to establish a list, which is a set of distinct elements. In a PRINT or INPUT statement, each element is separated from the next by a comma.

16. Every variable appearing in the program whose value is directly obtained through input must be listed in an INPUT statement before it is used elsewhere in the program.

17. In a PRINT statement, such as PRINT X, the PC displays the value of X and not the letter X.

18. The PRINT statement can be used to display messages as well as the values of variables.

19. In a PRINT statement, the semicolon separator instructs the system to maintain the current position of the cursor.

20. The CLS statement causes all the information on the output screen to be erased and places the cursor in the upper left corner of the screen.

21. A null list in a PRINT statement causes the PC to display a blank line.

22. A line in a program can contain more than one statement if colons are used to separate them.

23. Spaces should appear in a QuickBASIC statement in the same places that spaces appear in an English sentence.

24. The REM statement, used to document a program, has no effect on the execution of the program. The apostrophe (') is an abbreviation for REM. It may also be used to insert a comment on the right-hand side of a QuickBASIC statement.

25. Grammatical and syntactical errors can be corrected by editing the QuickBASIC program. For example, you can correct errors while keying in a line. Lines can also be replaced, inserted or deleted.

26. There are four parts to the QB (QuickBASIC) screen — the view window, menu bar, immediate window, and the status line.

27. In the view window, you can enter, modify, and display programs.

28. The menu bar displays a list of menu names. Each menu name has a *pull-down menu* of commands. Press the Alt key to activate the menu bar. Many of the commands in the pull-down menus can be selected by typing the highlighted letter in the command name.

29. The immediate window is used to execute statements as soon as they are entered.

30. The status line displays important information, such as special keys, and the cursor line and column location on the screen.

31. Use the cursor movement keys or the mouse device to move the cursor on the screen.

32. QuickBASIC uses dialog boxes to display messages and request information.

33. To use the QB Advisor on-line help facility, press F1 for context-sensitive help or Shift + F1 for general help.

34. Editing is the process of entering and altering a program.

35. A file specification, also called a filespec, is used to identify programs and data files placed in auxiliary storage. A filespec is made up of a device name, file name and extension.

36. To execute the current program, press Shift + F5.

37. Select the Print command in the File menu to list all or part of the current program to the printer.
38. The output results of a program are displayed on the output screen. To print a hard copy of the output screen, press Print Screen (Shift + PrtSc on older keyboards).
39. Select the Save command in the File menu to save the current program to disk under the same file name.
40. Select the Save As command in the File menu to save the current program to disk under a new file name.
41. Select the Open command in the File menu to load a program from disk into main storage.
42. Select the New command in the File menu to erase the current program from main storage and begin a new program.
43. Select the Exit command in the File menu to quit QuickBASIC and return control to DOS.

2.12 TEST YOUR BASIC SKILLS (Even-numbered answers are in Appendix E)

1. Identify the eight major components of the QB screen shown in Figure 2.19.

FIGURE 2.19
The QB screen

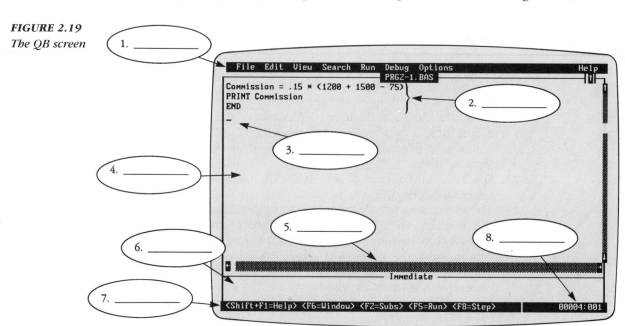

2. Put yourself in the place of the PC and record for each line the current values of W, X, and Y. (**Hint:** The value of a variable does not change until the program instructs the PC to change it.)

```
1   W = 4
2   X = 2
3   Y = 6
4   PRINT Y
5   W = W + 1
6   X = W * Y
7   PRINT X
8   X = 9
9   Y = Y - 2
10  PRINT Y
11  X = X - 9
12  PRINT X
13  END
```

Line	W	X	Y	Displayed
1				
2				
3				
4				
5				
6				
7				
8				
9				
10				
11				
12				
13				

3. For each program below, construct a table similar to the one in Exercise 2. Record for each line the current values of the variables and the results displayed by the PRINT statements.

a.
```
1   A = 1
2   B = 3
3   PRINT A
4   A = A + 1
5   B = B - 1
6   PRINT B
7   A = A + 1
8   B = B - 1
9   PRINT A
10  END
```

b. A is assigned the value 4, and B is assigned the value 2.
```
1   C = 4
2   PRINT C
3   INPUT A, B
4   C = A \ B + C + 8 MOD 4
5   A = A - 3
6   B = C ^ A
7   PRINT B
8   END
```

c. A is assigned the value 7, and B is assigned the value 2.
```
1   INPUT A, B
2   C = A * A
3   PRINT C
4   D = A - B
5   PRINT D
6   E = 1
7   PRINT E
8   D = D - 3
9   X = E / D
10  PRINT X
11  END
```

d. Principal is assigned the value 500, and Rate is assigned the value 10.
```
1   INPUT Principal, Rate
2   Rate = Rate / 100
3   Discount = Principal * Rate
4   Rate = Rate * 100
5   ' Display Results
6   PRINT "Discount rate"; Rate; "%"
7   PRINT "Price"; Principal; "Dollars"
8   PRINT "Discount"; Discount; "Dollars"
9   END
```

4. Write LET statements for each of the following:
   a. Assign T the value of 3.
   b. Assign X the value of T less 2.
   c. Assign P the product of T and X.
   d. Triple the value of T.
   e. Assign A the quotient of P divided by X.
   f. Increment X by 1.
   g. Cube the value of R.

5. What does the following program display when the value 10 is entered in response to the first and 8 in response to the second INPUT statement?

```
' Exercise 2.5
INPUT "What is the length"; Lng
INPUT "What is the width"; Wide
Area = Lng * Wide
PRINT "A rectangle with dimensions"; Lng; "and"; Wide
PRINT "has an area of"; Area; "."
END
```

6. Indicate three techniques presented in Chapter 2 for integrating data into a program.
7. In a QuickBASIC program, how do you instruct the PC to display two consecutive blank lines as part of the output results?
8. Explain in one sentence each the purpose of the following commands: Exit, New, Open, Print, Save As, and Start.
9. What is wrong with the following program?

```
' Exercise 2.9
INPUT X
X = A / B
PRINT "The answer is"; X
END
```

10. A program requests the user to input the hours worked (40) and the rate of pay ($6.75). The program determines the gross pay by multiplying the two values together, and then displays the gross pay. Is the following program solution logically correct for the problem stated?

```
' Exercise 2.10
INPUT "Hours worked ===> ", Hours
INPUT "Rate of pay ====> ", Rate
Pay = Rate * Hours ' Compute the Gross Pay
PRINT "The gross pay is 270"
END
```

11. List the function of the following keys when a dialog box is active:
    a. Esc
    b. Tab
    c. Enter

12. List the function of the following keys when the view window is active:

    a. Alt   b. Shift + Delete
    c. Enter   d. Home
    e. End   f. Ctrl + Home
    g. Ctrl + Q, X   h. Shift + F5
    i. F4   j. F6
    k. Backspace   l. Delete
    m. Insert   n. Shift + Insert
    o. Page Up

13. **PC Hands-On Exercise:** Boot the PC and load the QuickBASIC program as described earlier in this chapter. Insert the Student Diskette that accompanies this book into the default drive. With the QB screen on your monitor, do the following:
    a. Load Program 2.7 (PRG2-7) from the Student Diskette.
    b. Print a hard copy of the program.
    c. Run the program and see what happens.
    d. Use the Print Screen key to print a copy of the output screen.
    e. Quit QuickBASIC. Remove the Student Diskette and turn the PC off.

14. **PC Hands-On Exercise:** To gain experience with the QB Advisor, do the following:
    a. Start QuickBASIC and press the Enter key when the initial dialog box appears on the screen. Read the screen over and use the Print Screen key to obtain a hard copy. Press the Esc key.
    b. Type the keyword INPUT. With the cursor in or near the keyword INPUT, press the F1 key or click the right mouse button. When the help screen appears, read it over and print a hard copy. Press the Esc key.
    c. Press Shift + F1. When the help screen displays, read the information and scroll downward. Scroll back up to the top and move the cursor into the hyperlink Contents. Press the Enter key. Navigate around the QB Advisor by selecting hyperlinks and pressing the F1 key or clicking the mouse.

2.13   BASIC PROGRAMMING PROBLEMS

So that your computer programs will be documented properly, use the following identification format at the beginning of each QuickBASIC program:

```
' Problem Number
' A Short Description of the Problem
' Your Name, Course Number, Course Division
' Today's Date
' *****************************************
```

In line 1, use the comment "Problem 2-1" to represent the first problem in Chapter 2. In line 2, use the title of the problem as the comment. (See Program 2.8 on page 48.)

Upon completion of each problem, turn in to your instructor:

1. A logic diagram in flowchart form or in pseudocode as required
2. A listing of the program
3. The output results

(See Section 2.7 on how to obtain a hard copy of your program and output results.) Use meaningful variable names in all programs. Each major section of the program should be documented with appropriate remark lines.

Be sure to save the program solutions to auxiliary storage. Use file names of the form "LABc-n" where c represents the chapter number and n represents the problem number.

NOTE: All programming problems in this book include partial or complete sample output results and, when applicable, sample input data. Learn to select good test data to evaluate the logic of your program. Check your design and program against the sample output and select your own data for additional testing purposes.

---

1. Computation of a Sum

Purpose: To gain confidence in keying and executing your first QuickBASIC program.

Problem: Key in and execute the following program, which determines the sum of three numbers. Replace the verbiage in lines 3 and 4 with your name, course number, course division, and today's date as described earlier. After the program has displayed the proper output results, save the program as LAB2-1 and obtain a hard copy of the program and output results.

```
1      ' Problem 2-1
2      ' Computation of a Sum
3      ' Your Name, Course Number, Course Division
4      ' Today's Date
5      ' *****************************************
6      CLS ' Clear Screen
7      Sum = 25.65 + 13.75 + 15.25
8      PRINT "The sum is"; Sum
9      END
```

Input Data: None.

Output Results: The following results are displayed:

```
The sum is 54.65
```

2. Determining the Selling Price

Purpose: To become familiar with elementary uses of the INPUT, PRINT, and LET statements.

Problem: Merchants are in the retail business to buy goods from producers, manufacturers and wholesalers, and to sell the merchandise to their customers. To make a profit, they must sell their merchandise for more than the cost plus the overhead (taxes, store rent, upkeep, salaries and so forth). The margin is the sum of the overhead and profit. The selling price is the sum of the margin and cost. Write a program following the steps outlined in Section 2.10 on page 46, that will determine the selling price of an item that costs $48.27 and has a margin of 25%. Develop your solution by loading and modifying PRG2-8 on the Student Diskette. Save the program solution as LAB2-2. Use the following formula:

$$\text{Selling Price} = \left(\frac{1}{1 - \text{Margin}}\right) \times \text{Cost}$$

Input Data: Use the following data in response to INPUT statements:

Cost: $48.27
Margin: 25%

Output Results: The following results are displayed:

```
Cost =================> 48.27
Margin in percent ====> 25

Selling price ========> 64.36
```

3. The Optimal Investment

Purpose: To familiarize the student with the use of the CLS INPUT, PRINT, and LET statements and to perform multiple runs on the same program.

Problem: Three local banks have undertaken an advertising campaign to attract savings account customers. The specifics of their advertisements are shown in Table 2.13.

Construct a single program, following the steps outlined in Section 2.10 on page 46, that will be executed three times, once for each bank. The program is to compute and display the amount of a $500 investment for a period of one year. A comparison of the results will show the optimal investment. Develop your solution by loading and modifying PRG2-8 on the Student Diskette. Save the program solution as LAB2-3. Use the following formula:

Amount = Principal * (1 + Rate/T)^T

where T = number of times the investment is compounded per year (that is, the conversions).

TABLE 2.13 Interest Rates Charged by Three Local Banks		
BANK 1	**BANK 2**	**BANK 3**
Interest 6–7/8%	Interest 6–3/4%	Interest 6–5/8%
Compounded annually	Compounded semiannually	Compounded quarterly

Input Data: Enter the data found in Table 2.13 in response to INPUT statements. For example, for Bank 1 enter:

Bank: 1
Principal: $500.00
Rate: 0.06875
Conversions: 1

Output Results: The following results are displayed for Bank 1:

```
Please enter:
        Bank number =============> 1
        Principal ===============> 500
        Rate in decimal =========> 0.06875
        Number of conversions ===> 1

Amount of investment after one year for bank 1 ====> 534.375
```

4. Payroll Problem II — Gross Pay Computations

Purpose: To become familiar with some of the grammatical and logical rules of Quick-BASIC and to demonstrate some fundamental concepts of executing a QuickBASIC program.

Problem: Construct a program, following the steps outlined in Section 2.10 on page 46, that will clear the screen, then compute and display the gross pay for an employee working 80 hours during a biweekly pay period at an hourly rate of $12.50.

> **Version A:** Insert the data, 80 and 12.50, directly into a LET statement that determines the gross pay.

> **Version B:** Assign the data, 80 and 12.50, to variables in LET statements and then compute the gross pay in a separate LET statement.

> **Version C:** Enter the data, 80 and 12.50, in response to INPUT statements.

Output Results: The following results are displayed for Version B. For Version A, display only the last line.

```
Hours worked ===> 80
Rate of pay ====> 12.5
Gross pay ======> 1000
```

3

Calculations, Strings, and the PRINT Statement

3.1 INTRODUCTION

In Chapter 2 you were introduced to a few simple computer programs that demonstrated some of the grammatical rules of QuickBASIC. Also presented were examples of programs that interact with the user through the use of the INPUT and PRINT statements. This chapter continues to develop straight-line programs, with more complex computations and manipulation of data.

The focus of this chapter is on constants, variables, expressions, functions, rounding and truncation techniques, and the LET statement. This chapter also expands on the type of data that can be assigned to variables by introducing string values, examples of which include a word, phrase, or a sentence.

Finally, this chapter presents additional information about the PRINT statement, including use of the comma separator, the TAB function, and the SPC function.

Upon successful completion of this chapter, you will be able to write programs that manipulate string expressions and numeric expressions. You will also be able to control the spacing and formatting of the desired output.

Programming Case Study 3 | Tailor's Calculations

Program 3.1 determines the average neck, hat and shoe sizes of a male customer. The program uses the following formulas:

$$\text{Neck Size} = 3\left(\frac{\text{Weight}}{\text{Waistline}}\right) \qquad \text{Hat Size} = \frac{3 \times \text{Weight}}{2.125 \times \text{Waistline}} \qquad \text{Shoe Size} = 50\left(\frac{\text{Waistline}}{\text{Weight}}\right)$$

Program 3.1 on the next page computes the average neck size (15), hat size (7.058824) and shoe size (10) for Mike, who has a 35-inch waistline and weighs 175 pounds. Even though it is not used in the computations, the customer name is requested in the program because it helps identify the measurements when more than one set of computations is involved.

PROGRAM 3.1

```
 1    ' Program 3.1
 2    ' Tailor's Calculations
 3    ' Determine Neck Size, Hat Size and Shoe Size
 4    ' *********************************************
 5    CLS  ' Clear Screen
 6    INPUT "Customer's first name"; First.Name$
 7    INPUT "Waistline"; Waist
 8    INPUT "Weight"; Weight
 9    Neck.Size = 3 * Weight / Waist
10    Hat.Size  = 3 * Weight / (2.125 * Waist)
11    Shoe.Size = 50 * Waist / Weight
12    PRINT
13    PRINT First.Name$; "'s neck size is"; Neck.Size
14    PRINT First.Name$; "'s hat size is";  Hat.Size
15    PRINT First.Name$; "'s shoe size is"; Shoe.Size
16    END

      [run]

      Customer's first name? Mike
      Waistline? 35
      Weight? 175

      Mike's neck size is 15
      Mike's hat size is 7.058824
      Mike's shoe size is 10
```

Program 3.1 contains a sequence of LET statements (lines 9 through 11) with expressions that are more complex than those encountered in Chapter 2. Furthermore, line 6 contains a variable First.Name$ that is assigned a string of letters, Mike, rather than a numeric value. The value of First.Name$ is displayed along with the results because of lines 13 through 15. The following sections introduce some additional, formal definitions and special rules for constructing constants, variables, and LET statements, and for manipulating strings.

3.2   CONSTANTS

You will recall from Chapter 2 that constants are values that do not change during the execution of a program. Two different kinds of constants are valid for use in QuickBASIC programs: numeric constants and string constants. **Numeric constants** represent ordinary numbers that can be used in computations. A **string constant** is a sequence of letters, digits, and special characters enclosed in quotation marks. String constants are used for such nonnumeric purposes as representing an employee name, Social Security number, an address, or a telephone number.

Numeric Constants

A numeric constant can have one of three forms in QuickBASIC:

1. **Integer:** A positive or negative whole number with no decimal point, such as 174, 5903, 0, or −32768.
2. **Fixed Point:** A positive or negative real number with a decimal point, such as 713.1417, 0.0034, 0.0, −35.1, or 1923547463.34.
3. **Exponential form:** A number written as an integer or fixed point constant, followed by the letter D or E and an integer. D or E stands for "times 10 to the power." (An explanation of the difference between using a D or E follows shortly.) Examples are 793E19, 62E-23, 1E0, +12.34789564129D+7, and −2.3D−3.

Examples of numeric constants in Program 3.1 are 3, 2.125 and 50, found in lines 9, 10, and 11. Furthermore, the numeric data 35 and 175, entered in response to the INPUT statements in lines 7 and 8 of Program 3.1, must take the form of numeric constants. This leads to the following rule:

INPUT RULE 2 *Numeric data assigned to numeric variables through the use of the* INPUT *statement must take the form of numeric constants.*

Table 3.1 lists some ordinary numbers and shows how they may be expressed as valid numeric constants in QuickBASIC. Examples 1, 2, and 3 of Table 3.1 show that special characters such as $, ¢, and comma (,) are not allowed in numeric constants.

TABLE 3.1 Examples of Numeric Constants		
EXAMPLE	**ORDINARY NUMBERS**	**NUMERIC CONSTANTS IN QuickBASIC**
1.	$3.14	3.14
2.	+1,512.71	1512.71 or +1512.71 or 1.51271E3
3.	4¢	4 or 4. or 4E0
4.	−29.7822	-29.7822 or -2.97822E1
5.	0	0 or 0. or 0E0 or 0D0
6.	6.02257×10^{23}	6.02257E23 or +6.02257D+23

Examples 3 and 5 show that you may write an integer in any of the three forms. If a number is negative as in example 4, the minus sign must precede the number. If a number is positive as in example 2, the plus sign is optional.

Example 2 indicates that *commas must not be inserted into numeric constants.* Finally, spaces should not occur within numeric constants.

Numeric Constants in Exponential Form

Numeric constants may be written in **exponential form**. This form is similar to **scientific notation**. It is a shorthand way of representing very large and very small numbers in a QuickBASIC program.

Using exponential form, a constant, regardless of its magnitude, is expressed as a value between 1 and 10 multiplied by a power of 10. For example, 1,500,000 can be expressed as 1.5×10^6 in scientific notation. The positive power of ten in 1.5×10^6 shows that the decimal point was previously moved 6 places to the left, that is

1.500000.

6 places to left

In order to write 1.5×10^6 as a QuickBASIC constant in exponential form, the letter D or E, which stands for "times 10 to the power," is substituted for the "x 10." Hence, the exponential form constant may be written as 1.5E6 or 1.5D6.

In the same way, a small number such as 0.000000001234 can be expressed in scientific notation as 1.234×10^{-9} and in exponential form in QuickBASIC as 1.234E−9 or 1.234D–9. The negative power of 10 in 1.234 x 10⁻⁹ represents that the decimal point was previously moved nine places to the right, that is

9 places to right

Table 3.2 lists some ordinary numbers and shows how they may be expressed in scientific notation and as constants in exponential form in QuickBASIC.

TABLE 3.2	Examples of Scientific Notation and Exponential-Form Constants	
ORDINARY NUMBERS	**SCIENTIFIC NOTATION**	**POSSIBLE EXPONENTIAL-FORM CONSTANTS**
10,000,000	1×10^7	1E7 or 1.E+7 or 0.01E9
0.0000152	1.52×10^{-5}	1.52E-5 or +152D-7
0.001	1×10^{-3}	1E-3 or 0.001E0
−6000000000000	-6×10^{12}	-6E+12 or -6D12 or -0.6E13
−0.005892	-5.892×10^{-3}	-5.892E-3 or -5892E-6
186,000	1.86×10^5	1.86E+5 or 0.186D6

Type and Range of Numeric Constants

Numeric constants are stored in main storage in one of four forms: short integer, long integer, single precision, or double precision. The PC requires 2 bytes of main storage to store a short integer, 4 bytes to store a long integer, 4 bytes to store a single-precision constant, and 8 bytes to store a double-precision constant.

We tell the PC how to store a numeric constant by the way we write it. For example, a numeric constant is stored in short integer form if it is between −32768 and +32767 and does not contain a decimal point or if it contains a trailing percent sign (%).

For the most part, you can let the PC decide how to store the numeric constants in your program; that is, *write the numeric constants the same way you would in algebra.* However, if desired, you can control the way a numeric constant is stored by appending a special character to it (Table 3.3). Experienced programmers often use these special characters to improve the efficiency, accuracy, and speed of their programs.

TABLE 3.3	Declaring the Type of Numeric Constant	
SPECIAL CHARACTER	**TYPE**	**EXAMPLE**
%	Short Integer	25%
&	Long Integer	343&
!	Single Precision	23!
#	Double Precision	87.3#
E	Single Precision (exponential form)	3.456E4
D	Double Precision (exponential form)	3.281937465746D-24

Table 3.4 summarizes the ranges of the different types of numeric constants and numeric variables in QuickBASIC.

TABLE 3.4 Range and Precision of Numeric Constants and Numeric Variables

TYPE	RANGE AND PRECISION
Short Integer	-32,768 to +32,767
Long Integer	-2,147,483,648 to +2,147,483,647
Single Precision	-3.37E+38 to +3.37E+38 with up to 7 digits of significance
Double Precision	-1.67D+308 to +1.67D+308 with up to 15 digits of significance

String Constants

A string constant has as its value the string of all characters between surrounding quotation marks. The length of a string constant may be from 0 to 32,767 characters. A string with a length of zero is a **null string** or **empty string**. The quotation marks indicate the beginning and end of the string constant and are not considered to be part of the value.

The messages that have been incorporated in INPUT statements to prompt for the required data and in PRINT statements to identify results are examples of string constants. For example, string constants appear in lines 6, and 13 of Program 3.1 as shown below:

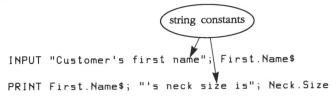

```
INPUT "Customer's first name"; First.Name$

PRINT First.Name$; "'s neck size is"; Neck.Size
```

Note that the apostrophe (') is different from quotation marks (''). While quotation marks have special meaning to QuickBASIC, the apostrophe is just another character that you can include in a string constant.

String constants can be assigned to variables in a LET statement, as is shown in Program 3.2.

PROGRAM 3.2

```
 1     ' Program 3.2
 2     ' Examples Of String Constants
 3     ' ***************************
 4     Model$ = "Q1937A"
 5     Part$  = "12AB34"
 6     Description$ = "Nylon, Disc"
 7     PRINT "Model number: "; Model$
 8     PRINT "Part number: "; Part$
 9     PRINT "Description: "; Description$
10     END

       [run]

       Model number: Q1937A
       Part number: 12AB34
       Description: Nylon, Disc
```

In line 4 of Program 3.2, the variable Model$ is assigned the value Q1937A. In line 5, Part$ is assigned the value 12AB34, and in line 6, Description$ the value Nylon, Disc.

String constants are used in a program to represent values that name or identify a person, place or thing. They are also used to represent report and column headings and output messages. The capability to manipulate data of this type is important, especially in the field of business information systems. As you will see later in this chapter as well as in Chapter 9, QuickBASIC also includes **string functions** for manipulating strings.

Table 3.5 lists sequences of letters, digits and special characters and shows how they may be expressed as valid string constants.

	TABLE 3.5 Examples of String Constants	
EXAMPLE	**STRING OF CHARACTERS**	**CORRESPONDING STRING CONSTANT IN QUICKBASIC**
1.	989-2545 (telephone number)	`"9892545"`
2.	Nikole Rai	`"Nikole Rai"`
3.	blank (space)	`" "`
4.	EMPLOYEE FILE LIST	`"EMPLOYEE FILE LIST"`
5.	310-38-6024 (Social Security nbr.)	`"310386024"`
6.	She said, "No"	`"She said, 'No'"`
7.	A null or empty string	`""`

String data entered in response to the INPUT statement require quotation marks only if one of the following is true of the string data item:

1. The string contains leading or trailing spaces
2. The string contains a comma or colon

The following rule summarizes the assignment of string data items through the use of the INPUT statement:

**INPUT RULE 3**   *String data that is assigned to string variables through the use of the* INPUT *statement may be entered with or without surrounding quotation marks, provided the string contains no leading or trailing spaces or embedded commas or colons. If the string contains leading or trailing spaces or embedded commas or colons, it must be surrounded with quotation marks.*

3.3 VARIABLES

In Chapter 2 you learned that in programming a variable is a location in main storage whose value can change as the program is executed. In a program, the variable is referenced by a variable name. Variables are declared in a QuickBASIC program by incorporating variable names in statements. For example, the following LET statements

```
Rank = 4
School$ = "Purdue"
```

instruct QuickBASIC to set up independent storage areas for the variables Rank and School$, as well as the constants 4 and Purdue.

Although it may appear to you that Rank is being assigned the value 4 when you enter the statement through your keyboard, this does not occur until the program is executed.

Unlike a constant, a variable may be redefined; that is, its value may be changed during the execution of a program. However, its value may remain unchanged in a QuickBASIC program, if you so desire. For example, if in the previous partial program a third line is added as shown:

```
Rank = 4
School$ = "Purdue"
Rank = 2
```

then, the value of Rank changes from 4 to 2 when the third line is executed. QuickBASIC recognizes that the two variable names are the same and during translation does not attempt to create an independent storage location for the second variable name Rank. In other words, there can be only one variable in a program with the name Rank; however, it can be referenced and the value changed as often as needed.

Two categories of variables are valid for use in a QuickBASIC program. These are simple variables and subscripted variables. **Simple variables** are used to store single values, while **subscripted variables** are used to store groups of values. Our discussion here concerns simple variables. Subscripted variables will be discussed in Chapter 8.

As with constants, there are two types of simple variables: numeric and string. A **numeric variable** may only be assigned a numeric value, and a **string variable** may only be assigned a string of characters.

When you execute a program, all numeric variables are assigned an initial value of zero, and all string variables are assigned a null value. The LET statement may be used to assign a variable a constant value or the result of a calculation. Variables may also be assigned values through INPUT statements.

Selection of Variable Names

A QuickBASIC variable name can be up to 40 characters in length. It must begin with a letter. The letter may be followed by up to 39 characters (letters, digits, or periods).

If a variable name ends with a $, then QuickBASIC establishes a location in main storage to receive a string value. If a variable name does not end with a $, then Quick-BASIC establishes a location in main storage to receive a numeric value.

Keywords such as, LET, PRINT, and END, or any other **reserved word** that has special meaning to QuickBASIC, may not be used as a variable name. (See the back page of this book for a list of the QuickBASIC reserved words.)

QuickBASIC is not **case sensitive**. That is, the variable names COUNT, Count, count, and couNT all reference the same variable. In this book, all variable names are in lowercase with an initial capital letter, such as Employee, Commission, and Rate. Variable names made up of more than one word contain a capital letter at the beginning of each word, and each word is separated by a period, such as Pay.Rate, Marital.Status, and Cust.Num$.

Some examples of numeric and string variable names, invalid if written as given, are listed in Tables 3.6 and 3.7 on the next page.

TABLE 3.6 Invalid Numeric Variables and the Corresponding Valid Forms

INVALID NUMERIC VARIABLES	TYPE OF ERROR	VALID NUMERIC VARIABLES
1p	First character must be a letter.	Pay1 or Pay
Let	Let is a keyword.	Lets
Emp-Name	Special characters other than the period are invalid.	Emp.Name
Rate$	A numeric variable must not end with a $.	Rate

TABLE 3.7 Invalid String Variables and the Corresponding Valid Forms		
INVALID STRING VARIABLES	**TYPE OF ERROR**	**VALID STRING VARIABLES**
Emp.Address	Appended dollar sign necessary.	Emp.Address$
Width$	Width is a keyword.	Wide$
Cus Phone$	Blank characters not permitted.	Cus.Phone$

When you compose variable names, make them as meaningful as possible. It is far easier for a person to read the various statements in a program if meaningful names are used. For example, assume the formula for gross pay is given by

Gross Pay = Rate × Hours

The following statement may represent the formula in a QuickBASIC program:

```
A = B * C
```

However, it is more meaningful to write

```
G = R * H
```

It is even more meaningful to say

```
Gross = Rate * Hours
```

Some BASIC programmers use the period to separate words in the variable names or to group variable names as shown below:

Group name.Specific name

For example, if several variable names are needed to describe data in an employee record, then Emp may be used as the group name. That part of the variable name following the period differentiates between the variable names beginning with the group name as shown here:

```
Emp.Number$
Emp.Name$
Emp.Address$
Emp.Salary
Emp.Code$
```

Develop a disciplined style for choosing meaningful variable names for a program. During the program design stage, establish guidelines for how variable names will be selected, and rigorously follow these guidelines when coding the program. Of course, you must abide by the rules that may restrict or enhance the ways you make up variable names. (For additional programming style tips, see Section C.5 in Appendix C.)

Declaring Variable Types

The name of a variable determines whether it is string or numeric, and if numeric, what its precision is. If the dollar sign is absent at the end of the variable name, then the variable is declared to be numeric. As with numeric constants, numeric variables may be

TABLE 3.8 Declaring the Type of Numeric Variable

SPECIAL CHARACTER	TYPE	EXAMPLE
%	Short Integer	`Count%`
&	Long Integer	`Count&`
!	Single Precision	`Count!`
ƀ (Space)	Single Percision	`Count`
#	Double Precision	`Count#`

declared one of the following types by appending a special character to the variable name: short integer, long integer, single precision, or double precision. Table 3.8 summarizes the special characters used to define the variable type.

If there is no trailing special character in a variable name, then QuickBASIC defines it to be single precision as shown in Table 3.8. Variable names such as Sum, Emp.Salary and Product are single-precision numeric variables. As with numeric constants, experienced programmers often append these special characters to numeric variables to improve the efficiency, accuracy, and speed of their program.

An alternative to appending a special character to a variable name to declare its data type is to use the statements DEFINT (integer), DEFLNG (long integer), DEFSNG (single precision), DEFDBL (double precision), and DEFSTR (string) at the beginning of a program. These statements are used to define the data type for a group of variables whose names begin with a letter in the specified range. For example, the statement

```
DEFINT S-U
```

declares all variables whose names begin with S through U as integer type. (See Table 3.4 for the range of values that can be assigned to the different numeric variable types and their precision.)

3.4 THE LET STATEMENT

The LET statement in QuickBASIC is used to assign a value to a variable. The general form of the LET statement is given in Table 3.9. Each LET statement consists of the optional keyword LET, followed by a variable, followed by an equal sign, and then by an expression.

TABLE 3.9 The LET Statement

General Form:	LET numeric variable = numeric expression or LET string variable = string expression
Purpose:	Causes the evaluation of the expression, followed by the assignment of the resulting value to the variable to the left of the equal sign.

Examples:	`LET Perimeter = 2 * Side1 + 2 * Side2`
	`LET Q = (B + A) / 2 - Q + R`
	`Count = Count + 1`
	`Opposite = -Opposite`
	`Table(Y, 4) = 0`
	`Description$ = "Plier"`
	`Hypotenuse = (Base ^ 2 + Height ^ 2) ^ (1/2)`
	`P(I) = C(K) + P(J)`
	`E = M * C^2`
	`Number$ = Prefix$ + "0520"`

Note:	The keyword LET is optional.

The execution of the LET statement is not a one-step process for the PC. The execution of a LET statement requires two steps: evaluation of the expression, and assignment of the result to the variable to the left of the equal sign.

Although the equal sign is used in QuickBASIC, it does not carry all the properties of the equal sign in mathematics. For example, the equal sign in QuickBASIC does not allow for the symmetric relationship. That is,

```
LET A = B
```

cannot be written as

```
B = LET A
```

The equal sign in QuickBASIC can best be described as meaning "is replaced by". Therefore,

```
Interest = Principal * Rate * Time / 360
```

means that the old value of Interest is replaced by the value determined from the expression to the right of the equal sign.

| Programming Case Study 4A | Determining the Single Discount Rate

Program 3.3 determines the single discount rate equal to the series of discount rates of 40%, 20% and 10% using the following formula:

$$\text{Rate} = 1 - (1 - \text{rate}_1)(1 - \text{rate}_2)(1 - \text{rate}_3) \ldots (1 - \text{rate}_n)$$

where Rate is the single discount rate, and rate_1, rate_2 ...rate_n is the series of discount rates. The number of factors of $(1 - \text{rate}_n)$ that is used to determine the single discount rate is dependent on the number of discounts. Program 3.3 is written to determine the single discount rate of a series of three discount rates.

PROGRAM 3.3

```
 1    ' Program 3.3
 2    ' Determining the Single Discount Rate
 3    ' ***************************************
 4    CLS   ' Clear Screen
 5    PRINT "Enter in Decimal Form:"
 6    INPUT "          First Discount ======> ", Rate1
 7    INPUT "          Second Discount =====> ", Rate2
 8    INPUT "          Third Discount ======> ", Rate3
 9    Rate = 1 - (1 - Rate1) * (1 - Rate2) * (1 - Rate3)
10    PRINT
11    PRINT "Single Discount =================>"; Rate
12    END

[run]

Enter in Decimal Form:
          First Discount ======> 0.40
          Second Discount =====> 0.20
          Third Discount ======> 0.10

Single Discount =================> .568
```

After the three discount rates are assigned their decimal values in Program 3.3, line 9 determines the value of the single discount from the expression found to the right of the equal sign. Specifically, the expression is evaluated, and the final value 0.568 is assigned to the variable Rate. Line 11 displays the value for Rate before the program ends.

When dealing with rates that usually occur in percent form, it is often preferable to have the program accept the data and display the results in percent form. Program 3.4 shows you how to write a solution to Programming Case Study 4A that accomplishes this task.

PROGRAM 3.4

```
1     ' Program 3.4
2     ' Determining the Single Discount Rate
3     ' **********************************
4     CLS  ' Clear Screen
5     PRINT "Enter in Percent Form:"
6     INPUT "            First Discount ======> ", Rate1
7     INPUT "            Second Discount =====> ", Rate2
8     INPUT "            Third Discount ======> ", Rate3
9     Rate1 = Rate1 / 100
10    Rate2 = Rate2 / 100
11    Rate3 = Rate3 / 100
12    Rate  = 1 - (1 - Rate1) * (1 - Rate2) * (1 - Rate3)
13    Rate  = 100 * Rate
14    PRINT
15    PRINT "Single Discount ================>"; Rate; "%"
16    END


[run]

Enter in Percent Form:
            First Discount ======> 40
            Second Discount =====> 20
            Third Discount ======> 10

Single Discount ================> 56.8 %
```

In Program 3.4, the INPUT statements (lines 6 through 8) prompt the user to enter the discount rates in percent form. In lines 9 through 11, the rates are changed from percent form to decimal form by dividing Rate1, Rate2, and Rate3 by 100. The single discount is then determined by line 12. Line 13 replaces the assigned value of Rate (0.568) with 100 times Rate. That is, line 13 changes the value of Rate from decimal form to percent form. Line 15 then displays the value of Rate. The string constant % found at the end of line 15 helps identify the result as a percent value.

Program 3.4 includes two concepts that many beginners have difficulty understanding. The first is that the same variable — Rate1, for example, in line 9 — can be found on both sides of the equal sign. The second concerns the reuse of a variable that had been assigned a value through computations in an earlier LET statement. In Program 3.4, Rate1, Rate2 and Rate3 are reused in line 12 after being assigned values in earlier LET statements. At the end of this chapter, there are several exercises to help you better understand these important concepts.

3.5 EXPRESSIONS

Expressions may be either numeric or string. **Numeric expressions** consist of one or more numeric constants, numeric variables and numeric function references, all of which are separated from each other by parentheses and arithmetic operators.

The seven valid arithmetic operators and examples of their use are shown in Table 2.1 on page 23. They include exponentiation ($^$), multiplication ($*$), division ($/$), integer division ($\backslash$), modulo (MOD), addition ($+$) and subtraction ($-$).

Recall that exponentiation is the raising of a number to a power. For example, 4 ^ 2 is equal to 16, and 3 ^ 4 is equal to 81. In programming, the asterisk (*) means *times* and the slash means *divided by*. Therefore, 8 * 4 is equal to 32, and 8 / 4 is equal to 2. For addition and subtraction, the traditional symbols + and – are used.

Two arithmetic operators that may be unfamiliar to you are the backslash (\) and MOD. The backslash instructs the PC first to round the dividend and the divisor to integers and then truncate any decimal portion of the quotient. For example, 5 \ 3 is equal to 1, and 6.8 \ 3.2 is equal to 2.

The modulo operator returns the integer remainder of integer division. For example, 34 MOD 6 is equal to 4, and 23 MOD 12 is equal to 11.

String expressions consist of one or more string constants, string variables and string function references separated by the **concatenation operator (+)**, which combines two strings into one. No other operators are allowed in string expressions.

A programmer must be concerned with both the formation and the evaluation of an expression. It is necessary to consider what an expression is, as well as what constitutes validity in an expression, before it is possible to write valid QuickBASIC statements with confidence.

Formation of Numeric Expressions

The definition of a numeric expression dictates the manner in which a numeric expression is to be validly formed. For example, it may be perfectly clear to you that the following invalid statement has been formed to assign A twice the value of B:

```
A = 2B   ' Invalid Statement
```

However, the PC will reject the statement because a constant and a variable within the same expression must be separated by an arithmetic operator. The statement can validly be written

```
A = 2 * B
```

It is also invalid to use a string variable or string constant in a numeric expression. The following are invalid numeric expressions:

```
6 + "DEBIT" / C
A$ / B + C$ - 19
```

invalid numeric expressions

Evaluation of Numeric Expressions

Formation of complex expressions involving several arithmetic operations can sometimes create problems. For example, consider the statement

```
A = 8 / 4 / 2
```

Does this assign a value of 1 or 4 to A? The answer depends on how the PC evaluates the expression. If the PC completes the operation 8 / 4 first and only then 2 / 2, the expression yields the value 1. If the PC completes the second operation, 4 / 2, first and only then 8 / 2, it yields 4.

The PC follows the normal algebraic rules. Therefore, the expression 8 / 4 / 2 yields a value of 1.

The order in which the operations in an expression are evaluated is given by the following rule:

PRECEDENCE RULE 1   *Unless parentheses dictate otherwise, reading from left to right in a numeric expression, all exponentiations are performed first, then all multiplications and/or divisions, then all integer divisions, then all modulo arithmetic, and finally all additions and/or subtractions.*

This order of operations is sometimes called the rules of precedence, or the hierarchy of operations. The meaning of these rules can be made clear with some examples.

For example, the expression 18 / 3 ^ 2 + 4 * 2 is evaluated as follows:

```
18 / 3 ^ 2 + 4 * 2 = 18 / 9 + 4 * 2
                   = 2       + 4 * 2
                   = 2       + 8
                   = 10
```

If you had trouble following the logic behind this evaluation, use the following technique. Whenever a numeric expression is to be evaluated, *look* or *scan* from left to right five different times meanwhile applying Precedence Rule 1. On the first scan, every time you encounter an ^ operator, you perform exponentiation. In this example, 3 is raised to the power of 2, yielding 9.

On the second scan, moving from left to right again, every time you encounter the operators * and /, perform multiplication and division. Hence, 18 is divided by 9, yielding 2, and 4 and 2 are multiplied, yielding 8.

On the third scan, from left to right, perform all integer division. On the fourth scan, from left to right, perform all modulo arithmetic. In this example, there is no integer division or modulo arithmetic.

On the fifth scan, moving again from left to right, every time you detect the operators + and −, perform addition and subtraction. In this example, 2 and 8 are added to form 10.

The following expression includes all seven arithmetic operators and yields a value of 2:

```
3 * 9 MOD 2 ^ 2 + 5 \ 4.8 / 2 - 3 = 3 * 9 MOD 4 + 5 \ 4.8 / 2 - 3 ◄── (at end of first scan)
                                  = 27 MOD 4 + 5 \ 2.4 - 3 ◄──── (at end of second scan)
                                  = 27 MOD 4 + 2 - 3 ◄──── (at end of third scan)
                                  = 3 + 2 - 3 ◄──── (at end of fourth scan)
                                  = 2 ◄──── (at end of fifth scan)
```

The expression below yields the value of −2.73, as follows:

```
2 - 3 * 4/5 ^ 2 + 5/4 * 3 - 2 ^ 3 = 2 - 3 * 4/25 + 5/4 * 3 - 8 ◄──── (at end of first scan)
                                  = 2 - 0.48 + 3.75 - 8 ◄──── (at end of second scan)
                                  = -2.73 ◄──── (at end of fifth scan)
```

The Effect of Parentheses in the Evaluation of Numeric Expressions

Parentheses may be used to change the order of operations. In QuickBASIC, parentheses are normally used to avoid ambiguity and to group terms in a numeric expression; they do not imply multiplication. The order in which the operations in an expression containing parentheses are evaluated is given in the following rule:

PRECEDENCE RULE 2   *When parentheses are inserted into an expression, the part of the expression within the parentheses is evaluated first, and then the remaining expression is evaluated according to Precedence Rule 1.*

If the first example contained parentheses, as does (18 / 3) ^ 2 + 4 * 2, then it would be evaluated in the following manner:

```
(18 / 3) ^ 2 + 4 * 2 = 6 ^ 2 + 4 * 2
                     = 36 + 4 * 2
                     = 36 + 8
                     = 44
```

The rule is as follows: *Make five scans from left to right within each pair of parentheses, and only after doing this make the standard five passes over the entire numeric expression.*

The expression below yields the value of 1.41, as follows:

```
(2 - 3 * 4 / 5) ^ 2 + 5 / (4 * 3 - 2 ^ 3) = (2 - 3 * 4 / 5) ^ 2 + 5 / (4 * 3 - 8)
                                          = (2 - 2.4) ^ 2 + 5 / (12 - 8)
                                          = (-0.4) ^ 2 + 5 / 4
                                          = 0.16 + 5 / 4
                                          = 0.16 + 1.25
                                          = 1.41
```

Use parentheses freely when in doubt as to the formation and evaluation of a numeric expression. For example, if you wish to have the PC divide 8 * D by 3 ^ P, the expression may correctly be written as 8 * D / 3 ^ P, but you may also write it as (8 * D) / (3 ^ P).

For more complex expressions, QuickBASIC allows parentheses to be contained within other parentheses. When this occurs, the parentheses are said to be **nested**. In this case, QuickBASIC evaluates the innermost parenthetical expression first, and then goes on to the outermost parenthetical expression. Thus, 18 / 3 ^ 2 + (3 * (2 + 5)) is broken down in the following manner:

```
18 / 3 ^ 2 + (3 * (2 + 5)) = 18 / 3 ^ 2 + (3 * 7)
                           = 18 / 3 ^ 2 + 21
                           = 18 / 9 + 21
                           = 2 + 21
                           = 23
```

Table 3.10 gives examples of the QuickBASIC equivalent of some algebraic statements. Study each example carefully. There are two common errors beginners make. Often, beginners surround the wrong part of an expression with parentheses and fail to balance the parentheses. Be sure that an expression has as many closed parentheses as open parentheses. When operations of the same precedence are encountered, Precedence Rule 1 applies. For example,

```
A - B - C is interpreted as (A - B) - C
A / B / C is interpreted as (A / B) / C
A ^ B ^ C is interpreted as (A ^ B) ^ C
A \ B \ C is interpreted as (A \ B) \ C
A MOD B MOD C is interpreted as (A MOD B) MOD C
```

TABLE 3.10 QuickBASIC Equivalent Statements	
ALGEBRAIC STATEMENTS	**EQUIVALENT LET STATEMENTS**
1. $H = \sqrt{X^2 + Y^2}$	`H = (X ^ 2 + Y ^ 2) ^ 0.5`
2. $S = AL^P K^{I-P}$	`S = A * L ^ P * K ^ (1 - P)`
3. $Q = \dfrac{-b + \sqrt{b^2 - 4ac}}{2a}$	`Q = (-B + (B ^ 2 - 4 * A * C) ^ 0.5) / (2 * A)`
4. $A = F\left[\dfrac{r}{(1 + r)^n - 1}\right]$	`A = F * (R / (((1 + R) ^ N) - 1))`
5. $P = \sqrt[3]{(x - p)^2 + y^2}$	`P = ((X - P) ^ 2 + Y ^ 2) ^ (1 / 3)`
6. $Z = \dfrac{ab}{x + \sqrt{x^2 - a^2}}$	`Z = A * B / (X + (X ^ 2 - A ^ 2) ^ 0.5)`

To illustrate the order of operations and the use of parentheses, here is yet a third solution to Programming Case Study 4A.

PROGRAM 3.5

```
1    'Program 3.5
2    ' Determining the Single Discount Rate
3    ' ****************************************
4    CLS   ' Clear Screen
5    PRINT "Enter in Percent Form:"
6    INPUT "          First Discount ======> ", Rate1
7    INPUT "          Second Discount ======> ", Rate2
8    INPUT "          Third Discount ======> ", Rate3
9    Rate = 1 - (1 - Rate1 / 100) * (1 - Rate2 / 100) * (1 - Rate3 / 100)
10   Rate = 100 * Rate
11   PRINT
12   PRINT "Single Discount ================>"; Rate; "%"
13   END

[run]

Enter in Percent Form:
          First Discount ======> 40
          Second Discount ======> 20
          Third Discount ======> 10

Single Discount ================> 56.8 %
```

Program 3.5 is similar to Program 3.4 in that both the data entered and the result displayed are in percent form. The major difference is that in this new solution all the computations have been incorporated into a single LET statement. Lines 9 through 12 in Program 3.4 have been replaced by a new line 9 in Program 3.5.

The programmer's ability to control the sequence of operations with the use of parentheses is obvious in Program 3.5. If you have a mathematical background, you may find the method used in Program 3.5 to your liking. If you have less confidence in your mathematical ability, you may find it easier to use the technique of multiple LET statements, as shown in Program 3.4.

The following summarizes the arithmetic rules discussed in this section:

ARITHMETIC RULE 2   *A numeric expression may not contain string variables or string constants.*

ARITHMETIC RULE 3   *The formation and evaluation of numeric expressions follow the normal algebraic rules.*

Construction of Error-Free Numeric Expressions

Once you have written a numeric expression observing the precedence rules, the PC is capable of translating it; no error messages will be generated. However, this is no guarantee the PC will actually be able to evaluate it. In other words, although a numeric expression may be validly formed, your PC may not be able to evaluate it because of the numbers involved. In situations where error conditions arise during execution, Quick-BASIC will halt the program and display a dialog box informing you of the error. Applying the following rules to your program should help you avoid such hazards:

1. Do not attempt to divide by zero.
2. Do not attempt to determine the square root of a negative value.
3. Do not attempt to raise a negative value to a nonintegral value.
4. Do not attempt to compute a value that is greater than the largest permissible value or less than the smallest nonzero permissible value for your PC system.

By way of a dramatic summary, Figure 3.1 illustrates some of the combinations to be avoided in numeric expressions written in a QuickBASIC program.

FIGURE 3.1
Numeric
expressions
that cannot be
evaluated.

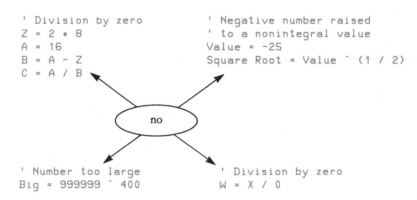

Numeric Functions

QuickBASIC includes many **numeric functions** to handle common mathematical calculations. These numeric functions are discussed in detail in Chapter 9. Two of the more used numeric functions are the INT function and the SQR functions. The INT function returns the largest integer not greater than the argument. The **argument** is a number or numeric expression surrounded by parentheses that immediately follows the word INT. Table 3.11 gives some examples of the INT function.

TABLE 3.11 The INT Function		
VALUE OF VARIABLE	**THE STATEMENT**	**RESULTS IN**
Q = 10.8	Q = INT(Q)	Q = 10
X = 1.6543	X = INT(X + .5)	X = 2
Y = -3.45	W = INT(Y)	W = -4

The SQR function returns the square root of the positive argument. Table 3.12 gives some examples of the SQR function.

TABLE 3.12 The SQR Function

VALUE OF VARIABLE	THE STATEMENT	RESULTS IN
	`Root = SQR(9)`	`Root = 3`
`X = 3, Y = 4`	`Hypo = SQR(X ^ 2 + Y ^ 2)`	`Hypo = 5`
`Cube = 625`	`Answ = SQR(SQR(Cube))`	`Answ = 5`
`Num = -25`	`Comp = SQR(Num)`	`Illegal Function Call`

The following section illustrates the use of the `INT` function to round and truncate a value before it is displayed.

Rounding and Truncation

Many applications require that computation results be rounded or truncated before being displayed. Consider the result displayed for Mike's hat size in Program 3.1:

```
Mike's hat size is 7.058824
```

Let's assume that it is desired to display the result 7.058824 to the nearest hundredths place—rounded to 7.06 or truncated to 7.05. There are various ways to round or truncate a result in QuickBASIC. In this section, a generalized procedure for rounding and truncating positive numbers will be developed.

Developing a Rounding and Truncation Procedure

Recall from your earlier years in school that the rounding operation involves two steps. Assuming you are dealing with positive numbers, you first add five to the digit to the right of the digit to be retained. For example,

STEP 1.   7.058824 + 0.005 = 7.063824

Second, you truncate (drop) the digits to the right of the digit to be retained. For example,

STEP 2.   7.063824 = 7.06

This second step of the rounding operation is the most complex part of the procedure for a beginner using QuickBASIC to grasp. However, we can handle this in the following way:

STEP 2a. Multiply the value 7.638824 by 100: 7.063824 × 100 = 706.3824

STEP 2b. Truncate the digits to the right of the decimal: 706.3824 = 706

STEP 2c. Divide the resultant value by 100: 706 / 100 = 7.06 (rounded result)
Combining the steps, we may write the QuickBASIC code in the following way:

```
Hat.Size = Hat.Size + .005       step 1
Hat.Size = Hat.Size * 100
Hat.Size = INT(Hat.Size)         step 2
Rounded  = Hat.Size / 100
```

With parentheses, the four lines of QuickBASIC code in steps 1 and 2 can be rewritten as a single statement for rounding a value as follows:

```
Rounded = INT((Hat.Size + .005) * 100) / 100
```

Recall from our earlier discussions that the operations found in the innermost set of parentheses are completed first. Therefore, the number 0.005 is added to the value of Hat.Size first, and only then is the sum multiplied by 100. The INT function returns the largest integer not greater than the argument, which in turn, is divided by 100.

Similarly, the QuickBASIC code can be written as a single statement for truncating a value:

```
Truncated = INT(Hat.Size * 100) / 100
```

Program 3.6, which is similar to Program 3.1 except that only the hat size is computed and displayed, illustrates the use of the procedures developed for rounding and truncating to the nearest hundredth, before displaying them.

The rounding and truncation procedures developed here work only for positive numbers. Chapter 9 presents procedures that work for both positive and negative numbers.

PROGRAM 3.6

```
1    ' Program 3.6
2    ' Tailor's Calculations
3    ' Determine Hat Size Rounded and Truncated
4    ' ****************************************
5    CLS  ' Clear Screen
6    INPUT "Customer's first name"; First.Name$
7    INPUT "Waistline"; Waist
8    INPUT "Weight"; Weight
9    Hat.Size  = 3 * Weight / (2.125 * Waist)
10   Rounded   = INT((Hat.Size + .005) * 100) / 100
11   Truncated = INT(Hat.Size * 100) / 100
12   PRINT
13   PRINT First.Name$; "'s hat size is"; Hat.Size
14   PRINT First.Name$; "'s hat size is"; Rounded; "(Rounded)"
15   PRINT First.Name$; "'s hat size is"; Truncated; "(Truncated)"
16   END

[run]

Customer's first name? Mike
Waistline? 35
Weight? 175

Mike's hat size is 7.058824
Mike's hat size is 7.06 (Rounded)
Mike's hat size is 7.05 (Truncated)
```

String Expressions

The capability to process strings of characters is an essential part of any programming language that is to be used for business applications. Letters, words, names, and a combination of letters and numbers all play an important role in generating readable reports and easing communication between nontechnical personnel and the computer.

In QuickBASIC, string expressions include string constants, string variables, string function references, and a combination of the three separated by the concatenation operator (+).

Do not be confused by the dual function of the symbol + in QuickBASIC. When dealing with numeric expressions, the + symbol represents the operation of addition. When dealing with strings, the + symbol represents the operation of concatenation; that is, the joining of two strings into one string. Consider the following program:

PROGRAM 3.7

```
1     ' Program 3.7
2     ' Examples of String Expressions
3     ' ******************************
4     CLS   ' Clear screen
5     INPUT "Area code ===============> ", Area.Code$
6     INPUT "Local number ============> ", Local.No$
7     Comment$  = "Telephone number "
8     Phone.No$ = Area.Code$ + "-" + Local.No$
9     PRINT
10    PRINT Comment$; "========> "; Phone.No$
11    END

[run]

Area code ===============> 219
Local number ============> 844-0520

Telephone number ========> 219-844-0520
```

Examples of string expressions in Program 3.7 include the string Telephone number in line 7, which is assigned to Comment$ and the string expression Area.Code$ + "–" + Local.No$ in line 8, which is assigned to Phone.No$.

In line 8 the plus sign is the **concatenation operator** (+). When strings are concatenated, they are joined in the order they are found. The result is a single string. The value of Phone.No$, which is displayed by line 10, is illustrated in the output results of Program 3.7.

Use of LEFT$, LEN, MID$ and RIGHT$ String Functions

Although concatenation is the only valid string operation, QuickBASIC includes functions that allow for additional string manipulation. The most often used string functions are presented in Table 3.13. Other string functions are presented in Chapter 9.

TABLE 3.13 Common String Functions

FUNCTION	FUNCTION VALUE
LEFT$(X$, N)	Returns the leftmost N characters of the string argument X$.
LEN(X$)	Returns the number of characters in the value associated with the string argument X$.
MID$(X$, P, N)	Returns N characters of the string argument X$ beginning at P.
RIGHT$(X$, N)	Returns the rightmost N characters of the string argument X$.
Where X$ is a string expression, and N and P are numeric expressions.	

Program 3.8 illustrates the use of the functions found in Table 3.13.

PROGRAM 3.8

```
1     ' Program 3.8
2     ' Example of Referencing String Functions
3     ' ****************************************
4     CLS   ' Clear screen
5     INPUT "Complete telephone number =====> ", Number$
6     Area.Code$ = LEFT$(Number$, 3)
7     Prefix$ = MID$(Number$, 5, 3)
8     Last.Four.Digits$ = RIGHT$(Number$, 4)
9     Char.Cnt = LEN(Number$)
10    PRINT
11    PRINT "Area code ============> "; Area.Code$
12    PRINT "Prefix ===============> "; Prefix$
13    PRINT "Last four digits =====> "; Last.Four.Digits$
14    PRINT "Character count in "; Number$; " =====>"; Char.Cnt
15    END

[run]

Complete telephone number =====> 219-989-2545

Area code ============> 219
Prefix ===============> 989
Last four digits =====> 2545
Character count in 219-989-2545 =====> 12
```

In Program 3.8, the function LEFT$ in line 6 assigns the three leftmost characters of Number$ to Area.Code$. Area.Code$ is assigned the string 219. In line 7, the MID$ function assigns three characters beginning with the fifth character 9 in Number$ to Prefix$. Prefix$ is assigned the string 989. In line 8, the function RIGHT$ assigns the last four characters of Number$ to Last.Four.Digits$. Last.Four.Digits$ is assigned the string 2545. Finally, in line 9, the LEN function is used to assign the numeric variable Char.Cnt a value equal to the number of characters in Number$. Char.Cnt is assigned the numeric value 12. (For a more detailed discussion on the operation of concatenation and the LEFT$, LEN, MID$, and RIGHT$ functions, see Chapter 9.)

3.6   THE PRINT STATEMENT

The PRINT statement is used to write information to the screen. It is commonly used to display the results from computations, to display headings and labeled information, and to plot points on a graph. In addition, the PRINT statement allows you to control the spacing and the format of the desired output.

The general form of the PRINT statement is given with examples in Table 3.14. The PRINT statement consists of the keyword PRINT. It may also have an optional list of **print items** separated by mandatory commas or semicolons. The print items may be numeric or string constants, variables, expressions, or null items. In addition, the print items may include useful function references, such as the Integer and Square Root functions, INT and SQR.

TABLE 3.14	The PRINT Statement
General Form:	PRINT item pm item pm . . . pm item
	where each **item** is a constant, variable, expression, function reference, or null, and where each **pm** is a comma or semicolon.
Purpose:	Writes information to the screen.
Examples:	PRINT
	PRINT Emp.Name$
	PRINT Count; Discount, Employee$; Number
	PRINT Sex.Code$; " "; Time; " "; Marital.Status$
	PRINT , , Height, Weight; Race$; Job(8);
	PRINT "X = "; X, "Y = "; Y
	PRINT "The answer is $"; H,
	PRINT TAB(10); (X + Y) / 4, INT(A)
	PRINT "The interest rate is"; Interest; "%"
	PRINT X; " "; 2 * X; " "; 3 * X; " "; 4 * X
Note:	Enter the question mark (?), and QuickBASIC changes it to the keyword PRINT when the cursor is moved off the line. Enter one or more spaces between print items, and QuickBASIC inserts a semicolon between the print items when the cursor is moved off the line.

Print Zones and Print Positions

The most common use of the PRINT statement is to display values defined earlier in a program. Every sample program presented so far includes a PRINT statement. Listing items separated by commas within a PRINT statement

```
PRINT Product$, Original.Price, Rate, Discount, Sale.Price
```

causes the values of Product$, Original.Price, Rate, Discount and Sale.Price to be displayed on a single line. QuickBASIC displays the five values in print zones.

In the 80-column display, there are five print zones per line. Each **print zone** has 14 positions for a total of 70 positions per line. The **print positions** are numbered consecutively from the left, starting with position one, as shown in Figure 3.2.

FIGURE 3.2

In the 80-column display mode, the print line is divided into five print zones.

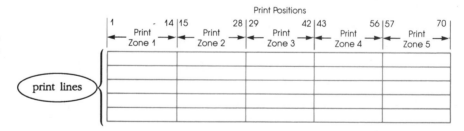

Representation of Numeric Output

Numeric constants, variables, expressions, and function references are evaluated to produce a string of characters consisting of a sign, the decimal representation of the number, and a trailing space. The sign is a leading space if the number is positive, or a leading minus sign if the number is negative.

Representation of String Output

String constants, string variables, string expressions, and string function references are displayed without any leading or trailing spaces. For example, when the following line

```
PRINT "Quick"; "BASIC"
```

is executed, the PC displays QuickBASIC in print positions 1 through 10. Unlike the way it treats numeric output, the PC does not insert a trailing space following the string constants in the output.

Use of the Comma Separator

Punctuation marks, such as the comma and semicolon, are placed between print items. In this section the role of the comma separator is examined. As illustrated by lines 9 through 15 of Program 3.9 in Figure 3.3, the **comma separator** allows you to display values that are automatically positioned in tabular format. Each PRINT statement executed displays one line of information, unless one of the following conditions are true:

1. The number of print zones required by the PRINT statement exceeds five.
2. The PRINT statement ends with a comma or semicolon. (See Program 3.9 in Figure 3.3, lines 9 and 10.)

Two or more consecutive commas may be included in a PRINT statement (lines 14 and 15 in Figure 3.3) as a means of tabulating over print zones.

Use of the Semicolon Separator

In this section, the role of the semicolon separator in the PRINT statement is examined. While the comma separator allows you to tab to the next print zone, the **semicolon separator** does not. Instead, the semicolon in a PRINT statement causes the display of the value immediately to the right of the previous one. The semicolon allows you to display more than five items per line. Use of the semicolon separator is referred to as displaying values in a **packed**, or **compressed format**.

Lines 18 and 19 in Figure 3.3 show the use of the semicolon separator. While each numeric value displayed is preceded by a leading sign and a trailing space, string values are displayed with no spaces separating them.

In line 19, all five print items are separated by the semicolon, and the values are all displayed within the first 18 print positions.

If a PRINT statement ends with a semicolon, the first item in the next PRINT statement displays on the same line in compressed form.

Creating Blank Lines

If a PRINT statement contains a null list, then a blank line results. For example,

```
PRINT
```

contains no print items and results in the display of a blank line. Line 24 in Figure 3.3 displays a blank line before the values displayed by line 25.

Use of the TAB Function

So far, PRINT statements have contained the comma and semicolon as separators among numeric and string expressions to display the values of these expressions in a readable format with correct spacing. Compact and exact spacing of output results also can be achieved by the use of the TAB and SPC functions.

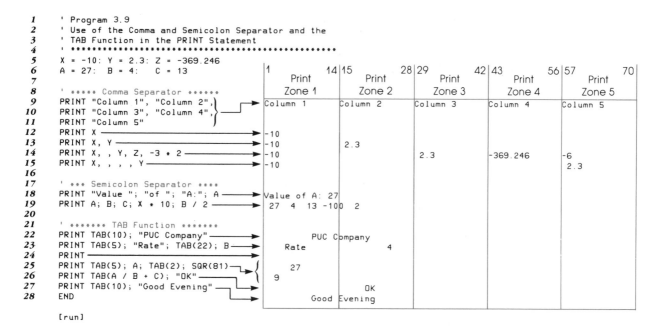

[run]

FIGURE 3.3

The effect of commas, semicolons, and the TAB function in PRINT statements with numeric and string expressions.

The TAB function is used in the PRINT and LPRINT statements to specify the exact print positions for the various output results on a given line. The LPRINT statement is discussed shortly. Use of the TAB function

```
PRINT TAB(10); "PUC Company"
```

causes the string to be displayed beginning in exactly print position 10, as shown in line 22 in Figure 3.3.

The general form of the TAB function is

```
TAB(numeric  expression);
```

where the numeric expression, the argument, may be a numeric constant, variable, expression, or function reference. The value of the argument determines the position on the line of the next character to be displayed. QuickBASIC automatically appends a semicolon to the TAB function if you don't.

Line 25 in Figure 3.3 shows that backspacing is not permitted. If the argument is less than the current column position on the output device, then the PC positions the cursor or print head mechanism on the next line at a column position equal to the argument.

Study closely the remaining examples of the TAB function in lines 22 through 27 in Figure 3.3. Note that noninteger arguments are rounded. The following rules summarize the use of the TAB function:

TAB RULE 1   *The argument must be less than or equal to 32,767. An argument that is less than 1 is set equal to 1.*

TAB RULE 2   *A decimal argument is rounded to the nearest integer.*

TAB RULE 3   *Backspacing is not permitted with the TAB function. If the cursor or print head mechanism is beyond the print position that equates to the argument, then the PC moves to the next line.*

TAB RULE 4   *If the argument is greater than the output width, then it is divided by the output width, and the remainder is used as the argument.*

Displaying Spaces — The SPC Function

The function SPC is similar to the Spacebar on a typewriter. It may be used to insert spaces between print items. The general form of the SPC function is

SPC(numeric expression)

Consider the following:

```
PRINT "Column 1"; SPC(3); "Column 2"; SPC(5); "Column 3"
```

The SPC(3) causes the insertion of three spaces between Column 1 and Column 2. The SPC(5) inserts five spaces between Column 2 and Column 3. The spaces inserted between results displayed are often called **filler**. The function SPC may be used any number of times in the same PRINT statement. However, it may be used only in a PRINT or LPRINT statement.

Calculations within the PRINT Statement

QuickBASIC permits calculations to be made within the PRINT statement. For instance, the sum, difference, product, quotient, modulo, and exponentiation of two numbers, such as 4 and 2, may be made in the conventional way by using LET statements or by using the PRINT statement, as is in Program 3.10.

PROGRAM 3.10

```
1   ' Program 3.10
2   ' Calculations Within a PRINT Statement
3   ' ***************************************
4   PRINT 4 + 2; SPC(4); 4 - 2; SPC(4); 4 * 2; SPC(4); SQR(121)
5   PRINT 4 / 2; SPC(4); 4 \ 2; SPC(4); 4 MOD 2; SPC(4); 4 ^ 2
6   END

    [run]

    6        2        8        11
    2        2        0        16
```

Using the Immediate Window

As described earlier in Chapter 2, QuickBASIC has a narrow window at the bottom of the screen, called the immediate window, that permits your PC to act as a powerful desk calculator. To activate the immediate window, press the F6 key. Press it again, and the view window is activated. If you have a mouse, move the pointer to the inactive window and click the mouse button.

Through the immediate window, statements like the PRINT statement can be executed individually without being incorporated into a program. You merely enter the keyword PRINT followed by any numeric expression. As soon as you press the Enter key, the PC immediately computes and displays the value of the expression on the output screen.

The following example illustrates the computation of a complex expression in the immediate window:

```
PRINT (2 - 3 * 4 / 5) ^ 2 + 5 / (4 * 3 - 2 ^ 3)
 1.41
```

The value 1.41 is displayed on the output screen.

You can enter up to 10 lines in the immediate window, and each line can contain multiple statements separated by colons. Each line is executed independently of the others when the Enter key is pressed. You can move back and forth among the lines in the immediate window, executing them in any order.

Some programmers use the immediate window to test screen output before incorporating it into a large program. Once the code is executing properly, it can be copied into the view window and made part of the current program.

You can also use the immediate window to **debug** the program in the view window. For example, if a program terminates unexpectedly, the PRINT statement can be used in the immediate window to display the values of variables used in the program in the view window. This use of the immediate window can be of great benefit in clearing up logical errors in a program. (See Appendix C for a discussion of debugging a program that has errors.)

The LPRINT Statement

While the PRINT statement displays results on the screen, the LPRINT statement prints the results on the printer. Everything that has been presented with respect to the PRINT statement in this chapter applies to the LPRINT statement as well. Obviously, to use this statement, you must have a printer attached to your PC, and it must be in the Ready mode.

3.7   WHAT YOU SHOULD KNOW

The following list summarizes this chapter:

1. Constants are values that do not change during the execution of a program.
2. There are two types of constants — numeric constants and string constants.
3. Numeric constants represent ordinary numbers. A numeric constant may be written in one of three forms—integer, fixed point or exponential form.
4. An integer constant is a positive or negative whole number with no decimal point.
5. A fixed point constant is one with a decimal point.
6. A numeric constant written in exponential form is one written as an integer or fixed point constant, followed by the letter D or E and an integer. D or E stands for ''times 10 to the power.''

7. Depending on how it is written in a program, a numeric constant is stored as one of the following types: short integer, long integer, single precision, or double precision.

8. The only special characters allowed in a numeric constant are a leading sign (+ or − or blank), the decimal point and the letter D or E.

9. String constants represent strings of characters enclosed in quotation marks. A string constant can have from 0 to 32,767 characters.

10. In programming, a variable is a location in main storage that can be referenced by a variable name and whose value can change as the program is executed.

11. There are two types of variables in QuickBASIC, simple variables and subscripted variables. Simple variables are used to store single values. Subscripted variables are used to store groups of values. Either of the two can be defined as numeric or string.

12. A variable name can be up to 40 characters in length. It must begin with a letter. The letter can be followed by letters, digits, and periods.

13. You should develop a disciplined style for choosing meaningful variable names in a program.

14. The name of a variable determines whether it is string or numeric. As the last character in a variable name, the dollar sign declares that the variable will represent a string. If the last character is not a dollar sign ($), then the variable is numeric.

15. If a variable name ends with an exclamation point (!) or no special character, then it is declared single precision. Other special characters appended to variable names are as follows: percent sign (%) declares it short integer, ampersand (&) declares it long integer, and number sign (#) declares it double precision. The statements DEFINT (integer), DEFLNG (long integer), DEFSNG (single precision), DEFDBL (double precision), and DEFSTR (string) may be used to declare the data types for groups of variables.

16. While short integer variables and constants take up 2 bytes of main storage, long integer and single-precision variables take up 4 bytes, and double-precision variables take up 8 bytes of main storage.

17. Numeric data assigned to numeric variables through the use of the INPUT statement must take the form of numeric constants.

18. String data assigned to string variables through the use of the INPUT statement must be surrounded with quotation marks when the string contains leading or trailing blanks or embedded commas or colons.

19. The LET statement causes evaluation of the expression to the right of the equal sign, followed by assignment of the resulting value to the variable to the left of the equal sign.

20. The equal sign in QuickBASIC can best be described as meaning "is replaced by".

21. It is invalid to assign a string expression to a numeric variable or a numeric expression to a string variable.

22. A numeric expression is a sequence of one or more numeric constants, numeric variables and numeric function references separated from each other by parentheses and arithmetic operators.

23. A string expression is a sequence of one or more string constants, string variables or string function references separated by the concatenation operator.

24. The formation and evaluation of numeric expressions follow the normal algebraic rules.

25. Unless parentheses dictate otherwise, reading from left to right in a numeric expression, all exponentiations are performed first, then all multiplications and/or divisions, then all integer divisions, then all modulo arithmetic, and finally all additions and/or subtractions. This order is called the hierarchy of operations or the rules of precedence.

26. When parentheses are inserted into an expression, the part of the expression within the parentheses is evaluated first, and then the remaining expression is evaluated according to the rules of precedence.

27. No numeric expression can be evaluated if it requires a value that is not mathematically defined. For example, do not divide a number by zero in your program.
28. INT(N) returns the largest integer that is less than or equal to the argument N.
29. SQR(N) returns the square root of the positive argument N.
30. To round X to the nearest hundredths place, use the expression: INT((X + 0.005) * 100) / 100.
31. To truncate X to the nearest hundredths place, use the expression: INT((X * 100) / 100.
32. Concatenation generates a single string value, which is the result of combining the values of each of the terms in the order they are found in the expression.
33. The string functions LEFT$, LEN, MID$, and RIGHT$ are used to access and manipulate groups of characters (substrings) within a string.
34. The PRINT statement consists of the keyword PRINT. It may also have an optional list of print items separated by mandatory commas or semicolons. The print items may be numeric or string constants, variables, expressions or null items. In addition, the print items may include useful functions such as INT or SQR.
35. The comma separator in a PRINT statement allows you to display output automatically positioned in a tabular format determined by five print zones in the 80-column display mode and two print zones in the 40-column display mode. Each print zone in the 80-column display mode has 14 positions. In the 40-column display mode, print zone 1 has 14 positions, and print zone 2 has 26 characters.
36. If a PRINT statement contains no list of print items, then a blank line results.
37. The semicolon separator can be used to generate output in a compressed or packed format.
38. The TAB function is used in the PRINT statement to specify the exact print positions for the various output results on a given print line.
39. The SPC function is used to insert spaces (filler) between print items.
40. QuickBASIC allows calculations to be made within the PRINT statement.
41. QuickBASIC permits the PC to be used as a powerful desk calculator through the use of the immediate window. The immediate window may also be used to debug programs in the view window, as well as test lines of code before they are moved into the view window.

3.8   TEST YOUR BASIC SKILLS (Even-numbered answers are in Appendix E)

1. Which of the following are invalid constants if each appeared exactly as written in a valid location in a QuickBASIC statement?

   a. 6.4   b. 7$ c. +.319#   d. 0
   e. 1,976!   f. 179F4   g. 9%   h. $1.75
   i. 1E1   j. 987.6D-25   k. 0E0   l. 4.56-

2. Write the number 568,962,482,176 to the greatest possible accuracy using a precision of seven significant digits. What is the error in this value?

3. Which one of the arithmetic operations are performed first in the following numeric expressions?

   a. 9 / 5 * 6   b. X - Y + A
   c. 3 * (A + 8)   d. (X * (2 + Y)) ^ 2 + Z ^ (2 ^ 2) - 6 MOD 3
   e. X / Y \ Z   f. (B ^ 2 - 4 * A * C) / (2 * A)

4. Evaluate each of the following:

   a. 4 * 5 * 3 / 6 - 7 ^ 2 / 3   b. (2 - 4) + 5 ^ 2
   c. 12 \ 6 / 2 + 7 MOD 3 + 3

5. Calculate the numeric value for each of the following valid numeric expressions if
   A = 3, B = 4, C = 5, W = 3, T = 4, X = 1, and Y = 2.

   a. `(A + B / 2) + 6.2`   b. `(A / (C + 1) * 4 - 5) / 2 + ( 4 MOD 3 \ 3)`
   c. `3 * (A ^ B) / C`   d. `X + 2 * Y * W / 3 - 7 / (T - X / Y) - W ^ T`
   e. `SQR(A ^ 2 + B ^ 2)`   f. `INT(1012.346 + .005) * 100) / 100`
   g. `INT(1012.346 * 100) / 100`

6. Which of the following are invalid variables in QuickBASIC? Why?

   a. `A`   b. `Sale!`   c. `Int`   d. `P.1#`   e. `39`
   f. `Print`   g. `7f`   h. `For$`   i. `Q$`   j. `Q9%`

7. Consider the valid programs below. What is displayed if each is executed?

   a. ```
      ' Exercise 3.7a
      A = 2.5
      B = 4 * A / 2 * A + 5
      PRINT B
      B = 4 * A / (2 * A + 5)
      PRINT B
      A = -A
      PRINT A
      A = -A
      PRINT A
      END
      ```

   b. ```
      ' Exercise 3.7b
      CLS  ' Clear Screen
      Count = 0
      Count = Count + 1
      PRINT Count
      Count = Count + 1
      PRINT Count
      Count = Count + 1
      PRINT Count
      Count = Count - 3
      PRINT Count, Count + 1,
      PRINT Count + 2, Count + 3
      END
      ```

   c. ```
      ' Exercise 3.7c
      X = 4
      Y = 1
      A = X + Y
      B = Y - X
      C = A + B - X
      D = 2 * (A + B + C) / 4
      PRINT A, B, C, D
      END
      ```

   d. Assume Seed is assigned the value 1.
      ```
      ' Exercise 3.7d
      INPUT "Enter seed number ===> ", Seed
      Seed = Seed * (Seed + 1)
      PRINT Seed
      Seed = Seed * (Seed + 1)
      PRINT Seed
      Seed = Seed * (Seed + 1)
      PRINT Seed
      Seed = Seed * (Seed + 1)
      PRINT Seed
      END
      ```

8. What is the distinction between the formulation of a numeric expression and the
   evaluation of a numeric expression?

9. Can a validly formed numeric expression always be executed by a computer?

10. Calculate the numeric value for each of the following numeric expressions if X = 2,
    Y = 3, and Z = 6.

    a. `X + Y ^ 2`
    b. `Z / Y/ X`
    c. `12 / (3 + Z) - X`
    d. `X ^ Y ^ Z`
    e. `X * Y + 2.5 * X + Z`
    f. `(X ^ (2 + Y)) ^ 2 + Z ^ (2 ^ 2)`

11. Repeat Exercise 10 for the case of  X = 4,  Y = 6, and  Z = 2.

12. Write a valid `LET` statement for each of the following algebraic statements:

    a. $q = (d + e)^{1/3}$

    b. $d = (A^2)^{3.2}$

    c. $b = \dfrac{20}{6 - S}$

    d. $Y = a_1x + a_2x^2 + a_3x^3 + a_4x^4$

    e. $h = \sqrt{X} + \dfrac{X}{X - Y}$

    f. $S = \sqrt{19.2X^3}$

    g. $V = 100 - (2/3)^{100 - B}$

    h. $t = \sqrt{76,234/(2.37 + D)}$

    i. $V = 0.12340005M - \left[ \dfrac{(0.123458)^3}{M - N} \right]$

    j. $Q = \dfrac{(F - M1000)^{2B}}{4M} - \dfrac{1}{E}$
      ```

13. If necessary, insert parentheses so that each numeric expression results in the value indicated on the right-hand side of the arrow.

a. 8 / 2 + 2 + 12 --> 14
b. 8 ^ 2 - 1 --> 8
c. 3 / 2 + 0.5 + 3 ^ 1 --> 5
d. 12 MOD 5 \ 2 + 1 ^ 2 + 1 * 2 * 3 / 4 - 3 / 2 --> 0
e. 12 - 2 - 3 - 1 - 4 --> 10
f. 7 * 3 + 4 ^ 2 - 3 / 13 --> 22
g. 3 * 2 - 3 * 4 * 2 + 3 --> -60
h. 3 * 6 - 3 + 2 + 6 * 4 - 4 / 2 ^ 1 --> 33

14. Which of the following are invalid LET statements?

a. X = 9 / B(A + C)
b. X + 5 = Y
c. 17 = X
d. P = 4 * 3 -+6
e. For = SQR(16)
f. X = -X * (((1 + R) ^ 2 - N) ^ 2 + (2 + X)
g. Get Q = R ^ S ^ Q ^ T
h. P = +4
i. G = 4(-2 + A)
j. X = X + 1

15. Consider the valid programs below. What is displayed if each program is executed? Assume A is assigned the value 2 and B the value 3.

a.
```
' Exercise 3.15a
INPUT A, B
D = (A ^ 6 / A * B) - (8 * B / 4)
D = D + 1
PRINT D
END
```

b.
```
' Exercise 3.15b
INPUT A, B
B  = 3
E1 = A * B
E1 = A ^ (6 / E1)
E2 = B * 8
E3 = 4 + 1
E2 = E2 / E3
A  = E1 - E2
PRINT A
END
```

16. Repeat Exercise 15 for the case where A is assigned 1 and B is assigned 2.

17. If the string John R. Blakely is entered in response to the INPUT statement, what is displayed by the following program?

```
' Exercise 3.17
CLS  ' Clear Screen
INPUT "Name ===> ", Name$
First.Name$  = LEFT$(Name$, 4)
Last.Name$   = RIGHT$(Name$, 7)
Mid.Initial$ = MID$(Name$, 6, 2)
Abrev.Name$  = LEFT$(Name$, 1) + MID$(Name$, 7, 1)
Abrev.Name$  = Abrev.Name$ + " " + MID$(Name$, 6, 3) + RIGHT$(Name$, 7)
Char.Cnt = LEN(Name$)
PRINT Name$
PRINT First.Name$, Last.Name$, Mid.Initial$, Abrev.Name$, Char.Cnt
END
```

18. Consider the valid programs listed below. What is displayed if each is executed?

a.
```
' Exercise 3.18a
CLS  ' Clear Screen
PRINT "Net"; "      "; "Pay"
PRINT TAB(11); "Net Pay"
PRINT
PRINT "N"; SPC(3); "e"; SPC(3); "t"; SPC(3); "P";
PRINT SPC(3); "a"; SPC(3); "y"
END
```

```
b. ' Exercise 3.18b
   CLS  ' Clear Screen
   PRINT "Hours", "Gross", "FICA", "FIT"
   PRINT "Hours"; "Gross"; "FICA"; "FIT"
   PRINT : PRINT 10, 20, 30, 30 - 10
   PRINT 10; 20; 30; 30 - 10
   PRINT : PRINT TAB(10); "Hours"
   PRINT "Hours"; TAB(40); "Gross"
   END
```

19. What does the following program print.

```
' Exercise 3.19
CLS  ' Clear Screen
Average1 = 4 + 5 + 6 + 7 + 8 / 5
Average2 = (4 + 5 + 6 + 7 + 8) / 5
LPRINT "Is the average of 4, 5, 6, 7, and 8 ";
LPRINT "equal to"; Average1; "or"; Average 2; "?"
END
```

20. Evaluate each of the following:

a. INT(3.8)   b. INT(-3.8)

c. SQR(400)   d. SQR(-400)

21. **PC Hands-On Exercise:** Load Program 3.1 (PRG3-1) from the Student Diskette. Execute the program. Enter your name and measurements in place of Mike's. How close did Program 3.1 come in estimating your neck, hat and shoe size?

22. **PC Hands-On Exercise:** Load Program 3.4 (PRG3-4) from the Student Diskette. In lines 9 through 11, rather than dividing the discounts by 100, multiply them by 0.01. Execute the program. Enter the same data used with Program 3.4. Are the results the same for the modified version of Program 3.4 as they were for the original?

3.9   BASIC PROGRAMMING PROBLEMS

1. Service Charge Computations

Purpose: To become familiar with the use of constants and variables, and the INPUT, PRINT, and LET statements.

Problem: Write a straight-line program to determine the new service charge. Use the formula

New Service Charge = Old Service Charge + 2% × Old Service Charge

(**Hint:** See Program 3.1 on page 58 or PRG3-1 on the Student Diskette.)

Input Data: Use the old service charge, 114.26, as the sample data in response to the appropriate INPUT statement.

Output Results: The following output results are displayed:

```
Old service charge ====> 114.26
New service charge ====> 116.5452
```

2. Maturity Value of an Investment Converted Quarterly

Purpose: To become familiar with the concepts associated with arithmetic operations, with parentheses in expressions, and with the use of INPUT, LET, and PRINT statements.

Problem: Write a straight-line program to determine the maturity value of an investment of D dollars for Y years at P percent converted quarterly. Use the following formula:

$$S = D \left(1 + \frac{P}{M}\right)^{YM}$$

where S = maturity value
D = investment in dollars
P = nominal rate of interest
Y = time in years
M = number of conversions per year

(**Hint:** See Program 3.4 on page 67 or PRG3-4 on the Student Diskette. The program solution must include a statement to change the rate from percent form to decimal form.)

Input Data: Use the following sample data in response to the appropriate INPUT statements:

Investment: $10,500
Interest: 11.5%
Time: 4 years 6 months
Conversions: 4

Output Results: The following results display. Depending on the computer you use, you may end up with a 5 or 6 as the last digit in the maturity value result.

```
Please enter the:
        Investment in $ ======> 10500
        Nominal rate in % ====> 11.5
        Time in years ========> 4.5
        No. of Conversions ===> 4

Maturity value ==============> $ 17489.06
```

3. Determining the Monthly Payment on a Loan

Purpose: To become familiar with the hierarchy of operations in a LET statement, the use of the INPUT and PRINT statements, and the procedure for rounding a value.

Problem: Write a program to determine the monthly payment for a loan where the annual interest rate (expressed in percent), the amount of the loan, and the number of years are entered via INPUT statements. The monthly payment for the loan is computed from the following relationship:

$$P = \left(\frac{r(1 + r)^n}{(1 + r)^n - 1}\right) \times L$$

where P = payment
L = amount of the loan
r = monthly interest rate
n = number of payments

Display the payment rounded to the nearest cent. Also determine the total interest paid by using the following formula:

Total Interest Paid = nP − L

(**Hint:** The annual interest rate must be divided by 1,200, and the time must be multiplied by 12. Also see Program 3.6 on page 74 or PRG3-6 on the Student Diskette.)

Input Data: Use the following sample data:

Loan: $8,000.00
Interest rate: 12.8%
Time: 4 years

Output Results: The following results are displayed:

```
Amount of loan ================> 8000
Interest rate (in percent) ====> 12.8
Time in years =================> 4

Monthly payment ===============> $ 213.83
Total interest paid ===========> $ 2263.84
```

4. Extracting Substrings

Purpose: To become familiar with the string functions.

Problem: Construct a program to prompt you to enter the alphabet and assign it to a string variable. Using the MID$ string function and concatenation operator, have the program string the selected letters from the alphabet together to form and display your first name. Use the LEN function to determine the number of characters in your first name.

(**Hint:** See Program 3.8 on page 76 or PRG3-8 on the Student Diskette.)

Input Data: Prepare and use the following data:

ABCDEFGHIJKLMNOPQRSTUVWXYZ

Output Results: The following results are displayed for a person with the first name JOHN:

```
Enter the alphabet: ABCDEFGHIJKLMNOPQRSTUVWXYZ

My first name is: JOHN
The number of letters in my first name is: 4
```

NOTE: Answers will vary.

5. English to Metric Conversion

Purpose: To become familiar with the use of the INT function, declaring double-precision variables and constants to specify double-precision arithmetic, and a procedure for rounding.

Problem: Write a program to convert an English measurement in miles, yards, feet and inches to a metric measurement in kilometers, meters and centimeters. Use the following formula to change the English measurement to inches:

Total Inches = 63360 * Miles + 36 * Yards + 12 * Feet + Inches

Use the following formula to determine the equivalent meters:

$$\text{Meters} = \frac{\text{Total Inches}}{39.37}$$

The variable used to represent the number of meters and the numeric constant 39.37 must be declared double precision — add a trailing number sign (#) to each or use the statement DEFDBL to declare the variable to double precision. (This instructs the PC to carry out double-precision arithmetic.)

Use the INT function to determine the number of kilometers, meters and centimeters. Round the centimeters to two decimal places.

(**Hint:** Once the number of meters has been determined, the maximum number of kilometers can be computed from: Kilometers = INT(Meters/1000). Next, the remaining meters can be determined from: Remaining Meters = Meters – 1000 * Kilometers. The number of integer meters in Remaining Meters can then be determined from: Integer Meters = INT(Remaining Meters). Continue with the same technique to compute the number of centimeters.)

Input Data: Use the following sample data:

Miles:	3	Feet:	2
Yards:	2	Inches:	6

Output Results: The following results are displayed.

```
English to Metric Conversion

Miles: 3
Yards: 2
Feet: 2
Inches: 6

Kilometers: 4
Meters: 830
Centimeters: 63.25
```

6. Payroll Problem III: Federal Withholding Tax Computations

Purpose: To become familiar with the procedure for rounding a value and executing a program a multiple number of times.

Problem: Modify Payroll Problem II (Problem 4) in Chapter 2 to accept by means of INPUT statements an employee number, number of dependents, hourly rate of pay, and hours worked during a biweekly pay period. Use the following formulas to compute the gross pay, federal withholding tax, and net pay:

1. Gross pay = hours worked × hourly rate of pay
2. Federal withholding tax = 0.2 × (gross pay – dependents × 38.46)
3. Net pay = gross pay – federal withholding tax

Round the gross pay and federal withholding tax following their computation. Execute the program for each employee described under Input Data for this problem. Have the program clear the screen before accepting any data.

(**Hint:** See Program 3.6 on page 74 or PRG3-6 on the Student Diskette.)

Input Data: Use the following sample data:

Employee Number	Number of Dependents	Hourly Rate of Pay	Hours Worked
123	2	$12.50	80
124	1	8.00	100
125	1	13.00	80
126	2	4.50	20

Output Results: The following results are displayed for employee number 123:

```
Employee number ===========> 123
Number of dependents ======> 2
Hourly rate of pay ========> 12.50
Hours worked ==============> 80

Gross pay =================> 1000
Federal withholding tax ===> 184.62
Net pay ===================> 815.38
```

Use the Print Screen key to print the output results for each employee.

The Top-Down Approach to Problem Solving Using Subprograms

4.1 INTRODUCTION

This chapter presents the top-down (modular) approach to solving problems. The top-down approach is a useful methodology for solving larger and more complex problems than those presented in the previous chapters. The objective of the **top-down approach** is to take the original problem and break it into smaller and more manageable subproblems, each of which is easier to solve than the original one. In other words, to solve a problem top-down, you divide and conquer.

The idea of solving a problem by dividing it into smaller subproblems is not new. In his *Discourse on Method*, more than 300 years before the first computer was built, Rene Descartes made this same point. In essence, he says that the resolution of a problem can be achieved if a person does the following: (1) divides each of the difficulties into as many parts as possible; and (2) thinks in an orderly fashion, beginning with those matters which are simplest and easiest to understand, and gradually working toward those which are more complex.

At first the top-down approach may appear to be cumbersome, especially for the simple problems discussed so far. However with large, complex problems, it is the only logical way to develop programs. We are introducing this methodology early because most programmers find it difficult to change their plan of attack, that is, unlearn less sophisticated program development habits. By the time we get to the more sophisticated problems, we want to be sure that you are solving problems top-down by habit.

The top-down approach to problem solving involves four major steps: (1) problem analysis, (2) top-down design, (3) top-down programming, and (4) top-down testing and debugging. **Top-down design** is a strategy that breaks large, complex problems into smaller, less complex problems and then decomposes each of these into even smaller problems. **Top-down programming** is a strategy that codes high-level modules as soon as they are designed and generally *before* the low-level modules have been designed. **Top-down testing and debugging** is a strategy that tests and debugs the high-level modules of a system *before* the low-level modules have been coded and possibly before they have been designed.

The top-down approach to problem solving is a methodology recommended by nearly all computer professionals. The claim is that a program developed top down is reliable, has simplicity of design, and is easy to read and maintain or modify. The steps in the program development life cycle described in Table 1.4 on page 13 should follow the top-down approach as shown in Figure 4.1 on the next page.

FIGURE 4.1

*The steps in the
program devel-
opment life
cycle (Table 1.4)
can be grouped
to fit into the
top-down
approach to
problem
solving.*

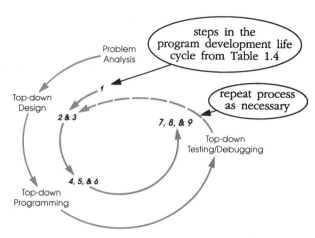

This chapter uses Programming Case Study 4A to illustrate the top-down approach to problem solving. Review the problem analysis for Programming Case Study 4A on page 66 before continuing.

4.2   TOP-DOWN DESIGN

Solutions to problems should be designed in a top-down fashion. The top-down design strategy is performed in two stages: (1) high-level design and (2) detailed design. High-level design identifies *what* tasks need to be performed, while detailed design addresses *how* the tasks should be performed.

High-Level Design

Top-down design takes a telescopic approach, beginning with the big picture and then zooming on the details. First, you identify the overall problem. Then, you identify the subproblems. Each subproblem may be further subdivided. This process continues until a level is reached where each problem identified is easily comprehended.

A graphical representation of the top-down design approach is a **top-down chart**, also called a **hierarchy chart** or **Visual Table of Contents — VTOC**. Figure 4.2 represents a top-down chart in which the problem or task presented in Programming Case Study 4A is broken down into subtasks. The overall task and each of the subtasks are represented by a process symbol with a short description written inside it. The top-down chart is read from top to bottom, and in general, from left to right.

FIGURE 4.2

*A top-down
chart for the
problem pre-
sented in Pro-
gramming Case
Study 4A.*

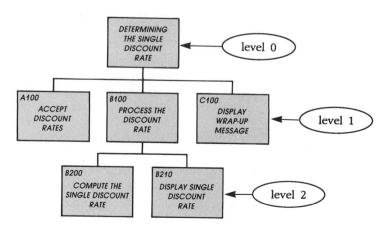

A top-down chart differs from a program flowchart, pseudocode, or other logic tools, in that it does not show decision-making logic or flow of control. A program flowchart, or pseudocode, shows *procedure*, but a top-down chart shows *organization* and *functionality*. A top-down chart allows you to concentrate on defining *what* needs to be done in the program before deciding *how* and *when* it is to be done, which is represented in a program flowchart, pseudocode, or other logic tools.

A top-down chart is very similar to a company's organization chart; each subtask carries out a function for its superior. Think of the higher level subtasks as vice presidents of the organization, who do the controlling functions of that organization. The top-down chart in Figure 4.2 resembles a small company with only two levels below the president. As a company grows and becomes more complex, additional levels are appended to the organizational chart to carry out the tasks for that organization. Likewise, as problems become larger and more complex, additional levels are added to the top-down chart.

As you design from top to bottom (general to specific), the subtasks are connected to their superior tasks by vertical lines. Each subtask is subordinate to the one above it and superior to any that are below it.

Notice that each task in the top-down chart in Figure 4.2 is identified with a capital letter and a number; for example, A100 for Accept Discount Rates. The letter identifies the branch of the top-down chart from left to right; the first digit of the number represents the level of the task within the branch. Collectively, the letter and the number are called a **level number**, which represents the placement of the task within the program. Subordinate tasks have the same letter as their superior with a higher number than their superior. In our example, level zero represents the highest task in the program; level one has three tasks; and level two, the lowest level, has two tasks.

In Figure 4.2, we adopted the technique of representing level one tasks as A100, B100, and C100. Because the two tasks in level two are subordinate to B100, we assigned task numbers in increments of ten; for example, B200 and B210 are subordinate to B100. If task C100 had three subordinate tasks at level two, they would be numbered as C200, C210, and C220. If task B200 had three subordinate tasks at level three, they would be numbered as B300, B310, and B320.

The same subtask may be subordinate to more than one superior task. Recurring subtasks are identified by darkening the upper right-hand corner of the process symbol as shown in Exercise 1 on page 114. At implementation, recurring subtasks are coded once and called as often as needed.

A top-down chart is not a program flowchart, nor does it replace the program flowchart or other logic tools in designing algorithms. A top-down chart is a tool that is used early in the design stage to decompose, in an orderly fashion, a large task into subtasks, and to some extent to show the flow of control between these subtasks. The result is a graphic view of what must be done to solve the overall problem. Therefore, creating top-down charts is referred to as **high-level design**.

The emphasis in the top-down approach is on careful analysis. The first top-down chart a programmer thinks of is seldom the one that is implemented. Typically, a top-down chart is reviewed and refined several times before it is considered acceptable. In many companies, top-down charts are submitted to a **peer review group**, composed of programmers and analysts, for further review and refinement before a programmer is allowed to proceed with the next step of program development. This process of review and refinement is sometimes referred to as a **structured walk-through**.

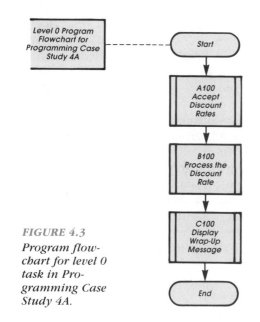

FIGURE 4.3

Program flow-chart for level 0 task in Programming Case Study 4A.

Detailed Design

The next step is to design *how* the tasks in the top-down chart should be performed. In the top-down approach, the higher level tasks are designed, coded, and tested generally *before* the lower level tasks are even designed. This technique ensures correctness at each level before proceeding. Our next step, then, is to develop the logic for the level zero task in the top-down chart, Determining the Single Discount Rate. The logic is quite simple. As shown in the flowchart in Figure 4.3, the level 0 task performs no detail work; it only invokes (*or calls*) the lower level tasks.

4.3   TOP-DOWN PROGRAMMING USING SUBPROGRAMS

Once the flowchart for a higher level task has been designed, its solution should be coded and tested *before* the lower level tasks are designed. Each task in the top-down chart is called a **module**. The highest level module in a program (level 0) is called the **Main module**. Our first programming step is to code the Main module as represented by the flowchart in Figure 4.3. Programming Case Study 4A, Determining the Single Discount Rate, calls three lower level modules: (1) A100 Accept Discount Rates, (2) B100 Process the Discount Rate, and (3) C100 Display Wrap-Up Message. For many practical problems, properly coded modules have one entry point, one exit point, no dead (unexecuted) code, and no infinite (endless) loops; however, exceptions exist. For additional information on properly coded modules, see Section 4.5 in Appendix A.

The Main module may be implemented in a QuickBASIC program as three CALL statements. The function of the first CALL is to invoke the A100 Accept Discount Rates module. At the completion of its prescribed task, the A100 Accept Discount Rates module returns control to the Main module. The second CALL invokes the B100 Process the Discount Rate module, which maintains control until the rate is processed. The final CALL in the Main module references the C100 Display Wrap-Up Message module. Upon completion of its task, the C100 Display Wrap-Up Message module returns control to the Main module and the program terminates. Once coded, the Main module is called the Main Program; that is, the term *module* refers to design and the terms *program* or *subprogram* refer to QuickBASIC code.

The lower level modules are implemented in QuickBASIC as **subprograms**. A **subprogram** is a separate section of code intended to accomplish a specific task. A subprogram begins with the keyword SUB, followed immediately by a subprogram name. Like a variable name, a **subprogram name** can be up to 40 characters in length. The subprogram is invoked by a CALL statement. The keyword CALL is immediately followed by the subprogram name to which control is transferred. Once control transfers, the instructions following the subprogram name are executed one after the other until the END SUB statement is encountered. The END SUB statement transfers control back to the next executable statement following the corresponding CALL statement in the superior program or subprogram (Figure 4.4).

FIGURE 4.4
A physical view of control transferring from the Main Program to a subprogram and eventually returning to the Main Program.

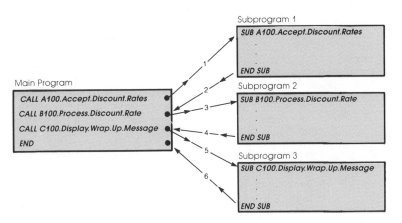

The general forms of the SUB and CALL statements are given in Tables 4.1 and 4.2.

TABLE 4.1   The SUB Statement

General Form: SUB subprogramname (p₁, ..., pₙ) STATIC
$$\cdot$$
$$\cdot$$

END SUB

where **subprogramname** is the name of the subprogram (up to 40 characters long); and

p₁ through pₙ is an optional list of parameters (variables), separated by commas, that show the number and type of arguments to be passed to the subprogram from the CALL statement. If present, STATIC instructs the PC to retain the values of the local variables between calls.

If STATIC is not present, then local variables are initialized to zeros or null strings each time the subprogram is called.

Purpose: Defines a subprogram. The subprogram is called (invoked) by a CALL statement from the Main Program or from another subprogram.

Examples: SUB statements without END SUB statements. See the corresponding CALL statements in Table 4.2 on the next page.

1. SUB C100.Wrap.Up
2. SUB B300.Compute.Gross (Gross, Hours, Rate, Dependents)
3. SUB B320.Print.Detail (E.Name$, Age, Date.In$) STATIC
4. SUB B400.Accumulate (Gross.Total, Hours.Total) STATIC
5. SUB B510.Print.Message (Month, Message$)
6. SUB A110.Binary.Sort (Array())

Note: The END SUB causes control to transfer from the subprogram back to the first executable statement immediately following the CALL statement that called (invoked) the subprogram.

TABLE 4.2	The CALL Statement

General Form: CALL subprogramname (a_1, ..., a_n)

where **subprogramname** is the name of a subprogram; and

a_1 **through** a_n is an optional list of arguments (variables, constants, expressions, array elements, or entire arrays), separated by commas, that must agree in number and type with the parameter list in the corresponding SUB statement.

Purpose: Causes control to transfer to a subprogram represented by subprogramname. Causes the location of the next executable statement following the CALL to be retained. If an argument list is included, then the arguments are *passed* to the parameters in the order specified.

Examples: These CALL statements reference the SUB statements in Table 4.1.

```
1. CALL C100.Wrap.Up
2. CALL B300.Compute.Gross(G, 46.5, Job * Class, D)
3. CALL B320.Print.Detail(E.Name$, Age, Date.In$)
4. CALL B400.Accumulate(Gr.Total, Hrs.Total)
5. CALL B510.Print.Message(Month(1), "does not")
6. CALL A110.Binary.Sort(Cost())
```

Note: You can call a subprogram by using the name of the subprogram without the keyword CALL. For example, B400.Accumulate Gr.Total, Hrs.Total calls the subprogram B400.Accumulate the same as in example 4. If the keyword CALL is not present, then don't surround the argument list with parentheses. This form of the CALL statement will not be used in this book.

Types of Subprograms

There are two types of subprograms — internal and external. An **internal subprogram**, also called an **associated subprogram**, is one that belongs to the same unit of code as the Main Program. When you save a program that has internal subprograms, they are all saved to disk under a given name. Furthermore, when you load a program into main storage, all internal subprograms are also loaded. How to enter and edit internal subprograms will be discussed later in Section 4.4.

An **external subprogram** is independent from the calling program and resides in auxiliary storage in one of the following three forms:

1. A separate and distinct program
2. Part of another program
3. A QuickBASIC library

With regards to external subprograms, we will cover only the first type, which requires the use of the CHAIN statement (see Appendix C). For information on how to call subprograms located in another program or located in a QuickBASIC library, see the QuickBASIC user's manual or select *Modules and Procedures* under *Contents* in the Help menu.

Stubs

Because we have not yet designed the logic for the three lower level modules in Programming Case Study 4A, we must implement these subprograms as stubs. A **stub** is a skeleton version of the final subprogram. It does not contain details or fulfill program tasks; it simply exists as the target of a CALL statement. Often programmers place one PRINT statement inside a stub. For example, a Process module stub might be coded as shown at the top of the next page.

```
SUB B100.Process
    PRINT "You are now inside the B100 subprogram"
END SUB
```

Through the use of these *dummy* PRINT statements, stubs help demonstrate that a program flows as intended. With stubs, you can test and debug a program *as it is being built*. When the program is complete and functional, the *dummy* PRINT statements are removed.

Program 4.1

Consider the following top-down code for the level 0 module in Programming Case Study 4A, Determining the Single Discount Rate. The code corresponds to the flowchart in Figure 4.3 on page 94.

PROGRAM 4.1

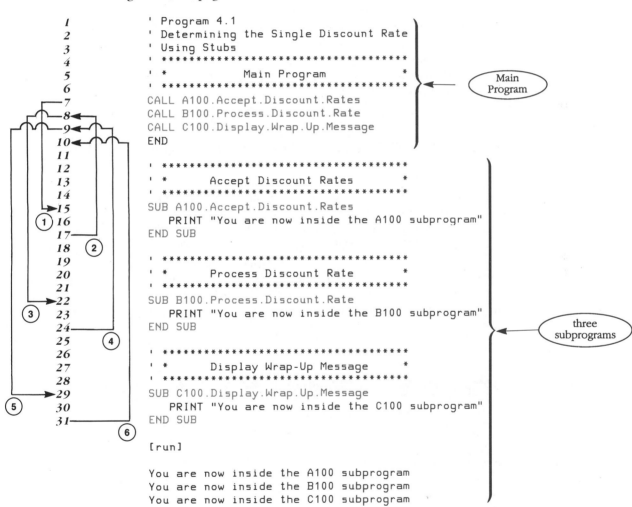

```
 1    ' Program 4.1
 2    ' Determining the Single Discount Rate
 3    ' Using Stubs
 4    ' **************************************
 5    ' *            Main Program            *
 6    ' **************************************
 7    CALL A100.Accept.Discount.Rates
 8    CALL B100.Process.Discount.Rate
 9    CALL C100.Display.Wrap.Up.Message
10    END
11
12    ' **************************************
13    ' *        Accept Discount Rates       *
14    ' **************************************
15    SUB A100.Accept.Discount.Rates
16        PRINT "You are now inside the A100 subprogram"
17    END SUB
18
19    ' **************************************
20    ' *        Process Discount Rate       *
21    ' **************************************
22    SUB B100.Process.Discount.Rate
23        PRINT "You are now inside the B100 subprogram"
24    END SUB
25
26    ' **************************************
27    ' *        Display Wrap-Up Message     *
28    ' **************************************
29    SUB C100.Display.Wrap.Up.Message
30        PRINT "You are now inside the C100 subprogram"
31    END SUB

[run]

You are now inside the A100 subprogram
You are now inside the B100 subprogram
You are now inside the C100 subprogram
```

When you execute Program 4.1, the CALL statement in line 7 transfers control to the A100.Accept.Discount.Rates subprogram (line 15). This stub displays the message You are now inside the A100 subprogram. The END SUB statement in line 17 returns control to line 8.

The CALL statement in line 8 invokes the B100.Process.Discount.Rate subprogram, which begins at line 22. Once the message You are now inside the B100 subprogram displays, the END SUB statement in line 24 returns control to line 9 in the Main Program.

Line 9, in turn, transfers control to the C100.Display.Wrap.Up.Message subprogram (line 29). Following the display of `You are now inside the C100 subprogram`, the END SUB statement in line 31 returns control to line 10 of the Main Program.

The END statement in line 10 halts the execution of the program. Prior to Program 4.1, all programs used the END statement as the physical end of the program. It should be apparent now that QuickBASIC does not require that the END statement be the last physical statement in the program.

Recommended Style and Tips When Coding Subprograms

Consider the following tips when coding subprograms in QuickBASIC:

1. Start each subprogram with a comment box. A **comment box** consists of three or more remark lines with asterisks surrounding a brief comment.
2. Use a level number as part of the subprogram name, such as A100.
3. Indent the statements between the SUB and the END SUB by three spaces.
4. Position subprograms below their superior, and in the order in which they are called, so that subprograms can be located easily in a printout for debugging purposes. As we shall see shortly, QuickBASIC prints subprograms in alphabetical order by their name.

4.4   USING THE QUICKBASIC EDITOR TO ENTER SUBPROGRAMS

The QuickBASIC editor includes all the tools you need to enter, modify, and print subprograms. Program 4.1 will be used to illustrate the development of subprograms with the QuickBASIC editor.

To initiate a subprogram, type the statement SUB A100.Accept.Discount.Rates below the last line of the Main Program in the view window (Figure 4.5). When you press the Enter key, the Main Program disappears, and QuickBASIC displays the screen shown in Figure 4.6. The Main Program is still active and available, but is not in the view window. As shown in Figure 4.6, QuickBASIC automatically includes the SUB and END SUB statements with a blank line between them. The cursor is positioned on the blank line.

FIGURE 4.5
The initiation of a new subprogram via Alternative 1 — entering the SUB *statement in the view window.*

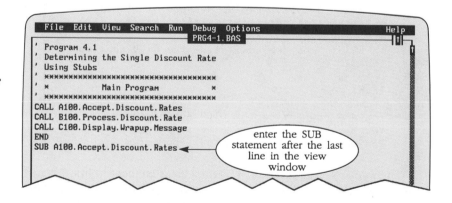

FIGURE 4.6
The display by QuickBASIC of the SUB *statement followed by a blank line and the* END SUB *statement.*

According to Program 4.1, we need to add a comment box above the first SUB statement. Use the Up Arrow key to move the cursor to the S in SUB. Press the Enter key. QuickBASIC displays a dialog box cautioning you that only comments may be placed above a SUB statement. Press the Enter key and enter the comment box for the subprogram A100.Accept.Discount.Rates (lines 12 to 14 of Program 4.1). Next, move the cursor back to the blank line between SUB and END SUB and enter the dummy PRINT statement in the subprogram.

To begin the second subprogram, enter the SUB statement below the END SUB statement. QuickBASIC again displays the screen shown in Figure 4.6. At this point, you can enter the dummy PRINT statement in the second subprogram.

Another way to initiate a new subprogram is to select the New SUB command in the Edit menu shown in Figure 4.7. Recall that you activate the Edit menu by pressing the Alt key and typing the letter E. If you have a mouse, click Edit in the menu bar.

When you initiate a subprogram using the New SUB command, QuickBASIC displays a dialog box requesting that you enter the subprogram name. Once the subprogram name is entered, the screen shown in Figure 4.6 displays.

FIGURE 4.7

The initiation of a new subprogram via Alternative 2 — selecting the command New SUB in the Edit menu.

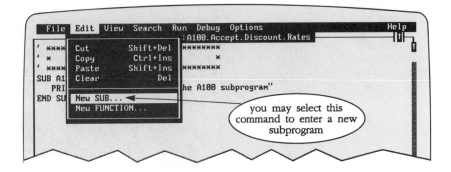

Editing Subprograms

After entering the Main Program and the associated subprograms, the view window will display the last subprogram. At this point, you may want to review and correct entries in the Main Program and the associated subprograms. QuickBASIC allows you to display and edit the different units of code in two ways:

1. Select the SUBs command (F2) in the View menu (Figure 4.8) and then select the name of the Main Program or subprogram to display.
2. Press Shift + F2 to display the next subprogram in alphabetical order by name. Press Ctrl + F2 to display the previous subprogram in alphabetical order by name.

FIGURE 4.8

Selection of the SUBs command (function key F2) in the View menu allows for the display and editing of the Main Program or any associated subprograms.

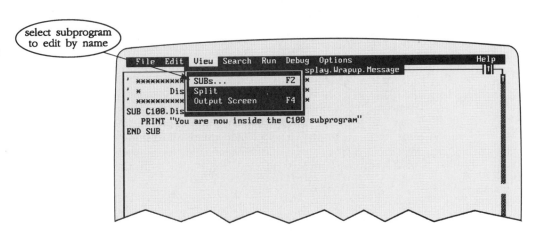

When you select the SUBs command in the View menu, QuickBASIC displays the dialog box shown in Figure 4.9. This dialog box has several features. First of all, it displays the names of the Main Program and associated subprograms. The subprogram names are indented below the Main Program name. In Figure 4.9, the name of the Main Program is PRG4-1 because we saved it under this name before entering the first SUB statement. The Main Program would be identified as <Untitled> if it had not been saved before displaying this screen.

To display the Main Program or any one of the associated subprograms, use the arrow keys to select the desired name and press the Enter key. If you have a mouse, click the name twice. QuickBASIC immediately displays the selected program in the view window.

Note in Figure 4.9 that there are buttons below the box containing the program names. Table 4.3 summarizes the function of these buttons. To use them, highlight the desired program, select the button using the Tab key and press the Enter key. If you have a mouse, click the program name and then click the button. Edit in Active is the default button if you don't select one before you press the Enter key or click the mouse.

FIGURE 4.9

The dialog box display of the names of the Main Program and associated subprograms.

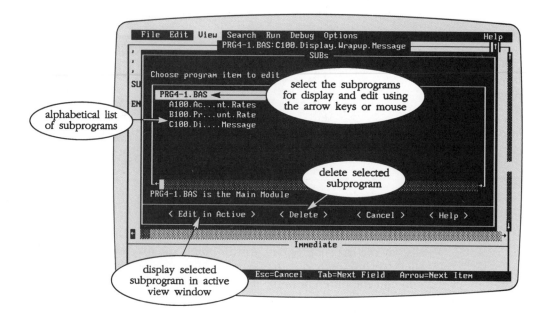

TABLE 4.3   Function of the Buttons in the Dialog Box when the SUBs Command is Selected in the View Menu

BUTTON	FUNCTION
Edit in Active	Causes the highlighted program to replace the program in the active window. If the view window is split, the program in the inactive window remains where it is on the screen.
Delete	Causes the deletion of the highlighted subprogram.
Cancel	Cancels the dialog box and activates the view window.
Help	Displays a help window with information on using the SUBs dialog box.

Splitting the View Window

To split the view window horizontally into two view windows (Figure 4.10) so that you can display and edit the Main Program and a subprogram or two subprograms, do the following:

1. Select the Split command in the View menu (Figure 4.8).
2. Press F6 to activate the lower window.
3. Press F2 or select the SUBs command in the View window (Figure 4.8). When the dialog box shown in Figure 4.9 displays, select the subprogram you want to display in the second window and press the Enter key.

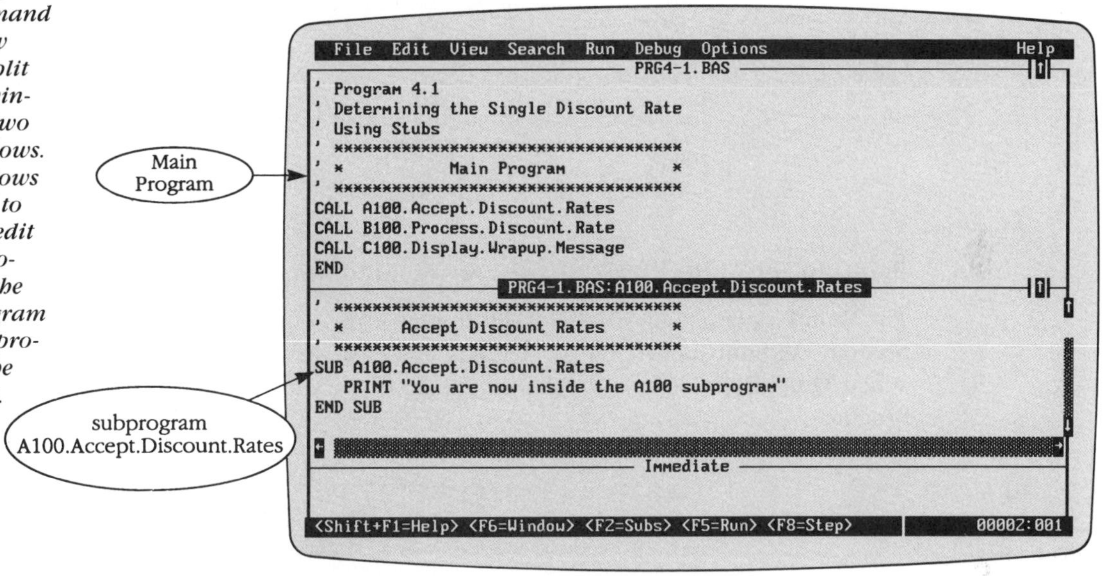

FIGURE 4.10

Selection of the Split command in the View menu to split the view window into two view windows. Split windows allow you to view and edit two subprograms or the Main Program and a subprogram at the same time.

Once the two programs display, use the F6 key to deactivate one window and activate the other. To increase the size of the active window by one line, press Alt + Plus(+); to decrease the size one line, press Alt + Minus(–). When changing the size of a window, you must use the Plus and Minus Keys on the numeric keypad. To return to a single view window, activate the window you want to keep. Next, select the Split command in the View window. The Split command is like a toggle switch. Select it once, and the view window is divided into two view windows. Select it again, and the inactive window disappears.

Saving, Loading, and Executing the Main Program and Associated Subprograms

Use the Save command in the File menu to save the Main Program and associated subprograms. This command causes the Main Program and all associated subprograms to be saved under the same file name.

When you save a program that includes subprograms, QuickBASIC automatically appends a DECLARE statement for each subprogram to the beginning of the Main Program. The DECLARE statements for Program 4.1 are shown in Figure 4.11. If you make changes to the parameter list in any subprogram, then change the DECLARE statements so that their parameter lists agree with the parameter lists in the SUB statements. (Parameter lists are discussed in the next section).

Use the Open command in the File menu to load the Main Program and associated subprograms from disk into main storage.

To execute a program with subprograms, press Shift + F5 while the Main Program or any one of the associated subprograms is in the view window. Execution begins with the first executable statement in the Main Program. Because our subprograms are only stubs, the output displays the information contained in the dummy PRINT statements (see Program 4.1 on page 97).

FIGURE 4.11

The display of the DECLARE *statements for Program 4.1, one for each subprogram.*

Printing the Main Program and Associated Subprograms

The Main Program and associated subprograms are printed the same way that you print a program without subprograms. That is, first select the Print command in the File menu. When QuickBASIC displays the Print dialog box shown in Figure 4.12, select Entire Program.

FIGURE 4.12

The display of the Print dialog box.

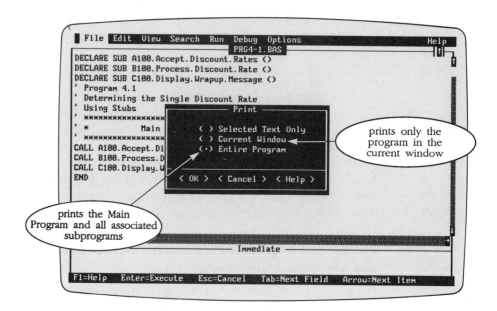

QuickBASIC prints the Main Program first, followed by the subprograms in alphabetical order by name. The use of a level number, such as A100 or B100, as part of the subprogram name should now be obvious to you. If you want to control the order in which the subprograms are printed, you must select appropriate names or print the Main Program and subprograms one at a time. To print the subprograms one at a time, do the following:

1. Load the subprogram into the view window.
2. Issue the Print command from the File menu and select Current Window in the Print dialog box (Figure 4.12).

4.5 DESIGNING THE LOGIC FOR SUBPROGRAMS

We have completed one full cycle in the top-down approach to solving Programming Case Study 4A using top-down design, top-down programming, and top-down testing and debugging. After defining the problem, we composed a top-down chart. Then, we designed the logic in the highest level module, Determining the Single Discount Rate. Next, we coded the logic using stubs to implement the lower level modules. Finally, we entered the code using the QuickBASIC editor, and we executed the program.

We are now ready to design the logic for the lower level modules in Programming Case Study 4A. According to the top-down method, you should design one module at a time — entering each one using the QuickBASIC editor and executing the new program *before* designing the logic for the next module. This technique enables you to isolate any errors to the module just entered and saves you a lot of time debugging, especially in large, complex programs. Although we will show you the logic for multiple lower level modules at once, we strongly recommend you code and test your programs one module at a time.

According to the top-down chart in Figure 4.2 on page 92, level one contains three modules: A100 Accept Discount Rates, B100 Process the Discount Rate and C100 Display Wrap-Up Message. Notice the B100 Process the Discount Rate module invokes two lower level modules: B200 Compute the Single Discount Rate and B210 Display Single Discount Rate. These two modules will initially be coded as stubs. Figure 4.13 shows the logic for the level-one modules in our top-down chart.

FIGURE 4.13

General flow-charts for the level one modules: Accept Discount Rates, Process the Discount Rate, and Display Wrap-Up Message.

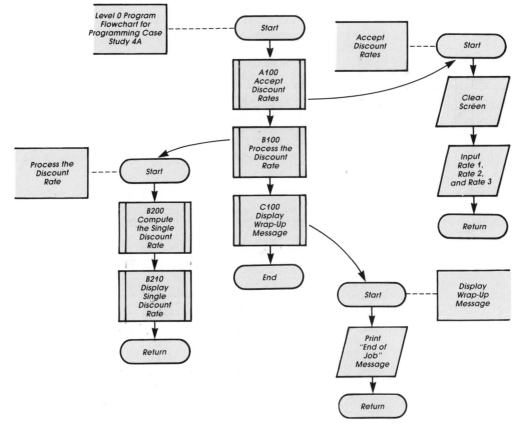

Program 4.2

The following QuickBASIC program corresponds to the flowchart in Figure 4.13, illustrating the completed code for the level-one modules.

PROGRAM 4.2

```
 1    ' Program 4.2
 2    ' Determining the Single Discount Rate
 3    ' With the Level One Modules Coded
 4    ' **********************************
 5    ' *            Main Program              *
 6    ' **********************************
 7    CALL A100.Accept.Discount.Rates
 8    CALL B100.Process.Discount.Rate
 9    CALL C100.Display.Wrap.Up.Message
10    END
11
12    ' **********************************
13    ' *        Accept Discount Rates          *
14    ' **********************************
15    SUB A100.Accept.Discount.Rates
16       CLS   ' Clear Screen
17       PRINT "Enter in Percent Form:"
18       INPUT "          First Discount ======> ", Rate1
19       INPUT "          Second Discount =====> ", Rate2
20       INPUT "          Third Discount ======> ", Rate3
21    END SUB
22
23    ' **********************************
24    ' *        Process Discount Rate          *
25    ' **********************************
26    SUB B100.Process.Discount.Rate
27       CALL B200.Compute.Single.Rate
28       CALL B210.Display.Single.Rate
29    END SUB
30
31    ' **********************************
32    ' *        Compute Single Rate            *
33    ' **********************************
34    SUB B200.Compute.Single.Rate
35       PRINT "You are now inside the B200 subprogram"
36    END SUB
37
38    ' **********************************
39    ' *         Display Single Rate           *
40    ' **********************************
41    SUB B210.Display.Single.Rate
42       PRINT "You are now inside the B210 subprogram"
43    END SUB
44
45    ' **********************************
46    ' *        Display Wrap-Up Message        *
47    ' **********************************
48    SUB C100.Display.Wrap.Up.Message
49       PRINT
50       PRINT "*********** End of Job ***********"
51    END SUB
```

nested subprograms

```
[run]

Enter in Percent Form:
              First Discount ======> 40
              Second Discount =====> 20
              Third Discount ======> 10
You are now inside the B200 subprogram
You are now inside the B210 subprogram

*********** End of Job ***********
```

The flow of Program 4.2 is nearly identical to Program 4.1. The difference is that we have implemented the level-one modules. Recall that the CALL statement in line 7 transfers control to the A100.Accept.Discount.Rates subprogram (line 15). Notice this subprogram is now completely coded; it clears the screen and accepts three discounts. The END SUB statement in line 21 returns control to the next executable statement following the CALL in the Main Program (line 8).

The CALL statement in line 8 invokes the B100.Process.Discount.Rate subprogram (line 26), which invokes two subprograms. When one subprogram calls another subprogram, the lower level subprogram is called a **nested subprogram**. The CALL statement in line 27 transfers control to the B200.Compute.Single.Rate subprogram (line 34). This nested subprogram is actually a stub, which displays the message You are now inside the B200 subprogram. The END SUB statement in line 36 returns control to line 28.

The CALL statement in line 28 invokes the B210.Display.Single.Rate stub, which begins at line 41. After the message You are now inside the B210 subprogram displays, the END SUB statement in line 43 returns control to line 29. The END SUB statement in line 29 returns control to line 9 in the Main Program.

Line 9 transfers control to the C100.Display.Wrap.Up.Message subprogram (line 48), which is now completely coded. It displays a blank line and the End of Job message. The END SUB statement in line 51 returns control to line 10 of the Main Program. Line 10 halts execution of the Main Program.

Sharing Variables with All Associated Subprograms

We are now ready to design the level-two modules in our program. According to Figure 4.2 on page 92, level two contains the B200 Compute Single Discount Rate and B210 Display Single Discount Rate modules. The flowcharts in Figure 4.14 show the logic for these two modules in our top-down chart.

FIGURE 4.14
Flowcharts for the level-two modules.

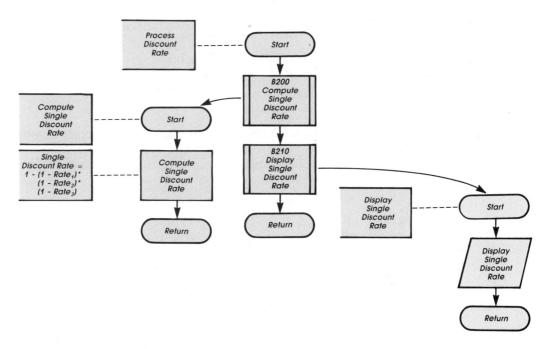

The B200 Compute Single Discount Rate module uses the three rates entered in the A100 Accept Discount Rates module. The B210 Display Single Discount Rate module uses the discount rate calculated in the B200 Compute Single Discount Rate module. Both of these modules require variables created in previous modules.

With subprograms, variables are by default **local variables**; that is, available only to the subprogram that created them. To share variables between the Main Program and all associated subprograms, you must use the COMMON statement with the attribute SHARED in the Main Program to list the variables that are available to all associated subprograms. Hence, through the COMMON statement, we can make variables **global** to all associated subprograms. The general form of the COMMON is given in Table 4.4.

TABLE 4.4 The COMMON Statement	

General Form:	COMMON attribute v_1, ..., v_n where **attribute** is one of the following: SHARED, /blockname/, or null; and v_1 **through** v_n is the list of variables to share. If the attribute SHARED is included, then the COMMON statement declares that the variable list is to be shared with all associated subprograms. If the attribute is **/blockname/** or null, then the variables that follow are identified as a group to be passed to an external subprogram that includes a similar COMMON statement.
Purpose:	Identifies variables that are to be shared globally between the Main Program and all associated subprograms.
Examples:	COMMON SHARED Sum, Count, Amount COMMON /AreaValues/Length, Width COMMON Rate(), Cost
Note:	1. The keyword SHARED may also be used in a DIM or REDIM statement to share variables between a Main Program and subprograms. 2. If attribute is /blockname/, then the COMMON statement is called a **named COMMON block**. If attribute is null, then it is called a **blank COMMON block**.

Any number of COMMON statements may appear in a program. For example, the following statement

```
COMMON SHARED Gross, Tax, Dependents
```

is the same as the following list of statements:

```
COMMON SHARED Gross
COMMON SHARED Tax
COMMON SHARED Dependents
```

However, it is invalid to list the same variable name in more than one COMMON statement in the same program.

The COMMON statement must be located at the beginning of the Main Program as illustrated in Program 4.3.

Program 4.3

Consider the following completed code for Programming Case Study 4A. The stubs from Program 4.2 (B200 and B210) have been converted to working subprograms, and all of the variables have been made global with the COMMON SHARED statement in line 7. The output results due to the execution of Program 4.3 are shown below the program code.

PROGRAM 4.3

```
1    ' Program 4.3
2    ' Determining the Single Discount Rate
3    ' Sharing Variables with Subprograms
4    ' **********************************
5    ' *           Main Program          *
6    ' **********************************
7    COMMON SHARED Rate1, Rate2, Rate3, Rate
8    CALL A100.Accept.Discount.Rates
9    CALL B100.Process.Discount.Rate
10   CALL C100.Display.Wrap.Up.Message
11   END
12
13   ' **********************************
14   ' *        Accept Discount Rates       *
15   ' **********************************
16   SUB A100.Accept.Discount.Rates
17      CLS   ' Clear Screen
18      PRINT "Enter in Percent Form:"
19      INPUT "            First Discount ======> ", Rate1
20      INPUT "            Second Discount =====> ", Rate2
21      INPUT "            Third Discount ======> ", Rate3
22   END SUB
23
24   ' **********************************
25   ' *        Process Discount Rate        *
26   ' **********************************
27   SUB B100.Process.Discount.Rate
28      CALL B200.Compute.Single.Rate
29      CALL B210.Display.Single.Rate
30   END SUB
31
32   ' **********************************
33   ' *          Compute Single Rate         *
34   ' **********************************
35   SUB B200.Compute.Single.Rate
36      Rate1 = Rate1 / 100
37      Rate2 = Rate2 / 100
38      Rate3 = Rate3 / 100
39      Rate = 1 - (1 - Rate1) * (1 - Rate2) * (1 - Rate3)
40      Rate = 100 * Rate
41   END SUB
42
43   ' **********************************
44   ' *          Display Single Rate          *
45   ' **********************************
46   SUB B210.Display.Single.Rate
47      PRINT
48      PRINT "Single Discount ================>"; Rate; "%"
49   END SUB
50
51   ' **********************************
52   ' *       Display Wrap-Up Message       *
53   ' **********************************
54   SUB C100.Display.Wrap.Up.Message
55      PRINT
56      PRINT "*********** End of Job ************"
57   END SUB
```

COMMON statement makes variables global

```
[run]

Enter in Percent Form:
             First Discount ======> 40
             Second Discount =====> 20
             Third Discount ======> 10

Single Discount ================> 56.8 %

*********** End of Job ************
```

Parameters and Arguments

An alternative to making all variables global with the COMMON SHARED statement is to pass the values of variables to the subprograms that need them. Values are passed to subprograms by assigning them to the arguments in the CALL statement. When the call is made, the arguments are assigned to the corresponding parameters in the SUB statement, where the first argument is passed to the first parameter, the second argument to the second parameter, and so on. With respect to the number of arguments in the CALL statement, the following can be stated:

> **SUB RULE 1**   *The number of arguments in the* CALL *statement must agree exactly with the number of parameters in the* SUB *statement.*

This capability of *passing* only the required values to a subprogram is considered to be one of the major advantages over the COMMON statement. Whereas a **parameter** in a SUB statement must be a variable, an **argument** in a CALL statement can be a constant, variable, expression, array element, or entire array. (Arrays are discussed in Chapter 8). Figure 4.15 illustrates the subprogram terminology and argument assignments.

FIGURE 4.15
The terminology used to describe the elements of a subprogram and argument assignments.

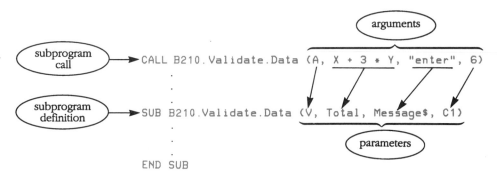

Passing Constants and Expressions.   Both constants and expressions can appear in the argument list of a CALL statement. Numeric constants and expressions can only be passed to numeric variables. Likewise, string constants and expressions can only be passed to string variables. If an attempt is made to pass a numeric value to a string variable, the PC will display a dialog box with the diagnostic message Type mismatch before terminating execution of the program.

Consider the argument list in line 5 and the parameter list in line 11 of Program 4.4. The first argument, 4.67, is passed to the integer variable X%. Because the constant 4.67 is real and X% is an integer variable, the PC forces the constant to the type of X% and passes it as the value 5. The second argument is a numeric expression, and it is passed to the variable Y. When control transfers to the subprogram A100.Print.Detail.Line, Y is equal to 7.5. Finally, the string QuickBASIC is passed to the string variable S$. In line 12 of subprogram A100.Print.Detail.Line, the PRINT statement displays the values of the three parameters X%, Y, and S$.

The following rule summarizes the preceding discussion:

> **SUB RULE 2**   *Arguments in the* CALL *statement must agree with the corresponding parameters in type. If an argument and a parameter are numeric, but do not agree in type, then the argument is forced to agree with the parameter.*

PROGRAM 4.4

```
1     ' Program 4.4
2     ' Passing Constants and Expressions
3     ' *********************************
4     CLS   ' Clear Screen
5     CALL A100.Print.Detail.Line(4.67, (5 * 6) / 4, "QuickBASIC")
6     END
7
8     ' *********************************
9     ' *        Print Detail Line      *
10    ' *********************************
11    SUB A100.Print.Detail.Line (X%, Y, S$)
12        PRINT X%, Y, S$
13    END SUB
```

```
[run]

      5               7.5             QuickBASIC
```

The remainder of this section is divided into subsections that illustrate the different ways QuickBASIC allows you use of this argument-parameter-list technique to pass values between a calling program and subprograms. Our discussion focuses on Program 4.5 on the next page and the corresponding output results in Figure 4.16. Program 4.5 is an alternative solution to Programming Case Study 4A.

Passing No Values to a Subprogram.   Not all subprograms require that the calling program pass values. For example, in Program 4.5 on the next page, the SUB statement that defines the subprogram C100.Display.Wrap.Up.Message (line 57) does not have a parameter list. Therefore, the CALL statement in line 9 does not have an argument list. The C100.Display.Wrap.Up.Message subprogram simply displays the End of Job message and returns control to line 10 in the Main Program.

Passing Values Between the Main Program and Subprograms or Between Nested Subprograms.   In Program 4.5, the CALL statement in line 7 transfers control to A100.Accept.Discount.Rates (line 16). As we explained, this subprogram clears the screen and accepts three discounts. The difference in this program is that these three discounts are *returned* to the Main Program. Notice that line 16 has a parameter list: (Rate1, Rate2, Rate3). When the END SUB statement in line 22 returns control to the the Main Program, it also returns the values of Rate1, Rate2, and Rate3 due to the parameter list in line 16 and the argument list in line 7.

After control passes back to line 8, Main Program calls B100.Process.Discount.Rate, which in turn invokes two lower level subprograms. Notice the CALL statement in line 8 has an argument list: (Rate1, Rate2, Rate3). Current values of each of these variables are *sent to* the parameter list in line 28, which defines the B100.Process.Discount.Rate subprogram.

PROGRAM 4.5

```
 1    ' Program 4.5
 2    ' Determining the Single Discount Rate
 3    ' Passing Values Between Subprograms
 4    ' ***********************************************
 5    ' *                 Main Program                *
 6    ' ***********************************************
 7    CALL A100.Accept.Discount.Rates(Rate1, Rate2, Rate3)
 8    CALL B100.Process.Discount.Rate(Rate1, Rate2, Rate3)
 9    CALL C100.Display.Wrap.Up.Message
10    END
11
12    ' ***********************************************
13    ' *            Accept Discount Rates            *
14    ' *          Returns Rate1, Rate2, Rate3        *
15    ' ***********************************************
16    SUB A100.Accept.Discount.Rates (Rate1, Rate2, Rate3)
17       CLS  ' Clear Screen
18       PRINT "Enter in Percent Form:"
19       INPUT "          First Discount ======> ", Rate1
20       INPUT "          Second Discount =====> ", Rate2
21       INPUT "          Third Discount ======> ", Rate3
22    END SUB
23
24    ' ***********************************************
25    ' *            Process Discount Rate            *
26    ' *          Receives Rate1, Rate2, Rate3       *
27    ' ***********************************************
28    SUB B100.Process.Discount.Rate (Rate1, Rate2, Rate3)
29       CALL B200.Compute.Single.Rate(Rate1, Rate2, Rate3, Rate)
30       CALL B210.Display.Single.Rate(Rate)
31    END SUB
32
33    ' ***********************************************
34    ' *            Compute Single Rate              *
35    ' * Receives Rate1, Rate2, Rate3; Returns Rate *
36    ' ***********************************************
37    SUB B200.Compute.Single.Rate (Rate1, Rate2, Rate3, Rate)
38       Rate1 = Rate1 / 100
39       Rate2 = Rate2 / 100
40       Rate3 = Rate3 / 100
41       Rate = 1 - (1 - Rate1) * (1 - Rate2) * (1 - Rate3)
42       Rate = 100 * Rate
43    END SUB
44
45    ' ***********************************************
46    ' *            Display Single Rate              *
47    ' *              Receives Rate                  *
48    ' ***********************************************
49    SUB B210.Display.Single.Rate (Rate)
50       PRINT
51       PRINT "Single Discount =================>"; Rate; "%"
52    END SUB
53
54    ' ***********************************************
55    ' *            Display Wrap-Up Message          *
56    ' ***********************************************
57    SUB C100.Display.Wrap.Up.Message
58       PRINT
59       PRINT "*********** End of Job ***********"
60    END SUB

      [run]
```

arguments

parameters

FIGURE 4.16

Output results due to execution of Program 4.5

```
Enter in Percent Form:
              First Discount ======> 40
              Second Discount =====> 20
              Third Discount ======> 10


Single Discount ================> 56.8 %

*********** End of Job ************
```

Because the values of Rate1, Rate2, and Rate3 are required to compute the single discount rate, these three values are then sent to the B200.Compute.Single.Rate subprogram. Notice that line 29 has an argument list of (Rate1, Rate2, Rate3, Rate). Likewise, line 37 has a parameter list of (Rate1, Rate2, Rate3, Rate). B200.Compute.Single.Rate *receives* the current values of the first three variables in the parameter list: Rate1, Rate2, and Rate3. The subprogram then computes the single discount rate and *returns* the value of the variable Rate to B100.Process.Discount.Rate because the variable Rate is listed in both the parameter list in line 37 and the argument list in line 29.

After control passes back to line 30, the program calls B210.Display.Single.Rate (line 49), which receives the value of the variable Rate so it can be displayed.

When using the argument-parameter-list technique to pass values of variables between the Main Program and subprograms or between subprograms, maintain consistency in variable placement. In this book, the variables listed first in an argument list are being *sent* to the subprogram. Any variables being *received* are placed at the end of the list. Likewise, in a parameter list *received* variables are listed first and *returned* variables are listed last. In addition, we place a comment above the subprogram indicating which variables are being received and which are being sent (lines 14, 26, 35, and 47).

Sharing Variables with Individual Subprograms. An alternative to passing values between the Main Program and subprograms using the argument-parameter-list technique is to share the values from the subprogram to the Main Program. Figure 4.17 shows the Main Program and the A100.Accept.Discount.Rates subprogram, sharing the values of Rate1, Rate2 and Rate3, rather than passing them.

FIGURE 4.17

Sharing variables between a subprogram and the Main Program.

```
1    ' Program 4.5
2    ' Determining the Single Discount Rate
3    ' Passing Values Between Subprograms
4    ' *************************************************
5    ' *                 Main Program                  *
6    ' *************************************************
7    CALL A100.Accept.Discount.Rates
8    CALL B100.Process.Discount.Rate(Rate1, Rate2, Rate3)
9    CALL C100.Print.Wrap.Up.Message
10   END
11
12   ' *************************************************
13   ' *           Accept Discount Rates               *
14   ' *           Shares Rate1, Rate2, Rate3          *
15   ' *************************************************
16   SUB A100.Accept.Discount.Rates
17       SHARED Rate1, Rate2, Rate3      ← variables shared with Main Program
18       CLS  ' Clear Screen
19       PRINT "Enter in Percent Form:"
20       INPUT "            First Discount ======> ", Rate1
21       INPUT "            Second Discount ======> ", Rate2
22       INPUT "            Third Discount ======> ", Rate3
23   END SUB
```

In Figure 4.17, the three discount rates accepted in the A100.Accept.Discount.Rates subprogram are shared with the Main Program because these rates are required in other subprograms (B100, B200, and B210). Because B100.Process.Discount.Rate is called from the Main Program, these discount rates must be available to the Main Program.

A SHARED statement or a group of SHARED statements placed immediately after the SUB statement at the beginning of a subprogram can be used to declare a list of variables that you want to share in either direction between the Main Program and the subprogram. The general form of the SHARED statement is given in Table 4.5.

TABLE 4.5   The SHARED Statement

General Form: SHARED v_1, ..., v_n
   where **v_1 through v_n** is a list of variables to share between the Main Program
   and the subprogram in which the SHARED statement resides.

Purpose: Shares the values of variables in both directions between a subprogram and
   the Main Program.

Examples: SHARED A, B, C
   SHARED Factor()

Note: The SHARED statement can also be used to define the type of variables in the
   list using the keyword AS. For example, SHARED K AS INTEGER, P AS DOUBLE
   declares K as an integer variable and P as a double-precision variable.

Line 7 in Figure 4.17 calls A100.Accept.Discount.Rates. This subprogram accepts the data from the user via INPUT statements and passes the values back to the Main Program due to the SHARED statement in line 17.

In QuickBASIC we cannot share values between subprograms; that is, the value of a variable created in one subprogram cannot be shared with another subprogram. This leads to the following rule:

SHARED RULE 1   *The SHARED statement can be used only to share variables defined in the Main Program or the subprogram in which the SHARED statement resides. The SHARED statement cannot be used to share variables between two subprograms.*

At first you may find the concept of passing variables a bit confusing. So, you might begin writing programs using the COMMON SHARED statement discussed earlier. However, passing values makes a program more efficient and less prone to error because variables are created and stored only when needed. For the programs in the remaining chapters in this book, we will alternate between the two techniques to better acquaint you with each one.

4.6   WHAT YOU SHOULD KNOW

1. The top-down approach to problem solving is a popular method of solving large, complex problems. It involves four major steps: (1) problem analysis, (2) top-down design, (3) top-down programming, and (4) top-down testing and debugging.
2. Top-down design is a strategy that breaks large, complex problems into smaller, less complex problems and then decomposes each of these into even smaller problems. Top-down design is performed in two stages: (1) high-level design and (2) detailed design.

3. High-level design is implemented through a top-down chart, which is a graphical representation of the task broken down into subtasks. Top-down charts show organization and functionality.

4. Each task in a top-down chart should be assigned a level number, such as A100, which represents the placement of the task within the program.

5. In many organizations, top-down charts are submitted to a peer review group for further review and refinement before a programmer is allowed to proceed to detailed design. This process of review and refinement is sometimes referred to as a structured walk-through.

6. Detailed design is implemented through program flowcharts, pseudocode, or other logic tools, which show how the tasks in the top-down chart should be performed. The higher level tasks are designed, coded, and tested generally before the lower level ones are even designed.

7. Top-down programming is a strategy that codes high-level modules as soon as they are designed and generally *before* the low-level modules have been designed.

8. Top-down testing and debugging is a strategy that tests and debugs the high-level modules of a system *before* the low-level modules have been coded and possibly before they have been designed.

9. Each task in the top-down chart is called a module.

10. Properly coded modules have one entry point, one exit point, no dead code, and no infinite loops; however, exceptions exist.

11. One method of implementing lower level modules in QuickBASIC is through subprograms.

12. A subprogram is a unit of code delimited by the SUB and END SUB statements and called (invoked) by the CALL statement.

13. The CALL statement transfers control to a subprogram and retains the location of the next executable statement following the CALL statement.

14. There are two types of subprograms — internal and external. Internal means that the subprogram belongs to the same unit of code as the Main Program. External means that the subprogram is independent from the calling program. That is, the subprogram is stored on disk under another name.

15. Subprograms are initially implemented as stubs. A stub is a skeleton version of the final subprogram. With stubs, you can test and debug a program as it is being built.

16. A subprogram may call another subprogram, which may in turn call another, and so on.

17. Subprogram names follow the same rules as for variable names.

18. The QuickBASIC editor includes all the tools you need to enter, modify, and print subprograms.

19. The COMMON statement with the attribute SHARED identifies variables that are to be shared between the Main Program and all internal (associated) subprograms.

20. Values are passed to subprograms by assigning them to the arguments in the CALL statement. The arguments are then passed to the corresponding parameters in the SUB statement.

21. The arguments in the CALL statement must agree in type and number with the parameters in the SUB statement.

22. A parameter in a SUB statement must be a variable. An argument in a CALL statement may be a constant, variable, expression, array element, or entire array.

23. The SHARED statement placed in a subprogram shares the values of the variables in both directions between the subprogram and the Main Program.

4.7   TEST YOUR BASIC SKILLS (Even-numbered answers are in Appendix E)

1. Consider the following top-down chart.

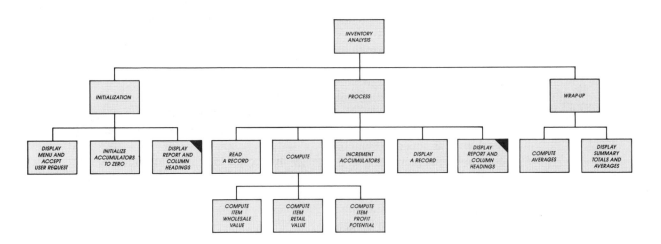

a. What is the name of the Main module?
b. How many levels are in the top-down chart?
c. What is(are) the name(s) of the modules in level 1?
d. Assign level numbers to each module, beginning with A100 for INITIALIZATION.

2. Consider the valid program listed below. What is displayed once it is executed?

```
' Exercise 4.2
CLS  ' Clear Screen
B = 20
CALL B210.Compute(10, B, "Subprogram", C)
PRINT "The value of C ="; C
END

SUB B210.Compute (X, Y, Term$, Z)
   Z = 3 * X ^ 2 + Y / 2 + LEN(Term$)
END SUB
```

3. Match each SUB statement to a CALL statement on the basis of type and number in the argument and parameter lists.

CALL Statements

a. CALL A300.SUBR(X, Y, Z)
b. CALL A300.SUBR
c. CALL A300.SUBR(U, X, Y, "Z")
d. CALL A300.SUBR(X)
e. CALL A300.SUBR("X", Y, Z)
f. CALL A300.SUBR("X", "Y")
g. CALL A300.SUBR(3, 5, "Z")

SUB Statements

1. SUB A300.SUBR (A)
2. SUB A300.SUBR (A, B, C$)
3. SUB A300.SUBR (A, B, C, D)
4. SUB A300.SUBR (A$, B, C)
5. SUB A300.SUBR
6. SUB A300.SUBR (A, B, C, D$)
7. SUB A300.SUBR (A$, B$, C)
8. None of the above.

4. Consider the valid program listed below. What is displayed when it is executed? Assume that Principal is assigned the value 100 and Rate is assigned 15.

```
' Exercise 4.4
' **********************************
' *            Main Program         *
' **********************************
COMMON SHARED Principal, Rate, Amount
CALL Accept.Input
CALL Compute.Amt
CALL Display.Amt
END


' **********************************
' *          Accept User Input      *
' **********************************
SUB Accept.Input
   CLS  ' Clear Screen
   INPUT "Principal ===> ", Principal
   INPUT "Rate in % ===> ", Rate
END SUB


' **********************************
' *            Compute Amount       *
' **********************************
SUB Compute.Amt
   Rate = Rate / 100
   Amount = Principal + Rate * Principal
END SUB


' **********************************
' *            Display Amount       *
' **********************************
SUB Display.Amt
   PRINT "Amount ======>"; Amount
END SUB
```

5. Rewrite the following program so that the input, computations, and output are done in separate subprograms. Use the COMMON statement to share variables.

```
' Exercise 4.5
' *************
CLS
INPUT "Gallons ===> ", Gallons
INPUT "Quarts ====> ", Quarts
INPUT "Pints =====> ", Pints
Ounces = 128 * Gallons + 32 * Quarts + 16 * Pints
PRINT : PRINT "Ounces ====>"; Ounces
END
```

6. Explain how the SHARED statement is used to pass values between a Main Program and subprogram. Is this statement placed in the Main Program or subprogram?
7. Rewrite the solution for exercise 4 by passing values of variables.
8. Rewrite your solution for exercise 5 by passing values of variables.
9. Which function keys are used to move from one subprogram to another in the QuickBASIC editor?

10. **PC Hands-On Exercise:** Load Program 4.3 (PRG4-3) from the Student Diskette. Execute the program in the step mode by continuously pressing the F8 key. See Appendix C for information on the step mode in QuickBASIC. When requested, enter the same data that was entered for Program 4.3. Now do you understand how the CALL statement transfers control to a subprogram and the END SUB statement returns control to the calling program?

11. **PC Hands-On Exercise:** Load Program 4.4 (PRG4-4) from the Student Diskette. In line 5, change the argument list to (3.4, 12, ''Book''). Execute the program and compare the results to those displayed by Program 4.4.

4.8   BASIC PROGRAMMING PROBLEMS

1. Service Charge Computations Using the COMMON Statement

Purpose: To become familiar with the top-down approach to problem solving using subprograms; and the CALL, SUB, END SUB, and COMMON statements.

Problem: Solve BASIC Programming Problem 1 in Chapter 3 on page 86 using the top-down chart shown in Figure 4.18.

Part 1:   Design a program flowchart for the Main module. Code the lower level modules using stubs. (**Hint:** See Program 4.1 on page 97 or PRG4-1 on the Student Diskette.) Test and debug the Main Program.

FIGURE 4.18

A top-down chart for the Service Charge Computations problem.

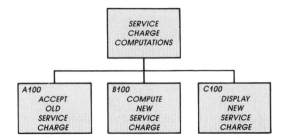

Part 1 Output Results: The following results are displayed when the program is coded with stubs:

```
You are now inside the A100 subprogram
You are now inside the B100 subprogram
You are now inside the C100 subprogram
```

Part 2:   Design program flowcharts for the lower level modules. Test and debug the subprograms one at a time. (**Hint:** See Program 4.3 on page 107 or PRG4-3 on the Student Diskette.)

Part 2 Output Results: Refer to BASIC Programming Problem 1 in Chapter 3 on page 86.

2. Service Charge Computations Passing Values Between Subprograms

Purpose: To become familiar with the top-down approach to problem solving using subprograms; the CALL, SUB, and END SUB statements; and passing values through a parameter list.

Problem: Solve BASIC Programming Problem 1 in Chapter 3 on page 86 using the top-down chart shown in Figure 4.18.

Part 1:   Design a program flowchart for the Main module. Code the lower level modules using stubs. (**Hint:** See Program 4.1 on page 97 or PRG4-1 on the Student Diskette.) Test and debug the Main Program. See Problem 1, Part 1, on opposite page for output results.

Part 2:   Design program flowcharts for the lower level modules. Pass all values to the subprograms through a parameter list. Test and debug the subprograms one at a time. (**Hint:** See Program 4.5 on page 110 or PRG4-5 on the Student Diskette.) See Problem 1, Part 2, on the opposite page for output results.

3. Determining the Monthly Payment on a Loan Using the COMMON Statement

Purpose: To become familiar with the top-down approach to problem solving using subprograms; and the CALL, SUB, END SUB, and COMMON statements.

Problem: Solve BASIC Programming Problem 3 in Chapter 3 on page 87 using the top-down chart shown in Figure 4.19.

Part 1:   Design a program flowchart for the Main module. Code the lower level modules using stubs. (**Hint:** See Program 4.1 on page 97 or PRG4-1 on the Student Diskette.) Test and debug the Main Program.

FIGURE 4.19

A top-down chart for Determining the Monthly Payment on a Loan problem.

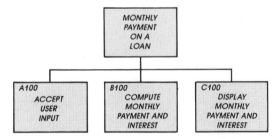

Part 1 Output Results: The following results are displayed when the program is coded with stubs:

```
You are now inside the A100 subprogram
You are now inside the B100 subprogram
You are now inside the C100 subprogram
```

Part 2:   Design program flowcharts for the lower level modules. Test and debug the subprograms one at a time. (**Hint:** See Program 4.3 on page 107 or PRG4-3 on the Student Diskette.)

Part 2 Output Results: Refer to BASIC Programming Problem 3 in Chapter 3 on page 87.

4. Determining the Monthly Payment on a Loan Passing Values Between Subprograms

Purpose: To become familiar with the top-down approach to problem solving using subprograms; the CALL, SUB, and END SUB statements; and passing values through a parameter list.

Problem: Solve BASIC Programming Problem 3 in Chapter 3 on page 87 using the top-down chart shown in Figure 4.19.

Part 1:   Design a program flowchart for the Main module. Code the lower level modules using stubs. (**Hint:** See Program 4.1 on page 97 or PRG4-1 on the Student Diskette.) Test and debug the Main Program. See Problem 3, Part 1, on previous page for output results.

Part 2:   Design program flowcharts for the lower level modules. Pass all values to the subprograms through a parameter list. Test and debug the subprograms one at a time. (**Hint:** See Program 4.5 on page 110 or PRG4-5 on the Student Diskette.) See Problem 3, Part 2, on the previous page for output results.

5. Payroll Problem IV: Federal Withholding Tax Computations Using the COMMON Statement

Purpose: To become familiar with the top-down approach to problem solving using subprograms; and the CALL, SUB, END SUB, and COMMON statements.

Problem: Solve BASIC Programming Problem 6 in Chapter 3 on page 89 using the top-down chart shown in Figure 4.20.

Part 1:   Design a program flowchart for the Main module. Code the lower level modules using stubs. (**Hint:** See Program 4.1 on page 97 or PRG4-1 on the Student Diskette.) Test and debug the Main Program.

FIGURE 4.20

A top-down chart for Payroll problem IV.

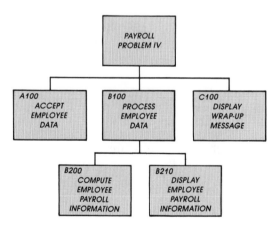

Part 1 Output Results: The following results are displayed when the program is coded with stubs:

```
You are now inside the A100 subprogram
You are now inside the B100 subprogram
You are now inside the C100 subprogram
```

Part 2:   Design program flowcharts for the lower level modules. Test and debug the subprograms one at a time. (**Hint:** See Program 4.3 on page 107 or PRG4-3 on the Student Diskette.)

Part 2 Output Results: Refer to BASIC Programming Problem 6 in Chapter 3 on page 90.

6. Payroll Problem IV: Federal Withholding Tax Computations Passing Values Between Subprograms

Purpose: To become familiar with the top-down approach to problem solving using subprograms; the CALL, SUB, and END SUB statements; and passing values through a parameter list.

Problem: Solve BASIC Programming Problem 6 in Chapter 3 on page 89 using the top-down chart shown in Figure 4.20.

Part 1: Design a program flowchart for the Main module. Code the lower level modules using stubs. (**Hint:** See Program 4.1 on page 97 or PRG4-1 on the Student Diskette.) Test and debug the Main Program. See Problem 5, Part 1, on the opposite page for output results.

Part 2: Design program flowcharts for the lower level modules. Pass all values to the subprograms through a parameter list. Test and debug the subprograms one at a time. (**Hint:** See Program 4.5 on page 110 or PRG4-5 on the Student Diskette.) See Problem 5, Part 2, on the opposite page for output results.

5

Looping and Input/Output

5.1 INTRODUCTION

The programs we have discussed so far are classified as **straight-line programs**. Up to this point, therefore, we have not yet utilized the complete power of the PC; essentially, we have used it as a high-speed calculator. However, the power of a PC is derived both from its speed and its capability to do repetitive tasks. One of the purposes of this chapter is to introduce you to the DO, and LOOP statements. These statements allow you to instruct the PC to loop and repeat a task in a program.

The programs developed in Chapters 2, 3, and 4 processed only small amounts of data. In this chapter we present a technique for integrating data into a program through the use of the READ and DATA statements. The READ and DATA statements are usually preferred over the INPUT statement when a program has to process large amounts of data that are part of the program itself.

The third topic to be discussed in this chapter is the generation of formatted reports. In Chapter 3, you learned about the PRINT statement. In this chapter, you will learn about the PRINT USING and LOCATE statements. These statements give you even more control over the output than the PRINT statement does.

Upon successful completion of this chapter, you should be able to write programs that can process data that is part of the program itself, and you will be able to generate formatted reports. Furthermore, you will be able to write programs that can repeat the same task over and over.

Programming Case Study 5 | Determining the Sale Price

Program 5.1 computes the discount amount and sale price for each of a series of products. The discount amount is determined from the following formula:

$$\text{Discount Amount} = \frac{\text{Discount Rate}}{100} \times \text{Original Price}$$

The sale price is determined from the following formula:

$$\text{Sale Price} = \text{Original Price} - \text{Discount Amount}$$

The product data includes a product number, original price, and discount rate, as shown below:

Product Number	Original Price	Discount Rate in Percent
112841A	$115.00	14
213981B	100.00	17
332121A	98.00	13
586192X	88.00	12
714121Y	43.00	8
EOF	0	0

trailer record → (to EOF row)

The top-down chart and flowchart that correspond to Program 5.1 are given in Figure 5.1. For your convenience in following the logic of the program, numbers have been placed on the top, left-hand corner of the symbols to illustrate the relationship between the flowchart and the program.

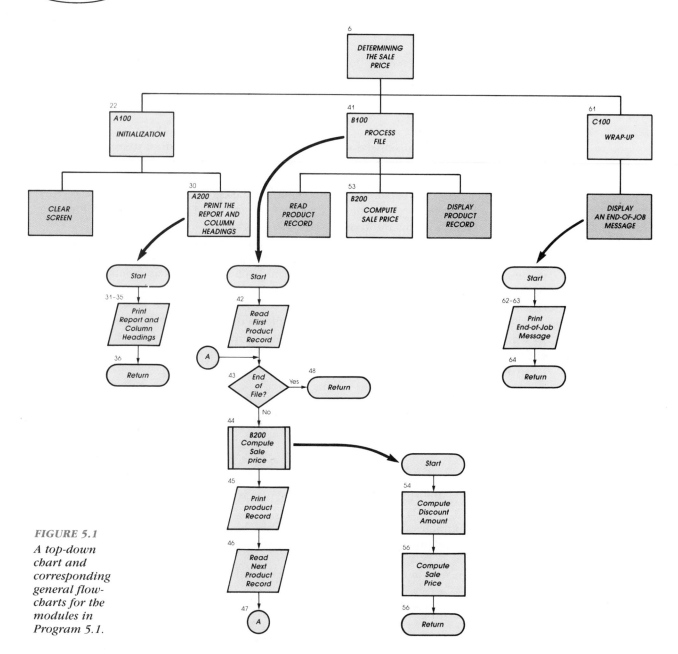

FIGURE 5.1

A top-down chart and corresponding general flow-charts for the modules in Program 5.1.

Program 5.1

The following program corresponds to the top-down chart and flowcharts in Figure 5.1. The colored modules in Figure 5.1 are implemented in Program 5.1 as subprograms. The grey modules represent tasks that have been moved into their superior subprogram in Program 5.1.

PROGRAM 5.1

```
1    ' Program 5.1
2    ' Determining the Sale Price
3    ' *********************************************
4    ' *                Main Program               *
5    ' *********************************************
6    COMMON SHARED Product$, Original.Price, Rate, Discount, Sale.Price
7    CALL A100.Initialization
8    CALL B100.Process.File
9    CALL C100.Wrap.Up
10   ' *************** Data Follows ****************
11   DATA 112841A, 115, 14
12   DATA 213981B, 100, 17
13   DATA 332121A,  98, 13
14   DATA 586192X,  88, 12
15   DATA 714121Y,  43,  8
16   DATA EOF,       0,  0  :  ' This is the Trailer Record
17   END
18
19   ' *********************************************
20   ' *               Initialization              *
21   ' *********************************************
22   SUB A100.Initialization
23      CLS  ' Clear Screen
24      CALL A200.Print.Headings
25   END SUB
26
27   ' *********************************************
28   ' *               Print Headings              *
29   ' *********************************************
30   SUB A200.Print.Headings
31      PRINT TAB(21); "Determine the Sale Price"
32      PRINT
33      PRINT "Product", "Original", "Discount", "Discount", "Sale"
34      PRINT "Number", "Price", "Rate in %", "Amount", "Price"
35      PRINT
36   END SUB
37
38   ' *********************************************
39   ' *                Process File               *
40   ' *********************************************
41   SUB B100.Process.File
42      READ Product$, Original.Price, Rate
43      DO WHILE Product$ <> "EOF"
44         CALL B200.Compute.Sale.Price
45         PRINT Product$, Original.Price, Rate, Discount, Sale.Price
46         READ Product$, Original.Price, Rate
47      LOOP
48   END SUB
49
50   ' *********************************************
51   ' *              Compute Sale Price           *
52   ' *********************************************
53   SUB B200.Compute.Sale.Price
54      Discount = Rate / 100 * Original.Price
55      Sale.Price = Original.Price - Discount
56   END SUB
57
```

Annotations:
- creates a sequence of data for use by the READ statements (lines 11–16)
- reads first product record (line 42)
- reads remaining product records (line 46)

(continued)

```
58      ' *************************************************
59      ' *                   Wrap-Up                     *
60      ' *************************************************
61      SUB C100.Wrap.Up
62         PRINT
63         PRINT "End of Report"
64      END SUB
```

[run]

Determine the Sale Price

Product Number	Original Price	Discount Rate in %	Discount Amount	Sale Price
112841A	115	14	16.1	98.9
213981B	100	17	17	83
332121A	98	13	12.74	85.26
586192X	88	12	10.56	77.44
714121Y	43	8	3.44	39.56

End of Report

Program 5.1 begins by declaring variables with the COMMON SHARED statement in line 6, so they may be accessed by all of the subprograms. Then the Main Program includes three CALL statements. Each CALL invokes a subprogram that carries out a particular subtask. The CALL in line 7 invokes A100.Initialization beginning at line 22. A100.Initialization clears the screen and calls A200.Print.Headings, which begins at line 30. This nested subprogram displays the report and column headings before the END SUB statement in line 36 returns control to A100.Initialization. The END SUB statement in A100.Initialization (line 25), in turn, returns control to line 8 in the Main Program.

The PRINT statement in line 31 of A200.Print.Headings includes the TAB function that specifies the report heading is to begin exactly in column 21. The two PRINT statements in lines 33 and 34, and the one in line 45, contain a comma separator after each string constant or variable, which causes the PC to produce output in a tabular format.

The second CALL statement in the Main Program, line 8, calls B100.Process.File, which begins at line 41. Lines 42 and 46 contain READ statements that instruct the PC to assign values to Product$, Original.Price, and Rate from the sequence of data created from DATA statements that begin at line 11. Note, this data is part of Program 5.1 itself. The rules regarding the READ and DATA statements are presented in Section 5.3.

Following the first READ statement in line 42, lines 43 through 47 establish a Do loop. A **Do loop** begins with a DO statement and ends with a LOOP statement. The DO WHILE statement in line 43 (one form of the DO statement) and the LOOP statement in line 47, cause the range of statements between them to be executed repeatedly as long as Product$ does not equal the string constant EOF. The expression Product$ <> "EOF", following DO WHILE in line 43, is called a **condition**. A condition can be true or false. In the case of the DO WHILE, the statements within the loop are executed while the condition is true.

When Product$ does equal EOF, the condition in line 43 is false. Therefore, the PC skips the statements within the loop and continues execution at the first statement following the LOOP statement. The first statement following the LOOP statement is the END SUB statement in line 48. This statement transfers control to line 9 in the Main Program.

One execution of a Do loop is called a **pass**. Note that the statements within the loop, lines 44 through 46, are indented by three spaces for the purpose of readability. Collectively, lines 44 through 46 are called the **range** of statements in the Do loop.

B100.Process.File contains two READ statements located in lines 42 and 46. The first READ statement in line 42, is executed only once. (This READ statement is called the **primary read** or **lead read**.) The other READ statement in line 46 is executed in each pass through the Do loop. Although many program styles exist, the programming style of using two READ statements and a Do loop will be used often in this book.

Testing for the End-of-File

Lines 11 through 15 contain data for only five products. The sixth product in line 16 is the **trailer record**. It represents the end-of-file and is used to determine when all the valid data has been processed. To incorporate an end-of-file test, a variable must be selected and a trailer record added to the data. In Program 5.1, we selected the product number as the test for end-of-file and the data value EOF. Because it guards against reading past end-of-file, the trailer record is also called the **sentinel record**. And the value EOF is called the **sentinel value**. The value EOF is clearly distinguishable from all the rest of the data assigned to Product$. This sentinel value is the same as the string constant found in the condition in line 43.

After the READ statement in line 46 assigns Product$ the value EOF, the LOOP statement returns control to the DO WHILE statement. Because Product$ is equal to the value EOF, the DO WHILE statement causes the PC to pass control to line 48, which follows the corresponding LOOP statement.

The END SUB statement in line 48 returns control to the Main Program. Line 9 then calls C100.Wrap.Up, which displays the message End of Report, and control is returned to the Main Program. Because the DATA statements are nonexecutable, lines 11 through 16 are ignored and line 17 causes the PC to terminate execution of the program. Lines 61 through 64 are also referred to as an **end-of-file routine**.

Three other points are worthy to note about establishing a test for end-of-file in a Do loop:

1. It is important that the trailer record contain enough values for all the variables in the READ statement. In Program 5.1, if we only added the sentinel value EOF to line 16, there would not be enough data to fulfill the requirements of the three variables in the READ statement. We arbitrarily assigned zero values to each.

2. The Do loop requires the use of two READ statements. The first READ statement (line 42) reads the first product record, before the PC enters the Do loop. The second READ statement, found at the bottom of the Do loop (line 46), causes the PC to read the next data record. This READ statement reads the remaining data records, one at a time, until there are no more data records left. Note that if the first record contains the product EOF, the DO WHILE statement will immediately transfer control to the statement below the corresponding LOOP statement.

3. Program 5.1 can process any number of products by simply placing each in a DATA statement prior to the trailer record.

5.2 THE DO and LOOP STATEMENTS

By now the potential of the DO and LOOP statements should be apparent. As we indicated earlier, the DO WHILE statement used in Program 5.1 to control the loop is just one form of the DO statement. This section describes the alternative forms of the DO statement and how to select one over the others when implementing a loop.

The general forms for the DO and LOOP statements are shown in Tables 5.1 and 5.2.

TABLE 5.1   The DO Statement

General Form: DO

or

DO WHILE condition

or

DO UNTIL condition

where **condition** is a relational expression.

Purpose: Causes the statements between DO and LOOP to be executed repeatedly. The three general forms work in the following way:

1. With the first general form, DO, the loop is controlled by a condition in the corresponding LOOP statement.
2. DO WHILE causes the loop to be executed while the condition is true.
3. DO UNTIL causes the loop to be executed until the condition becomes true.

In the latter two cases, the condition is tested before the range of statements is executed. (See Figures 5.2a and 5.2b.)

Examples:
```
DO
DO WHILE Emp.Name$ <> "EOF"
DO WHILE Side1 + Side2 < 5
DO UNTIL Discount >= 500
DO UNTIL Amount <= 125.25
```

TABLE 5.2   The LOOP Statement

General Form: LOOP

or

LOOP WHILE condition

or

LOOP UNTIL condition

where **condition** is a relational expression.

Purpose: Identifies the end of a Do loop. The three general forms work in the following way:

1. If the condition is in the corresponding DO statement, then the LOOP statement automatically returns control to the DO statement.
2. LOOP WHILE causes the loop to be executed while the condition is true.
3. LOOP UNTIL causes the loop to be executed until the condition becomes true.

In the latter two cases, the test to continue the loop is made after each pass. (See Figures 5.2c and 5.2d.)

Examples:
```
LOOP
LOOP WHILE Control$ = "Y"
LOOP UNTIL Control$ = "Y"
```

Figure 5.2 illustrates the four ways you can formulate a Do loop. The DO or LOOP statement that contains the condition is represented in a flowchart by the diamond-shape symbol. When you flowchart the branch to the top of the loop, you may wish to use a connector symbol, such as the circled A in Figure 5.1, rather than flowlines shown in the flowcharts in Figure 5.2.

Selecting the Proper Do Loop for a Program

Your program flowchart should tell you the type of Do loop to use in your program. The type you choose is dependent on the following two points:

1. If the decision to terminate is at the top of the loop, use the DO WHILE or DO UNTIL. (See Figures 5.2a and 5.2b.) If the decision to terminate is at the bottom of the loop, use the LOOP WHILE or LOOP UNTIL. (See Figures 5.2c and 5.2d.)
2. Use the keyword WHILE if you want to continue execution of the loop *while* the condition is true. Use the keyword UNTIL if you want to continue execution of the loop *until* the condition is true.

In this book, we will use two of the four Do loops. When the decision to terminate is at the top of the loop, we will use the DO WHILE statement shown in Figure 5.2a. This form was used earlier in Program 5.1. When the decision to terminate is at the bottom of the loop, we will use the LOOP UNTIL statement shown in Figure 5.2d. (For an example of a program that uses the LOOP UNTIL statement, see Program 5.3 later in this chapter.)

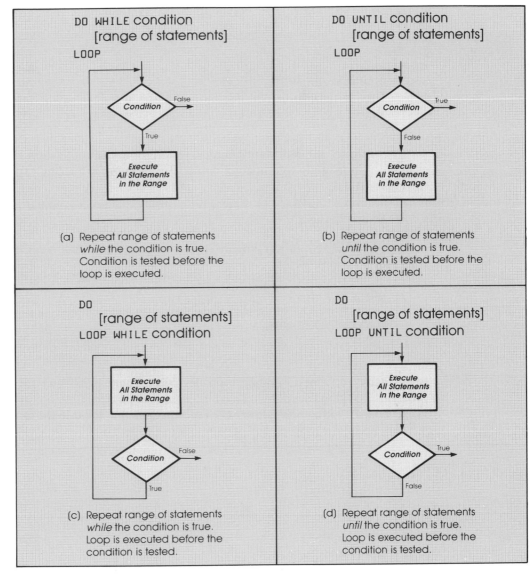

FIGURE 5.2
The four ways to write a Do loop and their corresponding general flowcharts.

Conditions

In line 43 of Program 5.1, the DO WHILE statement contains the condition

```
Product$ <> "EOF"
```

The condition is made up of two expressions and a **relational operator**. The condition specifies a relationship between expressions that is either true or false. If the condition is true, execution continues with the line following the DO WHILE statement. If the condition is false, then control is transferred to the line following the corresponding LOOP statement.

The PC makes a comparison between the two operators based upon the relational operator. Table 5.3 lists the six valid relational operators.

	TABLE 5.3 Relational Operators Used in Conditions		
RELATIONS	**MATH SYMBOL**	**QuickBASIC SYMBOL**	**EXAMPLES**
Equal To	=	=	Code$ = "1"
Less Than	<	<	Gross < 1000
Greater Than	>	>	Rate > 0.05
Less Than Or Equal To	≤	<= or =<	Tax <= 250
Greater Than Or Equal To	≥	>= or =>	Count >= 10
Not Equal To	≠	<> or ><	Same$ <> "End"

There are several important points to watch for in the application of conditions. For example, it is invalid to compare a numeric expression to a string expression. The following is invalid:

```
DO WHILE Dollars$ > 100     ' Invalid
```

Furthermore, the condition should ensure termination of the loop. If a logical error such as

```
DO WHILE 3 > 1        ← this condition is always true

    [range of statements]

LOOP
```

is not detected, a never-ending loop develops. There is no way to stop the endless program execution except by manual intervention, such as pressing Ctrl + Break on your PC keyboard. (For additional examples of programs that include Do loops, see Programs 5.2 and 5.3 in this chapter, and Section 6.4 in Chapter 6.)

5.3 THE READ, DATA, AND RESTORE STATEMENTS

In Section 5.1 the READ and DATA statements were briefly introduced. Like the INPUT statement, these two statements are used in tandem to assign data items to variables. They differ from the INPUT statement in that you enter the data as part of the program rather than keying the data in after execution. The INPUT statement is the preferred form of input when processing small amounts of data, while the READ and DATA statements are preferred when processing large amounts of data that are part of the program itself.

This section illustrates the rules of the READ, DATA, and RESTORE statements and gives further examples of their use, as well as their limitations.

The DATA Statement

The DATA statement provides for the creation of a sequence of data items for use by the READ statement. The general form of the DATA statement and some examples are given in Table 5.4.

TABLE 5.4   The DATA Statement

General Form: DATA data item, . . ., data item

where each data item is either a numeric constant or a string constant.

Purpose: Provides for the creation of a sequence of data items for use by the READ statement.

Examples (with READ statements):

```
DATA 2, -3.14, 0.025, -95
READ Month$, Discount, Commission, Returns
------------------------------------------------
DATA 0.24E33, 0, -2.5D-12, 1.23#, 2.46!, 5
READ Dist, Fac, Adjust (J), X# Y, Z%
------------------------------------------------
DATA 15, , ",", YES, "2 + 7 = ", NO, 2.2, ""
READ H, A$, B$(3), C$, D$, E$, I, F$
```

Note: In the last example, A$ and F$ are both assigned the null character.

The DATA statement consists of the keyword DATA followed by a list of data items separated by mandatory commas. The data items may be numeric or string and are formulated according to the following rules:

DATA RULE 1   *Numeric data items placed in a DATA statement must be formulated as numeric constants.*

DATA RULE 2   *String data items placed in a DATA statement may be formulated with or without surrounding quotation marks, provided the string contains no trailing or leading blanks or embedded commas or colons. A string that contains a trailing or leading blank or an embedded comma or colon must be surrounded with quotation marks.*

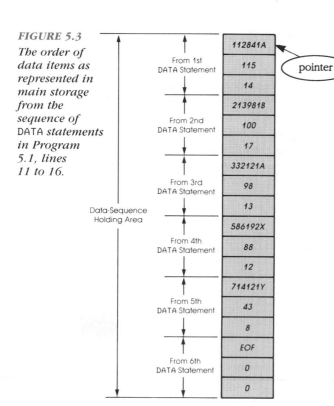

FIGURE 5.3

The order of data items as represented in main storage from the sequence of DATA statements in Program 5.1, lines 11 to 16.

Data items from all DATA statements in a program are collected in main storage into a single **data-sequence holding area**. The order in which the data items appear in the DATA statements determines their order in the single data sequence (Figure 5.3). In other words, the ordering of the data items is based on two considerations: the sequence of the DATA statements, and the order from left to right of the data items within each DATA statement.

The number of data items that can be represented in a DATA statement depends not only on the type of problem but also on the programming style adopted by the programmer. Some programmers prefer to write one DATA statement for each data item, like this:

```
DATA 310386024
DATA JOE NIKOLE
DATA -3.85
DATA -1E-15
READ Soc.Sec$, Emp.Name$, Amount, Standard
```

Others prefer to write as many data items in a DATA statement as there are variables in the READ statement that refer to that DATA statement. For example, the previous DATA and READ statements can be rewritten in this way:

```
DATA 310386024, JOE NIKOLE, -3.85, -1E-15
READ Soc.Sec$, Emp.Name$, Amount, Standard
```

The DATA statement, like the REM statement, is a nonexecutable statement; that is, if the execution of a program reaches a line containing a DATA statement, it proceeds to the next line with no other effect. In this book, all DATA statements are placed at the end of the Main Program as shown in Program 5.1 because of the following rule:

DATA RULE 3   DATA *statements can be placed only in the Main Program. They cannot be placed in subprograms.*

The READ Statement

The READ statement provides for the assignment of values to variables from a sequence of data items created from DATA statements. The general form of the READ statement is given in Table 5.5. The READ statement consists of the keyword READ followed by a list of variables separated by mandatory commas. The variables may be numeric or string variables.

TABLE 5.5	The READ Statement

General Form: READ variable, . . ., variable

                 where each variable is either a numeric variable or a string variable.

Purpose: Provides for the assignment of values to variables from a sequence of data items created from DATA statements.

Examples (with DATA statements):   See Table 5.4.

The READ statement causes the variables in its list to be assigned specific values, in order, from the data sequence formed by all of the DATA statements. In order to visualize the relationship between the READ statement and its associated DATA statement, you may think of a **pointer** associated with the data-sequence holding area, as shown in Figure 5.3. When a program is first executed, this pointer points to the first data item in the data sequence. Each time a READ statement is executed, the variables in the list are assigned specific values from the data sequence, beginning with the data item indicated by the pointer, and the pointer is advanced one value per variable, in a downward fashion, to point beyond the data used.

Figure 5.4 illustrates the data-sequence holding area and pointer for a partial program containing multiple READ and DATA statements. The pointer initially points to the location of 565.33 in the holding area. When line 4 is executed, the value of 565.33 is assigned to the variable Mon.Sales; the pointer is advanced to the location of the next value 356.45, which is assigned to the variable Tue.Sales; and the pointer is advanced to the location of the next value, 478.56. When line 5 is executed, the variable Wed.Sales is assigned the value of 478.56, Thur.Sales the value of 756.23, and Fri.Sales the value of 342.23.

As this assignment occurs, the pointer advances one value per variable to point to a location beyond the data used, which is recognized by the PC as the end of the data-sequence holding area.

```
1     ' Determining the Average Daily Sales
2     ' with Multiple READ and Multiple DATA Statements
3     ' ***************************************************
4     READ Mon.Sal, Tue.Sal
5     READ Wed.Sal, Thur.Sal, Fri.Sal
6     Average = (Mon.Sal + Tue.Sal + Wed.Sal + Thur.Sal + Fri.Sal) / 5
7     PRINT Mon.Sal, Tue.Sal, Wed.Sal, Thur.Sal, Fri.Sal
8     PRINT "The average is"; Average
9     ' ************** Data Follows ****************
10    DATA 565.33, 356.45, 478.56
11    DATA 756.23, 342.23

      [run]

      565.33          356.45          478.56          756.23          342.23
      The average is 499.76
```

FIGURE 5.4

Partial program and the corresponding data-sequence holding area.

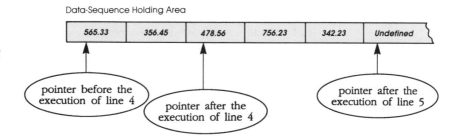

In the partial program in Figure 5.4, the PC is unable to calculate Average correctly until it has the value of Mon.Sales, Tues.Sales, Wed.Sales, Thur.Sales, and Fri.Sales. The READ statement should occur somewhere before the LET statement in the program. This example can be generalized to give the following:

 **READ RULE 1**   *Every variable appearing in the program whose value is directly obtained by a* READ *should be listed in a* READ *statement before it is used elsewhere in the program.*

Like the DATA statements, the placement of the READ statement is important. Furthermore, more than one DATA statement may be used to satisfy one READ statement, and more than one READ statement may be satisfied from one DATA statement.

READ RULE 2   *A program containing a* READ *statement must also have at least one* DATA *statement.*

If there is an insufficient number of data items to be assigned to the variables of a READ statement, a dialog box appears in the middle of the screen with the diagnostic message Out of DATA. However, excessive data items in a program are ignored.

Finally, the type of data item in the data sequence must correspond to the type of variable to which it is to be assigned. If they do not agree, a dialog box appears in the middle of the screen with the diagnostic message Syntax error.

READ RULE 3   *Numeric variables in* READ *statements require numeric constants as data items in* DATA *statements, and string variables require quoted strings or unquoted strings as data.*

The RESTORE Statement

Usually data items from a DATA statement are processed by a READ statement only once. If you want the PC to read all or some of the same data items later, you must use the RESTORE statement to restore the data.

The RESTORE statement allows the data in a given program to be reread as often as necessary by other READ statements. The general form of the RESTORE statement is given with an example in Table 5.6. The RESTORE statement consists of the keyword RESTORE optionally followed by a label. If no label follows the keyword RESTORE, then the next READ statement accesses the first data item in the first DATA statement. If a label follows RESTORE, the next READ statement accesses the first data item in the DATA statement that immediately follows the specified label.

TABLE 5.6   The RESTORE Statement

General Form:	RESTORE label
	where **label** is blank, a label name, or a line number.
Purpose:	Allows the data in the program to be reread. If no label follows the keyword RESTORE, then the next READ statement accesses the first data item in the first DATA statement.
	If a label follows RESTORE, the next READ statement accesses the first data item in the first DATA statement that immediately follows the specified label.
Examples:	RESTORE
	RESTORE Record

The RESTORE statement causes the pointer to be moved backward or forward to a specified area in the data-sequence holding area. This is done so that the next READ statement executed will read the data from some other point in the sequence.

The RESTORE statement is generally used when it is necessary to perform several types of computations on the same data items. It can also be used to randomly access data located in DATA statements that have labels. The partial program in Figure 5.5 illustrates the use of the RESTORE statement.

<table>
<tr><td>

FIGURE 5.5

An example of using the RESTORE *statement.*

</td><td>

```
1     ' Use of the RESTORE Statement
2     ' ***************************
3     READ Item.1, Item.2, Item.3
4     Sum = Item.1 + Item.2 + Item.3
5     RESTORE  ' Reset data pointer to first data item
6     READ Item.4, Item.5, Item.6
7     Product = Item.4 * Item.5 * Item.6
8     PRINT Item.1, Item.2, Item.3, Sum
9     PRINT Item.4, Item.5, Item.6, Product
10    ' ******* Data Follows *******
11    DATA 1, 3, 9

[run]

1           3           9           13
1           3           9           27
```

</td></tr>
</table>

When the first READ statement in line 3 is executed in the partial program in Figure 5.5, Item.1 is assigned the value of 1, Item.2 the value of 3, and Item.3 the value of 9 from the DATA statement in line 11. After a value for Sum is computed in line 4, the RESTORE statement in line 5 is executed. This resets the pointer to the beginning of the data-sequence holding area so that it points at the value of 1 again. When the second READ statement in line 6 is executed, the values of 1, 3, and 9 are reread and assigned to Item.4, Item.5, and Item.6.

5.4   THE PRINT USING STATEMENT FOR FORMATTED OUTPUT

The PRINT USING statement is far more useful than the PRINT statement in exactly controlling the format of a program's output. In Chapter 3 you were introduced to the comma, the semicolon, and the TAB and SPC functions for print-control purposes. For most applications, these print-control methods will suffice. However, when you are confronted with generating readable reports for nontechnical personnel, more control over the format of the output is essential. The PRINT USING statement gives you the desired capabilities to display information according to a predefined format instead of the free format provided by the PRINT statement.

Through the use of the PRINT USING statement, you can do the following:

1. Specify the exact image of a line of output.
2. Force decimal-point alignment when displaying numeric tables in columnar format.
3. Control the number of digits displayed for a numeric result.

4. Specify that commas be inserted into a number. (Starting from the units position of a number and progressing toward the left, digits are separated into groups of three by a comma.)
5. Specify that the sign status of the number be displayed along with the number (**+** or blank if positive, **–** if negative).
6. Assign a fixed or floating dollar sign (\$) to the number displayed.
7. Force a numeric result to be displayed in exponential form.
8. **Left-** or **right-justify** string values in a formatted field. (That is, align the leftmost or rightmost characters, respectively.)
9. Specify that only the first character of a string be displayed.
10. Round a value automatically to a specified number of decimal digits.

The general form of the PRINT USING statement is given with examples in Table 5.7.

TABLE 5.7   The PRINT USING Statement

General Form: PRINT USING string expression; list

where **string expression** (sometimes called the descriptor field or format field) is either a string constant or a string variable, and,

list is a list of items to be displayed in the format specified by the descriptor field.

Purpose: Provides for controlling exactly the format of a program's output by specifying an image to which that output must conform.

Examples:
```
PRINT USING "The answer is #,###.##"; Cost
PRINT USING "## divided by # is #.#"; Num; Den; Quot

Format$ = "Total cost =======> $$,###.##-"
PRINT USING Format$; Total

Total.Line1$ = "**,###.##"
PRINT USING Total.Line1$; Check;

PRINT USING "\   \"; Cust.Name$

PRINT USING "!, !, \       \"; First$; Middle$; Last$

PRINT USING "Example _##"; Number

PRINT USING "#.##^^^^"; Dis.1; Dis.2; Dis.3; Dis.4
```

Declaring the Format of the Output

To control the format of the displayed values, the PRINT USING statement is used in conjunction with a string expression that specifies exactly the image to which the output must conform. The string expression is placed immediately after the words PRINT USING in the form of a string constant or string variable. If the format is described by a string variable, then the string variable must be assigned the format by a LET statement before the PRINT USING statement is executed in the program. Figure 5.6 illustrates the two methods for specifying the format for the PRINT USING statement.

FIGURE 5.6

The two methods for defining the format for a PRINT USING *statement.*

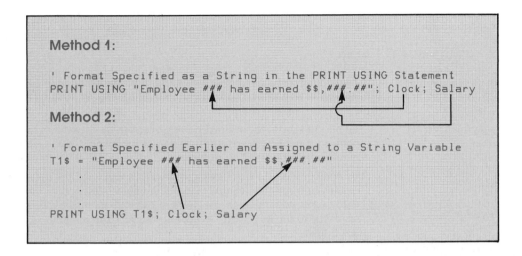

In Method 1 of Figure 5.6, the string following the keywords PRINT USING instructs the PC to display the values of Clock and Salary using the format found in that statement. In Method 2, the string constant has been replaced by the string variable T1$ that was assigned the desired format in the previous statement. If Clock is equal to 000105 and Salary is equal to 4563.20, then the results displayed from the execution of either PRINT USING statement in Method 1 or Method 2 are as follows:

Format Symbols

Table 5.8 on the next page includes the format symbols available with QuickBASIC. One or more consecutive format symbols appearing in a string expression is a **descriptor field**, or **format field**.

The Number Sign Symbol

The number sign (#) is the format symbol used to define a numeric descriptor field. Grouped number signs indicate exactly how many positions are desired in a numeric result during output. A number sign reserves space for a digit or sign. For example,

    # indicates one position in a numeric result
    ## indicates two positions in a numeric result
    #### indicates four positions in a numeric result
    ####.## indicates six positions, two of which are to the right of the decimal point.

It is your responsibility to ensure that enough number signs are in the descriptor field to fit the output results in the prescribed format.

TABLE 5.8   Format Symbols

SYMBOL	FUNCTION	EXAMPLES
#	Grouped number signs define a numeric descriptor field and cause the display of a numeric value in integer form.	# ### ####
.	The period is used for decimal-point placement. A decimal point in a numeric descriptor field causes the display of a numeric value in fixed point form.	###. ###.## .###
,	The comma is used for automatic-comma placement. A comma in front of a decimal point in a numeric descriptor field causes the display of a numeric value with commas displayed to the left of the decimal point every three significant digits.	#,###,### ###,###.## ######,.##
^ ^ ^ ^	Four consecutive circumflexes to the right of a numeric descriptor field causes the display of a value in exponential notation (D or E format).	##^^^^ #.###^^^^ +##.###^^^^
+	A single plus sign to the left or right of a numeric descriptor field causes the display of a numeric value with a sign (plus or minus) immediately before or after the number.	+##,###.## ###+ #,###.##+
–	A single minus sign to the right of a numeric descriptor field causes the display of negative numbers with a trailing minus sign and positive numbers with a trailing space.	##.##– ###– ###,###.##–
$	A single leading dollar sign in a numeric descriptor field causes the display of a fixed dollar sign in that position, followed by a numeric value. (Note: The dollar sign may be substituted for any valid QuickBASIC character listed in Table D.3 in Appendix D. Format symbols must be preceded by the underscore character.)	$### $##.## $#,###.##+
$ $	Two leading dollar signs in a numeric descriptor field cause the display of a single dollar sign immediately to the left of the first significant digit of a numeric value.	$$##.## $$###.##– $$,###.##
* *	Two leading asterisks in a numeric descriptor field cause the display of a numeric value with leading spaces, filled with asterisks, to the left of the numeric value.	**###.### **,###.## **.##
* * $	Two leading asterisks followed by a single dollar sign in a numeric descriptor field combine the effects of the previous two symbols. These symbols (**$) cause the display of a numeric value with leading spaces filled with asterisks, followed by a floating dollar sign immediately to the left of the numeric value.	**$######## **$#,###.##+
&	The ampersand causes the display of a complete string value left-justified.	&
!	The exclamation point causes the display of the first character of a string value.	!
_	The underscore causes the display of the next character in the descriptor field as if the character were a string constant. Any of the format symbols in this table can be displayed as a string constant.	_& _! _# #_# _$$##.##_#
\n spaces\	Two backslashes separated by n spaces cause the display of a string of characters left-justified and equal in length to 2 plus the number of spaces (n).	\\ \ \ \ \ \ \

Consider the example in Figure 5.7, where A = 10, B = −11, C = 12.75, and
D = 4565.

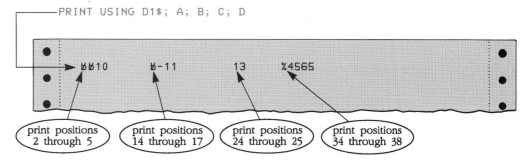

FIGURE 5.7

*Displaying
numeric values
through the use
of the* PRINT
USING *statement. The
character ƀ represents a blank
character in the
output results.*

```
                    ' Format Specified Earlier and Assigned to a String Variable
                    D1$ = " ####          ####        ##          ###"


                    PRINT USING D1$; A; B; C; D
```

```
            ƀƀ10         ƀ-11         13      %4565
```

print positions
2 through 5

print positions
14 through 17

print positions
24 through 25

print positions
34 through 38

Table 5.9 summarizes the use of the number sign in various descriptor fields. The
partial program in Figure 5.8 on page 139 gives examples of the use of the number sign.

TABLE 5.9   Use of the Number Sign (#) in a Descriptor Field

DESCRIPTOR FIELD	DATA	OUTPUT	REMARKS
####	10	ƀƀ10	Right-justify the digits in the field with leading
####	−11	ƀ-11	spaces. Note the floating minus sign.
##	12.75	13	The data is rounded to an integer, since only integers are specified by the descriptor field.
###	4565	%4565	Because the data is too large for the specified descriptor field, the value is displayed but is preceded by a percent sign (%) to indicate that an insufficient number of positions were reserved for this descriptor field.

If the string expression referenced in a PRINT USING statement contains fewer
descriptor fields than print items in the list, QuickBASIC reuses the string expression.
For example, when the following line is entered in the immediate screen

```
PRINT USING "##    "; -5; -7; -9
```

the PC displays

```
-5    -7    -9
```

If the string expression contains more descriptor fields than print items in the list,
QuickBASIC ignores the excess. For example,

```
PRINT USING "##      ##      ##      ##"; −5
```

results in −5 being displayed in print positions 1 and 2.

The Decimal Point (Period) Symbol

The period (.) in a numeric descriptor field places a decimal point in the output record at that character position in which it appears, and the format of the numeric result is aligned with the position of the decimal point. When number signs (#) precede the decimal point in a descriptor field, any leading zeros appearing in the data are replaced by spaces, except for a single leading zero immediately preceding the decimal point.

When number signs follow the decimal point, unused positions to the right of the decimal point are filled with trailing zeros. When the data contains more digits to the right of the decimal point than the descriptor field allows, the data is displayed rounded to the limits of the descriptor field.

Table 5.10 and the partial program in Figure 5.8 illustrate the use of the decimal point in various descriptor fields.

TABLE 5.10   Use of the Decimal Point (.) in a Descriptor Field

DESCRIPTOR FIELD	DATA	OUTPUT	REMARKS
####.##	217.5	ƀ217.50	Unspecified decimal fraction positions are filled
#####.##	-40	ƀƀ-40.00	with trailing zeros.
#####.##	23.458	ƀƀƀ23.46	Decimal fractional digits are rounded.
####.##	0.027	ƀƀƀ0.03	The last leading zero before the decimal point is not suppressed.

The Comma Symbol

A comma (,) to the left of the decimal point in a numeric descriptor field places a comma in front of every third digit to the left of the decimal point. A comma specifies a digit position within the descriptor field. If there are less than four significant digits to the left of the decimal point, the PC displays a space in place of the comma symbol. Table 5.11 and the partial program in Figure 5.8 illustrate the use of the comma in various descriptor fields.

If the descriptor field containing a comma has too few number signs, the comma is replaced by a digit.

TABLE 5.11   Use of the Comma (,) in a Descriptor Field

DESCRIPTOR FIELD	DATA	OUTPUT	REMARKS
#,###	4000	4,000	Comma displayed.
#,###,###	999999	ƀƀ999,999	Comma displayed.
#,###.##	-30.5	ƀƀ-30.50	Space displayed for comma when leading digits are blank.
########,.##	9876543.21#	9,876,543.21	Comma in front of a decimal point in descriptor field.

FIGURE 5.8

*An example
of using the
number (#)
sign, decimal
point (.), and
comma (,) for-
mat symbols.*

```
 1   ' Examples of the Use of the Number Sign
 2   ' Decimal Point and Comma in a Descriptor Field
 3   ' **********************************************
 4   CLS  ' Clear Screen
 5   DL1$ = "####    #,###    #,###.##    #########,.##"
 6   READ Value, Constant#
 7   PRINT USING DL1$; Value; Value; Value; Constant#
 8   PRINT USING "####"; Value
 9   PRINT USING "#,###"; Value
10   PRINT USING "#,###.##"; Value
11   ' ************* Data Follows ****************
12   DATA 1234.56, -1234567.87

     [run]

     1235    1,235    1,234.56    -1,234,567.87
     1235
     1,235
     1,234.56
```

The Plus and Minus Sign Symbols

A plus sign (+) as either the first or last character in a numeric descriptor field causes a + to be displayed before the number if the data item is positive, or a – if the data item is negative. If the plus sign is the first character in the descriptor field, it is called a **floating sign**. If the plus sign is the last character in the descriptor field, it is called a **fixed sign**.

A minus sign (–) at the end of a numeric descriptor field, also called a fixed sign, causes negative numbers to be displayed with a trailing minus sign and positive numbers to be displayed with a trailing space.

Table 5.12 gives examples of the use of the plus and minus sign symbols in various numeric descriptor fields.

TABLE 5.12   Use of the Plus (+) or Minus (–) Sign in a Descriptor Field

DESCRIPTOR FIELD	DATA	OUTPUT	REMARKS
FIXED SIGNS			
###.##-	000.01	ƀƀ0.01ƀ	The last leading zero before the decimal point is not suppressed.
###.##+	20.5	ƀ20.50+	
###.##+	-8.236	ƀƀ8.24-	Automatic rounding when length of data exceeds descriptor-field specification.
###.##-	-456.0	456.00-	
FLOATING SIGNS			
+##.##	40.5	+40.50	
+##.##	7.07	ƀ+7.07	
+###.##	-0.236	ƀƀ-0.24	
+##.##	-456.0	%-456.00	

The Dollar Sign Symbol

A single dollar sign ($) appearing to the left of a numeric descriptor field causes a $ to be displayed in that position of the output record. A single dollar sign is called a **fixed dollar sign**.

Two leading dollar signs ($$) at the left of a numeric descriptor field causes a single dollar sign to float. The dollar sign will appear at the left of the first significant digit. Two leading dollar signs appearing together are called a **floating dollar sign**. The leading dollar signs specify two positions in the numeric descriptor field. One position is filled by the dollar sign; the second sign reserves a digit position. Table 5.13 gives examples of the use of the dollar sign in various numeric descriptor fields.

TABLE 5.13   Use of the Dollar Sign ($) in a Descriptor Field

DESCRIPTOR FIELD	DATA	OUTPUT	REMARKS
FIXED DOLLAR SIGN			
$###.##	123.45	$123.45	
$###.##	98.76	$ƀ98.76	
$###.##-	40.613	$ƀ40.61ƀ	
$#,###.##-	-40.613	$ƀƀƀ40.61-	
$#,###.##+	40.613	$ƀƀƀ40.61+	
FLOATING DOLLAR SIGN			
$$###.##	1.23	ƀƀƀ$1.23	
$$,###.##	1234.68	$1,234.68	Second $ sign replaced by digit.
$$##.##-	-1.0	ƀƀ$1.00-	

The Asterisk Symbol

Two asterisks (**) starting at the left side of a numeric descriptor field cause the value to be displayed in asterisk-filled format. The left side of the numeric field is filled with leading asterisks rather than leading spaces.

Leading asterisks are often used when monetary checks are being printed or when the result must be protected. Hence, leading asterisks are sometimes called **check-protection asterisks**, and their use prevents someone from physically adding digits to the left side of a number. Table 5.14 gives examples of the use of the asterisk in various numeric descriptor fields.

TABLE 5.14   Use of the Asterisk (*) in a Descriptor Field

DESCRIPTOR FIELD	DATA	OUTPUT	REMARKS
**,###.##	10.15	****10.15	Asterisk displayed for comma when leading digits are zero.
**##-	-6.95	***7-	Data is rounded to an integer.
**###.##	4.58	****4.58	
**$#,###.##	50.258	*****$50.26	Dollar sign floats, and leading zeros are displayed as asterisks.

Formatted Character String Output

Descriptor fields for string values are defined in terms of the ampersand (&), two backslashes (\\), the exclamation point (!), or the underscore (_), rather than the number sign (#). Table 5.8 summarizes these four symbols.

As a descriptor field, the ampersand represents a variable-length string field. The number of positions used to display the string is dependent on the internal size of the string. The ampersand indicates the beginning position in which the string is displayed, and expansion is to the right in the line. Table 5.15 summarizes the use of the ampersand. The partial program in Figure 5.9 gives examples of the use of the ampersand. Note that the underscore (_) is used in line 10 to precede the exclamation point (!). This informs the PC that the exclamation point is a string constant to be displayed, not a descriptor field.

TABLE 5.15 Use of the Ampersand (&) as a Descriptor Field

DESCRIPTOR FIELD	DATA	OUTPUT	REMARKS
&	ABC	ABC	The character A is placed exactly in the line at the location specified by the ampersand. The B and C are placed in & + 1 and & + 2 positions of the line, respectively.
&	ABCDE	ABCDE	
&	A	A	

FIGURE 5.9

An example of using the ampersand (&) and underscore (_) format symbols.

```
1     ' Use of the Ampersand and the
2     ' Underscore as Descriptor Fields
3     ' *****************************
4     CLS  ' Clear Screen
5     Short$ = "REM"
6     Middle$ = "Remark"
7     Long$ = "Remarkable"
8     PRINT USING "The keyword &"; Short$
9     PRINT USING "represents  &."; Middle$
10    PRINT USING "Isn't that  &_!"; Long$
11    PRINT USING "So &"; Short$;
12    PRINT USING "&"; "arkable"

[run]

The keyword REM
represents  Remark.
Isn't that  Remarkable!
So REMarkable
```

The exact number of positions to use for displaying a string value can be specified by using two backslashes separated by zero or more spaces. The number of positions in the descriptor field, including the two backslashes, indicate how many positions are to be used to display the string value. The string value is aligned in the descriptor field left-justified. If the internal value of the string contains fewer characters than the descriptor field, the string value is filled with spaces on the right in the print line. If the internal value of the string contains more characters than the descriptor field, the string value is truncated on the right. Table 5.16 on the next page summarizes the use of the backslash, and the partial program in Figure 5.10 gives examples of its use.

TABLE 5.16   Use of the Backslash (\) in a Descriptor Field

DESCRIPTOR FIELD	NUMBER OF SPACES BETWEEN BACKSLASHES	DATA	OUTPUT	REMARKS
\ \	3	ABCDE	ABCDE	Size of descriptor field and string value the same.
\ \	1	ABCDE	ABC	The last two characters are truncated.
\\	0	ABCDE	AB	The last three characters are truncated.
\ \	6	ABCDE	ABCDEƀƀƀ	Three spaces are appended to the right of the string value in the print line.

FIGURE 5.10

An example of using the backslash (\) format symbol.

```
1    ' Use of Two Backslashes in a Descriptor Field
2    ' *********************************************
3    CLS   ' Clear Screen
4    H1$ = "Name      Address      City-State     Zip Code"
5    H2$ = "----      -------      ----------     --------"
6    D1$ = "\         \ \          \ \            \ \        \"
7    PRINT H1$
8    PRINT H2$
9    READ Cust.Name$, Cust.Street$, Cust.City$, Cust.Zip$
10   PRINT USING D1$; Cust.Name$; Cust.Street$; Cust.City$; Cust.Zip$
11   ' *************** Data Follows **************
12   DATA Jones J., 451 W 45th, "Munster, IN", 46321-0452

[run]

Name      Address    City-State    Zip Code
----      -------    ----------    --------
Jones J.  451 W 45th  Munster, IN   46321-0452
```

Study closely the method used in lines 4 through 6 in the partial program in Figure 5.10 to align the fields. Collectively the three statements give you a good idea of what the output will eventually look like. This technique will be used throughout this book. Lines 7 and 8 print H1$ and H2$. These two variables are equal to the column headings as defined in lines 4 and 5. Line 10 displays the customer information using the format assigned to D1$ in line 6.

The exclamation point is used as a descriptor field to specify a one-position field in the print line. If the internal value of the string to be displayed is longer than one character, only the leftmost character is displayed. Table 5.17 summarizes the use of the exclamation point, and the partial program in Figure 5.11 illustrates its use.

TABLE 5.17   Use of the Exclamation Point (!) as a Descriptor Field

DESCRIPTOR FIELD	DATA	OUTPUT	REMARKS
!	JOE	J	First initial of name displayed.
!	XYZ	X	

FIGURE 5.11

An example of using the exclamation point (!) format symbol.

```
1   ' Use of the Exclamation Point as a Descriptor Field
2   ' ******************************************************
3   CLS  ' Clear Screen
4   READ First.Name$, Middle.Name$, Last.Name$
5   PRINT USING "!. !. \        \"; First.Name$; Middle.Name$; Last.Name$
6   ' *************** Data Follows ******************
7   DATA George, Alfred, Smith

    [run]

    G. A. Smith
```

The LPRINT USING Statement

Like the LPRINT statement, the LPRINT USING statement prints the results on the printer. Everything that has been presented with respect to the PRINT USING statement also applies to the LPRINT USING statement. This statement gives you the capacity to print results according to a predefined format on the printer.

Programming Case Study 6 | Determining the Accounts Receivable Balance

This problem and its program solution incorporate much of the information discussed so far in this chapter, including the following useful techniques for formatting a report:

1. Align the detail lines with the column headings.
2. Force decimal-point alignment.
3. Control the number of digits displayed in a result.
4. Specify that commas and decimal points be appropriately displayed in numeric results.

Problem: Ron's Family Discount House would like its PC to generate a management report on the printer for the accounts receivable balance for a monthly billing period. The following formula is used to determine the balance:

End-of-Month Balance = Beginning of Month Balance–
Payments + Purchases – Credits +
Service Charge on Ending Unpaid Balance

The following formula is used to compute the Service Charge:

Service Charge = 19.5% Annually on the Unpaid Balance
or
= 0.01625 * (Beginning-of-Month Balance–
Payments – Credits) per Month

Round the Service Charge to ensure consistency between the Beginning-of-Month Balance and End-of-Month Balance.

The input data for each customer includes customer number, beginning-of-month balance, payments, purchases, and credits. The following accounts receivable data is to be processed:

Customer Number	Beginning Balance	Payment	Purchases	Credit
14376172	$1,112.32	$35.00	$56.00	$ 0.00
16210987	30.00	30.00	15.00	0.00
18928384	125.50	25.00	0.00	12.50
19019293	120.00	12.00	12.00	23.00
19192929	10.00	7.00	2.50	1.50
EOF	0	0	0	0

The program should generate a report on the printer that includes report and column headings and a line of information for each customer. Each line is to include the five values read for each customer, the service charge, and end-of-month balance as described on the **printer spacing chart** shown in Figure 5.12. Lines 1 through 4 of the printer spacing chart define the report and column headings. Lines 1 through 4 are called **heading lines**. Line 6 defines the **detail line** that is displayed for each record processed: the row of Xs on line 6 describes an area for a string value, and the groups of 9s with commas and decimal points describe areas for numeric values. Finally, line 8 describes the end-of-job message. A line that includes summaries or end-of-job messages is called a **total line**. Total lines that include summaries are presented in later chapters.

FIGURE 5.12

Output for Program 5.2, designed on a printer spacing chart.

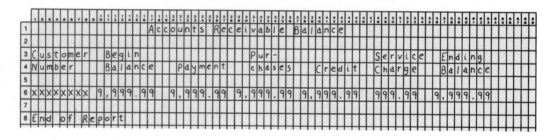

Following are a top-down chart (Figure 5.13), a list of the program tasks in outline form that correspond to the top-down chart, a program solution, and a discussion of the program solution.

FIGURE 5.13

A top-down chart for Program 5.2.

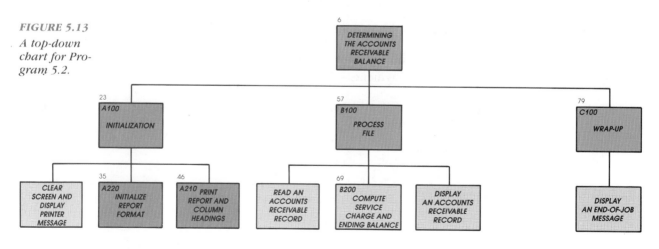

Program Tasks

The following program tasks correspond to the top-down chart in Figure 5.13:

1. A100.Initialization

   a. Clear the screen.
   b. Display a message on the screen that instructs the user to set the paper in the printer to the top of the page. After the user aligns the paper and turns the printer on, accept the Enter key response via the INPUT statement to continue.
   c. Call A200.Initialize.Report.Format. In this subprogram initialize the report format described on the printer spacing chart in Figure 5.12 to string variables. Use the string variables H1\$, H2\$, and H3\$ for the heading lines, D1\$ for the detail line, and T1\$ for the total line.
   d. Call A210.Print.Headings. In this subprogram, use the LPRINT statement to display the heading lines H1\$, H2\$, and H3\$.

2. B100.Process.File

   a. Read the first accounts receivable record; use the following variable names:

      Cus.No\$ = Customer Number
      Beg.Bal = Beginning Balance
      Pay   = Payments
      Pur   = Purchases
      Cr   = Credits

   b. Use a DO WHILE statement to establish a Do loop. The condition within the DO WHILE statement should allow the loop to be executed as long as Cus.No\$ does not equal the sentinel value EOF (Cus.No\$ < > "EOF").

      (1) Call B200.Compute.Service.Charge, which performs the following tasks:

         (a) Compute the unpaid balance from this formula:

            Unp.Bal = Beg.Bal − Pay − Cr

         (b) Compute the service charge from this formula:

            Serv.Chg = 0.01625 * Unp.Bal

            Round the service charge to the nearest cent using this formula:

            Serv.Chg = INT((Serv.Chg + 0.005) * 100) / 100

         (c) Compute the end-of-month balance from this formula:

            End.Bal = Unp.Bal + Pur + Serv.Chg

      (2) Use the LPRINT USING statement to print the seven values pertaining to the customer.
      (3) Read the next accounts receivable record.

3. C100.Wrap.Up — use the LPRINT statement to print T1\$.

Program Solution

Program 5.2 on the next page corresponds to the top-down chart in Figure 5.13 and the preceding tasks. The colored modules in Figure 5.13 are implemented in Program 5.2 as the Main Program with subprograms. The grey modules represent subtasks that have been moved into their superior modules in Program 5.2.

PROGRAM 5.2

```
1      ' Program 5.2
2      ' Determining the Accounts Receivable Balance
3      ' ***********************************************
4      ' *                 Main Program                *
5      ' ***********************************************
6      COMMON SHARED Beg.Bal, Pay, Pur, Cr, Serv.Chg, End.Bal
7      COMMON SHARED H1$, H2$, H3$, D1$, T1$
8      CALL A100.Initialization
9      CALL B100.Process.File
10     CALL C100.Wrap.Up
11     ' ************** Data Follows *****************
12     DATA 14376172, 1112.32, 35,   56,    0
13     DATA 16210987,      30, 30,   15,    0
14     DATA 18928384,   125.5, 25,    0, 12.5
15     DATA 19019293,     120, 12,   12,   23
16     DATA 19192929,      10,  7,  2.5,  1.5
17     DATA EOF,            0,  0,    0,    0
18     END
19
20     ' ***********************************************
21     ' *              Initialization                 *
22     ' ***********************************************
23     SUB A100.Initialization
24        CLS ' Clear Screen
25        PRINT "Set the paper in the printer to the top of page."
26        PRINT
27        INPUT "Press the Enter key when the printer is ready...", Control$
28        CALL A200.Initialize.Report.Format
29        CALL A210.Print.Headings
30     END SUB
31
32     ' ***********************************************
33     ' *          Initialize Report Format           *
34     ' ***********************************************
35     SUB A200.Initialize.Report.Format
36        H1$ = "             Accounts Receivable Balance"
37        H2$ = "Customer  Begin                    Pur-          Service  Ending"
38        H3$ = "Number    Balance  Payment   chases  Credit  Charge  Balance"
39        D1$ = "\        \ #,###.##  #,###.## #,###.## #,###.##  ###.## #,###.##"
40        T1$ = "End of Report"
41     END SUB
42
43     ' ***********************************************
44     ' *              Print Headings                 *
45     ' ***********************************************
46     SUB A210.Print.Headings
47        LPRINT H1$
48        LPRINT
49        LPRINT H2$
50        LPRINT H3$
51        LPRINT
52     END SUB
53
```

string expression used in LPRINT and LPRINT USING statements

```
54    ' ********************************************
55    ' *                Process File              *
56    ' ********************************************
57    SUB B100.Process.File
58       READ Cus.No$, Beg.Bal, Pay, Pur, Cr
59       DO WHILE Cus.No$ <> "EOF"
60          CALL B200.Compute.Service.Charge
61          LPRINT USING D1$; Cus.No$; Beg.Bal; Pay; Pur; Cr; Serv.Chg; End.Bal
62          READ Cus.No$, Beg.Bal, Pay, Pur, Cr
63       LOOP
64    END SUB
65
66    ' ********************************************
67    ' *          Compute Service Charge          *
68    ' ********************************************
69    SUB B200.Compute.Service.Charge
70       Unp.Bal = Beg.Bal - Pay - Cr
71       Serv.Chg = .01625 * Unp.Bal
72       Serv.Chg = INT((Serv.Chg + .005) * 100) / 100
73       End.Bal = Unp.Bal + Pur + Serv.Chg
74    END SUB
75
76    ' ********************************************
77    ' *                 Wrap-Up                  *
78    ' ********************************************
79    SUB C100.Wrap.Up
80       LPRINT
81       LPRINT T1$
82    END SUB
```

FIGURE 5.14
The report generated on the printer by Program 5.2.

```
                    Accounts Receivable Balance

   Customer  Begin                  Pur-            Service  Ending
   Number    Balance    Payment     chases  Credit  Charge   Balance

   14376172  1,112.32    35.00      56.00    0.00    17.51  1,150.83
   16210987     30.00    30.00      15.00    0.00     0.00     15.00
   18928384    125.50    25.00       0.00   12.50     1.43     89.43
   19019293    120.00    12.00      12.00   23.00     1.38     98.38
   19192929     10.00     7.00       2.50    1.50     0.02      4.02

   End of Report
```

Discussion of the Program Solution

When Program 5.2 is executed by pressing Shift + F5, it begins by declaring variables and the string expressions globally in lines 6 and 7. Then, control transfers to A100.Initialization, which begins by performing basic housekeeping tasks. (We tend not to place housekeeping statements in separate subprograms because they do not relate directly to the problem at hand.) The PC clears the screen and then displays the following message to the user due to lines 25 through 27:

```
Set the paper in the printer to the top of page.
Press the Enter key when the printer is ready...
```

Note that the INPUT statement temporarily halts the program until the user presses the Enter key in response to the message in the second line. Once the user aligns the paper in the printer and presses the Enter key, line 28 transfers control to A200.Initialize.Report.Format. Lines 36 through 40 assign the heading lines, detail line, and total line described on the printer spacing chart in Figure 5.12 to string variables.

Next, line 29 in A100.Initialization transfers control to A210.Print.Headings. The LPRINT statements (lines 47 through 51) print the report and column headings by referencing the string variables defined in A200.Initialize.Report.Format.

After A100.Initialization is complete, the CALL statement in line 9 invokes B100.Process.File. In line 58, the READ statement instructs the PC to read the first record found in line 12. Because the first record is not the end-of-file, the DO WHILE statement in line 59 passes control to line 60, and customer 14376172 is processed.

After the second record is read, the LOOP statement in line 63 instructs the PC to loop back to line 59 to test for end-of-file. The second record is processed and displayed before the PC reads the next record. This process continues until all of the accounts receivable records have been processed. When the trailer record is read, control returns to the Main Program, which then calls C100.Wrap.Up. After the message End of Report is printed, control returns to the Main Program which is terminated by line 18.

The report (Figure 5.14) shows that through the use of the LPRINT USING statement in line 61, Program 5.2 prints all monetary values rounded to the nearest cent, with decimal points aligned and right-justified below the column headings. The customer number, which is defined to be a string variable, is displayed left-justified. The significance of taking the time to lay out the report on a printer spacing chart should be apparent in this Programming Case Study. Once the printer spacing chart is complete, the format of the report can be copied directly into the program, as shown in lines 36 through 40 of Program 5.2.

Note, in A200.Initialize.Report.Format that the report format lines call for printing the first column of the report beginning in print position 1 — the position next to the left, perforated edge of the paper. To print the report several positions from the left edge as shown in Figure 5.14, move the paper in the printer to the left prior to running the program. You can also add several spaces to the left side of each of the report format lines in A200.Initialize.Report.Format.

With the output techniques discussed so far in this chapter, you may now begin to dress up your output. Programmers often forget that most people using the results of computer-generated reports are unfamiliar with computers and are confused by poorly formatted output. You now have the capability in QuickBASIC to produce high quality reports that are meaningful and easy to read.

5.5   THE LOCATE STATEMENT

The LOCATE statement may be used to position the cursor on the screen. It also may be used to turn the cursor on and off. Standard screens have 24 vertical lines (rows) and 80 horizontal print positions (columns). The LOCATE statement can position the cursor precisely on any one of the 1,920 positions on the screen.

The general form of the LOCATE statement is shown in Table 5.18. The values that follow the keyword LOCATE are called **parameters**.

| **TABLE 5.18** The LOCATE Statement | | |

General Form: LOCATE row, column, cursor

where **row** represents the row and is a numeric expression between 1 and 24 for a standard screen;

column represents the column and is a numeric expression between 1 and 80 in the 80-column display and between 1 and 40 in the 40-column display; and

cursor is a numeric expression equivalent to 0 or 1. Zero makes the cursor invisible, and 1 makes the cursor visible.

Purpose: To position the cursor precisely on the screen and to make the cursor visible or invisible.

Examples:
1. LOCATE 5, 10
2. LOCATE 1, 1
3. LOCATE 7
4. LOCATE , 50
5. LOCATE 4, 6, 0
6. LOCATE , , 1

Note: The LOCATE statement also may be used to control the size of the cursor. (For further information on controlling the size of the cursor, see the QuickBASIC user's manual.)

In Table 5.18, example 1 moves the cursor to column 10 on line 5. It makes no difference whether the cursor is above or below line 5 or to the right or left of column 10; when the statement is executed, the cursor is moved to line 5, column 10.

Example 2 moves the cursor to the **home position**: the leftmost column on line 1. Example 3 in Table 5.18 moves the cursor directly up or down to the same column on line 7. In example 4 the row is left blank, and in this case, the PC moves the cursor to column 50 of the current line. When the row, column or cursor are left blank, the PC uses the current value.

Example 5 of Table 5.18 causes the PC to position the cursor in column 6 of line 4. Furthermore, the third parameter zero instructs the PC to make the cursor invisible. Example 6 makes the cursor visible at the current position.

The following revised version of Programming Case Study 4A illustrates the use of the PRINT USING and LOCATE statements. In addition, a new procedure for displaying messages on the screen is presented.

| Programming Case Study 4B | Determining the Single Discount Rate with a Fixed Screen Format and End-of-File Test |

Let's consider a refined program solution to Programming Case Study 4A, Determining the Single Discount Rate. Add the following to the original program specifications presented in Chapters 3 and 4:

1. Redesign the output results to agree with the format shown on the **screen layout form** in Figure 5.15. A screen layout form is similar to a printer spacing chart in that it allows you to construct a skeleton of the output results for a screen, rather than the printer.
2. Format the single discount as shown on line 16 in Figure 5.15.
3. Allow the user to decide whether he or she wants to enter another series of discounts or terminate execution of the program (line 20, Figure 5.15).

FIGURE 5.15

Output for Program 5.3 designed on a screen layout form.

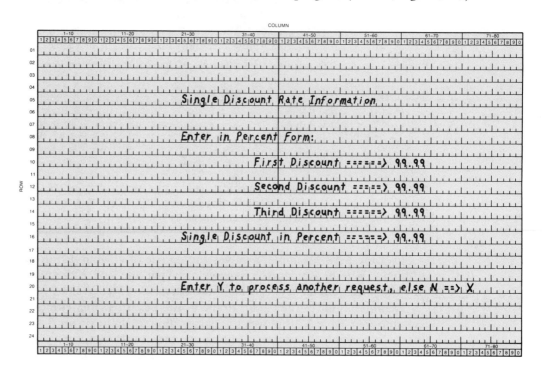

Following are a top-down chart (Figure 5.16), a list of the additional program tasks, a program solution, and a discussion of the program solution.

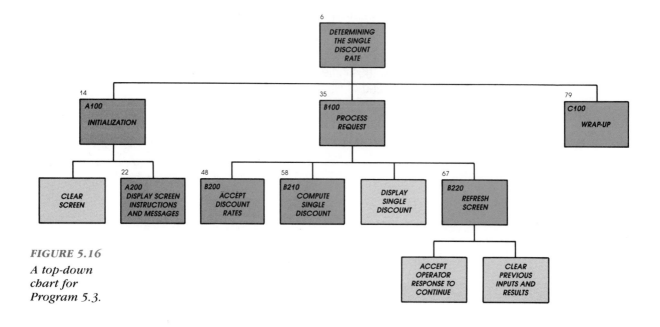

FIGURE 5.16

A top-down chart for Program 5.3.

Additional Program Tasks

1. Use the LOCATE statement to position the cursor for each line displayed. Display all instructions and messages once in A100.Initialization. Leave the instructions and messages on the screen for the duration of execution of the program. Use the LOCATE statement and SPC function to blank out the results to the right of the instructions and messages before processing another series of discounts.

2. Use the PRINT USING statement to format the single discount.

3. Establish a Do loop within B100.Process.Request that executes the range of statements *before* testing for termination of the loop. That is, use a DO...LOOP UNTIL. (See Figure 5.2d on page 127.)

4. Use the condition UCASE$ (Control$) = "N" in the LOOP statement to determine whether to terminate the loop described in 3. The UCASE$ function converts the value of Control$ to uppercase. (See Section 9.2 in Chapter 9 for more details on the UCASE$ function.) After displaying the single discount and before the LOOP statement, call upon a subprogram that uses the INPUT statement to accept a response from the user as to whether he or she wants to determine another single discount. Assign the response to Control$ (Y to continue, N to terminate execution). Note, we are assuming that the user will not enter any responses other than Y, y, N, or n. After accepting the response, clear the screen of the results from the previous inputs and results.

5. Use the argument-parameter-list technique to pass values between a calling program and subprograms.

PROGRAM 5.3

```
1    ' Program 5.3
2    ' Determining the Single Discount Rate
3    ' ***************************************************
4    ' *                 Main Program                    *
5    ' ***************************************************
6    CALL A100.Initialization
7    CALL B100.Process.Request
8    CALL C100.Wrap.Up
9    END
10
11   ' ***************************************************
12   ' *                Initialization                   *
13   ' ***************************************************
14   SUB A100.Initialization
15       CLS   ' Clear Screen
16       CALL A200.Display.Prompt.Messages
17   END SUB
18
19   ' ***************************************************
20   ' *            Display Prompt Messages              *
21   ' ***************************************************
22   SUB A200.Display.Prompt.Messages
23       LOCATE 5, 25: PRINT "Single Discount Rate Information"
24       LOCATE 8, 25: PRINT "Enter in Percent Form:"
25       LOCATE 10, 37: PRINT "First Discount ======> "
26       LOCATE 12, 37: PRINT "Second Discount =====> "
27       LOCATE 14, 37: PRINT "Third Discount ======> "
28       LOCATE 16, 25: PRINT "Single Discount in Percent ======>"
29       LOCATE 20, 25: PRINT "Enter Y to process another request, else N ==>"
30   END SUB
31
```

(continued)

```
32      ' ***********************************************
33      ' *              Process Request              *
34      ' ***********************************************
35      SUB B100.Process.Request
36         DO
37            CALL B200.Accept.Rates(Rate1, Rate2, Rate3)
38            CALL B210.Compute.Single.Discount(Rate1, Rate2, Rate3, Rate)
39            LOCATE 16, 59: PRINT USING " ##.##"; Rate
40            CALL B220.Refresh.Screen(Control$)
41         LOOP UNTIL UCASE$(Control$) = "N"
42      END SUB
43
44      ' ***********************************************
45      ' *            Accept Discount Rates          *
46      ' *           Returns Rate1, Rate2, Rate3     *
47      ' ***********************************************
48      SUB B200.Accept.Rates (Rate1, Rate2, Rate3)
49         LOCATE 10, 60: INPUT "", Rate1
50         LOCATE 12, 60: INPUT "", Rate2
51         LOCATE 14, 60: INPUT "", Rate3
52      END SUB
53
54      ' ***********************************************
55      ' *          Compute Single Discount          *
56      ' * Receives Rate1, Rate2, Rate3; Returns Rate *
57      ' ***********************************************
58      SUB B210.Compute.Single.Discount (Rate1, Rate2, Rate3, Rate)
59         Rate = 1 - (1 - Rate1 / 100) * (1 - Rate2 / 100) * (1 - Rate3 / 100)
60         Rate = 100 * Rate
61      END SUB
62
63      ' ***********************************************
64      ' *               Refresh Screen              *
65      ' *              Returns Control$             *
66      ' ***********************************************
67      SUB B220.Refresh.Screen (Control$)
68         LOCATE 20, 72: INPUT "", Control$
69         LOCATE 10, 60: PRINT SPC(7);
70         LOCATE 12, 60: PRINT SPC(7);
71         LOCATE 14, 60: PRINT SPC(7);
72         LOCATE 16, 60: PRINT SPC(7);
73         LOCATE 20, 72: PRINT SPC(7);
74      END SUB
75
76      ' ***********************************************
77      ' *                  Wrap-Up                  *
78      ' ***********************************************
79      SUB C100.Wrap.Up
80         CLS  ' Clear Screen
81         LOCATE 12, 25: PRINT "End of Program - Have a Nice Day"
82      END SUB
```

keeps user in a loop until an N or n is pressed

Discussion of the Program Solution

When Program 5.3 is executed, the CALL statement in line 6 transfers control to A100.Initialization. In the top-down chart in Figure 5.16, A100.Initialization has two subtasks: clear the screen, and display *all* of the messages specified on the screen layout form described in Figure 5.15. Line 15 carries out the first subtask. Line 16 transfers control to A200.Display.Prompt.Messages in lines 22 through 30 to accomplish the second subtask. The display from these lines is shown in Figure 5.17.

FIGURE 5.17

*The display
from Program
5.3 due to the
execution of
lines 23
through 29.*

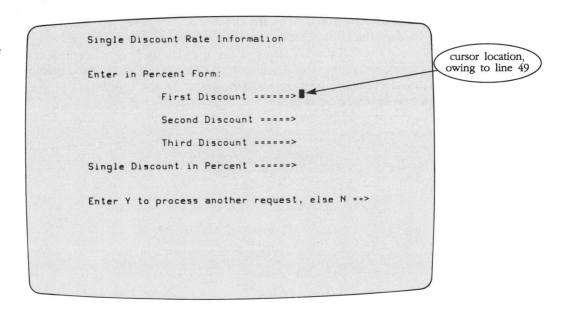

```
         Single Discount Rate Information


    Enter in Percent Form:

                      First Discount ======>█

                     Second Discount =====>

                      Third Discount ======>

        Single Discount in Percent ======>


        Enter Y to process another request, else N ==>
```

cursor location,
owing to line 49

Note that we did not place the first subtask of A100.Initialization in Figure 5.16 in a separate subprogram in Program 5.3. Recall that a top-down chart, such as the one in Figure 5.16, shows *what* must be done to solve the problem. At coding time, potential subprograms that are only a few lines of code or perform housekeeping tasks may be placed directly in the superior module. The decision as to whether a subtask in a top-down chart should be a separate subprogram in a program becomes easier to make with experience.

After A100.Initialization displays the messages shown in Figure 5.17, control returns to line 7 in the Main Program. Line 7, in turn, transfers control to B100.Process.Request. The DO statement in line 36 does not include a condition. Therefore, the range of statements (lines 37 through 40) is executed before testing for termination of the loop.

The first statement in the loop (line 37) transfers control to B200.Accept.Rates. In this lower level subprogram, lines 49 through 51 employ the LOCATE and INPUT statements to accept the three discounts from the user. You'll recall that the LOCATE statement is capable of moving the cursor back to the end of the corresponding message that is already displayed on the screen. Each INPUT statement has the null string as the prompt message. The null string followed by the comma eliminates the question mark that is displayed when no prompt message is used. The three discount rates are then returned to B100.Process.Request due to the arguments in line 37 and the parameters in line 48.

After control passes back to line 38, Program 5.3 calls the subprogram B210.Compute.Single.Discount, which received the three discount rates and uses these rates to compute the single rate. The single discount rate is then returned to the subprogram B100.Process.Request due to the arguments in line 38 and the parameters in line 58. Next, the single rate is displayed (line 39). Line 40 then transfers control to B220.Refresh.Screen. The INPUT statement in line 68 of B220.Refresh.Screen causes the PC to halt execution until a response to continue is entered by the user. This gives the user time to read the results. When the user finishes reading the results, he or she enters a response. This response, Control$, is returned to B100.Process.Request because of the argument in line 40 and the parameter in line 67.

If the user enters a Y or any other character other than N or n, as shown in Figure 5.18, then the PC will make another pass through the Do loop because of the condition in line 41. On the other hand, if the user enters N or n, control returns to the Main Program, and C100.Wrap.Up displays a message before the END statement in line 9 terminates execution of the program. Note in line 81 of C100.Wrap.Up, a pleasant message to the user is displayed as part of the end-of-job routine.

FIGURE 5.18

Screen display from Program 5.3 when entering discounts of 40%, 20%, and 10%.

```
Single Discount Rate Information


Enter in Percent Form:

           First Discount ======> 40

           Second Discount =====> 20

           Third Discount ======> 10

Single Discount in Percent ======> 56.80


Enter Y to process another request, else N ==> Y
```

The last important point regarding Program 5.3 concerns lines 69 through 73 in B220.Refresh.Screen. These lines are used to refresh the screen in preparation for the next set of data to be entered by the user. In each of these lines, the LOCATE statement is used to move the cursor to the exact position where previous data entered by the user is displayed on the screen. Following each LOCATE statement, the SPC function is used in a PRINT statement to blank out the previous data. SPC(7) blanks out seven positions to the right, beginning with the location of the cursor. If you plan to use this procedure to build screens, it is important to remember that the LOCATE statement does not clear the screen. Any old data will remain on the screen unless it is cleared. This is the purpose of B220.Refresh.Screen.

5.6   WHAT YOU SHOULD KNOW

1. A loop in a program instructs the PC to repeat a series of instructions.
2. A loop defined by the DO and LOOP statements is called a Do loop. The DO statement indicates the beginning of the loop and the LOOP statement the end of the loop. The condition can be placed in the DO or LOOP statement. (See Figure 5.2 for examples of the different ways a Do loop can be constructed in QuickBASIC.)
3. One execution of a loop is a pass.

4. A condition is a relationship that is either true or false. A condition is made up of two expressions separated by a relational operator. There are six valid relational operators: greater than (>); less than (<); equal to (=); greater than or equal to (>=); less than or equal to (<=), and not equal to (<>).

5. The DATA statement provides for the creation of a sequence of data items for use by the READ statement.

6. The DATA statement consists of the keyword DATA followed by a list of data items, which can be either numeric or string. If string data contains a leading or trailing blank or an embedded comma or colon, the data must be enclosed in quotation marks.

7. The DATA statement is a nonexecutable statement. DATA statements can be placed only in the Main Program. They cannot be placed in subprograms.

8. Data items from all DATA statements are collected and placed into one single data-sequence holding area. The order in which the data items appear among all DATA statements determines the order of the data items in the single data- sequence holding area.

9. The READ statement provides for the assignment of values to variables from a sequence of data items created from DATA statements.

10. The READ statement consists of the keyword READ followed by a list of variables separated by mandatory commas.

11. Every variable appearing in the program whose value is directly obtained by a READ must be listed in a READ statement before it is used in the program.

12. A program containing a READ statement must also have at least one DATA statement.

13. The RESTORE statement allows the data in a given program to be reread by READ statements as often as necessary.

14. The RESTORE statement consists of the keyword RESTORE followed by an optional label. If the label is not present, the pointer is restored to the first data item in the first DATA statement. If the label is present, then the pointer is set to the first data item in the DATA statement referenced by the specified label.

15. The PRINT USING statement is useful in controlling the output format.

16. One or more consecutive format symbols appearing in a string expression are a descriptor field, or field format.

17. Depending on the type of editing desired, numeric descriptor fields can include a number sign, decimal point, comma, dollar sign, plus or minus sign, asterisk, and four consecutive circumflexes. (See Table 5.9.)

18. Descriptor fields for string values use the exclamation point, ampersand, underscore, and two backslashes separated by n spaces, which reserve n + 2 positions in the line, to display a string.

19. While the PRINT USING statement displays results on the screen, the LPRINT USING statement prints the results on a printer.

20. The LOCATE statement is used to position the cursor on the screen. It also may be used to make the cursor visible or invisible.

5.7   TEST YOUR BASIC SKILLS (Even-numbered answers are in Appendix E)

1. Consider the valid programs listed below. What is displayed if each is executed?

a.
```
' Exercise 5.1a
' MPG Comparison
READ Car.Model$, Miles, Gallons
DO WHILE Car.Model$ <> "EOF"
    Mpg = Miles / Gallons
    PRINT "Car model ===> "; Car.Model$
    PRINT "Miles =======>"; Miles
    PRINT "Gallons =====>"; Gallons
    PRINT "Mpg =========>"; Mpg
    PRINT
    READ Car.Model$, Miles, Gallons
LOOP
PRINT "Job Finished"
' **** Data Follows ****
DATA A,    1275, 41.7
DATA B,     685,  23.2
DATA C,    1650, 62.5
DATA EOF, 0,      0
END
```

b.
```
' Exercise 5.1b
READ X, Y
DO WHILE X <> -1
    PRINT "Old value of X ="; X
    PRINT "Old value of Y ="; Y
    T = X
    X = Y
    Y = T
    PRINT "New value of X ="; X
    PRINT "New value of Y ="; Y
    PRINT
    READ X, Y
LOOP
LOCATE 13, 7: PRINT "Job Finished"
' ***** Data Follows *****
DATA  4, 6
DATA  3, 7
DATA -1, 0
END
```

c.
```
' Exercise 5.1c
' ******** Main Program *******
COMMON SHARED A, B, Count, X, Y
CALL A100.Initialization
CALL B100.Process.File
CALL C100.Wrap.Up
' ******** Data Follows *******
DATA 4, 9, 6, 10, 8, 12, 0, -1
END

' ****** Initialization *******
SUB A100.Initialization
    CLS  ' Clear Screen
    A = 0
    B = 0
    Count = 0
END SUB

' ******* Process File ********
SUB B100.Process.File
    READ X, Y
    DO WHILE Y >= 0
        A = A + X
        B = B + Y
        Count = Count + 1
        PRINT Count; A; B
        READ X, Y
    LOOP
END SUB

' ********* Wrap-Up **********
SUB C100.Wrap.Up
    LOCATE 1, 14, 0
    PRINT USING "Count ====> ###"; COUNT
    LOCATE 3, 14, 1: PRINT "FINIS"
END SUB
```

d.
```
' Exercise 5.1d
' Displaying Hi!
CLS  ' Clear Screen
Row = 12
Column = 31
Cursor = 0
DO
    Column = Column + 4
    LOCATE Row, Column, Cursor: PRINT "Hi!"
    Row = Row + 1
LOOP UNTIL Row = 20
END
```

e.
```
' Exercise 5.1e
' Nested Do Loops
CLS  ' Clear Screen
Row = 0
DO
    Row = Row + 1
    Column = 0
    DO
        Column = Column + 1
        LOCATE Row, Column: PRINT "*"
    LOOP UNTIL Column > 40
LOOP UNTIL Row > 10
END
```

2. Correct the errors in the following programs:

   a.
   ```
   ' Exercise 5.2a
   READ S, B,
   D = S - B
   SPC(5)
   LOCATE 26, 14, -1 : PRANT D
   END
   DATA 4, 6 ' Data for READ
   ```

   b.
   ```
   ' Exercise 5.2b
   DATA 1, 2, 5, 6, 8, 7, 1, 3, 2, 0
   READ X, Y, Z
   DO WHILE X > 0
     X1 = X * Y
     X1 = X1 * Z
     READ X, Y, Z
   LOOP WHILE X > 0
   PRINT X2
   END
   ```

3. Consider the following types of Do loops.
   a. DO WHILE...LOOP
   b. DO UNTIL...LOOP
   c. DO...LOOP WHILE
   d. DO...LOOP UNTIL

   Answer the following questions for each type of Do loop:

   (1) Is the test made before or after the range of statements is executed?
   (2) What is the *minimum* number of times the range of statements is executed?
   (3) Does the Do loop terminate when the condition is true or false?

4. Write a sequence of LOCATE and PRINT statements that will display the value of A in column 7 of the first line and the value of B in column 45 of the fourth line.

5. Write a single PRINT statement in the immediate window to compute and display:

   a. $\sqrt{Y}$ b. $\sqrt[3]{Y}$ c. $\sqrt[4]{Y}$

6. Write a PRINT USING statement that includes the string constant for the purpose of displaying the message The amount is followed by the value of Amount. Include a numeric descriptor field with the following characteristics:
   a. Five digit positions, two to the right of the decimal point
   b. A floating dollar sign
   c. A sign status to the right of the number
   d. Three or more check-protection asterisks

7. Determine whether the conditions below are true or false, given the following: Credit.Union = 25, Ins.Ded = 20, and Salary = 900
   a. Credit.Union >= 25
   b. Salary / Ins.Ded < Credit.Union
   c. Ins.Ded = Credit.Union - 5
   d. Salary <> 800
   e. 875 + Credit.Union <= Salary
   f. Ins.Ded > 20

8. Write a sequence of statements that will clear the screen and display the value 6 in print position 6 of line 6.

9. Write a LOCATE and PRINT statement that will cause the following to be displayed starting in column 20 of line 7: Customer name =====>

10. Indicate the location of the cursor immediately after the following two lines are executed:

```
LOCATE 5, 12, 1 : PRINT "PC"
LOCATE 14
```

11. What kind of graphic output displays from this program?

```
' Exercise 5.11
CLS  ' Clear Screen
LOCATE 10, 38: PRINT "VVVVV"
LOCATE 11, 37: PRINT "X"; TAB(43); "X"
LOCATE 12, 36: PRINT "X"; TAB(39); "O"; TAB(41); "O"; TAB(44); "X"
LOCATE 13, 36: PRINT "X"; TAB(44); "X"
LOCATE 14, 36: PRINT "X"; TAB(40); "U"; TAB(44); "X"
LOCATE 15, 36: PRINT "X"; TAB(38); "("; TAB(42); ")"; TAB(44); "X"
LOCATE 16, 36: PRINT "X"; TAB(40); "-"; TAB(44); "X"
LOCATE 17, 37: PRINT "X"; TAB(43); "X"
LOCATE 18, 38: PRINT "XXXX"
END
```

12. Write a program that will generate the following graphic output. Use the LOCATE statement to position the upper left most asterisk in column 33 of line 8.

```
* * * * * * * * * * * * *
*  B  A  S  I  C  *
B  L          N  B
A     E     R     A
S        A        S
I     E     R     I
C  L          N  C
*  B  A  S  I  C  *
* * * * * * * * * * * * *
```

13. Write a PRINT USING statement that displays the value of Last.Name$ beginning in position 1 for each of the following:
    a. Only the first character of Last.Name$ is displayed.
    b. All of Last.Name$ is displayed.
    c. The first six characters of Last.Name$ are displayed.
    d. The first two characters of Last.Name$ are displayed.

14. Write a sequence of LOCATE and PRINT statements to display the following figure with the vertex at print position 20 on line 9. Clear the screen and make the cursor invisible before displaying the figure.

15. For each of the following descriptor fields and corresponding data, indicate what the PC displays. Use the letter ƀ to indicate the space character.

	Descriptor Field	Data	Result		Descriptor Field	Data	Result
a.	###	25		b.	#,###.##	38.4	
c.	$$,###.##-	-22.6		d.	$#,###.##-	425.89	
e.	**#,###.##	88.756		f.	#,###.#	637214	
g.	##.##-	3.975		h.	###.##	-123.8	
i.	##,###.###	12.6143		j.	##.##^^^^	265.75	
k.	!	ABCD		l.	&	ABCD	
m.	\\ (zero spaces)	ABCD		n.	\ \ (2 spaces)	ABCD	

16. **PC Hands-On Exercise**: Load Program 5.1 (PRG5-1) from the Student Diskette and do the following:
    a. Execute Program 5.1 and note the results displayed. Move the trailer record (line 16) to the top of the list of DATA statements (between lines 10 and 11). Execute the program and see what happens.
    b. Reload PRG5-1. Delete the trailer record; execute the program and see what happens. Note the importance of the trailer record.

17. **PC Hands-On Exercise**: Load Program 5.3 (PRG5-3) from the Student Diskette. Display and execute the program. Enter the following sets of data:

    Set 1: 10%, 15%, 25%
    Set 2: 2%, 4%, 6%
    Set 3: 2.25%, 34.55%, 46.99%
    Set 4: 99.99%, 99.99%, 99.99%

    Step through the program and try to determine which statement the PC is attempting to execute when it suspends execution to accept the data.

5.8 BASIC PROGRAMMING PROBLEMS

1. Determining the Price/Earnings (P/E) Ratio

Purpose: To become familiar with the top-down approach, READ and DATA statements, and Do loops.

Problem: Construct a top-down program to compute and display the P/E ratio for companies whose current stock prices and earnings per share are known. Process the companies listed in the table below until the Stock Name is equal to EOF.

The P/E ratio is a useful tool employed by stock market analysts in evaluating the investment potential of various companies. The P/E ratio is determined by dividing the price of a share of stock by the company's latest earnings per share.

Declare variables globally using the COMMON SHARED statement.

(Hint: Use the top-down chart illustrated in Figure 5.1 and Program 5.1 — PRG5-1 on the Student Diskette — as a guide to solving this problem.)

Input Data: Prepare and use the following sample data:

Stock Name	Price per Share	Latest Earnings
Apple	59 1/4	2.72
Cray	37 1/2	4.17
Digital	46	3.83
IBM	90 5/8	6.92
Tandem	13 7/8	0.31
EOF	0	0

(trailer record → points to EOF row)

Output Results: The following results are displayed:

```
                      P/E Ratio Report

       Stock          Price Per     Latest        P/E
       Name           Share         Earnings      Ratio
       -----          ---------     --------      -----
       Apple          59.25         2.72          21.78309
       Cray           37.5          4.17          8.992805
       Digital        46            3.83          12.01044
       IBM            90.625        6.92          13.0961
       Tandem         13.875        .31           44.75806

       End of Stock Report
```

2. Inflation Gauge

Purpose: To become familiar with printing a report on the printer and the use of the DO WHILE, LOOP, READ, DATA, and LPRINT USING statements.

Problem: Write a top-down program to read today's current price, the previous price and the number of weeks between price quotes from DATA statements. Compute the sample annual inflation rate and the expected price of the item one year from today's current price. Use the following formulas:

Price Change = (Current Price – Beginning Price) / Weeks * 52
Annual Inflation = Price Change / Beginning Price
Expected Price = Current Price + Inflation Rate * Current Price

Round the inflation rate to the nearest cent before determining the expected price of the item in one year. For each item processed, print the item, current price, computed inflation rate and expected price in one year. For the current price and expected price in one year, use the descriptor field #,###.##. For the inflation rate, use the descriptor field ###.##.

Before printing the first line of the report, display a message on the screen requesting that the operator turn on the printer.

Declare variables globally using the COMMON SHARED statement.

(**Hint:** Use the top-down chart illustrated in Figure 5.16 and Program 5.2 — PRG5-2 on the Student Diskette — as a guide to solving this problem.)

Input Data: Prepare and use the following sample data:

Item	Current Price	Beginning Price	Number Weeks
1 doz. eggs	$0.93	$0.92	13
1 lb. butter	2.59	2.50	15
1 gal. milk	1.92	1.85	18
1 loaf bread	1.10	1.07	6

Output Results: The following results are printed:

```
   Inflation Gauge Report

              Current    Inflation    Price
   Item       Price      Rate in %    in 1 Yr
   ----       -------    ---------    -------
   1 doz. eggs   0.93        4.35        0.97
   1 lb. butter  2.59       12.48        2.91
   1 gal. milk   1.92       10.93        2.13
   1 loaf bread  1.10       24.30        1.37

   Job Finished
```

3. Determining the Point of Intersection

Purpose: To become familiar with Do loops, testing for end-of-file, and the READ and DATA statements.

Problem: Maximum profit or minimum cost can often be determined from equations based on known facts concerning a product. The point of intersection of the equations is significant. Write a top-down program to find the point of intersection for two first-degree equations in two variables (that is, two equations and two unknowns). The general form for two equations is as follows:

$$a_1x + b_1y = c_1 \qquad a_2x + b_2y = c_2$$

Its solutions are expressed as follows:

$$x = \frac{c_1b_2 - c_2b_1}{a_1b_2 - a_2b_1} \qquad y = \frac{c_2a_1 - c_1a_2}{a_1b_2 - a_2b_1}$$

The program should read the coefficients (a_1, b_1, c_1, a_2, b_2 and c_2, in this order) from a DATA statement; solve for x and y; display the values of a_1, b_1 and c_1 on one line, and a_2, b_2, c_2, x and y on the next line. The program should loop back to read a set of data for the next system of equations.

Terminate the Do loop within the Process File subprogram when a_1 is equal to –999.999. Make your program efficient by computing the denominator of x and y only once.

Declare variables globally using the COMMON SHARED statement.

(Hint: Use the top-down chart illustrated in Figure 5.1 and Program 5.1 — PRG5-1 on the Student Diskette — as a guide to solving this problem.)

Input Data: Prepare and use the following sample data:

System	*Equation 1 Coefficients*			*Equation 2 Coefficients*		
	a	*b*	*c*	*a*	*b*	*c*
1	1	1	5	1	–1	1
2	2	–7	8	3	1	–8
3	0.6	–0.75	–8	0.6	–0.125	2

Output Results: The following results are displayed:

```
<-----------Equations------------>      <----Intersection--->
Coeff A      Coeff B      Coeff C      X Value      Y Value
-------      -------      -------      -------      -------
   1            1            5
   1           -1            1            3            2

   2           -7            8
   3            1           -8        -2.086957    -1.73913

  .6          -.75          -8
  .6          -.125          2         6.666667       16

End of Report
```

4. Determining the Eventual Cash Value of an Annuity

Purpose: To become familiar with the LOCATE statement, looping, the hierarchy of operations in a complex LET statement, the UCASE$ function, and building a screen for data entry.

Problem: An annuity or installment plan is a series of payments made at equal intervals of time. Examples of annuities are pensions and premiums on life insurance. More often than not, the interest conversion period is unequal to the payment interval. The following formula determines the eventual cash value of an annuity of R dollars paid per year in P installments for N years, at an interest rate of J percent converted M times a year.

$$S = R \left[\frac{\left(1 + \dfrac{J}{M}\right)^{MN} - 1}{P\left[\left(1 + \dfrac{J}{M}\right)^{M/P} - 1\right]} \right]$$

where S = eventual cash value
R = payment per year
P = number of installments per year
N = duration of the annuity in years
J = nominal interest rate
M = conversions per year

Write a top-down program to determine the eventual cash value of an annuity rounded to the nearest dollar. After processing the first annuity, loop back to process the next annuity.

Prior to processing the first annuity, clear the screen and use the LOCATE statement to center the instructions and messages. Display the instruction and message portions only *once*. After the results for the first set of data are displayed, request that the operator enter Y to process another set of data and N to terminate the program. If Y is entered, use the SPC function to clear the results, and then request the operator to enter the next set of data.

Use the argument-parameter-list technique to pass variables between a calling program and subprograms.

(Hint: Use the top-down chart illustrated in Figure 5.16 and Program 5.3 — PRG5-3 on the Student Diskette — as a guide to solving this problem.)

Input Data: Prepare and use the following sample data:

Data

Description	*Set 1*	*Set 2*	*Set 3*
Payment per year	$2,000	$3,000	$4,000
Installments per year	12	12	12
Time in years	20	20	20
Interest rate in %	13	14	15
Conversions per year	2	4	6

Output Results: The results for Set 1 are shown in Figure 5.19. Begin the screen title on line 5, column 25. After that, skip a line between each line displayed. Skip three lines prior to the last line. When the operator requests that the program terminate, clear the screen and display an appropriate message. The Eventual Cash Value for Sets 2 and 3 are $318,120.00 and $492,592.00, respectively.

FIGURE 5.19

Output results for Data Set 1 for Problem 4.

```
Eventual Cash Value of an Annuity

Payment per year ==========> 2000

Installments per year ======> 12

Time in years =============> 20

Interest rate in % ========> 13

Conversions per year ======> 2

Cash value ===============> $180,330.00



Enter Y to process another request, else N ==> Y
```

5. Check Digit Calculation

Purpose: To become familiar with using the INT function to separate the digits in a number and to learn about elementary check-digit calculations.

Problem: Companies that issue credit cards often use algorithms to create credit card numbers that people will have difficulty generating at random. One approach is to add the digits of a number and add 0 or 1 to make the sum of the digits even. For example, the number 45931 (that is, $4 + 5 + 9 + 3 + 1 = 22$ and even) would be acceptable but the number 37230 (that is, $3 + 7 + 2 + 3 + 0 = 15$ and odd) would not. The last digit in the number, either a 1 or a 0, is called the **check digit**.

Write a top-down program that accepts a four-digit number, generates the check digit, and displays the original number, check-digit number, and five-digit credit card number.

Use the argument-parameter-list technique to pass variables between a calling program and subprograms.

(**Hint:** Use the top-down chart illustrated in Figure 5.1 and Program 5.1 — PRG5-1 on the Student Diskette — as a guide to solving this problem. Use the function INT to determine the individual digits that make up the four-digit number and the check digit.)

Input Data: Prepare and use the following sample data in DATA statements: 4631, 4737, 2222, 9998

Output Results: The following output results are displayed:

```
           Check Digit Calculation

  Four Digit      Check          Credit Card
  Number          Digit          Number

     4631           0               46310
     4737           1               47371
     2222           0               22220
     9998           1               99981

  End of Check Digit Calculation
```

6. Payroll Problem V: Biweekly Payroll Report

Purpose: To become familiar with looping and the use of the LPRINT USING, READ and DATA statements.

Problem: Modify the top-down Payroll Problem IV (Problem 5) in Chapter 4, to generate a report on the printer. Include in the report a line of information for each employee. Each line is to include employee number, gross pay, federal withholding tax and net pay.
Declare variables globally using the COMMON SHARED statement.

(**Hint:** Use the top-down chart illustrated in Figure 5.13 and Program 5.2 — PRG5-2 on the Student Diskette — as a guide to solving this problem.)

Input Data: Use the sample data found in Payroll Problem IV. Add a trailer record. Select your own sentinel value.

Output Results: The following results are printed:

```
                 Biweekly Payroll Report

    Employee
    Number        Gross Pay      Fed. Tax      Net Pay
    --------      ---------      --------      -------
       123        1,000.00        184.62        815.38
       124          800.00        152.31        647.69
       125        1,040.00        200.31        839.69
       126           90.00          2.62         87.38

    End of Payroll Report
```

Structured Programming and Menu-Driven Programs

6.1 STRUCTURED PROGRAMMING

It is appropriate at this time that we introduce you to some important concepts related to structured programming.

Structured programming is a methodology according to which all program logic can be constructed from a combination of the following three basic control structures:

1. **Sequence.** The most fundamental of the structures, it provides for two or more actions to be executed in the order in which they appear.
2. **If-Then-Else** or **Selection.** Provides a choice between two alternatives.
3. **Do-While** or **Repetition.** Provides for the repeated execution of a loop.

The following are two extensions to these control structures:

Do-Until. An extension of the Do-While structure.
Case. An extension of the If-Then-Else structure, in which the choice includes more than two alternatives.

So far in this book, the Sequence, Do-While, and Do-Until control structures have been used, even though they have not been identified by their formal names.

The use of structured programming offers definite advantages. Computer professionals have found that when it is applied correctly in the construction of programs, structured programming confers the following benefits:

1. Programs are clearer and more readable.
2. Less time is spent debugging, testing, and modifying the program.
3. The programmer's productivity is increased.
4. The quality, reliability, and efficiency of the program are improved.

Clearly, there are important payoffs in the use of structured programming.

Control Structures

In the previous chapter, the programs performed precisely the same computations for every set of data items that was processed. In some applications, it is not always desirable to process each set of data items in exactly the same way. For example, in a program that computes gross pay, some employees may be eligible for overtime, while others may not. Therefore, a decision must be made concerning which of two gross pay formulas to use.

The sequential flow of control within modules used in previous programs and shown in Figure 6.1 is not sufficient to solve problems that involve **decision making**. To develop an algorithm that requires deviation from sequential control, we need another control structure. This new structure, called If-Then-Else, is shown in Figure 6.2. It is also described in detail in Appendix A, Section A.4.

FIGURE 6.1
Sequence
structure.

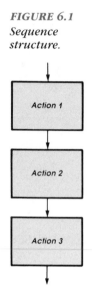

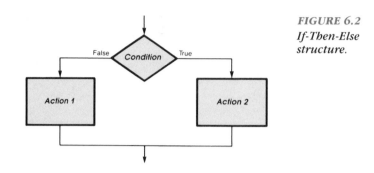

FIGURE 6.2
If-Then-Else
structure.

The flowchart representation of a decision is the diamond-shaped symbol. One flowline will always be shown entering the symbol, and two lines will always be shown leaving the symbol. A condition that must be either true or false is written within the decision symbol. Such a condition asks, for example, whether two variables are equal or whether an expression is within a certain range. If the condition is true, one path is taken; if not, the other path is taken. In Figure 6.2 we have adopted the convention of placing all the actions to the left of the diamond-shaped-symbol when the condition is false and all the actions to the right when the condition is true.

To instruct the PC to select actions on the basis of the values of variables, as illustrated in Figure 6.2, QuickBASIC includes the IF statement. This chapter presents a number of examples to illustrate how IF statements are used to implement If-Then-Else structures.

The SELECT CASE statement may be used to implement an extension of the If-Then-Else structure, in which there are more than two alternatives. This extended version of the If-Then-Else structure is called the Case structure; it is illustrated in Figure 6.3 and described in Appendix A, Section A.4. As we shall see later in this chapter, the Case structure is commonly used to implement menu-driven programs. A **menu-driven program** is one in which a menu or series of menus is used to guide a user through a multifunction interactive program. The **menu** itself lists the functions that a program or a section of a program can perform.

FIGURE 6.3
Case structure.

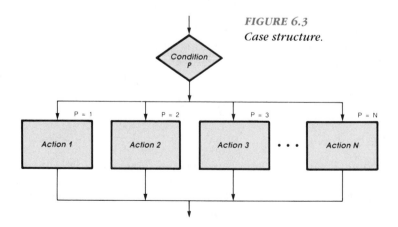

As we saw in Chapter 5, with looping, it is necessary to include a decision to terminate the loop after a sufficient number of repetitions has occurred. Most computer professionals agree that the decision to terminate a loop should be located at the very top or very bottom of the loop. A loop that has the termination decision at the top is called a Do-While structure (Figure 6.4). We implement a Do-While structure in Quick-BASIC by using the DO WHILE and LOOP statements.

A loop that has the termination decision at the bottom is called a Do-Until structure (Figure 6.5). We implement a Do-Until structure by using the DO and LOOP UNTIL statements. (For additional information on the Do-While and Do-Until structures, see Figure 5.2 in Chapter 5 and Section A.4 in Appendix A.)

FIGURE 6.4
Do-While
structure.

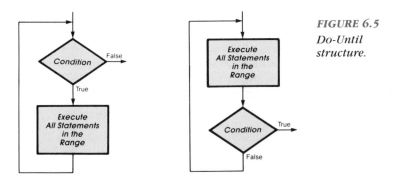

FIGURE 6.5
Do-Until
structure.

Combining Conditions

Logical operators, such as AND, OR, and NOT, may be used to combine conditions to reduce the number of statements required to implement certain If-Then-Else structures. In this chapter, we will discuss these three logical operators and three others — XOR, EQV, and IMP.

Logical operators are often used in the conditions of decision statements that verify the data entered by the user is within a range that will generate valid results when the program is executed. This is called **data validation**.

Top-Down Versus Structured

In Chapter 4, you studied concepts associated with the top-down, or modular, approach. In this chapter, you will study structured programming. Do not confuse structured programming with top-down programming; they are not the same. In designing a top-down solution, we use a top-down chart to determine *what must be done*, as described in Chapter 4. In designing a structured programming solution for a subtask, we use a program flowchart or some other logic tool to resolve the question of *how to implement* the subtask. Emphasis is placed on decision making and looping.

Upon successful completion of this chapter, you will be able to apply concepts related to structured programming and top-down programming. You will also be able to develop algorithms and write programs that include decisions, accumulators, logical operators, data-validation techniques, and menus.

6.2 THE IF STATEMENT

The IF statement is commonly regarded as one of the most powerful statements in QuickBASIC. The function of this statement is to perform selection. In selection, the IF statement is used to let a program choose between two alternative paths, as illustrated in Figure 6.2. The general form of the IF statement is given in Table 6.1.

TABLE 6.1   The IF Statement

General Form: IF condition THEN clause ELSE clause
or
IF condition THEN
  clause
ELSE
  clause
END IF

where **condition** is a relation that is either true or false, and **clause** is a statement or series of statements.

Purpose: If the condition is true, the PC executes the clause following the keyword THEN. If the condition is false and an ELSE clause is included, the PC executes the ELSE clause. After either clause is executed, control passes to the statement following the IF in the first form, known as a single-line IF statement, and to the statement following the corresponding END IF in the second form, known as a block IF statement.

Examples:

```
1.  IF Age > 65 THEN PRINT Age ELSE Switch$ = "Y"

2.  IF Tax >= 0 THEN
        Switch1$ = "Y"
        PRINT Gross.Pay
    ELSE
        Switch1$ = "N"
    END IF

3.  IF Mar.Status$ = "M" THEN
        PRINT "Married"
    END IF

4.  IF Sex.Code$ = "M" THEN
        IF Age >= 18 THEN
            PRINT "Male adult"
        ELSE
            PRINT "Male minor"
        END IF
    ELSE
        IF Age >= 18 THEN
            PRINT "Female adult"
        ELSE
            PRINT "Female minor"
        END IF
    END IF
```

Note: The IF statement may include the keyword ELSEIF to test for a series of different conditions. In situations where the ELSEIF may be used, we will use the SELECT CASE. (See Section 6.8 for a comparison between an IF statement using the keyword ELSEIF and the SELECT CASE statement.)

As indicated in Table 6.1, the IF statement is used to specify a decision. The condition appears between the keywords IF and THEN. In determining whether the condition is true or false, the PC first determines the single value of each expression in the condition and then evaluates them both with respect to the relational operator. Table 5.3 on page 128 lists the relational operators used to indicate the type of comparison.

If the condition in an IF statement is true, then the PC acts upon the THEN clause. If the condition is false, the PC acts upon the ELSE clause. In either case, after executing the statements making up the clause, control passes to the statement following the IF in the **single-line** IF statement, and to the statement following the corresponding END IF in the **block** IF statement. If no ELSE clause is present and the condition is false, then control passes immediately to the statement following the IF or corresponding END IF.

In Example 1 in Table 6.1, if Age is greater than 65, then the value of Age is displayed, and control passes to the statement following the IF statement. If Age is less than or equal to 65, Switch$ is assigned the value Y, and control passes to the statement following the IF statement. Note that the single-line IF statement does not include the END IF statement.

In Example 2 in Table 6.1, if Tax is greater than or equal to zero, the PC assigns Switch1$ the value Y and displays Gross.Pay. On the other hand, if Tax is less than zero, the PC assigns Switch1$ the value N. In either case, control passes to the statement following the corresponding END IF. Note that the block IF statement allows you to include as many statements as necessary in either clause.

In Example 3 in Table 6.1, if Mar.Status$ equals the value M, then the word Married displays, and control passes to the statement following the END IF. This IF statement does not include an ELSE clause. Hence, if the condition is false, control passes to the statement following the corresponding END IF without executing a clause.

Example 4 in Table 6.1 includes a nested IF statement. A **nested** IF statement is one in which a second IF statement is found within the THEN or ELSE clause. In Example 4, the nest of IF statements causes the PC to print one of the four possible messages. The message displayed depends on the value of Sex.Code$ and Age. Note that each IF statement in Example 4 ends with a corresponding END IF statement.

Structured programming permits the nesting of the five control structures to any reasonable level. For example, you may nest an IF statement within a loop formed by a DO WHILE statement, and this may be nested within a loop formed by a DO UNTIL statement.

Comparing Numeric Expressions

If the condition in an IF statement includes two numeric expressions, the comparison is based on the algebraic values of the two expressions. That is, the PC evaluates not only the magnitude of each resultant expression but also its sign. Examples 1 and 2 in Table 6.2 include conditions made up of numeric expressions.

Comparing String Expressions

If the condition in an IF statement includes two string expressions, the PC evaluates the two strings from left to right, one character at a time. As soon as one character in an expression is different from the corresponding character in the other expression, the comparison stops, and the PC decides which expression has a lower value, generally on the basis of numerical and alphabetical order. In other words, the PC evaluates two string expressions the same way you would. For example,

DOE is less than JOE	NO is not equal to No
JEFF is greater than JAFF	YES is equal to YES
TAPE is greater than TAP	

Two string expressions are considered equal if they are of the same length and contain an identical sequence of characters.

The PC determines which characters are *less than* other characters on the basis of the code that is used to store data in main storage. The code is called the **American Standard Code for Information Interchange (ASCII)**. A total of 256 different characters can be entered into main storage. The ASCII code and the collating sequence is shown in Appendix D, Table D.3. The **collating sequence** is the position of the character in relation to other characters. As Table D.3 shows, numbers are less than uppercase letters in value, which are in turn less than lowercase letters in value. The null character is considered to have the least value in the collating sequence. Examples 4 and 5 in Table 6.2 illustrate IF statements that include conditions made up of string expressions.

If you compare a numeric expression to a string expression in an IF statement, QuickBASIC will display a dialog box with the diagnostic message Type mismatch when you attempt to execute the program.

TABLE 6.2   Examples of IF Statements

EXAMPLE	STATEMENT	VALUES OF VARIABLES	RESULT
1	IF Z = 0 THEN S = 4	Z = 0	The variable S is assigned the value 4, and control passes to the line following the IF statement.

2	IF X < Y THEN
	  PRINT A
	  Tax = Tax + 10
	ELSE
	  PRINT B
	  Tax = Tax + 5
	END IF
		X = 7
		Y = 9
			The value of A is displayed; Tax is incremented by 10, and control passes to the line following the END IF.

3	IF D <> A - B - 6 THEN
	  PRINT S
	END IF
		D = 23
		A = 14
		B = -15
			Control passes to the line following the END IF.

4	IF B$ > C$ + D$ THEN
	ELSE
	  PRINT Y
	END IF
		B$ = ''WINE''
		C$ = ''WA''
		D$ = ''TER''
			The THEN clause is null and control passes to the line following the END IF.

5	IF A$ = "NO" THEN
	  PRINT A$
	END IF
		A$ = ''no''	Control passes to the line following the END IF. ''NO'' and ''no'' are not the same string.

Values of Conditions

Conditions are evaluated by the arithmetic-logic unit (ALU) in the PC. When the ALU evaluates a condition, it returns to the program a -1 if the condition is true, or 0 if the condition is false. This is illustrated in the following program, which displays the values of the three conditions X < Y, X = Y, and X > Y. Prior to the PRINT statement, the program assigns X the value 10, and Y the value 20.

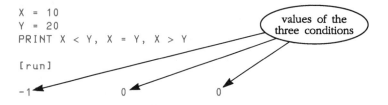

```
X = 10
Y = 20
PRINT X < Y, X = Y, X > Y

[run]

-1          0          0
```

values of the three conditions

Because X is less than Y, the first condition is equal to -1. The last two conditions are false; and therefore, zeros display.

Hence, each time an IF statement in a program executes, the ALU checks the condition. If the condition is true, the ALU returns a -1 (true) to the program, and the PC executes the THEN clause. If the condition is false, the ALU returns a 0 (false), and the PC executes the ELSE clause.

6.3 ACCUMULATORS

Most programs require **accumulators**, which are used to develop totals. Accumulators are numeric variables that are initialized to a predetermined value, such as zero, in the Initialization module, then incremented within the loop in the Process File module, and then manipulated or displayed in the Wrap-Up module. Although QuickBASIC automatically initializes numeric variables to zero, good programming practice demands this be done prior to the loop in which they are incremented.

There are two types of accumulators: counters and running totals. Both types are discussed in the sections that follow.

Counters

A **counter** is an accumulator that is used to count the number of times some action or event is performed. For example, appropriately placed within a loop, the statement

```
Emp.Count = Emp.Count + 1
```

causes the counter Emp.Count to increment by 1 each time a record is read. Associated with a counter is a statement placed in the Initialization module, which initializes the counter to some value. In most cases the counter is initialized to zero.

Running Totals

A **running total** is an accumulator that is used to sum the different values a variable is assigned during the execution of a program. For example, appropriately placed within a loop, the statement

```
Total.Gross = Total.Gross + Emp.Gross
```

causes Total.Gross to increase by the value of Emp.Gross. Total.Gross is called a running total. If a program is processing an employee file and the variable Emp.Gross is assigned the employee's gross pay each time a record is processed, then the variable Total.Gross represents the running total of the gross pay paid to all the employees in the file. As with a counter, a running total must be initialized to some predetermined value in the Initialization module.

Programming Case Study 7A   Weekly Payroll and Summary Report

The following example incorporates both a counter and a running total, as well as some of the concepts discussed earlier in this chapter.

Problem: A payroll application requires that the employee number, the hours worked, the rate of pay, and the gross pay be printed for each of the following employees:

Employee Number	Hours Worked	Rate of Pay
124	40	$5.60
126	56	5.90
128	38	4.60
129	48.5	6.10

Also, the total gross pay, the total number of employees, and the average gross pay for this payroll are to be printed. The required report is described on the printer spacing chart shown in Figure 6.6 on the next page.

FIGURE 6.6

Output for Program 6.1 designed on a printer spacing chart.

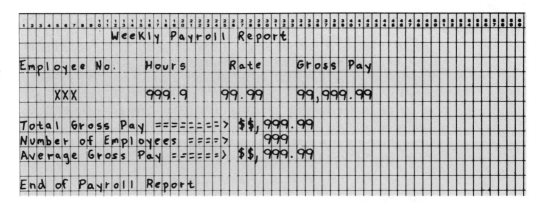

The gross pay is determined by multiplying the hours worked by the hourly rate of pay. Overtime, hours in excess of 40, is paid at 1.5 times the hourly rate.

Following are a top-down chart with two program flowcharts of subtasks (Figure 6.7) and the program tasks in outline form, a program solution in Program 6.1, followed by the program output results (Figure 6.8), and a discussion of the program solution.

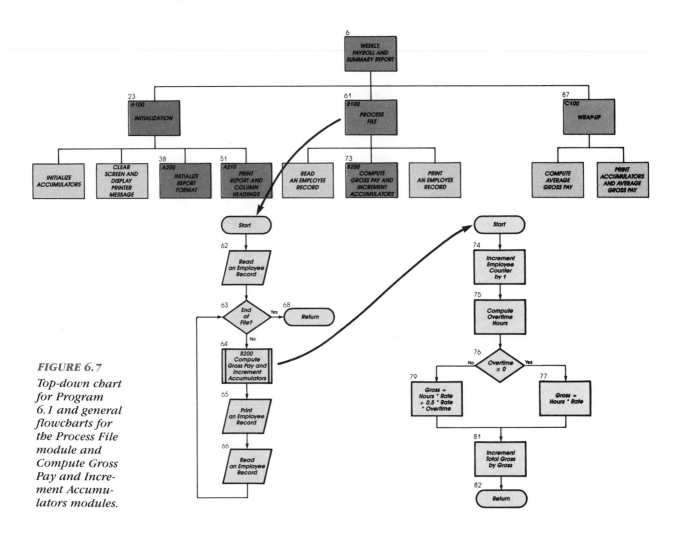

FIGURE 6.7

Top-down chart for Program 6.1 and general flowcharts for the Process File module and Compute Gross Pay and Increment Accumulators modules.

Program Tasks

The following program tasks correspond to the top-down chart in Figure 6.7.

1. A100.Initialization

   a. Initialize a counter (Emp.Count) and running total (Total.Gross) to zero. Use the counter to determine the total number of employees processed. Use the running total to determine the total gross pay.
   b. Clear the screen and display a message informing the user the report will print on the printer. After the user aligns the paper and turns the printer on, accept the Enter key response via the INPUT statement to continue.
   c. Initialize the report format — assign the heading lines, the detail line, and the total lines, described in Figure 6.6, to string variables.
   d. Print the report and column headings.

2. B100.Process.File

   a. Read an employee record. Use the following variable names for the employee record:

      Emp.Number$:   employee number
      Emp.Hours: employee hours
      Emp.Rate: employee hourly rate

   b. Use a DO WHILE statement to establish a loop for processing the employee records when Emp.Number$ does not equal the value EOF. If end-of-file, return control to the Main Program. If not end-of-file, do the following:
   (1) Determine the gross pay and increment accumulators.
       (a) Increment the counter Emp.Count by 1.
       (b) Compute the employee overtime (Emp.Overtime).
       (c) Determine the gross pay (Emp.Gross). If Emp.Overtime is less than or equal to zero, use this formula:

           Emp.Gross = Emp.Hours * Emp.Rate

           If Emp.Overtime is greater than zero, use this formula:

           Emp.Gross = Emp.Hours * Emp.Rate + 0.5 * Emp.Rate * Emp.Overtime

       (d) Increment the running total (Total.Gross) by the employee gross pay (Emp.Gross).
   (2) Print an employee record.
   (3) Read the next employee record.

3. C100.Wrap.Up

   a. Compute the average employee gross pay (Average.Gross).
   b. Print the values of the accumulators (Total.Gross and Emp.Count) and average employee gross pay (Average.Gross).
   c. Print an end-of-job message.
   d. Display an end-of-job message on the screen.

Program Solution

The following program and output results (Figure 6.8) corresponds to the preceding tasks and to the top-down chart in Figure 6.7:

PROGRAM 6.1

```
1    ' Program 6.1
2    ' Weekly Payroll and Summary Report
3    ' **************************************************
4    ' *                    Main Program                *
5    ' **************************************************
6    COMMON SHARED Emp.Count, Total.Gross
7    COMMON SHARED Emp.Hours, Emp.Rate, Emp.Gross
8    COMMON SHARED H1$, H2$, D1$, T1$, T2$, T3$, T4$
9    CALL A100.Initialization
10   CALL B100.Process.File
11   CALL C100.Wrap.Up
12   ' ************** Data Follows ****************
13   DATA 124, 40,   5.60
14   DATA 126, 56,   5.90
15   DATA 128, 38,   4.60
16   DATA 129, 48.5, 6.10
17   DATA EOF, 0,    0    : ' This is the trailer record
18   END
19
20   ' **************************************************
21   ' *                  Initialization                *
22   ' **************************************************
23   SUB A100.Initialization
24      Emp.Count = 0
25      Total.Gross = 0
26      CLS  ' Clear Screen
27      LOCATE 10, 20
28      PRINT "Set the paper in the printer to the top of page."
29      LOCATE 12, 20
30      INPUT "Press Enter when the printer is ready...", Control$
31      CALL A200.Initialize.Report.Format
32      CALL A210.Print.Headings
33   END SUB
34
35   ' **************************************************
36   ' *              Initialize Report Format          *
37   ' **************************************************
38   SUB A200.Initialize.Report.Format
39      H1$ = "              Weekly Payroll Report"
40      H2$ = "Employee No.   Hours      Rate     Gross Pay"
41      D1$ = "    \ \          ###.#     ##.##    ##,###.##"
42      T1$ = "Total Gross Pay ========> $$,###.##"
43      T2$ = "Number of Employees ====>    ###"
44      T3$ = "Average Gross Pay ======> $$,###.##"
45      T4$ = "End of Payroll Report"
46   END SUB
47
48   ' **************************************************
49   ' *          Print Report and Column Headings      *
50   ' **************************************************
51   SUB A210.Print.Headings
52      LPRINT H1$
53      LPRINT
54      LPRINT H2$
55      LPRINT
56   END SUB
57
```

values of these variables are available to all subprograms

set accumulators to 0 in the A100.Initialization subprogram

```
58    ' *********************************************************
59    ' *                    Process File                       *
60    ' *********************************************************
61    SUB B100.Process.File
62       READ Emp.Number$, Emp.Hours, Emp.Rate
63       DO WHILE Emp.Number$ <> "EOF"
64          CALL B200.Compute.Gross.And.Accumulate
65          LPRINT USING D1$; Emp.Number$; Emp.Hours; Emp.Rate; Emp.Gross
66          READ Emp.Number$, Emp.Hours, Emp.Rate
67       LOOP
68    END SUB
69
70    ' *********************************************************
71    ' *   Compute Gross Pay & Increment Accumulators   *
72    ' *********************************************************
73    SUB B200.Compute.Gross.And.Accumulate
74       Emp.Count = Emp.Count + 1
75       Emp.Overtime = Emp.Hours - 40
76       IF Emp.Overtime <= 0 THEN
77          Emp.Gross = Emp.Hours * Emp.Rate
78       ELSE
79          Emp.Gross = Emp.Hours * Emp.Rate + .5 * Emp.Rate * Emp.Overtime
80       END IF
81       Total.Gross = Total.Gross + Emp.Gross
82    END SUB
83
84    ' *********************************************************
85    ' *                     Wrap-Up                           *
86    ' *********************************************************
87    SUB C100.Wrap.Up
88       Average.Gross = Total.Gross / Emp.Count
89       LPRINT
90       LPRINT USING T1$; Total.Gross
91       LPRINT USING T2$; Emp.Count
92       LPRINT USING T3$; Average.Gross
93       LPRINT
94       LPRINT T4$
95       LOCATE 14, 20: PRINT "End of Job"
96    END SUB

      [run]
```

increment Emp.Count by 1 each time a record is processed

increment Total.Gross by Emp.Gross

display accumulators before the program terminates

FIGURE 6.8
The Weekly Payroll and Summary Report printed due to the execution of Program 6.1.

```
            Weekly Payroll Report

   Employee No.    Hours     Rate      Gross Pay

        124         40.0     5.60         224.00
        126         56.0     5.90         377.60
        128         38.0     4.60         174.80
        129         48.5     6.10         321.77


   Total Gross Pay ========> $1,098.17
   Number of Employees ====>         4
   Average Gross Pay ======>    $274.54


   End of Payroll Report
```

Discussion of the Program Solution

The solution to the Weekly Payroll and Summary Report, as represented by the top-down chart in Figure 6.7 and the corresponding Program 6.1, includes a few significant points that did not appear in previous programs. They are as follows:

1. The use of a counter (Emp.Count) and a running total (Total.Gross). Both are initialized to zero (lines 24 and 25) and are incremented each time an employee record is read. The counter is used to keep track of the total number of employees and is incremented in line 74. The running total is used to sum the gross pay and is incremented by the individual employee gross pay in line 81.

2. The A100.Initialization subprogram calls two subprograms. The first one, A200.Initialize.Report.Format (lines 38 through 46), assigns each output line, described on the printer spacing chart in Figure 6.6, to a string variable. Later, these string variables are used in LPRINT and LPRINT USING statements to print the required output. The second subprogram (lines 51 through 56) prints the report and column headings according to the format established in the subprogram A200.Initialize.Report.Format.

3. A decision is made in line 76 to determine which one of the two formulas is to be used to compute the gross pay. If Emp.Overtime is less than or equal to zero, the PC uses the THEN clause. If Emp.Overtime is greater than zero, the PC uses the ELSE clause.

4. The C100.Wrap.Up subprogram (lines 87 to 96) involves calculating an average that is based on the total gross pay (Total.Gross) and the number of employees (Emp.Count) and printing these totals and the average.

5. We are able to eliminate the recomputation of this value by calculating the overtime in line 75 and assigning it to the variable Emp.Overtime. Whenever a value is required several times in a program, it is better to compute it once and assign it to a variable, as in line 75, than to recompute it every time it is needed.

Programming Styles

You should be aware that there are several ways to modularize and code Program 6.1. For example, some programmers prefer to place the single statement that reads a record (line 62 or line 66 in Program 6.1) and the statement that prints the detail line (line 65 in Program 6.1) in separate subprograms. We did not follow this programming style because it tends to increase the complexity of a program and creates confusion by containing too many unnecessary levels of subprograms.

We believe a program should be easy to read and understand while still maintaining its structure. We do not believe in using unnecessary subprograms merely for the sake of subprogram usage.

6.4 IMPLEMENTING THE DO-WHILE AND DO-UNTIL STRUCTURES

In designing and implementing a Do loop, think carefully about where to place the decision to terminate the loop. As mentioned earlier in Section 5.2 of Chapter 5, the decision to terminate should be at the very top or very bottom of the loop.

If, in the design of a solution, the logic requires that you test to terminate before making a pass on the loop (Do-While structure), then use the DO WHILE and LOOP statements to implement the loop. If, on the other hand, the design calls for a pass on the loop before testing for termination (Do-Until structure), use the DO and LOOP UNTIL statements. The flowcharts and partial programs in Figures 6.9 and 6.10 illustrate two different solutions to the same problem — summing the first 100 integers:

(1 + 2 + 3 + ... + 100)

In Figure 6.9, the DO WHILE and LOOP statements are used to implement the Do-While structure. In Figure 6.10, the DO and LOOP UNTIL statements are used to implement the Do-Until structure. Both partial programs generate identical results.

FIGURE 6.9

A Do-While control structure implemented using the DO WHILE and LOOP statements.

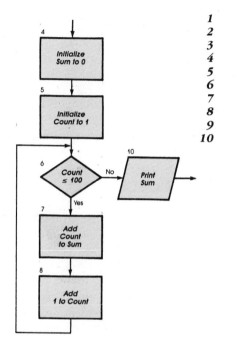

```
 1   ' Summing the First One Hundred Integers
 2   ' Using DO WHILE and LOOP Statements
 3   ' ****************************************
 4   Sum = 0
 5   Count = 1
 6   DO WHILE Count <= 100
 7      Sum = Sum + Count
 8      Count = Count + 1
 9   LOOP
10   PRINT "The sum is"; Sum

     [run]

     The sum is 5050
```

Do-While structure

FIGURE 6.10

A Do-Until control structure implemented using the DO and LOOP UNTIL statements.

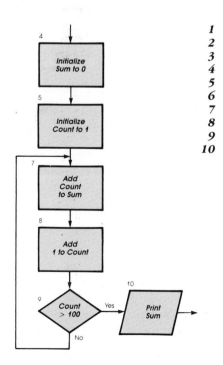

```
 1   ' Summing the First One Hundred Integers
 2   ' Using DO and LOOP UNTIL Statements
 3   ' ****************************************
 4   Sum = 0
 5   Count = 1
 6   DO
 7      Sum = Sum + Count
 8      Count = Count + 1
 9   LOOP UNTIL Count > 100
10   PRINT "The sum is"; Sum

     [run]

     The sum is 5050
```

Do-Until structure

The WHILE and WEND Statements

QuickBASIC also includes the WHILE and WEND statements for the purpose of implementing a Do-While loop in a program. This pair of statements works exactly the same as the DO WHILE and LOOP statements. The WHILE statement initiates a Do-While loop, and the WEND statement terminates it. Hence, in Figure 6.9, we can replace the DO WHILE statement in line 6 with the WHILE statement and the LOOP statement in line 9 with the WEND statement, and the program would function the same way as shown here:

```
6     WHILE Count <= 100
7         Sum = Sum + Count
8         Count = Count + 1
9     WEND
```

In this book we will use the DO WHILE and LOOP statements to implement the Do-While structure. However, because of their popularity in earlier dialects of Microsoft BASIC, you should be aware that the WHILE and WEND statements exist.

6.5   IMPLEMENTING THE IF-THEN-ELSE STRUCTURE

This section describes the various forms of the If-Then-Else structure and the implementation of IF statements in QuickBASIC.

Simple Forms of the If-Then-Else Structure

Consider the If-Then-Else structure in Figure 6.11 and the corresponding methods of implementing the logic in QuickBASIC. Assume that Reg$ represents a person's voter registration status. If Reg$ is equal to the value Y, the person is registered to vote. If Reg$ does not equal Y, the person is not registered to vote. Reg.Cnt and Not.Reg.Cnt are counters that are incremented as specified in the flowchart.

FIGURE 6.11

Implementation of the If-Then-Else structure, with alternative processing for the true and false cases.

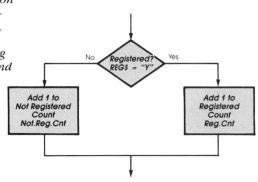

Method 1: Using a single IF statement.

```
IF Reg$ = "Y" THEN
    Reg.Cnt    = Reg.Cnt    + 1
ELSE
    Not.Reg.Cnt = Not.Reg.Cnt + 1
END IF
```

Method 2: Using two separate IF statements.

```
IF Reg$ = "Y" THEN
    Reg.Cnt    = Reg.Cnt    + 1
END IF
IF Reg$ <> "Y" THEN
    Not.Reg.Cnt = Not.Reg.Cnt + 1
END IF
```

In the first method of solution shown in Figure 6.11, an IF statement resolves the logic indicated in the partial flowchart. The first line compares Reg$ to the value Y. If Reg$ is equal to Y, then Reg.Cnt is incremented by 1 in the THEN clause. If Reg$ does not equal Y, Not.Reg.Cnt is incremented by 1 in the ELSE clause. Regardless of the counter incremented, control passes to the statement following the END IF.

Note that the first method could have been written as a single-line IF statement without the END IF. We recommend for readability purposes that you do not use the single-line IF statement.

In method 2, Reg$ is compared to the value Y twice. In the first IF statement, the counter Reg.Cnt is incremented by 1 if Reg$ is equal to Y. In the second IF statement, the counter Not.Reg.Cnt is incremented by 1 if Reg$ does not equal Y.

Although both methods are valid and both satisfy the If-Then-Else structure, the first method is more efficient, as it involves fewer lines of code and less execution time. Therefore, the first method is recommended over the second.

As shown in Figures 6.12, 6.13 and 6.14, the If-Then-Else structure can take on a variety of appearances. In Figure 6.12, there is a task only if the condition is true.

FIGURE 6.12

Implementation of an If-Then-Else structure with alternative processing for the true case.

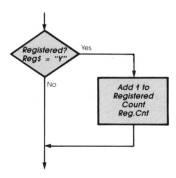

Method 1: Using an IF statement with no ELSE clause.

```
IF Reg$ = "Y" THEN
    Reg.Cnt = Reg.Cnt + 1
END IF
```

Method 2: Using an IF statement with a null ELSE clause.

```
IF Reg$ = "Y" THEN
    Reg.Cnt = Reg.Cnt + 1
ELSE
END IF
```

FIGURE 6.13

Implementation of an If-Then-Else structure with alternative processing for the false case.

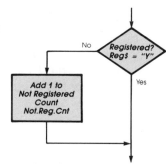

Method 1: Negating the condition in the decision symbol and using an IF statement.

```
IF Reg$ <> "Y" THEN
    Not.Reg.Cnt = Not.Reg.Cnt + 1
END IF
```

Method 2: Using an IF statement with a null THEN clause.

```
IF Reg$ = "Y" THEN
ELSE
    Not.Reg.Cnt = Not.Reg.Cnt + 1
END IF
```

FIGURE 6.14

Implementation of an If-Then-Else structure with several statements for both the true and false cases.

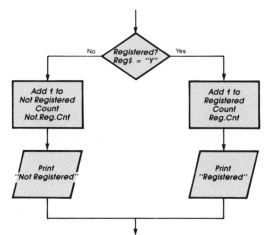

```
IF Reg$ = "Y" THEN
    Reg.Cnt = Reg.Cnt + 1
    PRINT "Registered"
ELSE
    Not.Reg.Cnt = Not.Reg.Cnt + 1
    PRINT "Not Registered"
END IF
```

In Figure 6.12, the first method is preferred over the second, because it is more straightforward and involves fewer lines of code. Note that the second method involves a null ELSE clause.

The If-Then-Else structure in Figure 6.13 illustrates the incrementation of the counter Not.Reg.Cnt when the condition is false. In method 1, the relation in the condition found in the partial flowchart has been negated. The condition Reg$ = "Y" has been modified to read Reg$ <> "Y" in the QuickBASIC code. Negating the relation is usually preferred when additional tasks must be done as a result of the condition being false.

In method 2, the relation is the same as in the decision symbol. When the condition Reg$ = Y is true, the null THEN clause simply passes control to the statement following the END IF. Either method is acceptable. Some programmers prefer always to include both a THEN and an ELSE clause, even when one of them is null. On the other hand, some prefer to negate the condition rather than include a null clause.

In Figure 6.14, each task in the If-Then-Else structure is made up of multiple statements. We have included in the figure a suggested method of implementation. If the condition Reg$ = "Y" is true, the two statements in the THEN clause are executed. If the condition is false, the two statements in the ELSE clause are executed.

Although there are alternative methods for implementing the If-Then-Else structure, the method presented is more straightforward and involves fewer lines of code.

Nested Forms of the If-Then-Else Structure

A nested If-Then-Else structure is one in which the action to be taken for the true or false case includes yet another If-Then-Else structure. The second If-Then-Else structure is considered to be nested, or layered, within the first.

Study the partial program that corresponds to the nested If-Then-Else structure in Figure 6.15. In the partial program in Figure 6.15, if the condition Age >= 18 is true, control passes to the true task beginning with line 2. If the condition is false, the ELSE clause in line 9 is executed. If control does pass to line 2, then a second IF tests to determine if Reg$ equals the value Y. If the condition in line 2 is true, lines 3 and 4 are executed. If the condition is false, then the PC executes lines 6 and 7.

FIGURE 6.15

Implementation of a nested If-Then-Else structure.

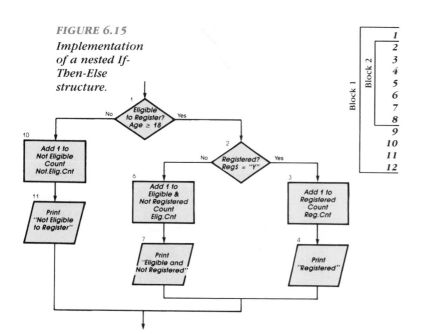

```
 1    IF Age >= 18 THEN
 2        IF Reg$ = "Y" THEN
 3            Reg.Cnt = Reg.Cnt + 1
 4            PRINT "Registered"
 5        ELSE
 6            Elig.Cnt = Elig.Cnt + 1
 7            PRINT "Eligible and Not Registered"
 8        END IF
 9    ELSE
10        Not.Elig.Cnt = Not.Elig.Cnt + 1
11        PRINT "Not Eligible to Register"
12    END IF
```

QuickBASIC requires that you end each block IF statement with an END IF. Hence, the IF in line 1 has a corresponding END IF in line 12, and the IF in line 2 has a corresponding END IF in line 8. This leads to the rule at the top of the next page.

IF RULE 1 *Each block* IF *statement must have a corresponding* END IF.

Note in Figure 6.15 that only one of the three alternative tasks is executed for each record processed. Regardless of the path taken, control eventually passes to the statement immediately following the last END IF in line 12.

If-Then-Else structures can be nested to any depth, but readability decreases as nesting increases. Consider the nested structure in Figure 6.16 and the corresponding implementation in QuickBASIC. Figure 6.16 contains three nests of If-Then-Else structures and six counters. The counters can be described in the following manner:

NE.Male:	totals the number of males not eligible to register
NE.Fem:	totals the number of females not eligible to register
NR.Male:	totals the number of males who are old enough to vote but have not registered
NR.Fem:	totals the number of females who are old enough to vote but have not registered
N.Vote:	totals the number of individuals who are eligible to vote but did not vote
Vote:	totals the number of individuals who voted

In the partial program in Figure 6.16, line 1 corresponds to the decision at the very top of the flowchart. Lines 2 through 14 handle the true case to the right in the flowchart. Lines 16 through 20 fulfill the false case to the left in the flowchart. Incorporating the logic and concepts found in Figure 6.16 into a complete program is left as an exercise for you at the end of this chapter. (See BASIC Programming Problem 3 at the end of this chapter.)

FIGURE 6.16

Implementation of a nested If-Then-Else structure with several layers.

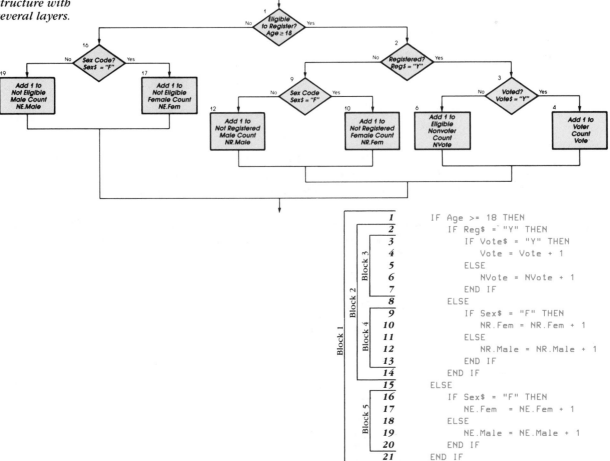

```
 1    IF Age >= 18 THEN
 2        IF Reg$ = "Y" THEN
 3            IF Vote$ = "Y" THEN
 4                Vote = Vote + 1
 5            ELSE
 6                NVote = NVote + 1
 7            END IF
 8        ELSE
 9            IF Sex$ = "F" THEN
10                NR.Fem = NR.Fem + 1
11            ELSE
12                NR.Male = NR.Male + 1
13            END IF
14        END IF
15    ELSE
16        IF Sex$ = "F" THEN
17            NE.Fem = NE.Fem + 1
18        ELSE
19            NE.Male = NE.Male + 1
20        END IF
21    END IF
```

6.6   LOGICAL OPERATORS

In many instances, a decision to execute one alternative or another is based upon two or more conditions. In previous examples that involved two or more conditions, we tested each condition in a separate decision statement. In this section, we will discuss combining conditions within one decision statement by means of the logical operators AND, OR, XOR, EQV, and IMP. When two or more conditions are combined by these logical operators, the expression is called a **compound condition**. The logical operator NOT allows you to write a condition in which the truth value is **complemented**, or reversed.

The NOT Logical Operator

A condition made up of two expressions and a relational operator is sometimes called a **relational expression**. A relational expression that is preceded by the logical operator NOT forms a condition that is false when the relational expression is true. If the relational expression is false, then the condition is true. Consider the following IF statements:

Method 1: Using the NOT logical operator.

```
IF NOT A > B THEN
   READ A
END IF
```

Method 2: Using other relations to complement.

```
IF A <= B THEN
   READ A
END IF
```

Method 3: Using a null THEN.

```
IF A > B THEN
ELSE
   READ A
END IF
```

If A is greater than B, meaning the relational expression is true, then the condition NOT A > B is false. If A is less than or equal to B, meaning the relational expression is false, then the condition is true. All three methods are equivalent; however, methods 1 and 2 are preferred.

Because the logical operator NOT can increase the complexity of the decision statement significantly, use it sparingly. As illustrated in Table 6.3, with QuickBASIC you may write the complement, or reverse, of a condition by using other relations.

TABLE 6.3   Use of Other Relations to Complement a Condition

CONDITION	COMPLEMENT OF CONDITION METHOD 1	METHOD 2
A = B	A <> B	NOT A = B
A < B	A >= B	NOT A < B
A > B	A <= B	NOT A > B
A <= B	A > B	NOT A <= B
A >= B	A < B	NOT A >= B
A <> B	A = B	NOT A <> B

The following rule summarizes the use of the logical operator NOT:

LOGICAL OPERATOR RULE 1 *The logical operator* NOT *requires that the relational expression be false for the condition to be true. If the relational expression is true, then the condition is false.*

The AND Logical Operator

The AND operator requires that both conditions be true for the compound condition to be true. Consider the following IF statements:

Method 1: Using the AND logical operator.

```
IF Sex$ = "M" AND Age > 20 THEN
    PRINT Emp.Name$
END IF
```

Method 2: Using nested IF statements.

```
IF Sex$ = "M" THEN
    IF Age > 20 THEN
        PRINT Emp.Name$
    END IF
END IF
```

If Sex$ is equal to the value M and Age is greater than 20, then Emp.Name$ is displayed before control passes to the line following the END IF. If either one of the conditions is false, then the compound condition is false, and control passes to the line following the END IF without Emp.Name$ being displayed. Although both methods are equivalent, method 1 is more efficient, more compact, and more straightforward than method 2.

Like a single condition, a compound condition can be only true or false. To determine the truth value of the compound condition, the PC must evaluate and assign a truth value to each individual condition. Then the truth value is determined for the compound condition.

For example, if Count equals 4 and Code$ equals ''A'', the PC evaluates the following compound condition in the manner shown:

```
IF Count = 3 AND Code$ = "A" THEN PRINT Emp.Soc.Sec
```
    1. false   2. true
              3. false

The PC first determines the truth value for each condition, then concludes that the compound condition is false because of the AND operator.

A compound condition can be made up of several conditions separated by AND operators. The flowchart in Figure 6.17 on the next page indicates that all three variables (T1, T2, and T3) must equal zero to increment Count by 1. The IF statement in Figure 6.17 illustrates the use of a compound condition to implement the logic. The AND operator requires that all three conditions be true for Count to be incremented by 1. If any one of the three conditions is false, control is transferred to the line following the END IF, and Count is not incremented by 1.

FIGURE 6.17
Use of two AND *operators.*

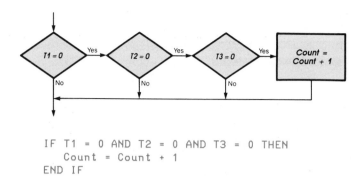

```
IF T1 = 0 AND T2 = 0 AND T3 = 0 THEN
    Count = Count + 1
END IF
```

The following rule summarizes the use of the logical operator AND:

LOGICAL OPERATOR RULE 2	*The logical operator* AND *requires that* **all** *conditions be true for the compound condition to be true.*

The OR Logical Operator

The OR operator requires only one of the two conditions be true for the compound condition to be true. If both conditions are true, the compound condition is also true. Likewise, if both conditions are false, the compound condition is false. The use of the OR operator is illustrated below:

Method 1: Using the OR logical operator.

```
IF Div = 0 OR Expo > 1E30 THEN
    PRINT "WARNING" : STOP
END IF
```

Method 2: Using two IF statements.

```
IF Div = 0 THEN
    PRINT "WARNING" : STOP
END IF
IF Expo > 1E30 THEN
    PRINT "WARNING" : STOP
END IF
```

FIGURE 6.18
Use of two OR *operators.*

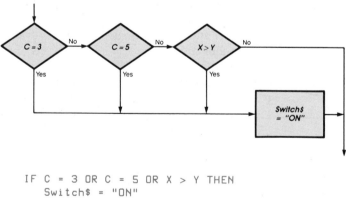

```
IF C = 3 OR C = 5 OR X > Y THEN
    Switch$ = "ON"
END IF
```

In method 1, if either Div equals 0 or Expo is greater than 1E30, the THEN clause is executed. If both conditions are true, the THEN clause is also executed. If both conditions are false, the THEN clause is bypassed, and control passes to the line following the END IF.

Method 2 uses two IF statements to resolve the same problem. Again, both methods are equivalent. However, method 1 is more straightforward than method 2. Can you write a single nested IF statement without a logical operator that results in the same logic described in methods 1 and 2?

Figure 6.18 illustrates a partial flowchart and the use of two OR operators to implement it.

As with the logical operator AND, the truth values of the individual conditions in the IF statement in Figure 6.18 are first determined, and then the truth values for the conditions containing the logical operator OR are evaluated. For example, if C equals 4, X equals 4.9, and Y equals 4.8, the following condition is true:

```
IF   C = 3   OR   C = 5   OR   X > Y   THEN Switch$ = "ON"
      1. false      2. false    3. true
                4. false
                      5. true
```

In this IF statement, the PC first evaluates the individual conditions (steps 1, 2, and 3). The first and second conditions are false, and the third condition is true. Next, the PC evaluates the leftmost OR (step 4). Because the truth values of the first two conditions are false, the truth value of C = 3 OR C = 5 is also false.

Finally, the PC evaluates the truth value of the condition resulting from step 4 and the condition resulting from step 3 for the rightmost logical operator OR. Because the condition resulting from step 3 has a truth value of true, the entire condition is determined to be true.

The following rule summarizes the use of the logical operator OR:

LOGICAL OPERATOR RULE 3   *The logical operator OR requires **only one** of the conditions be true for the compound condition to be true. If both conditions are true, the compound condition is also true.*

The Logical Operators XOR, EQV, and IMP

Three logical operators not used very often but are a part of QuickBASIC are XOR (exclusive OR), EQV (equivalence), and IMP (implication).

The XOR operator requires one of the two conditions be true for the compound condition to be true. If both conditions are true, the compound condition is false. Likewise, if both conditions are false, the compound condition is also false. For example, if C = 3 and D = 4, then the following compound condition is false:

```
C = 3 XOR D > 3
 1. true    2. true
      3. false
```

The EQV operator requires both conditions be true or both conditions be false for the compound condition to be true. For example, if C = 4 and D = 3, then the following compound condition is true:

```
C = 3 EQV D > 3
 1. false    2. false
      3. true
```

The IMP operator requires that both conditions be true or both conditions be false, or the first condition be false and the second condition be true for the compound condition to be true. For example, if C = 4 and D = 5, then the following compound condition is true:

```
C = 3 IMP D > 3
1. false    2. true
      3. true
```

Truth Tables

Truth tables for the six logical operators discussed in this section are summarized in Table 6.4. A summary of the order of precedence of all QuickBASIC operators, including arithmetic, relational, and logical, can be found on page 4 of the reference card in the back of this book.

TABLE 6.4   Truth Tables for Logical Operators Where A and B Represent Conditions, T Represents True, and F Represents False

LOGICAL OPERATOR NOT

VALUE OF A	VALUE OF NOT A
T	F
F	T

LOGICAL OPERATOR XOR

VALUE OF A	VALUE OF B	VALUE OF A XOR B
T	T	F
T	F	T
F	T	T
F	F	F

LOGICAL OPERATOR AND

VALUE OF A	VALUE OF B	VALUE OF A AND B
T	T	T
T	F	F
F	T	F
F	F	F

LOGICAL OPERATOR EQV

VALUE OF A	VALUE OF B	VALUE OF A EQV B
T	T	T
T	F	F
F	T	F
F	F	T

LOGICAL OPERATOR OR

VALUE OF A	VALUE OF B	VALUE OF A OR B
T	T	T
T	F	T
F	T	T
F	F	F

LOGICAL OPERATOR IMP

VALUE OF A	VALUE OF B	VALUE OF A IMP B
T	T	T
T	F	F
F	T	T
F	F	T

Combining Logical Operators

Logical operators can be combined in a decision statement to form a compound condition. The formation of compound statements that involve more than one type of logical operator can create problems unless you fully understand the order in which the PC evaluates the entire condition. Consider the following decision statement:

```
IF X > Y OR T = D AND H < 3 OR NOT Y = R THEN
    Count = Count + 1
END IF
```

Does the PC evaluate operators from left to right or right to left or one type of operator before another?

The order of evaluation is a part of what is called the **rules of precedence**. Just as we have rules of precedence for arithmetic operations (Chapter 3), we also have rules of precedence for logical operators.

> **PRECEDENCE RULE 3**
>
> *Reading from left to right, unless parentheses dictate otherwise, conditions containing arithmetic operators are evaluated first; then those containing relational operators; then those containing* NOT *operators; then those containing* AND *operators; then those containing* OR *or* XOR *operators; then those containing* EQV *operators, and finally those containing* IMP *operators.*

The compound condition in the previous IF statement, then, is evaluated as follows. Assume that D = 3, H = 3, R = 2, T = 5, X = 3, and Y = 2:

```
  X > Y   OR   T = D   AND   H < 3   OR   NOT  Y = R
  1. true      2. false       3. false       4. true
                     6. false            5. false
              7. true
                          8. true
```

If you have trouble following the logic behind this evaluation, use this technique: Applying the rules of precedence, look, or scan, from *left to right* four different times. On the first scan, determine the truth value of each condition that contains a relational operator. On the second scan, moving from left to right again, evaluate all conditions that contain NOT operators. Y = R is true and NOT Y = R is false. On the third scan, moving again from left to right, evaluate all conditions that contain AND operators. T = D is false, as is H < 3; therefore, T = D and H < 3. is false. On the fourth scan, moving from left to right, evaluate all conditions that contain OR operators. The first OR yields a truth value of true. The second OR yields, for the entire condition, a final truth value of true.

The Effect of Parentheses in the Evaluation of Compound Conditions

Parentheses may be used to change the order of precedence. In QuickBASIC, parentheses are normally used to avoid ambiguity and to group conditions with a desired logical operator. When there are parentheses in a compound condition, the PC evaluates that part of the compound condition within the parentheses first and then continues to evaluate the remaining compound condition according to the rules of precedence. For example, suppose variable C (below) has a value of 6, and D has a value of 3. Consider the following compound condition:

```
  C = 7   AND   D < 4   OR   D <> 0
  1. false      2. true        3. true
            4. false
                     5. true
```

Following the order of precedence for logical operators, the compound condition yields a truth value of true. If parentheses surround the latter two conditions in the compound condition, then the OR operator is evaluated before the AND condition, and the compound condition yields a truth value of false, as shown below:

```
C = 7   AND   (D < 4   OR   D <> 0)
‾‾‾‾‾          ‾‾‾‾‾          ‾‾‾‾‾‾
4. false       1. true       2. true
                    ‾‾‾‾‾‾‾‾‾‾‾
                      3. true
‾‾‾‾‾‾‾‾‾‾‾‾‾‾‾‾‾‾‾‾‾‾‾‾‾‾‾‾
          5. false
```

Parentheses may be used freely when the evaluation of a compound condition is in doubt. For example, if you wish to evaluate the compound condition

```
C > D AND S = 4 OR X < Y AND T = 5
```

you may incorporate it into a decision statement as it stands. You may also write it as

```
(C > D AND S = 4) OR (X < Y AND T = 5)
```

and feel more certain of the outcome of the decision statement.

6.7   DATA-VALIDATION TECHNIQUES

Up to this point, we have assumed the data used in the various programs is valid. However, a good program always checks the data to be sure it is accurate at initial input, especially when the INPUT statement is used. In information processing, Garbage In — Garbage Out (GIGO, pronounced GE-GO) is used to describe the generation of inaccurate information from the input of invalid data.

In this section, some definitions and techniques for testing data will be formalized so you will write programs that are characterized by Garbage Doesn't Get In (GDGI) rather than GIGO. **Data validation** is the process of ensuring that valid data is assigned to a program. The following, four data-validation techniques are used:

1. The reasonableness check
2. The range check
3. The code check
4. The digit check

Before describing these data-validation techniques, we will examine the BEEP statement and its use in validation routines.

The BEEP Statement

When executed, the BEEP statement causes the PC's speaker to beep for a quarter of a second; several successive BEEP statements produce a constant beeping sound. For example, the following statement causes the PC to beep for one second.

```
BEEP : BEEP : BEEP : BEEP
```

The BEEP statement is often used in validation routines to alert the user something is wrong. The general form of the BEEP statement is given in Table 6.5.

TABLE 6.5 The BEEP Statement	
General Form:	BEEP
Purpose:	Causes the PC speaker to beep for a quarter of a second.
Examples:	BEEP
	BEEP : BEEP : BEEP : BEEP

Additional examples of the BEEP statement are presented in the remainder of this section.

The Reasonableness Check

The **reasonableness check** ensures the legitimacy of data items that are entered from an external source, such as the keyboard. For example, a program may check a string variable to ensure a specific number of characters is assigned to it. Or a program may check a numeric variable representing a person's age to ensure that it is positive. If the data is not reasonable, the program can request the data be reentered, or it can note the error in a report.

The following partial program requests that the user enter a five-character part number. If the string data item does not contain five characters, the user is requested to reenter the part number.

```
1    INPUT "Five character Part Number =====> "; Part$
2    DO WHILE LEN(Part$) <> 5
3       BEEP : BEEP : BEEP : BEEP
4       PRINT "Part Number "; Part$; " in error, please reenter"
5       INPUT "Five character Part Number =====> "; Part$
6    LOOP

[run]

Five character Part Number =====> 436A
Part Number 436A in error, please reenter
Five character Part Number =====> 436A2
```

an invalid part number

Line 1 requests the user enter a part number. Line 2 uses the LEN function to test the length of the entry. If the length of Part$ is 5, control transfers to the line following the LOOP statement in line 6. If the length of Part$ is not 5, the PC enters the body of the Do-While loop. Within the loop, the speaker is beeped for one second; a diagnostic message is displayed, and the user is requested to reenter the part number. The PC remains in the loop until a valid part number is entered or until the program is manually terminated.

If the LOCATE statement is used to specify exactly where the prompt message in the first INPUT statement is displayed on the screen, the following routine may be used in place of the previous one:

```
1    LOCATE 14, 10 : INPUT "Five character Part Number =====> "; Part$
2    DO WHILE LEN(Part$) <> 5
3       BEEP : BEEP : BEEP : BEEP
4       LOCATE 15, 10
5       PRINT "Part Number "; Part$; " in error, please reenter"
6       LOCATE 14, 44 : PRINT SPC(10)
7       LOCATE 14, 44 : INPUT "", Part$
8       LOCATE 15, 10 : PRINT SPC(40)
9    LOOP
```

In this example, if an invalid entry is made, line 5 displays the diagnostic message, line 6 erases the previous user entry, and line 7 positions the cursor to the right of the prompt message displayed earlier by line 1. Following the next user entry, line 8 erases the diagnostic message displayed earlier by line 5.

The Range Check

The **range check** ensures data items entered from an external device fall within a range of valid values. A company may have a rule all purchase order amounts must be less than $500.00. If so, then the program that processes the purchase order should check the amount on the order to verify that it is greater than zero and less than $500.00. This range check is shown in the following partial program:

```
1   INPUT "Purchase Order Amount ($0.00 < Amount < $500.00) =====> "; Amt
2   DO WHILE Amt <= 0 OR Amt >= 500
3      BEEP : BEEP : BEEP : BEEP
4      PRINT "Amount"; Amt; "is in error, please reenter"
5      INPUT "Purchase Order Amount ($0.00 < Amount < $500.00) =====> "; Amt
6   LOOP
```

[run]

```
Purchase Order Amount ($0.00 < Amount < $500.00) =====> 525.45
Amount 525.45 is in error, please reenter
Purchase Order Amount ($0.00 < Amount < $500.00) =====> 425.45
```

an out-of-range purchase order amount

The range check, defined by the condition in the DO WHILE statement in line 2, verifies that the value of the purchase order amount is positive and less than $500.00. If the purchase amount is within range, the Do-While loop is bypassed, and control transfers to the line following the LOOP statement in line 6. If the purchase amount is out of range, the PC enters the body of the loop. Line 3 beeps the speaker for one second. Line 4 displays a diagnostic message, and line 5 requests the user enter a valid amount. Note, the PC remains in the loop while invalid amounts are entered or until the program is manually terminated.

The Code Check

The **code check** ensures codes entered from an external source are valid. In a school registration system, for example, the value for class standing may be F for freshman, S for sophomore, J for junior, and G for senior, with all other codes considered invalid.

The following partial program requests that the user enter the class standing:

```
1   INPUT "Class Standing (F, S, J, OR G) =====> "; Class$
2   DO WHILE Class$ <> "F" AND Class$ <> "S" AND Class$ <> "J" AND Class$ <> "G"
3      BEEP : BEEP : BEEP : BEEP
4      PRINT "Class Standing "; Class$; " is invalid, please reenter"
5      INPUT "Class Standing (F, S, J, OR G) =====> "; Class$
6   LOOP
```

an invalid class-standing code

[run]

```
Class Standing (F, S, J, OR G) =====> B
Class Standing B is invalid, please reenter
Class Standing (F, S, J, OR G) =====> J
```

As illustrated in the compound condition in line 2, and because the codes are seldom contiguous (meaning they seldom follow one another in the alphabet or, for that matter, in sequence), the logical operator AND and the relational operator <> are normally used to form the compound condition. If Class$ equals F, S, J, or G, control does not enter the Do-While loop; rather, it transfers to the line following the LOOP statement in line 6.

Any other value assigned to Class$ causes the PC to enter the Do-While loop. Line 3 beeps the speaker, line 4 displays the diagnostic message, and line 5 requests the user to enter a valid class standing.

The Digit Check

The **digit check** verifies the assignment of a special digit to a number. A company may use a procedure whereby all part numbers of items sold begin with the digit 2. The partial program below illustrates how the string function LEFT$ can be used to accept only part numbers that begin with a 2.

```
1    INPUT "Part Number =====> "; Part$
2    DO WHILE LEFT$(Part$, 1) <> "2"
3       BEEP : BEEP : BEEP : BEEP
4       PRINT "Part Number must begin with a 2, please reenter"
5       INPUT "Part Number =====> "; Part$
6    LOOP


[run]


Part Number =====> 12389
Part Number must begin with a 2, please reenter
Part Number =====> 22389
```

an invalid part number

In line 2, the expression LEFT$(Part$, 1) is equal to the first character of Part$. If the first character in Part$ is a 2, control bypasses the Do-While loop. If the first character is not a 2, control enters the Do-While loop. The PC beeps the speaker and displays a diagnostic message, and the user is requested to reenter the part number.

6.8 THE SELECT CASE STATEMENT AND MENU-DRIVEN PROGRAMS

The SELECT CASE statement is used to implement the Case structure. The Case structure is an extension of the If-Then-Else structure. It is illustrated in Figure 6.19 on the next page and described in Appendix A, Section A.4.

Figure 6.19 shows two methods for implementing a Case structure, which determines a letter grade (Letter.Grade$) from a grade point average (GPA) using the following grading scale:

Grade Point Average	Letter Grade
GPA ≥ 90	A
80 ≤ GPA < 90	B
70 ≤ GPA < 80	C
60 ≤ GPA < 70	D
0 ≤ GPA < 60	F
GPA < 0	Error

FIGURE 6.19

Implementation of a Case structure.

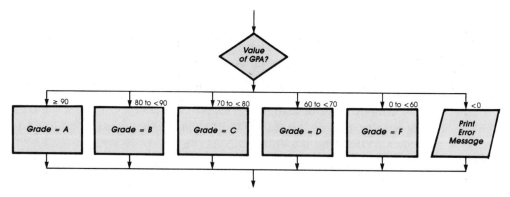

Method 1: Using an `IF` statement with an `ELSEIF` clause.

```
IF GPA >= 90 THEN
    Letter.Grade$ = "A"
ELSEIF GPA >= 80 THEN
    Letter.Grade$ = "B"
ELSEIF GPA >= 70 THEN
    Letter.Grade$ = "C"
ELSEIF GPA >= 60 THEN
    Letter.Grade$ = "D"
ELSEIF GPA >= 0 THEN
    Letter.Grade$ = "F"
ELSE
    PRINT "Negative grade average"
END IF
```

Method 2: Using a `SELECT CASE` statement.

```
SELECT CASE GPA
  CASE IS >= 90
     Letter.Grade$ = "A"
  CASE IS >= 80
     Letter.Grade$ = "B"
  CASE IS >= 70
     Letter.Grade$ = "C"
  CASE IS >= 60
     Letter.Grade$ = "D"
  CASE IS >= 0, IS < 60
     Letter.Grade$ = "F"
  CASE ELSE
     PRINT "Negative grade average"
END SELECT
```

For example, if your GPA is 89.6, your letter grade is a B. The first method of implementation in Figure 6.19 uses the `IF` statement with the `ELSEIF` clause, and the second method uses the `SELECT CASE` statement.

In method 1 of Figure 6.19, an `IF` statement with several `ELSEIF` clauses is used to implement the Case structure. Each `ELSEIF` is followed by a condition and a `THEN` clause. Only one of the `THEN` clauses or the `ELSE` clause, just before the `END IF`, is executed for each pass. For example, if the variable GPA is equal to 74, then the condition in the second `ELSEIF` clause is true, and Letter.Grade$ is assigned the value C. After executing the `THEN` clause, the PC transfers control to the statement below the `END IF`. It does not test any of the conditions below the first condition that is true.

In method 2 of Figure 6.19, the `SELECT CASE` statement is used to implement the grading scale. Notice how much easier it is to read through the `SELECT CASE` than the `IF` statement in method 1. When the PC executes the `SELECT CASE` statement, it compares the variable GPA, which follows the keywords `SELECT CASE`, to the expressions following the keyword CASE in each CASE clause. A CASE clause is also called a **case**. It begins the comparison with the first case and continues through the remaining ones until it finds a match. When a match is found, the range of statements immediately following the keyword CASE is executed. Following execution of the case, control transfers to the statement following the END SELECT. The PC does not search for additional matches in the remaining cases.

For example, if GPA is equal to 89.6, then the PC finds a match in the second case. Therefore, it assigns Letter.Grade$ the value B and passes control to the statement following the END SELECT. If GPA equals a negative value, then no match is found, and the PRINT statement following the CASE ELSE is executed.

The general form of the SELECT CASE statement is given in Table 6.6.

TABLE 6.6 The SELECT CASE Statement

General Form:
```
SELECT CASE testexpression
    CASE matchexpression
        [range of statements]
        .
        .
        .
    CASE ELSE
        [range of statements]
END SELECT
```
where **testexpression** is a string or numeric expression that is matched with the matchexpression in the corresponding CASE clauses; and, **matchexpression** is a numeric or string expression or a range of numeric or string expressions of the following form:
1. expression, expression, . . . ,expression
2. expression TO expression
3. IS relational expression where relation is <, >, >=, <=, =, or <>.

Purpose: Causes execution of the range of statements that follow the CASE clause whose matchexpression matches the testexpression. If there is no match, then the range of statements in the CASE ELSE clause is executed. Following the execution of a range of statements, control passes to the statement following the END SELECT.

Examples: (Also see Table 6.7 for additional examples of the matchexpression in CASE clauses.)

```
1. SELECT CASE Age                 2. SELECT CASE Code$
       CASE IS = 0                        CASE "A", "B", "D"
          CALL B200.Baby                     Interest = .015
       CASE IS < 2                           Time = 24
          CALL B210.Toddler               CASE "C", "G" TO "K"
       CASE IS < 14                          Interest = .014
          CALL B220.Youngster                Time = 36
       CASE IS < 21                       CASE "L" TO "Z"
          CALL B230.Young.Adult              Interest = .013
       CASE IS >= 21                         Time = 48
          CALL B240.Adult                 CASE "E", "F"
       CASE ELSE                             Interest = .012
          PRINT "INVALID AGE"                Time = 60
   END SELECT                          END SELECT
```

Note: If the CASE ELSE clause is not included, as in Example 2, in a SELECT CASE statement, then it is the programmer's responsibility to ensure the testexpression falls within the range of one of the matchexpressions found in the accompanying CASE clauses, otherwise the diagnostic message CASE ELSE expected displays in a dialog box when a match is not found.

As indicated in Table 6.6, with the SELECT CASE, you place the variable or expression you want to test after the keywords SELECT CASE. Next, you assign the group of values that make each alternative case true after the keyword CASE. Each case contains the range of statements to execute, and you may have as many cases as required. After the last case, end the SELECT CASE with an END SELECT.

Example 1 in Table 6.6 tests the variable Age against the matchexpressions, beginning with the first CASE clause and continuing downward until a match is found. If Age is equal to 0, then a match occurs on the first case, and control transfers to the subprogram B200.Baby. The keyword IS is required when a relational operator, such as =, is used. When the END SUB statement in B200.Baby executes, control returns to the statement following the END SELECT. If Age is greater than or equal to 2, but less than 14, control transfers to the subprogram B220.Youngster. If Age is greater than or equal to 14, but less than 21, control transfers to the subprogram B230.Young.Adult. If Age is less than 0, the CASE ELSE is executed, and the message INVALID AGE displays. Note that the CASE ELSE clause is the last one in the list of cases. The placement of the CASE ELSE clause can be stated as follows:

SELECT CASE RULE 1   *If a CASE ELSE clause is included, then it must be the last case.*

Note that in Example 1, if Age is equal to a value of 0, then all cases are true. However, only the range of statements that correspond to the first match is executed. This leads to the following rule:

SELECT CASE RULE 2   *Only the first matched case in a SELECT CASE is executed.*

In Example 2 of Table 6.6, the variable Code$ is matched against several different categories of letters. The first case is executed if Code$ is equal to the value A, B, or D. The commas in a list of expressions following the keyword CASE are mandatory. If Code$ is equal to the value C or the letters G through K, then the second case is executed. The keyword TO is required when specifying a range, such as "G" TO "K". If Code$ is equal to the values L through Z, the third case is executed. Finally, if Code$ is equal to the value E or F, then the last case is executed.

Note in this example that there is no CASE ELSE. The assumptions here are that Code$ contains no lowercase letters between A to Z; Code$ is validated prior to the execution of the SELECT CASE, and that Code$ is equal to an uppercase letter between A and Z. Hence, the CASE ELSE is not required. However, if you don't validate the expression, then always include a CASE ELSE. This leads to the following rule:

SELECT CASE RULE 3   *If there is no match and no CASE ELSE, then Quick-BASIC halts execution of the program and displays a diagnostic message in a dialog box.*

When specifying a range in a CASE clause, make sure the smaller value is listed first. For example, CASE 3 TO -1 is invalid. It should be stated as CASE -1 TO 3. The same applies to string values. Whereas, CASE "Jeff" TO "Jim" is valid, CASE "Jim" TO "Jeff" is not.

Valid Match Expressions

As indicated in Table 6.6, there are several ways to construct valid match expressions. Consider the match expressions in Table 6.7.

In Example 1 in Table 6.7, the match expression is a list made up of the letters F to H, the letter S, and the value of the variable Emp.Code$. In Example 2, the match expression includes Emp.Salary and the expression Max.Salary – 2000. Note that if a relational operator is used, then the keyword IS is required. The second value in the list of Example 2 shows that expressions with arithmetic operators are allowed. The third example includes a list with the keywords IS and TO.

	TABLE 6.7 Valid Match Expressions
EXAMPLE	**MATCH EXPRESSION**
1.	CASE "F" TO "H", "S", Emp.Code$
2.	CASE IS = Emp.Salary, IS = Max.Salary - 2000
3.	CASE IS < 12, 20 TO 30, 48.6, IS > 100

It is easy to see why programmers use the SELECT CASE statement. A SELECT CASE statement is used when the design of a program includes a Case structure. Furthermore, nesting of Case structures is permitted as with the other structures. The following Programming Case Study illustrates a major use of the SELECT CASE statement — menu-driven programs.

| Programming Case Study 8 | A Menu-Driven Program

It is common for programs to have multiple functions. A menu, a list of the functions that a program can perform, is often used to guide a user through a multifunction program. We call programs that display a menu of functions a menu-driven program. Such a program displays a menu like the one illustrated on the screen layout form in Figure 6.20. The user can then choose the desired function from the list by entering a corresponding code. Once the request is satisfied, the program again displays the menu. As illustrated in Figure 6.20, one of the codes (in this case 7) terminates execution of the program.

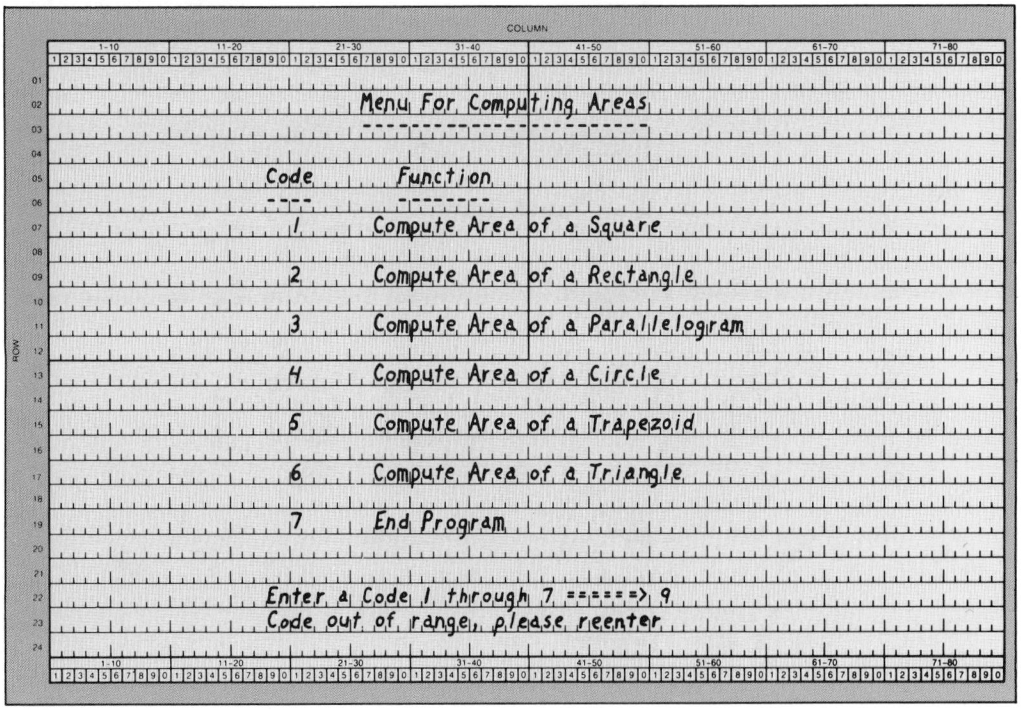

FIGURE 6.20

A menu of program functions designed on a screen layout form.

The following problem uses the menu illustrated in Figure 6.20:

Problem: A menu-driven program is to compute the area of a square, rectangle, parallelogram, circle, trapezoid and triangle. The program should display the menu shown in Figure 6.20. Once a code is entered, the program must do a range check to ensure that the code corresponds to one of the menu functions. After the selection of the proper function, the program should prompt the user for the necessary data, compute the area, and display it accordingly. The displayed results are to remain on the screen until the Enter key on the keyboard is pressed. After that, the program should display the menu again.

1. Area of a square: $A = S * S$ where S is the length of a side of the square.
2. Area of a rectangle: $A = L * W$ where L is the length and W is the width of the rectangle.
3. Area of a parallelogram: $A = B * H$ where B is the length of the base, and H is the height of the parallelogram.
4. Area of a circle: $A = 3.141598 * R * R$ where R is the radius of the circle.
5. Area of a trapezoid: $A = H(B1 + B2)/2$ where H is the height, B1 is the length of the primary base, and B2 is the length of the secondary base of the trapezoid.
6. Area of a triangle: $A = B * H/2$ where B is the base, and H is the height of the triangle.

FIGURE 6.21

A top-down chart and general flowchart for the Process Request module for Program 6.2.

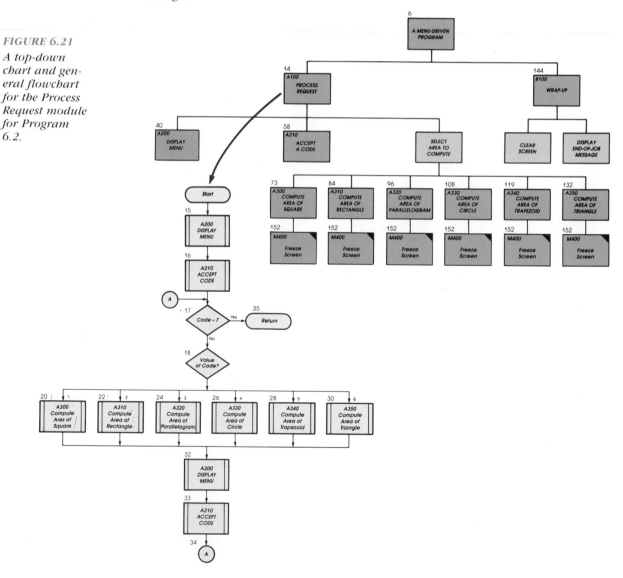

The Freeze Screen module at the fourth level of the top-down chart in Figure 6.21 has more than one superior. Recall from Chapter 4 that we identify lower level modules with more than one superior by darkening the upper right-hand corner of the process symbol. Furthermore, we assign a module with more than one superior the letter M for multiple superiors. The letter M is then followed by a level number that corresponds to its level in the top-down chart. At coding time, modules that begin with the letter M physically end up at the bottom of the list of subprograms.

The general flowchart of the Process Request module in Figure 6.21 illustrates the six independent functions of Program 6.2. Each module reference includes its own output, processing, and output statements.

Program Tasks

The following program tasks correspond to the top-down chart in Figure 6.21:

1. A100.Process.Request

   a. Display the menu shown in Figure 6.20 using the LOCATE and PRINT statements.
   b. Accept a value for Code.
      (1) Request the user to enter a code. Assign the code to the integer variable Code%. (Make the variable an integer type to ensure that the code entered is an integer. If a decimal number is entered, the PC will only assign Code% the whole number portion of the number.)
      (2) Use a Do-While loop to validate the code. If the code is invalid, beep the speaker, display an appropriate diagnostic message and again ask the user to select a function.
      (3) When a valid code is entered, clear the screen and return control to A100.Process.Request.
   c. Establish a Do-While loop that executes while Code does not equal 7. Within the loop, use a SELECT CASE statement to transfer control to the subprogram that carries out the requested function. In this case, implement each of the 6 different area computations in separate subprograms. Within each subprogram do the following:
      (1) Request the data using one or more INPUT statements.
      (2) Compute the area. For efficiency, multiply by 0.5, rather than divide by 2, in the formulas that determine the areas of a trapezoid and triangle.
      (3) Display the results.
      (4) Prior to returning to A100.Process.Request, call a subprogram (M400. Freeze.Screen) to keep the information on the screen. Beep the speaker to alert the user to press the Enter key. Use the following prompt message to redisplay the menu:
          Press Enter key to return to menu....
   d. Display the menu as described earlier in 1a and accept a value for Code.

2. B100.Wrap.Up

   a. Clear the screen.
   b. Display a pleasant message prior to terminating the program.

Program Solution

The following program corresponds to the preceding tasks and to the top-down chart in Figure 6.21:

PROGRAM 6.2

```
1     ' Program 6.2
2     ' A Menu-Driven Program
3     ' ******************************************************
4     ' *                     Main Program                   *
5     ' ******************************************************
6     COMMON SHARED Code%, Control$
7     CALL A100.Process.Request
8     CALL B100.Wrap.Up
9     END
10
11    ' ******************************************************
12    ' *                   Process Request                  *
13    ' ******************************************************
14    SUB A100.Process.Request
15       CALL A200.Display.Menu
16       CALL A210.Accept.Code
17       DO WHILE Code% <> 7
18          SELECT CASE Code%
19             CASE 1
20                CALL A300.Area.Square
21             CASE 2
22                CALL A310.Area.Rectangle
23             CASE 3
24                CALL A320.Area.Parallelogram
25             CASE 4
26                CALL A330.Area.Circle
27             CASE 5
28                CALL A340.Area.Trapezoid
29             CASE 6
30                CALL A350.Area.Triangle
31          END SELECT
32          CALL A200.Display.Menu
33          CALL A210.Accept.Code
34       LOOP
35    END SUB
36
37    ' ******************************************************
38    ' *                   Display Menu                     *
39    ' ******************************************************
40    SUB A200.Display.Menu
41       CLS  ' Clear Screen
42       LOCATE 2, 27: PRINT "Menu For Computing Areas"
43       LOCATE 3, 27: PRINT "------------------------"
44       LOCATE 5, 19: PRINT "Code      Function"
45       LOCATE 6, 19: PRINT "----      --------"
46       LOCATE 7, 19: PRINT " 1        Compute Area of a Square"
47       LOCATE 9, 19: PRINT " 2        Compute Area of a Rectangle"
48       LOCATE 11, 19: PRINT " 3        Compute Area of a Parallelogram"
49       LOCATE 13, 19: PRINT " 4        Compute Area of a Circle"
50       LOCATE 15, 19: PRINT " 5        Compute Area of a Trapezoid"
51       LOCATE 17, 19: PRINT " 6        Compute Area of a Triangle"
52       LOCATE 19, 19: PRINT " 7        End Program"
53    END SUB
54
```

Code% and Control$ available to all subprograms

```
55    ' **********************************************************
56    ' *                    Accept a Code                      *
57    ' **********************************************************
58    SUB A210.Accept.Code
59       LOCATE 22, 19: INPUT "Enter a Code 1 through 7 =======> ", Code%
60       DO WHILE Code% < 1 OR Code% > 7
61          BEEP: BEEP: BEEP: BEEP
62          LOCATE 23, 19: PRINT "Code out of range, please reenter"
63          LOCATE 22, 52: PRINT SPC(10);
64          LOCATE 22, 52: INPUT "", Code%
65          LOCATE 23, 19: PRINT SPC(40);
66       LOOP
67       CLS
68    END SUB
69
70    ' **********************************************************
71    ' *              Compute Area of a Square                 *
72    ' **********************************************************
73    SUB A300.Area.Square
74       LOCATE 5, 24: PRINT "Compute Area of a Square"
75       LOCATE 8, 24: INPUT "Length of Side of Square ====> ", Side
76       Area = Side * Side
77       LOCATE 10, 24: PRINT "Area of Square ==============>"; Area; "Square Units"
78       CALL M400.Freeze.Screen
79    END SUB
80
81    ' **********************************************************
82    ' *             Compute Area of a Rectangle               *
83    ' **********************************************************
84    SUB A310.Area.Rectangle
85       LOCATE 5, 24: PRINT "Compute Area of a Rectangle"
86       LOCATE 8, 24: INPUT "Length of Rectangle =====> ", Length
87       LOCATE 10, 24: INPUT "Width of Rectangle ======> ", Wide
88       Area = Length * Wide
89       LOCATE 12, 24: PRINT "Area of Rectangle =======>"; Area; "Square Units"
90       CALL M400.Freeze.Screen
91    END SUB
92
93    ' **********************************************************
94    ' *           Compute Area of a Parallelogram             *
95    ' **********************************************************
96    SUB A320.Area.Parallelogram
97       LOCATE 5, 24: PRINT "Compute Area of Parallelogram"
98       LOCATE 8, 24: INPUT "Base of Parallelogram =====> ", Base1
99       LOCATE 10, 24: INPUT "Height of Parallelogram ===> ", Height
100      Area = Base1 * Height
101      LOCATE 12, 24: PRINT "Area of Parallelogram =====>"; Area; "Square Units"
102      CALL M400.Freeze.Screen
103   END SUB
104
105   ' **********************************************************
106   ' *              Compute Area of a Circle                 *
107   ' **********************************************************
108   SUB A330.Area.Circle
109      LOCATE 5, 24: PRINT "Compute Area of a Circle"
110      LOCATE 8, 24: INPUT "Radius of Circle =====> ", Radius
111      Area = 3.141598 * Radius * Radius
112      LOCATE 10, 24: PRINT "Area of Circle =======>"; Area; "Square Units"
113      CALL M400.Freeze.Screen
114   END SUB
115
```

(continued)

```
116   ' *************************************************************
117   ' *              Compute Area of a Trapezoid                 *
118   ' *************************************************************
119   SUB A340.Area.Trapezoid
120      LOCATE 5, 24: PRINT "Compute Area of a Trapezoid"
121      LOCATE 8, 24: INPUT "Primary Base of Trapezoid =====> ", Base1
122      LOCATE 10, 24: INPUT "Secondary Base of Trapezoid ===> ", Base2
123      LOCATE 12, 24: INPUT "Height of Trapezoid ===========> ", Height
124      Area = Height * (Base1 + Base2) * .5
125      LOCATE 14, 24: PRINT "Area of Trapezoid ============>"; Area; "Square Units"
126      CALL M400.Freeze.Screen
127   END SUB
128
129   ' *************************************************************
130   ' *              Compute Area of a Triangle                  *
131   ' *************************************************************
132   SUB A350.Area.Triangle
133      LOCATE 5, 24: PRINT "Compute Area of a Triangle"
134      LOCATE 8, 24: INPUT "Base of Triangle =====> ", Base1
135      LOCATE 10, 24: INPUT "Height of Triangle ===> ", Height
136      Area = Base1 * Height * .5
137      LOCATE 12, 24: PRINT "Area of Triangle =====>"; Area; "Square Units"
138      CALL M400.Freeze.Screen
139   END SUB
140
141   ' *************************************************************
142   ' *                       Wrap-Up                            *
143   ' *************************************************************
144   SUB B100.Wrap.Up
145      CLS
146      LOCATE 12, 24: PRINT "End of Program - Have a Nice Day!"
147   END SUB
148
149   ' *************************************************************
150   ' *                    Freeze Screen                         *
151   ' *************************************************************
152   SUB M400.Freeze.Screen
153      BEEP: BEEP: BEEP: BEEP
154      LOCATE 20, 24
155      INPUT "Press Enter key to return to menu....", Control$
156   END SUB

[run]
```

When Program 6.2 is first executed, line 7 calls A100.Process.Request. In this sub-program, line 15 calls A200.Display.Menu, and line 16 calls A210.Accept.Code.

In A200.Display.Menu, line 41 clears the screen, and lines 42 through 52 display the menu illustrated in Figure 6.22. The last line of Figure 6.22 is displayed by line 59 in A210.Accept.Code. Assume function 3 is selected, as shown in the lower right corner of Figure 6.22.

FIGURE 6.22

The menu displayed by A200.Display. Menu and A210.Accept. Code subprograms in Program 6.2.

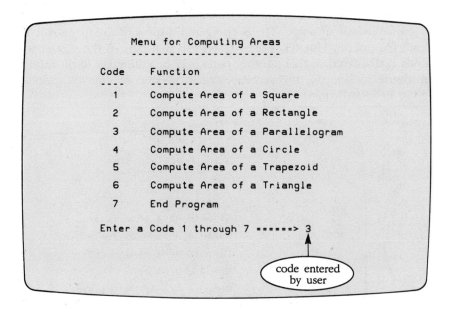

When the Enter key is pressed, lines 60 through 66 validate the code. Once a valid code is entered, line 67 again clears the screen before control is returned to the calling subprogram A100.Process.Request.

Because Code is not equal to 7, the DO WHILE statement in line 17 allows control to pass to the SELECT CASE statement in line 18. With Code equal to 3, control passes to A320.Area.Parallelogram (lines 96 through 103). Figure 6.23, for example, shows a base of 10 units and a height of 4 units to have been entered, which results in an area of 40 square units for the parallelogram. The subprogram (M400.Freeze.Screen) called by line 102 allows the user to view the results on the screen for as long as desired. Note that the speaker is beeped four times. Four beeps produces a constant beep that lasts for approximately a second. Once the Enter key is pressed in response to line 155, the PC returns control to line 32. Line 32 redisplays the menu shown in Figure 6.22.

FIGURE 6.23

The display from the selection of code 3 (Compute Area of a Parallelogram).

```
Compute Area of a Parallelogram


Base of Parallelogram =====> 10

Height of Parallelogram ===> 4

Area of Parallelogram =====> 40 Square Units



Press Enter key to return to menu...
```

Figure 6.24 shows an out-of-range code which causes the PC to beep before displaying a diagnostic message. The beeping and display of the diagnostic message are due to lines 61 and 62. Line 63 is used to refresh that part of the screen where the incorrect code is displayed so that another code may be entered. After a valid code is entered in response to line 64, the screen is again cleared by line 67, and control returns to A100.Process.Request.

FIGURE 6.24

Diagnostic message displayed by line 62 owing to the invalid code 9.

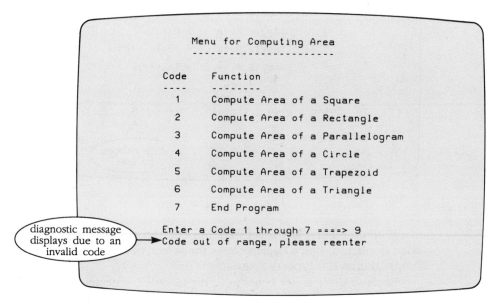

```
                    Menu for Computing Area
                    -----------------------

             Code     Function
             ----     --------
              1       Compute Area of a Square

              2       Compute Area of a Rectangle

              3       Compute Area of a Parallelogram

              4       Compute Area of a Circle

              5       Compute Area of a Trapezoid

              6       Compute Area of a Triangle

              7       End Program

             Enter a Code 1 through 7 ====> 9
             Code out of range, please reenter
```

diagnostic message displays due to an invalid code

If the user enters a code of 5 to compute the area of a trapezoid with a primary base of 18, secondary base of 9 and a height of 5, the display shown in Figure 6.25 occurs.

FIGURE 6.25

The display from the selection of code 5 (Compute Area of a Trapezoid).

```
     Compute Area of a Trapezoid

     Primary Base of Trapezoid =====> 18

     Secondary Base of Trapezoid ===> 9

     Height of Trapezoid ===========> 5

     Area of Trapezoid =============> 67.5 Square Units

     Press Enter key to return to menu...
```

To terminate execution of Program 6.2, enter a code of 7. Line 8 in the Main Program calls B100.Wrap.Up, which displays an appropriate message before line 9 terminates execution of the program.

The preceding problem could have been solved by replacing the SELECT CASE statement with an IF statement containing ELSEIF clauses. Usually, however, when a series of three or more tests is to be performed in succession, the SELECT CASE statement is the better alternative for purposes of readability.

6.9   WHAT YOU SHOULD KNOW

1. Structured programming is a methodology according to which all program logic can be constructed from a combination of the following three basic control structures: Sequence, Selection (If-Then-Else or Case), and Repetition (Do-While or Do-Until).

2. The If-Then-Else structure is used in program design to specify a selection between two alternative paths.

3. The Case structure is an extension of the If-Then-Else structure, in which the choice includes more than two alternatives.

4. Most computer professionals agree the decision statement to terminate a loop should be located at the top or bottom of the loop.

5. A loop that has the termination decision statement at the top is called a Do-While structure. A loop that has the termination decision statement at the bottom is called a Do-Until structure.

6. Top-down programming and structured programming are not the same. Top-down programming describes a strategy for solving large, complex problems. To solve a problem top-down, you divide and conquer. Structured programming is used within modules to generate disciplined code. We improve the clarity and reduce the complexity by using only the five control structures — Sequence, If-Then-Else, Case, Do-While, and Do-Until.

7. The IF statement is used to implement the If-Then-Else structure.

8. The IF statement has two general forms — single line and block. A single-line IF statement must fit on one line, and the END IF statement is not required. The block IF statement can include multiple lines in each clause and must end with an END IF statement.

9. In an IF statement, if the condition is true, the PC executes the THEN clause, and control passes to the statement following the corresponding END IF. If the condition is false, the PC executes the ELSE clause, and control passes to the statement following the corresponding END IF. If the condition is false and no ELSE clause is included in the IF statement, then the PC passes control to the statement following the corresponding END IF.

10. If the condition in an IF statement contains two numeric expressions, then the comparison is based on the algebraic values of the two expressions.

11. If the condition in an IF statement contains two string expressions, the PC evaluates the two strings from left to right, one character at a time. As soon as one character in one expression is different from the corresponding character in the other expression, the PC decides which expression has a lower value.

12. QuickBASIC uses the ASCII code. It is the collating sequence of the ASCII code that determines the position of a character in relation to other characters.

13. A null THEN or null ELSE clause in an IF statement is valid.

14. A counter is an accumulator used to count the number of times some action or event is performed.

15. A running total is an accumulator used to sum the different values a variable is assigned during the execution of a program.

16. All accumulators should be initialized to some value before they are used in a statement that tests the accumulator or adds to its value.

17. Depending on the problem to be solved, an If-Then-Else structure can have alternative processing for both the true case and the false case, alternative processing only for the true case, or alternative processing only for the false case.

18. Negating the relation in the condition of an If-Then-Else structure can sometimes simplify and clarify the IF statement.

19. A nested If-Then-Else structure is one in which the action to be taken for the true or false case includes yet another If-Then-Else structure.

20. In a nested block IF statement, each IF must have a corresponding END IF statement.

21. The truth value of the relational expression in a condition is complemented by the logical operator NOT.

22. The logical operator NOT requires the relational expression be false for the condition to be true. If the relational expression is true, then the condition is false.

23. When two or more conditions are combined by the logical operators AND, OR, XOR, EQV, or IMP, the expression is a compound condition.

24. The logical operator AND requires both conditions be true for the compound condition to be true.

25. The logical operator OR requires only one of the two conditions be true for the compound condition to be true. If both conditions are true, the compound condition is also true.

26. The XOR (exclusive OR) operator requires one of the two conditions be true for the compound condition to be true. If both are true, the condition is false.

27. The EQV (equivalence) operator requires both conditions be true or both conditions be false for the compound condition to be true.

28. The IMP (implication) operator requires both conditions be true or both conditions be false, or the first condition be false and the second true for the compound condition to be true.

29. Unless parentheses dictate otherwise, reading from left to right, conditions containing arithmetic operators are evaluated first, then those containing relational operators, then those containing NOT operators, then those containing AND operators, then those conditions containing OR and XOR operators, then those containing EQV operators, and finally those containing IMP operators.

30. The BEEP statement causes the PC's speaker to beep for one-fourth of one second.

31. Data validation is a technique used to ensure valid data is assigned to a program. Data can be validated, or checked, for reasonableness, range, code, and digit.

32. A reasonableness check is a technique used to ensure data items entered from an external device, such as the keyboard, are of reasonable and valid magnitudes.

33. A range check is a technique used to ensure data items entered from an external device fall within a range of valid values.

34. A code check is a technique used to ensure codes entered from an external source are valid.

35. A digit check is a technique used to verify the assignment of a special digit to a number. A check digit is an addition (that is, suffix) to a number that requires validation; this addition can be used to verify the rest of the digits.

36. Use the SELECT CASE statement to implement a case structure.

37. The SELECT CASE statement includes a test expression. When the test expression is evaluated, the PC attempts to match it to the match expressions in the corresponding CASE clauses. If a match is found, the range of statements for that CASE clause is executed. If a match is not found, the statements contained in the CASE ELSE are executed. Following the execution of one of the cases, control transfers to the statement following the corresponding END SELECT.

38. Match expressions can include a list of values separated by commas, a range of values using the keyword TO, or a relational operator preceded by the keyword IS and followed by a value.

39. A menu is a list of the functions that a program can perform. When a menu-driven program is first executed, it displays a menu of functions. Each time a requested function is satisfied, the program redisplays the menu.

6.10 TEST YOUR BASIC SKILLS (Even-numbered answers are in Appendix E)

1. Consider the valid programs below. What is displayed if each is executed?

a.
```
' Exercise 6.1a
' ******* Main Program *******
COMMON SHARED Count1, Count2, Age, Weight
CALL A100.Initialization
CALL B100.Process.File
CALL C100.Wrap.Up
' ******* Data Follows *******
DATA 10, 125, 24, 110, 21, 150, 30, 120
DATA 51, 225, 47, 95, 18, 130, -1, 0
END

' ****** Initialization ******
SUB A100.Initialization
   CLS   ' Clear Screen
   Count1 = 0
   Count2 = 0
END SUB

' ******* Process File *******
SUB B100.Process.File
   READ Age, Weight
   DO WHILE Age > 0
      CALL B200.Accumulate
      READ Age, Weight
   LOOP
END SUB

' ******* Accumulate *********
SUB B200.Accumulate
   Count1 = Count1 + 1
   IF Age >= 21 AND Weight >= 120 THEN
      Count2 = Count2 + 1
   END IF
END SUB

' ********* Wrap-Up **********
SUB C100.Wrap.Up
   PRINT "Number of people evaluated:"; Count1
   PRINT "Number of adults weighing "
   PRINT "120 pounds or more:"; Count2
END SUB
```

b.
```
' Exercise 6.1b
' *************
A = 1
PRINT A
DO WHILE A > 0
   IF A - 2  0 THEN
      A = 2
   ELSE
      CALL Sub1(A)
   END IF
   PRINT A
LOOP
END

' *** Subprogram 1 ***
SUB Sub1 (A)
   IF A - 2 = 0 THEN
      A = 3
   ELSE
      CALL Sub2(A)
   END IF
END SUB

' *** Subprogram 2 ***
SUB Sub2 (A)
   IF A - 4 < 0 THEN
      A = 4
   ELSE
      CALL Sub3(A)
   END IF
END SUB

' *** Subprogram 3 ***
SUB Sub3 (A)
   IF A - 4 = 0 THEN
      A = 5
   ELSE
      A = 1
   END IF
END SUB
```

c. Assume I is assigned the values 1, 4, 7, 2, 21, 20, -99.
```
' Exercise 6.1c
INPUT I
DO WHILE I <> -99
   SELECT CASE I
      CASE 1, 4, 7
         PRINT "Case 1"
      CASE IS < 8
         PRINT "Case 2"
      CASE 14 TO 21
         PRINT "Case 3"
      CASE ELSE
         PRINT "Case 4"
   END SELECT
   INPUT I
LOOP
```

d.
```
' Exercise 6.1d
READ X, Y
DO WHILE X > 0
   IF X = Y AND Y >= 10 THEN
      PRINT "Both Conditions are True"
   END IF
   IF X = Y XOR Y >= 10 THEN
      PRINT "Only One of the Two Conditions is True"
   END IF
   IF NOT X = Y AND NOT Y >= 10 THEN
      PRINT "Neither Condition is True"
   END IF
   READ X, Y
LOOP
PRINT "End of Job"
' ********* Data Follows **********
DATA 3, 5, 8, 10, 15, 15, 4, 4, -1, 0
END
```

2. Write a QuickBASIC statement that will initialize X to 0 and another that will initialize T to 10. Also, write additional QuickBASIC statements that will consecutively increment these variables by the following:

   a. 1   b. 7   c. 2   d. double each value   e. minus 1

3. Given the following:

   Employee number E = 500
   Salary S = $700
   Job code J = 1
   Tax T = $60
   Insurance deduction I = $40

   Determine the truth value of the following compound conditions:

   a. E < 400 OR J = 1   b. S = 700 AND T = 50

   c. S - T = 640 AND J = 1   d. T + I = S - 500 OR J = 0

   e. NOT J < 0   f. NOT S > 500 AND NOT T > 80

   g. NOT (J = 1 OR T = 60)   h. J = 1 XOR E >= 500

   i. I <> 40 EQV S > 500   j. S = 700 IMP T = 60

   k. S < 300 AND I < 50 OR J = 1   l. S < 300 AND (I < 50 OR J = 1)

   m. NOT (NOT J = 1)

4. Determine the value of Q that will cause the condition in the IF statements below to be true:

   a. IF Q > 8 OR Q = 3 THEN   b. IF Q + 10 >= 7 AND NOT Q < 0 THEN
          Z = Z / 10   PRINT "The answer is"; A
      END IF   END IF

   c. IF Q / 3 < 9 THEN   d. IF Q <> 3 XOR Q = 3 THEN
          Count = Count + 1   Sum = Sum + Amt
      END IF   END IF

5. Write a series of statements to perform the logic indicated below:

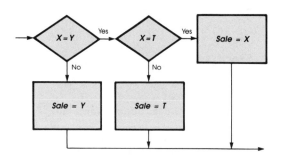

6. Construct IF statements for each of the structures found below:

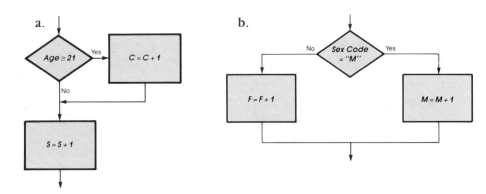

7. Construct IF statements for each of the logic structures found below:

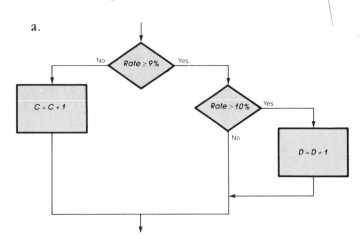

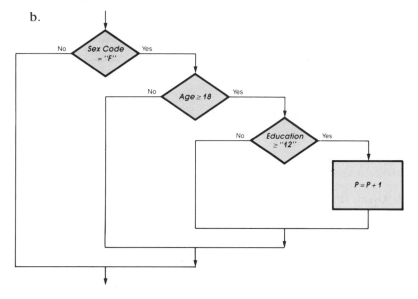

c.

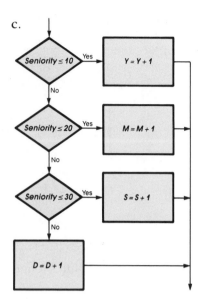

d.

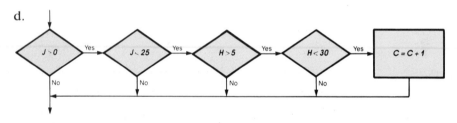

e.

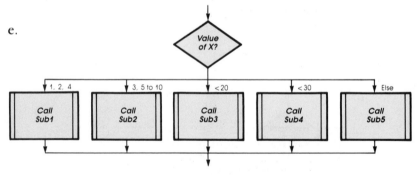

8. Construct a partial flowchart for each of the following:

   a. `NOT(S = Q) AND (X > 1 OR C < 3)`

   b. `(K = 9 AND Q = 2) OR NOT Z = 3 OR T = 0`

9. Given the following: S = 0, Y = 4, B = 7, T = 8, and X = 3

   Determine the action taken for each of the following:

   a.
   ```
   IF S > 0 THEN
       CALL B200.Compute
   END IF
   ```

   b.
   ```
   IF B = 4 OR T > 7 THEN
       IF X > 1 THEN
           CALL B200.Compute
       END IF
   END IF
   ```

   c.
   ```
   IF X = 3 OR T > 2 THEN
       IF Y > 7 THEN
           CALL B200.Compute
       END IF
   END IF
   ```

   d.
   ```
   IF X + 2 < 5 THEN
       IF B < Y + X THEN
           CALL B200.Compute
       END IF
   END IF
   ```

```
e. IF B <> 7 AND NOT(T = 6) THEN      f. IF T > X OR B <> S THEN
      CALL B200.Compute                     CALL B200.Compute
   END IF                                END IF
```

10. Write a subprogram (A200.Accept.Value) for each of the following situations that request the user to enter a value. After the value is entered, validate the value using a Do-While loop. If the value is invalid, display an appropriate diagnostic message and request the entry be reentered. In the SUB statement, include the specified variable as a parameter. For example, for the first problem begin with the SUB statement SUB A200.Accept.Value(Percent).

   a. Request a percent (Percent). If the percent is negative or greater than 25, request the user to reenter the value.
   b. Request a balance (Balance). Check if the balance is between \$550.99 and \$765.50 inclusive. If the balance is outside the range, request the user to reenter the value.
   c. Request a customer code (Code\$). Check to ensure the code is an A, D, E or F. If the code is invalid, request the user to reenter the code.
   d. Request a customer number (Customer\$) and check to ensure the third leftmost digit is a 4. If the third digit is not a 4, request the user to reenter the number.

11. Assume P and Q are simple conditions. The following logical equivalences are known as DeMorgan's Laws:

    NOT (P OR Q) is equivalent to NOT P AND NOT Q
    NOT (P AND Q) is equivalent to NOT P OR NOT Q

    Use DeMorgan's Laws to find a logical equivalent for each of the following:

    a. NOT(P OR (NOT Q))
    b. NOT((NOT P) OR Q)
    c. NOT(NOT P AND Q)
    d. NOT((NOT P) AND (NOT Q))

12. Write a subprogram that determines and prints the number of negative values (Negative), number of zero values (Zero) and number of positive values (Positive) in the following data set: 4, 2, 3, –9, 0, 0, –4, –6, –8, 3, 2, 0, 0, 8, –3, 4. Use the sentinel value –1E37 to test for the end-of-file. Include Negative, Zero, and Positive as parameters in the SUB statement.

13. Given four variables W, X, Y, and Z with previously defined values, write a sequence of IF statements to increment the variable Count by 1 if all four variables have the exact value of 100.

14. The sequence of Fibonacci numbers begins with 1, 1 and continues endlessly, each number being the sum of the preceding two:

    1, 1, 2, 3, 5, 8, 13, 21, 34, ...

    Construct a partial program to compute and print the first X% numbers of the sequence where the value of X% is entered in response to an INPUT statement. Accept only values for X% greater than 0 and less than or equal to 185.

15. Given two positive valued variables A and B, write a sequence of statements to assign the variable with the larger value to Greater and the variable with the smaller value to Smaller. If A and B are equal, assign either to Equal.

16. The values of three variables U, V, and W are positive and not equal to each other. Using IF statements, determine which has the smallest value and assign this value to Small.

17. The symbol N! represents the product of the first N positive integers:

    N! = N * (N − 1) * (N − 2) * ... * 1

    When a result is defined in terms of itself, we call it a recursive definition. Construct a subprogram that receives a positive integer (Number) and returns its factorial (Factor). Use the argument-parameter-list technique to pass values. The recursive definition is as follows:

    If N = 1, then N! = 1; otherwise N! = N(N − 1)!.

18. Consider the following program:

```
' Exercise 6.18
' ******* Main Program *******
COMMON SHARED Count, Sum, X, Y, Z
CALL A100.Initialization
CALL B100.Process.File
CALL C100.Wrap.Up
' ******* Data Follows *******
DATA 4, 1, 15, 12, 7, 1, 8, 4, 7
DATA 6, 8, 3, 1, 7, 2, -1, 0, 0
END

' ****** Initialization ******
SUB A100.Initialization
   CLS ' Clear Screen
   Count = 0
   Sum = 0
END SUB

' ******* Process File *******
SUB B100.Process.File
   READ X, Y, Z
   DO WHILE X > 0
      CALL B200.Evaluate
      READ X, Y, Z
   LOOP
END SUB

' ********* Evaluate *********
SUB B200.Evaluate
   IF X   Y + 2 THEN
      Count = Count - 1
   ELSE
      IF X >= Z + 1 THEN
         Sum = Sum + X * Z
         Count = Count + 1
         PRINT Sum
      ELSE
         Count = Count - 2
      END IF
   END IF
END SUB

' ********* Wrap-Up **********
SUB C100.Wrap.Up
   PRINT Count, Sum
   PRINT "End of Report"
END SUB
```

a. Which variable is used to test for end-of-file?
b. What are the values of Count and Sum just before the LOOP statement is executed for the third time?

c. How many lines are displayed by this program?

d. What is the maximum value of Sum displayed?

e. What is the maximum value of Count displayed?

19. The WESAVU National Bank computes its monthly service charge on checking accounts by adding $0.25 to a value computed from the following:

$0.09 per check for the first ten checks

$0.08 per check for the next ten checks

$0.07 per check for the next ten checks

$0.06 per check for all the rest of the checks

Write a subprogram (B200.Compute.Charge) that includes a SELECT CASE statement and a PRINT statement to display the account number (Account), the number of checks cashed (Checks), and the computed monthly charge (Charge). Assume the account number and the number of checks cashed are passed to the subprogram via the argument-parameter-list technique.

20. Write a partial program to set A = −1 if C and D are both zero, set A = −2 if neither C nor D is zero and set A = −3 if either, but not both, C or D is zero.

21. In each of the following compound conditions, indicate the order of evaluation by the PC. (See the examples on page 187. Beginning with 1, use numbers and truth values to show the order of evaluation.)

a. S > 0 OR A > 0 OR T > 0

b. S > 0 AND A > 0 AND NOT T > 0

c. S > 0 IMP A > 0 EQV T > 0 AND P > 0

d. NOT S > 0 AND T > 0 XOR P > 0

22. **PC Hands-On Exercise:** Load Program 6.1 (PRG6-1) from the Student Diskette. Display the program and execute it. After the results are displayed, modify the program by changing lines 32 and 65 to comments so that PRG6-1 displays only the summary totals.

Reload PRG6-1. Modify it by changing lines 13 through 17 to comments. Execute the modified version of Program 6.1. Now do you understand why it is important to have at least one line of data, in addition to the trailer record, for this program?

23. **PC Hands-On Exercise:** Load Program 6.2 (PRG6-2) from the Student Diskette. List the program, and then execute it. When requested, enter the following data:

Data Set 1:   Code = 4, Radius = 5

Data Set 2:   Code = 0 (A diagnostic message should display.)

Data Set 3:   Code = 6, Base = 4, Height = 6

Data Set 4:   Code = 7 (End program.)

6.11   BASIC PROGRAMMING PROBLEMS

1. Employee Average Yearly Salary

Purpose: To illustrate the concepts of counter and running total initialization, counter and running total incrementation, looping, and testing for the last value in a set of data.

Problem: Construct a top-down program to read records, count records, accumulate salaries and print a sequence of data consisting of employee numbers and salaries for various employees in a payroll file. Use the COMMON SHARED statement to declare variables globally. After the sentinel value (EOF) is processed, print the total number of employees and the average yearly salary of all the employees processed. Before processing the file, display a message that requests the user to turn on the printer.

(**Hint:** Use the top-down chart illustrated in Figure 6.7 and Program 6.1 — PRG6-1 on the Student Diskette — as a guide to solving this problem.)

Input Data: Prepare and use the following sample data in DATA statements:

Employee Number	Employee Salary	Employee Number	Employee Salary
123	$16,000	196	17,400
148	8,126	201	18,950
184	14,800	EOF	0

Output Results: The following results are printed:

```
Employee Salary Report

Employee      Employee
Number        Salary
--------      --------
  123         16,000.00
  148          8,126.00
  184         14,800.00
  196         17,400.00
  201         18,950.00

Number of Employees ===>   5
Average Salary ========> $15,055.20

End of Employee Salary Report
```

2. Selecting the Best and Worst Salesperson

Purpose: To become familiar with decision-making logic, exchanging the values of string variables, and using the RESTORE statement.

Problem: Construct a top-down program that will determine and display the best and worst salesperson on the basis of total sales from a salesperson file. If necessary, use the argument-parameter-list technique to pass values between subprograms.

(**Hint:** After determining and printing the best salesperson, use the RESTORE statement and reread the data to determine and display the worst salesperson.)

Input Data: Prepare and use the following sample data in DATA statements:

Salesperson Name	Total Sales
Franklin, Ed	$96,185
Smith, Susan	18,421
Stankie, Jim	97,856
Runaw, Jeff	32,146
Ray, Kathy	13,467
Doolittle, Frank	11,316
Zachery, Louis	48,615

Output Results: The following results are displayed:

```
Best Salesperson ======> Stankie, Jim
Total Sales ===========> $97,856.00

Worst Salesperson =====> Doolittle, Frank
Total Sales ===========> $11,316.00
```

3. Voter Analysis

Purpose: To become familiar with nested If-Then-Else structures.

Problem: Construct a top-down program that will clear the screen, analyze a citizen file and generate the following totals:

1. Number of males not eligible to register
2. Number of females not eligible to register
3. Number of males who are old enough to vote but have not registered
4. Number of females who are old enough to vote but have not registered
5. Number of individuals who are eligible to vote but did not vote
6. Number of individuals who did vote
7. Number of records processed

Declare required variables globally using the COMMON SHARED statement.

(Hint: Use the variable names described on page 181 and the If-Then-Else structure shown in Figure 6.16.)

Input Data: Prepare and use the following sample data in DATA statements:

Number	Age in Years	Sex Code	Registered	Voted
1614	18	F	N	N
1321	21	M	N	N
1961	33	M	Y	Y
1432	46	F	Y	Y
1721	25	M	Y	Y
1211	16	M	N	N
1100	38	F	Y	Y
4164	34	M	Y	N
2139	19	M	Y	N
8647	25	F	Y	Y
9216	13	M	N	N
7814	15	F	N	N

Output Results: The following results are displayed:

```
Voter Analysis

Males Not Eligible to Register =================> 2
Females Not Eligible to Register ==============> 1

Males Old Enough to Vote but Not Registered =====> 1
Females Old Enough to Vote but Not Registered ===> 1

Individuals Eligible to Vote but Did Not Vote ===> 2
Individuals that Voted ==========================> 5

Total Number of Records Processed ===============> 12

End of Report
```

4. Stockbroker's Commission

Purpose: To become familiar with the If-Then-Else structure and methods used to determine a stockbroker's commission.

Problem: Write a top-down program that will read a stock transaction and determine the stockbroker's commission. Each transaction includes the following data: the stock name, price per share, number of shares involved, and the stockbroker's name. Declare required variables globally using the COMMON SHARED statement.

The stockbroker's commission is computed in the following manner: if price per share P is less than or equal to $40.00, the commission rate is $0.15 per share; if P is greater than $40.00, the commission rate is $0.25 per share. If the number of shares sold is less than 125, the commission is 1.5 times the rate per share.

Each detail line of output to the printer is to include the stock transaction data set and the commission paid the stockbroker. Test the stock name for the EOF. Print the total commission earned.

(**Hint:** Use the top-down chart illustrated in Figure 6.7 and Program 6.1 — PRG6-1 on the Student Diskette — as a guide to solving this problem.)

Input Data: Prepare and use the following sample data in DATA statements:

Stock Name	Price per Share	Number of Shares	Stockbroker Name
Crane	$32.50	200	Baker, G.
FstPa	17.50	100	Smith, J.
GenDyn	56.25	300	Smith, A.
Harris	40.00	125	Lucas, M.
BellCd	48.00	160	Soley, K.
BellHow	22.00	300	Jones, D.

Output Results: The following results are printed:

```
              Stockbroker's Commission

  Stock          Price      Number      Stockbroker
  Name         Per Share   Of Shares    Name            Commission
  -----        ---------   ---------    -----------     ----------
  Crane          32.50        200       Baker, G.           30.00
  FstPa          17.50        100       Smith, J.           22.50
  GenDyn         56.25        300       Smith, A.           75.00
  Harris         40.00        125       Lucas, M.           18.75
  BellCd         48.00        160       Soley, K.           40.00
  BellHow        22.00        300       Jones, D.           45.00

  Total Commission Earned                                 $231.25

  End of Report
```

5. Aging Accounts

Purpose: To become familiar with data validation and with the concepts of aging accounts receivable using Julian Calendar dates (that is, using a number between 1 and 365 to signify a date).

Problem: Write a top-down program to compute the total amount due and percentage of the total amount of receivables that are as follows:

1. Less than 30 days past due (accounts due < 30 days)
2. Past due between 30 and 60 days (30 < = accounts due < = 60)
3. Past due over 60 days (accounts due > 60)

Include in the output the number of accounts in each category. The first input value will be today's Julian date from the keyboard. Verify the Julian date is a value between 1 and 365 inclusive. Assume no leap years.

The account number, amount due and the date due for each customer should be stored in one or more DATA statements. Use the COMMON SHARED statement to declare required variables globally.

(**Hint:** See Program 6.1 on page 174 or PRG6-1 on the Student Diskette.)

Input Data: Prepare and use the sample data at the top of the next page. Assume today's Julian date is 155 (that is, 155th day of the year).

Account Number	Amount Due	Date Due
1168	1495.67	145
2196	3211.16	15
3485	1468.12	130
3612	1896.45	98
7184	5.48	126
8621	965.10	75
9142	613.50	105

Output Results: The following prompts and messages are displayed:

```
Please enter the Julian Date =====> 155

Set the paper in the printer to the top of page.

Press the Enter key when the printer is ready...
```

The following results are printed:

```
                    Aging Accounts For Day 155

Accounts            Number of        Total            Percent of
Past Due            Accounts         Amount Due       Total Amount
--------            ---------        ----------       ------------
Less Than 30 Days       3            2,969.27             30.75
30 To 60 Days           2            2,509.95             26.00
Over 60 Days            2            4,176.26             43.25

Job Complete
```

6. Money Changer

Purpose: To illustrate the concepts of multiple loops and data validation.

Problem: Construct a top-down program that will make change from a one dollar bill on a sale of less than or equal to one dollar. Have the program request the amount of the sale. If the sale amount is less than 1 cent or greater than 100 cents, display a diagnostic message and request the amount of the sale be re-entered. The program is to display the number of half dollars, quarters, dimes, nickels, and pennies that are to be returned to the customer. Have the program return as many half dollars as possible, then as many quarters as possible, and so on. A sale amount of –99 indicates end-of-job. Use the argument-parameter-list technique to pass the variables between subprograms.

Input Data: Enter the following sample data via INPUT statements:

$0.13, –$0.29, $0.0, $0.72, $1.04, $0.25, $1.00, $0.01, $0.99, $0.47

Output Results: The following results are displayed for a sale amount of $0.13.

```
Money Changer

Enter Amount of Sale as a Whole Number
Between 1 Cent and 100 Cents Inclusive ====> 13

Return to the Customer -   1 Half Dollar
                           1 Quarter
                           1 Dime(s)
                           0 Nickel
                           2 Pennies

Press Enter to Initiate a New Sale...
```

7. The Check Digit Problem

Purpose: To illustrate the concepts of generating check digits.

Problem: Construct a top-down program to verify a six-digit part number by validating the units position for a check digit. The computation of the check digit involves multiplying every other digit of the original number by 2 and adding these values and the remaining digits of the number together. The units digit of the result obtained is then subtracted from 10 to obtain the check digit.

To illustrate the process used, let us form the part number by computing the check digit for the number 72546. The alternate digits are first multiplied by 2:

```
    7     5     6
          ×     2
   ────────────────
   14    10    12
```

Then the remaining digits (2 and 4) are included, and all the above digits are added:

$$1 + 4 + 1 + 0 + 1 + 2 + 2 + 4 = 15$$

The 5 is subtracted from 10 to give a check digit of 5, so the part number becomes 725465.

This algorithm is sophisticated in that it can detect invalid part numbers that have digits reversed, such as 752465 instead of 725465.

Use the argument-parameter-list technique to pass the variables between subprograms.

(Hint: The six digits in the part number must be separated. You may separate digits through the use of the INT function. For example, the leftmost digit [D6] can be determined from the following, where PART is the six-digit value:

```
D6 = INT(PART / 100000)
```

and the second leftmost digit [D5] is equal to:

```
D5 = INT((PART - D6 * 100000) / 10000)
```

Continue in this fashion, until all six digits are extracted.)

Input Data: Prepare and use the following part numbers. Check to see if the rightmost digit is the correct check digit.

725465, 752465, 033332, 098792, 098798, 089798, 000000, 000001, 999999, 999995

Output Results: The following results are displayed for 725465:

```
Validation of Check Digit

Enter Part Number =====> 725465

Part Number is Valid

To continue validation enter Y, else N... N
```

8. A Menu-Driven Program with Multifunctions

Purpose: To become familiar with the SELECT CASE statement, a multifunction program, data validation, and the use of a menu.

Problem: Use top-down programming techniques to write a menu-driven program to compute the volume of a box, cylinder, cone, and sphere. Use the COMMON SHARED statement to declare required variables globally.

The program should display the menu that is shown under Output Results. Once a code is entered, it must be validated. After the selection of the proper function, the program should prompt the user for the necessary data, compute the volume, and display it accordingly. The displayed results are to remain on the screen until the Enter key on the keyboard is pressed. After that, the program should redisplay the menu.

Use the following formulas for the volumes V:

1. Volume of a box: $V = L * W * H$ where L is the length, W is the width and H is the height of the box.
2. Volume of a cylinder: $V = \pi * R * R * H$, where π equals 3.14159, R is the radius and H is the height of the cylinder.
3. Volume of a cone: $V = (\pi * R * R * H)/3$, where π equals 3.14159, R is the radius of the base and H is the height of the cone.
4. Volume of a sphere: $V = 4 * \pi * R * R * R/3$, where π equals 3.14159 and R is the radius of the sphere.

(Hint: See program 6.2 on page 198 or PRG6-2 on the Student Diskette.)

Input Data: Use the following sample data:

```
Code — 3, Radius = 7, Height = 9
Code — 4, Radius = 10
Code — 1, Length = 4.5, Width = 6.7, Height = 12
Code — 2, Radius = 8, Height = 15
Code — 7  (This code should return a diagnostic message.)
Code — 5  (End Program.)
```

Output Results: The following menu is displayed:

```
Menu For Computing Volumes
- - - - - - - - - - - - - - - - - - - - - - - - - -

Code      Function
- - - -   - - - - - - - -
   1      Compute Volume of a Box
   2      Compute Volume of a Cylinder
   3      Compute Volume of a Cone
   4      Compute Volume of a Sphere
   5      End Program

Enter a Code 1 through 5 =======>
```

9. Payroll Problem VI — Biweekly Payroll Computations with Time and a Half for Overtime

Purpose: To become familiar with decision making and some payroll concepts.

Problem: Modify in a top-down fashion Payroll Problem V (Problem 6) in Chapter 5, to include the following conditions:

1. Overtime (hours worked > 80) is paid at 1.5 times the hourly rate.
2. Federal withholding tax is determined in the same manner as indicated in Payroll Problem III in Chapter 3. However, assign a value of $0.00 if the gross pay less the product of the number of dependents and $38.46 is not positive.
3. After processing the employee records, print the total gross pay, federal withholding tax and net pay.
4. Print the payroll report on the printer.

Use the COMMON SHARED statement to declare required variables globally.

(**Hint:** Use the top-down chart illustrated in Figure 6.7 and Program 6.1 — PRG6-1 on the Student Diskette — as a guide to solving this problem.)

Input Data: Use the sample data found in Payroll Problem III (Problem 6) in Chapter 3. Modify the DATA statement representing employee 126 so that the number of dependents equals 9.

Output Results: The following results are printed:

```
                    Biweekly Payroll Report

    Employee
    Number        Gross Pay        Fed. Tax        Net Pay
    --------      ----------       --------        -------
      123         1,000.00          184.62         815.38
      124           880.00          168.31         711.69
      125         1,040.00          200.31         839.69
      126            90.00            0.00          90.00

    Total Gross Pay ========>     3,010.00
    Total Withholding Tax ==>       553.23
    Total Net Pay ===========>    2,456.77

    End of Payroll Report
```

Sequential Files, Paging Reports, and Control-Break Processing

7.1 INTRODUCTION

In the first six chapters of this book, we stressed the importance of integrating data into the program. You learned that data may be entered into a program through the use of the LET statement, the INPUT statement, or the READ and DATA statements. This chapter presents a fourth method for entering data — the use of data files. With data files, the data is stored in auxiliary storage rather than in the program itself. This technique is used primarily for dealing with large amounts of data.

Processing large amounts of data often involves generating reports that are many pages in length. When the length of a report exceeds one page, the report and column headings, as well as a page number, should be printed at the top of each page. This chapter introduces you to writing programs that generate reports of more than one page.

The third topic presented in this chapter is **control breaks**. A control break is a technique used to generate subtotals within a report. Most businesses today are divided into units for the purpose of better management. To evaluate the performance of the units within each level, managerial reports are generated that show summaries, or minor totals for each subunit. This chapter illustrates programming techniques for generating these types of reports.

At the conclusion of this chapter, you should be able to design programs that write reports to auxiliary storage, build data files, process data files, and generate reports with paging and control breaks.

7.2 DATA FILES

In previous chapters, top-down program development was emphasized. Of equal concern are the organization and processing of data in the form of files. This is especially true in a business environment for the following three reasons:

1. Business applications, such as payroll, billing, order entry, and inventory, involve the processing of extensive amounts of data.
2. Data must be continually updated if management reports are to be useful.
3. The same data is often required for several applications such as payroll, personnel, pension plans, and insurance reporting.

Computer manufacturers have applied a great deal of effort in developing both hardware, such as auxiliary storage devices, and software, such as **file-handling statements**, to deal directly with the organization and processing of large amounts of data.

In programs in previous chapters, the LET statement, the INPUT statement, or the READ and DATA statements were used to enter data into the PC. A more efficient and convenient method of organizing data is to store it on an auxiliary storage device, such as a diskette or hard disk, and keep it separate from the programs that will process the data. Data stored in this fashion is a **file**, a group of related records. The number of records making up a file may range from just a few, to thousands or millions. Each record within the file contains related data items.

Figure 7.1 illustrates a partial list of data items that can be found within the records of a payroll file. Common data items occupy the same position in each record. This sequence within a record is important both for processing and updating a file.

FIGURE 7.1

A conceptual view of a file stored on a diskette, with each data item separated by a comma and each record separated by a carriage return character<cr>.

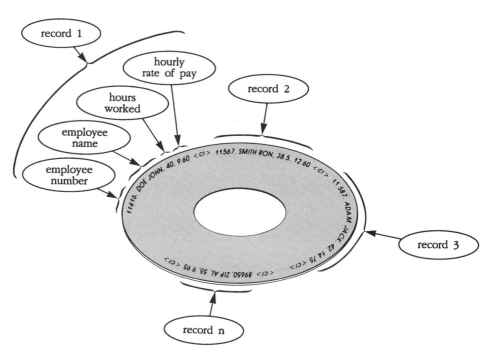

Creating a data file that is separate from the program yet accessible to it means the following:

1. Data can be used by different programs without having to be reentered each time.
2. Records can be easily updated.
3. Many data files can be processed by a single program.
4. Programs can process a particular file for one run and another file for the next, provided the data items in the records of the files have some common order.

QuickBASIC includes a set of file-handling statements that allow a user to do the following:

1. Create data files.
2. Define the data files to be used by a program.
3. Open a file.
4. Read data from a file.
5. Write data to a file.
6. Test for the end-of-file.
7. Close a file.

File Organization

File organization is a method of arranging records on an auxiliary storage device. QuickBASIC provides for two types of file organization—sequential and random.

A file organized sequentially is called a **sequential file** and is limited to sequential processing. This means the records can be processed only in the order in which they are placed in the file. Conceptually, a sequential file is identical to the use of DATA statements within a QuickBASIC program. For example, the fourteenth record in a sequential file cannot be processed until after the previous thirteen records have been processed. Similarly, the fourteenth data item in a DATA statement of a QuickBASIC program cannot be processed until the previous thirteen data items have been processed.

Sequential organization can also be used to write reports to auxiliary storage instead of to the screen or printer. Once the report is in auxiliary storage, it can be displayed at any time and as often as needed. Writing reports to auxiliary storage is a common practice, especially with programs that generate multiple reports. In such programs, each report is written to a separate file.

The second type of file organization, random files, will be discussed in Chapter 10.

7.3 SEQUENTIAL FILE PROCESSING

This section presents the file-handling statements required to create and process sequential files. And we also present sample programs to illustrate the following:

1. How reports can be written to auxiliary storage instead of to the screen or to the printer.
2. How to build sequential files that other programs can process.
3. How reports can be generated from data that is located in sequential files.

Later, in Chapter 10, we will show you how to update sequential files.

Opening Sequential Files

Before any file can be read from or written to, it must be opened by the OPEN statement. When executed, the OPEN statement carries out the following five basic functions:

1. Requests the PC to allocate a **buffer**. A buffer is a part of main storage through which data is passed between the program and auxiliary storage.
2. Identifies by name the file to be processed.
3. Indicates whether the file is to be read from or written to.
4. Assigns the file a filenumber.
5. Sets the "pointer" to the beginning of the file or to the end of the file.

The general form of the OPEN statement is shown in Table 7.1 on the next page.

As described in Table 7.1, a sequential file may be opened for input, output, or append. Example 1 in Table 7.1 opens the file EMPLOYEE.DAT for input as filenumber 1. The file is located on the B drive. Since EMPLOYEE.DAT is opened for **input**, the program can only read records from it. An attempt to write a record to EMPLOYEE.DAT will result in the display of a dialog box with the following diagnostic message:

```
Bad file mode
```

If an attempt is made to open a nonexistent file for input, the following diagnostic message displays in a dialog box:

```
File not found
```

TABLE 7.1   The OPEN Statement for Sequential Files

General Form: OPEN filespec FOR mode AS #filenumber

where **filespec** is the name of the file;

mode is one of the following:

APPEND specifies sequential output mode, where the pointer is positioned to the end of the file;

INPUT specifies sequential input mode, where the pointer is positioned at the beginning of the file,

OUTPUT specifies sequential output mode, where the pointer is positioned at the beginning of the file; and

filenumber is a numeric expression whose value is between 1 and 255. The filenumber is associated with the file (filespec) for as long as it is open. The filenumber is used by other file-handling statements to refer to the specific file.

Purpose: Allows a program to read records from or write records to a sequential data file.

Examples:
1. OPEN "B:EMPLOYEE.DAT" FOR INPUT AS #1
2. OPEN "payroll.lis" FOR OUPUT AS #2
3. OPEN "ACCOUNTS.DAT" FOR APPEND AS #3
4. OPEN Filename$ FOR INPUT AS #3

Note:
1. The OPEN statement also includes an ACCESS parameter for controlling access of files on a network. This parameter will not be used in this book.
2. QuickBASIC provides for a second general form for the OPEN statement:

OPEN mode, #filenumber, filespec

This second general form is less contemporary than the general form specified at the top of this table, and therefore, will not be used in this book.

Example 2 in Table 7.1 opens PAYROLL.LIS on the default drive for output. Because PAYROLL.LIS is opened for **output**, the program can only write records to the sequential file.

Opening a sequential file for output always creates a new file. If, for example, PAYROLL.LIS already exists, then it is deleted before it is opened. Because there are never any records in a newly opened file, the data pointer is positioned at the beginning of the file.

In the third example in Table 7.1, the OPEN statement opens ACCOUNTS.DAT on the default drive for appending records to the end of the file. If ACCOUNTS.DAT exists, the data pointer is positioned after the last record. If ACCOUNTS.DAT does not exist, the PC creates it and positions the data pointer at the beginning of the file.

The **append mode** (APPEND) should be used in the OPEN statement whenever records are being added to a sequential file. For example, with an order-entry application, it may be desirable to maintain a weekly customer order file. Orders entered on a daily basis are appended to those which have been previously entered. At the end of the week, the customer order file will contain the orders for the week in the sequence entered.

The last example in Table 7.1 illustrates how the filespec may be defined in an OPEN statement as a string variable. This allows you to write an OPEN statement in a program without knowing the name of the sequential file. Of course, when the program is executed, the user must supply the filespec. This is usually done through the use of an INPUT statement. Consider the following partial program:

```
INPUT "Please enter filespec to process ====> ", Filename$
OPEN Filename$ FOR INPUT AS #3
```

The OPEN statement opens for input the file that corresponds to the string constant assigned to the string variable Filename$. Note that the user is responsible for the entire file specification — device name, file name, and file extension. Through the use of the concatenation operator, which is discussed in Chapters 3 and 9, we can simplify the user entry as shown here:

```
INPUT "Name of the File to Process ====> ", Filename$
OPEN "B:" + Filename$ + ".DAT" FOR INPUT AS #3
```

In this case, the user enters only the file name. The concatenation operators in the OPEN statement append the device name to the front of the file name and the file extension to the back of the file name.

The filenumber in an OPEN statement must be an integer expression whose value is between 1 and 255.

The following rules summarize the use of the OPEN statement:

OPEN RULE 1 *A sequential file must be opened before it can be read from or written to.*

OPEN RULE 2 *A program can read only records from a sequential file that has been opened for input.*

OPEN RULE 3 *A sequential file must already exist if it is opened for input.*

OPEN RULE 4 *A program can write only records to a sequential file that has been opened for output or append.*

OPEN RULE 5 *A filenumber can be assigned to only one sequential file at a time.*

Closing Sequential Files

When a program is finished reading or writing to a file, it must close the file with the CLOSE statement. The CLOSE statement terminates the association between the file and the filenumber assigned in the OPEN statement and deallocates the part of main storage that is assigned to the buffer. If a file is being written to, the CLOSE statement ensures that the last record is transferred from the buffer in main storage to auxiliary storage.

The general form of the CLOSE statement is shown in Table 7.2.

TABLE 7.2 The CLOSE Statement

General Form:	CLOSE or CLOSE #filenumber$_1$, ..., #filenumber$_n$
Purpose:	Terminates the association between a filenumber and a file that was established in a previously executed OPEN statement. If the file is opened for output, the CLOSE statement ensures that the last record is transferred from main storage to auxiliary storage. If no filenumbers follow the keyword CLOSE, then all opened files are closed.
Examples:	CLOSE #1, #2, #3 CLOSE #1 CLOSE #2, #1 CLOSE

The CLOSE statement terminates access to a file. For example,

```
CLOSE #2, #3
```

causes the files assigned to filenumbers 2 and 3 to be closed. Any other files previously opened by the program remain open.

Following the close of a specified file, the filenumber may be assigned again to the same file or to a different file by an OPEN statement. Opening and closing a file more than once in a program is quite common. For example, many applications involve reading and processing the records in a sequential data file to compute an average. The file is then processed a second time to evaluate each record against the average. The term **rewind** is sometimes used to describe the technique of closing and then opening the file to begin processing again with the first record.

Note that when executed, the END statement closes all opened files before terminating execution of the program. In our opinion, it is good programming practice to close all opened files with the CLOSE statement, instead of relying on the execution of the END statement.

The following rule summarizes the CLOSE statement:

CLOSE RULE 1   *A file must be opened before it can be closed.*

Writing Reports to a Sequential File

The PRINT #n and PRINT #n, USING statements are used to write reports to sequential files. Once it has been written to a file, the report can be displayed or printed as often as desired without the program being reexecuted. The general forms of the PRINT #n and PRINT #n, USING statements are shown in Tables 7.3 and 7.4, respectively.

TABLE 7.3 The PRINT #n Statement	
General Form:	PRINT #n, item pm item pm ... pm item
	where **n** is a filenumber assigned to a file defined in an OPEN statement;
	item is a constant, variable, expression, function reference, or null; and
	pm is a comma or semicolon.
Purpose:	Writes information to a sequential file in auxiliary storage.
Examples:	PRINT #1, PRINT #2, Emp.Name$, Age, Weight PRINT #1, "Total Sales ======>"; Total PRINT #2, X + Y/4, C * B PRINT #3, Q1.Tax, Q2.Tax, Q3.Tax, Q4.Tax PRINT #2, Sum;
Note:	Type the question mark (?), and QuickBASIC changes it to the keyword PRINT when the cursor is moved off the line.

The PRINT #n and PRINT #n, USING statements work in exactly the same way as the PRINT and PRINT USING statements except that information is written to a sequential file in auxiliary storage rather than to the screen. For example, the statement

```
PRINT Record.Count, Total.Amount, Average
```

displays the values of Record.Count, Total.Amount, and Average on the screen in print zones 1, 2, and 3. Similarly, the statement

```
PRINT #1, Record.Count, Total.Amount, Average
```

creates and transmits a record image to the sequential file assigned to filenumber 1, with the values of Record.Count, Total.Amount, and Average beginning in zones 1, 2, and 3 of the record.

TABLE 7.4 The PRINT #n, USING Statement

General Form:	PRINT #n, USING string expression; list
	where **n** is a filenumber assigned to a file defined in an OPEN statement;
	string expression (sometimes called the descriptor field, or format field) is either a string constant or a string variable; and
	list is a list of items to be displayed in the format specified by the format field.
Purpose:	Provides for controlling exactly the format of a program's output to a sequential file in auxiliary storage by specifying an image to which that output must conform.
Examples:	PRINT #3, USING "The answer is #,###.##"; Cost
	PRINT #2, USING "## divided by # is #.#"; Num; Den; Quot
	T1$ = "Total cost =======> $$,###.##-"
	PRINT #7, USING T1$; Total
	D1$ = "**,###.##"
	PRINT #1, USING D1$; Check;
	PRINT #2, USING "\ \"; Cust.Name$
	PRINT #4, USING "Example _##"; NUMBER
	PRINT #9, USING "#.##^^^^"; Dis.1; Dis.2; Dis.3; Dis.4
Note:	For more information on the descriptor field, see Table 5.8 on page 136.

Programming Case Study 7B	Writing the Weekly Payroll and Summary Report to Auxiliary Storage

In Chapter 6, the Weekly Payroll and Summary Report (Programming Case Study 7A) was introduced. In the solution (Program 6.1 on page 174), the LPRINT and LPRINT USING statements printed the report. In the following modified solution, the report is written to a sequential file in auxiliary storage using the PRINT #n and PRINT #n, USING statements.

Program 7.1 is identical to Program 6.1, except for the inclusion of the following:

1. Line 29, which displays a message on the screen indicating that the report is being written to auxiliary storage
2. Line 30, which opens for output the sequential file REPORT.LIS on the default drive
3. Inclusion of filenumber 1 in each PRINT#n and PRINT#n, USING statement writing the report
4. Line 51, the subprogram name is changed from Display.Headings to Print.Headings
5. Line 95, which closes REPORT.LIS
6. Lines 96 and 97, which display end-of-job information on the screen.

Program Solution

The following program writes the weekly payroll and summary report to auxiliary
storage:

PROGRAM 7.1

```
1    ' Program 7.1
2    ' Writing the Weekly Payroll and Summary Report
3    ' to Auxiliary Storage
4    ' Report File Name = REPORT.LIS
5    ' *************************************************
6    ' *                 Main Program                  *
7    ' *************************************************
8    COMMON SHARED Emp.Count, Total.Gross
9    COMMON SHARED Emp.Hours, Emp.Rate, Emp.Gross
10   COMMON SHARED H1$, H2$, D1$, T1$, T2$, T3$, T4$
11   CALL A100.Initialization
12   CALL B100.Process.File
13   CALL C100.Wrap.Up
14   ' ************** Data Follows *****************
15   DATA 124, 40,    5.60
16   DATA 126, 56,    5.90
17   DATA 128, 38,    4.60
18   DATA 129, 48.5, 6.10
19   DATA EOF,  0,    0    : ' This is the trailer record
20   END
21
22   ' *************************************************
23   ' *                Initialization                 *
24   ' *************************************************
25   SUB A100.Initialization
26      Emp.Count = 0
27      Total.Gross = 0
28      CLS  ' Clear Screen
29      LOCATE 10, 20: PRINT "Writing Payroll Report to Auxiliary Storage..."
30      OPEN "REPORT.LIS" FOR OUTPUT AS #1
31      CALL A200.Initialize.Report.Format
32      CALL A210.Print.Headings
33   END SUB
34
35   ' *************************************************
36   ' *            Initialize Report Format           *
37   ' *************************************************
38   SUB A200.Initialize.Report.Format
39      H1$ = "          Weekly Payroll Report"
40      H2$ = "Employee No.   Hours      Rate     Gross Pay"
41      D1$ = "    \   \         ###.#     ##.##     ##,###.##"
42      T1$ = "Total Gross Pay ========> $$,###.##"
43      T2$ = "Number of Employees ====>     ###"
44      T3$ = "Average Gross Pay ======> $$,###.##"
45      T4$ = "End of Payroll Report"
46   END SUB
47
48   ' *************************************************
49   ' *        Print Report and Column Headings       *
50   ' *************************************************
51   SUB A210.Print.Headings
52      PRINT #1, H1$
53      PRINT #1,
54      PRINT #1, H2$
55      PRINT #1,
56   END SUB
57
```

```
58      ' ***************************************************
59      ' *                  Process File                   *
60      ' ***************************************************
61      SUB B100.Process.File
62         READ Emp.Number$, Emp.Hours, Emp.Rate
63         DO WHILE Emp.Number$ <> "EOF"
64            CALL B200.Compute.Gross.And.Accumulate
65            PRINT #1, USING D1$; Emp.Number$; Emp.Hours; Emp.Rate; Emp.Gross
66            READ Emp.Number$, Emp.Hours, Emp.Rate
67         LOOP
68      END SUB
69
70      ' ***************************************************
71      ' *  Compute Gross Pay & Increment Accumulators  *
72      ' ***************************************************
73      SUB B200.Compute.Gross.And.Accumulate
74         Emp.Count = Emp.Count + 1
75         Emp.Overtime = Emp.Hours - 40
76         IF Emp.Overtime <= 0 THEN
77            Emp.Gross = Emp.Hours * Emp.Rate
78         ELSE
79            Emp.Gross = Emp.Hours * Emp.Rate + .5 * Emp.Rate * Emp.Overtime
80         END IF
81         Total.Gross = Total.Gross + Emp.Gross
82      END SUB
83
84      ' ***************************************************
85      ' *                   Wrap-Up                       *
86      ' ***************************************************
87      SUB C100.Wrap.Up
88         Average.Gross = Total.Gross / Emp.Count
89         PRINT #1,
90         PRINT #1, USING T1$; Total.Gross
91         PRINT #1, USING T2$; Emp.Count
92         PRINT #1, USING T3$; Average.Gross
93         PRINT #1,
94         PRINT #1, T4$
95         CLOSE #1,
96         LOCATE 12, 20: PRINT "Report Stored Under File Name REPORT.LIS"
97         LOCATE 14, 20: PRINT "End of Job"
98      END SUB

        [run]
```

Discussion of the Program Solution

When the Shift + F5 is pressed to execute Program 7.1, the information shown in Figure 7.2 displays on the screen to inform the user the report is being written to a sequential file in auxiliary storage under the name REPORT.LIS.

FIGURE 7.2

The display from the execution of Program 7.1.

```
Writing Payroll Report to Auxiliary Storage...

Report Stored Under File Name REPORT.LIS

End of Job
```

The report written to auxiliary storage by Program 7.1 is illustrated in Figure 7.3. To view the report, use the Open command in the File menu to display REPORT.LIS in the view window, or quit QuickBASIC and use the MS-DOS TYPE or PRINT commands.

```
            Weekly Payroll Report

Employee No.    Hours      Rate    Gross Pay

    124         40.0       5.60      224.00
    126         56.0       5.90      377.60
    128         38.0       4.60      174.80
    129         48.5       6.10      321.77

Total Gross Pay ========> $1,098.17
Number of Employees =====>         4
Average Gross Pay ======>    $274.54

End of Payroll Report
```

Flowchart of the OPEN and CLOSE Statements

The I/O symbol is used to represent the OPEN and CLOSE statements. The flowchart symbol below on the left represents the OPEN statement in line 30 of Program 7.1, and the flowchart symbol on the right represents the CLOSE statement in line 95 of Program 7.1.

Writing Data to a Sequential File

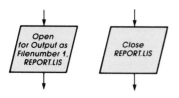

In Program 7.1, the PRINT #n and PRINT #n, USING statements were used to write a *report* to a sequential file in auxiliary storage. To write *data* to a sequential file, we use the WRITE #n statement. The WRITE #n statement writes data in a format required by the INPUT #n statement. The format requirement is similar to that of the READ and DATA statements — all data items are separated by commas. The WRITE #n statement even goes one step better by surrounding all string data items with quotation marks.

The following WRITE #n statement writes a record in the format required by the INPUT #n statement:

```
WRITE #1, Stock$, Location$, Desc$, Cost, Price, Quantity
```

This WRITE #n statement causes a comma to be placed between the data items in the record. Quotation marks are placed around the values of Stock$, Location$, and Desc$, and a carriage return character <cr> is appended to the last data item written to form the record. For example, if Stock$ = C101, Location$ = 1, Desc$ = Roadhandler, Cost = 97.56, Price = 125.11, and Quantity = 25, then the previous WRITE #1, statement transmits the following record to the sequential file assigned to filenumber 1:

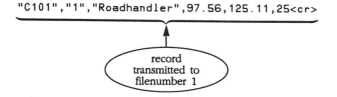

```
"C101","1","Roadhandler",97.56,125.11,25<cr>
```

record
transmitted to
filenumber 1

Note that the string values are delimited with the quotation marks and that the usual leading and trailing spaces surrounding positive numbers are compressed out.

The general form of the WRITE #n statement is given in Table 7.5.

TABLE 7.5 The WRITE #n Statement

General Form:	WRITE #n, list of variables
	where **n** is a filenumber assigned to a sequential file opened for output.
Purpose:	Writes data items separated by commas to a sequential file in auxiliary storage.
Examples:	WRITE #1, Cost, Margin, Price
	WRITE #2, Amount, Description$
	WRITE #3, Dependents, Tax,

Programming Case Study 9 | Creating a Sequential File

Problem: The PUC Company has requested that a sequential file (INVNTORY.DAT) be created from the inventory data below Figure 7.4. The data must be written in a format that is consistent with the INPUT #n statement. Use a series of LOCATE and INPUT statements to display the screen shown in Figure 7.4.

FIGURE 7.4

The screen design for requesting user entry of inventory records for Program 7.2.

In the following inventory data, each line represents an inventory record:

Stock Number	Warehouse Location	Description	Unit Cost	Selling Price	Quantity on Hand
C101	1	Roadhandler	97.56	125.11	25
C204	3	Whitewalls	37.14	99.95	140
C502	2	Tripod	32.50	38.99	10
S209	1	Maxidrill	88.76	109.99	6
S416	2	Normalsaw	152.55	179.40	1
S812	2	Router	48.47	61.15	8
S942	4	Radialsaw	376.04	419.89	3
T615	4	Oxford-Style	26.43	31.50	28
T713	2	Moc-Boot	24.99	29.99	30
T814	2	Work-Boot	22.99	27.99	56

Following are a list of the program tasks in outline form, a program solution, and a discussion of the program solution:

Program Tasks

1. A100.Initialization

    a. Set Record.Count to zero.
    b. Open INVNTORY.DAT.

2. B100.Build.File — create a Do-Until loop that executes *until* the uppercase value of Control$ equals N.

    a. Call B200.Accept.Record.
    b. If the uppercase value of Add.Rec$ is equal to the value Y, then call the subprogram B210.Write.Record. In B210.Write.Record, do the following:
        (1) Write the record to INVNTORY.DAT.
        (2) Increment Record.Count by 1.

3. C100.Wrap.Up

    a. Close the file.
    b. Display Record.Count and an end-of-job message.

Program Solution

The following program corresponds to the preceding tasks.

PROGRAM 7.2

```
1     ' Program 7.2
2     ' Creating a Sequential File
3     ' Output File Name = INVNTORY.DAT
4     ' ****************************************************************
5     ' *                        Main Program                        *
6     ' ****************************************************************
7     COMMON SHARED Record.Count, Add.Rec$, Control$
8     COMMON SHARED Stock$, Location$, Desc$, Cost, Price, Quantity
9     CALL A100.Initialization
10    CALL B100.Build.File
11    CALL C100.Wrap.Up
12    END
13
14    ' ****************************************************************
15    ' *                        Initialization                      *
16    ' ****************************************************************
17    SUB A100.Initialization
18       Record.Count = 0
19       OPEN "INVNTORY.DAT" FOR OUTPUT AS #1
20    END SUB
21
22    ' ****************************************************************
23    ' *                          Build File                        *
24    ' ****************************************************************
25    SUB B100.Build.File
26       DO
27          CALL B200.Accept.Record
28          IF UCASE$(Add.Rec$) = "Y" THEN
29             CALL B210.Write.Record
30          END IF
31       LOOP UNTIL UCASE$(Control$) = "N"
32    END SUB
33
```

```
34    '  ****************************************************************
35    '  *                  Accept an Inventory Record                 *
36    '  ****************************************************************
37    SUB B200.Accept.Record
38       CLS   ' Clear Screen
39       LOCATE 5, 25: PRINT "Inventory File Build"
40       LOCATE 6, 25: PRINT "--------------------"
41       LOCATE 8, 25: INPUT "Stock Number =========> ", Stock$
42       LOCATE 10, 25: INPUT "Warehouse Location ===> ", Location$
43       LOCATE 12, 25: INPUT "Description ==========> ", Desc$
44       LOCATE 14, 25: INPUT "Unit Cost ============> ", Cost
45       LOCATE 16, 25: INPUT "Selling Price ========> ", Price
46       LOCATE 18, 25: INPUT "Quantity On Hand =====> ", Quantity
47       LOCATE 21, 25: INPUT "Enter Y to add record, else N ===> ", Add.Rec$
48       LOCATE 23, 25: INPUT "Enter Y to add ANOTHER record, else N ===> ", Control$
49    END SUB
50
51    '  ****************************************************************
52    '  *                   Write an Inventory Record                 *
53    '  ****************************************************************
54    SUB B210.Write.Record
55       WRITE #1, Stock$, Location$, Desc$, Cost, Price, Quantity
56       Record.Count = Record.Count + 1
57    END SUB
58
59    '  ****************************************************************
60    '  *                            Wrap-Up                          *
61    '  ****************************************************************
62    SUB C100.Wrap.Up
63       CLOSE #1
64       CLS   ' Clear Screen
65       LOCATE 10, 15: PRINT "Creation of Sequential File is Complete"
66       LOCATE 14, 15
67       PRINT "Total Number of Records in INVNTORY.DAT ===>"; Record.Count
68    END SUB

[run]
```

Discussion of the Program Solution

When Program 7.2 is executed, line 19 opens INVNTORY.DAT for output as filenumber 1.

In B100.Build.File, line 27 in the Do loop calls B200.Accept.Record. Figure 7.5 on the next page shows the display due to the execution of this subprogram for the first record entered by the user. Note the two messages at the bottom of the screen. The first message (line 47) gives the user the opportunity to reject the transaction by assigning Add.Rec$ a value other than Y or y (line 28). The second message (line 48) requests the user enter a Y to add another record to the inventory file.

Owing to line 29, the inventory record is added by B210.Write.Record if the upper-case value of Add.Rec$ is equal to Y.

Line 31 controls the Do loop. If the uppercase value of Control$ equals N, then the Do loop terminates, and control returns to line 11 of the Main Program. If the uppercase value of Control$ is equal to any other value, then the Do loop continues.

FIGURE 7.5
The display after the first record is entered due to the execution of Program 7.2.

```
Inventory File Build
--------------------

Stock Number =========> C101

Warehouse Location ===> 1

Description ==========> Roadhandler

Unit Cost ============> 97.56

Selling Price ========> 125.11

Quantity on Hand =====> 25


Enter Y to add record, else N ===> Y

Enter Y to add ANOTHER record, else N ===> Y
```

In B210.Write.Record, line 55 includes the `WRITE #n` statement. This statement writes the record to the sequential file INVNTORY.DAT in a format consistent with the `INPUT #n` statement in Table 7.6. Figure 7.6 shows the format of the data written to INVNTORY.DAT by Program 7.2.

FIGURE 7.6
A listing of INVNTORY.DAT created by Program 7.2.

```
"C101","1","Roadhandler",97.56,125.11,25
"C204","3","Whitewalls",37.14,99.95,140
"C502","2","Tripod",32.5,38.99,10
"S209","1","Maxidrill",88.76,109.99,6
"S416","2","Normalsaw",152.55,179.4,1
"S812","2","Router",48.47,61.15,8
"S942","4","Radialsaw",376.04,419.89,3
"T615","4","Oxford-Style",26.43,31.5,28
"T713","2","Moc-Boot",24.99,29.99,30
"T814","2","Work-Boot",22.99,27.99,56
```

In C100.Wrap.Up, line 63 closes INVNTORY.DAT. This ensures the last record entered by the user is moved from the buffer to the file in auxiliary storage. Figure 7.7 shows the display due to lines 65 through 67 of C100.Wrap.Up.

FIGURE 7.7
The display due to the execution of the subprogram C100.Wrap.Up in Program 7.2.

```
Creation of Sequential File Is Complete

Total Number of Records in INVNTORY.DAT ===> 10
```

Data validation was purposely left out of this case study to present a clear-cut example of how to create a sequential file. In a production environment, reasonableness checks should always be considered for the stock number (Stock$), warehouse location (Location$), unit cost (Cost), selling price (Price), quantity on hand (Quantity), and user responses (Add.Rec$ and Control$). Data should always be validated before it is placed in a file.

The INPUT #n Statement

The INPUT #n statement is used to read data from a sequential file that has been created with the WRITE #n statement. The statement is the same as the READ statement, except that it reads data from a file instead of from DATA statements. The following partial program,

```
OPEN "INVNTORY.DAT" FOR INPUT AS #1
  .
  .
  .
INPUT #1, Stock$, Location$, Desc$, Cost, Price, Quantity
```

reads six data items from the sequential file INVNTORY.DAT.

For data to be read from a sequential file, the following must be true:

1. The file must already exist.
2. The file must be opened for input.
3. The data items in the file must be separated by a comma or by a carriage return character <cr>.

The general form of the INPUT #n statement is shown in Table 7.6.

TABLE 7.6 The INPUT #n Statement

General Form:	INPUT #n, list of variables where **n** is a filenumber assigned to an existing sequential file opened for input.
Purpose:	Reads data items from a sequential file in auxiliary storage and assigns them to variables.
Examples:	INPUT #1, Sum, Fix, Desc$, Price INPUT #3, Amount INPUT #2, Code$, Salary, Tax, Dependents

---

The INPUT #n statement causes the variables in its list to be assigned specific values, in order, from the data sequence found in the sequential file assigned to filenumber n. In order to visualize the relationship between the INPUT #n statement and the associated file, think of a **pointer** associated with the data items, as discussed in Chapter 5, page 129. When the OPEN statement is executed, this pointer points to the first data item in the data-sequence holding area. Each time an INPUT #n statement is executed, the variables in the *list* are assigned values from the data-sequence holding area, beginning with the data item that is indicated by the pointer, and the pointer is advanced one value per variable. Hence, the pointer points to the next data item to be assigned when the INPUT #n statement is executed.

If the data type of the data item to be assigned does not agree with the variable in the INPUT #n statement, then the PC displays within a dialog box the diagnostic message

```
Type mismatch
```

For example, it is invalid to assign a string value to a numeric variable. In determining the actual value of a data item, the PC scans in the following manner:

1. For a numeric value: Leading spaces and carriage return characters <cr> are ignored. The first character that is not a space or a carriage return character is assumed to be the start of the numeric data item. A comma, carriage return, or space terminates the numeric value.

2. For a string value: Leading spaces and carriage return characters are ignored. The first character that is not a space or a carriage return character is assumed to be the start of the string data item. Spaces within a string are valid characters. If the first character is a quotation mark, the string data item will consist of all characters between the first quotation mark and the second. Also, if the first character is a quotation mark, the string cannot include a quotation mark. If the string is unquoted, the value terminates with a comma or a carriage return character.

The following rules summarize the material discussed in this section:

 *Before the* INPUT #n *statement is executed, the filenumber n must be assigned to a sequential file that is opened for input.*

 *Numeric variables in* INPUT #n *statements require numeric constants as data items, and string variables require quoted strings or unquoted strings as data.*

The EOF Function

When a sequential file that was opened for output is closed, the PC automatically adds an **end-of-file mark** after the last record written to the file. Later, when the same sequential file is opened for input, you can use the EOF(n) function to test for the end-of-file mark. The n indicates the filenumber assigned to the file in the OPEN statement.

If the EOF function senses the end-of-file mark, it returns a value of –1 (true). Otherwise, it returns a value of 0 (false). The EOF function can be used to control a Do loop. For example, consider the following partial program:

```
OPEN "INVNTORY.DAT" FOR INPUT AS #1
 .
 .
 .
DO WHILE NOT EOF(1)
   INPUT #1, Stock$, Location$, Desc$, Cost, Price, Quantity
   CALL B200.Compute.And.Accumulate
   CALL B210.Print.Record
LOOP
```

In the DO WHILE statement, the EOF(1) function is used to control the Do loop. Each time the DO WHILE statement is executed, the PC checks to see whether the data pointer is pointing to the end-of-file mark in INVNTORY.DAT.

When using the EOF function, it is important to organize your program so that the test for the end-of-file precedes the execution of the INPUT #n statement. Therefore, note in the previous partial program that only one INPUT #n statement is used, and that this statement is placed inside at the top of the Do loop. This is different from our previous programs which used READ statements — one prior to the Do loop and one at the bottom of the Do loop.

The logic exhibited by the Do loop also works when the file is empty (that is, when the file contains no records). If the INVNTORY.DAT file is empty, the OPEN statement in the partial program above still opens the file for input. However, when the DO WHILE statement is executed, the EOF function immediately detects the end-of-file mark on the empty file, thereby causing the Do loop to pass control to the statement following the corresponding `LOOP` statement.

Two additional points must be considered regarding the `EOF` function:

1. It is invalid to precede the filenumber with a number sign (#). For example, the following is invalid:

```
WHILE NOT EOF(#1)   ' Invalid due to #
```

2. Filenumber n must be opened for input. It is invalid to test for the end-of-file mark on a file that is opened for output.

The following rule summarizes the placement of the `EOF` function in a program.

EOF FUNCTION RULE 1   *The* `EOF` *function should test for the end-of-file mark prior to the execution of an* `INPUT` #n *statement.*

(See Programs 7.3, 7.4, and 7.5, later in this chapter, for examples on the use of the `EOF` function.)

7.4 PAGING A REPORT

Processing large amounts of data often results in generating reports that are many pages long. In multiple-page reports, the report title, the column headings, and a page number should be printed at the top of every page. This is called **paging** the report. Optionally, the current date and time may be printed on each page.

Additional programming logic is required for paging a report. For example, immediately after a detail or total line is printed, a **line counter** should be incremented to keep track of what line the printer is on. Prior to printing a detail or a series of total lines, an `IF` statement should be used to determine whether the paper in the printer should be advanced to the top of the next page. The condition in the `IF` statement compares the line counter to the maximum number of lines per page. The maximum number of lines per page is usually assigned to a variable in the Initialization module.

Here is the logic for single-spacing detail lines in a report:

1. If the line counter is greater than or equal to the maximum lines per page, call the Print Report and Column Headings module.
2. Print the detail line.
3. Increment the line counter by 1. (Increment the line counter by 2 for double-spacing and by 3 for triple-spacing.)

Here is the logic for the Print Report and Column Headings module:

1. Increment the page counter by 1.
2. Advance the paper to the top of the page.
3. Print the report title, column headings, and page counter.
4. Set the line counter equal to the number of lines printed in this module plus 1.

It is also important to be aware of some of the characteristics associated with most dot matrix and letter-quality printers attached to PCs.

1. The paper in a printer is normally 8.5 inches wide and 11 inches long on continuous forms.
2. Printers print 6 or 8 lines per inch. The default value is 6 lines per inch.
3. When the printer is turned on, it establishes as the top of the page the line on the paper that the print-head mechanism (or the ribbon) is at. To ensure that the paper is aligned properly for a program, it is good practice to request in the Initialization module that the user align the paper to the top of the page.

To **align the paper**, turn the printer off and use the platen knob to advance the paper so the perforation between sheets is approximately one inch above the top of the print-head mechanism. Next, turn the printer back on. Remember, if the paper is not aligned properly, the page breaks will not align with the top of the page.

4. In the Print Report and Column Headings module, we instruct the printer to advance to the top of the page by printing a Form Feed character. The ASCII code for the **Form Feed character** is 12. There is no single key on the keyboard for this code; however, we can transmit the Form Feed character by using the CHR$ function. This function is discussed in detail in Chapter 9 on page 332. The following LPRINT statement advances the paper to the top of the page:

```
LPRINT CHR$(12);  ' Advance the paper to top of page
```

Once the paper has ejected, the semicolon following the CHR$ function instructs the printer to stay on the current line rather than move down a line.

The following problem requires data to be read and processed from the sequential file created by Program 7.2. The program solution illustrates printing a report on the printer, paging a report, the INPUT #n statement, and the use of the EOF function.

Programming Case Study 10   Processing a Sequential Data File and Paging a Report

In this case study, we want to generate a report using the data in the sequential file INVNTORY.DAT. This file was created by Program 7.2, and its contents are shown in Figure 7.6 on page 234.

For each record in INVNTORY.DAT, the following are to be printed on the printer by means of the LPRINT and LPRINT USING statements:

1. Stock number
2. Description
3. Unit cost
4. Selling price
5. Quantity on hand
6. Total item cost of a stock item (unit cost times quantity on hand)
7. Total selling price of a stock item (selling price times quantity on hand)

Print the total inventory cost and the total inventory selling price after all records have been processed.

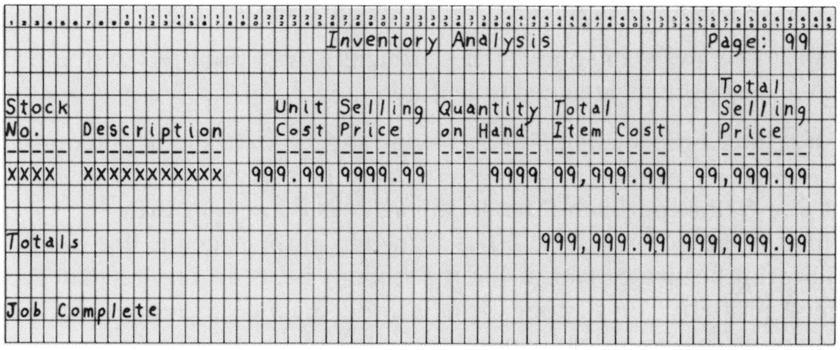

FIGURE 7.8

The output for Program 7.3, designed on a printer-spacing chart.

Print the report title, column headings, and a page number at the top of each page. Print the inventory records on every other line. That is, double-space the report. Print a maximum of 20 lines per page. (We selected 20 lines per page to ensure a page break with the small data file used in this case study. Normally, the maximum lines per page is set at around 60.)

The printer-spacing chart in Figure 7.8 illustrates the design of the report to be printed.

Following are the program tasks in outline form, a program solution, and a discussion of the program solution.

Program Tasks

1. A100.Initialization

    a. Set Page.Count to zero.
    b. Set Max.Lines.Per.Page to 20.
    c. Set Grand.Tot.Cost and Grand.Tot.Price to zero.
    d. Display a message to align the paper in the printer.
    e. Open INVNTORY.DAT.
    f. Call A200.Initialize.Report.Format.
    g. Call M300.Print.Headings. Because this subprogram is also called from any other subprogram that prints lines on the printer, assign a level number beginning with the letter M, which stands for multiple, followed by a number representing the lowest level at which it exists. Additionally, we place this subprogram below C100.Wrap.Up so it may be easily located. In M300.Print.Headings, do the following:
        (1) Increment Page.Count by 1.
        (2) If Page.Count is greater than 1, then advance the paper to the top of the page.
        (3) Print the report title and Page.Count.
        (4) Print the column headings.
        (5) Set Line.Count to 7.

2. B100.Process.File — Establish a Do-While loop that executes while the EOF function does not detect the end-of-file mark in INVNTORY.DAT. In this loop do as follows:

    a. Read an inventory record.
    b. Call B200.Compute.Accumulate.
        (1) Compute the total cost (Tot.Cost) and total price (Tot.Price).
        (2) Increment Grand.Tot.Cost and Grand.Tot.Price.
    c. Call B210.Print.Record. In this subprogram, do the following:
        (1) Compare Line.Count to Max.Lines.Per.Page + 1. If the condition is true, call M300.Print.Headings.
        (2) Print the inventory record.
        (3) Increment Line.Count by 2.

3. C100.Wrap.Up

    a. Close INVNTORY.DAT.
    b. Compare Line.Count to Max.Lines.Per.Page − 1. If the condition is true, then call M300.Print.Headings.
    c. Print Grand.Tot.Cost and Grand.Tot.Price.
    d. Print an end-of-job message to conclude the report.
    e. Display an end-of-job message on the screen.

Program Solution

The following program corresponds to the requirements of the printer-spacing chart in Figure 7.8 and to the preceding program tasks:

PROGRAM 7.3

```
1    ' Program 7.3
2    ' Processing a Sequential Data File
3    ' Input File Name = INVNTORY.DAT
4    ' *****************************************************
5    ' *                 Main Program                      *
6    ' *****************************************************
7    COMMON SHARED Page.Count, Max.Lines.Per.Page, Grand.Tot.Cost
8    COMMON SHARED Grand.Tot.Price, Tot.Cost, Tot.Price, Line.Count
9    COMMON SHARED H1$, H2$, H3$, H4$, H5$, D1$, T1$, T2$
10   COMMON SHARED Stock$, Location$, Desc$, Cost, Price, Quantity
11   CALL A100.Initialization
12   CALL B100.Process.File
13   CALL C100.Wrap.Up
14   END
15
16   ' *****************************************************
17   ' *                Initialization                     *
18   ' *****************************************************
19   SUB A100.Initialization
20      Page.Count = 0
21      Max.Lines.Per.Page = 20
22      Grand.Tot.Cost = 0
23      Grand.Tot.Price = 0
24      CLS  ' Clear Screen
25      LOCATE 10, 20
26      PRINT "Set the paper in the printer to the top of page."
27      LOCATE 12, 20
28      INPUT "Press the Enter key when the printer is ready...", Control$
29      OPEN "INVNTORY.DAT" FOR INPUT AS #1
30      CALL A200.Initialize.Report.Format
31      CALL M300.Print.Headings
32   END SUB
33
34   ' *****************************************************
35   ' *          Initialize Report Format                 *
36   ' *****************************************************
37   SUB A200.Initialize.Report.Format
38      H1$ = "                    Inventory Analysis          Page: ##"
39      H2$ = "                                                    Total"
40      H3$ = "Stock                    Unit Selling Quantity Total      Selling"
41      H4$ = "No.   Description   Cost Price   On Hand Item Cost   Price"
42      H5$ = "----- ------------ ---- ------- -------- --------- -------"
43      D1$ = "\   \  \            \ ###.## ####.##     #### ##,###.## ##,###.##"
44      T1$ = "Totals                               ###,###.## ###,###.##"
45      T2$ = "Job Complete"
46   END SUB
47
48   ' *****************************************************
49   ' *                Process File                       *
50   ' *****************************************************
51   SUB B100.Process.File
52      DO WHILE NOT EOF(1)
53         INPUT #1, Stock$, Location$, Desc$, Cost, Price, Quantity
54         CALL B200.Compute.And.Accumulate
55         CALL B210.Print.Record
56      LOOP
57   END SUB
58
```

```
59    ' ***************************************************
60    ' *        Compute and Increment Accumulators       *
61    ' ***************************************************
62    SUB B200.Compute.And.Accumulate
63       Tot.Cost = Cost * Quantity
64       Tot.Price = Price * Quantity
65       Grand.Tot.Cost = Grand.Tot.Cost + Tot.Cost
66       Grand.Tot.Price = Grand.Tot.Price + Tot.Price
67    END SUB
68
69    ' ***************************************************
70    ' *            Print an Inventory Record            *
71    ' ***************************************************
72    SUB B210.Print.Record
73       IF Line.Count >= Max.Lines.Per.Page + 1 THEN
74          CALL M300.Print.Headings
75       END IF
76       LPRINT USING D1$; Stock$; Desc$; Cost; Price; Quantity; Tot.Cost; Tot.Price
77       LPRINT
78       Line.Count = Line.Count + 2
79    END SUB
80
81    ' ***************************************************
82    ' *                    Wrap-Up                      *
83    ' ***************************************************
84    SUB C100.Wrap.Up
85       CLOSE #1
86       IF Line.Count >= Max.Lines.Per.Page - 1 THEN
87          CALL M300.Print.Headings
88       END IF
89       LPRINT
90       LPRINT USING T1$; Grand.Tot.Cost; Grand.Tot.Price
91       LPRINT
92       LPRINT T2$
93       LPRINT CHR$(12); ' Advance the paper to top of page
94       LOCATE 14, 20: PRINT "Job Complete"
95    END SUB
96
97    ' ***************************************************
98    ' *        Print Report and Column Headings         *
99    ' ***************************************************
100   SUB M300.Print.Headings
101      Page.Count = Page.Count + 1
102      IF Page.Count > 1 THEN
103         LPRINT CHR$(12); ' Advance the paper to top of page
104      END IF
105      LPRINT USING H1$; Page.Count
106      LPRINT
107      LPRINT H2$
108      LPRINT H3$
109      LPRINT H4$
110      LPRINT H5$
111      Line.Count = 7
112   END SUB

      [run]
```

Discussion of the Program Solution

When Program 7.3 is executed, the report illustrated in Figure 7.9 is printed on the printer. The following points should be noted concerning the program solution represented by Program 7.3:

1. In line 20, Page.Count is initialized to zero; later, in line 101, it is incremented by 1 just prior to printing the report title. In line 21, Max.Lines.Per.Page is set equal to 20, the number of lines to be printed per page.

2. In line 29, the OPEN statement opens INVNTORY.DAT for input as filenumber 1. The remaining file-handling statements, which are lines 53 and 85, reference INVNTORY.DAT by specifying the filenumber 1.

3. The Do-While loop, lines 52 through 56 in B100.Process.File, processes records while the EOF function does not detect the end-of-file mark.

4. The activity of printing an inventory record is in a separate subprogram (lines 72 through 79) because it involves several lines of code. This subprogram is called from line 55 in the Do-While loop. Study B210.Print.Record closely. Whenever a program pages a report, the line counter must be tested (line 73) before the detail line is printed. After printing the detail line and double-spacing, the line counter is incremented by 2 (line 78).

   Note that the line counter (Line.Count) is compared against a value that ensures that the required lines to be printed in the subprogram will fit on the page. The problem specifications indicated that only 20 physical lines were to be printed per page. Because Line.Count is initialized to 7 (line 111) and incremented by two each time a detail line is printed (line 78), Line.Count takes on the values 7, 9, 11, 13, 15, 17, 19, 21. When Line.Count is 19, there is enough room on the page to print another detail line. When Line.Count is 21, there is no more room on the page. Hence, in line 73 when Line.Count is greater than or equal to Max.Lines.Per.Page + 1, that is 21, we transfer control to M300.Print.Headings.

5. M300.Print.Headings is called from lines 31, 74, and 87. Top-down programming requires that a module called from two or more different places in a program be placed below the last call. Calls should always be made in a downward direction in the program. Additionally, since this module is called from several points in the program, its level number begins with M which stands for multiple, followed by a number denoting the lowest level at which the module exists.

   M300.Print.Headings, beginning at line 100, increments the page number (line 101), advances the paper to the top of the page, prints the report and column headings (lines 105 through 110), and finally sets the line counter to 7 (line 111). Line.Count is set equal to the number of the next line to be printed.

6. Although the warehouse location is not manipulated or displayed by Program 7.3, it is necessary to include a variable (Location$) that represents the warehouse location in the list of the INPUT #n statement (line 53) because the data item is part of the record. You cannot be selective and input from a sequential data file, only those data items which you plan to manipulate or display. All data items within the record must be assigned to variables in the INPUT #n statement, as shown in line 53.

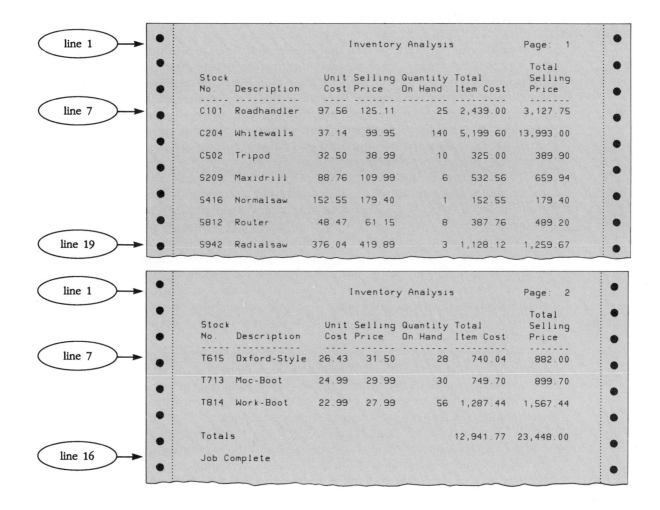

```
line 1 →                    Inventory Analysis              Page:   1

                                                         Total
              Stock             Unit Selling Quantity Total    Selling
              No.   Description Cost Price   On Hand  Item Cost Price
              ----- ----------- ---- ------- -------- --------- -------
line 7 →      C101  Roadhandler 97.56 125.11      25  2,439.00  3,127.75

              C204  Whitewalls  37.14  99.95     140  5,199.60 13,993.00

              C502  Tripod      32.50  38.99      10    325.00    389.90

              S209  Maxidrill   88.76 109.99       6    532.56    659.94

              S416  Normalsaw  152.55 179.40       1    152.55    179.40

              S812  Router      48.47  61.15       8    387.76    489.20

line 19 →     S942  Radialsaw  376.04 419.89       3  1,128.12  1,259.67


line 1 →                    Inventory Analysis              Page:   2

                                                         Total
              Stock             Unit Selling Quantity Total    Selling
              No.   Description Cost Price   On Hand  Item Cost Price
              ----- ----------- ---- ------- -------- --------- -------
line 7 →      T615  Oxford-Style 26.43 31.50      28    740.04    882.00

              T713  Moc-Boot    24.99  29.99      30    749.70    899.70

              T814  Work-Boot   22.99  27.99      56  1,287.44  1,567.44

              Totals                                 12,941.77 23,448.00

line 16 →     Job Complete
```

FIGURE 7.9

The report generated by Program 7.3.

7.5   CONTROL-BREAK PROCESSING

Most businesses today are divided into smaller units for the purpose of better management. A retail company doing business on a national scale may have several levels of management with the levels headed by such people as a district manager, a store manager, and a department manager. To evaluate the performance of the units within each level, managerial reports are generated showing summaries, or minor totals, for each subunit. For example, a sales analysis report generated for the manager of a company often shows a summary sales total for each district within the company, as well as a grand sales total for the company.

Programs that are written to generate levels of subtotals use a technique involving control fields and control breaks. A **control field** contains data that is to be compared from record to record. A **control break** occurs when the data in the control field changes.

A control break may be used to display a summary line each time a selected data item, common to all records in the file, changes value. The variable assigned to the selected data item is called the **control variable**. For this technique to work successfully, it is essential that the records be processed in sequence, according to the data item that determines the break. For example, to generate the Sales Analysis Report shown in Figure 7.10, all the records that belong to District 1 must precede all the District 2 records.

With the sales records in sequence, the program solution can check each sales record to see whether it is the first record of a new district. If the sales record represents an item from the *old* district (that is, if the current item and the previous one belong to the same district), then selected contents of that record are printed, and the PC adds the sales amount for that item to a district sales accumulator.

When a sales record that belongs to a *new* district is read, a control break occurs, and the current value of the district sales accumulator is printed. In addition, asterisks are usually printed to the right of the totals to indicate a summary. One asterisk indicates the lowest level, two asterisks the next level, and so on. Before processing the sales record that caused the control break, the PC must add the district sales to the company sales total, which is displayed after all records in the file have been processed.

Furthermore, the control variable must be assigned the value of the next district number before the processing of the record is resumed. Finally, the variable that is used to sum the district sales must be reset to zero after each control break so that it can be used to sum the sales for the next district.

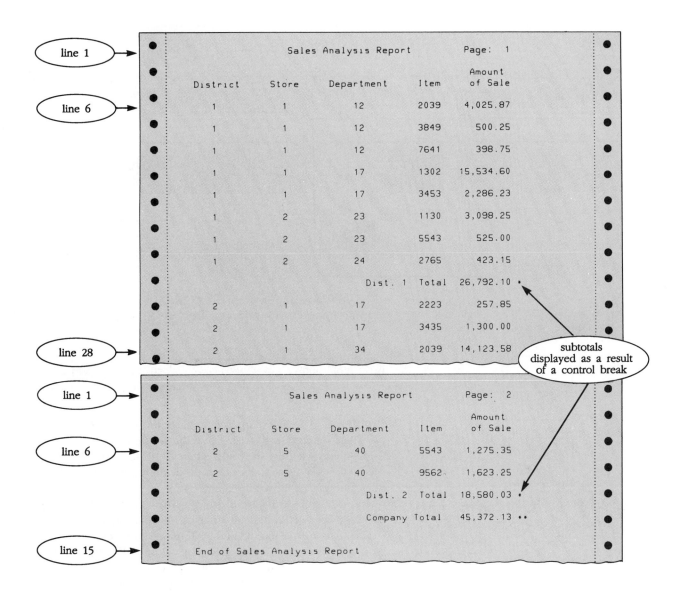

line 1

line 6

line 28

```
                    Sales Analysis Report          Page:   1

                                                 Amount
   District       Store      Department     Item   of Sale

      1             1            12         2039   4,025.87

      1             1            12         3849     500.25

      1             1            12         7641     398.75

      1             1            17         1302  15,534.60

      1             1            17         3453   2,286.23

      1             2            23         1130   3,098.25

      1             2            23         5543     525.00

      1             2            24         2765     423.15

                                Dist. 1  Total  26,792.10 *

      2             1            17         2223     257.85

      2             1            17         3435   1,300.00

      2             1            34         2039  14,123.58
```

subtotals displayed as a result of a control break

line 1

line 6

line 15

```
                    Sales Analysis Report          Page:   2

                                                 Amount
   District       Store      Department     Item   of Sale

      2             5            40         5543   1,275.35

      2             5            40         9562   1,623.25

                                Dist. 2  Total  18,580.03 *

                                Company Total   45,372.13 **


End of Sales Analysis Report
```

FIGURE 7.10

Sales Analysis Report (report with a single-level control break).

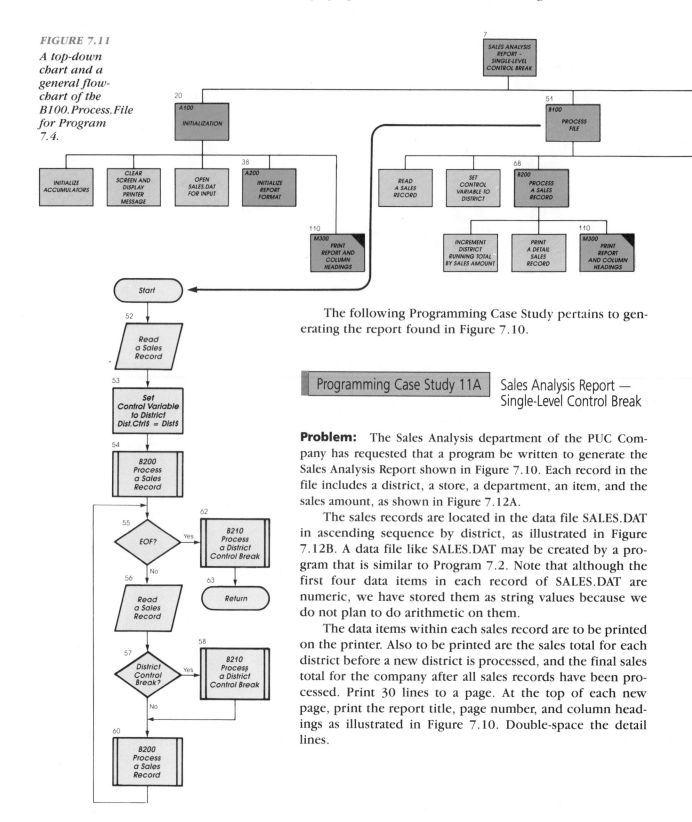

The following Programming Case Study pertains to generating the report found in Figure 7.10.

Programming Case Study 11A Sales Analysis Report — Single-Level Control Break

Problem: The Sales Analysis department of the PUC Company has requested that a program be written to generate the Sales Analysis Report shown in Figure 7.10. Each record in the file includes a district, a store, a department, an item, and the sales amount, as shown in Figure 7.12A.

The sales records are located in the data file SALES.DAT in ascending sequence by district, as illustrated in Figure 7.12B. A data file like SALES.DAT may be created by a program that is similar to Program 7.2. Note that although the first four data items in each record of SALES.DAT are numeric, we have stored them as string values because we do not plan to do arithmetic on them.

The data items within each sales record are to be printed on the printer. Also to be printed are the sales total for each district before a new district is processed, and the final sales total for the company after all sales records have been processed. Print 30 lines to a page. At the top of each new page, print the report title, page number, and column headings as illustrated in Figure 7.10. Double-space the detail lines.

FIGURE 7.11
(continued)

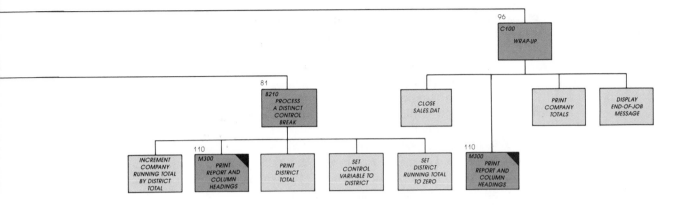

FIGURE 7.12

(A) The sales data in ascending sequence by department within store within district. (B) A listing of the sales data stored in SALES.DAT.

District	Store	Dept.	Item	Amt. of Sale	
1	1	12	2039	$ 4,025.87	"1","1","12","2039",4025.87
1	1	12	3849	500.25	"1","1","12","3849",500.25
1	1	12	7641	398.75	"1","1","12","7641",398.75
1	1	17	1302	15,534.60	"1","1","17","1302",15534.6
1	1	17	3453	2,286.23	"1","1","17","3453",2286.23
1	2	23	1130	3,098.25	"1","2","23","1130",3098.25
1	2	23	5543	525.00	"1","2","23","5543",525
1	2	24	2765	423.15	"1","2","24","2765",423.15
2	1	17	2223	257.85	"2","1","17","2223",257.85
2	1	17	3435	1,300.00	"2","1","17","3435",1300
2	1	34	2039	14,123.58	"2","1","34","2039",14123.58
2	5	40	5543	1,275.35	"2","5","40","5543",1275.35
2	5	40	9562	1,623.25	"2","5","40","9562",1623.25
				(A)	**(B)**

Figure 7.11 shows a top-down chart for the Sales Analysis report and a general flowchart of B100.Process.File. Following are a list of the program tasks in outline form, a program solution, and a discussion of the program solution.

Program Tasks

The following program tasks correspond to the top-down chart in Figure 7.11:

1. A100.Initialization

   a. Set Page.Count to zero.
   b. Set Max.Lines.Per.Page to 30.
   c. Set Dist.Total and Cmpy.Total to zero.
   d. Clear the screen.
   e. Display a message instructing the user to align the paper in the printer.
   f. Open SALES.DAT.
   g. Initialize report format and print the report headings.

2. B100.Process.File, if not end-of-file

    a. Read a sales record.

    b. Assign the value of Dist$ to Dist.Ctrl$.

    c. Call B200.Process.Record. Within this subprogram, do the following:

        (1) Increment Dist.Total by Amount.

        (2) If Line.Count is greater than or equal to Max.Lines.Per.Page, then print the report headings.

        (3) Print the detail line.

        (4) Increment Line.Count by 2.

    d. Establish a Do-While loop that executes while not end-of-file. Within this loop, do the following:

        (1) Read the next sales record.

        (2) Test for a control break (`Dist$ <> Dist.Ctrl$`). If a control break occurs, then call B210.Process.District.Break. This subprogram must do the following:

            (a) Increment Cmpy.Total by Dist.Total.

            (b) If Line.Count is greater than or equal to Max.Lines.Per.Page, then print the report headings.

            (c) Print Dist.Total.

            (d) Set Dist.Ctrl$ equal to Dist$.

            (e) Reset Dist.Total to zero.

        (3) Call B200.Process.Record described in step 2c.

    e. Following the Do-While loop, process the last district.

3. C100.Wrap.Up

    a. Close SALES.DAT.

    b. If Line.Count is greater than or equal to Max.Lines.Per.Page – 2, then print the report headings.

    c. Print Cmpy.Total and an end-of-job message.

    d. Display an end-of-job message on the screen.

Program Solution

Program 7.4 corresponds to the preceding program tasks and to the top-down chart in Figure 7.11.

PROGRAM 7.4

```
 1     ' Program 7.4
 2     ' Sales Analysis Report -- Single Level Control Break
 3     ' Input File Name = SALES.DAT
 4     ' *********************************************************
 5     ' *                   Main Program                        *
 6     ' *********************************************************
 7     COMMON SHARED Page.Count, Max.Lines.Per.Page, Dist.Total, Cmpy.Total
 8     COMMON SHARED Line.Count, H1$, H2$, H3$, D1$, T1$, T2$, T3$
 9     COMMON SHARED Dist$, Store$, Dept$, Item$, Amount, Dist.Ctrl$
10     CALL A100.Initialization
11     IF NOT EOF(1) THEN
12         CALL B100.Process.File
13     END IF
14     CALL C100.Wrap.Up
15     END
16
```

```
17    ' ******************************************************
18    ' *                    Initialization                  *
19    ' ******************************************************
20    SUB A100.Initialization
21        Page.Count = 0
22        Max.Lines.Per.Page = 30
23        Dist.Total = 0
24        Cmpy.Total = 0
25        CLS  ' Clear Screen
26        LOCATE 10, 20
27        PRINT "Set the paper in the printer to the top of page."
28        LOCATE 12, 20
29        INPUT "Press the Enter key when the printer is ready...", Control$
30        OPEN "SALES.DAT" FOR INPUT AS #1
31        CALL A200.Initialize.Report.Format
32        CALL M300.Print.Headings
33    END SUB
34
35    ' ******************************************************
36    ' *              Initialize Report Format              *
37    ' ******************************************************
38    SUB A200.Initialize.Report.Format
39        H1$ = "                    Sales Analysis Report              Page: ##"
40        H2$ = "                                                            Amount"
41        H3$ = "District        Store        Department      Item      Of Sale"
42        D1$ = "    \\          \\               \\           \ \   ##,###.##"
43        T1$ = "                                Dist. \\ Total ###,###.## *"
44        T2$ = "                                Company Total ####,###.## _**"
45        T3$ = "End of Sales Analysis Report"
46    END SUB
47
48    ' ******************************************************
49    ' *                   Process File                     *
50    ' ******************************************************
51    SUB B100.Process.File
52        INPUT #1, Dist$, Store$, Dept$, Item$, Amount
53        Dist.Ctrl$ = Dist$
54        CALL B200.Process.Record
55        DO WHILE NOT EOF(1)
56            INPUT #1, Dist$, Store$, Dept$, Item$, Amount
57            IF Dist$ <> Dist.Ctrl$ THEN
58                CALL B210.District.Break ' Call Process a District Control Break
59            END IF
60            CALL B200.Process.Record
61        LOOP
62        CALL B210.District.Break
63    END SUB
64
65    ' ******************************************************
66    ' *               Process a Sales Record               *
67    ' ******************************************************
68    SUB B200.Process.Record
69        Dist.Total = Dist.Total + Amount
70        IF Line.Count >= Max.Lines.Per.Page THEN
71            CALL M300.Print.Headings
72        END IF
73        LPRINT USING D1$; Dist$; Store$; Dept$; Item$; Amount
74        LPRINT
75        Line.Count = Line.Count + 2
76    END SUB
77
```

(continued)

```
78      ' ****************************************************
79      ' *            Process a District Control Break      *
80      ' ****************************************************
81      SUB B210.District.Break
82         Cmpy.Total = Cmpy.Total + Dist.Total
83         IF Line.Count >= Max.Lines.Per.Page THEN
84            CALL M300.Print.Headings
85         END IF
86         LPRINT USING T1$; Dist.Ctrl$; Dist.Total
87         LPRINT
88         Line.Count = Line.Count + 2
89         Dist.Ctrl$ = Dist$
90         Dist.Total = 0
91      END SUB
92
93      ' ****************************************************
94      ' *                     Wrap-Up                      *
95      ' ****************************************************
96      SUB C100.Wrap.Up
97         CLOSE #1
98         IF Line.Count >= Max.Lines.Per.Page - 2 THEN
99            CALL M300.Print.Headings
100        END IF
101        LPRINT USING T2$; Cmpy.Total
102        LPRINT : LPRINT : LPRINT T3$
103        LPRINT CHR$(12); ' Advance the paper to top of page
104        LOCATE 14, 20: PRINT "Job Complete"
105     END SUB
106
107     ' ****************************************************
108     ' *          Print Report and Column Headings        *
109     ' ****************************************************
110     SUB M300.Print.Headings
111        Page.Count = Page.Count + 1
112        IF Page.Count > 1 THEN
113           LPRINT CHR$(12); ' Advance the paper to top of page
114        END IF
115        LPRINT USING H1$; Page.Count
116        LPRINT
117        LPRINT H2$
118        LPRINT H3$
119        LPRINT
120        Line.Count = 6
121     END SUB

        [run]
```

Discussion of the Solution

When Program 7.4 is executed, the PC prints the report shown in Figure 7.10 on page 245. Note these important points regarding the control break process in Program 7.4.

1. In A100.Initialization, lines 23 and 24 initialize the district and the company accumulators.

2. In the Main Program, B100.Process.File is called by line 12 only if SALES.DAT is not empty. The IF statement is required in line 11 because the first statement in B100.Process.File (line 52) is the INPUT #n statement.

3. In B100.Process.File, line 52 reads the first sales record. Line 53 sets the control variable (Dist.Ctrl$) equal to the first district (Dist$). Line 54 causes the first sales record to be processed.

The DO WHILE statement in line 55 tests to determine whether there are any records left in SALES.DAT. Within the Do-While loop, line 56 reads the next sales record. Line 57 compares the district of the most recently read sales record to the control variable. If they are different, a control break has occurred, and B210.District.Break is called. Whether or not a control break occurs, line 60 processes the sales record last read by line 56.

Following the processing of a record, line 61 returns control to the DO WHILE statement in line 55. When the end-of-file mark is finally detected, the DO WHILE statement transfers control to line 62, and the totals for the last district in the file are processed.

4. In B210.District.Break, the four requirements for processing a control break are fulfilled in the following way:

   a. Line 82 increments the company sales accumulator (Cmpy.Total) by the district sales accumulator (Dist.Total).

   b. Line 83 tests for a page break. Lines 86 through 88 print the value of the district sales accumulator and increment Line.Count. Note that line 86 uses the control variable (Dist.Ctrl$) rather than the variable Dist$ to print the district number. Can you explain why we don't print Dist$?

   c. Line 89 assigns the control variable (Dist.Ctrl$) the value of the new district.

   d. Line 90 sets the district sales accumulator (Dist.Total) to zero in preparation for processing the next district.

5. In C100.Wrap.Up, the company sales total (Cmpy.Total) is printed.

Programming Case Study 11B | Sales Analysis Report — Two Levels of Control Breaks

There are four classifications of control breaks: minor, intermediate, major, and multiple. A report may include one break (minor), as was the case in the previous example; two breaks (intermediate); three breaks (major); or multiple (more than three breaks).

The next program solution illustrates the generation of a sales analysis report that is the same as the one shown in Figure 7.10, except that it includes two levels of control breaks. The control breaks are stored within district, within company. Each control break causes a number of summaries to be displayed, depending on the level of the break. A store change (minor) causes one summary to be displayed. A district change (major) causes both the last store total and the district total to be displayed. When the end-of-file mark is sensed, all summaries that relate to the last store and district are displayed, along with the grand total sales for the company.

The logic employed in a program involving multilevel control breaks is similar to that shown in Program 7.4. It makes little difference whether there are two, three, or more levels to consider. The program need only include additional decision statements and accumulators for each control-break summary. The comparison should be structured so that the major level is considered first, then the intermediate levels, and so forth down to the minor level.

Finally, it is important that the sales records be in ascending sequence by store within district. That is, within each district, the stores must be in ascending sequence. Study carefully the sequence of the sales records in SALES.DAT shown in Figure 7.12A on page 247.

A list of the additional program tasks required to modify Program 7.4 so that it will generate the new report are listed below. The program solution, the Sales Analysis Report, and a discussion of the program solution follow.

Program Tasks in Addition to Those Listed for Programming Case Study 11A

1. A100.Initialization

    a. Set Max.Lines.Per.Page to 36 rather than 30.
    b. Set Store.Total to zero.
    c. In A200.Initialize.Report.Format, add an extra total line to print the value of Store.Total when a minor control break occurs.

2. B100.Process.File

    a. Set Store.Ctrl$ equal to Store$ after the first record is read.
    b. Within the Do-While loop, add a test for a minor control break (Store$ <> Store.Ctrl$) immediately after the test for the major control break (Dist$ <> Dist.Ctrl$).
    c. As the first statement in B210.District.Break, add a call to B220.Store.Break. (Whenever there is a district control break, there is a store control break.)
    d. Add the subprogram B220.Store.Break. This subprogram is nearly identical to B210.District.Break; the only difference is that the reference to all variables is at the store level rather than at the district level.

Program Solution

PROGRAM 7.5

The following Program 7.5 contains the modifications to Program 7.4 described by the preceding additional tasks:

```
 1   ' Program 7.5
 2   ' Sales Analysis Report -- Two Levels of Control Breaks
 3   ' Input File Name = SALES.DAT
 4   ' *******************************************************
 5   ' *                  Main Program                       *
 6   ' *******************************************************
 7   COMMON SHARED Page.Count, Max.Lines.Per.Page, Line.Count
 8   COMMON SHARED Store.Total, Dist.Total, Cmpy.Total
 9   COMMON SHARED H1$, H2$, H3$, D1$, T1$, T2$, T3$, T4$
10   COMMON SHARED Dist$, Store$, Dept$, Item$, Amount, Dist.Ctrl$, Store.Ctrl$
11   CALL A100.Initialization
12   IF NOT EOF(1) THEN
13       CALL B100.Process.File
14   END IF
15   CALL C100.Wrap.Up
16   END
17
18   ' *******************************************************
19   ' *                  Initialization                     *
20   ' *******************************************************
21   SUB A100.Initialization
22       Page.Count = 0
23       Max.Lines.Per.Page = 36
24       Store.Total = 0
25       Dist.Total = 0
26       Cmpy.Total = 0
27       CLS   ' Clear Screen
28       LOCATE 10, 20
29       PRINT "Set the paper in the printer to the top of page."
30       LOCATE 12, 20
31       INPUT "Press the Enter key when the printer is ready...", Control$
32       OPEN "SALES.DAT" FOR INPUT AS #1
33       CALL A200.Initialize.Report.Format
34       CALL M300.Print.Headings
35   END SUB
36
```

```
37      ' ********************************************************
38      ' *              Initialize Report Format               *
39      ' ********************************************************
40      SUB A200.Initialize.Report.Format
41          H1$ = "                  Sales Analysis Report          Page: ##"
42          H2$ = "                                                   Amount"
43          H3$ = "District      Store        Department      Item    Of Sale"
44          D1$ = "    \\           \\             \\           \ \    ##,###.##"
45          T1$ = "                                  Store \\ Total ###,###.## *"
46          T2$ = "                                  Dist. \\ Total ###,###.## *_*"
47          T3$ = "                                  Company Total ####,###.## *_**"
48          T4$ = "End of Sales Analysis Report"
49      END SUB
50
51      ' ********************************************************
52      ' *                    Process File                     *
53      ' ********************************************************
54      SUB B100.Process.File
55          INPUT #1, Dist$, Store$, Dept$, Item$, Amount
56          Dist.Ctrl$ = Dist$
57          Store.Ctrl$ = Store$
58          CALL B200.Process.Record
59          DO WHILE NOT EOF(1)
60              INPUT #1, Dist$, Store$, Dept$, Item$, Amount
61              IF Dist$ <> Dist.Ctrl$ THEN
62                  CALL B210.District.Break
63              END IF
64              IF Store$ <> Store.Ctrl$ THEN
65                  CALL B220.Store.Break
66              END IF
67              CALL B200.Process.Record
68          LOOP
69          CALL B210.District.Break
70      END SUB
71
72      ' ********************************************************
73      ' *               Process a Sales Record                *
74      ' ********************************************************
75      SUB B200.Process.Record
76          Store.Total = Store.Total + Amount
77          IF Line.Count >= Max.Lines.Per.Page THEN
78              CALL M300.Print.Headings
79          END IF
80          LPRINT USING D1$; Dist$; Store$; Dept$; Item$; Amount
81          LPRINT
82          Line.Count = Line.Count + 2
83      END SUB
84
85      ' ********************************************************
86      ' *            Process a District Control Break         *
87      ' ********************************************************
88      SUB B210.District.Break
89          CALL B220.Store.Break
90          Cmpy.Total = Cmpy.Total + Dist.Total
91          IF Line.Count >= Max.Lines.Per.Page THEN
92              CALL M300.Print.Headings
93          END IF
94          LPRINT USING T2$; Dist.Ctrl$; Dist.Total
95          LPRINT
96          Line.Count = Line.Count + 2
97          Dist.Ctrl$ = Dist$
98          Dist.Total = 0
99      END SUB
100
```

(continued)

```
101    ' *********************************************************
102    ' *              Process a Store Control Break            *
103    ' *********************************************************
104    SUB B220.Store.Break
105       Dist.Total = Dist.Total + Store.Total
106       IF Line.Count >= Max.Lines.Per.Page THEN
107          CALL M300.Print.Headings
108       END IF
109       LPRINT USING T1$; Store.Ctrl$; Store.Total
110       LPRINT
111       Line.Count = Line.Count + 2
112       Store.Ctrl$ = Store$
113       Store.Total = 0
114    END SUB
115
116    ' *********************************************************
117    ' *                      Wrap-Up                          *
118    ' *********************************************************
119    SUB C100.Wrap.Up
120       CLOSE #1
121       IF Line.Count >= Max.Lines.Per.Page - 2 THEN
122          M300.Print.Headings
123       END IF
124       LPRINT USING T3$; Cmpy.Total
125       LPRINT : LPRINT : LPRINT T4$
126       LPRINT CHR$(12); ' Advance paper to top of page
127       LOCATE 14, 20: PRINT "Job Complete"
128    END SUB
129
130    ' *********************************************************
131    ' *            Print Report and Column Headings           *
132    ' *********************************************************
133    SUB M300.Print.Headings
134       Page.Count = Page.Count + 1
135       IF Page.Count > 1 THEN
136          LPRINT CHR$(12); ' Advance paper to top of page
137       END IF
138       LPRINT USING H1$; Page.Count
139       LPRINT
140       LPRINT H2$
141       LPRINT H3$
142       LPRINT
143       Line.Count = 6
144    END SUB

    [run]
```

Discussion of the Program Solution

When Program 7.5 is executed, the report shown in Figure 7.13 is generated.

The main difference between the report in Figure 7.13 and the one in Figure 7.10 is that in Figure 7.13 there are two levels of control breaks. Following the processing of all Store 1, District 1 records, a total for Store 1 prints. Following a district control break, both the totals for the store and district print. Printing the store and district totals each time they change continues until the entire file has been processed.

The following specific points should be noted concerning Program 7.5:

1. In B100.Process.File, line 61 tests for a district control break. If a district control break occurs, control transfers to the subprogram beginning at line 88. The first instruction in this subprogram, line 89, transfers control to B220.Store.Break. Once the store control break has been processed, control returns to the subprogram B210.District.Break, and the district control break is processed. Line 89 ensures that a store control break is processed whenever a district control break occurs.

2. After testing for a district control break in line 61, line 64 tests to determine whether there is a store control break. If there is a minor control break, control transfers to B220.Store.Break.

When a sales record causes a district control break, the condition in line 64 that tests for a store control break can never be true because Store.Ctrl$ is equal to Store$, owing to the major control break.

As an addition to this program solution, in BASIC Programming Problem 6 on page 262 you are asked to generate a triple-control-break report with the same file SALES.DAT that was used in Programming Case Studies 11A and 11B. The report requires three control breaks that include department within store, within district. A close look at SALES.DAT in Figure 7.10 reveals that the file is in ascending sequence by department, within store, within district.

FIGURE 7.13
Sales Analysis Report (report with two levels of control breaks).

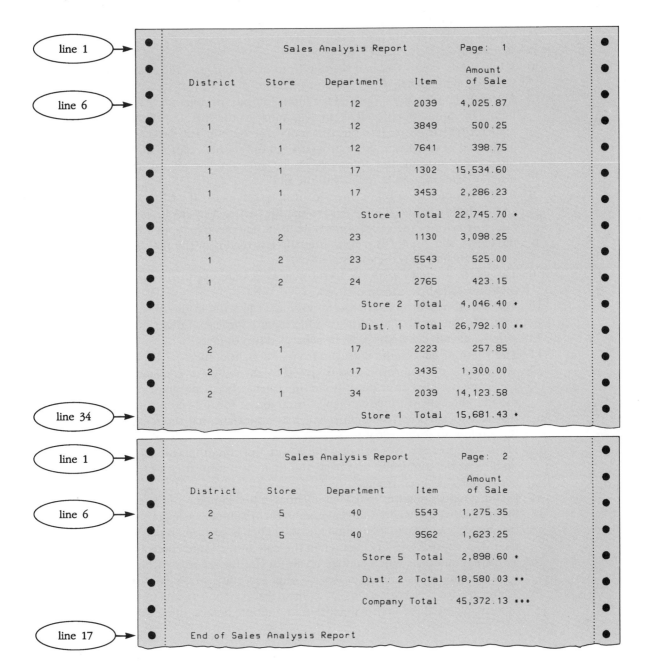

7.6   WHAT YOU SHOULD KNOW

1. In QuickBASIC, the four following techniques can be used to integrate data into a program:
   a. The INPUT statement and keyboard or any other external input device
   b. The READ and DATA statements
   c. The INPUT #n statement and data files
   d. The LET statement

2. A file is a group of related records. Each record within the file contains related data items.

3. QuickBASIC provides for two types of file organization—sequential and random. A file that is organized sequentially is limited to sequential processing. Random files will be discussed in Chapter 10.

4. A filespec identifies a file in auxiliary storage.

5. Before a file can be read from or written to, it must be opened by the OPEN statement.

6. When a program is finished reading from or writing to a file, it must close the file with the CLOSE statement.

7. A sequential file can be opened for input, output, or append. If a file is opened for input, the pointer is placed at the beginning of the file, and the program can only read records from it. If a file is opened for output, the pointer is placed at the beginning of the file, and the program can only write records to the file. If a file is opened for append, the pointer is placed after the last record in the file, and the program can only write records to the file.

8. If a file is opened for input, the file must already exist. If a file is opened for output and it already exists, the PC deletes the file before it opens it. The file may or may not exist prior to the execution of the OPEN statement for appending records. If the file exists, the pointer is placed after the last record in the file. If the file does not exist, then APPEND is the same as OUTPUT.

9. The PRINT #n and PRINT #n, USING statements are used to write information to a sequential file in the form of a report.

10. The WRITE #n statement is used to write data to a file in the format required by the INPUT #n statement. The format requirement is similar to that of the READ and DATA statements: all data items must be separated by commas.

11. The INPUT #n statement reads data from a sequential file.

12. When a file opened for output is closed by the CLOSE or END statement, an end-of-file mark is added after the last record. Later, when a program reads records from the file, the EOF(n) function may be used to test for the end-of-file mark on the file that is associated with filenumber n. It is important that the test be made prior to the attempt to read a record.

13. Paging a report involves printing the report and column headings along with a page number at the top of the first page and then each time after a predetermined number of lines has been printed.

14. Paging a report requires two accumulators: a line counter and a page counter.

15. Programs that are written to generate levels of subtotals use control fields and control breaks. A control field contains data that is to be compared from record to record. A control break occurs when the data in the same control field changes.

16. To display subtotals when control breaks occur, the records within a file must be in sorted sequence, ascending or descending, according to the control field.

17. There are four classifications of control breaks: one break (minor); two breaks (intermediate); three breaks (major); and multiple breaks (more than three).

7.7 TEST YOUR BASIC SKILLS (Even-numbered answers are in Appendix E)

1. Consider the valid partial program below and to the right, then explain its function. Assume that the values in the table below and to the left are entered in response to the INPUT statements in the program.

Stock Item	Selling Price	Discount Code
138	$ 78.56	2
421	123.58	3
617	475.65	2
812	23.58	1
917	754.56	4

```
' Exercise 7.1
OPEN "EX71.DAT" FOR OUTPUT AS #1
DO
    CLS   ' Clear Screen
    INPUT "Stock Item ======> ", Item$
    INPUT "Selling Price ===> ", Price
    INPUT "Discount Code ===> ", Code$
    WRITE #1, Item$, Price, Code$
    INPUT "Add ANOTHER record? (Y or N)", Control$
LOOP UNTIL UCASE$(Control$) = "N"
CLOSE #1
PRINT : PRINT "Job Complete"
```

2. Fill in the blanks in the following sentences:
   a. The _____ statement with a mode of _____ or _____ must be executed before a PRINT #n, PRINT #n, USING, or WRITE #n statement is executed.
   b. The _____ statement with a mode of _____ must be executed before an INPUT #n statement is executed.
   c. A file can be opened as often as required, provided it is _____ before each subsequent open.
   d. The function _____ is used to test for the end-of-file mark with a sequential file.
   e. When records are to be added to the end of a sequential file, the _____ mode is used in the OPEN statement.

3. Explain the purpose of the EOF function. Also indicate where it should be located in a program in relation to the INPUT #n statement.

4. A program is to read records from one of three sequential data files, SALES1.DAT, SALES2.DAT, and SALES3.DAT. The three files are stored on the diskette in the B drive. Write three OPEN statements that would allow the program to read records from any of the three sequential files.

5. Construct a WRITE #n statement that would write the values of A, B, X$, and D to a sequential file in the format required by the INPUT #n statement.

6. Which of the following are invalid file-handling statements? Why?
   a. OPEN FOR OUTPUT "B:SAL.DAT" AS #1
   b. OPEN File$ FOR APPEND AS #3
   c. PRINT #1,
   d. PRINT #1, A,
   e. PRINT #1 USING "####.##"; Cost
   f. CLOSE
   g. DO WHILE NOT EOF(#2)
   h. INPUT #2, Amount,

7. Assume that the following line is located in the Print a Detail Line subprogram and prints the detail line for a report:

   `LPRINT Emp.Number$, Emp.Name$, Emp.Soc.Sec$, Emp.Salary`

   Write the line that would immediately follow it if
   a. Double-spacing were required.
   b. Triple-spacing were required.

8. Write a statement that would properly increment the line counter (Line.Count) for each of the requirements below. This statement would follow the LPRINT statement in Exercise 7 in the Print a Detail Line subprogram.
   a. Single-space the detail line.
   b. Double-space the detail line.
   c. Triple-space the detail line.

9. Write the IF statement that would test to determine whether the report title and column headings should be printed for each of the requirements below. This IF statement would precede the LPRINT statement in Exercise 7 in the Print a Detail Line subprogram. Assume Line.Count was initialized to 2 in the Print Report and Column Headings subprogram.
    a. Max.Lines.Per.Page = 10 and triple-spacing
    b. Max.Lines.Per.Page = 45 and double-spacing
    c. Max.Lines.Per.Page = 54 and single-spacing

10. **PC Hands-On Exercise:** Do the following:
    a. Load Program 7.3 (PRG7-3) from the Student Diskette. Delete line 78. Execute the program. Compare the results to those in Figure 7.9. Now do you understand why it is important to increment the line counter in line 78?
    b. Load Program 7.3 again. In line 20, initialize Page.Count to 99. Execute the program and examine the page numbers on the report. How would you adjust line 38 to ensure that page numbers up to 999 will print correctly?
    c. Load Program 7.3 again. In line 21, set Max.Lines.Per.Page to 14. Execute the program and compare the report to Figure 7.9. Do you agree that by modifying the value of this variable you can change the number of lines printed per page?

11. **PC Hands-On Exercise:** Load Program 7.4 (PRG7-4) from the Student Diskette. Display and execute Program 7.4. Delete line 62 and execute the program a second time. Study the output results and explain the function of line 62.

12. **PC Hands-On Exercise:** Load Program 7.5 (PRG7-5) from the Student Diskette. Display and execute Program 7.5. Delete line 89 and execute the program a second time. Study the output results. Do you understand that when there is a major control break, all lower level control breaks must also be processed?

7.8   BASIC PROGRAMMING PROBLEMS

1. Creating a Master File

Purpose: To become familiar with creating a sequential file that is consistent with the format required by the INPUT #n statement. Use of the OPEN, CLOSE, and WRITE #n statements is required.

Problem: Construct a top-down program to create a sequential file named EX71PAY.DAT that represents the payroll master file for the PUC Company. A **master file** is one that is, for the most part, permanent or includes data that is required each time an application such as payroll is processed. Each record in the file describes an employee, including the year-to-date (YTD) payroll information, as shown under the Input Data.

Write the data to the file in the format required by the INPUT #n statement. Have the user enter a Y (or y) to add the record entered and displayed on the screen before writing it to the file. After completing each record entry, have the user enter a Y (or y) to add another record, or an N (or n). As part of the end-of-job routine, display a message indicating that the file was created as well as the total number of records written to the file. Use the COMMON SHARED statement to declare all required variables globally.

(**Hint:** See Program 7.2 on page 232 or PRG7-2 on the Student Diskette.)

Input Data: Prepare and use the sample data at the top of the next page.

| Employee | | Depend- | Marital | Rate | Year-to-Date | | |
| | | | | | Gross | Federal | Soc. Sec. |
No.	Name	ents	Status	of Pay	Pay	With. Tax	Tax
123	Col, Joan	2	M	12.50	25,345.23	10,256.45	1,938.91
124	Fiel, Don	1	S	18.00	50,725.00	15,546.45	3,880.46
125	Dit, Lisa	1	S	13.00	52,115.23	14,035.78	3,924.45
126	Snow, Joe	9	M	4.50	11,510.05	854.34	880.52
134	Hi, Frank	0	M	8.75	9,298.65	2,678.25	711.35
167	Bri, Edie	3	S	10.40	8,190.45	2,017.50	626.57
210	Liss, Ted	6	M	8.80	7,098.04	2,120.55	543.00
234	Son, Fred	2	M	6.75	0.00	0.00	0.00

Output Results: The sequential file EX71PAY.DAT is created in auxiliary storage on the default drive. The results are shown below for the first payroll record on the left. The results below and to the right are displayed prior to the termination of the program

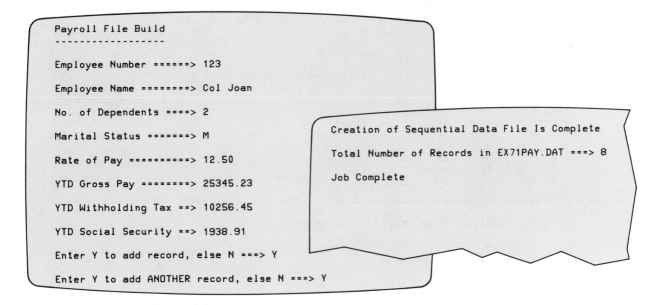

```
Payroll File Build
------------------

Employee Number ======> 123

Employee Name ========> Col Joan

No. of Dependents =====> 2

Marital Status ========> M

Rate of Pay ==========> 12.50

YTD Gross Pay ========> 25345.23

YTD Withholding Tax ==> 10256.45

YTD Social Security ==> 1938.91

Enter Y to add record, else N ===> Y

Enter Y to add ANOTHER record, else N ===> Y
```

```
Creation of Sequential Data File Is Complete

Total Number of Records in EX71PAY.DAT ===> 8

Job Complete
```

2. Master File List

Purpose: To become familiar with reading records in a sequential file, printing the records on the printer, and paging a report. Use of the OPEN, CLOSE, INPUT #n, LPRINT, and LPRINT USING statements and the EOF function is required.

Problem: Write a top-down program that prints the data items found in each employee record of the sequential file EX71PAY.DAT created in BASIC Programming Problem 1. Page the report. Print a maximum of 17 lines to a page. Double-space the detail lines and single-space the total lines. As part of the end-of-job routine, display the following totals: employee-record count, YTD gross pay, YTD federal withholding tax, and YTD social security tax.

(Hint: See Program 7.3 on page 240 or PRG7-3 on the Student Diskette. Define the YTD gross pay as a double-precision variable.)

Input Data: Use the sequential file EX71PAY.DAT created in Problem 1 on the previous page. (If you did not complete BASIC Programming Problem 1, then use EX71PAY.DAT found on the Student Diskette.)

Output Results: The following results are displayed.

```
 ●                                   Payroll File List                Page:   1        ●

 ●      Employee            Marital Rate of  <-------Year-to-Date-------->            ●
        No. Name       Dep. Status  Pay      Gross Pay With. Tax Soc. Sec.
 ●      --- --------    ---- ------- -------  --------- --------- ---------          ●

 ●      123 Col Joan     2     M        12.50  25,345.23 10,256.45  1,938.91         ●

 ●      124 Fiel Don     1     S        18.00  50,725.00 15,546.45  3,880.46         ●

 ●      125 Dit Lisa     1     S        13.00  52,115.23 14,035.78  3,924.45         ●

 ●      126 Snow Joe     9     M         4.50  11,510.05    854.34    880.52         ●

 ●      134 Hi Frank     0     M         8.75   9,298.65  2,678.25    711.35         ●

 ●      167 Bri Edie     3     S        10.40   8,190.45  2,017.50    626.57         ●
```

```
 ●                                   Payroll File List                Page:   2        ●

 ●      Employee            Marital Rate of  <-------Year-to-Date-------->            ●
        No. Name       Dep. Status  Pay      Gross Pay With. Tax Soc. Sec.
 ●      --- --------    ---- ------- -------  --------- --------- ---------          ●

 ●      210 Liss Ted     6     M         8.80   7,098.04  2,120.55    543.00         ●

 ●      234 Son Fred     2     M         6.75       0.00      0.00      0.00         ●

 ●      Total Number of Records ========>        8                                   ●
        Total YTD Gross Pay ============> 164,282.67
 ●      Total YTD Wihtholding Tax ======>  47,509.32                                 ●
        Total YTD Social Security ======>  12,505.26
 ●      Job Complete                                                                 ●
```

3. Writing a Report to Auxiliary Storage

Purpose: To become familiar with writing a report to a sequential file. Use of the OPEN, CLOSE, INPUT #n, PRINT #n, and PRINT #n, USING statements and the EOF function is required.

Problem: Same as BASIC Programming Problem 2, except write the report to the sequential file EX73RPT.LIS. Later, use the MS-DOS command TYPE to display the report on the screen and the PRINT command to print the report on the printer.

Input Data: Use the sequential file EX71PAY.DAT that was created in BASIC Programming Problem 1. (If you did not complete BASIC Programming Problem 1, then use EX71PAY.DAT found on the Student Diskette.)

Output Results: The sequential file EX73RPT.LIS is created in auxiliary storage. The following is displayed at the end-of-job:

```
Report complete and stored under the file name EX73RPT.LIS.

Job Complete
```

4. Appending Records to the End of a File

Purpose: To become familiar with appending records to the end of a sequential file. Use of the OPEN, CLOSE, and WRITE #n statements is required.

Problem: The sequential file EX74PAY.DAT found on the Student Diskette is a duplicate of EX71PAY.DAT, created by BASIC Programming Problem 1. Append to EX74PAY.DAT the new employee records described under Input Data.

Input Data: Prepare and use the following sample data:

Employee Number	Employee Name	Dependents	Marital Status	Rate of Pay
345	Lie Jeff	2	M	6.60
612	Abe Mike	1	S	8.75

Because these are new employees, assign all year-to-date items a value of zero.

Output Results: The screen display should be the same as shown in the Output Results for BASIC Programming Problem 1. The following is displayed at the end-of-job:

```
Total Number of Records Added to EX74PAY.DAT ===> 2

Job Complete
```

5. Computing the Average Age of Employees with a Minor Control Break

Purpose: To become familiar with a method of testing for a control break in a file. Use of the OPEN, CLOSE, and INPUT #n statements and the EOF function is required.

Problem: Construct a top-down program that will find the average age of those employees less than 40 years old and the average age of those greater than or equal to 40 years old. The program should do the following:

1. Read a department number and an employee's age from the sequential data file EX75EMP.DAT found on the Student Diskette. The employee records found in EX75EMP.DAT are shown under Input Data.
2. Test to see whether the department number is the same as the previous one.
3. If the department number is the same, determine whether the age is greater than or equal to 40, or less than 40. Use an IF statement to transfer control so that the age is added to an appropriate total, and a variable representing a counter has its value incremented by 1.
4. If the department number changes (control break occurs), transfer control to determine the average ages of those employees below 40, and of those 40 and above; display a summary line; then, reset counters and the control variable, and continue processing the next department.

(**Hint:** Use the top-down chart illustrated in Figure 7.12 and Program 7.4 — PRG7-4 on the Student Diskette — as a guide to solving this problem.)

Input Data: The sequential data file EX75EMP.DAT is stored on the Student Diskette. The file contains the following sample data:

Dept. No.	Age	Dept. No.	Age	Dept. No.	Age	Dept. No.	Age
1	26	1	64	2	65	2	25
1	38	1	19	2	18	3	21
1	22	1	38	2	37	3	23
1	40	2	46	2	41	3	34
1	51	2	48	2	43	3	56

Output Results: The following results are displayed:

```
              Employee Average Age

              Below    Average Age    40 and    Average Age
 Dept. No.    40       Below 40       Above     40 and Above
 --------     -----    -----------    ------    ------------

    1           5         28.6          3           51.7
    2           3         26.7          5           48.6
    3           3         26.0          1           56.0

 Employee Age Analysis Report Complete
```

6. Sales Analysis Report with Three Levels of Control Breaks

Purpose: To become familiar with paging a report, the LPRINT and LPRINT USING statements, and the concepts of multilevel control breaks and sequential file processing.

Problem: Write a top-down program that prints a report with three levels of control breaks. The program is to process the sequential data file SALES.DAT used earlier in the chapter by Program 7.4 and stored on the Student Diskette. Print totals for department, store, district, and company. A listing of SALES.DAT is shown in Figure 7.12 on page 247. Note that the records are in sequence by department, within store, within district. The report should be similar to the one shown in Figure 7.13 on page 255. Page the report. Print a maximum of 36 lines per page.

(Hint: See Program 7.5 on page 252 or PRG7-5 on the Student Diskette.)

Input Data: Use the sequential data file SALES.DAT that is located on the Student Diskette.

Output Results: The output results should be similar to the report shown in Figure 7.13.

7. Checking the Sequence of Customer Numbers

Purpose: To devise an efficient method of checking the sequence in ascending order of records in a sequential data file.

Problem: A sequential data file EX77CUS.DAT on the Student Diskette contains customer records. Each record contains a customer number and the balance due. The records must be checked to ensure that all are in ascending sequence on the basis of the customer number. The program must not compare the first customer number against the customer number of 0 or 1, or any predetermined fixed number. Beginning with the second record, each customer number should be compared to the previous customer number in sequence.

If a customer record is out of order, the following is to be displayed:

```
Out of Order =====> XXXXX
```

where the Xs represent the customer number of the record that is out of order. If a duplicate customer number is detected, the following is to be displayed:

```
Duplicate ========> XXXXX
```

If the customer record is in ascending order, processing continues. Duplicate customer numbers are not out of order. When the last customer number is processed, display the total customer records that have been sequence-checked in ascending order.

Input Data: Use the sequential data file EX77CUS.DAT on the Student Diskette. Listed below are the first five records. You can use the Open command in the File menu to display the entire file.

Customer Number	*Balance Due*
03000	$ 43.25
03012	132.00
03013	5.65
03015	354.98
03014	99.80

Output Results: The following partial results are shown:

```
Out of Order =====> 3014
Duplicate ========> 3018
Out of Order =====> 3037

          .

          .

Out of Order =====> 3078
Out of Order =====> 3095

Customer Numbers in Sequence =====> 31

Job Finished
```

8. Payroll Problem VII: Social Security Computations and Multiple-File Processing

Purpose: To become familiar with multiple-file processing and paging a report.

Problem: Modify Payroll Problem VI (Problem 7) in Chapter 6 to determine the social security deduction. The social security deduction is equal to 7.65% of the gross pay, to a maximum of $3,924.45 (7.65% of $51,300) for the year. Modify the solution to Payroll Problem VI by adding this additional computation as a subprogram. Include the following:

1. Use the master payroll file EX71PAY.DAT created in BASIC Programming Problem 1 of this chapter to obtain year-to-date information and the rate of pay for each employee. (If you did not complete BASIC Programming Problem 1, then use EX71PAY.DAT found on the Student Diskette.)
2. Use the transaction file EX78TRA.DAT on the Student Diskette. A **transaction file** is one that contains temporary data. In this case, the temporary data is the employee number and hours worked for the pay period, as shown under Input Data.
3. Write a new master file EX78PAY.DAT that includes the updated year-to-date values for each employee.
4. Page the report. Print a maximum of 17 lines to a page.
5. Round the social security tax and withholding tax to the nearest cent.

You may assume that the records in EX71PAY.DAT and EX78TRA.DAT are in ascending sequence and that there is exactly one record in each file per employee. That is, each record in EX71PAY.DAT has a match in EX78TRA.DAT.

Input Data: Use the sequential data files described below. Both files are stored on the Student Diskette.

1. EX71PAY.DAT as the master payroll file (See the Input Data for BASIC Programming Problem 1).
2. EX78TRA.DAT as the transaction file. EX78TRA.DAT contains the following data:

Employee Number	Hours Worked
123	88
124	96
125	72
126	80
134	80
167	70.5
210	80
234	32

Output Results: A new master payroll file is created as EX78PAY.DAT.   The following report is printed on the printer.

```
                    Biweekly Payroll Report              Page:   1

  Employee
  Number        Gross Pay       Fed. Tax      Soc. Sec.      Net Pay
  --------      ---------       --------      ---------      -------
    123         1,150.00         214.62          87.98        847.40

    124         1,872.00         366.71          43.99      1,461.30

    125           936.00         179.51           0.00        756.49

    126           360.00           2.77          27.54        329.69

    134           700.00         140.00          53.55        506.45

    167           733.20         123.56          56.09        553.55
```

```
                    Biweekly Payroll Report              Page:   2

  Employee
  Number        Gross Pay       Fed. Tax      Soc. Sec.      Net Pay
  --------      ---------       --------      ---------      -------
    210           704.00          94.65          53.86        555.49

    234           216.00          27.82          16.52        171.66

  Total Gross Pay ========>     6,671.20
  Total Withholding Tax ==>     1,149.64
  Total Social Security ==>       339.52
  Total Net Pay ==========>     5,182.04

  End of Payroll Report
```

FOR Loops, Arrays, Sorting, and Table Processing

8.1 INTRODUCTION

In earlier chapters, loops were implemented (coded) with the DO and LOOP statements. This chapter presents a second method for implementing certain types of loops by means of the FOR and NEXT statements.

Also in the previous chapters, the programs used simple variables such as Amount, Price, and Code$ to store and access data. Each variable was assigned a single value in an INPUT, LET, or READ statement. Another technique that can make a program shorter, easier to code, and more general is the use of arrays. In this chapter, we will discuss the advantages gained by grouping similar data into an array. In QuickBASIC, an **array** is a string or numeric variable that is allocated a specified number of storage locations, each of which can be assigned a unique value. In other words, an array allows a programmer to store more than one value under the same variable name. Arrays are commonly used in programming for sorting and table processing, in which related data items are organized into rows and columns.

A report is usually easier to work with and more meaningful if the information is generated in some sequence such as first to last, largest to smallest, or oldest to newest. Arranging data according to order or sequence is called **sorting**.

In data processing terminology, a **table** is a collection of data in which each item is uniquely identified by a label, by its position relative to other items, or by some other means. Income tax tables, insurance tables, airline schedules, and telephone directories are examples of tables that present data that is concise yet easy to read and understand. Storing table elements in arrays allows a programmer to organize the entries and to write efficient code for retrieving each individual element.

Upon successful completion of this chapter, you will be able to code certain types of loops more efficiently. You also will be able to develop programs that demand that large amounts of data, stored in an orderly fashion, be available to the PC during the entire execution of the program.

8.2 THE FOR AND NEXT STATEMENTS

The FOR and NEXT statements make it possible to execute a section of a program repeatedly, with automatic changes in the value of a variable between repetitions.

In Chapters 5, 6, and 7, the DO and LOOP statements were used to implement a loop structure that executed a section of a program repeatedly. Whenever you have to develop a **counter-controlled loop**, a loop that executes based on the value of a counter, the coding requires statements for initializing, incrementing, and testing for a counter. Any counter-controlled loop may be written with the FOR and NEXT statements. When these two statements are used to establish a loop, called a **For loop**.

The Do-While Loop Versus the For Loop

The two partial programs in Figure 8.1 illustrate the similarity between the use of the DO WHILE and LOOP statements and the FOR and NEXT statements. Both partial programs compute the sum of the integers from 1 to 100.

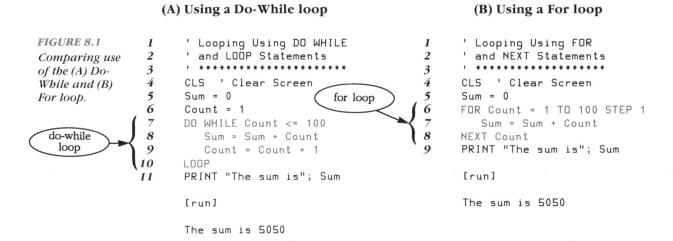

(A) Using a Do-While loop   **(B) Using a For loop**

FIGURE 8.1

Comparing use of the (A) Do-While and (B) For loop.

```
 1    ' Looping Using DO WHILE
 2    ' and LOOP Statements
 3    ' *********************
 4    CLS  ' Clear Screen
 5    Sum = 0
 6    Count = 1
 7    DO WHILE Count <= 100
 8        Sum = Sum + Count
 9        Count = Count + 1
10    LOOP
11    PRINT "The sum is"; Sum

[run]

The sum is 5050
```

```
 1    ' Looping Using FOR
 2    ' and NEXT Statements
 3    ' ******************
 4    CLS  ' Clear Screen
 5    Sum = 0
 6    FOR Count = 1 TO 100 STEP 1
 7        Sum = Sum + Count
 8    NEXT Count
 9    PRINT "The sum is"; Sum

[run]

The sum is 5050
```

The partial program in Figure 8.1A uses the DO WHILE and LOOP statements. Lines 5 and 6 initialize the running total (Sum) to 0 and the counter (Count) to 1. Line 7 tests to determine whether the value of Count is less than or equal to 100. If the condition is true, Sum is incremented by Count, and Count is incremented by 1 before control transfers back to line 7. When the condition in the DO WHILE statement is false, the PC terminates the loop, and line 11 displays the value of Sum.

The partial program in Figure 8.1B incorporates the FOR and NEXT statements to define the For loop (lines 6 through 8). Read through this partial program carefully and note how compact it is and how superior it is to the partial program in Figure 8.1A. Using a single FOR statement, as in line 6 of Figure 8.1B, we can consolidate the functions of lines 6, 7, and 9 of the partial program in Figure 8.1A.

As well as using less main storage and being easier to read than the one in Figure 8.1A, the For loop is also more efficient; it executes faster than the Do-While loop. In Chapter 9, we will illustrate performance difference between various versions of a For loop.

The Execution of a For Loop

The execution of the For loop in Figure 8.1B involves the following:

1. When the FOR statement is executed for the first time, the For loop becomes active, and Count is set equal to 1.
2. Count is compared to 100. Because it is less than or equal to 100, the statements in the For loop, in this case line 7, are executed.
3. Control returns to the FOR statement, where the value of Count is incremented by 1, the value that follows the keyword STEP.
4. If the value of Count is less than or equal to 100, execution of the For loop continues.

5. When the value of Count is greater than 100, control transfers to the statement (line 9) following the corresponding NEXT statement.

The general forms of the FOR and NEXT statements are given in Tables 8.1 and 8.2.

TABLE 8.1   The FOR Statement

General Form:	FOR k = initial value TO limit value STEP increment value
	or
	FOR k = initial value TO limit value
	where **k** is a simple numeric variable called the **loop variable**, and the **initial value**, **limit value**, and **increment value** are numeric expressions.
Purpose:	Causes the statements between the FOR and NEXT statements to be executed repeatedly until the value of k exceeds the limit value. When k exceeds the limit value, control transfers to the line immediately following the corresponding NEXT statement.
	If the increment value is negative, the test is reversed. The value of k is decremented each time through the loop, and the loop is executed until k is less than the limit value.
Examples:	``` FOR Item = 1 TO 20
FOR Amount = -5 TO 15 STEP 2
FOR Count = 10 TO -5 STEP -3
FOR Tax = 0 TO 10 STEP 0.1
FOR Total = Start TO Finish STEP Increment
FOR S = A + 5 TO C / D STEP F * B
FOR I = 20 TO 20
FOR J = 20 TO 1 ```
Note:	If the keyword STEP is not used, then the increment value defaults to 1.

TABLE 8.2   The NEXT Statement

General Form:	NEXT k
	where **k** is the same variable as the loop variable in the corresponding FOR statement.
Purpose:	Identifies the end of a For loop.
Examples:	``` NEXT Amount
NEXT Item ```

The terminology used to describe the FOR statement is shown in Figure 8.2.

FIGURE 8.2

The terminology used to describe the FOR *and* NEXT *statements.*

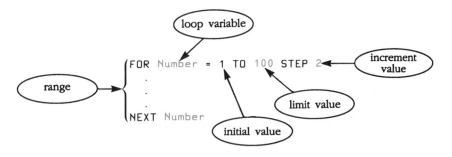

As shown in Figure 8.2, the **range** of a For loop is the set of repeatedly executed statements, beginning with the FOR statement and continuing up to and including the NEXT statement that has the same loop variable.

Flowchart Representation of a For Loop

The flowchart representation of a For loop is the Do-While structure (Figure 8.3). In the first process symbol, the loop variable is assigned the initial value. Next a test is made. If the condition is true, the loop is terminated, and control transfers to the statement that follows the NEXT statement.

If the condition is false, control passes into the body of the For loop. After the statements in the For loop are executed, the loop variable is incremented by the increment value, and control transfers back up to the decision symbol again to test whether the loop variable exceeds the limit value.

If the increment value is negative, the test is reversed. The value of the loop variable is decremented each time through the loop, and the loop is executed while the loop variable is equal to or greater than the limit value. Figure 8.4 illustrates the flowchart that corresponds to the partial program in Figure 8.1B.

FIGURE 8.3

General flow-chart representation of a For Loop.

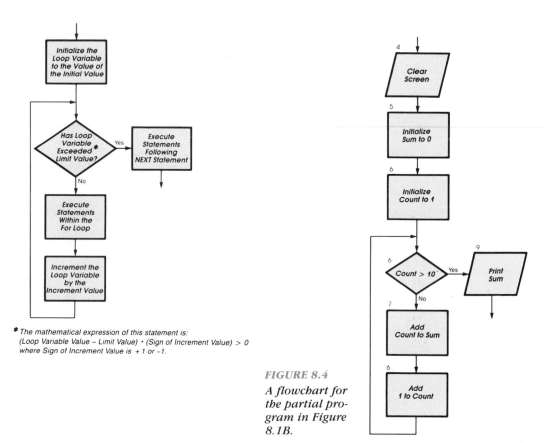

FIGURE 8.4

A flowchart for the partial program in Figure 8.1B.

Valid Values in the FOR Statement

The examples presented in Table 8.1 indicate that the initial, limit, and increment values of a FOR statement can take on a variety of representations. This section is divided into subsections that illustrate these representations.

Stepping by 1.   Many applications call for incrementing, or **stepping**, the loop variable by 1 each time the For loop is executed. You may write such a FOR statement as follows:

```
FOR Rate = 1 TO 12 STEP 1
```

or

```
FOR Rate = 1 TO 12
```

Subprogram B300.Determine.Amount includes a FOR statement without the STEP parameter. The subprogram receives a value called Principal and computes the amount of an investment (Amount), compounded annually, for whole number interest rates (Rate) between 1% and 12%, inclusive. Assume the value 500 is passed to Principal in Figure 8.5.

FIGURE 8.5

Using a For loop to determine various amounts.

```
1    ' Stepping by 1 in a FOR Statement
2    ' *********************************
3    SUB 300.DETERMINE.AMOUNT (Principal)
4       PRINT USING "Principal: #,###.##"; Principal
5       PRINT
6       PRINT "Rate          Amount"
7       D1$ = "##.#      ##,###.##"
8       FOR Rate = 1 TO 12
9          Amount = Principal * (1 + Rate / 100)
10         PRINT USING D1$; Rate, Amount
11      NEXT Rate
12      PRINT "Job Complete"
13   END SUB

[run]

Principal:  500.00

Rate          Amount
 1.0          505.00
 2.0          510.00
 3.0          515.00
 4.0          520.00
 5.0          525.00
 6.0          530.00
 7.0          535.00
 8.0          540.00
 9.0          545.00
10.0          550.00
11.0          555.00
12.0          560.00
Job Complete
```

Line 4 in the subprogram in Figure 8.5 displays the value of Principal, which is received from the calling program. Line 8 activates the For loop and assigns Rate a value of 1 (1%). Line 9 computes the amount of the investment, and line 10 displays the interest rate and amount. The loop variable Rate is incremented by 1, and the loop is executed repeatedly until Rate exceeds 12. When this occurs, control transfers to line 12.

As with Do-While loops, the statements between FOR and NEXT should be indented by three spaces for the purpose of readability. (See lines 9 and 10 in Figure 8.5.) This style allows you to scan a For loop quickly, and it simplifies the debugging effort.

Stepping by a Value Other Than 1.   Some applications call for the loop variable to be incremented by a value other than 1. If line 8 of Figure 8.5 is modified to

```
FOR Rate = 1 TO 12 STEP 3
```

the program computes the amount of an investment, compounded annually, for interest rates of 1%, 4%, 7%, and 10%. The loop terminates when the loop variable Rate becomes 13 because this is greater than the value of the limit.

Initializing the Loop Variable to a Value Other Than 1.   It is not necessary to initialize the loop variable to 1. If line 8 in Figure 8.5 is modified to

```
FOR Rate = 8 TO 16 STEP 2
```

the program generates a report that shows the even-valued interest rates between 8% and 16%, inclusive.

Some applications call for initializing the loop variable to zero or some negative value. For example, the statements

```
FOR Temp = 0 TO 10
```

or

```
FOR Temp = -6 TO 12
```

are both valid. The first example causes the For loop to execute 11 times. The second example causes the For loop to execute 19 times.

Decimal Fraction Values in a FOR Statement.   The values in a `FOR` statement can be decimal fraction numbers. If line 8 in Figure 8.5 is modified to

```
FOR Rate = 11.5 TO 12.5 STEP .1
```

the program computes the amount of an investment compounded annually for interest rates between 11.5% and 12.5%, inclusive, in increments of one-tenth of one percent.

Be careful with decimal fraction parameters because the PC cannot always store the exact binary representation of a decimal number. Stepping by a decimal fraction can, in some instances, result in one less or one more time through the For loop than you expect.

Negative Values in a FOR Statement.   The values in a `FOR` statement can be negative. If line 8 in Figure 8.5 is modified to

```
FOR Rate = 8 TO 0 STEP -1
```

the program generates a report in which the interest rates are decremented from 8% to 0%. The negative step value in the `FOR` statement causes the test to be reversed, and the loop variable is decremented until it is less than the limit value.

Variables in a FOR Statement.   The subprogram in Figure 8.6 shows the values in a `FOR` statement can be variables as well as numeric constants. Lines 4 through 7 display the initial, terminal, and increment values. Assume the following `CALL` statement called subprogram B340.Determine.Amount:

```
CALL B340.Determine.Amount (10, 12.5, .5, 3000)
```

FIGURE 8.6

Variable values in a FOR statement.

```
 1    ' Variable Values in a FOR Statement
 2    ' **********************************
 3    SUB B340.Determine.Amount (Rate1, Rate2, Increment, Principal)
 4       PRINT USING "Initial Rate:   ###.##%"; Rate1
 5       PRINT USING "Limit Rate:     ###.##%"; Rate2
 6       PRINT USING "Increment Rate: ###.##%"; Increment
 7       PRINT USING "Principal:    #,###.##"; Principal
 8       PRINT
 9       PRINT "Rate        Amount"
10       D1$ = "##.#      ##,###.##"
11       FOR Rate = Rate1 TO Rate2 STEP Increment
12          Amount = Principal * (1 + Rate / 100)
13          PRINT USING D1$; Rate; Amount
14       NEXT Rate
15       PRINT "Job Complete"
16    END SUB

      [run]
```

```
Initial Rate:      10.00%
Limit Rate:        12.50%
Increment Rate:     0.50%
Principal:      3,000.00

Rate          Amount
10.0          3,300.00
10.5          3,315.00
11.0          3,330.00
11.5          3,345.00
12.0          3,360.00
12.5          3,375.00
Job Complete
```

Be sure that the increment value is assigned a value other than zero. An increment value of zero creates an infinite loop, endless loop, and forces you to press Ctrl + Break to terminate further processing of the program on the PC.

Expressions as Values in a FOR Statement.   The values in a FOR statement may be complex numeric expressions. For example, the following FOR statements are valid:

```
FOR X = A * B TO S    T STEP C * 2
FOR Y = (A + B) / C TO P * (F - G)    C STEP 5 * V
```

If C is zero, what do you think happens in the two FOR statements above?

Redefining For Loop Values

Once the FOR statement is executed, the initial, limit, and increment values are set and cannot be altered while the For loop is active. QuickBASIC simply disregards any attempt to redefine them. For example, the following For loop executes ten times, even though the variables in the FOR statement are changed by lines 6 through 8:

```
1        Initial = 1
2        Limit = 10
3        Increment = 1
4        FOR Loop.Variable = Initial TO Limit STEP Increment
5            PRINT Loop.Variable, Initial, Limit, Increment
6            Initial = 5
7            Limit = 1
8            Increment = 4
9        NEXT Loop.Variable
```

does not change the values in the FOR statement → { 6 7 8

On the second pass, the values displayed for Initial, Limit, and Increment by line 5 are 5, 1, and 4. However, the initial, limit, and increment values in the FOR statement are assigned 1, 10, and 1, by lines 1 to 3, respectively.

Exiting a For Loop Prematurely — the EXIT Statement

There are certain looping situations that require a premature exit from the For loop. QuickBASIC includes the EXIT statement for terminating a For loop early. Consider the partial program in Figure 8.7 on the next page, which requests the user to enter five values for Amount, one each time through the For loop. If the user enters a value that is less than or equal to zero, the For loop terminates prematurely due to the EXIT FOR statement in line 8.

FIGURE 8.7

Use of the EXIT
FOR statement
to terminate a
For loop pre-
maturely.

```
1    ' Premature Exit from a For Loop
2    ' ******************************
3    Total.Amount = 0
4    FOR Loop.Variable = 1 TO 5
5       INPUT "Amount value"; Amount
6       IF Amount <= 0 THEN
7          PRINT "Amount <= 0 ...Program terminating"
8          EXIT FOR
9       END IF
10      Total.Amount = Total.Amount + Amount
11   NEXT Loop.Variable
12   PRINT : PRINT "Value of Loop.Variable is"; Loop.Variable

[run]

Amount value? 23
Amount value? 12
Amount value? -6
Amount <= 0 ...Program terminating

Value of Loop.Variable is 3
```

When the partial program in Figure 8.7 executes, the condition in the IF statement in line 6 is false for the first two Amount values, 23 and 12. When the user enters the third value (–6), the condition in line 6 is true, and the diagnostic message displays due to line 7. Next, line 8 causes the PC to exit the For loop and continue execution with the PRINT statement in line 12. This is called a **premature exit** from the For loop. Note that when the PC exits the For loop, the value of the loop variable is available for further processing, as shown by the last output line displayed due to line 12.

The general form of the EXIT statement is given in Table 8.3.

TABLE 8.3   The EXIT Statement

General Form: EXIT statement
where statement is FOR, DO, DEF, FUNCTION, SUB.

Purpose: Exit a For or Do loop, function, or subprogram prematurely.

Examples: EXIT FOR
EXIT DO

Rules that summarize the FOR statement are listed below.

FOR RULE 1   *If the increment value following the keyword* STEP *is positive, or if the keyword* STEP *is not used, then the PC executes the For loop while the loop variable is less than or equal to the limit value. If the increment value is negative, the test is reversed. The value of the loop variable is decremented each time through the loop, and the loop is executed until the loop variable is less than the limit value.*

FOR RULE 2   *The value of the increment value must not be zero.*

FOR RULE 3   *A valid initial entry into a For loop can be accomplished only by transferring control to the* FOR *statement.*

FOR RULE 4 *A normal exit from a For loop leaves the current value of the loop variable equal to its value the last time the NEXT statement was executed plus the increment value.*

FOR RULE 5 *A premature exit from a For loop leaves the current value of the loop variable equal to its value the last time the NEXT statement was executed.*

FOR RULE 6 *Statements located in the range of a For loop cannot change the initial, limit, and increment values.*

Iterations in a For Loop

The number of **iterations**, or repetitions, specified by a FOR statement may be computed with the following formula:

$$\text{No. of Iterations} = \frac{\text{Limit value} - \text{Initial value}}{\text{Increment value}} + 1$$

where the ratio is performed in integer arithmetic so that the quotient is truncated to the next lowest integer.

How many iterations are performed by a For loop with the following FOR statement?

```
FOR TEMP = -73 TO 987 STEP 7
```

Using the formula, the number of iterations is

$$\frac{987 - (-73)}{7} + 1 = 151 + 1 = 152$$

Note that the initial quotient was 151.42, but the decimal fraction 0.42 was truncated.

Another Look at the For Loop

The For loop in QuickBASIC corresponds to a Do-While structure. (See Figure 8.3 on page 268.) The test for whether the value of the loop variable exceeds the limit value is carried out at the beginning of the loop. This means that the body of the For loop will not be executed if the initial value is greater than the limit value.

For example, in the following partial program, when the FOR statement is encountered, control immediately transfers to the line below the NEXT statement. The For loop is executed zero times, and the loop variable is equal to the initial value.

```
Count = 0
FOR I = 10 TO 1 STEP 2
   Count = Count + 1
NEXT I
PRINT "The loop variable is equal to"; I
PRINT "The For loop is executed"; Count; "times"

[run]

The loop variable is equal to 10
The For loop is executed 0 times
```

On the other hand, if the increment value is −2 in the FOR statement, the loop variable is equal to 0 when the For loop is deactivated, and the For loop is executed five times.

Re-examine Figure 8.3 and note that the mathematical expression used to terminate the looping in a For loop is

(Loop Variable Value – Limit Value) * (Sign of Increment Value) > 0

where the sign of the increment value is either +1 or –1.

Nested For Loops

Just as there are nested expressions and nested subroutines in QuickBASIC, there are nested For loops. When the statements of one For loop lie within the range of another For loop, the loops are said to be **nested**, or **embedded**. Furthermore, the outer For loop may be nested in the range of still another For loop, and so on.

The partial program in Figure 8.8 utilizes two nested For loops. The inner For loop, formed by lines 5 through 7, is written so that all the statements in its range also lie within the range of the outer For loop, lines 3 through 9.

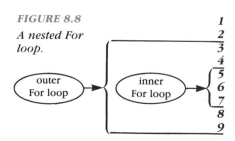

FIGURE 8.8

A nested For loop.

```
1    ' Nested For Loops
2    ' ****************
3    FOR X = 1 TO 4
4        PRINT "OUTER LOOP ---- X ="; X
5        FOR Y = 1 TO 3
6            PRINT "    Inner Loop - X ="; X; "AND Y ="; Y
7        NEXT Y
8        PRINT
9    NEXT X

[run]

OUTER LOOP ---- X = 1
    Inner Loop - X = 1 AND Y = 1
    Inner Loop - X = 1 AND Y = 2
    Inner Loop - X = 1 AND Y = 3

OUTER LOOP ---- X = 2
    Inner Loop - X = 2 AND Y = 1
    Inner Loop - X = 2 AND Y = 2
    Inner Loop - X = 2 AND Y = 3

OUTER LOOP ---- X = 3
    Inner Loop - X = 3 AND Y = 1
    Inner Loop - X = 3 AND Y = 2
    Inner Loop - X = 3 AND Y = 3

OUTER LOOP ---- X = 4
    Inner Loop - X = 4 AND Y = 1
    Inner Loop - X = 4 AND Y = 2
    Inner Loop - X = 4 AND Y = 3
```

When line 3 is executed in the partial program in Figure 8.8, the outer For loop becomes active. The loop variable X is set to 1, and line 4 displays that value. When line 5 is executed, the inner For loop becomes active. The loop variable Y is set to 1, and line 6 displays the values of both X and Y. With X equal to 1, control remains within the inner loop, which is executed three times, until Y exceeds 3. At this point, the inner loop is satisfied, and control passes to the outer For loop, which executes line 8.

Control then passes back to line 3, where the loop variable X is incremented by 1 to become 2. After line 4 displays the new value of X, line 5 is executed, and the inner For loop becomes active again. The loop variable Y is initialized to 1, and the process repeats itself.

When the outer loop is satisfied, control passes to line 10. In Figure 8.8, the outer For loop executes a total of four times, and the inner For loop executes a total of 3 * 4, or 12, times.

As another example of a program with nested For loops, consider the partial program in Figure 8.9, which generates the multiplication table. Each time the loop variable in the outer For loop (lines 6 through 12) is assigned a new value, the inner For loop (lines 8 through 10) computes and displays one row of the table. The two loop variables, Row and Column, are multiplied together in line 9 to form the various products in the multiplication table.

FIGURE 8.9

Generating the multiplication table using a nested For loop.

```
1    ' Generating the Multiplication Table
2    ' ************************************
3    CLS  ' Clear Screen
4    PRINT "  ×  !   0   1   2   3   4   5   6   7   8   9  10  11  12"
5    PRINT "-----+--------------------------------------------------"
6    FOR Row = 0 TO 12
7       PRINT USING "###  _!"; Row;
8       FOR Column = 0 TO 12
9          PRINT USING "####"; Row * Column;
10      NEXT Column
11      PRINT
12   NEXT Row
13   PRINT
14   PRINT "End of Multiplication Table"
```

[run]

× !	0	1	2	3	4	5	6	7	8	9	10	11	12
0 !	0	0	0	0	0	0	0	0	0	0	0	0	0
1 !	0	1	2	3	4	5	6	7	8	9	10	11	12
2 !	0	2	4	6	8	10	12	14	16	18	20	22	24
3 !	0	3	6	9	12	15	18	21	24	27	30	33	36
4 !	0	4	8	12	16	20	24	28	32	36	40	44	48
5 !	0	5	10	15	20	25	30	35	40	45	50	55	60
6 !	0	6	12	18	24	30	36	42	48	54	60	66	72
7 !	0	7	14	21	28	35	42	49	56	63	70	77	84
8 !	0	8	16	24	32	40	48	56	64	72	80	88	96
9 !	0	9	18	27	36	45	54	63	72	81	90	99	108
10 !	0	10	20	30	40	50	60	70	80	90	100	110	120
11 !	0	11	22	33	44	55	66	77	88	99	110	121	132
12 !	0	12	24	36	48	60	72	84	96	108	120	132	144

End of Multiplication Table

The PRINT statements in lines 7 and 9 end with the semicolon separator. Recall from Chapter 3 that when a PRINT statement ends with a semicolon, the cursor remains on the same line. Each time the inner loop is satisfied, the null PRINT statement in line 11 moves the cursor to the beginning of the next line.

Valid Nesting of For Loops

When nesting occurs, all statements in the range of the inner For loop also must be in the range of the outer For loop. QuickBASIC does not allow the range of an inner For loop to extend past the end of the range of an outer For loop. If this type of error occurs, QuickBASIC displays a dialog box with the diagnostic message NEXT without FOR.

When one For loop is nested within another, the name of the loop variable for each For loop must be different. Figure 8.10 illustrates valid and invalid nesting of For loops.

FIGURE 8.10

Valid and invalid nesting of For loops.

The usefulness of the FOR and NEXT statements for looping purposes should be apparent from the examples and illustrations presented so far. However, you will see an even greater use for them in applications involving the manipulation of arrays, which are discussed in the following sections of this chapter. The material in this section can be summarized in the following rules:

> **FOR RULE 7**   *If the range of a For loop includes another For loop, all statements in the range of the inner For loop also must be within the range of the outer For loop.*

> **FOR RULE 8**   *When one For loop is within another, the name of the loop variable for each For loop must be different.*

8.3   ARRAYS VERSUS SIMPLE VARIABLES

Arrays permit a programmer to represent many values with one variable name. The variable name assigned to represent an array is called the **array name**. The elements in the array are distinguished from one another by subscripts. In QuickBASIC, the subscript is written inside a set of parentheses and is placed immediately to the right of the array name. Recall from Chapter 3, page 63, that QuickBASIC allows two different types of variables: simple and subscripted. While simple variables are used to store and reference values that are independent of one another, subscripted variables are used to store and reference values that have been grouped into an array.

Consider the problem of writing a program that is to manipulate the 12 monthly sales for a company and generate a year-end report. Figure 8.11 illustrates the difference between using an array to store the 12 monthly sales and using simple variables.

FIGURE 8.11

Utilizing an array (A) versus simple variables (B).

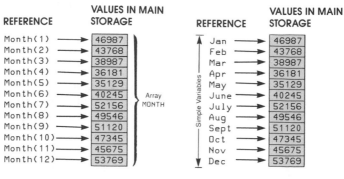

(A) Storing monthly sales in the array Month.

(B) Storing monthly sales in simple variables.

The monthly sales stored in an array require the same storage allocation as the sales represented as independent variables. The difference lies in the programming techniques that can access the different values. For example, the programmer may assign the values of simple variables in a READ statement in this manner:

```
READ Jan, Feb, Mar, Apr, May, June, July, Aug, Sept, Oct, Nov, Dec
```

Each simple variable must explicitly appear in a LET or PRINT statement if the monthly sales are to be summed or displayed. Not only will the programming consume time, but also the variables *must* be properly placed in the program.

The same function can be accomplished by entering all 12 values into the array Month:

```
FOR Number = 1 TO 12
    READ Month(Number)
NEXT Number
```

In the FOR statement, Number is initialized to 1. The READ statement assigns the first value in the data holding area to Month(1) and is read as "Month sub 1". Then Number is incremented to 2, and the next value is assigned to Month(2). This continues until Month(12) is assigned to the twelfth value in the data holding area.

Month2 and Month(2) are different from each other. Month2 is a simple variable, no different from Sale, Increment, Digit, or Cost. Whereas, Month(2) is the second element in the array Month, and the manner in which it is called upon in a program differs from the fashion in which a simple variable is called.

8.4 DECLARING ARRAYS

Before arrays can be used, the amount of main storage to be reserved must be declared in the program. This is the purpose of the DIM statement. The keyword DIM is an abbreviation of **dimension**. The DIM statement also declares the **lower-bound value** and **upper-bound value** of the subscript. The upper- and lower-bound values define the **range** of permissible values to which a subscript may be assigned.

The DIM Statement

The main function of the DIM statement is to declare to the PC the necessary information about the allocation of storage locations for arrays used in a program. Good programming practice dictates that every program that utilizes array elements should have a DIM statement that properly defines the arrays.

The general forms of the DIM statement are given in Table 8.4 on the next page.

In Table 8.4, Example 1 reserves storage for a one-dimensional numeric array Balance, which consists of five elements, or storage locations. These elements — Balance(0), Balance(1), Balance(2), Balance(3), and Balance(4) — can be used in a program in much the same way as a simple variable can be used. For this DIM statement, elements Balance(5), Balance(6), and Balance(−4) are considered not valid.

Example 2 in Table 8.4 establishes a one-dimensional array named Code$. Code$ has eight elements — Code$(1), Code$(2), Code$(3), Code$(4), Code$(5), Code$(6), Code$(7), and Code$(8). In this DIM statement, both the lower-bound value (1) and the upper-bound value (8) are specified using the keyword TO.

Example 3 declares two one-dimensional arrays, Pick and Job$, and one two-dimensional array, Time. The DIM statement reserves storage locations for 10 elements for the array Pick, which has negative lower and upper bounds; 201 elements for the array Job$, and 400 elements for the array Time.

The fourth example in Table 8.4 declares three arrays. The first array, Cost, is a one-dimensional array consisting of a negative lower bound and 51 elements. The last two, K$ and Amount, are three-dimensional arrays. Multidimensional arrays, such as K$ and Amount, are discussed in Section 8.6.

TABLE 8.4   The DIM Statement

General Form: DIM [SHARED] array name(size) ..., array name(size)

or

DIM [SHARED] array name(lb_1 TO ub_1), ..., array name(lb_1 TO ub_1, ..., lb_n TO ub_n)

where SHARED is an optional attribute that instructs QuickBASIC to share the arrays in the list with all subprograms,

array name represents a numeric or string variable name,

size in the first general form defines the upper-bound value of each subscript of the array.

Size may be a positive integer or numeric variable for one-dimensional arrays. Size may be a series of positive integers or a series of numeric variables separated by commas for multidimensional arrays.

In the second general form, **lb_n** may be a positive or negative integer or numeric variable that serves as the lower-bound value of the array, and **ub_n** may be a positive or negative integer or numeric variable that serves as the upper-bound value.

Purpose: To reserve storage locations for arrays.

Examples:
1. DIM Balance(4)
2. DIM SHARED Code$(1 TO 8)
3. DIM Pick(-10 TO -1), Job$(200), Time(1 TO 20, 1 TO 20)
4. DIM SHARED Cost(-5 TO 45), K$(X TO 50, Y, Z), Amount(2, 1 TO 75, 7)

Notes:
1. In the first general form, the lower bound of each dimension is 0, unless you include an OPTION BASE statement.
2. In QuickBASIC, the maximum number of dimensions is 60.
3. The DIM statement can declare the type of array (that is, integer, single precision, etc.). For additional information, load QuickBASIC, press Shift + F1, select the hyperlink Index, and select the keyword DIM.

If you plan to use the SHARED attribute in the DIM statement to share the arrays between subprograms, then place the DIM SHARED statement in the Main Program immediately below the COMMON SHARED statements. If you plan to share the arrays using some other method of passing values, then place the DIM statement in the Initializion module. In any case, follow this rule:

DIM RULE 1   *The DIM statement can be located anywhere before the first use of an array element in a program.*

A single DIM statement will be sufficient for most programs in this chapter. If four different arrays are to be declared, all four arrays can be listed in the same DIM statement as follows:

a

```
DIM X(1 TO 20), Code(15 TO 28), Temp(Row, Column, Plane), Desc$(25)
```

Four separate DIM statements can also be used in the program to declare the arrays individually:

```
DIM X(1 TO 20)
DIM Code(15 TO 28)
DIM Temp(Row, Column, Plane)
DIM Desc$(25)
```

The OPTION BASE Statement

When only the upper bound is specified, QuickBASIC allocates the zero element for each one-dimensional array. For two-dimensional arrays, an extra row — the zero row — and an extra column — the zero column — are reserved. Thus,

```
DIM SHARED Month(12), Time(20, 20)
```

actually reserves 13 elements for the array Month and 21 rows and 21 columns or 441 elements for the array Time. The extra array element is Month(0) for the array Month, and the extra row and column is the 0th (read "zeroth") row and the 0th column for the array Time. Although an additional element, row, or column will not present a problem to your program, the OPTION BASE statement allows you to control the lower bound of arrays that are declared when you specify only the upper-bound value in a DIM statement.

An alternative to using the OPTION BASE statement is to use the TO option in the DIM statement and specify both the upper- and lower-bound values for each array.

The general form of the OPTION BASE statement is found in Table 8.5.

TABLE 8.5   The OPTION BASE Statement

General Form:	OPTION BASE n where **n** is either 0 or 1.
Purpose:	To assign a lower bound of 0 or 1 to all arrays in a program.
Examples:	OPTION BASE 0 OPTION BASE 1
Note:	If the OPTION BASE statement is not used, the lower-bound value is set to zero for all arrays declared with only an upper-bound value.

When considering the placement of an OPTION BASE statement in a program, the following rules can be stated:

OPTION BASE RULE 1   *The OPTION BASE statement can be used only once in a program, and it must precede any DIM statement in a program.*

OPTION BASE RULE 2   *The OPTION BASE statement affects only dimensions within arrays that are declared without a lower-bound value.*

Dynamic Allocation of Arrays

Some applications call for dynamically dimensioned arrays. A **dynamically dimensioned array** is one that has a variable or expression, rather than a constant, as the lower bound or upper bound. For example, a program may manipulate 60 elements of a one-dimensional array during one run, 100 elements the next time, and so on. Rather than modify the value of the size of a `DIM` statement each time the number of elements changes, QuickBASIC permits the size of an array in a `DIM` statement to be written as a simple variable, as in

```
DIM Code(Size)
```

This `DIM` statement reserves a variable number of elements for the one-dimensional array Code.

Usually an `INPUT` or `READ` statement is used before the `DIM` statement to assign a value to the variable used to determine the size of the array. Once Size is assigned a value, the `DIM` statement allocates the actual number of elements to the array Code. Any `FOR` statements involved in the manipulation of the array must contain as their limit value the same simple variable Size.

Variables may also be used as the lower- and upper-bound values for an array dimensioned using the keyword `TO`. For example, the following `DIM` statement is valid:

```
DIM Code(Lower TO Upper)
```

Here again, the variables Lower and Upper must be assigned values prior to the execution of the `DIM` statement.

In this book, when a variable is used as the size in a `DIM` statement, it will be placed in the Initialization module and the arrays will be passed through the `COMMON SHARED` statement. This way the `READ` or `INPUT` statement that assigns the variable a value is not in the Main Program. (See Program 8.2 for an example of a dynamically dimensioned array.)

8.5   MANIPULATING ARRAYS

In this section, several sample programs that manipulate the elements of arrays will be discussed. Before the programs are presented, however, it is important that you understand the syntax and limitations of subscripts.

Subscripts

As indicated in Section 8.3, the elements of an array are referenced by assigning a subscript to the array name. The subscript is written within parentheses and is placed immediately to the right of the array name. The subscript may be any valid number, variable, or numeric expression within the range of the array. This leads to the following rule:

 **DIM RULE 2**   *Subscripts must be within the lower and upper bounds of an array.*

If an array Tax is declared as

```
DIM SHARED Tax(1 TO 50)
```

it is invalid to reference Tax(−3), Tax(51), or any others that are outside the lower and upper bounds of the array.

Noninteger subscripts are rounded to the nearest integer to determine the element to be manipulated. Table 8.6 illustrates some additional examples of subscripts.

TABLE 8.6 Examples of Subscripts

ARRAY REFERENCE	COMMENT
Tax(1)	Valid, provided 1 is within the range of the array.
Tax(-3)	Valid, provided –3 is within the range of the array.
Tax(X + Y)	Valid, provided X + Y is within the range of the array.
Tax(-X)	Valid, provided –X is within the range of the array.
Tax(12.7)	Valid, provided the array has been declared with an upper bound of at least 13.
Tax(0)	Valid, provided the zero element exists.
Tax(Cost(2))	Valid, provided Cost(2) is within the range of the array. Subscripted subscripts are allowed to any valid dimension level in QuickBASIC.
Tax(X(2, 3), Y(1, 3))	Valid, provided X(2, 3) and Y(1, 3) are within the range of the array.
Tax(X + Y/3 + 5^X)	Valid, provided $X + Y / 3 + 5 ^ X$ is within the range of the array.

You must decide which variables will be subscripted in any program and then use them consistently throughout the program. For example, if the array element is Month(Number), the subscript Number should not be dropped to form the name Month, and the subscript Number should not be replaced by multiple subscripts to form Months(Number1, Number2) in the same program. On the PC, either of these two actions would cause the program to halt and display a dialog box with a diagnostic message indicating the type of error.

The partial program in Figure 8.12 reads data into an array and then displays the value of each element in the array.

FIGURE 8.12

Declaring, loading, and printing the elements of an array.

```
1    ' Monthly Sales Analysis I
2    ' ************************
3    DIM Month(1 TO 12)
4    CLS   ' Clear Screen
5    ' ****** Read Monthly Sales Into Month ******
6    FOR Number = 1 TO 12
7       READ Month(Number)
8    NEXT Number
9    ' ********** Display Monthly Sales **********
10   FOR Number = 1 TO 12
11      PRINT Month(Number),
12   NEXT Number
13   ' ************** Data Follows **************
14   DATA 46987, 43768, 38987, 36181, 35129, 40245
15   DATA 52156, 49546, 51120, 47345, 45675, 53769

[run]

     46987         43768         38987     36181       35129
     40245         52156         49546     51120       47345
     45675         53769
```

In Figure 8.12, line 3 reserves 12 elements or storage locations for the array Month. Valid subscripts for Month range from 1 to 12. Line 6 activates the first For loop and assigns Number a value of 1. Line 7 reads the first data item, 46987, from the data holding area and assigns it to Month(1). Number is incremented to 2, and line 8 returns control to the FOR statement in line 6. The READ statement in line 7 then assigns the second data item to Month(2). This loop continues until Month(12) is assigned the twelfth data item, 53769.

Line 10 activates the second For loop and resets Number to 1. This For loop then proceeds to display the values assigned to the array Month, as shown.

Summing the Elements of an Array

FIGURE 8.13

Summing the elements of an array.

Many applications call for summing the elements of an array. In the partial program in Figure 8.13, the monthly sales are summed; an average is computed; and the sales are displayed, four to a line.

```
1    ' Monthly Sales Analysis II
2    ' ************************
3    DIM Month(1 TO 12)
4    CLS  ' Clear Screen
5    Total.Sales = 0
6    ' ****** Read Monthly Sales Into Month and Sum Monthly Sales ******
7    FOR Number = 1 TO 12
8       READ Month(Number)
9       Total.Sales = Total.Sales + Month(Number)
10   NEXT Number
11   ' ************ Compute and Display Average Monthly Sales ************
12   Avg.Sales = Total.Sales / 12
13   PRINT USING "The average of the monthly sales is $$##,###.##"; Avg.Sales
14   PRINT
15   ' ****************** Display Monthly Sales **********************
16   FOR Number = 1 TO 12 STEP 4
17      PRINT Month(Number), Month(Number + 1), Month(Number + 2), Month(Number + 3)
18   NEXT Number
19   PRINT
20   PRINT "Job Complete"
21   ' ********************** Data Follows **********************
22   DATA 46987, 43768, 38987, 36181, 35129, 40245
23   DATA 52156, 49546, 51120, 47345, 45675, 53769
24   END

[run]

The average of the monthly sales is   $45,075.67

    46987         43768         38987         36181
    35129         40245         52156         49546
    51120         47345         45675         53769

Job Complete
```

In Figure 8.13, line 9 is used to sum the values of the array elements. For example, when line 7 activates the For loop, Number is assigned the value of 1. Line 8 reads the first data item, 46987, and assigns it to Month(1). Line 9 increments Total.Sales by Month(1). Number is incremented to 2, and line 10 returns control to the FOR statement in line 7.

After the READ statement, Total.Sales is assigned the sum of Total.Sales and Month(2). This process continues until the twelfth element is added to the sum of the first 11 elements of the array Month. Line 12 computes the average, and line 13 displays it.

The For loop found in lines 16 through 18 displays the monthly sales, four to a line. The first time through the loop, Number is equal to 1; and Month(1), Month(2), Month(3), and Month(4) display on one line. The next time through the loop, Number is equal to 5; and Month(5), Month(6), Month(7), and Month(8) display on the next line. Finally, Number is set equal to 9; and Month(9), Month(10), Month(11), and Month(12) display on the third line. The subscripts in line 17 are in the form of numeric expressions.

Programming Case Study 12 | Analysis of Monthly Sales

The following programming case study illustrates the use of parallel arrays and the selection of elements that meet a certain criterion. **Parallel arrays** are two or more arrays that have corresponding elements. This case study also shows how arrays may be used to store data is used many times during the execution of a program.

Problem

Ray's Roofing Company has stored the past year's monthly sales on a diskette in a sequential file called MONTHSAL.DAT. The file is made up of 12 records as shown below:

"January",46987	"May",35129	"September",51120
"February",43768	"June",40245	"October",47345
"March",38987	"July",52156	"November",45675
"April",36181	"August",49546	"December",53769

The company would like to have a program that displays annual sales information. The following is to be included in the report:

1. The average monthly sales for the previous year
2. A list of the months in which the sales exceeded the average monthly sales (Include the sales figures for these months and their deviation from the average sales.)
3. The month name with the greatest sales and the month name with the least sales (Assume that no two months have equal monthly sales.)

A partial top-down chart, showing the first level of decomposition, and a flowchart for each subtask are illustrated in Figure 8.14 on the next page. The program tasks that correspond to the top-down chart, a program solution, and a discussion of the program solution follow.

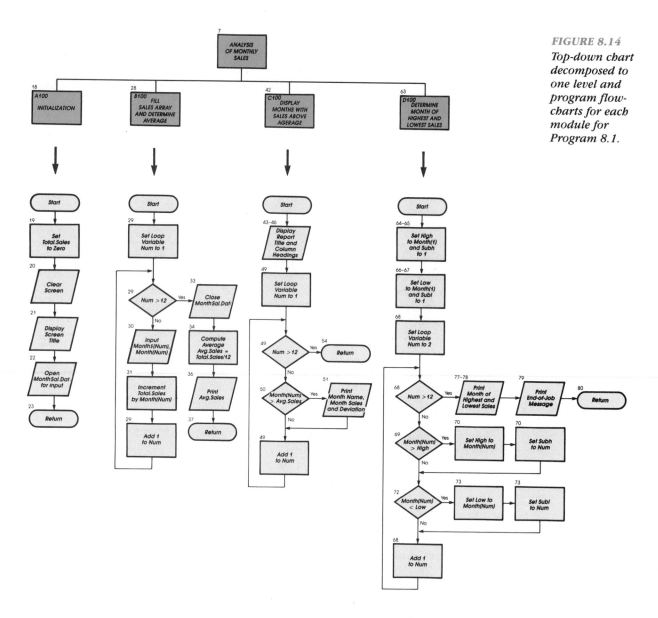

Program Tasks

The following program tasks correspond to the top-down chart in Figure 8.14.

1. Main Program

   a. Use the COMMON SHARED statement to pass simple variables between subprograms.

   b. Use the DIM SHARED statement to dimension two parallel arrays, Month$ and Month, to 12 elements (1 to 12). Use the array Month$ to store the 12 month names and the array Month to store the 12 monthly sales.

   c. Call subordinate subprograms.

2. A100.Initialization

   a. Initialize a running total (Total.Sales) to zero. Use Total.Sales to sum the 12 monthly sales.

   b. Clear the screen and display a screen title.

   c. Open the sequential data file MONTHSAL.DAT for input as filenumber 1.

3. B100.Fill.Sales.Array.and.Determine.Avg

   a. Use a For loop with an initial value of 1 and a limit value of 12 to read the 12 month names and corresponding sales into the parallel arrays Month$ and Month. Within the loop, increment Total.Sales by each monthly sales.

   b. Close the MONTHSAL.DAT file.

   c. Determine the average monthly sales (Avg.Sales) by dividing Total.Sales by 12.

   d. Display the average monthly sales.

4. C100.Display.Months.With.Sales.Above.Avg

   a. Display report title and column headings.

   b. With an initial value of 1 and limit value of 12, use a For loop to test each month's sales against the average monthly sales. If the month's sales are greater than the average monthly sales, display the month name, the month's sales, and deviation of the month's sales from the average monthly sales.

5. D100.Determine.High.and.Low.Sales

   a. Assume that the first month has the highest and lowest sales.

      (1) Set the variable High to the first month's sales. Initialize the variable Subh to the value 1. Subh is used later as a subscript to access the month name with the greatest sales.

      (2) Set the variable Low to the first month's sales. Initialize the variable Subl to the value 1. Subl is used later as a subscript to access the month name with the least sales.

   b. Use a For loop with an initial value 2 and limit value 12 to test the sales of the second through twelfth months against the value of the variable High. If a month's sales are greater than the value of High, assign the month's sales to High and the value of the loop variable (Num) to Subh. Also include within the For loop a test in which the month's sales are compared against the value of Low. If the month's sales are less than the value of Low, assign the month's sales to Low and the value of the loop variable (Num) to Subl.

   c. Display the month with the greatest sales — Month$(Subh).

   d. Display the month with the least sales — Month$(Subl).

Program Solution

Program 8.1 corresponds to the previously defined tasks and to the top-down chart in Figure 8.14.

PROGRAM 8.1

```
1    ' Program 8.1
2    ' Analysis of Monthly Sales
3    ' Input File Name = MONTHSAL.DAT
4    ' *************************************************************
5    ' *                        Main Program                       *
6    ' *************************************************************
7    COMMON SHARED Total.Sales, Avg.Sales
8    DIM SHARED Month$(1 TO 12), Month(1 TO 12)
9    CALL A100.Initialization
10   CALL B100.Fill.Sales.Array.and.Determine.Avg
11   CALL C100.Display.Months.With.Sales.Above.Avg
12   CALL D100.Determine.High.and.Low.Sales
13   END
14
```

declares and shares arrays between all subprograms

(continued)

```
15    ' *************************************************************
16    ' *                      Initialization                       *
17    ' *************************************************************
18    SUB A100.Initialization
19       Total.Sales = 0
20       CLS   ' Clear Screen
21       LOCATE 1, 8: PRINT "Analysis of Monthly Sales"
22       OPEN "MONTHSAL.DAT" FOR INPUT AS #1
23    END SUB
24
25    ' *************************************************************
26    ' *          Fill Sales Array and Determine Average           *
27    ' *************************************************************
28    SUB B100.Fill.Sales.Array.and.Determine.Avg
29       FOR Num = 1 TO 12
30          INPUT #1, Month$(Num), Month(Num)
31          Total.Sales = Total.Sales + Month(Num)
32       NEXT Num
33       CLOSE #1
34       Avg.Sales = Total.Sales / 12
35       LOCATE 3, 1
36       PRINT USING "The average monthly sales is $$##,###.##"; Avg.Sales
37    END SUB
38
39    ' *************************************************************
40    ' *          Display Months with Sales Above Average          *
41    ' *************************************************************
42    SUB C100.Display.Months.With.Sales.Above.Avg
43       LOCATE 6, 1
44       PRINT "Months in Which Sales Are Above Average"
45       PRINT
46       PRINT "Month              Sales            Deviation"
47       PRINT
48       D1$ = "\              \      ##,###.##            ##,###.##"
49       FOR Num = 1 TO 12
50          IF Month(Num) > Avg.Sales THEN
51             PRINT USING D1$; Month$(Num); Month(Num); Month(Num) - Avg.Sales
52          END IF
53       NEXT Num
54    END SUB
55
56    ' *************************************************************
57    ' *         Determine Month of Highest and Lowest Sales       *
58    ' *                                                           *
59    ' * Assume First Month has the Highest and Lowest Sales       *
60    ' * Subh = Subscript of Highest Sales, High = Highest Sales   *
61    ' * Subl = Subscript of Lowest Sales,  Low  = Lowest Sales    *
62    ' *************************************************************
63    SUB D100.Determine.High.and.Low.Sales
64       High = Month(1)
65       Subh = 1
66       Low = Month(1)
67       Subl = 1
68       FOR Num = 2 TO 12
69          IF Month(Num) > High THEN
70             High = Month(Num): Subh = Num
71          END IF
72          IF Month(Num) < Low THEN
73             Low = Month(Num): Subl = Num
74          END IF
75       NEXT Num
76       PRINT
77       PRINT "Month of Highest Sales - "; Month$(Subh)
78       PRINT "Month of Lowest Sales  - "; Month$(Subl)
79       PRINT : PRINT "Job Complete"
80    END SUB

      [run]
```

FIGURE 8.15

The display due to the execution of Program 8.1.

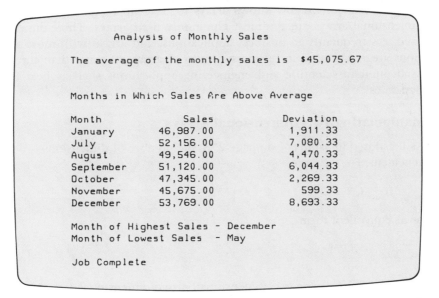

```
              Analysis of Monthly Sales

   The average of the monthly sales is  $45,075.67


   Months in Which Sales Are Above Average

   Month           Sales           Deviation
   January         46,987.00        1,911.33
   July            52,156.00        7,080.33
   August          49,546.00        4,470.33
   September       51,120.00        6,044.33
   October         47,345.00        2,269.33
   November        45,675.00          599.33
   December        53,769.00        8,693.33

   Month of Highest Sales - December
   Month of Lowest Sales  - May

   Job Complete
```

Discussion of the Program Solution

In Program 8.1, the arrays Month$ and Month are declared in the Main Program by the DIM SHARED statement in line 8. The DIM SHARED statement shares the arrays between the Main Program and all subprograms. The B100.Fill.Sales.Array.and.Determine.Avg subprogram is similar to the partial program in Figure 8.13. The For loop (lines 29 through 32) loads the two arrays with values and sums the monthly sales. Line 33 closes MONTHSAL.DAT. At this point, the entire file is loaded into the parallel arrays Month$ and Month. Line 34 computes the average; line 36 displays the average monthly sales (Figure 8.15).

The For loop, lines 49 through 53, tests each of the monthly sales found in the array Month against the average monthly sales, Avg.Sales. If the value of an element in the array is greater than the average, then the PC is instructed to display the corresponding month name, the monthly sales, and the monthly sales deviation from the average—Month(Num) - Avg.Sales.

In the last subprogram of Program 8.1, lines 64 through 78 illustrate a technique that determines and displays the month in which the sales are the highest and the month in which the sales are the lowest. In lines 64 through 67, the first month's sales are assumed to be the highest as well as the lowest. The For loop, lines 68 through 75, tests the remaining months against the highest sales (line 69) and the lowest sales (line 72).

If a month's sales—Month(Num)—are greater than the current highest sales (High), the month's sales are assigned as the current highest sales, and the variable Subh is assigned the value of the subscript Num. When the For loop is satisfied, Subh is the subscript that represents the element in the array Month that has the highest sales. Subl is the subscript that represents the element in the array Month that has the lowest sales. Because Month$ and Month are parallel arrays, the corresponding month with the highest and lowest sales can be obtained by referencing Month$(Subh) and Month$(Subl).

8.6 MULTIDIMENSIONAL ARRAYS

The dimension of an array is the number of subscripts required to reference an element in an array. Up to now, all the arrays were one dimensional, and an element was referenced by an integer, a variable, or a single expression in the parentheses following the array name. QuickBASIC allows arrays to have up to 60 dimensions. One- and two-dimensional arrays are the most commonly used arrays. Three-dimensional arrays are used less frequently in business applications, and arrays with more than three dimensions are rarely used in business. However, arrays of more than three dimensions are used often in scientific and engineering applications such as heat transfer and fluid dynamics.

Manipulating Two-Dimensional Arrays

As illustrated in Table 8.4 on page 278, the number of dimensions is declared in the `DIM` statement. For example,

```
DIM SHARED Cost(1 TO 2, 1 TO 5)
```

or its equivalent form

```
OPTION BASE 1
DIM SHARED Cost(2, 5)
```

declares an array to be two dimensional. A two-dimensional array usually takes the form of a table. The first subscript tells how many rows there are, and the second subscript tells how many columns. Figure 8.16 shows a 2 × 5 array (read "2 by 5 array"). Cost(1, 1) is read as "Cost sub one one" and references the element found in the first row and first column.

FIGURE 8.16

Conceptual view of the storage locations reserved for a 2 × 5 two-dimensional array called Cost, with the name of each element specified.

ROWS \ COLUMNS	1	2	3	4	5
1	COST(1, 1)	COST(1, 2)	COST(1, 3)	COST(1, 4)	COST(1, 5)
2	COST(2, 1)	COST(2, 2)	COST(2, 3)	COST(2, 4)	COST(2, 5)

Cost(2, 3) is read as "Cost sub two three" and references the element found in the second row and third column.

FIGURE 8.17

A 2 × 5 array with each element assigned a value.

ROWS \ COLUMNS	1	2	3	4	5
1	6	12	-52	3.14	0.56
2	8	2	5	6	2

Assuming that the elements of the array Cost are assigned the values shown in Figure 8.17, the following statements are true:

Cost(1, 2) is equal to 12.
Cost(2, 4) is equal to 6.
Cost(2, 2) is equal to 2.
Cost(1, 1) is equal to Cost(2, 4).
Cost(3, 5) is outside the range of the array; it does not exist.
Cost(2, 6) is outside the range of the array; it does not exist.
Cost(−2, −5) is outside the range of the array; it does not exist.

Initializing Arrays

You may write the code at the top of the next page to initialize to 0, row by row, all the elements in a 4 × 3 array called Area.

```
DIM Area(1 TO 4, 1 TO 3)
FOR Row = 1 TO 4
   FOR Column = 1 TO 3
      Area(Row, Column) = 0
   NEXT Column
NEXT Row
```

To initialize to 1 all elements on the main diagonal of a 5 × 5 array called Table, you may write the following:

```
DIM Table(1 TO 5, 1 TO 5)
FOR Row = 1 TO 5
   Table(Row, Row) = 1
NEXT Row
```

As a result, elements Table(1, 1), Table(2, 2), Table(3, 3), Table(4, 4), and Table(5, 5) are assigned the value of 1.

Two-dimensional arrays often are used to classify data. For example, if a company makes five models of a particular product and the production of each model involves a certain amount of processing time on six different machines, the processing time can be summarized in a table of five rows and six columns, as illustrated in Figure 8.18.

FIGURE 8.18

A table showing the processing time each model spends on a machine.

PRODUCT PROCESSING TIME IN MINUTES	MACHINE					
	1	2	3	4	5	6
MODEL NUMBER 1	13	30	5	17	12	45
2	23	12	13	16	0	20
3	45	12	28	16	10	13
4	21	16	15	22	19	26
5	23	50	17	43	15	18

The following statement reserves storage for the two-dimensional array in Figure 8.18:

```
DIM Time(1 TO 5, 1 TO 6)
```

If Model represents the model number (row of the table) and Machine represents the machine (column of the table), then the subscripted variable Time(Model, Machine) gives the time it takes for a model to be processed on a particular machine. The value of Model can range from 1 to 5, and the value of Machine can range from 1 to 6. If Model is equal to 4 and Machine is equal to 5, the table tells us the product processing time is 19 minutes. That is, model number 4 involves 19 minutes of processing on machine 5.

To sum all the elements in row 4 of the table in Figure 8.18 into a running total Sum4 and to sum all the elements in column 2 into a running total Sum2, you can write the following:

```
DIM Time(1 TO 5, 1 TO 6)
Sum2 = 0
Sum4 = 0
FOR Model = 1 TO 5
   Sum2 = Sum2 + Time(Model, 2)
NEXT Model
FOR Machine = 1 TO 6
   Sum4 = Sum4 + Time(4, Machine)
NEXT Machine
```

The last three short partial programs should give you an idea of how to handle elements that appear in various rows and columns of two-dimensional arrays.

Arrays with More Than Two Dimensions

The table in Figure 8.18 is for one product with five different models. Now suppose we want to consider comparable tables for two different products, each of which has five different model numbers and all of which utilize the six machines. To construct such a table, we can modify the array Time so it is a three-dimensional array:

```
DIM Time(1 TO 5, 1 TO 6, 1 TO 2)
```

Now the subscripted variable Time(Model, Machine, Product) refers to the time it takes for a given model number (Model) on a particular machine (Machine) for a specific product (Product).

Figure 8.19 represents a conceptual view of some of the storage locations for a 5 × 6 × 2 array called Time. This three-dimensional array contains five rows, six columns, and two planes, for a total of 60 elements.

If we want to take into account the production differences at three different sites, we can make Time a four-dimensional array:

```
DIM Time(1 TO 5, 1 TO 6, 1 TO 2, 1 TO 3)
```

Now the subscripted variable Time(Model, Machine, Product, Site) refers to the processing time it takes for a given model number, on a particular machine, for a specific product, at a given site. If factors other than site, product, model, and machine are required, we can add even more dimensions.

FIGURE 8.19

Conceptual view of some of the storage locations reserved for a 5 × 6 × 2 three-dimensional array called Time.

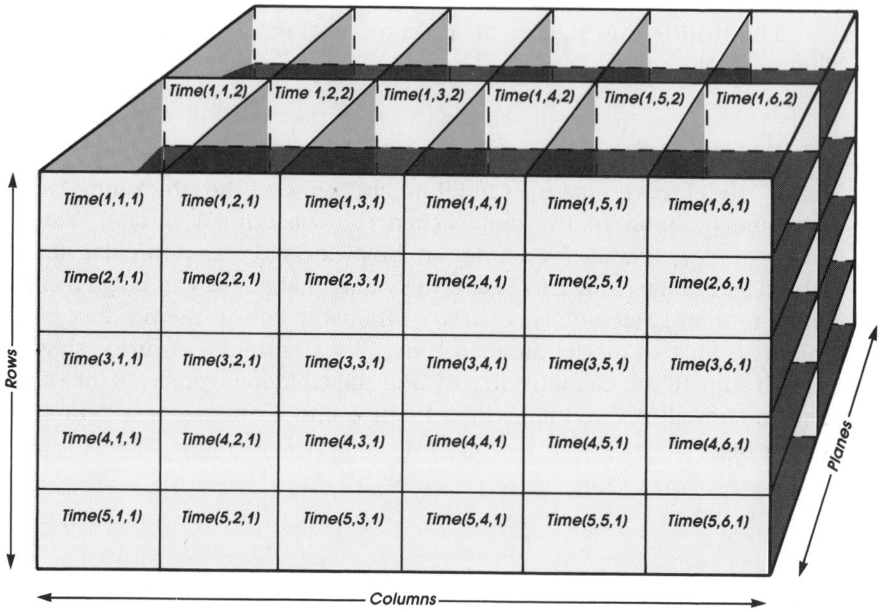

Determining the Lower- and Upper-Bound Subscript Values of an Array

QuickBASIC includes two functions that allow you to determine during the execution of a program the lower- and upper-bound subscript values of an array. LBOUND(array name, N)

FIGURE 8.20

*Using the
UBOUND and
LBOUND
functions.*

returns the lower-bound subscript value, and UBOUND(array name, N) returns the upper-bound subscript value. N specifies the Nth dimension. If N is omitted, QuickBASIC uses 1. As an example of these two functions, consider the partial program in Figure 8.20, which is self-explanatory.

```
1     ' Displaying the Lower- and Upper-Bound
2     ' Subscript Values of Arrays
3     ' ************************************
4     OPTION BASE 5
5     DIM S(-5 TO 4), T(5 TO 10, 8), A(7, 3, 4 TO 7)
6     PRINT "Array S:"
7     PRINT TAB(3); "Upper-bound value ===>", UBOUND(S, 1)
8     PRINT TAB(3); "Lower-bound value ===>", LBOUND(S, 1)
9     PRINT
10    PRINT "Array T:"
11    PRINT TAB(3); "Upper-bound values ==>", UBOUND(T, 1), UBOUND(T,2)
12    PRINT TAB(3); "Lower-bound values ==>", LBOUND(T, 1), LBOUND(T,2)
13    PRINT
14    PRINT "Array A:"
15    PRINT TAB(3); "Upper-bound values ==>", UBOUND(A, 1), UBOUND(A,2), UBOUND(A, 3)
16    PRINT TAB(3); "Lower-bound values ==>", LBOUND(A, 1), LBOUND(A,2), LBOUND(A, 3)

[run]

Array S:
   Upper-bound value ===>      4
   Lower-bound value ===>     -5

Array T:
   Upper-bound values ==>     10           8
   Lower-bound values ==>      5           1

Array A:
   Upper-bound values ==>      7           3           7
   Lower-bound values ==>      1           1           4
```

8.7 SORTING

Sorting data into alphabetical or numerical order is one of the more frequently executed operations in a business data processing environment. It is a time-consuming operation, especially when large amounts of data are involved. Computer professionals have spent a great deal of time developing algorithms to speed up the sorting process. Usually, the faster the process is, the more complex the algorithm. In this section, we will discuss two of the more common sort algorithms: the **bubble sort** and the **Shell sort**, named after its author, Donald Shell.

Figure 8.21 illustrates the difference between unsorted data and the same data in ascending and descending sequence. Data that is in sequence from lowest to highest in value is in **ascending sequence**. Data that is in sequence from highest to lowest in value is in **descending sequence**.

FIGURE 8.21

Data in various sequences.

Data in No Particular
Sequence

Data in Ascending
Sequence

Data in Descending
Sequence

The Bubble Sort

The bubble sort is a straightforward method of sorting data items that have been placed in an array. To illustrate the logic of a bubble sort, we will sort the data found in Figure 8.21 into ascending sequence. Assume that the data has been assigned to the array B, as illustrated in Figure 8.22.

FIGURE 8.22

Original order of unsorted data in the array B.

B(1)	8
B(2)	6
B(3)	9
B(4)	4
B(5)	1

The bubble sort involves comparing adjacent elements and **swapping** (that is, interchanging) the values of those elements when they are out of order. For example, B(1) is compared to B(2). If B(1) is less than or equal to B(2), no swap occurs. If B(1) is greater than B(2), the values of the 2 elements are swapped. B(2) is then compared to B(3), and so on, until B(4) is compared to B(5). One complete time through the array is called a **pass**. At the end of the first pass, the largest value is in the last element of the array B, as illustrated in Figure 8.23. Its box has been shaded to show that it is in its final position and will not move again.

FIGURE 8.23

First pass through the array B.

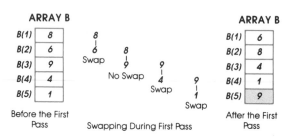

The maximum number of passes necessary to sort the elements in an array is equal to the number of elements in the array less 1. Because array B has 5 elements, four passes at most are made on the array. Keep in mind that the minimum number of passes to sort the elements in an array may be one. This occurs when the array elements are initially stored in sorted sequence.

Figures 8.24, 8.25, and 8.26 illustrate the second, third, and fourth passes made on the array B. On the fifth pass, no values are swapped. The swapping pushes the larger values down in the illustrations, and as a side effect, the smaller numbers *bubble* up to the top of the array.

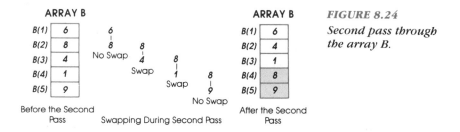

FIGURE 8.24

Second pass through the array B.

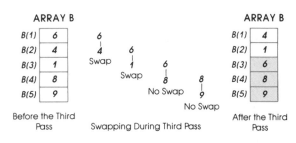

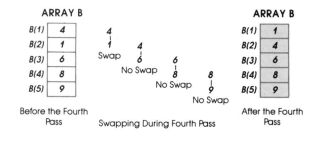

FIGURE 8.25

Third pass through the array B.

FIGURE 8.26

Fourth pass through the array B, which is now in ascending sequence.

The SWAP Statement

To exchange the values of two storage locations in a program, we use the **SWAP** statement. The general form of the **SWAP** statement is shown in Table 8.7.

TABLE 8.7   The SWAP Statement

General Form:	SWAP variable$_1$, variable$_2$ where **variable$_1$** and **variable$_2$** are of the same type.
Purpose:	Exchanges the values of two variables or two elements of an array.
Examples:	1. `SWAP Old.Balance, New.Balance` 2. `SWAP Array(Size), Array(Size + 1)` 3. `SWAP Code1$(Row, Col), Code2$(Row, Col)`

In Table 8.7, Example 1 exchanges the values of the two simple variables Old.Balance and New.Balance. Prior to the execution of the SWAP statement, if Old.Balance is equal to 500 and New.Balance is equal to 600, then after its execution, Old.Balance is equal to 600, and New.Balance is equal to 500.

In Example 2 of Table 8.7, the values of the two subscripted variables Array(Size) and Array(Size + 1) are exchanged. Exchanging the values of two adjacent elements of an array is a common practice with sort algorithms.

Finally, in Example 3 of Table 8.7, the SWAP statement exchanges the values of the two corresponding string elements of tables Code1$ and Code2$.

Implementing the Bubble Sort

The statement that compares two adjacent elements in an array and exchanges them when necessary is

```
IF B(I) > B(I + 1) THEN
   SWAP B(I), B(I + 1)
END IF
```

One pass on the array, which compares all adjacent elements, can be implemented by using the following For loop:

```
FOR I = 1 TO 4
   IF B(I) > B(I + 1) THEN
      SWAP B(I), B(I + 1)
   END IF
NEXT I
```

Finally, as illustrated in Figures 8.23 through 8.26, the elements of the array are sorted by completing four passes on the array. This can be accomplished with a pair of nested For loops. To make the routine more general, we have also included an expression for the limit parameters in each For loop as follows:

```
Limit = 5
FOR J = 1 TO (Limit - 1)
   FOR I = 1 TO (Limit - 1)
      IF B(I) > B(I + 1) THEN      ⟵  inefficient
         SWAP B(I), B(I + 1)            algorithm
      END IF
   NEXT I
NEXT J
```

Although the nested For loops sort the values of the elements in the array B, the algorithm is highly inefficient for the two following reasons. First, the values of the elements in the array may already be in ascending sequence before the sort routine is initiated. This inefficient technique would still make four passes on the sorted array.

Second, during a pass, all the values of the elements in the array beyond the last interchange may be in sequence. For example, assume 100 numbers are being sorted, and on the first pass the *last interchange* is made between the fifty-ninth and sixtieth elements in the list. On the next pass, elements beyond the fifty-eigth and fifty-ninth need not be compared because they will be in the proper sequence.

To minimize the number of passes it takes to sort an array, a variable called a switch is required. The switch is used to halt the sort routine when the array is sorted. The **switch** is a simple string variable that takes on two values during the duration of the loop. If Switch$ is the variable that represents the switch, then when the switch is on, meaning Switch$ equals the value ON, another pass is required. When the switch is off, meaning Switch$ equals the value OFF, the array is sorted, and the loop is terminated. The switch is turned on whenever two adjacent elements are exchanged, and this means that another pass is required. If a pass is made, meaning all adjacent elements are compared, and the switch remains off, then the array is sorted.

In the previous algorithm, the outer For loop controlled the number of passes. If a switch is used to control the number of passes, then the For loop should be replaced by a Do-While loop. To sort on the next pass only to the point where the last interchange occurred, a variable called Last is required. Last is assigned the current value of the loop variable I whenever an interchange is made. When the For loop is satisfied, the value of Last is assigned to the Limit value of the For loop.

The following partial program will *efficiently* sort the elements of the array B into ascending sequence:

```
31        ' *****************************
32        ' *          Bubble Sort          *
33        ' *****************************
34        SUB B100.Bubble.Sort
35            Limit = Number
36            Switch$ = "ON"
37            DO WHILE Switch$ = "ON"
38                Switch$ = "OFF"
39                FOR I = 1 TO (Limit - 1)
40                    IF B(I) > B(I + 1) THEN
41                        SWAP B(I), B(I + 1)
42                        Switch$ = "ON"
43                        Last = I
44                    END IF
45                NEXT I
46                Limit = Last
47            LOOP
48        END SUB
```

these two statements substantially improve the efficiency of the sort, especially when some of the data is already in order

The variable Switch$ controls whether another pass will be done on the array. Line 36 assigns Switch$ a value of ON. Because Switch$ equals ON, line 37 passes control into the body of the Do-While loop. Line 38 assigns Switch$ a value of OFF just before the For loop makes a pass on the loop. If Switch$ is not modified later in the loop (line 42), the values in the array are in sequence, and the next time that line 37 is executed control transfers to line 48.

The FOR statement in line 39 initializes I to 1. The first element B(1) is then compared to B(2). If B(1) is greater than B(2), the THEN clause swaps the values of the two elements and assigns Switch$ a value of ON. Next, B(2) is compared to B(3) and so on.

The number of comparisons per pass is equal to the number of elements to compare minus 1. Because the number of data items to sort is five, the limit parameter in the FOR statement is set to 4.

Program 8.2 incorporates the logic found in this partial program to sort the values 8, 6, 9, 4, and 1. To make the sort algorithm more general, a variable can be used for the size of the array. Line 21 dynamically allocates storage for array B. Because array B is dynamically allocated on the basis of Number, we placed the DIM statement in A100.Initialization instead of using the DIM SHARED statement in the Main Program. The array B is shared across the subprograms due to line 7.

The For loop, made up of lines 24 through 27, loads and displays the unsorted elements of the array. The B100.Bubble.Sort subprogram (lines 34 through 48) sorts the numeric array. The C100.Display.Sorted.Array subprogram (lines 53 through 58) displays the elements after the array has been sorted.

PROGRAM 8.2

```
1    Program 8.2
2    ' Sorting Numeric Data Using the
3    ' Bubble Sort Technique
4    ' *****************************
5    ' *         Main Program         *
6    ' *****************************
7    COMMON SHARED Number, B()
8    CALL A100.Initialization
9    CALL B100.Bubble.Sort
10   CALL C100.Display.Sorted.Array
11   ' ******** Data Follows ********
12   DATA 5 : ' Number of values to sort
13   DATA 8, 6, 9, 4, 1
14   END
15
16   ' *****************************
17   ' *         Initialization       *
18   ' *****************************
19   SUB A100.Initialization
20      READ Number
21      DIM B(1 TO Number)
22      CLS  ' Clear Screen
23      PRINT "Unsorted -";
24      FOR I = 1 TO Number
25         READ B(I)
26         PRINT B(I);
27      NEXT I
28      PRINT : PRINT
29   END SUB
30
31   ' *****************************
32   ' *         Bubble Sort         *
33   ' *****************************
34   SUB B100.Bubble.Sort
35      Limit = Number
36      Switch$ = "ON"
37      DO WHILE Switch$ = "ON"
38         Switch$ = "OFF"
39         FOR I = 1 TO (Limit - 1)
40            IF B(I) > B(I + 1) THEN
41               SWAP B(I), B(I + 1)
42               Switch$ = "ON"
43               Last = I
44            END IF
45         NEXT I
46         Limit = Last
47      LOOP
48   END SUB
49
```

Line 7 annotation: Number and array B are shared across subprograms

Line 21 annotation: array B declared

(continued)

```
50    ' *****************************
51    ' *      Display Sorted Array       *
52    ' *****************************
53    SUB C100.Display.Sorted.Array
54       PRINT "Sorted   -";
55       FOR I = 1 TO Number
56          PRINT B(I);
57       NEXT I
58    END SUB

[run]

Unsorted - 8  6  9  4  1

Sorted   - 1  4  6  8  9
```

The advantage to studying sort algorithms is that they raise the question of algorithm efficiency. In the next section, we will discuss the Shell sort, which offers a vast improvement over the bubble sort algorithm.

The Shell Sort

The bubble sort algorithm works well for a small number of data items, but it can take too much processing time for a large number of data items. The problem with this algorithm is that the smaller data items move only one position at a time because only adjacent elements are compared. The Shell sort provides a faster means of sorting a large number of data items. For example, in tests we have run with five hundred data items, the Shell sort reduces the processing time by a factor of five. In tests we have run with a thousand data items, it reduces the processing time by a factor of 10. The longer the list to be sorted, the greater the advantage of the Shell sort over the bubble sort.

The Shell sort is similar to the bubble sort, but instead of comparing and swapping adjacent elements B(I) and B(I + 1), it compares and swaps nonadjacent elements B(I) and B(I + Gap), where Gap starts out considerably greater than 1.

Prior to the loop that swaps the elements, Gap is set to one-half the length of the array. When a swap is made, a big improvement takes place. When no swap is made on a pass, the Gap is halved again for the next pass. Finally, the Gap becomes 1, as in the bubble sort, and adjacent elements are compared and swapped.

The Shell sort is used in Program 8.3 to sort a list of fifteen data items. In the B100.Shell.Sort subprogram, line 36 begins by assigning the Gap to one-half the size of the list. Line 37 initiates a loop that has as its body the bubble sort with some minor modifications. Within the For loop (lines 42 through 48), the integer 1 in the bubble sort algorithm is replaced by the variable Gap.

To make the Shell sort even faster, all the numeric variables could have been declared as integer data type for the limited data that required sorting.

PROGRAM 8.3

```
1     Program 8.3
2     Sorting Numeric Data Using the
3     Shell Sort Technique
4     ' *****************************
5     ' *         Main Program           *
6     ' *****************************
7     COMMON SHARED Number, B()
8     CALL A100.Initialization
9     CALL B100.Shell.Sort
10    CALL C100.Display.Sorted.Array
11    ' ******** Data Follows ********
12    DATA 15 : ' Number of Values to Sort
13    DATA 18, 13, 6, 4, 19, 12, 67, 1
14    DATA 11, 13, 27, 32, 2, 17, 55
15    END
16
```

Number and array B are shared across subprograms

```
17     ' *****************************
18     ' *        Initialization       *
19     ' *****************************
20     SUB A100.Initialization
21       READ Number
22       DIM B(1 TO Number)
23       CLS  ' Clear Screen
24       PRINT "Unsorted -";
25       FOR I = 1 TO Number
26         READ B(I)
27         PRINT B(I);
28       NEXT I
29       PRINT : PRINT
30     END SUB
31
32     ' *****************************
33     ' *         Shell Sort          *
34     ' *****************************
35     SUB B100.Shell.Sort
36       Gap = Number \ 2
37       DO WHILE Gap > 0
38         Limit = Number
39         Switch$ = "ON"
40         DO WHILE Switch$ = "ON"
41           Switch$ = "OFF"
42           FOR I = 1 TO Limit - Gap
43             IF B(I) > B(I + Gap) THEN
44               SWAP B(I), B(I + Gap)
45               Switch$ = "ON"
46               Last = I
47             END IF
48           NEXT I
49           Limit = Last
50         LOOP
51         Gap = Gap \ 2
52       LOOP
53     END SUB
54
55     ' *****************************
56     ' *    Display Sorted Array     *
57     ' *****************************
58     SUB C100.Display.Sorted.Array
59       PRINT "Sorted   -";
60       FOR I = 1 TO Number
61         PRINT B(I);
62       NEXT I
63     END SUB
```

array B declared

```
[run]

Unsorted - 18  13  6  4  19  12  67  1  11  13  27  32  2  17  55

Sorted   - 1  2  4  6  11  12  13  13  17  18  19  27  32  55  67
```

8.8   TABLE PROCESSING

Many applications call for the use of data that arranged in tabular form. Rates of pay, tax brackets, part costs, and insurance rates are examples of tables that contain systematically arranged data. Arrays make it easier to write programs for applications involving tables.

Table Organization

Tables are organized on the basis of how the data items, also called **table functions**, are to be referenced. In **positionally organized tables**, table functions can be accessed by their position in the table. In **argument-organized tables**, table functions are accessed by the value that corresponds to the desired table function.

Positionally Organized Tables

To illustrate a positionally organized table, a program can be written that displays the name of the month in response to a month number, 1 through 12. Figure 8.27 shows the basic concept behind accessing a table function in a positionally organized table.

In Figure 8.27, the month name is selected from the table on the basis of its location. A value of 1, entered by the user, equates to January, 2 to February, and so on. To write a program that uses table processing techniques, you must do the following:

1. Define the table by declaring an array.
2. Load the table functions into the array.
3. Write statements to access the table entries.

FIGURE 8.27

Accessing a table function in a positionally organized table.

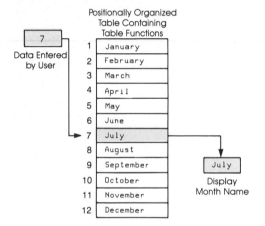

Program 8.4 illustrates how to declare, load, and access the table of month names described in Figure 8.27. Line 6 defines the table by declaring the one-dimensional string array Month$ to 12 and sharing it between subprograms. Lines 19 through 21 load the table functions — in this case, the month names — into the array. Line 57 in B210.Access.Table.Function subprogram accesses the desired table function.

The routine to access the table function in Program 8.4 is straightforward. The user enters a value for Num. A range check (lines 42 through 48) ensures the value is between 1 and 12. Once a valid value is entered, line 57 references the corresponding element of the array that contains the table functions. Figures 8.28 and 8.29 show the results displayed as a result of entering the month numbers 7 and 12 in response to a request by Program 8.4.

Notice in Program 8.4, that we mixed the methods of passing values between subprograms. In this program, we shared array Month$ using the DIM SHARED statement in line 6 and passed the variables Num and Control$ using the argument-parameter-list technique in the B200 and B210 subprograms. Some programmers use the following rule: If variables are used across legs (for example, between A and B subprograms), then use the COMMON SHARED statement or the DIM SHARED statement. If variables are used only within a leg (such as within the B subprograms), then use the argument-parameter-list technique. Program 8.4 illustrates this rule.

PROGRAM 8.4

```
1    ' Program 8.4
2    ' Accessing Functions in a Positionally Organized Table
3    ' ********************************************************
4    ' *                    Main Program                      *
5    ' ********************************************************
6    DIM SHARED Month$(1 TO 12)           ' Declare the Table
7    CALL A100.Initialization
8    CALL B100.Process.Request
9    CALL C100.Wrap.Up
10   ' ************* Table Entries Follow ****************
11   DATA January, February, March, April, May, June, July
12   DATA August, September, October, November, December
13   END
14
15   ' ********************************************************
16   ' *                   Initialization                    *
17   ' ********************************************************
18   SUB A100.Initialization
19      FOR Number = 1 TO 12
20         READ Month$(Number)                ' Load the Table
21      NEXT Number
22   END SUB
23
24   ' ********************************************************
25   ' *                  Process a Request                   *
26   ' ********************************************************
27   SUB B100.Process.Request
28      DO
29         CALL B200.Accept.User.Input(Num)
30         CALL B210.Access.Table.Function(Num, Control$)
31      LOOP UNTIL UCASE$(Control$) = "N"
32   END SUB
33
34   ' ********************************************************
35   ' *                  Accept User Input                   *
36   ' *                     Returns Num                      *
37   ' ********************************************************
38   SUB B200.Accept.User.Input (Num)
39      CLS  ' Clear Screen
40      LOCATE 3, 15
41      INPUT "Month Number (Enter 1 through 12) =====> ", Num
42      DO WHILE Num < 1 OR Num > 12
43         LOCATE 5, 15: PRINT "Month Number Invalid, Please Reenter"
44         BEEP: BEEP: BEEP: BEEP
45         LOCATE 3, 56: PRINT SPC(15);
46         LOCATE 3, 56: INPUT "", Num
47         LOCATE 5, 15: PRINT SPC(40);
48      LOOP
49   END SUB
50
51   ' ********************************************************
52   ' *             Access the Table Function                *
53   ' *           Receives Num    Returns Control$           *
54   ' ********************************************************
55   SUB B210.Access.Table.Function (Num, Control$)
56      LOCATE 5, 15
57      PRINT "Month Name ============================> "; Month$(Num)
58      LOCATE 7, 15
59      INPUT "Enter Y to process another month number, else N... ", Control$
60   END SUB
61
```

(continued)

```
62    ' *********************************************************
63    ' *                        Wrap-Up                        *
64    ' *********************************************************
65    SUB C100.Wrap.Up
66       CLS  ' Clear Screen
67       PRINT : PRINT "Job Complete"
68    END SUB

      [run]
```

FIGURE 8.28

The display by Program 8.4 due to entering the month number 7.

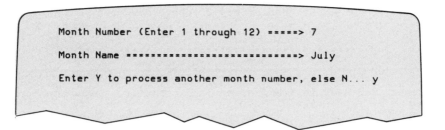

```
    Month Number (Enter 1 through 12) =====> 7

    Month Name ============================> July

    Enter Y to process another month number, else N... y
```

FIGURE 8.29

The display by Program 8.4 due to entering the month number 12.

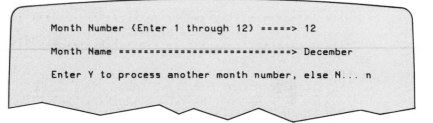

```
    Month Number (Enter 1 through 12) =====> 12

    Month Name ===========================> December

    Enter Y to process another month number, else N... n
```

Positionally organized tables, such as Month$ in Program 8.4, are not difficult to understand. Unfortunately, few tables can be constructed on the basis of the relative position of the table functions. Months, days of the week, and job classes are examples of systematic data that can be organized into positional tables.

Argument-Organized Tables

In most applications, tables are characterized by entries made up of multiple functions. Multiple-function entries are accessed by means of a **search argument**. The search argument is entered by the user much as the month number was in Program 8.4. The search argument is compared to the **table argument**, a table entry, to retrieve the corresponding table function. Figure 8.30 illustrates the composition of a table that is organized by arguments.

FIGURE 8.30

Conceptual view of an argument-organized table.

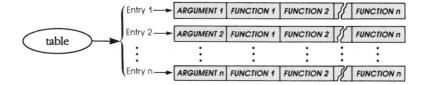

The table argument is assigned to a one-dimensional array. Functions are assigned to parallel arrays. Unlike a positionally organized table, in which the value entered is used to obtain the table function, an argument-organized table must be searched until the search argument agrees with one of the table arguments. This search is a **table search**, or a **table lookup**.

There are two methods for searching a table: the serial search and the binary search. A **serial search** begins by comparing the search argument to the first table argument. If the two agree, the search is over. If they do not agree, then the search argument is compared to the second table argument, and so on until the table argument either is found or not found. In the serial search, the table arguments may be either in sorted or unsorted order, or arranged in a predetermined order based on frequency of use.

In general, a **binary search** begins the search in the middle of the table and determines whether the table argument that agrees with the search argument is in the upper half or the lower half of the table. The half that contains this table argument is then halved again. This process continues until there is nothing left to divide in half. At that point, the binary search is complete; the table argument either has been found or not found. The binary search, which requires that the table arguments be in sorted order, that is in ascending or descending sequence, will be discussed in greater detail later.

Serial Search

A serial search, sometimes called a **linear search**, is a procedure that all of us use in everyday life. Suppose, for example, that you have a parts list that contains the part numbers and corresponding part descriptions and part costs. If you have a part number, one method for finding the part description and cost is to read through the part number list until you find the part number for which you are searching. You can then read off the description and cost that correspond to the part number. Figure 8.31 illustrates the basic concept of a serial search.

FIGURE 8.31

Conceptual view of a serial search.

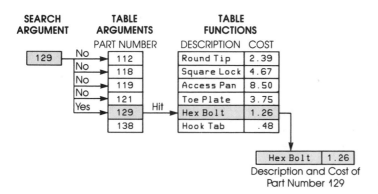

The search argument is tested against each of the table arguments, beginning with the first, until a *hit* is made. At that point, the corresponding part description and part cost are selected from the table.

A program that completes the serial search illustrated in Figure 8.31 first needs to have the table defined. Because each entry is made up of a table argument and two functions, we declare three parallel arrays — Part, Desc$, and Cost, as shown in line 25 of the partial program below. The variable Entries is assigned the number of parts in the parts list by line 24.

```
24    READ Entries
25    DIM Part(1 TO Entries), Desc$(1 TO Entries), Cost(1 TO Entries)
```

The array Part is assigned the part numbers, the array Desc$ the part descriptions, and the array Cost the part costs. A For loop is used to load the table, as follows:

```
26        FOR Number = 1 TO Entries
27            READ Part(Number), Desc$(Number), Cost(Number)
28        NEXT Number
```

Each time the READ statement is executed, one entry is loaded into the parallel arrays. Each entry in the table consists of an argument and two functions.

The following partial program searches the argument table and causes either the part description and part cost or a diagnostic message to be displayed. Assume that the user has assigned the part number that is to be looked up to the variable Search.Argument.

```
51    ' ********************************************************
52    ' *              Access the Table Function              *
53    ' *        Receives Search.Argument   Returns Control$    *
54    ' ********************************************************
55    SUB B210.Access.Table.Function (Search.Argument, Control$)
56       FOR Number = 1 TO Entries
57           IF Search.Argument = Part(Number) THEN
58               EXIT FOR  ' Process a Table Hit
59           END IF
60       NEXT Number
61       IF Number <= Entries THEN
62           CALL B300.Display.Table.Function(Number)
63       ELSE
64           LOCATE 7, 15
65           PRINT "Part Number"; Search.Argument; "NOT FOUND"
66       END IF
67       LOCATE 11, 15
68       INPUT "Enter Y to look up another part number, else N.... ", Control$
69    END SUB
70
71    ' ********************************************************
72    ' *              Display Table Function                 *
73    ' *                 Receives Number                     *
74    ' ********************************************************
75    SUB B300.Display.Table.Function (Number)
76       LOCATE 7, 15
77       PRINT "Description =====> "; Desc$(Number)
78       LOCATE 9, 15
79       PRINT USING "Cost ============> $$#.##"; Cost(Number)
80    END SUB
```

A For loop (lines 56 through 60) is used to implement the serial search algorithm. The IF statement in line 57 compares Search.Argument against the part numbers in the table Part(Number). When a hit occurs, the EXIT FOR statement in line 58 causes a premature exit from the For loop. In this case, Number is equal to the desired subscript. If no hit occurs, then the For loop runs its normal course, and Number is greater than the limit value Entries.

　　　　The IF statement following the For loop in line 61 compares Number to Entries. If Number is less than or equal to Entries, then the search was successful, and control transfers to the B300.Display.Table.Function subprogram. Number is used in lines 77 and 79 to display the corresponding part description and part cost found in the parallel arrays. If Number is greater than Entries in line 61, then the search was unsuccessful, and the diagnostic message in line 65 displays. The complete program follows.

PROGRAM 8.5

```
1    Program 8.5
2    ' Serial Search of an Argument Organized Table
3    ' *******************************************************
4    ' *                    Main Program                     *
5    ' *******************************************************
6    COMMON SHARED Entries, Part(), Desc$(), Cost()
7    CALL A100.Initialization
8    CALL B100.Process.Request
9    CALL C100.Wrap.Up
10   ' ****************** Table Entries ******************
11   DATA 6 : ' Number of Table Entries
12   DATA 112, Round Tip,    2.39
13   DATA 118, Square Lock,  4.67
14   DATA 119, Access Pan,   8.5
15   DATA 121, Toe Plate,    3.75
16   DATA 129, Hex Bolt,     1.26
17   DATA 138, Hook Tab,      .48
18   END
19
20   ' *******************************************************
21   ' *                  Initialization                    *
22   ' *******************************************************
23   SUB A100.Initialization
24      READ Entries
25      DIM Part(1 TO Entries), Desc$(1 TO Entries), Cost(1 TO Entries)
26      FOR Number = 1 TO Entries
27         READ Part(Number), Desc$(Number), Cost(Number)
28      NEXT Number
29   END SUB
30
31   ' *******************************************************
32   ' *                 Process a Request                  *
33   ' *******************************************************
34   SUB B100.Process.Request
35      DO
36         CALL B200.Accept.User.Input(Search.Argument)
37         CALL B210.Access.Table.Function(Search.Argument, Control$)
38      LOOP UNTIL UCASE$(Control$) = "N"
39   END SUB
40
41   ' *******************************************************
42   ' *                 Accept User Input                  *
43   ' *             Returns Search.Argument                *
44   ' *******************************************************
45   SUB B200.Accept.User.Input (Search.Argument)
46      CLS   ' Clear Screen
47      LOCATE 5, 15
48      INPUT "Part Number =====> ", Search.Argument
49   END SUB
50
```

(continued)

```
51    ' ************************************************************
52    ' *              Access the Table Function             *
53    ' *     Receives Search.Argument   Returns Control$     *
54    ' ************************************************************
55    SUB B210.Access.Table.Function (Search.Argument, Control$)
56       FOR Number = 1 TO Entries
57          IF Search.Argument = Part(Number) THEN
58             EXIT FOR   ' Process a Table Hit
59          END IF
60       NEXT Number
61       IF Number <= Entries THEN
62          CALL B300.Display.Table.Function(Number)
63       ELSE
64          LOCATE 7, 15
65          PRINT "Part Number"; Search.Argument; "NOT FOUND"
66       END IF
67       LOCATE 11, 15
68       INPUT "Enter Y to look up another part number, else N.... ", Control$
69    END SUB
70
71    ' ************************************************************
72    ' *               Display Table Function               *
73    ' *                  Receives Number                   *
74    ' ************************************************************
75    SUB B300.Display.Table.Function (Number)
76       LOCATE 7, 15
77       PRINT "Description =====> "; Desc$(Number)
78       LOCATE 9, 15
79       PRINT USING "Cost ============> $$#.##"; Cost(Number)
80    END SUB
81
82    ' ************************************************************
83    ' *                       Wrap-Up                      *
84    ' ************************************************************
85    SUB C100.Wrap.Up
86       CLS   ' Clear Screen
87       PRINT : PRINT "Job Complete"
88    END SUB

[run]
```

Figure 8.32 illustrates the display that is due to a part number of 129, and Figure 8.33 illustrates the display that is due to the invalid part number 122.

FIGURE 8.32

The display from Program 8.5 due to a part number of 129.

```
    Part Number =====> 129

    Description =====> Hex Bolt

    Cost ============> $1.26

    Enter Y to look up another part number, else N... Y
```

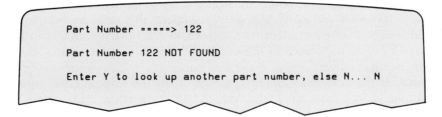

```
Part Number ======> 122

Part Number 122 NOT FOUND

Enter Y to look up another part number, else N... N
```

Ordering the Table Arguments for a Serial Search

For a serial search, it is not always necessary that the table arguments be in sequence. If it is known that some table entries are requested more often than others, then the table entries requested most often should be placed at the beginning of the table. For example, assume that a frequency analysis uncovered the following pattern of requests regarding the part-number table entries illustrated earlier in Figure 8.31:

Part Number	% Requested
112	10
118	4
119	15
121	40
129	25
138	6

According to the frequency analysis, the description and cost for part number 121 are requested 40% of the time, and the description and cost for part number 118 are requested only 4% of the time.

If we load the table according to the frequency analysis, then the table entry for part number 121 is at the beginning of the table, and the table entry for part number 118 is at the end of the table. This is shown in Figure 8.34. In contrast to the search done earlier in Figure 8.31, the same search takes three fewer comparisons in Figure 8.34. If we load the table according to the frequency analysis, 65% of the requests will require, at most, two comparisons.

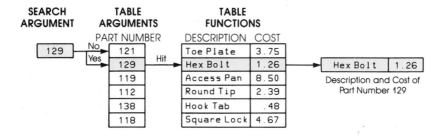

Binary Search

A serial search is useful for short tables, but not for long ones. For example, suppose the names in a telephone book were not listed alphabetically. If there were 15,000 names, it would take on the average 7,500 comparisons to find a specific telephone number. Some numbers might require only a few comparisons to find, while others might require nearly 15,000 comparisons.

Because telephone books are arranged alphabetically, any name listed therein can be located quickly and easily. When the arguments in a table are in alphabetical or numerical order, an efficient algorithm, known as the binary search, can be used. A binary search begins the search in the middle of the table. If the search argument is less than the middle table argument, the search continues by halving the lower valued half of the table. If the search argument is greater than the middle table argument, the search continues by halving the higher valued half of the table. If the search argument is equal to the middle table argument, the search is over. The binary search algorithm continues to narrow the table until it either finds a match or determines there is no match.

Figure 8.35 illustrates how the binary search algorithm works with a table of part numbers and corresponding part costs. Follow carefully the arrows numbered 1 to 4.

FIGURE 8.35

A conceptual view of a binary search.

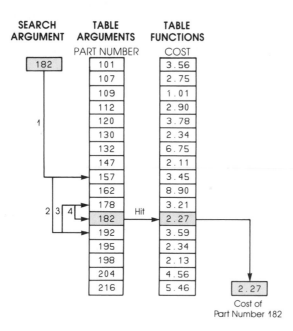

Part number 182 is first compared against the ninth element of the 17-element array. Because 182 is greater than 157, the match is located in the higher valued half of the table. Part number 182 is next compared to the thirteenth element, halfway between 10 and 17. The part number is less than 192, and the confined area between 10 and 13 is halved again. On the next comparison, 182 is greater than 178, and the area is reduced by half. On the fourth comparison, a match is found. A serial search for part number 182 would have taken 12 comparisons before a match had been found. The difference in the number of comparisons between the two algorithms becomes even greater as the size of the table increases.

Program 8.6 employs the binary search algorithm to search the table described in Figure 8.35. In the B210.Access.Table.Function subprogram (lines 53 through 74), the variables Low and High are initialized to the beginning and end of that section of the array Part to which the search is confined. Line 54 initializes Low to 1. Line 55 initializes High to Entries, which is equal to the number of entries in the table. Line 56 initializes Middle to 1 to ensure that Part(Middle) in line 57 is within the range of the array.

The Do-While loop (lines 57 through 65) carry out the search. The compound condition in line 57 terminates the Do-While loop when Search.Argument is equal to Part(Middle) or when Low exceeds High. Immediately following the Do-While loop, line 67 tests to determine which of the two conditions caused the Do-While loop to terminate. If the search ends because Search.Argument is equal to Part(Middle), the search is successful. If the search ends because Low exceeds High, the search is unsuccessful.

PROGRAM 8.6

```
 1   ' Program 8.6
 2   ' Binary Search of an Argument-Organized Table
 3   ' ************************************************************
 4   ' *                    Main Program                        *
 5   ' ************************************************************
 6   COMMON SHARED Entries, Part(), Cost()
 7   CALL A100.Initialization
 8   CALL B100.Process.Request
 9   CALL C100.Wrap.Up
10   ' ************* Table Entries Follow *****************
11   DATA 17 : ' Number of Table Entries
12   DATA 101, 3.56, 107, 2.75, 109, 1.01, 112, 2.9,  120, 3.78
13   DATA 130, 2.34, 132, 6.75, 147, 2.11, 157, 3.45, 162, 8.9
14   DATA 178, 3.21, 182, 2.27, 192, 3.59, 195, 2.34, 198, 2.13
15   DATA 204, 4.56, 216, 5.46
16   END
17
18   ' ************************************************************
19   ' *                   Initialization                       *
20   ' ************************************************************
21   SUB A100.Initialization
22      READ Entries
23      DIM Part(1 TO Entries), Cost(1 TO Entries)  ' Declare the Table
24      FOR Number = 1 TO Entries
25         READ Part(Number), Cost(Number)                ' Load the Table
26      NEXT Number
27   END SUB
28
29   ' ************************************************************
30   ' *                  Process a Request                     *
31   ' ************************************************************
32   SUB B100.Process.Request
33      DO
34         CALL B200.Accept.User.Input(Search.Argument)
35         CALL B210.Access.Table.Function(Search.Argument, Control$)
36      LOOP UNTIL UCASE$(Control$) = "N"
37   END SUB
38
39   ' ************************************************************
40   ' *                  Accept User Input                     *
41   ' *               Returns Search.Argument                  *
42   ' ************************************************************
43   SUB B200.Accept.User.Input (Search.Argument)
44      CLS  ' Clear Screen
45      LOCATE 5, 15
46      INPUT "Part Number =====> ", Search.Argument
47   END SUB
48
```

(continued)

```
49    ' *******************************************************
50    ' *              Access the Table Function             *
51    ' *        Receives Search.Argument   Returns Control$  *
52    ' *******************************************************
53    SUB B210.Access.Table.Function (Search.Argument, Control$)
54       Low = 1
55       High = Entries
56       Middle = 1
57       DO WHILE Search.Argument <> Part(Middle) AND Low <= High
58          Middle = (Low + High) \ 2
59          IF Search.Argument < Part(Middle) THEN
60             High = Middle - 1
61          END IF
62          IF Search.Argument > Part(Middle) THEN
63             Low = Middle + 1
64          END IF
65       LOOP
66       LOCATE 7, 15
67       IF Search.Argument = Part(Middle) THEN
68          PRINT USING "Cost ==============> $$#.##"; Cost(Middle)
69       ELSE
70          PRINT "Part Number"; Search.Argument; "NOT FOUND"
71       END IF
72       LOCATE 9, 15
73       INPUT "Enter Y to look up another part number, else N... ", Control$
74    END SUB
75
76    ' *******************************************************
77    ' *                      Wrap-Up                        *
78    ' *******************************************************
79    SUB C100.Wrap.Up
80       CLS  ' Clear Screen
81       PRINT : PRINT "Job Complete"
82    END SUB
```

[run]

Figure 8.36 shows the results that are displayed when a part number of 182 is entered by the user. This corresponds to the example illustrated earlier in Figure 8.35. Figure 8.37 shows the results that are displayed when an invalid part number is entered.

FIGURE 8.36

The display from Program 8.6 due to entering the part number 182.

```
    Part Number =====> 182

    Cost ============>   $2.27

    Enter Y to look up another part number, else N... y
```

```
Part Number =====> 163

Part Number 163 NOT FOUND

Enter Y to look up another part number, else N... n
```

Combining Table-Access Methods

By itself, a binary search is not always the best method for searching large tables. This is especially true if the most sought after entries can be isolated. For example, the following frequency analysis of a part-number table with 650 table entries suggests that the table be divided into two tables — one small table in which the six most requested entries are ordered by request, and one large table containing 644 entries, in which the arguments are in ascending sequence.

Part Number	% Requested
112	8
118	4
119	10
121	40
129	25
138	6
Remaining 644 Part Numbers	7

A serial search is first used with the smaller table. If this search is unsuccessful, then a binary search is used on the larger table. This concept can be expanded further to include several tables and an algorithm that searches one table — a directory table — to determine the table that contains the entry and is to be searched next.

Some Formulae For Searching

When a serial search is used, the average number of searches may be found from the following formula:

s = n / 2

where n = total number of elements

    s = average number of searches

The table on the right illustrates the effects of this formula.

Total number of elements	Average number of searches
2	1
4	2
8	4
16	8
32	16
64	32
128	64
.	.
.	.
.	.

The word *binary* is given to the binary search algorithm because this algorithm keeps splitting into two sorted lists of elements until either a match has been found or not found, as illustrated earlier in the telephone book analogy. The following table illustrates the effects of the binary search algorithm:

Total number of elements	Average number of searches
2	1
4	2
8	3
16	4
32	5
64	6
128	7
.	.
.	.
.	.

The formula for determining the average number of searches when a binary search is used can be derived as follows:

$$n = 2^s$$
$$\log_2 n = s$$

or

$$s = \log_2 n$$

where n = total number of elements

s = average number of searches

Hence, on the average, a binary search is faster than a serial search when the size of the total number of elements increases.

8.9   WHAT YOU SHOULD KNOW

1. The FOR and NEXT statements are used to set up counter-controlled loops.
2. If the increment value following the keyword STEP is positive or the keyword STEP is not used, then the PC executes the For loop until the loop variable exceeds the limit value. If the increment value is negative, the test is reversed. The value of the loop variable is decremented each time through the loop, and the loop is executed until the loop variable is less than the limit value.
3. The FOR statement may be located anywhere before the corresponding NEXT statement.
4. A valid initial entry into a For loop can be accomplished only by transferring control to the FOR statement.
5. If the range of a For loop includes another For loop, all the statements that are in the range of the inner For loop must also be within the range of the outer For loop.
6. When one For loop is within another, the name of the control variable for each For loop must be different.
7. The EXIT statement may be used to prematurely exit a For loop.
8. An array is a variable that allocates a specified number of storage locations, each of which can be assigned a unique value.

9. The elements in the array are distinguished from one another by subscripts. The subscript, written in parentheses, can be a numeric constant, a numeric variable, or a numeric expression.

10. The dimension of an array is the number of subscripts required to reference an element in an array.

11. Before an array can be used in a program, the DIM statement should be used to declare the number of storage locations in main storage that must be reserved for the array.

12. The DIM statement may be located anywhere before the first occurrence of a sub-scripted variable in a program. If you use the DIM SHARED statement to share arrays with subprograms, place it immediately below the COMMON SHARED statement in the Main Program. If you use the DIM statement and share arrays with subprograms, using the COMMON SHARED statement, then place the DIM statement in the Initialization subprogram.

13. Several arrays may be dimensioned in the same DIM statement.

14. The programmer has the choice in a DIM statement of specifying only the upper bound of an array or both the lower and upper bounds. If only the upper bound is specified, then the lower bound is zero, unless the OPTION BASE statement is used. To specify both bounds, use the keyword TO.

15. The OPTION BASE statement is used to assign a lower bound of 0 or 1 to all arrays dimensioned with only an upper bound. If the OPTION BASE statement is not used, the lower bound for all arrays is set to zero.

16. The subscript that references an array element must be within the range of the array. The range is the number of elements in the array.

17. Noninteger subscripts are rounded to the nearest integer.

18. An array is usually loaded with data using a READ or INPUT statement inside a For loop.

19. Parallel arrays are two or more arrays that have corresponding elements.

20. QuickBASIC permits arrays to be dynamically allocated. In the DIM statement, a variable is placed within the parentheses to indicate the size of the array. Before the DIM statement, the variable is assigned a value to which the array is dimensioned.

21. A two-dimensional array is one that requires two subscripts to reference any element. The first subscript designates the row of that element, and the second subscript designates the column of that element.

22. QuickBASIC allows up to 60 dimensions. One- and two-dimensional arrays are the most commonly used arrays in business applications.

23. Sorting is the arranging of data in accordance with some certain order or sequence. Data in sequence from lowest to highest is in ascending sequence; data in sequence from highest to lowest is in descending sequence.

24. The LBOUND and UBOUND functions may be used to determine the lower- and upper-bound subscript values of an array.

25. The SWAP statement is used to interchange the values of two variables or elements of an array.

26. Both the bubble sort and Shell sort algorithms work on arrays that contain numeric or string data.

27. Regardless of the sort algorithm used, three steps are required in a program to sort data: dimension the array, load the array with data, and apply an algorithm to manipulate the elements in the array.

28. Tables are organized on the basis of how the data is to be referenced. In positionally organized tables, table functions can be accessed by their position in the table. In argument-organized tables, table functions are accessed by looking up a desired value that corresponds to them. To retrieve these corresponding table functions, a search argument is compared against the table argument. When the search argument matches the table argument, the corresponding table functions are selected and used.

29. To utilize table-processing techniques in a program, you must (1) declare the table by dimensioning arrays for the table entries, (2) use a READ or an INPUT statement inside a For loop to load the table entries, and (3) code appropriate statements to access the table entries.
30. Serial and binary search methods are normally used to access data stored in tables.
31. A serial search, which normally begins at the top of the table, does not require the data to be in any sequence.
32. A binary search, which begins in the middle of the table, requires the data to be in ascending or descending sequence.

8.10   TEST YOUR BASIC SKILLS (Even-numbered answers are in Appendix E)

1. Consider the four valid programs listed below. What is displayed if each program is executed?

a.
```
' Exercise 8.1a
Between0.50 = 0
Between50.100 = 0
Greater100 = 0
READ Num
FOR I = 1 TO Num
   READ Score
   IF Score >= 0 AND Score < 50 THEN
      Between0.50 = Between0.50 + 1
   END IF
   IF Score >= 50 AND Score <= 100 THEN
      Between50.100 = Between50.100 + 1
   END IF
   IF Score > 100 THEN
      Greater100 = Greater100 + 1
   END IF
NEXT I
PRINT Between0.50, Between50.100, Greater100
' ********** Data Follows **********
DATA 10
DATA 150, 99, 100, 50, 0, 25, 88
DATA 42, 101, 10
END
```

b.
```
' Exercise 8.1b
F = 0
FOR I = 1 TO 3
   G = 0
   F = F + 1
   FOR J = 1 TO 4
      G = G + F
      PRINT F, G
   NEXT J
NEXT I
END
```

c.
```
' Exercise 8.1c
CLS   ' Clear Screen
DIM A(1 TO 5), B(1 TO 5), C(1 TO 5)
FOR I = 1 TO 5
   READ A(I), B(I)
NEXT I
FOR I = 1 TO 5
   C(I) = A(I) * B(I)
   PRINT C(I);
NEXT I
' ******** Data Follows *********
DATA 1, 4, 2, 3, 4, 4, 2, 4, 3, 5
END
```

d.
```
' Exercise 8.1d
CLS   ' Clear Screen
OPTION BASE 1
READ X, Y
DIM A(X, Y)
FOR I = 1 TO X
   FOR J = 1 TO Y
      READ A(I, J)
      PRINT A(I, J);
   NEXT J
   PRINT
NEXT I
' **** Data Follows ****
DATA 4, 3
DATA 2, 1, 6, 9, 5
DATA 6, 2, 1, 3, 8, 4, 2
END
```

2. Assume the array L is dimensioned in a program by the statement DIM L(1 TO 5, 1 TO 5). The elements of the array L are assigned the following values via the READ statement.

ARRAY L

2	5	14	30	50
7	12	21	70	10
5	15	70	60	0
19	20	30	10	20
22	45	20	40	50

Write the subscripted variable name that references the following values found in the array L:

a. 12 b. 70 c. 15 d. 45 e. 60 f. 7 g. 14 h. 22

3. Identify the syntax and logic error(s), if any, in each of the following FOR statements:
   a. FOR Amount = -1 TO -10
   b. FOR Var = 1 TO 6 STEP -1
   c. FOR Vector = 1 TO SQR(25)
   d. FOR Pint$ = 0 TO 7
   e. FOR Value = 10 TO 1
   f. FOR Quad = A TO B STEP -B

4. Explain what the following partial program does:

```
Exercise 8.4
OPTION BASE 1
DIM A(3, 4), B(3, 4)
         .
         .
         .
FOR I = 1 TO 3
   FOR J = 1 TO 4
      B(I, J) = A(I, J)
   NEXT J
NEXT I
PRINT LBOUND(A, 1), UBOUND(A, 1), LBOUND(B, 2), UBOUND(B, 2)
```

5. Assume that the array A has 4 rows and 4 columns and that the elements of the array A are assigned the following values:

ARRAY A

1	2	3	4
5	6	7	8
9	10	11	12
13	14	15	16

Note: A(1, 1) = 1 and A(3, 2) = 10.

What will be the final arrangement of array A after the following partial program is executed? Select your answer from the choices below:

```
' Exercise 8.5
FOR I = 1 TO 4
   FOR J = 1 TO 4
      A(I, J) = A(J, I)
   NEXT J
NEXT I
```

a.

1	2	3	4
5	6	7	8
9	10	11	12
13	14	15	16

b.

16	15	14	13
12	11	10	9
8	7	6	5
4	3	2	1

c.

1	2	2	4
5	6	6	8
9	10	10	12
13	14	14	16

d.

1	5	9	13
5	6	10	14
9	10	11	15
13	14	15	16

e. None of these.

6. Refer to the initial array A given in Exercise 5. What will be the final arrangement of the array A after each of the following partial programs is executed? Select your answer from the choices given in Exercise 5.

a.
```
' Exercise 8.6a
FOR I = 1 TO 4
   A(I, 3) = A(I, 2)
NEXT I
```

b.
```
' Exercise 8.6b
J = 2
FOR I = 1 TO 4
    A(I, J + 1) = A(I, J)
NEXT I
```

c.
```
' Exercise 8.6c
FOR I = 1 TO 4
   A(I, I) = A(I - 2, I + 2)
NEXT I
```

d.
```
' Exercise 8.6d
FOR I = 1 TO 4
   FOR J = 1 TO 4
       A(I, J) = A(I, J)
   NEXT J
NEXT I
```

7. Refer to the initial array A given in Exercise 5. What will be the final arrangement of the array A after the following partial program is executed? Select your answer from the choices given in Exercise 5. Assume that the array B has been declared the same as the array A.

```
' Exercise 8.7
FOR I = 1 TO 4
   FOR J = 1 TO 4
       B(I, J) = A(I, J)
   NEXT J
NEXT I
X = 0
FOR I = 4 TO 1 STEP -1
   Y = 0
   X = X + 1
   FOR J = 4 TO 1 STEP -1
      Y = Y + 1
      A(X, Y) = B(I, J)
   NEXT J
NEXT I
```

8. Given the one-dimensional array Number, consisting of 50 elements, write a subprogram (B400.Count.Elements) that will count the number of elements in the array Number that have a value between 0 and 18, inclusive, between 26 and 29, inclusive, and between 42 and 47 inclusive. Use the following counters:

Low: count of elements with a value between 0 and 18, inclusive
Mid: count of elements with a value between 26 and 29, inclusive
High: count of elements with a value between 42 and 47, inclusive

Use the subscript I to help reference the elements. Use the argument-parameter-list technique to receive the array number.

9. Given an array F that has been declared to have 100 elements, assume that each element of the array F has been assigned a value and is passed using the argument-parameter-list technique. Write a subprogram (B350.Move.Up) to shift all the values up one location. That is, assign the value of F_1 to F_2, F_2 to F_3, and F_{100} to F_1. Do not use any array other than the array F. Be sure not to destroy a value before it is shifted.

10. Given the three arrays A, B, and C, each declared to have 50 elements, assume that the elements of the arrays A and B have been assigned values and are passed using the argument-parameter-list technique. Write a subprogram (B300.Check.Arrays)

that compares each element of the array A to its corresponding element in the array B. Assign a 1, 0, or –1 to the corresponding element in the array C, as follows:

1 if A is greater than B
0 if A is equal to B
–1 if A is less than B

11. Identify the error(s), if any, in each of the following partial programs:

a.
```
' Exercise 8.11a
DIM X(50 TO 300)
FOR I = 1 TO 500
    READ X(I)
NEXT I
```

b.
```
' Exercise 8.11b
DIM X(1 TO 700)
FOR K = 700 TO 1 STEP -1
    READ X(K)
NEXT K
```

12. Given the two two-dimensional arrays R and S, each of which has 10 rows and 10 columns. Write a subprogram (A200.Sum) that uses the argument-parameter-list technique to receive the arrays R and S and return Sum. Compute the sum (Sum) of the products of the elements of the arrays with common subscripts. That is, find the following:

$$\text{Sum} = \sum_{j=1}^{10} \left(\sum_{k=1}^{10} R_{jk} S_{jk} \right)$$

13. A program utilizes four arrays B(I), K(J), L(I), and M(Q, J). The maximum values for I, J, and Q are 15, 36, and 29. The minimum values for I, J, and Q are –10, 5, and 3. Write a correct `DIM` statement that shares the arrays between subprograms.

14. How many lines will be displayed by the following program?

```
' Exercise 8.14
FOR C = 1 TO 20
    FOR A = 1 TO 10
        FOR Q = 1 TO 8
            PRINT C, A, Q
        NEXT Q
    NEXT A
NEXT C
END
```

15. Write a subprogram (B600.Series) for each of the following expressions and display the result:
   a. $1 + 1/2 + 1/4 + 1/8 + ... + 1/2^{10}$ b. $1^1 + 2^2 + 3^3 + 4^4 + 5^5$

16. Given the one-dimensional array A, consisting of 50 elements, write the `DIM` statement and the For loop to count the number of elements with negative, positive, and zero values in the array.

17. Write a subprogram (B300.Greatest) to find the salesperson who has the greatest total sales for a given period. Assume that the total sales are in the array Sales, that the corresponding salespersons' names are in the array Person$, and that each array has been dimensioned to a lower bound of 1 and an upper bound of 50, using the `DIM SHARED` statement.

18. Write a subprogram (B300.Least) to find the salesperson who has the least total sales for a given period. Use the same arrays as in exercise 17. Assume the arrays were declared using the `DIM SHARED` statement.

19. Write a subprogram (B400.Pascal) to generate the first six rows of **Pascal's triangle**. Each entry in a given row of the triangle is generated by adding the two adjacent entries in the immediately preceding row. For example, the third entry in row 4 is the sum of the second and third entries in row 3. The first six rows of Pascal's triangle are shown to the right. To eliminate the complexity of spacing, display each row starting in column 1.

```
                    1
                  1   1
                1   2   1
              1   3   3   1
            1   4   6   4   1
          1   5  10  10   5   1
```

20. Write a partial program to display the item number and gross sales for all items that have gross sales greater than $3,000. Assume that the item number is stored in the array Item$ and that the corresponding gross sales are stored in the array Sales. Declare a lower bound of 1 and an upper bound of 200 for the arrays. Do not write the code to load the arrays.

21. Consider the valid program below. What displays when the program is executed?

```
' Exercise 8.21
DIM Fib(1 TO 10)
PRINT "N", "NTH FIBONACCI NO."
Fib(1) = 1
Fib(2) = 1
PRINT 1, Fib(1)
PRINT 2, Fib(2)
FOR Num = 3 TO 10
   Fib(Num) = Fib(Num - 2) + Fib(Num - 1)
   PRINT Num, Fib(Num)
NEXT Num
END
```

22. **PC Hands-On Exercise:** Enter the partial program in Figure 8.1B on page 266. Modify the initial, limit, and increment values in the FOR statement according to the sets listed below. Execute the program for each set. If the PC goes into an endless loop, press Ctrl + Break to terminate processing.

Set	Initial	Limit	Increment	Set	Initial	Limit	Increment
1	1	1000	2	6	1	10	0.1
2	25	75	5	7	1	−10	−1
3	5	5	1	8	1	10	0
4	5	1	1	9	−5	−20	
5	5	1	−1				

23. **PC Hands-On Exercise:** Enter the partial program in Figure 8.9 on page 275. Display and execute the program. Change the limit value to 15 in the FOR statements in lines 6 and 8. Execute the program and see what happens.

24. **PC Hands-On Exercise:** Enter the partial program in Figure 8.12 on page 281. Delete line 6. Execute the program and see what happens. Reenter line 3. In line 6, insert the following statement:

```
For Number = 12 TO 1 STEP -1
```

Execute the partial program. Compare the sequence of the monthly sales to the original results displayed in Figure 8.12 on page 281.

25. **PC Hands-On Exercise:** Load Program 8.2 (PRG8-2) from the Student Diskette. Change the relation in line 40 from "greater than" to "less than." Execute the program. Compare the sequence of the sorted numbers to the sequence originally displayed by Program 8.2. Do you understand the difference between ascending sequence and descending sequence?

26. **PC Hands-On Exercise:** Load Program 8.6 (PRG8-6) from the Student Diskette. Turn on the trace feature in the Debug menu. Execute the program and enter the same part numbers shown in Figures 8.36 and 8.37. See if you can follow the sequence of statements executed in Program 8.6 from the displayed results. (See Appendix C for a discussion of tracing and other debugging features of QuickBASIC.)

8.11 BASIC PROGRAMMING PROBLEMS

1. Sum of a Series of Numbers

Purpose: To become familiar with the implementation of counter-controlled loops by means of the FOR and NEXT statements.

Problem: Write five different partial programs (like the one in Figure 8.1B on page 266) as described below.

PART A: Construct a partial program to compute and display the sum of the following series: 1 + 2 + 3 + . . . + 100. Use a For loop to create these integers, and sum them.

PART B: Same as Part A, except sum all the even numbers from 2 to 100, inclusive.

PART C: Same as Part A, except input the lower and upper limits.

PART D: Same as Part C, except include a variable step.

PART E: Same as Part A, except construct a one-statement QuickBASIC program in the immediate window to compute directly, instead of iteratively, the sum of the numbers from 1 to 100.

Input Data: For Parts A, B, and E, there is no input. For C, input a lower limit of 15 and an upper limit of 42. For Part D, input a lower limit of 20, an upper limit of 75, and a step of 5.

Output Results: Display the result of each program in sentence form. For Parts A and E, the sum is 5050; for Part B, the sum is 2550; for Part C, the sum is 798; for Part D, the sum is 570.

2. Credit Card Verification

Purpose: To become familiar with declaring, loading, and serially searching a table.

Problem: Write a top-down program that will accept a six-digit credit card number and verify this number is in a table. If the credit card number is in the table, display a message indicating that the credit card number is valid. If the credit card number is not in the table, display a message indicating that the credit card is invalid, alert the manager, and beep the speaker several times. Declare the credit card number table to Number elements. Use the following 15 credit card numbers.

131416	238967	384512	583214	172319
345610	410001	672354	194567	351098
518912	691265	210201	372198	562982

The number of credit cards (15) and the credit card numbers are stored in a data file under the name EX82CARD.TBL on the Student Diskette.

Use the COMMON SHARED statement to declare the array globally. Use the argument-parameter passing technique to pass simple variables between subprograms.

Input Data: Use the following sample data:

372198   518912   102002   672354   210200   000000   999999

Output Results: The following results are shown for credit card numbers 372198 and 210200:

```
                    Credit Card Verification


Credit Card Number  •••••> 372198

Credit Card Number is valid

Enter Y to verify another Credit Card Number, else N... Y
```

```
                    Credit Card Verification


Credit Card Number  =====> 210200

•• Error •• Credit Card Number is invalid — Alert Your Manager

Enter Y to verify another Credit Card Number, else N... N
```

3. Windchill Table Lookup

Purpose: To become familiar with accessing data from a positionally organized table and the DIM SHARED statement.

Problem: As every resident of Alaska knows, the real enemy in terms of the weather is not the near-zero temperatures, but the windchill factor. Meteorologists in Alaska and in many other states give both the temperature and the windchill factor. So important is the windchill factor that calm air at −40° Fahrenheit is less likely to cause frostbite than air just below freezing that is blowing at gale forces. Basically, two factors determine the windchill factor: the velocity of wind and the temperature.

Write a top-down program that accepts from the user a temperature between −20°F and 15°F and a wind velocity between 5 mph and 30 mph, both in multiples of five. The program should look up the windchill factor in a positionally organized table and display it. Use the following table of windchill factors:

Table of Windchill Factors

Temperature in Fahrenheit	Wind Velocity in Miles per Hour					
	5	10	15	20	25	30
−20	−26	−46	−58	−67	−74	−79
−15	−21	−40	−51	−60	−66	−71
−10	−15	−34	−45	−53	−59	−64
−5	−10	−27	−38	−46	−51	−56
0	−5	−22	−31	−39	−44	−49
5	0	−15	−25	−31	−36	−41
10	7	−9	−18	−24	−29	−33
15	12	−3	−11	−17	−22	−25

In your program, use the INPUT #n statement and the data file EX83TABL.TBL on the Student Diskette to fill the table. Use the DIM SHARED statement in the Main Program to declare the two-dimensional array globally. Use the argument.parameter passing technique to pass simple variables between subprograms.

Input Data: Use the following sample data:

Temperature (°F)	Wind Velocity (mph)
–15	10
5	30
–5	40
–40	25
15	10

Output Results: The following results are shown for the first set of data items:

```
Windchill Table Lookup

Temperature (Between -20 and 15) ======>  -15

Velocity (Between 5 and 30) ==========>   10

Windchill Factor ====================>  -40

Enter Y to determine another windchill factor, else N... N
```

4. Week-Ending Department and Store Receipts

Purpose: To become familiar with the use of arrays for determining totals and the DIM SHARED statement.

Problem: Businesses are usually subdivided into smaller units for the purpose of better organization. The Tri-Quality retail store is subdivided into four departments. Each department submits its receipts at the end of the day to the store manager. Using an array consisting of 5 rows and 6 columns, write a top-down program that is assigned the daily sales. Use the fifth row and sixth column to accumulate the totals. After accumulating the totals, display the entire array.

Input Data: Use the following sample data:

Dept.	Monday	Tuesday	Wednesday	Thursday	Friday
1	$2,146	$6,848	$8,132	$8,912	$5,165
2	8,123	9,125	6,159	5,618	9,176
3	4,156	5,612	4,128	4,812	3,685
4	1,288	1,492	1,926	1,225	2,015

In your program, use the INPUT #n statement and the data file EX84SAL.DAT to fill the array. EX84SAL.DAT is stored on the Student Diskette. Use the DIM SHARED statement in the Main Program to declare the arrays globally.

Output Results: The following results are displayed:

```
                    Week-Ending Store Receipts

    Dept     Mon.      Tues.     Wed.      Thur.      Fri.     Total
    -----------------------------------------------------------------
     1      2,146     6,848     8,132     8,912     5,165    31,203
     2      8,123     9,125     6,159     5,618     9,176    38,201
     3      4,156     5,612     4,128     4,812     3,685    22,393
     4      1,288     1,492     1,926     1,225     2,015     7,946
     T     15,713    23,077    20,345    20,567    20,041    99,743

    Job Complete
```

5. Merging Lists

Purpose: To become familiar with the operation of merging.

Problem: Merging is the process of combining two sorted lists into a single sorted list. Obviously, one list can be appended to the other, and the new list can then be sorted. This process, however, is not always the most efficient. Write a top-down program that merges two arrays X and Y into array Z. Assume that the arrays X and Y have been presorted and are in ascending sequence. Declare the array X to have N elements, array Y to have M elements, and array Z to have N + M elements. Display the contents of the array Z as part of the end-of-job routine.

(Hint: Be sure to take into consideration that the two arrays are not the same size. That is, when the shorter of the two arrays has been processed, assign the remaining elements of the longer array to the array Z.)

Input Data: Use the following sample data.

Array X: 15 elements — 6, 9, 12, 15, 22, 33, 44, 66, 72, 84, 87, 92, 96, 98, 99

Array Y: 10 elements — 4, 8, 12, 16, 24, 31, 68, 71, 73, 74

Output Results: The following results are displayed. Note that the format of your results may vary slightly.

```
The merged array, Z, has 25 elements. Their values are:
  4   6   8   9   12   12   15   16   22   24   31   33   44   66   68   71   72
 73  74  84  87   92   96   98   99

Job Complete
```

6. Sorting Customer Numbers

Purpose: To become familiar with sorting data into ascending or descending sequence and to gain a better understanding of the bubble and Shell sort algorithms.

Problem: Write a top-down program that requests the selection from a menu of functions for sorting the customer records by customer number. Use the file EX77CUS.DAT described in Chapter 7, BASIC Programming Problem 7, page 262, and sort it into either ascending or descending sequence. Use the bubble sort algorithm to sort the customer numbers into ascending sequence. Use the Shell sort algorithm to sort the customer numbers into descending sequence. Declare the customer number array so that the program can sort up to a maximum of 100 records. Note that there are only 43 records in the customer file. Count the records as they are read into the arrays to determine the limit parameter for the For loops that sort the data.

Input Data: Use the data stored in the data file EX77CUS.DAT on the Student Diskette.

Output Results: The following is displayed on the screen:

```
Menu for Sorting Customer Numbers
---------------------------------

Code            Function
----            --------
  1             Ascending Sequence
  2             Descending Sequence
  3             End Program

Enter a Code 1 through 3 =====> 2

Press the Enter key when the printer is ready...
```

The following partial results for the descending sort of the customer records by customer number are printed on the attached printer.

```
Sorted Customer List
--------------------
Customer     Balance
--------     -------
  3096        27.95
  3095        56.75
   .            .

   .            .
   .            .
  3012       132.00
  3000        43.25
Report Complete
```

7. Determining the Mean, the Variance, and the Standard Deviation

Purpose: To apply the concepts of array elements to a statistical problem.

Problem: Construct a top-down program to find the mean (average), the variance, and the standard deviation of a variable number of student grades. Use the following three formulas:

$$\text{Mean} = \frac{\sum\limits_{j=1}^{n} X_j}{n} \qquad \text{Variance} = \frac{\sum\limits_{j=1}^{n} (X_j - \text{Mean})^2}{n - 1} \qquad \text{Standard Deviation} = \sqrt{\text{Variance}}$$

where n is the total number of grades and X_j is the student grades.

Input Data: Enter the number of students via the INPUT statement. Use DATA statements for the student grades.

Number of students: 10
Student grades: 97, 90, 87, 93, 96, 88, 78, 95, 96, 87

Output Results: The following results are displayed:

```
Statistical Analysis of Student Grades
----------------------------------------

Mean =================> 90.7
Variance ============> 35.12222
Standard Deviation ==> 5.9264

Job Complete
```

8. Payroll Problem VIII: Bonus Table Lookup Computations

Purpose: To become familiar with table utilization and program modification.

Problem: Modify Payroll Problem VII (Problem 8) in Chapter 7 to compute a bonus for each employee. Add the bonus to the gross pay defined in Payroll Problem VI. Adjust the report to include the bonus. Also, print the total bonus paid to all employees.

The bonus is computed by multiplying a factor times the original gross pay. The factor is based on a job class found in each employee payroll transaction record. After computing the gross pay for an employee, use the job class to search the bonus table for the bonus factor to multiply times the gross pay to determine the bonus. If the job class is not in the table, assign the employee a bonus of $25.00. The bonus table follows:

Job Class	Bonus Factor
01	.025
03	.0315
06	.04
07	.045
09	.05
10	.0525
12	.055

The data that makes up the bonus table is stored under the name EX88RATE.TBL on the Student Diskette. The very first data item in EX88RATE.TBL is 7, the number of table entries. Use this value to dimension the parallel arrays used to store the table.

Each record in the transaction file contains an employee number, the number of hours worked, and a job class. The transaction file contains the following eight records:

Employee Number	Hours Worked	Job Class
123	88	06
124	96	03
125	72	07
126	80	07
134	80	12
167	70.5	02
210	80	03
234	32	09

The transaction file is stored under the name EX88TRA.DAT on the Student Diskette. The employee master file EX71PAY.DAT is the same as for Payroll Problem VII in Chapter 7. You may assume the records in EX71PAY.DAT and EX88TRA.DAT are in ascending sequence and there is exactly one record in each file per employee. (That is, each record in EX71PAY.DAT has a match in EX88TRA.DAT.) Use the COMMON SHARED statement to declare all required variables globally.

Input Data: Use the following three sequential data files, described under **Problem** and stored on the Student Diskette:

File Name	Description
EX88RATE.TBL	Bonus Table Entries
EX71PAY.DAT	Employee Payroll Master File
EX88TRA.DAT	Employee Payroll Transaction File

Output Results: A master employee payroll file, as described in Payroll Problem VII in Chapter 7, is created as EX88PAY.DAT. The following report is printed on the printer:

```
                    Biweekly Payroll Report          Page:   1

  Employee
  Number     Bonus   Gross Pay   Fed. Tax   Soc. Sec.    Net Pay
  --------   -----   ---------   --------   ---------    -------
     123     46.00   1,196.00     223.82      91.49      880.69

     124     58.97   1,930.97     378.50      43.99    1,508.48

     125     42.12     978.12     187.93       0.00      790.19

     126     16.20     376.20       6.01      28.78      341.41

     134     38.50     738.50     147.70      56.50      534.30

     167     25.00     758.20     128.56      58.00      571.64
```

```
                    Biweekly Payroll Report          Page:   2

  Employee
  Number     Bonus   Gross Pay   Fed. Tax   Soc. Sec.    Net Pay
  --------   -----   ---------   --------   ---------    -------
     210     22.18     726.18      99.08      55.55      571.54

     234     10.80     226.80      29.98      17.35      179.47


  Total Bonus =============>      259.76
  Total Gross Pay =========>    6,930.96
  Total Withholding Tax ==>     1,201.58
  Total Social Security ==>       351.66
  Total Net Pay ===========>    5,377.72

  End of Payroll Report
```

Chapter

More on Strings and Functions

9.1 INTRODUCTION

Computers were originally built to perform mathematical calculations. They are still used for that purpose; however, today more and more computer applications process string data as well. Sections 3.5 and 5.5 briefly introduced five string functions — LEFT$, MID$, RIGHT$, LEN, and UCASE$ — giving some indication of the capability of QuickBASIC to manipulate string data. As you shall see in this chapter, QuickBASIC includes several additional string functions, string statements, and special variables that place it among the better programming languages for manipulating letters, numbers, words, and phrases.

QuickBASIC also includes numeric functions to handle common mathematical calculations. Section 3.5 introduced you to two numeric functions — INT and SQR. In this chapter, we discuss additional frequently used numeric functions.

A second type of function discussed in Chapter 9 is the **user-defined function**. With a function that is defined by the user, numeric or string functions can be created to perform a task often needed by the programmer. User-defined functions can be defined and called in the same program or defined as a distinct unit of code in the same fashion as a subprogram and called by any program.

Finally, this chapter introduces you to **system event trapping**. This activity requires the PC to check for the occurrence of an event — for example, the user pressing one of the function keys — as it executes a program. When the event occurs, the PC immediately transfers control to an event-assigned subroutine. Once the subroutine has been completed, the PC continues execution of the program where it left off when the event occurred.

9.2 STRING FUNCTIONS AND STATEMENTS

A list of the frequently used QuickBASIC string functions, along with their areas of use, are shown in Table 9.1 on the next page. To be used, these functions need only be referred to by name in a LET, PRINT, or IF statement. (For a complete listing of the string functions and statements, see the Reference Card at the back of this book.)

TABLE 9.1 Frequently Used QuickBASIC String Functions	
FUNCTION	**FUNCTION VALUE**
ASC(X$)	Returns a two-digit numeric value equivalent in ASCII code to the first character of the string argument X$.
CHR$(N)	Returns a single string character equivalent in ASCII code to the numeric argument N.
DATE$	Returns the system date as a string in the form mm-dd-yyyy.
INKEY$	Accepts a single character from the keyboard without suspending execution of the program or waiting for the Enter key to be pressed.
INPUT$(N)	Suspends execution of the program until N number of characters from the keyboard are entered.
INSTR(P,X$,S$)	Returns the beginning position of the substring S$ in string X$. P indicates the position the search begins in X$ and may be omitted from the argument list. If the search for S$ in X$ is unsuccessful, INSTR returns a value of zero.
LCASE$(X$)	Returns X$ in lowercase.
LEFT$(X$, N)	Extracts the leftmost N characters of the string argument X$.
LEN(X$)	Returns the length of the string argument X$.
LTRIM$(X$)	Returns X$ with leading blanks trimmed away.
MID$(X$, P, N)	Extracts N characters of the string argument X$ beginning at position P.
RIGHT$(X$, N)	Extracts the rightmost N characters of the string argument X$.
RTRIM$(X$)	Returns X$ with trailing blanks trimmed away.
SPACE$(N)	Returns N number of spaces.
SPC(N)	Displays N spaces. May be used only in a PRINT or LPRINT statement.
STR$(N)	Returns the string equivalent of the numeric argument N.
STRING$(N, X$)	Returns N times the first character of X$.
TIME$	Equals the time of day in 24-hour notation as a string in the form hh:mm:ss.
UCASE$(X$)	Returns X$ in uppercase.
VAL(X$)	Returns the numeric equivalent of the string argument X$.

Concatenation, Substrings, and Character Counting Revisited — +, LEN, LEFT$, RIGHT$ and MID$

The extraction of substrings from a large string and the combining of two or more strings are important in manipulating nonnumeric data. In Section 3.5, on page 75, the concatenation operation (+) and the LEN, LEFT$, RIGHT$, and MID$ functions were briefly introduced. You'll recall that concatenation (+) is the only string operation allowed in QuickBASIC. It joins two strings to form a new string. For example,

```
Join$ = "ABC" + "DEF"
```

assigns Join$ the value ABCDEF. The second string is joined to the right end of the first string to form the result, which is then assigned to Join$. More than one concatenation operator may appear in a single assignment statement.

For example, if Phrase1$ = Resist♭ and Phrase2$ = the urge♭ and Phrase3$ = to code where ♭ represents a blank character, then

Phrase$ = Phrase1$ + Phrase2$ + Phrase3$

assigns Phrase$ the string Resist the urge to code.

The LEN function returns the length of the argument. The argument may be a string constant, a string variable, or a string expression. Table 9.2 and the partial program in Figure 9.1 illustrate the use of the LEN function.

TABLE 9.2	Examples of the LEN Function	
VALUE OF VARIABLE	**THE STATEMENT**	**RESULTS IN**
Comp1$ = IBM PS/2	Len1 = LEN(Comp1$)	Len1 = 8
Comp2$ = Zenith	Len2 = LEN(Comp2$)	Len2 = 6
	Len3 = LEN("Clone")	Len3 = 5
	Len4 = LEN(" ")	Len4 = 0
Noth$ = null	Len5 = LEN(Noth$)	Len5 = 0

FIGURE 9.1

```
1     ' Examples of the use of the LEN function
2     ' ******************************************
3     CLS   ' Clear Screen
4     Word1$ = "Structured"
5     Word2$ = "Programming"
6     Length = LEN(Word1$)
7     PRINT Word1$; " has"; Length; "characters."
8     PRINT Word2$; " has"; LEN(Word2$); "characters."
9     PRINT Word1$ + " " + Word2$; " has";
10    PRINT LEN(Word1$ + " " + Word2$); "characters."

[run]

Structured has 10 characters.
Programming has 11 characters.
Structured Programming has 22 characters.
```

In Figure 9.1, LEN(Word1$) in line 6 assigns the variable Length a value of 10. In line 8, LEN(Word2$) is displayed as 11. In line 10, the LEN function returns the length of the string expression WORD1$ + " " + WORD2$ as 22.

The LEFT$, MID$, and RIGHT$ string functions may be used to extract substrings from a string constant, a string variable, or a string expression. A **substring** is a part of a string. For example, some substrings of Return of the Jedi are Return, Jedi, of t, and ed. All three functions reference substrings on the basis of the position of characters within the string argument, where the leftmost character of the string argument is position 1; the next is position 2, and so on. For example, in the string Return of the Jedi, the substring Return begins in position 1, and the substring Jedi begins in position 15.

LEFT$(X$, N) extracts a substring starting with the leftmost character (position 1) of the string X$. The length of the substring is determined by the integer value of the length argument N. For example, the following statement assigns a value of Return to Sub1$:

Sub1$ = LEFT$("Return of the Jedi", 6)

`Return` begins in position 1 and has a length of 6. The quotation marks are not part of the string.

`RIGHT$(X$, N)` extracts a substring starting with the rightmost character of the string argument X$. The length of the substring is determined by the value of the length argument N. For example, if Movie$ is equal to the string `Raiders of the Lost Ark`, then the following statement assigns Sub2$ the substring `Ark`:

```
Sub2$ = RIGHT$(Movie$, 3)
```

`MID$(X$, P, N)` extracts a substring beginning with the character in position P of X$. The length of the substring is determined by the value of the length argument N. For example, if Phrase$ is equal to the string `Every dog must have his day`, then the following statement assigns Sub3$ the substring `dog must have`:

```
Sub3$ = MID$(Phrase$, 7, 13)
```

If the length argument is not included in the list for the `MID$` function, then the PC returns a substring that begins with the position argument and ends with the last character in the string argument. For example, if Phrase$ is equal to the string

```
Today is the tomorrow I worried about yesterday
```

then the following statement assigns Sub4$ the substring `I worried about yesterday`:

```
Sub4$ = MID$(Phrase$, 23)
```

Table 9.3 illustrates the use of the `LEFT$`, `RIGHT$`, and `MID$` functions.

TABLE 9.3   Examples of the LEFT$, RIGHT$, and MID$ Functions

Assume S$ is equal to: `If something can go wrong, it will`

EXAMPLE	THE STATEMENT	RESULTS IN
1.	`C$ = LEFT$(S$, 12)`	`C$ = If something`
2.	`F$ = LEFT$(S$, 1.7)`	`F$ = If`
3.	`H$ = LEFT$(S$, 0)`	`H$ = null`
4.	`J$ = RIGHT$(S$, 7)`	`J$ = it will`
5.	`P$ = RIGHT$("to be", -1)`	`Illegal function call`
6.	`R$ = RIGHT$(S$, 50)`	`R$ = S$`
7.	`T$ = MID$(S$, -1, 6)`	`Illegal function call`
8.	`U$ = MID$(LEFT$(S$, 4), 2, 1)`	`U$ = f`
9.	`V$ = MID$(S$, 75, 4)`	`V$ = null`
10.	`X$ = MID$(S$, 18)`	`X$ = go wrong, it will`
11.	`Y$ = MID$(S$, 32768)`	`Illegal function call`

In Example 2 of Table 9.3, the argument 1.7 is rounded to 2. In Example 3, the numeric argument 0 causes the PC to assign H$ the null string. In Example 5, the negative argument (−1) causes the PC to display a dialog box with a diagnostic message. Example 6 shows that if the length argument is greater than the length of the string argument, the function returns a substring that begins at the specified position and includes the remaining portion of the string.

In Example 7, the position argument, −1, is invalid. Example 8 shows that you may include a string function as the string argument. Example 9 illustrates that a null string is returned when the specified beginning position in the `MID$` function is greater than the length of the argument string. Example 10 shows that when the length argument is not included in the MID$ function, the PC returns a substring beginning with the specified position and ending with the last character of the string argument. Finally, Example 11 causes a dialog box to display with a diagnostic message because the position argument is greater than 32,767. The position argument must be in the range 1 to 32,767.

QuickBASIC interprets the position argument P and the length argument N of the LEFT$, MID$, and RIGHT$ functions according to the following rules:

STRING FUNCTION RULE 1 *If the position argument P or the length argument N is a decimal fraction, the value of N or P is rounded to an integer.*

STRING FUNCTION RULE 2 *If the length argument N is less than 0 or greater than 32,767, then the function call is illegal. If N is equal to zero, the function returns a null string.*

STRING FUNCTION RULE 3 *If the length argument N is greater than the remaining length of the string argument, the function returns a substring that begins at the specified position and includes the remaining portion of the string.*

STRING FUNCTION RULE 4 *If the position argument P is greater than the length of the string argument, the function returns a null string. If the position argument P is less than 1 or greater than 32,767, then the function call is illegal.*

The partial program in Figure 9.2 makes use of the LEN and MID$ functions. The output results are shown on the next page. The basic purpose of the program is to search for words in a sentence. Each time a word is found, the program displays it on a separate line. The program assumes that each word, except for the last, is followed by a space.

FIGURE 9.2

```
1    ' Displaying Each Word in a Sentence
2    ' *********************************
3    CLS  ' Clear Screen
4    PRINT "Enter the sentence without punctuation:"
5    PRINT : INPUT "", Sentence$
6    Begin = 1
7    PRINT : PRINT "Words in the sentence:"
8    FOR Character = 1 TO LEN(Sentence$)
9       IF MID$(Sentence$, Character, 1) = " " THEN
10         PRINT TAB(23); MID$(Sentence$, Begin, Character - Begin)
11         Begin = Character + 1
12      END IF
13   NEXT Character
14   ' ******* Display the Last Word ******
15   PRINT TAB(23); MID$(Sentence$, Begin)
16   PRINT "Job Complete"

     [run]
```

(continued)

```
Enter the sentence without punctuation:

If an experiment works something has gone wrong

Words in the sentence:
                        If
                        an
                        experiment
                        works
                        something
                        has
                        gone
                        wrong
Job Complete
```

When the partial program in Figure 9.2 is executed, line 4 displays a prompt message. Line 5 accepts the sentence and assigns it to the variable Sentence$. In line 6, the variable Begin is assigned a value of 1. This variable is used later in line 10 to indicate the beginning position of each word and in line 15 to display the last word in the sentence.

Line 9 in the For loop tests each character in the sentence to determine whether it is a space. If a character is a space, then the word beginning at position Begin with length of Character – Begin is displayed, and Begin is set equal to a value that is equivalent to the beginning position of the next word. Because the last word in the sentence does not end with a space, line 15, instead of line 10, is used to display the last word.

Substring Searching and Replacement — INSTR Function and MID$ Statement

QuickBASIC includes the INSTR function to search a string argument for a particular substring. INSTR(P, X$, S$) returns the beginning position of the substring S$ in X$. The search begins at position P of X$. For example, the following partial program causes the variable Count1 to be assigned the value 4:

```
Phrase$ = "To be or not to be"
Count1 = INSTR(1, Phrase$, "be")
```

The second line in the partial program assigns Count1 the position of the first character of the substring be in string Phrase$. If there are no occurrences of the substring, INSTR returns the value zero.

The INSTR function always returns the leftmost position of the first occurrence of the substring. If the following statement is added to the previous partial program,

```
Count2 = INSTR(5, Phrase$, "be")
```

then Count2 is assigned a value of 17. The first occurrence of be is bypassed because the search begins at position 5, rather than position 1.

The position argument P may be omitted. For example, the statement Count1 = INSTR(Phrase$, "be") is identical to Count1 = INSTR(1, Phrase$, "be"). That is, the search begins at position 1, by default, and assigns Count1 a value of 4. Table 9.4 illustrates some additional examples of the INSTR function.

TABLE 9.4   Examples of the INSTR Function

Assume that S$ is equal to:
```
Rally 'round the flag, boys, rally once again
```

THE STATEMENT	RESULTS IN
Pos1 = INSTR(1, S$, ",")	Pos1 = 22
Pos2 = INSTR(Start, S$, "rally")	Pos2 = 30 (assume Start = 22)
Pos3 = INSTR(S$, " ' ")	Pos3 = 7

The MID$ statement is used for substring replacement. Do not confuse the MID$ statement with the MID$ function. The MID$ function returns a substring, but the MID$ statement replaces a series of characters within a string with a designated substring. The general form of the MID$ statement is given in Table 9.5.

TABLE 9.5   The MID$ Statement

General Form: `MID$(X$, P, N) = S$`

where **X$** is the string in which the replacement takes place;
   P is the position at which the replacement begins;
   N is the number of characters to replace; and
   S$ is the replacement substring.

Purpose: To replace a substring within a string.

Examples:
1. `MID$(Phrase$, 3, 4) = Substr$`
2. `MID$(Word1$, 1, 5) = "Y"`   (1 character replaced)
3. `MID$(Wd1$, 30, 2) = "abcde"` (2 characters replaced)
4. `MID$(E$, 4, 5) = A$ + B$`

As illustrated by the general form in Table 9.5, a substring of X$, specified by the beginning position P and the length N, is replaced by the substring S$. In Example 1 if Phrase$ is equal to `Inprocment` and Substr$ is equal to `vest`, then the following statement

```
MID$(Phrase$, 3, 4) = Substr$
```

assigns Phrase$ the value `Investment`. The substring `vest` replaces the substring `proc`.

Example 2 in Table 9.5 shows that if the replacement substring is shorter than the substring designated by the length argument in the MID$ statement, then only those characters that are designated by the replacement substring are actually replaced. For example, if Word1$ is equal to `Beast`, then the statement

```
MID$(Word1$, 1, 5) = "Y"
```

assigns Word1$ the value `Yeast`.

If the replacement substring has a length greater than that specified by N in the MID$ statement, then the PC replaces only N characters. The rightmost excess characters in the replacement substring are not used.

The partial program in Figure 9.3 modifies a line of text through the use of the INSTR function and the MID$ statement. The program searches for all occurrences of the substring ne. Each time the substring is found, it is replaced with the substring in.

FIGURE 9.3

```
1     ' Searching and Replacing Strings
2     ' ********************************
3     Phrase$ = "The rane in Spane stays manely in the plane"
4     PRINT "Old text ===> "; Phrase$
5     Position = INSTR(Phrase$, "ne")
6     DO WHILE Position < > 0
7        MID$(Phrase$, Position, 2) = "in"
8        Position = INSTR(Position + 2, Phrase$, "ne")
9     LOOP
10    PRINT
11    PRINT "New text ===> "; Phrase$

[run]

Old text ===> The rane in Spane stays manely in the plane

New text ===> The rain in Spain stays mainly in the plain
```

Line 5 in Figure 9.3 assigns the variable Position the value 7, which is the beginning position of the first occurrence of the substring ne. Line 7 replaces the substring ne that begins in position 7 with the substring in. Line 8 searches for the next occurrence of the substring ne. The search begins one position to the right of the previous occurrence. The next occurrence of the substring ne begins at position 16. Therefore, the INSTR function assigns Position a value of 16. The loop continues, with line 7 making the next replacement.

This process continues until all the occurrences of ne have been changed to in. At this point, line 8 assigns Position a value of zero, and the loop terminates. The modified value of Phrase$ is then displayed by line 11.

If Phrase$ is assigned a value without the substring ne, the Do-While loop (lines 6 through 9) will not execute. The INSTR function in line 5 returns a value of zero when the substring is not found. With Position equal to zero, the DO WHILE statement in line 6 causes execution to continue at line 10. In this case, the new text and old text are identical.

Converting Character Codes — ASC and CHR$

The ASC and CHR$ functions facilitate the manipulation of individual characters. The ASC(X$) function returns a two-digit numeric value that corresponds to the ASCII code for the first character of the string argument X$. As explained in Chapter 6 on page 169, each character in QuickBASIC has a corresponding ASCII numeric code the PC uses for storing the character in main storage or in auxiliary storage. For example, the character A has an ASCII code of 65; the character B has an ASCII code of 66, and so on. The following statement displays the result 67:

```
PRINT ASC("C")
  67
```

CHR$(N) can be described as the reverse of the ASC function. It returns a single string character equivalent in ASCII code to the numeric argument N. For example, the following statement displays the character B:

```
PRINT CHR$(66)
  B
```

A total of 256 different characters are represented by the ASCII code. (See Appendix D, Table D.3.) The CHR$ function allows you to enter any of the 256 characters by using the corresponding ASCII code as the argument. For example, the following partial program

```
FOR I = 1 TO 10
   PRINT CHR$(7);
NEXT I
PRINT CHR$(12)
```

causes the PC to beep 10 times and clear the first 24 lines of the screen because the ASCII code 7 corresponds to the character BEL (Bell), and the ASCII code 12 corresponds to the character FF (Form Feed).

Table 9.6 illustrates several examples of the ASC and CHR$ functions. Later, Programming Case Study 13 makes use of both functions to decipher a coded message.

TABLE 9.6   Examples of the ASC and CHR$ Functions

VALUE OF	THE STATEMENT	RESULTS IN
	Code1= ASC("5")	Code1 = 53
C$ = null	D1 = ASC(C$)	Illegal function call
D$ = ABC	E = ASC(D$)	E = 65
	Kay$ = CHR$(75)	Kay$ = K
D = -3	Y$ = CHR$(D)	Illegal function call

Changing Case — LCASE$ and UCASE$

The LCASE$ and UCASE$ functions are used to convert alphabetic characters in a string expression to uppercase or lowercase. For example, if Phrase$ is equal to 9946 REDBUD Road, then LCASE$(Phrase$) is equal to 9946 redbud road. Note that the digits 9946, the space between 9946 and REDBUD, and the lowercase characters oad are not affected by the LCASE$ function.

The UCASE$ function is the opposite of the LCASE$ function. UCASE$(Phrase$) returns the string 9946 REDBUD ROAD. Here again, the digits, space and uppercase characters in Phrase$ are not affected by the UCASE$ function. Only the lowercase characters oad are changed to uppercase.

Table 9.7 shows additional examples of the LCASE$ and UCASE$ functions.

TABLE 9.7   Examples of the LCASE$ and UCASE$ Functions

VALUE OF	THE STATEMENT	RESULTS IN
L$ = QuickBASIC	U$ = UCASE$(L$)	U$ = QUICKBASIC
	L$ = LCASE$("12A4B&3")	L$ = 12a4b&3
L$ = ms01Cr?	U$ = UCASE$(L$)	U$ = MS01CR?

Programming Case Study 4B on page 149, introduced the UCASE$ function. The user is asked to enter Y or N to control a looping process. For example,

```
LOOP UNTIL UCASE$(Control$) = "N"
```

determines if a Do-Until loop should continue.

| Programming Case Study 13 | Deciphering a Coded Message

Messages are often coded by having one letter represent another. The coded message is called a **cryptogram**, and an algorithm is used to decipher the message into readable form.

The objective here is to take a coded message and have the PC display the corresponding deciphered message in lowercase. The algorithm calls for subtracting 3 from the numeric code that represents each character in the coded message. After each character in the message is deciphered, it is to be displayed in lowercase. Obviously, the algorithm can be, and usually is, more complex. The coded message is W K H # V K D G R Z # N Q R Z V.

Following are an analysis of the problem, a program solution, and a discussion of the program solution.

Program Tasks

1. A100.Initialization

   a. Clear the screen.
   b. Accept the coded message.

2. B100.Process.Code — change and display the coded message. Use a For loop that includes the following:

   a. A limit parameter of LEN(Code$)
   b. The MID$ function to extract each character
   c. The ASC function to determine the numeric value equivalent to the ASCII code of the extracted character
   d. Subtraction of 3 from the numeric value determined in 2.c
   e. The CHR$ function to change the numeric value in 2.d to a character
   f. Displaying the character in lowercase using the LCASE$ function

3. C100.Wrap.Up — print End of Job message

Program Solution

The following program corresponds to the preceding tasks:

PROGRAM 9.1

```
 1    ' Program 9.1
 2    ' Deciphering a Coded Message
 3    ' ********************************************
 4    ' *              Main Program                *
 5    ' ********************************************
 6    CALL A100.Initialization(Code$)
 7    CALL B100.Process.Code(Code$)
 8    CALL C100.Wrap.Up
 9    END
10
11    ' ********************************************
12    ' *              Initialization              *
13    ' *              Returns Code$               *
14    ' ********************************************
15    SUB A100.Initialization (Code$)
16       CLS  ' Clear Screen
17       PRINT : INPUT "Coded message =======> ", Code$
18       PRINT : PRINT "The message is =======> ";
19    END SUB
20
```

```
21    ' ***********************************************
22    ' *              Process Code               *
23    ' *              Receives Code$             *
24    ' ***********************************************
25    SUB B100.Process.Code (Code$)
26       FOR Char = 1 TO LEN(Code$)
27          Number = ASC(MID$(Code$, Char, 1))
28          Number = Number - 3
29          Letter$ = CHR$(Number)
30          PRINT LCASE$(Letter$);
31       NEXT Char
32    END SUB
33
34    ' ***********************************************
35    ' *                 Wrap-Up                  *
36    ' ***********************************************
37    SUB C100.Wrap.Up
38       PRINT : PRINT
39       PRINT "End of Job"
40    END SUB

      [run]

      Coded message ========> WKH#VKDGRZ#NQRZV

      The message is =======> the shadow knows

      End of Job
```

Discussion of the Program Solution

Program 9.1 accepts a coded message, deciphers it one character at a time, and displays the corresponding message one character at a time in lowercase.

In line 26, LEN(Code$) is the limit value for the For loop. Line 27 determines the numeric value that corresponds to the ASCII code for the character selected by the MID$ function. It is valid for a string function to be part of the argument for another string function. Line 28 subtracts 3 from the value of Number, and in line 29 the CHR$ function returns the corresponding character. Finally, the LCASE$ function is used in the PRINT statement in line 30 to display the deciphered character in lowercase before the next character in the message is processed.

Modifying Data Types — STR$ and VAL

The PC cannot add a string value to a numeric value. The STR$ and VAL functions allow this restriction to be circumvented. The STR$(N) function returns the string equivalent of the numeric value N. VAL(X$) returns the numeric equivalent of the string X$. Thus, STR$(52.3) returns the string "52.3", and VAL("310.23") returns the numeric value 310.23. If the argument for the STR$ function is negative, the function returns a leading negative sign. If the argument for the VAL function does not represent a number, the function returns a value of 0. For example, the value displayed by the following statement is zero:

```
PRINT VAL("CHICAGO")
  0
```

Table 9.8 on the next page gives examples of both the STR$ and VAL functions. These two functions are used primarily in instances where a substring of numeric digits within an identification number — such as a credit card number or an invoice number — needs to be extracted for computational purposes, and the result has to be transformed back as a string value.

TABLE 9.8	Examples of the STR$ and VAL Functions	
VALUE OF	**THE STATEMENT**	**RESULTS IN**
	A$ = STR$(34)	A$ = 34
B = 64.543	S$ = STR$(B)	S$ = 64.543
C = -3.21	Z$ = STR$(C)	Z$ = -3.21
	F = VAL("766.321")	F = 766.321
K$ = 12E-3	Q = VAL(K$)	Q = 12E-3
P$ = ABC	W = VAL(P$)	W = 0

Note: Any numeric value assigned to a string variable is actually a string, not a number.

Duplicating Strings — SPACE$ and STRING$

The SPACE$ and STRING$ functions are used to duplicate string data. The SPACE$(N) function returns N spaces or blank characters. It is similar to the SPC function discussed in Chapter 3. For example, the two statements

```
PRINT "DEC"; SPC(4); "Micro VAX"
```

and

```
PRINT "DEC"; SPACE$(4); "Micro VAX"
```

display identical results. The advantage of the SPACE$ function over the SPC function is that SPACE$ may be used in statements other than the PRINT or LPRINT statements. For example, the following statement

```
Sp$ = SPACE$(25)
```

assigns Sp$ a string value of 25 spaces. If the argument is equal to or less than zero, the function returns the null string.

The STRING$(N, X$) function returns N times the first character of the string X$. The STRING$ function may be used to duplicate any character. For example, the following statement

```
PRINT STRING$(72, "*")
```

displays a line of 72 asterisks. The second argument may also be represented in ASCII code. That is, the statement

```
PRINT STRING$(72, 42)
```

is identical to the previous PRINT statement because 42 is the ASCII code representation for the asterisk character.

Table 9.9 gives examples of both the SPACE$ and STRING$ functions.

VALUE OF	THE STATEMENT	COMMENT
TABLE 9.9 Examples of the SPACE$ and STRING$ Functions		
N = 50	PRINT SPACE$(N); "A"	Displays 50 spaces, followed by the character A in position 51.
	Sp$ = SPACE$(12)	Assigns 12 spaces to Sp$.
	Null$ = SPACE$(0)	Assigns Null$ the null string.
C = 45	PRINT STRING$(C, "-")	Displays 45 minus signs.
	A$ = STRING$(5, 65)	Assigns A$ the string value AAAAA.

Trimming Blank Characters — LTRIM$ and RTRIM$

The LTRIM$ and RTRIM$ functions remove leading or trailing blank characters from a string expression. LTRIM$(X$) returns X$ with leading (left) blank characters removed. RTRIM$(X$) returns X$ with trailing (right) blank characters removed. For example, in the following partial program,

```
1    Phrase1$ = "    Leading Blanks"
2    Phrase2$ = "Trailing Blanks    "
3    Phrase.LTrim$ = LTRIM$(Phrase1$)
4    Phrase.RTrim$ = RTRIM$(Phrase2$)
```

line 3 assigns Phrase.LTrim$ the value Leading Blanks without the leading blank characters that were part of the string value in line 1. Line 4 assigns Phrase.RTrim$ the value Trailing Blanks without the trailing blank characters that were part of the string value in line 2.

Accessing the System Time and Date — DATE$ and TIME$

The DATE$ and TIME$ functions return the system date and system time, respectively. DATE$ is equal to the current system date as a string value in the form mm-dd-yyyy. The first two characters, mm, represent the month. The fourth and fifth characters, dd, represent the day. The last four characters, yyyy, represent the year. For example, if the system date is initialized to December 25, 1995, then the statement

```
Todays.Date$ = DATE$
```

assigns Todays.Date$ the string 12-25-1995.

TIME$ is equal to the system's time of day, in 24-hour notation, as a string value in the form hh:mm:ss. The first two characters, hh, represent the hours (range 00–23). The fourth and fifth characters, mm, represent the minutes (range 00–59). The last two characters, ss, represent the seconds (range 00–59). If the PC's internal clock is equal to 11:35:42 *at the instant* the statement

```
PRINT "The time is "; TIME$
```

executes, then the following displays:

```
The time is 11:35:42
```

The key phrase in the last sentence is *at the instant*, because as part of the start-up procedures, the PC's internal clock automatically maintains the time after it is entered by the user.

Table 9.10 gives examples of both the DATE$ and TIME$ functions.

TABLE 9.10   Examples of the DATE$ and TIME$ Functions

Assume DATE$ = 09-15-1995 and TIME$ = 15:26:32

THE STATEMENT	RESULTS IN
Td$ = DATE$	Td$ = 09-15-1995
Tt$ = TIME$	Tt$ = 15:26:32
Month$ = MID$(DATE$, 1, 2)	Month$ = 09
Day$ = MID$(DATE$, 4, 2)	Day$ = 15
Year$ = MID$(DATE$, 9, 2)	Year$ = 95
Hour$ = MID$(TIME$, 1, 2)	Hour$ = 15
Minute$ = MID$(TIME$, 4, 2)	Minute$ = 26
Second$ = MID$(TIME$, 7, 2)	Second$ = 32

Note: Any numeric value assigned to a string variable is actually a
string, not a number.

The DATE$ and TIME$ functions are frequently used to display the date and time as part of report headings. The DATE$ function may be also used in business-related applications to verify that a payment date, birth date, or hire date is valid.

Programming Case Study 14   Validating Payment Dates

The following program solution illustrates how to verify that a payment date is the present date or an earlier date, not a future date.

Problem: The following customer payment records are stored in the sequential file ACCREC.DAT. The payment dates are of the form mmddyy.

Customer Number	Customer Payment	Payment Date
31245381	$101.55	091595
46371230	95.25	061294
71209824	25.00	062494
96012567	38.00	053094

The accounts receivable department has requested a program to verify the payment date for each record in ACCREC.DAT is not a date in the future. The program should verify each payment date against today's date. If today's date is greater than or equal to the payment date, then the payment date is valid. If today's date is less than the payment date, then the payment date is invalid. For each record, print on the printer the customer number, the payment, the payment date, and a message indicating whether the payment date is valid or invalid. The results are to be in report form with one line printed for each record read. Assume that today's date is June 22, 1994. (Reboot the PC to enter this date or use the DATE$ statement, which is discussed in the next section.) To compare the two dates, the most significant part of the date (years) must be at the far left, followed by the next most significant part (months), followed by the least significant part (days). That is, the program must rearrange the two dates before it can compare them, as follows:

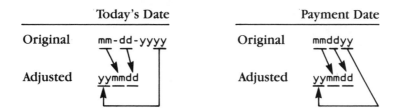

To rearrange the substrings within each date, the MID$ function and the concatenation operator may be used. Once the two fields have been adjusted, today's date can be compared against the customer payment date.

Following are a list of the program tasks, a program solution, and a discussion of the program solution.

Program Tasks

1. A100.Initialization

   a. Set To.Date$ to DATE$.
   b. Use this expression to rearrange today's date:

      Today$ = MID$(To.Date$, 9, 2) + MID$(To.Date$, 1, 2) + MID$(To.Date$, 4, 2)

   c. Request the user to turn on the printer.
   d. Call A200.Initialize.Report.Format
   e. Call A210.Print.Headings
   f. Open ACCREC.DAT.

2. B100.Process.File

   a. Read an accounts receivable record.
   b. Call B200.Validate.Payment.Date
      (1) Adjust the customer payment date (C.Date$). Use the following statement:

      Adj.Date$ = MID$(C.Date$, 5, 2) + MID$(C.Date$, 1, 2) + MID$(C.Date$, 3, 2)

      (2) If Today$ >= Adj.Date$, then Message$ equals Date OK. Otherwise, Message$ equals Date NOT OK.
   c. Print the customer number, the payment, the payment date, and the message. Format the payment date in the form mm-dd-yy.

3. C100.Wrap.Up

   a. Close ACCREC.DAT.
   b. Print an end-of-job message.
   c. Clear the screen and display an end-of-job message.

Program Solution

Program 9.2 corresponds to the preceding tasks.

PROGRAM 9.2

```
1    ' Program 9.2
2    ' Validating Payment Dates
3    ' Input File Name = ACCREC.DAT
4    ' ********************************************************
5    ' *                     Main Program                    *
6    ' ********************************************************
7    COMMON SHARED H1$, H2$, H3$, H4$, D1$, T1$, Today$
8    CALL A100.Initialization
9    CALL B100.Process.File
10   CALL C100.Wrap.Up
11   END
12
13       ' ****************************************************
14       ' *                 Initialization                  *
15       ' ****************************************************
16   SUB A100.Initialization
17      To.Date$ = DATE$
18      Today$ = MID$(To.Date$, 9, 2) + MID$(To.Date$, 1, 2)
19      Today$ = Today$ + MID$(To.Date$, 4, 2)
20      CLS  ' Clear Screen
21      LOCATE 12, 15: PRINT "Validating Payment Dates"
22      LOCATE 14, 15
23      INPUT "Press the Enter key when the printer is ready...", Control$
24      CALL A200.Initialize.Report.Format
25      CALL A210.Print.Headings
26      OPEN "ACCREC.DAT" FOR INPUT AS #1
27   END SUB
28
29       ' ****************************************************
30       ' *             Initialize Report Format            *
31       ' ****************************************************
32   SUB A200.Initialize.Report.Format
33      H1$ = "   Validating Payment Dates For "
34      H2$ = "Customer                    Payment"
35      H3$ = "Number      Payment        Date         Comment"
36      H4$ = "--------    -------        -------      -------"
37      D1$ = "\        \  #,###.##       \\-\\-\\      \           \"
38      T1$ = "End of Report"
39   END SUB
40
41       ' ****************************************************
42       ' *             Initialize Report Format            *
43       ' ****************************************************
44   SUB A210.Print.Headings
45      LPRINT H1$; DATE$
46      LPRINT SPC(3); STRING$(39, "-")
47      LPRINT
48      LPRINT H2$
49      LPRINT H3$
50      LPRINT H4$
51   END SUB
52
```

```
53    ' ***********************************************************
54    ' *                    Process File                         *
55    ' ***********************************************************
56    SUB B100.Process.File
57       DO WHILE NOT EOF(1)
58          INPUT #1, C.Num$, C.Pay, C.Date$
59          CALL B200.Validate.Payment.Date(C.Date$, Message$)
60          Month$ = LEFT$(C.Date$, 2)
61          Day$ = MID$(C.Date$, 3, 2)
62          Year$ = RIGHT$(C.Date$, 2)
63          LPRINT USING D1$; C.Num$; C.Pay; Month$; Day$; Year$; Message$
64       LOOP
65    END SUB
66
67    ' ***********************************************************
68    ' *                Validate Payment Date                    *
69    ' *          Receives C.Date$; Returns Message$             *
70    ' ***********************************************************
71    SUB B200.Validate.Payment.Date (C.Date$, Message$)
72       Adj.Date$ = MID$(C.Date$, 5, 2) + MID$(C.Date$, 1, 2)
73       Adj.Date$ = Adj.Date$ + MID$(C.Date$, 3, 2)
74       IF Today$ >= Adj.Date$ THEN
75          Message$ = "Date OK"
76       ELSE
77          Message$ = "Date NOT OK"
78       END IF
79    END SUB
80
81    ' ***********************************************************
82    ' *                      Wrap-Up                            *
83    ' ***********************************************************
84    SUB C100.Wrap.Up
85       CLOSE #1
86       LPRINT : LPRINT T1$
87       CLS  ' Clear Screen
88       LOCATE 12, 34: PRINT "Job Complete"
89    END SUB

      [run]
```

FIGURE 9.4

The report generated by Program 9.2.

```
    Validating Payment Dates For 06-22-1994
    --------------------------------------------

    Customer              Payment
    Number     Payment    Date        Comment
    --------   -------    -------     -------
    31245381   101.55     09-15-95    Date NOT OK
    46371230    95.25     06-12-94    Date OK
    71209824    25.00     06-24-94    Date NOT OK
    96012567    38.00     05-30-94    Date OK

    End of Report
```

Discussion of the Program Solution

In Program 9.2, line 17 assigns To.Date$ today's date. Lines 18 and 19 rearrange the substrings of To.Date$ in the format yymmdd and assigns the result to Today$. Lines 72 and 73 rearrange the substrings of the customer payment date into the same format. Line 74 compares today's date to the customer payment date. If Today$ is greater than or equal to Adj.Date$, then Message$ is set equal to Date OK. If Today$ is less than Adj.Date$, then the payment date is a future date, and Message$ is set equal to Date NOT OK. Pay particular attention to lines 18 and 19, and 72 and 73. Rearranging substrings is a common characteristic of programs that validate dates.

The report generated by Program 9.2 is shown in Figure 9.4. Note that the payment dates are formatted on the basis of the descriptor field in line 37 and the use of the string functions in lines 60 through 62.

Setting the Time and Date — The DATE$ and TIME$ Statements

While the DATE$ and TIME$ functions are equal to the **system's current date and time**, the DATE$ and TIME$ statements allow you to set the PC's date and time. These two statements override the date and time entered during start-up procedures. The general forms for the DATE$ and TIME$ statements are given in Tables 9.11 and 9.12.

TABLE 9.11   The DATE$ Statement

General Form:	DATE$ = string expression
	where **string expression** is one of the following forms:
	    mm-dd-yy
	    mm-dd-yyyy
	    mm/dd/yy
	    mm/dd/yyyy

Purpose:	To set the system date.
Examples:	DATE$ = "07-06-95" DATE$ = "7/6/1995" DATE$ = "06-22-2005" DATE$ = "1/25/96" DATE$ = Cur.Date$
Note:	The year must be in the range 1980 to 2099. If you enter a two-digit year, then the PC assumes 19yy. You may enter one digit for the month or day. If only one digit is entered, then the PC assumes a leading zero.

TABLE 9.12   The TIME$ Statement

General Form:	TIME$ = string expression
	where **string expression** is one of the following forms:

hh	Set the hour (range 0 to 23).
hh:mm	Set the hour and minute (minute range 0 to 59).
hh:mm:ss	Set the hour, minute, and second (second range 0 to 59).

Purpose:	To set the system time.
Examples:	TIME$ = "10"
	TIME$ = "1:23"
	TIME$ = "20:00:23"
	TIME$ = "0:25"
	TIME$ = Cur.Time$
Note:	You may enter one digit for the hour, minute, or second. If one digit is entered, then the system assumes a leading zero.

If you assign values that are out of the designated ranges described in Tables 9.11 and 9.12, the PC will display a dialog box with the following diagnostic message:

```
Illegal function call
```

If the expression assigned to the DATE$ or TIME$ statements is not a valid string, the PC displays a dialog box with the following diagnostic message:

```
Type mismatch
```

Accepting String Data — LINE INPUT Statement, INKEY$ and INPUT$ Functions

The LINE INPUT statement accepts a line entered from the keyboard as a string value and assigns it to a specified string variable. The LINE INPUT statement ignores the usual delimiters, namely, the quotation mark and the comma. That is, if the string value

```
She said, "Terminate the program!"
```

is entered in response to the statement

```
LINE INPUT "What did she say? "; Statement$
```

then Statement$ is assigned the entire string of characters

```
She said, "Terminate the program!"
```

including the comma and the quotation marks.

The general form of the LINE INPUT statement is shown in Table 9.13.

TABLE 9.13 The LINE INPUT Statement	
General Form:	LINE INPUT string variable or LINE INPUT ''input prompt message''; string variable or LINE INPUT #n, string variable
Purpose:	Provides for the assignment to a string variable of an entire line (up to 255 characters), including commas and quotation marks, entered from an external source such as the keyboard or auxiliary storage.
Examples:	**LINE INPUT Statement** / **Data from an External Source**

LINE INPUT Statement	**Data from an External Source**
LINE INPUT Cus.Rec$	"123","Adams Joe",44,0520
LINE INPUT "What? "; Stat$	"Don't do it", Amanda Said
LINE INPUT "Weight ===> "; Wgt$	126.5 lbs.
LINE INPUT #2, Complete.Line$	"John Smith", 46, "3", 12

Note:	A question mark is not displayed as part of the prompt unless it is included in the input prompt message.

The major differences between the LINE INPUT statement and the INPUT statement are:

1. The LINE INPUT statement does not automatically prompt the user with the question mark and trailing space, as the INPUT statement does.
2. The LINE INPUT statement can accept data for only one string variable. The INPUT statement can have more than one variable in the list, and the variables may be either numeric or string or both.

When executed, an INPUT or LINE INPUT statement instructs the PC to suspend execution of the program until the Enter key is pressed. That is, with these two statements, the PC must always be signaled by pressing the Enter key when you have finished entering the requested data. The INKEY$ and the INPUT$ functions do not require pressing the Enter key for the program to accept input.

The INKEY$ function *does not* suspend execution of the program; instead, it checks the keyboard to determine whether a character is pending — that is, whether a key was pressed since the last time it executed an expression with INKEY$ or since the beginning of the program if it is the first INKEY$ encountered. The following statement

```
Pending$ = INKEY$
```

assigns Pending$ the character that corresponds to the last key pressed. If no character is pending, then INKEY$ assigns the null string to Pending$.

Consider the following example, in which the INKEY$ function is used to control a looping process. The values of Number and Number MOD 7 are displayed until the user presses a key or until an overflow condition occurs.

```
Number = 1
DO WHILE INKEY$ = ""
    PRINT Number, Number MOD 7
    Number = Number + 1
LOOP
```

In this partial program, the INKEY$ function is used in the DO WHILE statement to control the loop. As long as there is no character pending from the keyboard, the PC continues to execute the loop.

The INKEY$ function is useful for applications requiring a program not to be interrupted and yet accept responses from the keyboard. This method of processing is essential for video game programs like Space Invaders or Missile Command. In these games, objects on the monitor are in constant motion, and at the same time, the games must check for user input such as the firing of a phaser or torpedo. Later in this chapter, we will study additional statements that can be used to trap similar events.

The INPUT$(N) function is even more sophisticated than the INKEY$ function because it accepts N characters from the keyboard. However, unlike INKEY$, INPUT$(N) suspends execution of the program until the user has pressed N number of keys. For example, the statement

```
Char$ = INPUT$(1)
```

causes the PC to suspend execution of the program and wait until a key is pressed.

The characters entered in response to the INPUT$ function are not displayed on the screen. To display the response, the statement that contains the function should be followed with a PRINT statement. For example,

```
CHAR$ = INPUT$(5)
PRINT CHAR$
```

displays the five characters entered by the user.

Table 9.14 illustrates examples of the INKEY$ and the INPUT$ functions.

TABLE 9.14 Examples of the INKEY$ and the INPUT$ Functions

THE STATEMENT	KEYBOARD RESPONSE	RESULTS IN
Pending$ = INKEY$	J	Pending$ = J
Keyboard$ = INKEY$	No Response	Keyboard$ = null
Char$ = INPUT$(4)	A1B2	Char$ = A1B2
One.Char$ = INPUT$(1)	3	One.Char$ = 3

A common use of the INPUT$ function is to suspend the execution of a program at the conclusion of a task so the information on the screen may be read before it disappears. For example, if a program is displaying a long list of items, you may want to suspend execution of the program after every 20 or so lines are displayed. The message

```
Press any key to continue...
```

is often used in this context. The INPUT$ simplifies the entry by not requiring the Enter key to be pressed. The following partial program shows how to incorporate this technique into a QuickBASIC program:

```
PRINT "Press any key to continue..."
Char$ = INPUT$(1)
```

The first line displays the message, and the second line suspends execution of the program. Execution continues when the user presses any key on the keyboard except Ctrl + Break.

9.3   NUMERIC FUNCTIONS

The most frequently used QuickBASIC numeric functions are listed in Table 9.15. (For a complete listing of the numeric functions, see the Reference Card at the back of this book.)

TABLE 9.15 Some QuickBASIC Numeric Functions	
FUNCTION	**FUNCTION VALUE**
ABS(N)	Returns the absolute value of the argument N.
ATN(N)	Returns the angle in radians whose tangent is the value of the argument N.
CINT(N)	Returns the value of N rounded to an integer.
COS(N)	Returns the cosine of the argument N where N is in radians.
CSRLIN	Returns the current cursor row position.
EXP(N)	Returns e(2.718281...) raised to the argument N.
FIX(N)	Returns the value of N truncated to an integer.
INT(N)	Returns the largest integer that is less than or equal to the argument N.
LOG(N)	Returns the natural log of the argument N where N is greater than 0.
POS(N)	Returns the current cursor column position.
RND	Returns a random number between 0 (inclusive) and 1 (exclusive).
SCREEN(R, C)	Returns the ASCII code for the character at the specified row (R) and column (C) on the screen.
SGN(N)	Returns the sign of the argument N: –1 if the argument N is less than 0; 0 if the argument N is equal to 0; or + 1 if the argument N is greater than 0.
SIN(N)	Returns the sine of the argument N where N is in radians.
SQR(N)	Returns the positive square root of the argument N.
TAN(N)	Returns the tangent of the argument N where N is in radians.
TIMER	Returns a value equal to the number of seconds elapsed since midnight.

In the discussion that follows, several examples of each numeric function are presented.

Arithmetic Functions — ABS, FIX, INT, CINT, and SGN

The functions classified as **arithmetic** include ABS (absolute value), FIX (fixed integer), INT (integer), CINT (rounded integer), and SGN (sign).

The ABS function takes any numeric expression and returns its positive value. For example, if N is equal to –4, then ABS(N) is equal to 4. Additional examples of the ABS function are shown in Table 9.16.

The FIX(N) function returns the truncated integer portion of the argument N. When the argument is positive, the FIX function is identical to the INT function. For example, if N is equal to 13.45, then FIX(N) returns 13. However, when the argument is negative, the two functions return a different result. For example, if N is equal to –4.45, then FIX(N) returns –4, and INT(N) returns –5. The INT function returns an integer less than or equal to the argument.

Like the FIX(N) and INT(N) functions, the CINT(N) function returns an integer. However, the CINT function returns the rounded integer portion of the argument. Additional examples of the FIX, INT, and CINT functions are shown in Table 9.16.

The SGN(N) function returns a value of +1 if the argument N is positive, 0 if the argument is 0, and −1 if the argument N is negative. Table 9.16 shows examples of the SGN function.

TABLE 9.16   Examples of the ABS, FIX, INT, CINT, and SGN Functions

VALUE OF VARIABLE	THE STATEMENT	RESULTS IN
N = -3	P = ABS(N)	P = 3
C = 4.5	M = ABS(C)	M = 4.5
C = 4, D = -6	A = C + ABS(D)	A = 10
G = 25.567	B = CINT(G)	B = 26
G = -25.567	C = CINT(G)	C = -26
G = 25.567	F = FIX(G)	F = 25
G = -25.567	X = FIX(G)	X = -25
G = -25.567	I = INT(G)	I = -26
G = -25.567	K = INT(ABS(G))	K = 25
D = 4	E = SGN(D)	E = 1
P = -5	F = 5 + SGN(P)	F = 4

Generalized Procedures for Rounding and Truncation

Although QuickBASIC allows for automatic rounding through the use of the PRINT USING statement, it is sometimes more convenient for the programmer to control the process of rounding and truncation. The CINT and FIX functions may be used to write generalized expressions for rounding or truncating a number to any decimal place. The generalized expression for rounding numbers is

```
CINT(N * 10 ^ E) / 10 ^ E
```

The generalized expression for truncating numbers is

```
FIX(N * 10 ^ E) / 10 ^ E
```

where N is the value to be rounded or truncated, and
       E is the number of decimal places desired

To determine what value should be assigned to E, begin counting from the decimal point as illustrated below.

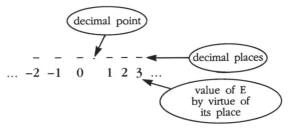

For example, if you want to round a result N to the nearest hundredths place, you assign E a value of 2. The generalized expression for rounding to the nearest hundredths place becomes the following:

```
CINT(N * 10 ^ 2) / 10 ^ 2
```

or

```
CINT(N * 100) / 100
```

For truncating a result N to the nearest hundredths place, the generalized expression becomes the following:

```
FIX(N * 10 ^ 2) / 10 ^ 2
```

or

```
FIX(N * 100) / 100
```

(See BASIC Programming Problem 3 at the end of this chapter for an example of the use of these generalized expressions for rounding and truncating values.)

Exponential Functions — SQR, EXP, and LOG

The functions classified as **exponential** include the SQR (square root), EXP (exponential), and LOG (logarithmic).

The SQR(N) function computes the square root of the argument N. Table 9.17 shows several examples of computing the square root of a number.

TABLE 9.17   Examples of the SQR Function

VALUE OF VARIABLE	THE STATEMENT	RESULTS IN
	Root = SQR(9)	Root = 3
Value = 0	R1 = SQR(Value)	R1 = 0
Cube = 625	R2 = SQR(SQR(Cube))	R2 = 5
Bus(1) = 1.15129	R3 = SQR(Bus(1))	R3 = 1.072982
X = 3, Y = 4	Hyp = SQR(X ^ 2 + Y ^ 2)	Hyp = 5
Neg = -49	Posi = SQR(ABS(Neg))	Posi = 7
N = -25	Root = SQR(N)	Illegal Function Call

The symbol **e** in mathematics represents the **Napierian base** (2.718281...), where the three dots show the fractional part of the constant is not a repeating sequence of digits. In QuickBASIC, the keyword EXP is used to represent this constant, which is raised to the power given as the argument in parentheses following the function name. The EXP function can be used, for example, to determine the value of $e^{1.14473}$. The following statement,

```
Pi = EXP(1.14473)
```

results in the variable Pi being assigned a value of 3.141593, which is a close approximation of π. If the value of the argument for the EXP function exceeds 88.72283, then an overflow condition occurs.

The natural log ($\log_e$ or ln) of a number can be determined by using the LOG function. For example, the value of X in the equation

$$e^x = 3.141593$$

can be determined by using the following statement:

```
X = LOG(3.141593)
```

The resulting value of X is 1.14473 and, therefore,

$$e^{1.14473} = 3.141593$$

This function can also be used to determine the logarithm to the base 10 by multiplying the LOG function by 0.434295. For example, in the statement

```
Log10 = 0.434295 * LOG(3)
```

Log10 is assigned the value 0.4771218, the base 10 logarithm of 3.

Of the three exponential functions, programmers use the square root function more than the exponential or logarithmic. However, the latter two functions are essential in some advanced applications. The following programming case study is an example of the use of the LOG function.

| Programming Case Study 15 | Determining the Time to Double an Investment

The formula for computing the amount of an investment compounded annually for a given number of years is $A = P(1 + J)^N$ where A is the total amount, P is the initial investment, J is the annual rate of interest, and N is the number of years.

This formula can be rewritten to solve for the number of years N:

$$N = \frac{\log\left(\frac{A}{P}\right)}{\log(1 + J)}$$

If the number of years it takes to double an investment is to be determined, then the amount A is equal to twice the investment P, or $A = 2P$. The formula for determining the number of years to double an investment can further be simplified to the following:

$$N = \frac{\log 2}{\log(1 + J)}$$

The ensuing problem uses the LOG function to compute the number of years it takes to double an investment.

Problem: The WESAVU National Bank requests that a program be written to display a table of annual interest rates and the corresponding years it will take to double an investment compounded annually for integer interests rates from 8% through 18%, inclusive. Display the number of years to the nearest tenths place.

Program Solution

Program 9.3 on the next page generates the specified report.

PROGRAM 9.3

```
1    ' Program 9.3
2    ' Determining the Time to Double an Investment
3    ' *********************************************
4    ' *                Main Program                *
5    ' *********************************************
6    COMMON SHARED H1$, H2$, H3$, H4$, H5$, D1$, T1$
7    CALL A100.Initialization
8    CALL B100.Generate.Table
9    CALL C100.Wrap.Up
10   END
11
12   ' *********************************************
13   ' *               Initialization               *
14   ' *********************************************
15   SUB A100.Initialization
16      CLS   ' Clear Screen
17      CALL A200.Initialize.Report.Format
18      CALL A210.Display.Headings
19   END SUB
20
21   ' *********************************************
22   ' *           Initialize Report Format          *
23   ' *********************************************
24   SUB A200.Initialize.Report.Format
25      H1$ = "Doubling an Investment"
26      H2$ = "----------------------"
27      H3$ = "Interest    Number"
28      H4$ = "Rate in %   of Years"
29      H5$ = "--------    --------"
30      D1$ = "   ##         ##.#"
31      T1$ = "End of Report"
32   END SUB
33
34   ' *********************************************
35   ' *     Display Report and Column Headings      *
36   ' *********************************************
37   SUB A210.Display.Headings
38      PRINT H1$
39      PRINT H2$
40      PRINT
41      PRINT H3$
42      PRINT H4$
43      PRINT H5$
44   END SUB
45
46   ' *********************************************
47   ' *              Generate Table                *
48   ' *********************************************
49   SUB B100.Generate.Table
50      Numerator = LOG(2)
51      FOR Interest = 8 TO 18
52         Time = Numerator / LOG(1 + Interest / 100)
53         PRINT USING D1$; Interest; Time
54      NEXT Interest
55   END SUB
56
57   ' *********************************************
58   ' *                 Wrap-Up                    *
59   ' *********************************************
60   SUB C100.Wrap.Up
61      PRINT : PRINT T1$
62   END SUB

[run]
```

FIGURE 9.5

The display due to the execution of Program 9.3.

```
Doubling an Investment
----------------------

Interest    Number
Rate in %   of Years
---------   --------
        8       9.0
        9       8.0
       10       7.3
       11       6.6
       12       6.1
       13       5.7
       14       5.3
       15       5.0
       16       4.7
       17       4.4
       18       4.2

End of Report
```

Discussion of the Program Solution

The results displayed by Program 9.3 are shown in Figure 9.5. With slight modifications to the values in the FOR statement (line 51) in Program 9.3, the number of years it takes to double an investment compounded annually can be determined for a variety of interest rates. The argument for the LOG function in line 50 may be changed to other numbers, such as 3 or 4, to determine how long it takes to triple or quadruple an investment compounded annually. (See BASIC Programming Problem 3 at the end of this chapter to determine the number of years it takes to double an investment compounded quarterly.)

Trigonometric Functions — SIN, COS, TAN, and ATN

In QuickBASIC the SIN, COS, and TAN functions can be used to determine the sine, cosine, and tangent of the angle X expressed in **radians**. For these functions to work correctly, the angle X *must* be expressed in radians. Because angles are usually expressed in degrees, the following statements relating angles and radians should prove helpful:

1 radian $= 180 / \pi$ degrees $= 180 / 3.141593$ degrees
1 degree $= \pi / 180$ radians $= 3.141593 / 180$ radians

When using these three functions, remember that if the argument is in units of degrees it must first be multiplied by 3.141593 / 180 to convert it into units of radians before the function can evaluate it. In mathematics, if the equation X = sin 30° is evaluated, then X = 0.5. Evaluating the same equation in QuickBASIC requires the following:

```
Rads = 30 * 3.141593 / 180
X = SIN(Rads)
```

or

```
X = SIN(30 * 3.141593 / 180)
```

QuickBASIC does not have corresponding functions for the cosecant, the secant and the cotangent. These three trigonometric functions must be evaluated by combinations of the SIN, COS, and TAN functions. Table 9.18 illustrates the combinations.

TABLE 9.18 Determining the Cosecant, Secant and Cotangent	
TO FIND THE	**USE**
Cosecant	1 / SIN(X)
Secant	1 / COS(X)
Cotangent	1 / TAN(X)

The fourth trigonometric function available in QuickBASIC is the arctangent. The ATN function returns a value that is the angle, in units of radians, that corresponds to the argument in the function. For example,

```
Angle = ATN(1)
```

results in Angle being assigned the value of 0.7853982 radians. Multiplying this number by 180/3.141593 yields an angle of 45°.

Utility Functions — POS, SCREEN, and CSRLIN

The POS function returns the current column position of the cursor relative to the left edge of the display screen. The value returned is an integer in the range 1 to 40, or 1 to 80, depending on the current screen width setting. For example,

```
PRINT TAB(15);
PRINT POS(0)
```

causes the PC to display the value 15. The value of the argument plays no role in the value returned by the POS function.

The CSRLIN function is equal to the current row (line) the cursor is on relative to the top of the display screen. The value of CSRLIN varies in the range 1 to 25. For example, the following statement entered in the immediate mode

```
LOCATE 5, 6 : PRINT CSRLIN
 5
```

displays the current line position.

The CSRLIN and POS functions are used in applications where a value must be displayed at a position on the screen other than the current one, followed by the return of the cursor to the former position. Consider the following partial program:

```
Row = CSRLIN
Col = POS(0)
LOCATE 1, 20 : PRINT "Aim the arrow carefully"
LOCATE Row, Col
```

The first line assigns Row the line the cursor is on. The second line assigns Col the column the cursor is in. The LOCATE statement in the third line moves the cursor to column 20 of line 1 and displays the message. The last line returns the cursor to its former position on the screen.

The SCREEN function allows you to determine which character is currently displayed at the intersection of a row and a column on the screen. The function returns the ASCII code for the character found at the specified location. For example, the following partial program assigns Char the value 66, because that is the ASCII code for the character B:

```
LOCATE 15, 16 : PRINT "B"
Char = SCREEN(15, 16)
```

This function may also be used to return the color attribute at the intersection of the specified row and column. For additional information on the SCREEN statement, load QuickBASIC, press Shift + F1, select the hyperlink Index, and select the keyword SCREEN.

Performance Testing — The TIMER Function

The TIMER function returns a single-precision numeric value representing the number of seconds that have elapsed since midnight. The following For loop illustrates values returned by the TIMER function:

```
TIME$ = "12:00:00"
FOR I = 1 TO 10
    PRINT "Time = "; TIME$, "Timer ="; TIMER
NEXT I

[run]

Time = 12:00:00        Timer = 43200.1
Time = 12:00:00        Timer = 43200.21
Time = 12:00:00        Timer = 43200.32
Time = 12:00:00        Timer = 43200.43
Time = 12:00:00        Timer = 43200.54
Time = 12:00:01        Timer = 43200.6
Time = 12:00:01        Timer = 43200.71
Time = 12:00:01        Timer = 43200.82
Time = 12:00:01        Timer = 43200.93
Time = 12:00:01        Timer = 43201.04
```

The first statement resets the system time to 12:00 noon (43,200 seconds past midnight). In the For loop, the PRINT statement displays both the system time and the number of seconds elapsed since midnight. A close look at the results shows that, on the average, it takes 0.11 seconds to make a pass on the For loop in this partial program on an IBM PC with 640K bytes of main storage.

The time it takes to make a pass on a given loop will vary slightly between runs and will depend on the type of PC used. For this reason, when benchmarking an algorithm, you should take the average duration of time it takes to accomplish the same task over many runs of the program under the same conditions. **Benchmarking** is the activity of comparing the performance of algorithms or applications that are running under similar conditions on one or more computer systems.

The following two partial programs make use of the TIMER function to determine the difference between using a single-precision variable and an integer variable as the loop variable in a For loop. Both partial programs execute empty For loops 32,766 times. The partial programs in Figure 9.6 and 9.7 on the next page were executed on a Gateway 2000 486DX/33 with 4 megabytes of main storage using MS-DOS Version 5.0 under Windows 3.1.

FIGURE 9.6   *FIGURE 9.7*

```
1      ' Timing a For Loop
2      ' in Single Precision
3      ' ********************
4      CLS  ' Clear Screen
5      '
6      Start = TIMER
7      FOR Count = 1 TO 32766
8      NEXT Count
9      Finish = TIMER
10     '
11     Duration = Finish - Start
12     PRINT "For loop time ==>";
13     PRINT USING "##.##"; Duration;
14     PRINT " seconds"

[run]

For loop time ==> 3.51 seconds
```

```
1      ' Timing a For Loop
2      ' in Integer Precision
3      ' ********************
4      CLS  ' Clear Screen
5      '
6      Start = TIMER
7      FOR Count% = 1 TO 32766
8      NEXT Count%
9      Finish = TIMER
10     '
11     Duration = Finish - Start
12     PRINT "For loop time ==>";
13     PRINT USING "##.##"; Duration;
14     PRINT " seconds"

[run]

For loop time ==>  .16 seconds
```

The duration of time it takes for the 486DX/33 to execute the For loop in the partial program in Figure 9.6 is 3.51 seconds. With the For loop in the partial program in Figure 9.7, the duration of time is 0.16 seconds. In other words, the For loop that uses an integer variable for the loop variable (Figure 9.7) executes 22 times faster than the same For loop that uses a single-precision variable for the loop variable (Figure 9.6). Hence, if you desire to speed up the execution of For loops in your program, you should declare the loop variable as type integer. From now on, we will declare all our loop variables to be type integer unless it takes on decimal fraction values.

In the partial programs in Figures 9.6 and 9.7, line 6 sets the variable Start to the value returned by the TIMER function. At the conclusion of each loop, the variable Finish is set equal to TIMER. In both programs, line 11 assigns Duration the time required to execute the particular loop.

Random Number Function and the RANDOMIZE Statement

The RND function is important to the programmer involved in the development of programs that simulate situations described by a random process. The owners of a shopping mall, for example, might want a program written to simulate the number of cars that would enter their parking lots during a particular period of the day. Or, the manager of a grocery store might want a program to model unpredictable values that represented people standing in line waiting to check out. The unpredictable values could be supplied by the RND function. Actually, the random numbers generated by the PC are provided by a repeatable process, and for this reason, they are often called **pseudo-random numbers**.

The RND function returns an unpredictable decimal fraction number between 0 (inclusive) and 1 (exclusive). Each time the function is referenced, any number between 0 and less than 1 has an equal probability of being returned by the function. For example, the statement

```
Number = RND
```

assigns Number a random number. The partial program in Figure 9.8 illustrates the generation of five random numbers.

FIGURE 9.8

```
1      ' Generating Random Numbers
2      '. *************************
3      CLS  ' Clear Screen
4      FOR I% = 1 TO 5
5         PRINT RND,
6      NEXT I%

       [run]

        .7151002      .683111      .4821425      .9992938      .6465093
```

Each time the RND function is referenced in line 5, a random number between 0 and < 1 is displayed.

The INT and RND functions can be combined to create random digits over a specified range. The following expression allows for the generation of random digits over the range C < n < D:

```
INT((D - C + 1) * RND + C)
```

For example, to generate random digits over the range 1 to 10, inclusive, change line 5 in Figure 9.8 to

```
PRINT INT((10 - 1 + 1) * RND + 1)
```

or

```
PRINT INT(10 * RND + 1)
```

The partial program in Figure 9.9 simulates tossing a coin 20 times. The expression INT(2 * RND) returns a zero (heads) or a one (tails). The expression in line 7 returned 13 zeros (heads) and 7 ones (tails).

FIGURE 9.9

```
1      ' Simulation of Coin Tossing
2      ' 0 is a Head and 1 is a Tail
3      ' The Coin is Tossed 20 Times
4      ' *************************
5      CLS  ' Clear Screen
6      FOR I% = 1 TO 20
7         PRINT INT(2 * RND);
8      NEXT I%

       [run]

        1  0  1  0  0  0  1  1  0  1  0  0  0  0  1  0  0  1  0  0
```

The partial program in Figure 9.9 can be enhanced to allow a user to enter the number of simulated coin tosses desired and to display the total number of heads and tails. This is illustrated in the partial program in Figure 9.10.

FIGURE 9.10

```
 1    ' Simulation of Coin Tossing
 2    ' 0 is a Head and 1 is a Tail
 3    ' User Enters Number of Times Coin Is Tossed
 4    ' *****************************************
 5    CLS ' Clear Screen
 6    Head = 0
 7    Tail = 0
 8    INPUT "How many tosses ===> ", Tosses
 9    FOR Number% = 1 TO Tosses
10       Rand.No = INT(2 * RND)
11       IF Rand.No = 0 THEN
12          Head = Head + 1
13       ELSE
14          Tail = Tail + 1
15       END IF
16    NEXT Number%
17    PRINT "Number of Heads ===>"; Head
18    PRINT "Number of Tails ===>"; Tail

[run]

How many tosses ===> 500
Number of Heads ===> 259
Number of Tails ===> 241
```

When executed, the partial program in Figure 9.10 requests the user to enter the number of coin tosses to be simulated. Depending on the value assigned to Rand.No, line 11 determines whether to increment Head (head counter) or Tail (tail counter) by 1. At the conclusion of the For loop, lines 17 and 18 display the total number of heads and total number of tails. As illustrated by the results of the partial program in Figure 9.10, out of 500 simulated coin tosses, 259 are heads and 241 are tails.

Every time this partial program is executed, it will display the same results because the PC generates random numbers from a starting value called the **seed**. Unless the seed is changed, the PC continues to generate the same set of random numbers in the same sequence each time the same program is executed. Once a program containing the RND function is ready for production, the RANDOMIZE statement can be used to instruct the PC to generate random numbers from a different seed each time the program is executed. The general form of the RANDOMIZE statement is shown in Table 9.19.

TABLE 9.19 The RANDOMIZE Statement	
General Form:	RANDOMIZE or RANDOMIZE numeric expression
Purpose:	To supply a new seed for the generation of random numbers by the RND function.
Examples:	RANDOMIZE RANDOMIZE TIMER RANDOMIZE 396.5 RANDOMIZE VAL(RIGHT$(TIME$,2))
Note:	If you do not include a parameter following the keyword RANDOMIZE, then the PC suspends execution of the program and requests a value between –32768 and 32767.

The rule for the execution of the RANDOMIZE statement in a program follows:

> **RANDOMIZE RULE 1** *The* RANDOMIZE *statement must be executed prior to any reference to the* RND *function.*

Programming Case Study 16   Guess a Number Between 1 and 100

The RND function can be used in a program to instruct the PC to simulate a popular guessing game in which the player attempts to guess a number between 1 and 100. Incorporating the RANDOMIZE statement ensures that the RND function will return a new set of random numbers each time the program is executed.

Following is a program solution and a discussion of the program solution:

PROGRAM 9.4

```
1    ' Program 9.4
2    ' Guess a Number Between 1 and 100
3    ' ***********************************************
4    ' *                 Main Program                *
5    ' ***********************************************
6    CALL A100.Initialization(Random.Number)
7    CALL B100.Guess.Number(Random.Number, Guess.Count)
8    CALL C100.Wrap.Up(Guess.Count)
9    END
10
11   ' ***********************************************
12   ' *               Initialization                *
13   ' *           Returns Random.Number             *
14   ' ***********************************************
15   SUB A100.Initialization (Random.Number)
16      CLS  ' Clear Screen
17      RANDOMIZE TIMER
18      Random.Number = INT(100 * RND + 1)
19      PRINT "**************************************"
20      PRINT "*                                    *"
21      PRINT "* Guess a number between 1 and 100.  *"
22      PRINT "* I will tell you if your guess is   *"
23      PRINT "* too high or too low.               *"
24      PRINT "*                                    *"
25      PRINT "**************************************"
26      PRINT
27   END SUB
28
29   ' ***********************************************
30   ' *               Guess a Number                *
31   ' * Receives Random.Number; Returns Guess.Count *
32   ' ***********************************************
33   SUB B100.Guess.Number (Random.Number, Guess.Count)
34      INPUT "Guess a number ====> ", Guess
35      Guess.Count = 1
36      DO WHILE Guess <> Random.Number
37         IF Guess > Random.Number THEN
38            PRINT "Too High"
39         ELSE
40            PRINT "Too Low"
41         END IF
42         INPUT "Guess a number ====> ", Guess
43         Guess.Count = Guess.Count + 1
44      LOOP
45   END SUB
46
```

(continued)

```
47    ' ***********************************************
48    ' *                  Wrap-Up                     *
49    ' *             Receives Guess.Count             *
50    ' ***********************************************
51    SUB C100.Wrap.Up (Guess.Count)
52       PRINT : PRINT "Your guess is correct."
53       PRINT "It took you"; Guess.Count; "guesses."
54    END SUB
```

[run]

FIGURE 9.11

The display due to the execution of Program 9.4.

```
*****************************************
*                                       *
* Guess a number between 1 and 100.  *
* I will tell you if your guess is   *
* too high or too low.                *
*                                       *
*****************************************

Guess a number ====> 50
Too Low
Guess a number ====> 75
Too Low
Guess a number ====> 87
Too Low
Guess a number ====> 95
Too High
Guess a number ====> 93
Too Low
Guess a number ====> 94

Your guess is correct.
It took you 6 guesses.
```

Discussion of the Program Solution

When Program 9.4 is executed, line 17 in A100.Initialization ensures that the program does not generate the same set of random numbers it generated the last time the program was executed. The seed is based on the value returned by the TIMER function. The chances of generating the same set of random numbers from one run of Program 9.4 to the next is very rare.

Line 18 assigns Random.Number the number to be guessed (94). Lines 19 through 25 display the instructions for the game as shown at the top of the screen in Figure 9.11. Line 34 in B100.Guess.Number accepts a value for Guess from the user. Line 35 sets the guess counter (Guess.Count) to 1. If Guess is equal to Random.Number in line 36, the program terminates after 1 guess. If Guess does not equal Random.Number, the PC executes the Do-While loop and displays an appropriate message before requesting the next guess and incrementing Guess.Count. When the user finally guesses the number, control passes to C100.Wrap.Up, and a message and the value of Guess.Count display.

9.4 USER-DEFINED FUNCTIONS

In addition to numeric and string functions, QuickBASIC allows you to define new string or numeric functions that relate to a particular application. This type of function, known as a **user-defined function**, is written directly into the program. The user-defined function may be written as a one-line statement or as a series of statements. One way QuickBASIC recognizes a user-defined function is by the keywords DEF FN, for *define function*, which initiate the function in the program. For example, the DEF FN statement

```
DEF FNY (X) = X * (X + 1) / 2
```

defines a one-line, user-defined function, x(x + 1) / 2, whose name is FNY. The parentheses following the name of the function surround a simple variable known as a **function parameter**. The expression to the right of the equal sign indicates which operations are to be performed with the value of X when the function is referenced in such statements as LET, PRINT, LPRINT, CASE SELECT, and IF. For example, either

```
Result = FNY(Value) + 5
```

or

```
PRINT FNY(Part / 3)
```

found in the same program with the user-defined function FNY described earlier will reference the FNY function.

Multiple-line, user-defined functions allow the user to define more complex algorithms. When more than one line is required, the user-defined function ends with the END DEF statement. The following user-defined function includes an IF statement that returns the value ON or OFF, depending on the value of Amount:

```
DEF FNSWITCH$ (Amount)
   IF Amount > 500 THEN
      FNSWITCH$ = "ON"
   ELSE
      FNSWITCH$ = "OFF"
   END IF
END DEF
```

The following statement uses the FNSWITCH$ function to assign Flag$ the value ON or OFF, depending on the value of the variable Cost:

```
Flag$ = FNSWITCH$(Cost)
```

Defining your own function reduces programming effort and makes your program compact and efficient. Instead of writing a common formula or algorithm over and over again, you simply define it once as a function, give it a name, and then reference it by that name whenever you need it.

The DEF FN Statement

Table 9.20 shows that the DEF FN statement permits the creation of user-defined functions. The name of the function follows DEF, and it must begin with the two letters FN, followed by a variable name that is consistent with the rules used for naming variables. The DEF FN must be placed in the Main Program; that is, you cannot define a function in a subprogram.

TABLE 9.20 The DEF Statement	
General Form:	DEF FNx(p_1, ..., p_n) = expression or DEF FNx(p_1, ..., p_n) [range of statements] END DEF where **x** is a simple variable that must agree in type with the expression, and **p_1** through **p_n** are simple variables called function parameters.
Purpose:	To define a function that is relevant to a particular application that can be referenced as frequently as needed in the program in which it is defined. In the second general form, the function FNx must be assigned a value by one of the statements within the multiple-line function.

Examples:	1. DEF FNCUBE(Y, Z) = Y ^ 3 + Z ^ 3
	2. DEF FNPI = 3.141593
	3. DEF FNSUB$(Stng$, P, N) = MID$(Stng$, P, N)
	4. DEF FNFUTUREVALUE (P, I, C, N)
	     I = R / C
	     M = C * N
	     FNFUTUREVALUE = P * (1 + I) ^ M
	  END DEF

Notes:	1. To be consistent with the QuickBASIC functions, capitalizing all letters in the name of the function is recommended. 2. A user-defined numeric function is declared integer, long integer, single precison, or double precision on the basis of the following:

Special Character Appended to Name	Type
Percent Sign (%)	Integer
Ampersand (&)	Long Integer
Exclamation Point (!) or no special character	Single precision
Number Sign (#)	Double precision

The parameters in a user-defined function are called **dummy variables** because they are assigned the values of the corresponding arguments when reference is made to the function. For example, the following partial program contains two user-defined functions. The first one rounds the value assigned to Number to the nearest cent. The second one truncates the value assigned to Number to the nearest cent.

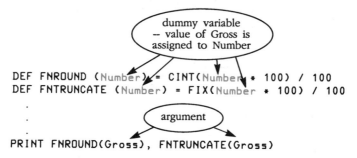

```
DEF FNROUND (Number) = CINT(Number * 100) / 100
DEF FNTRUNCATE (Number) = FIX(Number * 100) / 100
  .
  .
PRINT FNROUND(Gross), FNTRUNCATE(Gross)
```

The value of the variable Gross in the PRINT statement is used in place of the variable Number when the first user-defined function FNROUND is called. The same applies when the user-defined function FNTRUNCATE is called by the second item in the PRINT statement.

It is possible to define functions through the use of variables other than the parameters because variables used within the body of a DEF FN statement are global to the program. **Global** means that a variable name in both the user-defined function and in the calling program or subprogram references the same storage location. For example, in the following partial program

```
DEF FNC(A) = A * B * C
    .
    .
    .
READ A, B, C
```

the variables A, B, and C in the DEF FN are the same as the variables A, B, and C in the READ statement. That is, when the READ statement is executed, the variables A, B, and C in the DEF FN statement are assigned values.

A function with no parameters may be defined. Such functions may be used to define constants or expressions that do not require a variable, as shown below:

```
DEF FNPI#   = 3.14159265
DEF FNCENTI = 2.54
DEF FNRANDOM = INT(10 * RND + 1)
```

The first user-defined function defines FNPI# equal to pi (π) in double precision. FNCENTI is defined to be equal to the number of centimeters in an inch. FNRANDOM returns a random number between 1 and 10.

The rules regarding DEF FN statements in a program follows:

DEF FN RULE 1 *A user-defined function must be located in the Main Program in such a way that it is evaluated by the PC before it is called.*

DEF FN RULE 2 *The same user-defined function may be defined as often as required. The last definition executed is used.*

DEF FN RULE 3 *A user-defined function definition cannot reference itself.*

DEF FN RULE 4 *A multiple-line user-defined function must include a statement that assigns the function name a value.*

QuickBASIC also allows the user to define functions using the FUNCTION statement. (For a comparison between the DEF FN and FUNCTION statements, see Section 9.5.)

Referencing User-Defined Functions

User-defined functions are referenced in the same way as numeric functions.

The following program determines the effective rates of interest for the nominal rates 5.5%, 6.5%, 7.5%, 8.5%, and 9.5%, using the following formula:

$$R = \left(1 + \frac{J}{C}\right)^{C} - 1$$

where R is the effective rate;
C is the number of conversions per year; and
J is the nominal rate.

The partial program in Figure 9.12 calculates and displays the effective rates to two decimal places for nominal rates converted semiannually, quarterly, monthly, and daily. (Assume 365 days per year.)

FIGURE 9.12

```
1    ' Determining the Effective Rate of Interest
2    ' Using a User-Defined Function
3    ' ***********************************************
4    DEF FNRATE (Comp) = 100 * ((1 + Rate / (Comp * 100)) ^ Comp - 1)
5    CLS  ' Clear Screen
6    PRINT "                        Effective Rates Compounded"
7    PRINT "              ----------------------------------------"
8    PRINT "Nominal Rate   Semiannually  Quarterly  Monthly  Daily"
9    PRINT "------------   ------------  ---------  -------  -----"
10   D1$ = "    ##.##          ##.#       ##.##    ##.##   ##.##"
11   FOR Rate = 5.5 TO 9.5
12      PRINT USING D1$; Rate; FNRATE(2), FNRATE(4), FNRATE(12), FNRATE(365)
13   NEXT Rate
14   PRINT : PRINT "End of Report"
```

[run]

When the partial program in Figure 9.12 is executed, the display shown in Figure 9.13 is generated. The usefulness of the DEF FN statement is apparent in this program. Instead of having to code the formula four times to determine the corresponding effective rates for a nominal rate, the DEF FN statement allows you to code the formula once (line 4) and then reference it four times (line 12). The constant used as the argument in each function reference in line 12 is assigned to Comp in the DEF FN statement in line 4.

FIGURE 9.13

The display due to the execution of the partial program in Figure 9.12.

```
                   Effective Rates Compounded
              ----------------------------------------
Nominal Rate   Semiannually  Quarterly  Monthly  Daily
------------   ------------  ---------  -------  -----
    5.50          5.58         5.61      5.64    5.65
    6.50          6.61         6.66      6.70    6.72
    7.50          7.64         7.71      7.76    7.79
    8.50          8.68         8.77      8.84    8.87
    9.50          9.73         9.84      9.92    9.96

End of Report
```

Programming Case Study 17   Computer Simulation — Beat the House Roller

The following programming case study incorporates the use of both the RND function and a user-defined function.

Problem: Beat the House Roller is a simple but popular dice game in which the house roller throws a pair of dice. The customer then throws the dice, trying to roll a higher score. If the customer rolls a lower score or the same score as the house roller, the house wins. The bet is $5.00 for each game.

An accumulator is included to keep track of the customer's winnings. Also, the customer's winnings are displayed at the end of each roll. A means of temporarily stopping the game is included so that the customer can decide if he or she desires to continue playing. Following are an analysis of the problem, a program solution, and a discussion of the program solution.

Program Tasks

1. Main Program

    a. Declare variable Winnings as COMMON SHARED.
    b. Use the following user-defined function to generate random numbers between 1 and 6 to represent the sides of a die:

    DEF FNRANDOM = INT(6 * RND + 1)

    c. Call appropriate subprograms

2. A100.Initialization

    a. Reseed the random number generator.
    b. Set Winnings to zero.

3. B100.Roll.Dice — establish a Do-Until loop to do the following:

    a. Reference the user-defined function FNRANDOM twice in succession for the house roller. Determine the customer's score in the same manner. Display both scores.
    b. Determine the winner, and increment or decrement Winnings by $5.00.
    c. Display Winnings.

4. C100.Wrap.Up — Display a message on the basis of the customer's winnings. If the customer owes money, display the message Better luck next time! If the customer does not owe any money, display the message You are pretty lucky!

Program Solution

The following program solution corresponds to the preceding tasks:

PROGRAM 9.5

```
1    ' Program 9.5
2    ' Computer-Simulated Dice Game
3    ' ****************************************
4    ' *              Main Program            *
5    ' ****************************************
6    COMMON SHARED Winnings
7    CALL A100.Initialization
8    DEF FNRANDOM = INT(6 * RND + 1)
9    CALL B100.Roll.Dice
10   CALL C100.Wrap.Up
11   END
12
13   ' ****************************************
14   ' *              Initialization          *
15   ' ****************************************
16   SUB A100.Initialization
17       CLS  ' Clear Screen
18       RANDOMIZE TIMER
19       Winnings = 0
20   END SUB
21
```

DEF FN statement must be defined in Main Program

(continued)

```
22    ' ********************************************
23    ' *                Roll The Dice             *
24    ' ********************************************
25    SUB B100.Roll.Dice
26       DO
27          ' **** Determine House Roller Score ****
28          House = FNRANDOM + FNRANDOM
29          PRINT : PRINT "The house rolls ========>"; House
30          ' **** Determine the Customer's Score ****
31          Customer = FNRANDOM + FNRANDOM
32          PRINT "Your score =============>"; Customer
33          ' **** Determine the Winner ****
34          IF Customer > House THEN
35             Winnings = Winnings + 5
36          ELSE
37             Winnings = Winnings - 5
38          END IF
39          PRINT USING "Your winnings ==========>$$##.##"; Winnings
40          INPUT "Enter Y to roll the dice again, else N... ", Control$
41       LOOP UNTIL UCASE$(Control$) = "N"
42    END SUB
43
44    ' ********************************************
45    ' *                Wrap-Up                   *
46    ' ********************************************
47    SUB C100.Wrap.Up
48       PRINT : PRINT
49       IF Winnings > 0 THEN
50          PRINT "You are pretty lucky!"
51       ELSE
52          PRINT "Better luck next time!"
53       END IF
54    END SUB

[run]

The house rolls ========> 6
Your score =============> 9
Your winnings ==========>  $5.00
Enter Y to roll the dice again, else N... y

The house rolls ========> 7
Your score =============> 11
Your winnings ==========> $10.00
Enter Y to roll the dice again, else N... Y

The house rolls ========> 7
Your score =============> 4
Your winnings ==========>  $5.00
Enter Y to roll the dice again, else N... y

The house rolls ========> 9
Your score =============> 11
Your winnings ==========> $10.00
Enter Y to roll the dice again, else N... n

You are pretty lucky!
```

Discussion of the Program Solution

The solution to the Computer-Simulated Dice Game is represented by Program 9.5, which includes the following significant points:

1. Line 8 of the Main Program defines a function that is referenced four times (lines 28 and 31 of B100.Roll.Dice) for each pass through the loop.

2. Line 34 of B100.Roll.Dice tests to determine whether the running total Winnings should be incremented or decremented by $5.00.

3. Lines 49 through 53 of C100.Wrap.Up display an end-of-game message. The message displayed depends on the value of Winnings.

9.5 INDEPENDENT FUNCTIONS

The FUNCTION and END FUNCTION statements are similar to the DEF FN and END DEF statements in that they allow you to create user-defined functions. In both cases the functions are called by the function name in a LET, PRINT, LPRINT, or decision statement. If there are any arguments to pass to the function, they are passed in the same fashion as with subprograms. The arguments can be simple variables, expressions, constants, array elements, or entire arrays.

In the function definition, at least one statement must assign the function name a value. After the function is executed, the value assigned to the function name is returned to the statement that called the function.

Figure 9.13 illustrates the similarity between the use of the DEF FN and END DEF statements and the FUNCTION and END FUNCTION statements. Both partial programs call the function VOLUME. We use the style of capitalizing all letters in function names.

FIGURE 9.14

The DEF FN *statement versus the* FUNCTION *statement.*

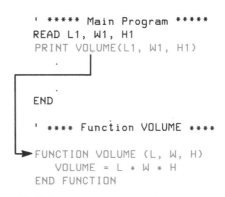

(A) Using DEF FN and END DEF.

(B) Using FUNCTION and END FUNCTION.

Although the two forms of defining user-defined functions appear similar, there are some significant differences as summarized in Table 9.21.

TABLE 9.21 Differences between using a DEF FN Statement and a FUNCTION Statement

DEF FN...END DEF	FUNCTION...END FUNCTION
1. Must be defined in the Main Program before a statement can reference it.	1. Defined as a distinct unit of code in the same fashion as a subprogram.
2. Name must begin with FN.	2. Name cannot begin with FN.
3. Variables are global.	3. Variables are local, unless shared.
4. Parameter list can only receive values using the pass-by-value method.	4. Parameter list can receive values using the pass-by-value or pass-by-reference method.
5. Cannot reference itself.	5. Can reference itself (recursive).
6. Single-line functions allowed.	6. Single-line functions not allowed.

All the methods for passing values discussed for subprograms in Chapter 4 work the same way for functions defined with the FUNCTION statement. All the rules regarding the SUB statement and SHARED statement apply as well.

The general form for the FUNCTION statement is shown in Table 9.22.

TABLE 9.22   The FUNCTION Statement

General Form: FUNCTION functionname (p₁, ..., pₙ) STATIC

.
.
.

END FUNCTION

where **functionname** is the name of the function (any QuickBASIC variable name is valid except those that begin with FN) ; and

p₁, ..., pₙ is an optional list of parameters, separated by commas, that shows the number and type of arguments to be passed to the function. If present, STATIC instructs the PC to retain the values of the local variables between calls. If STATIC is not present, then local variables are initialized to zeros or null strings each time the function is called.

Purpose: Defines a function that is relevant to a particular application that can be called as frequently as needed.

Examples:
1. FUNCTION AREA (Side1, Side2)
2. FUNCTION FVALUE (P, I, C, N)
3. FUNCTION TABLESEARCH (Search.Argument, Table()) STATIC

Notes:
1. A function is called by using the name of the function in a QuickBASIC statement.
2. The END FUNCTION causes control to transfer from the function back to the statement that called it.
3. To be consistent with the QuickBASIC functions, capitalize all letters in the name of the function.
4. A function is declared integer, long integer, single precision, or double precision on the basis of the following:

Special Character Appended to Name	Type
Percent Sign (%)	Integer
Ampersand (&)	Long Integer
Exclamation Point (!) or no special character	Single precision
Number Sign (#)	Double precision

Consider the partial program in Figure 9.15 which uses an independent function to determine the future value of a one-year investment. The function FUTUREVALUE is called in line 7 via a PRINT USING statement. The variables in the argument list are equal to 500, 0.0675, and 2. Thus, when control passes to the function FUTUREVALUE, the variables in the parameter list in line 11 are assigned the values 500, 0.0675, and 2. Like subprograms, the first argument is passed to the first parameter, the second argument to the second parameter, and so on.

The function name is assigned a value in line 12 of the function. When the END FUNCTION statement is executed, the value assigned to the function name (534.32) is returned to FUTUREVALUE(P, R, C) in line 7. Furthermore, the values of Principal, Rate, and Conversions are passed back to P, R, and C. In this function, however, the variables in the parameter list are not modified. Therefore, P, R, and C maintain their original values following the function call.

FIGURE 9.15

```
1      ' Computing the Future Value
2      ' **************************
3      CLS  ' Clear Screen
4      P = 500
5      R = .0675
6      C = 2
7      PRINT USING "The future value is $###.##"; FUTUREVALUE(P, R, C)
              .
              .
              .
8      ' ************************************************
9      ' *              Determine Future Value          *
10     ' ************************************************
11     FUNCTION FUTUREVALUE (Principal, Rate, Conversions)
12         FUTUREVALUE = Principal * (1 + Rate / Conversions) ^ Conversions
13     END FUNCTION

[run]

The future value is $534.32
```

An Example of a Recursive Function

The symbol n! is read *n factorial*. It is defined as the product of all the integers between 1 and n. Thus,

$$n! = n * (n - 1) * (n - 2) * \ldots * 2 * 1$$

For example,

$$5! = 5 * 4 * 3 * 2 * 1 = 120$$

n! can also be defined as n! = n * (n − 1)! This second representation of n! is called a **recursive definition**. For example,

5! = 5 * 4!	2! = 2 * 1!
4! = 4 * 3!	1! = 1 * 0!
3! = 3 * 2!	0! = 1 by definition

Recursive functions must have a condition that eventually stops the function from calling itself. With factorials, the function stops calling itself when 0! is evaluated. The partial program in Figure 9.16 on the next page illustrates a recursive function that determines the factorial of any integer between 1 and 10.

FIGURE 9.16

```
 1     ' Computing Factorials Using a Recursive Function
 2     ' ************************************************
 3     DO
 4        CLS  ' Clear Screen
 5        INPUT "Enter an Integer between 0 and 10 ===> ", Number%
 6        PRINT
 7        IF Number% >= 0 AND Number% <= 10 THEN
 8           PRINT USING "##_! = #,###,###"; Number%, FACTORIAL(Number%)
 9        ELSE
10           PRINT USING "## is outside the range, please reenter"; Number%
11           PRINT
12           INPUT "Press Enter key to continue...", Halt$
13        END IF
14        PRINT
15        INPUT "Enter Y to determine another factorial, else N ==> ", Control$
16     LOOP UNTIL UCASE$(Control$) = "N"
17
                 .
                 .
                 .

18     ' ************************************************
19     ' *                 Factorial Function           *
20     ' ************************************************
21     FUNCTION FACTORIAL (Number%)
22        IF Number% = 0 THEN
23           FACTORIAL = 1
24        ELSE
25           FACTORIAL = Number% * FACTORIAL(Number% - 1)
26        END IF
27     END FUNCTION
```

```
[run]

Enter an Integer between 0 and 10 ===> 8

 8! =    40,320

Enter Y to determine another factorial, else N ==> n
```

When the partial program in Figure 9.16 is executed, line 5 requests the user to enter an integer between 0 and 10. Line 7 validates the Number%. If Number% is between 0 and 10, then line 8 references the function FACTORIAL. If Number% is outside the range 0 to 10, a diagnostic message displays, and the user is requested to press the Enter key to continue. Whether or not Number% is valid, line 15 requests the user to enter Y or N to continue or terminate the program.

Let's return to line 8 and discuss the function call. When the function is called, control transfers to line 21, the first executable statement in FACTORIAL. Next, line 22 tests the value of Number%. If Number% equals zero, then FACTORIAL is assigned the value 1. If Number% is not equal to zero, then control transfers to line 25 and FACTORIAL is assigned the product of Number% and FACTORIAL(Number% - 1). It is here in line 25 that the function calls itself.

Each time FACTORIAL calls itself, the value of the parameter is decremented by 1. Thus, with Number% equal to 8,

FACTORIAL = 8 * 7 * 6 * 5 * 4 * 3 * 2 * 1 * 1

Hence, line 8 calls the function once, and line 25 calls itself eight times. Finally, line 27 returns the value of FACTORIAL to line 8.

To determine the factorial of integers greater than 10, change the function to double precision. For example, FUNCTION FACTORIAL# (Number%) returns a double-precision value with up to 15 digits of significance. When a function is declared by appending a special character to its name, any reference to the function must also include the special character. Note that upgrading the function to double precision would also require some minor changes to lines 5, 7, 8, and 10.

Using the QuickBASIC Editor to Enter Functions

A function is entered into the PC the same way as a subprogram except that you type the keyword FUNCTION instead of SUB. You can also initiate a function by selecting the New FUNCTION command in the Edit menu (Figure 4.7 on page 99).

To edit a function that is not active in the view window, use the same commands as described in Chapter 4 for subprograms. That is, select a specific function by using the SUBs (F2) command in the Edit menu or press Shift + F2 to display and edit the next function or subprogram in alphabetical order by name. Press Ctrl + F2 to display and edit the previous function or subprogram in alphabetical order by name.

Like subprograms, functions are saved to disk with the Main Program under a single file name. When you save the program, QuickBASIC appends a DECLARE statement at the beginning of the Main Program for each associated function. When the Main Program is loaded from disk into main storage, any associated functions and subprograms are also loaded into main storage.

To print the functions along with the Main Program, select Entire Program in the Print dialog box (Figure 4.12 on page 102). The PC prints functions and subprograms in alphabetical order by name after printing the Main Program. To print a function by itself, load the function into the view window, and select Current Window in the Print dialog box.

9.6 TRAPPING EVENTS

The GOSUB and RETURN Statements

This section discusses subroutines, which are different from subprograms. A subroutine begins with a name (label), followed immediately by a colon (:), and ends with a RETURN statement. Like a variable name, a **subroutine name** can be up to 40 characters. The subroutine is called by a GOSUB statement. The keyword GOSUB is immediately followed by the subroutine name to which control is transferred. Once control transfers, the instructions following the subroutine name are executed one after the other until the RETURN statement is executed. The RETURN statement returns control to the next executable statement following the corresponding GOSUB statement in the superior module (Figure 3.3). A subroutine, therefore, can only exit through a RETURN statement.

The general forms for the GOSUB and RETURN statements are shown in Tables 9.23 and 9.24 on the next page.

TABLE 9.23   The GOSUB Statement

General Form:	GOSUB label
	where **label** is a line label or line number that designates the beginning of a subroutine.
Purpose:	Causes control to transfer to the subroutine represented by label. Causes the location of the next executable statement following the GOSUB to be retained.
Examples:	GOSUB B220.Refresh.Time GOSUB C310.Change.Music GOSUB D420.Draw.Picture
Note:	If label is a line label, rather than a line number, then it must be followed immediately by a colon.

TABLE 9.24   The RETURN Statement

General Form:	RETURN
Purpose:	Causes control to transfer from the subroutine back to the first executable statement immediately following the GOSUB statement that referenced it.
Example:	RETURN
Note:	The RETURN statement may be followed by a label. This option is not used in this book.

Up to this point, we have avoided the use of subroutines and the GOSUB statement. We have concentrated on programming in a top-down fashion using subprograms instead of subroutines.

Some applications, however, require the PC to halt execution of a subprogram and execute a subroutine when a specific event has occurred. The RETURN statement in the subroutine transfers control back to the line label the PC was about to execute when control was transferred to the subroutine. Table 9.25 summarizes specific event-trapping statements that are available in QuickBASIC.

TABLE 9.25   A Summary of Event-Trapping Statements*

STATEMENT	PURPOSE
ON COM(n) GOSUB label	Transfers control to label when there is data filling the communications buffer (n).
ON KEY(n) GOSUB label	Transfers control to label when the function key or cursor control key (n) is pressed.
ON PEN GOSUB label	Transfers control to label when the light pen is activated.
ON PLAY(n) GOSUB label	Transfers control to label when a note (n) is sensed. Plays continuous background music.
ON STRIG(n) GOSUB label	Transfers control to label when one of the joystick buttons (n) is pressed.
ON TIMER(n) GOSUB label	Transfers control to label when the specified period of time (n) in seconds has passed.

* Label can be a line label or line number.

Execute event-trapping statements prior to the first possible occurrence of the event, and place the statement at the beginning of A100.Initialization.

All the statements in Table 9.25 require the execution of a second statement to activate the trap. The corresponding statement that activates the trap for the ON KEY(n) GOSUB statement is KEY ON(n). Consider the following:

```
ON KEY(3) GOSUB Function.Key.F3
KEY(3) ON
```

The first line informs the PC of the subroutine to branch to when the F3 key is pressed. The second line instructs the PC to begin checking for the event that is specified in the first line.

When the F3 key is pressed following the execution of the two lines, the PC saves the location of the line it was about to execute. It then executes the subroutine Function.Key.F3. The RETURN statement transfers control to the location of the line saved by the PC when the event was encountered.

As another example, consider the use of the ON TIMER (n) GOSUB statement. In some menu-driven applications, it is useful to display an accurate system time on the screen. The partial program in Figure 9.17 illustrates how you can instruct the PC to refresh the time displayed on the screen every five seconds without interfering with the interaction between the user and the program.

FIGURE 9.17

An example of refreshing the time displayed on the screen every five seconds.

```
1    ' ************************************************
2    ' *                   Main Program              *
3    ' ************************************************
4    CALL A100.Initialization
        .
        .
        .
5    END
6
7    ' ************************************************
8    ' *            Refresh Time Subroutine          *
9    ' ************************************************
10   Refresh.Time:        '   Start of subroutine
11      Row = CSRLIN
12      Col = POS(0)
13      LOCATE 1, 76: PRINT TIME$
14      LOCATE Row, Col
15   RETURN               '   End of subroutine
16
17   ' ************************************************
18   ' *                Initialization               *
19   ' ************************************************
20   SUB A100.Initialization
21      CLS  'Clear Screen
22      LOCATE 1, 76: PRINT TIME$
23      ON TIMER(5) GOSUB Refresh.Time
24      TIMER ON
25   END SUB
```

Line 21 clears the screen, and line 22 displays the system time in the format hh:mm:ss. Line 23 establishes the subroutine to branch to every five seconds. Note that n, the time interval, is specified in seconds. The value n may range between 1 and 86,400. The upper limit of n is equal to the number of seconds in 24 hours.

Line 24 activates the interval timer trap. Thereafter, as long as the program is executing, the PC branches to the subroutine Refresh.Time every five seconds and refreshes the time displayed on the screen.

If you desire, you may decrease the value of n, the time interval, to three seconds or something smaller to display the time more frequently and more accurately. However, be aware that if the value of n is too small, the performance of your program may degrade because the PC is being used to frequently update the time on the screen.

Note how the CSRLIN and POS functions are used in lines 11 and 12 to determine the current position of the cursor. Then in line 14, the cursor is moved back to the position it had before control passed to the subroutine.

You may also instruct the PC to turn off an event or to continue keeping track of the event but bypass trapping it. For example,

```
TIMER OFF
```

causes the PC to stop tracking TIMER activity, and no trapping takes place. The following statement

```
TIMER STOP
```

also instructs the PC to disregard trapping the interval timer. However, with the latter statement, TIMER activity is still tracked, so an immediate trap occurs when TIMER ON is later executed.

(For additional information on trapping events, including the restrictions placed on the parameter n, see the QuickBASIC manual.)

9.7   WHAT YOU SHOULD KNOW

1. QuickBASIC includes several string functions and string statements that place it among the better programming languages for manipulating letters, numbers, words, and phrases. (See Table 9.1 on page 326 for a list of the string functions.)
2. The MID$ statement replaces a substring within a string.
3. The DATE$ and TIME$ statements may be used to set the system time and date.
4. The LINE INPUT statement accepts an entire line from the keyboard as a string value and assigns it to a specified variable name.
5. QuickBASIC includes numeric functions to handle common mathematical calculations. (See Table 9.15 on page 346 for a list of the most frequently used numeric functions.)
6. The RANDOMIZE statement supplies a new seed for the generation of random numbers by the RND function.
7. In addition to the built-in functions, QuickBASIC allows you to define other numeric and string functions that relate to a particular application. This second type of function, known as a user-defined function, is written directly into the program.
8. User-defined functions begin with the keyword DEF FN. If the function is more than one-line long, then the definition ends with an END DEF statement.
9. All user-defined function names begin with the two letters FN, followed by a variable name that is consistent with the rules used for naming numeric variables.
10. User-defined functions must be defined in the same program in which they are called. Furthermore, when the program is executed, user-defined functions must be evaluated before they are called.
11. User-defined functions are called upon in a LET, PRINT, LPRINT, CASE SELECT or IF statement in the same way that numeric and string functions are called upon.
12. The FUNCTION and END FUNCTION statements are similar to the DEF FN and END DEF statements in that they allow you to create user-defined functions.

13. Table 9.21 on page 365 describes the differences between defining a function using the FUNCTION and DEF FN statements.

14. All the methods for passing values described in Chapter 4 for subprograms work the same way for functions defined with the FUNCTION statement.

15. A function defined with the FUNCTION statement may call itself. This type of function is called a recursive function.

16. A recursive function must include a condition that eventually stops the function from calling itself.

17. A function is entered into the PC the same as a subprogram except that you type the keyword FUNCTION instead of SUB.

18. QuickBASIC allows for subprograms and subroutines. A subroutine is referenced by a GOSUB statement. The keyword GOSUB is followed by a label that identifies the subroutine to which to transfer control.

19. A subroutine begins with a subroutine name followed immediately by a colon (:). In selecting a subroutine name, follow the rules for a variable name.

20. The RETURN statement is always the last statement executed in a subroutine. Its function is to cause control to transfer from the subroutine back to the first executable statement following the corresponding GOSUB statement.

21. QuickBASIC includes several event-trapping statements that instruct the PC to interrupt its normal execution of a program and execute a subroutine when a certain event has occurred.

9.8 TEST YOUR BASIC SKILLS (Even-numbered answers are in Appendix E)

1. Consider the valid programs below. What is displayed if each program is executed?

a.
```
' Exercise 9.1a
CLS  ' Clear Screen
State$ = "Mississippi"
FOR I% = 1 TO LEN(State$)
    LOCATE I%, I%: PRINT LEFT$(State$, I%)
NEXT I%
END
```

b. Assume that the system time is exactly 15:34:56.

```
' Exercise 9.1b
Clock = VAL(LEFT$(TIME$, 2))
IF Clock < 12 THEN
    Id$ = "am"
    IF Clock = 0 THEN
        Clock = 12
    END IF
ELSE
    Id$ = "pm"
    IF Clock <> 12 THEN
        Clock = Clock - 12
    END IF
END IF
Tim$ = STR$(Clock) + MID$(TIME$, 3, 6) + SPACE$(1) + Id$
PRINT "The time is "; Tim$
END
```

```
c. ' Exercise 9.1c
   Code$ = "08<NC74N0AA>FN20A45D;;H"
   CLS  ' Clear Screen
   PRINT "Coded message ======> "; Code$
   PRINT : PRINT "The message is =====> ";
   FOR I% = 1 TO LEN(Code$)
      Mesg = ASC(MID$(Code$, I%, 1))
      Mesg = Mesg + 17
      Char$ = CHR$(Mesg)
      PRINT LCASE$(Char$);
   NEXT I%
   END
```

```
d. ' Exercise 9.1d
   CLS  ' Clear Screen
   Phrase1$ = "TODAY IS THE TOMORROW YOU"
   Phrase2$ = " WORRIED ABOUT YESTERDAY"
   Phrase3$ = Phrase1$ + Phrase2$
   LOCATE 12, 15: PRINT LEFT$(Phrase3$, 1);
   FOR I% = 2 TO LEN(Phrase3$)
      Upper = ASC(MID$(Phrase3$, I%, 1))
      IF Upper <> 32 THEN
         Upper = Upper + 32
      END IF
      Lower$ = CHR$(Upper)
      PRINT Lower$;
   NEXT I%
   PRINT "."
   END
```

2. Evaluate each of the following. Assume that Phr$ is equal to the following string:

   `If I have seen further it is by standing upon the shoulders of giants`

   a. LEN(PHR$)
   b. RIGHT$(PHR$, 100)
   c. LEFT$(PHR$, 5)
   d. MID$(PHR$, 11, 4)
   e. VAL("36.8")
   f. ASC(MID$(PHR$, 4, 1))
   g. CHR$(71)
   h. STRING$(14, "A")
   i. STR$(-13.691)
   j. INSTR(10, PHR$, "i")
   k. MID$(PHR$, 64, 7) = "midgets"
   l. SPACE$(4)

3. Evaluate each of the following. Assume that Num is equal to 2 and that Phr$ is equal to the following string:

   `GOTO is a four-letter word`

   a. LEN(Phr$)
   b. RIGHT$(Phr$, 4)
   c. RIGHT$(Phr$, 30)
   d. LEFT$(Phr$, 50)
   e. LEFT$(Phr$, 1.5)
   f. LEFT$(Phr$, Num)
   g. MID$(Phr$, Num, 3)
   h. MID$(Phr$, Num ^ 3, 2)
   i. MID$(Phr$, 1, 5 * Num)
   j. INSTR(Phr$, "is")
   k. INSTR(Num, Phr$, "t")
   l. INSTR(2 * Num, Phr$, "r ")

4. Evaluate each of the following:

   a. VAL("99")
   b. ASC("+")
   c. CHR$(63)
   d. STR$(48.9)
   e. CLS : PRINT CSRLIN
   f. PRINT UCASE$("abc")
   g. CHR$(37)
   h. ASC(":")
   i. PRINT , POS(0)
   j. LOCATE 23, 46 : ? POS(0) + CSRLIN

5. What does the following program display when executed? What value must be assigned to Control$ to terminate the program?

```
' Exercise 9.5
Char$ = "a"
Control$ = ""
DO WHILE Control$ <> "&"
    FOR I% = 1 TO 80
        PRINT Char$;
    NEXT I%
    Control$ = INKEY$
    IF Control$ <> "" THEN
        Char$ = Control$
    END IF
LOOP
END
```

6. Using the concepts in this chapter, write a series of statements that will display the sum of the digits in the customer number Num$. Assume that Num$ is equal to the string value 1698.

7. Assuming that the system time is exactly 11:59:59 p.m. and that the system date is December 1, 1995, evaluate each of the following:

a. `Clock$ = TIME$`
b. `Day$ = DATE$`
c. `Sec = TIMER`

8. What does the following program display when executed? Explain the algorithm that is used in this program.

```
' Exercise 9.8
CLS  ' Clear Screen
PRINT "Prime numbers between 1 and 100 -";
PRINT 2;
FOR I% = 3 TO 100
    FOR K% = 2 TO INT(SQR(I%))
        IF I% MOD K% = 0
            K% = 12
        END IF
    NEXT K%
    IF K% < 12 THEN
        PRINT I%;
    END IF
NEXT I%
END
```

9. What does the following program display when executed?

```
' Exercise 9.9
CLS  ' Clear Screen
FOR K% = 1 TO 24
    FOR J% = 1 TO 10
        LOCATE 12, 36: PRINT "Wake Up ";
        FOR I% = 1 TO 5
            PRINT CHR$(7);
        NEXT I%
        LOCATE 12, 36: PRINT SPC(7);
    NEXT J%
    PRINT
NEXT K%
END
```

10. Write a single QuickBASIC statement for each of the following. Use numeric functions wherever possible. Assume that the value of X is a real number.

    a. $p = \sqrt{a^2 + b^2}$ b. $b = \sqrt{|\tan X - 0.51|}$

    c. $q = 8 \cos^2 X + 4 \sin X$ d. $y = e^x + \log_e (1 + X)$

11. What is the numeric value of each of the following?

    a. INT(-18.5)   b. ABS(-3)   c. INT(16.9)

    d. ABS(6.7)   e. EXP(1)   f. LOG(0)

12. Write separate QuickBASIC statements for each of the following:
    a. Determine the sign of $2X^3 + 3X + 5$.
    b. Determine the integer part of $4X + 5$.
    c. Round X to two decimal places, then to one decimal place.

13. Write a program that displays the values for X and SIN X where X varies between $0°$ and $180°$. Increment X in steps of 5.

14. Explain the purpose of the POS, SCREEN, and CSRLIN functions.

15. Characterize the four methods of accepting input through the keyboard — INPUT, LINE INPUT, INKEY$, and INPUT$(N) — in terms of suspension of program execution, type and length of data that may be assigned, and whether the Enter key must be pressed.

16. Write a program that will generate and display 100 random numbers between 1 and 52, inclusive.

17. Explain the purpose of the RANDOMIZE statement. Why is the TIMER function a good choice for determining the seed?

18. Write a user-defined function that will determine a 10% discount on the amount of purchase (Purchase) in excess of $200.00. The discount applies to the excess, not the entire purchase.

19. Explain the function of the following partial program:

```
ON KEY(5) GOSUB Function.Key.F5
KEY(5) ON
```

20. Is the following program valid or invalid? If it is invalid, indicate why.

```
' Exercise 9.20
DEF FNX(B) = FNA(B) + 5
DEF FNA(B) = FNW(B) * 7
DEF FNW(B) = B ^ 4
PRINT FNX(5)
END
```

21. Given the following program:

```
' Exercise 9.21
FOR I% = 1 TO 5
    READ X
    PRINT TAB(5); X,   (complete this portion)
NEXT I%
DATA 1.1, 10000.5, 100.3, 1000.4, 10.2
END
```

Complete the PRINT statement so that the results displayed in the second column are right-justified, as shown below:

```
1.1                    1.1
10000.5             10000.5
100.3                100.3
1000.4              1000.4
10.2                  10.2
```

Do not use the PRINT USING statement.

(**Hint:** Use the LOG function.)

22. Write a function using the FUNCTION statement that returns 1 if W is less than 10, 2 if W is between 10 and 100 inclusive, and 3 if W is greater than 100. Use the function name SWITCH.

23. **PC Hands-On Exercise:** Load Program 9.1 (PRG9-1) from the Student Diskette. Delete lines 27 through 29 and insert the following statement in place of line 30:

```
PRINT LCASE$(CHR$(ASC(MID$(CODE$, CHAR, 1)) - 3));
```

Execute the program and enter the following coded message:

KR#LV#WKH#VKDGRZB

Do you agree that it is valid to have functions as the arguments of other functions?

24. **PC Hands-On Exercise:** Load Program 9.3 (PRG9-3) from the Student Diskette. Change the argument of the LOG function in line 50 to 10 so the PC determines the number of years it takes to increase an investment tenfold at the given interest rates. Execute the program.

25. **PC Hands-On Exercise:** Load Program 9.4 (PRG9-4) from the Student Diskette and try your luck at guessing a number between 1 and 100. If you get bored with the game, modify PRG9-4, lines 18 and 21, to guess a number between 1 and 1,000.

26. **PC Hands-On Exercise:** Load Program 9.5 (PRG9-5) from the Student Diskette. Execute the program and try your luck at Beat the House Roller.

9.9   BASIC PROGRAMMING PROBLEMS

1. Palindromes

Purpose: To become familiar with the manipulation of strings through the use of the LEN and MID$ functions.

Problem: A palindrome is a word or phrase that is the same when read either backward or forward. For example, noon is a palindrome, but moon is not. Write a top-down program that requests the user to enter a string of uppercase characters and that determines whether the string is a palindrome.

Input Data: Use the following sample data:

```
9876556789
ABLE WAS I ERE I SAW ELBA
I
BOB DID BOB
WOW LIL DID POP
NUN
OTTO
RADAR
!@#$$@#!
( )
A PROGRAM IS A MIRROR IMAGE OF THE MIND
```

Output Results: The following partial results are shown:

```
String? 9876556789
9876556789 is a palindrome.
Enter Y to continue, else N... Y
          .
          .

          .

String? wow lil did pop
wow lil did pop is not a palindrome.

Enter Y to continue, else N... Y
```

2. English to Pig-Latin Conversion

Purpose: To become familiar with string manipulation.

Problem: In pig Latin, a word such as computer is converted to omputercay. For this BASIC Programming Problem, the translation from English to pig Latin calls for taking the first consonant of the word and moving it to the end of the word, followed by an appended "ay." If a word begins with a vowel, then the vowel remains in its beginning position, and the string "way" is appended to the end of the word. For example, apple becomes appleway.

Write a top-down program that displays the pig Latin translation for a string of English words (uppercase). Also display the number of words that begin with a vowel, the total number of words in the string, and the percentage of words that begin with a vowel. Do not include punctuation.

Input Data: Use the following sample data. Do not press the Enter key until you have entered the entire phrase.

> EVERY PROGRAM IS A SELF PORTRAIT OF THE PERSON WHO WROTE IT
> AUTOGRAPH YOUR WORK WITH EXCELLENCE

Output Results: The following results are displayed:

```
Enter the English Sentence Without Punctuation
-----------------------------------------------
EVERY PROGRAM IS A SELF-PORTRAIT OF THE PERSON WHO WROTE IT
AUTOGRAPH YOUR WORK WITH EXCELLENCE

The Sentence in Pig Latin is as follows:
-----------------------------------------------
EVERYWAY ROGRAMPAY ISWAY AWAY ELFSAY ORTRAITPAY OFWAY HETAY
ERSONPAY HOWAY ROTEWAY ITWAY AUTOGRAPHWAY OURYAY ORKWAY ITHWAY
EXCELLENCEWAY

Words beginning with a vowel ========>   7
Total number of words ===============>  17
Percentage beginning with a vowel ===>  41.17647

Job Complete
```

3. Time to Double an Investment Compounded Quarterly

Purpose: To become familiar with the use of numeric functions and user-defined functions, and the concepts of rounding and truncation.

Problem: Write a top-down program that will determine the time it takes to double an investment compounded quarterly for the following annual interest rates: 6%, 7%, 8% and 9%. The formula for computing the time is as follows:

$$N = \frac{\log 2}{M(\log(1+J)/M))}$$

where
N = time in years
J = annual interest rate
M = number of conversion periods

Once the time has been determined for a given interest rate, use the generalized expressions for rounding and truncation given in Section 9.3 on page 347 to round and truncate the answer to two decimal places. Define both expressions as user-defined functions in your program.

Input Data: None.

Output Results: The following results are displayed:

```
              Time to Double an Investment
                  Compounded Quarterly
              ------------------------------

                      Years              Years
       Annual         to Double          to Double
       Interest       (Rounded)          (Truncated)
       --------       ---------          -----------
         6%             11.64               11.63
         7%              9.99                9.98
         8%              8.75                8.75
         9%              7.79                7.78

       Job Complete
```

4. Order Entry Simulation

Purpose: To become familiar with the use of the random number function RND, the RANDOMIZE statement, the TIMER function, the INPUT$ function, and computer simulation.

Problem: Order entry is the process of receiving customer orders and producing shipping orders. The Oldtown Company has three clerks in its Order Entry Department. On the average, the three clerks can process 197 customer orders a day. Management has requested the Computer Information Systems Department to simulate the activities of the Order Entry Department over a four-week period (20 working days). The following statistics were compiled over the same four-week period during the previous year:

Customer Orders Received	Frequency in Days	Relative Frequency	Cumulative Frequency
185	1	0.05	0.05
190	5	0.25	0.30
195	6	0.30	0.60
200	4	0.20	0.80
205	3	0.15	0.95
210	1	0.05	1.00

Assuming that the four-week period (day 1 through day 20) begins with no backlog orders, write a top-down program that will print on the printer the simulation of the following:

1. Number of orders received each day
2. Number of orders processed (the day's order plus backlog orders)
3. Orders not processed
4. Number of days in which orders go unprocessed

The orders received are to be simulated by employing the RND function. Once the program is working properly, add the statement RANDOMIZE TIMER so a new seed will be used to generate the random numbers each time the program is executed.

The random number returned by the RND function should be passed through a SELECT CASE statement to determine whether it is less than or equal to the cumulative frequencies for orders compiled from the previous year. The logic for these tests is shown in Figure 9.18.

FIGURE 9.18

The logic for Order Entry Simulation.

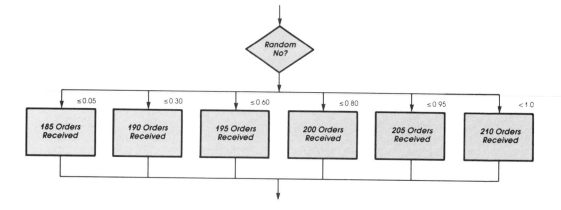

Input Data: None.

Output Results: Display the following message to the user:

```
Press any key when the printer is ready...
```

The following illustrates a sample run. Note that answers will vary, depending on the random numbers generated on the basis of the value of TIMER.

```
                    Order Entry Simulation
              Maximum Orders Processed per Day 197

                   Orders        Orders        Orders Not
         Day      Received      Processed       Processed
         ---      --------      ---------      ----------
          1         190           190              0
          2         200           197              3
          3         190           193              0
          .          .             .               .
          .          .             .               .
          .          .             .               .
         18         190           190              0
         19         195           195              0
         20         205           197              8

      Number of days orders went unprocessed ======> 10
```

5. Cryptograms

Purpose: To become familiar with concatenation, table searching, and string manipulation of cryptograms.

Problem: In Section 9.2, on page 334, you were introduced to a method of substituting characters in a coded message and determining the contents of the message. The direct substitution method, based on a table of substitutes, may also be used with cryptograms. Write a top-down program that uses the following table of substitutes to decode a given message:

Coded Characters: 9 G Q 6 V L P N W X A 8 T # H Z J M (U 3) R I S B F K D

Regular Characters: A B C D E F G H I J K L M N O P Q R S T U V W X Y Z – b .

The coded characters and their corresponding regular characters are stored in EX95CODE.TBL on the Student Diskette. Use the TYPE command to display the file EX95CODE.TBL to determine the order in which the data is stored. Assume that all coded messages are in uppercase. The character b represents the blank character.

Input Data: Use the following sample coded messages.

Message 1: G9(WQKW(KV9(S
Message 2: LW#6W#PKUNVK6VVZK(WTZ8WQWUWV(KW#K9K
            QHTZ8WQ9UV6KQH88VQUWH#KHLKUNW#P(K
            UHKGVK6H#VKW(KUNVKQMV9UW)WUSK#WUSK#K
            ZMHPM9TTW#PKFKND6DTW88(

Output Results: The following is shown for message 1:

```
Enter the coded message ====> G9(WQKW(KV9(S

The message is ==============> BASIC IS EASY

Job Complete
```

6. Soundex Code

Purpose: To become familiar with character transformation, Soundex, and the use of the LINE INPUT statement.

Problem: Companies that allow their customers to phone or write for information regarding their account status frequently have only the customer's name to aid them in locating a record in the account file. Sometimes the name itself is not clear, because of illegible handwriting or poor voice communications in a phone conversation. Also, when customers call to request information about their accounts, some companies like to ask as few questions as possible to give callers the impression that they are special customers.

Soundex is the name of a method for transforming the sound of a name into a successful and efficient search for a customer record. Developed by M. Odell and R. Russell, the method involves assigning a code, called the Soundex code, to a surname when a record is first added to a file, and placing this code in the record for access purposes. The Soundex code for a name is determined from the following rules:

1. Retain the first letter and drop all occurrences of a, e, h, i, o, u, w, and y in other positions of the name.

2. Assign the following digits to the remaining letters:

Digits	Letters
1	b,f,p,v
2	c,g,j,k,q,s,x,z
3	d,t
4	l
5	m,n
6	r

3. If two or more letters with the same code are adjacent in the original name, drop all but the first letter.
4. Convert the name to the form "letter, digit, digit, digit" by adding trailing zeros if there are less than three digits, or by dropping rightmost digits if there are more than three digits. The following examples of names have these corresponding Soundex codes:

Last Name	Code	Last Name	Code
Case	C200	Knuth	K530
Cash	C200	Smith	S530
Caise	C200	Smyth	S530
Gauss	G200	Smythe	S530

This system will work for most Anglo-Saxon names. Similar systems are available for other types of names such as Asian or Spanish. These systems may not always work, but they speed up the searching of many records.

Write a top-down program that builds an account file in which each record contains the customer number, customer name, Soundex code, and balance due. The program should request from the user the customer number, name, and balance due. From the last name, the program should determine the Soundex code and display it. Then the program should write the record to a sequential file EX96DATA.DAT.

Input Data: Use the following sample data. Be sure to include the comma (,) as part of the customer name.

Customer Number	Customer Name	Balance Due	Customer Number	Customer Name	Balance Due
1783	Allen, John	$55.00	3401	Smith, Amanda	$45.00
1934	Smit, Joan	0.00	3607	Cas, Louise	0.00
2109	Case, Jeff	5.00	4560	Smythe, Alice	4.00
2134	Alien, Bill	35.00	5590	Ellen, Boyd	7.80
2367	Allan, Fred	65.00	6498	Caes, Nikole	5.30
2568	Caise, Edie	87.00	7591	Kase, Judy	0.00

Output Results: The following partial results are displayed:

```
Customer Number =====> 1783
Customer Name =======> Allen, John
Balance =============> 55.00
Soundex Code ========> A450

Enter Y to add another account, else N... Y
```

The records are written to the sequential file EX96DATA.DAT.

7. Payroll Problem IX: Spelling Out the Net Pay

Purpose: To become familiar with table utilization, use of the zero element of an array, the INT and STR$ functions, and spelling out numbers.

Problem: Construct a top-down program that spells out the net pay for check-writing purposes. For example, the net pay $5,078.45 is written out on a check as follows:

Five Thousand Seventy-Eight Dollars and 45 Cents

Assume that the net pay does not exceed $9,999.99.

Hint: Use the INT function to separate the integer portion of the net pay into single digits. Use the single digits to access the words from one of two positionally organized tables. If the digit represents the thousands, hundreds, or units position, then access the word from the following table:

Digit	Word	Digit	Word
0	Null	10	Ten
1	One	11	Eleven
2	Two	12	Twelve
3	Three	13	Thirteen
4	Four	14	Fourteen
5	Five	15	Fifteen
6	Six	16	Sixteen
7	Seven	17	Seventeen
8	Eight	18	Eighteen
9	Nine	19	Nineteen

If the digit represents the tens position, then access the word from the following table:

Digit	Word	Digit	Word
0	Null	5	Fifty
1	Ten	6	Sixty
2	Twenty	7	Seventy
3	Thirty	8	Eighty
4	Forty	9	Ninety

The word entries for both tables are found in the sequential file EX97TAB.TBL on the Student Diskette. The entries for the thousands, hundreds, and units table are first in the sequential file, followed immediately by the entries for the tens table.

Use the INT and STR$ functions to determine the fraction portion of the net pay. Use the concatenation operator to string the words together. If there are no dollars or cents, display the word "No" accordingly.

Input Data: Use the sequential file EX97DATA.DAT found on the Student Diskette. The data file includes the following sample data:

Employee Number	Net Pay
123	$8,462.34
124	987.23
125	78.99
126	6,000.23
127	1,003.00
128	4,037.00
129	4.67
130	0.02

Output Results: The following results are displayed:

```
Employee
Number    Net Pay    Net Pay Spelled Out
--------  -------    -------------------
    123   8,462.34   Eight Thousand Four Hundred Sixty-Two Dollars and 34 Cents
    124     987.23   Nine Hundred Eighty-Seven Dollars and 23 Cents
    125      78.99   Seventy-Eight Dollars and 99 Cents
    126   6,000.23   Six Thousand  Dollars and 23 Cents
    127   1,003.00   One Thousand Three Dollars and No Cents
    128   4,037.00   Four Thousand Thirty-Seven Dollars and No Cents
    129       4.67   Four Dollars and 67 Cents
    130       0.02   No Dollars and 2 Cents

Job Complete
```

File Maintenance, Random File Processing, and Simulated-Indexed Files

10.1 INTRODUCTION

In Chapter 7, you were introduced to sequential file processing. Topics included writing reports to auxiliary storage and building and processing sequential data files. In this chapter, we discuss file maintenance. **File maintenance** means updating files in one or more of the following ways:

1. *Adding* new records
2. *Deleting* unwanted records
3. *Changing* data within records

This chapter also concentrates on two additional methods of file organization — random and simulated-indexed files.

Random Files

A file that is organized randomly is called a **random file**, or a **relative file**. The sequence of processing a random file has no relationship to the sequence in which the records are stored. If the tenth record in a file is required by a program, the record can be directly accessed without processing the previous nine records. However, the program must indicate to the PC the location of the record relative to the beginning of the file. For example, to access the tenth record instead of the third or fourth record, the program must explicitly indicate to the PC that the tenth record is requested for processing.

Indexed Files

A third type of file organization known as **indexed** is also widely used in data processing. A file organized by an index is an **indexed file**. An indexed file is organized around a specified data item called the **key**, which is common to each record. In an airline reservation file, the key may be the flight number. In an inventory file, the key may be the part number or a part description.

Indexed files have one advantage over random files: the program need only supply the key of the record to be accessed instead of the record's relative location. Although indexed files are not available with QuickBASIC, this method of organization may be simulated by using both a sequential file and a random file, as illustrated in Programming Case Study 22.

Indexed files and random files are used primarily for on-line activities where the applications call for random processing of the data. In airline reservation systems, inventory systems, management information systems, and customer credit checks, indexed or random organization of a file has important advantages over sequential organization.

10.2   FILE MAINTENANCE

File maintenance is one of the most important activities in data processing. The programming techniques that are used to update a file are usually based on the type of file organization under which the file was created. To update sequential files, the record additions, deletions, and changes are normally entered into another data file called a transaction file. A **transaction file**, therefore, contains data of a temporary, or transient nature. Once the updates have been completed, the transaction file can be archived and deleted.

The file that is updated is called the **master file**. A master file contains data that is usually permanent. **Current master file** refers to the master file before updating, and **new master file** refers to the updated version of the current master file. A file maintenance program that updates a sequential file must deal with at least three files, as illustrated in the system flowchart in Figure 10.1.

FIGURE 10.1

A system flowchart representing file maintenance of a sequential file.

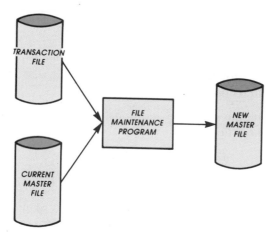

A **system flowchart** shows in graphic form the files, flow of data, equipment, and programs involved in a particular application. The cylinder-like symbols in Figure 10.1 symbolize auxiliary storage devices such as diskette units. The rectangle represents a computer system containing a program. The arrows in the system flowchart indicate that data is read from two files and that the results of the program are written to another file.

To use the file maintenance technique described in Figure 10.1, both the master and transaction files must be in the same sequence, based on one of the data items common to both files. For example, an inventory master file and a corresponding inventory transaction file may be in sorted ascending sequence by stock number.

For the sake of simplicity, the presentation of file maintenance has been divided into two problems and two corresponding program solutions. In the first set, Programming Case Study 18, a method of adding records to the current master file to form a new master file will be illustrated. In Programming Case Study 19, record deletion and changing data within records are illustrated. BASIC Programming Problem 10.1 at the end of this chapter requires the completion of all the file maintenance in one program.

File Maintenance I — Adding Records by Merging Files

Problem: Programming Case Study 9, on page 231 in Chapter 7, created a sequential data file called INVNTORY.DAT from the inventory data in Table 10.1.

TABLE 10.1 Inventory Data Used to Create the Master File INVNTORY.DAT

STOCK NUMBER	WAREHOUSE LOCATION	DESCRIPTION	UNIT COST	SELLING PRICE	QUANTITY ON HAND
C101	1	Roadhandler	97.56	125.11	25
C204	3	Whitewalls	37.14	99.95	140
C502	2	Tripod	32.50	38.99	10
S209	1	Maxidrill	88.76	109.99	6
S416	2	Normalsaw	152.55	179.40	1
S812	2	Router	48.47	61.15	8
S942	4	Radialsaw	376.04	419.89	3
T615	4	Oxford-Style	26.43	31.50	28
T713	2	Moc-Boot	24.99	29.99	30
T814	2	Work-Boot	22.99	27.99	56

New stock items are to be added to the inventory master file INVNTORY.DAT created in Programming Case Study 9. The new stock items are shown in Table 10.2 and are in the file TRAINV.DAT. The program should merge the records of the two files to create the new inventory master file. **Merging** is the process of combining two or more files that are *in the same sequence* into a single file that maintains that same sequence for a given data item found in each record. The two files are each in ascending sequence according to the stock number.

TABLE 10.2 Inventory Data in the Transaction File TRAINV.DAT

STOCK NUMBER	WAREHOUSE LOCATION	DESCRIPTION	UNIT COST	SELLING PRICE	QUANTITY ON HAND
C103	2	Saw-Blades	5.06	6.04	15
C206	1	Square	4.56	5.42	34
S210	3	Microscope	31.50	41.99	8
S941	2	Hip-Boot	26.95	32.50	12
T615	4	Oxford-Style	26.43	31.50	28
T731	1	Sandals	6.75	9.45	52

The transaction file can be created by modifying line 19 in Program 7.2 on page 232 as follows:

```
OPEN "TRAINV.DAT" FOR OUTPUT AS #1
```

and entering the records in Table 10.2 in response to the modified Program 7.2.

Also assume that the name of the current master file INVNTORY.DAT, has been changed to CURINV.DAT, using the MS-DOS command RENAME or the QuickBASIC NAME statement to change file names. (See Appendix D, Tables D.1 and D.2.) For example, use the MS-DOS command

```
RENAME INVNTORY.DAT CURINV.DAT
```

or the QuickBASIC statement

```
NAME "INVNTORY.DAT" AS "CURINV.DAT"
```

The NAME statement may be entered in the immediate window or placed in A100.Initialization.

By changing the name of the current master file, its former name INVNTORY.DAT can then be assigned to a new master file.

It is an error for a record in the transaction file to have the same stock number as a record in the current master file. If this happens, an appropriate diagnostic message, including the stock number and description, should display. Also, a count of the number of records in the new master file should display before the program is terminated.

A top-down chart showing what must be done to solve the problem is illustrated in Figure 10.2. Recall that recurring subtasks are identified by darkening the upper right-hand corner of the process symbol. At implementation time, recurring subtasks are coded once and called upon as often as needed. Following are the program tasks that specify how to solve the problem on the basis of the top-down chart, a program solution, and a discussion of the program solution.

Program Tasks

1. A100.Initialization

    a. Set Record.Count to zero.
    b. Set two end-of-file switches Master.Eof$ for the current master file and Transaction.Eof$ for the transaction file to the value OFF. Set either switch to the value ON when the end-of-file mark is sensed in the corresponding file.
    c. Open CURINV.DAT, TRAINV.DAT, and INVNTORY.DAT.
    d. Display an appropriate screen title.

FIGURE 10.2

Top down chart for Program 10.1.

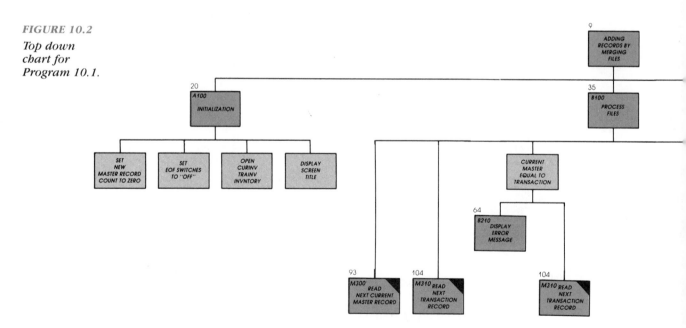

2. B100.Process.Files

    a. Read the first record in the current master file and the first record in the transaction file. Use the following variable names:

Current Master File		*Transaction File*	
M.Stock$	= stock number	T.Stock$	= stock number
M.Location$	= location	T.Location$	= location
M.Desc$	= description	T.Desc$	= description
M.Cost	= cost	T.Cost	= cost
M.Price	= price	T.Price	= price
M.Quantity	= quantity	T.Quantity	= quantity

    b. Establish a Do-While loop that executes while both Master.Eof$ and Transaction.Eof$ are equal to the value OFF. Within the loop, compare M.Stock$ to T.Stock$ and do the following:

       (1) If the stock number M.Stock$ is equal to the stock number T.Stock$, then display a diagnostic message and read the next transaction record.

       (2) If the stock number M.Stock$ is less than the stock number T.Stock$, then write the current master record to the new master file, increment counter Record.Count by 1, and read the next current master record.

       (3) If the stock number M.Stock$ is greater than the stock number T.Stock$, then write the transaction record to the new master file, increment counter Record.Count by 1, and read the next transaction record.

3. C100.Wrap.Up

    a. One of the two input files may still contain records that need to be written to the new master file. This procedure is often referred to as **flushing the files**.

    b. Close all files.

    c. Display the value of Record.Count as well as an end-of-job message.

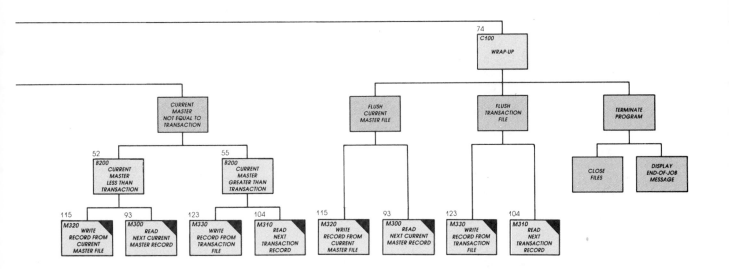

Program Solution

Program 10.1 corresponds to the top-down chart in Figure 10.2 and to the preceding program tasks.

```
1     ' Program 10.1
2     ' File Maintenance I  - Adding Records by Merging Files
3     ' Current Master File = CURINV.DAT
4     ' Transaction File    = TRAINV.DAT
5     ' New Master File      = INVNTORY.DAT
6     ' ***************************************************************
7     ' *                     Main Program                          *
8     ' ***************************************************************
9     COMMON SHARED Record.Count, Master.Eof$, Transaction.Eof$
10    COMMON SHARED M.Stock$, M.Location$, M.Desc$, M.Cost, M.Price, M.Quantity
11    COMMON SHARED T.Stock$, T.Location$, T.Desc$, T.Cost, T.Price, T.Quantity
12    CALL A100.Initialization
13    CALL B100.Process.Files
14    CALL C100.Wrap.Up
15    END
16
17    ' ***************************************************************
18    ' *                    Initialization                         *
19    ' ***************************************************************
20    SUB A100.Initialization
21       Record.Count = 0
22       Master.Eof$ = "OFF"
23       Transaction.Eof$ = "OFF"
24       OPEN "CURINV.DAT" FOR INPUT AS #1
25       OPEN "TRAINV.DAT" FOR INPUT AS #2
26       OPEN "INVNTORY.DAT" FOR OUTPUT AS #3
27       CLS ' Clear Screen
28       LOCATE 5, 15: PRINT "Adding Records to Inventory File"
29       LOCATE 6, 15: PRINT "--------------------------------"
30    END SUB
31
32    ' ***************************************************************
33    ' *                    Process Files                          *
34    ' ***************************************************************
35    SUB B100.Process.Files
36       CALL M300.Read.Master.Record
37       CALL M310.Read.Transaction.Record
38       DO WHILE Master.Eof$ = "OFF" AND Transaction.Eof$ = "OFF"
39          IF M.Stock$ <> T.Stock$ THEN
40             CALL B200.Determine.Record.To.Write
41          ELSE
42             CALL B210.Display.Error.Message
43             CALL M310.Read.Transaction.Record
44          END IF
45       LOOP
46    END SUB
47
48    ' ***************************************************************
49    ' *          Determine Record to Write to Master File         *
50    ' ***************************************************************
51    SUB B200.Determine.Record.To.Write
52       IF M.Stock$ < T.Stock$ THEN
53          CALL M320.Write.Master.Record
54          CALL M300.Read.Master.Record
55       ELSE
56          CALL M330.Write.Transaction.Record
57          CALL M310.Read.Transaction.Record
58       END IF
59    END SUB
60
```

```
61      ' ****************************************************************
62      ' *                  Display Error Message                     *
63      ' ****************************************************************
64      SUB B210.Display.Error.Message
65         PRINT
66         PRINT "********** Transaction Record Already in Current Master File"
67         PRINT "*  ERROR  * Stock Number = "; T.Stock$
68         PRINT "********** Description  = "; T.Desc$
69      END SUB
70
71      ' ****************************************************************
72      ' *                       Wrap-Up                              *
73      ' ****************************************************************
74      SUB C100.Wrap.Up
75         DO WHILE Master.Eof$ = "OFF"
76            CALL M320.Write.Master.Record
77            CALL M300.Read.Master.Record
78         LOOP
79         DO WHILE Transaction.Eof$ = "OFF"
80            CALL M330.Write.Transaction.Record
81            CALL M310.Read.Transaction.Record
82         LOOP
83         CLOSE
84         PRINT
85         PRINT "The number of records in the new master file is"; Record.Count
86         PRINT
87         PRINT "INVNTORY.DAT Update Complete"
88      END SUB
89
90      ' ****************************************************************
91      ' *              Read Next Current Master Record               *
92      ' ****************************************************************
93      SUB M300.Read.Master.Record
94         IF EOF(1) THEN
95            Master.Eof$ = "ON"
96         ELSE
97            INPUT #1, M.Stock$, M.Location$, M.Desc$, M.Cost, M.Price, M.Quantity
98         END IF
99      END SUB
100
101     ' ****************************************************************
102     ' *               Read Next Transaction Record                 *
103     ' ****************************************************************
104     SUB M310.Read.Transaction.Record
105        IF EOF(2) THEN
106           Transaction.Eof$ = "ON"
107        ELSE
108           INPUT #2, T.Stock$, T.Location$, T.Desc$, T.Cost, T.Price, T.Quantity
109        END IF
110     END SUB
111
112     ' ****************************************************************
113     ' *           Write Record from Current Master File            *
114     ' ****************************************************************
115     SUB M320.Write.Master.Record
116        WRITE #3, M.Stock$, M.Location$, M.Desc$, M.Cost, M.Price, M.Quantity
117        Record.Count = Record.Count + 1
118     END SUB
119
120     ' ****************************************************************
121     ' *             Write Record from Transaction File             *
122     ' ****************************************************************
123     SUB M330.Write.Transaction.Record
124        WRITE #3, T.Stock$, T.Location$, T.Desc$, T.Cost, T.Price, T.Quantity
125        Record.Count = Record.Count + 1
126     END SUB

        [run]
```

Discussion of the Program Solution

Because merging two files into one is a complex process, we recommend that you pay particular attention to the top-down chart in Figure 10.2. Stepping through both the program tasks and the top-down chart will give you a better understanding of the algorithm used to merge the two files.

Figures 10.3 and 10.4 show the contents of the current master file CURINV.DAT, and the transaction file TRAINV.DAT.

FIGURE 10.3
 	
A list of the records in the current master file, CURINV.DAT.
	`"C101","1","Roadhandler",97.56,125.11,25`
	`"C204","3","Whitewalls",37.14,99.95,140`
	`"C502","2","Tripod",32.5,38.99,10`
	`"S209","1","Maxidrill",88.76,109.99,6`
	`"S416","2","Normalsaw",152.55,179.4,1`
	`"S812","2","Router",48.47,61.15,8`
	`"S942","4","Radialsaw",376.04,419.89,3`
	`"T615","4","Oxford-Style",26.43,31.5,28`
	`"T713","2","Moc-Boot",24.99,29.99,30`
	`"T814","2","Work-Boot",22.99,27.99,56`

FIGURE 10.4
 	
A list of the records in the transaction file, TRAINV.DAT.
	`"C103","2","Saw-Blades",5.06,6.04,15`
	`"C206","1","Square",4.56,5.42,34`
	`"S210","3","Microscope",31.50,41.99,8`
	`"S941","2","Hip-Boot",26.95,32.50,12`
	`"T615","4","Oxford-Style",26.43,31.50,28`
	`"T731","1","Sandals",6.75,9.45,52`

When Program 10.1 is executed, line 12 in the Main Program calls the subprogram A100.Initialization. Line 21 initializes the counter Record.Count to zero. Record.Count is equal to the number of records written to the new master file INVNTORY.DAT. Lines 22 and 23 assign the end-of-file switches Master.Eof$ and Transaction.Eof$, the value of OFF. These two switches are used to control the Do-While loops in the program.

Lines 24 and 25 open for input the two files CURINV.DAT and TRAINV.DAT. Line 26 opens for output the new master file INVNTORY.DAT. Line 27 clears the screen, and lines 28 and 29 display a screen title.

Following the return of control to the Main Program, line 13 calls the subprogram B100.Process.Files. Lines 36 and 37 cause the PC to read the first record in each file. Within the Do-While loop, line 39 compares the stock number (M.Stock$) in the record read from the master file to the stock number (T.Stock$) in the record read from the transaction file. The comparison determines which record will be written to the new master file INVNTORY.DAT. The logic proceeds as follows:

1. If M.Stock$ is equal to T.Stock$, then control transfers to the subprogram B210.Display.Error.Message (lines 64 through 69), and a diagnostic message is displayed indicating that the record from TRAINV.DAT already exists in the data file CURINV.DAT. In line 43, the next record in TRAINV.DAT is read before control passes back to the top of the Do-While loop.

2. If M.Stock$ does not equal T.Stock$, then control passes to the subprogram B200.Determine.Record.To.Write beginning at line 51, and another comparison is made between the two variables to determine which record should be written to the new master file. The following procedure is used:

   a. If M.Stock$ is less than T.Stock$, then control transfers to the subprogram M300.Write.Master.Record (lines 115 through 118), which writes the record from CURINV.DAT. The counter Record.Count is incremented by 1 before control returns to line 54, and the next record in CURINV.DAT is read. Control then returns to B100.Process.Files.

b. If M.Stock$ is greater than T.Stock$, then control transfers to the subprogram M310.Write.Transaction.Record (lines 123 through 126), which writes the record from TRAINV.DAT. The counter Record.Count is incremented by 1 before control returns to line 57, and the next record in TRAINV.DAT is read. Control then returns to B100.Process.Files.

When the PC senses the end-of-file mark on either file, the end-of-file switch representing the exhausted file is assigned a value of ON, and control returns to the Main Program. Line 14 in the Main Program transfers control to C100.Wrap.Up.

If the end-of-file is sensed on TRAINV.DAT, then lines 75 through 78 flush any records remaining in CURINV.DAT. If the end-of-file is sensed on CURINV.DAT, then the Do-While loop (lines 79 through 82) flushes any records that remain in TRAINV.DAT.

It is important to note that the main Do-While loop in B100.Process.Files and both Do-While loops that flush the files in C100.Wrap.Up are controlled by switches and not by the EOF function. If you use the EOF function instead of the two switches to directly control the loops, the last record in each file may not be written to the new master file.

A close look at Figures 10.3 and 10.4 reveals that the fifth record in TRAINV.DAT has the same stock number as the eighth record in CURINV.DAT. This causes the display of a diagnostic message as shown in Figure 10.5.

FIGURE 10.5

The results displayed owing to the execution of Program 10.1.

```
                    Adding Records to Inventory File
                    --------------------------------

         ********** Transaction Record Already in Current Master File
         *  ERROR  * Stock Number = T615
         ********** Description   = Oxford-Style

         The number of records in the new master file is 15

         INVNTORY.DAT Update Complete
```

Figure 10.6 shows the contents of the new master file INVNTORY.DAT created by Program 10.1.

FIGURE 10.6

A list of the records in the merged, new master file INVNTORY.DAT.

```
"C101","1","Roadhandler",97.56,125.11,25
"C103","2","Saw-Blades",5.06,6.04,15
"C204","3","Whitewalls",37.14,99.95,140
"C206","1","Square",4.56,5.42,34
"C502","2","Tripod",32.5,38.99,10
"S209","1","Maxidrill",88.76,109.99,6
"S210","3","Microscope",31.5,41.99,8
"S416","2","Normalsaw",152.55,179.4,1
"S812","2","Router",48.47,61.15,8
"S941","2","Hip-Boot",26.95,32.5,12
"S942","4","Radialsaw",376.04,419.89,3
"T615","4","Oxford-Style",26.43,31.5,28
"T713","2","Moc-Boot",24.99,29.99,30
"T731","1","Sandals",6.75,9.45,52
"T814","2","Work-Boot",22.99,27.99,56
```

Programming Case Study 19 File Maintenance II — Deleting and Changing Records by Matching Records

In Programming Case Study 18, you were introduced to one category of file maintenance — adding new records to the master file. In the following programming case study, you are introduced to the two remaining categories of file maintenance — deletion of unwanted records and changing data within records in the master file. Here again, records will be read from two files, and a new master file will be created. A process known as **matching records** will be used. Matching records involves processing two or more related files that are in the same sequence according to a common data item.

As records are read from the two related files, the PC acts upon them in the following manner:

1. If the stock numbers in both records are equal, then the action indicated on the transaction record is carried out. Either the current master record is deleted by not writing it to the new master file, or the data is changed in the current master record, as indicated on the transaction record, and the modified current master record is written to the new master file.
2. If the stock number in the current master record is less than the stock number in the transaction record, that is, if the transaction file contains no modifications to the current master record, then the current master record is written to the new master file.
3. If the stock number in the current master file is greater than the stock number in the transaction record, that is, if the transaction record has no match, then the transaction record is in error, and a diagnostic message is displayed.

This process of matching records is illustrated in the following problem.

Problem: Given the current master file shown in Figure 10.6 and the transaction file shown in Table 10.3, a program that updates the current master file and creates a new master file will be illustrated. Both the current master file and the transaction file are in ascending sequence by stock number.

TABLE 10.3		Inventory Data in the Transaction File TRAINV–2.DAT				
STOCK NUMBER	**TRANSACTION CODE**	**WAREHOUSE LOCATION**	**DESCRIPTION**	**UNIT COST**	**SELLING PRICE**	**QUANTITY ON HAND**
C204	D	Null Char.	Null Char.	−1	−1	−1
C402	C	3	Null Char.	33.50	40.50	−1
S812	C	Null Char.	ROUTER-II	−1	−1	12
T615	D	Null Char.	Null Char.	−1	−1	−1
T731	C	Null Char.	Null Char.	6.50	−1	−1

Change the name of the current master file in Figure 10.6 to CURINV-2.DAT. Use the name TRAINV-2.DAT to identify the transaction file. Call the new master file INV-2.DAT.

With respect to the contents of the transaction file TRAINV-2.DAT, remember the following:

1. The transaction code D indicates that the corresponding record in the current master file is to be deleted, and the code C indicates changes. (Assume C and D are the only two transaction codes.)
2. Data items that are *not* to be changed in the current master file are designated in the transaction file with a value of −1 if the item is numeric, and by a null character if the item is a string.
3. In order for the INPUT statement to read the transaction file properly, all data items are assigned a value, including those within records representing a delete.
4. With minor modifications, Program 7.2, on page 232, can be used to build the transaction file.

If a record in the transaction file has no matching record in the current master file, then the diagnostic message

```
** ERROR ** Transaction record with stock number xxxx has no match
```

is displayed. As part of the end-of-job routine, the total number of records deleted and the number of records changed are displayed.

Because the algorithm for matching records is similar to the algorithm for merging files that was presented in Programming Case Study 18, a top-down chart and a list of the program tasks are not included in this programming case study. The program solution follows.

Program Solution

PROGRAM 10.2 Program 10.2 matches records between the current master file CURINV-2.DAT, and the transaction file TRAINV-2.DAT, and builds the new master file INV-2.DAT.

```
1     ' Program 10.2
2     ' File Maintenance II -- Deleting Records and Changing Fields
3     ' Current Master File =  CURINV-2.DAT
4     ' Transaction File    =  TRAINV-2.DAT
5     ' New Master File      = INV-2.DAT
6     ' *************************************************************
7     ' *                        Main Program                      *
8     ' *************************************************************
9     COMMON SHARED Delete.Count, Change.Count, Record.Count
10    COMMON SHARED Master.Eof$, Transaction.Eof$, T.Type$
11    COMMON SHARED M.Stock$, M.Location$, M.Desc$, M.Cost, M.Price, M.Quantity
12    COMMON SHARED T.Stock$, T.Location$, T.Desc$, T.Cost, T.Price, T.Quantity
13    CALL A100.Initialization
14    CALL B100.Process.Files
15    CALL C100.Wrap.Up
16    END
17
18    ' *************************************************************
19    ' *                      Initialization                      *
20    ' *************************************************************
21    SUB A100.Initialization
22       Delete.Count = 0
23       Change.Count = 0
24       Record.Count = 0
25       Master.Eof$ = "OFF"
26       Transaction.Eof$ = "OFF"
27       OPEN "CURINV-2.DAT" FOR INPUT AS #1
28       OPEN "TRAINV-2.DAT" FOR INPUT AS #2
29       OPEN "INV-2.DAT" FOR OUTPUT AS #3
30       CLS  ' Clear Screen
31       PRINT "Deleting Records and Changing Fields in Inventory File"
32       PRINT "------------------------------------------------------"
33    END SUB
34
35    ' *************************************************************
36    ' *                      Process Files                       *
37    ' *************************************************************
38    SUB B100.Process.Files
39       CALL M400.Read.Master.Record
40       CALL M410.Read.Transaction.Record
41       DO WHILE Master.Eof$ = "OFF" AND Transaction.Eof$ = "OFF"
42          IF M.Stock$ = T.Stock$ THEN
43             CALL B200.Determine.Maintenance.Type
44          ELSE
45             CALL B210.Write.Cur.Master.Or.Error.Message
46          END IF
47       LOOP
48    END SUB
49
```

(continued)

```
50      ' *****************************************************************
51      ' *                    Determine Maintenance Type                  *
52      ' *****************************************************************
53      SUB B200.Determine.Maintenance.Type
54         IF T.Type$ = "D" THEN
55            CALL B300.Delete.Record
56         ELSE
57            CALL B310.Change.Record
58         END IF
59      END SUB
60
61      ' *****************************************************************
62      ' *              Write Current Master or Error Message             *
63      ' *****************************************************************
64      SUB B210.Write.Cur.Master.Or.Error.Message
65         IF M.Stock$ < T.Stock$ THEN
66            CALL M420.Write.New.Master.Record
67            CALL M400.Read.Master.Record
68         ELSE
69            CALL M430.Display.Error.Message
70            CALL M410.Read.Transaction.Record
71         END IF
72      END SUB
73
74      ' *****************************************************************
75      ' *                         Delete Record                         *
76      ' *****************************************************************
77      SUB B300.Delete.Record
78         Delete.Count = Delete.Count + 1
79         CALL M400.Read.Master.Record
80         CALL M410.Read.Transaction.Record
81      END SUB
82
83      ' *****************************************************************
84      ' *                         Change Record                         *
85      ' *****************************************************************
86      SUB B310.Change.Record
87         IF T.Location$ <> "" THEN
88            M.Location$ = T.Location$
89         END IF
90         IF T.Desc$ <> "" THEN
91            M.Desc$ = T.Desc$
92         END IF
93         IF T.Cost <> -1 THEN
94            M.Cost = T.Cost
95         END IF
96         IF T.Price <> -1 THEN
97            M.Price = T.Price
98         END IF
99         IF T.Quantity <> -1 THEN
100           M.Quantity = T.Quantity
101        END IF
102        Change.Count = Change.Count + 1
103        CALL M420.Write.New.Master.Record
104        CALL M400.Read.Master.Record
105        CALL M410.Read.Transaction.Record
106     END SUB
107
```

```
108   ' ***************************************************************
109   ' *                        Wrap-Up                              *
110   ' ***************************************************************
111   SUB C100.Wrap.Up
112      DO WHILE Master.Eof$ = "OFF"
113         CALL M420.Write.New.Master.Record
114         CALL M400.Read.Master.Record
115      LOOP
116      DO WHILE Transaction.Eof$ = "OFF"
117         CALL M430.Display.Error.Message
118         CALL M410.Read.Transaction.Record
119      LOOP
120      CLOSE
121      PRINT
122      PRINT "Total Number of Records Deleted =========>"; Delete.Count
123      PRINT "Total Number of Records Changed =========>"; Change.Count
124      PRINT "Total Number of Records in New Master ====>"; Record.Count
125      PRINT
126      PRINT "INV-2.DAT Update Complete"
127   END SUB
128
129   ' ***************************************************************
130   ' *             Read Next Current Master Record                 *
131   ' ***************************************************************
132   SUB M400.Read.Master.Record
133      IF EOF(1) THEN
134         Master.Eof$ = "ON"
135      ELSE
136         INPUT #1, M.Stock$, M.Location$, M.Desc$, M.Cost, M.Price, M.Quantity
137      END IF
138   END SUB
139
140   ' ***************************************************************
141   ' *              Read Next Transaction Record                   *
142   ' ***************************************************************
143   SUB M410.Read.Transaction.Record
144      IF EOF(2) THEN
145         Transaction.Eof$ = "ON"
146      ELSE
147         INPUT #2, T.Stock$, T.Type$, T.Location$, T.Desc$, T.Cost, T.Price, T.Quantity
148      END IF
149   END SUB
150
151   ' ***************************************************************
152   ' *             Write Record to New Master File                 *
153   ' ***************************************************************
154   SUB M420.Write.New.Master.Record
155      WRITE #3, M.Stock$, M.Location$, M.Desc$, M.Cost, M.Price, M.Quantity
156      Record.Count = Record.Count + 1
157   END SUB
158
159   ' ***************************************************************
160   ' *                  Display Error Message                      *
161   ' ***************************************************************
162   SUB M430.Display.Error.Message
163      PRINT
164      PRINT "** ERROR ** Transaction record with stock number ";
165      PRINT T.Stock$; " has no match."
166   END SUB

   [run]
```

Discussion of the Program Solution

When Program 10.2 is executed, line 13 in the Main Program transfers control to A100.Initialization. Lines 22 through 26 initialize counters to zero and end-of-file switches to OFF. Line 27 opens for input the current master file CURINV-2.DAT shown in Figure 10.6. Line 28 opens for input the transaction file TRAINV-2.DAT. The file TRAINV-2.DAT contains the records shown in Figure 10.7. Line 29 opens the new master file INV-2.DAT. After the screen clears and the title displays, control returns to the Main Program.

FIGURE 10.7

A list of the records in the sequential file TRAINV-2.DAT.

```
"C204","D","","",-1,-1,-1
"C402","C", 3,"",33.50,40.50,-1
"S812","C","","ROUTER-II",-1,-1,12
"T615","D","","",-1,-1,-1
"T731","C","","",6.50,-1,-1
```

Next, line 14 in the Main Program transfers control to B100.Process.Files. Lines 39 and 40 call upon the subprograms to read the first current master record and the first transaction record. Within the Do-While loop, line 42 compares the two stock numbers M.Stock$ and T.Stock$. If M.Stock$ is equal to T.Stock$, then the transaction represents a change or delete, and control passes to B200.Determine.Maintenance.Type (lines 53 through 59). In line 54, the transaction type is compared to the value D. If the record represents a delete, then control transfers to B300.Delete.Record (lines 77 through 81). Otherwise, the record represents a change, and control transfers to B310.Change.Record (lines 86 through 106).

If in line 42 M.Stock$ does not equal T.Stock$, then control passes to line 64 — B210.Write.Cur.Master.Or.Error.Message. In this subprogram, the PC determines whether the current master record should be written to the new master or whether the transaction record is in error.

In B310.Change.Record lines 87 through 101 test each value assigned to the variables that correspond to the transaction record. If any of the numeric variables T.Cost, T.Price, or T.Quantity equal –1, then the corresponding variables in the current master file are *not* changed. If they equal any other value, the IF statements result in the assignment of new values to the variables making up the current master record. Line 87 compares T.Location$ to the null character. The null character signifies that the description field in the current master record is not to be changed. If T.Location$ does not equal a null character, then T.Location$ is assigned to M.Location$.

After each variable is tested, except for the stock number which cannot be changed, line 102 increments the change field counter (Change.Count) by 1, and line 103 causes the PC to write the modified current master record to the new master file. In M420.Write.New.Master.Record, line 156 increments the new master file record count (Record.Count) by 1. Finally, lines 104 and 105 read the next current master record and the next transaction record. Control then returns to B100.Process.Files.

Now let's go back to line 42 and discuss what happens if the current master record and transaction record do not match. If M.Stock$ does not equal T.Stock$, then control transfers to B210.Write.Curr.Master.Or.Error.Message (lines 64 through 72). Line 65 determines whether the stock number in the current master record M.Stock$ is less than the stock number T.Stock$ in the transaction record. If M.Stock$ is less than T.Stock$, then control transfers to M420.Write.New.Master.Record defined by lines 154 through 157, and the current master record is written to the new master file before Record.Count is incremented by 1. When control returns to the calling subprogram, line 67 reads the next record in the current master file.

In line 65, if M.Stock$ is not less than T.Stock$, then it is greater than T.Stock$. In this case, control transfers to M430.Display.Error.Message (lines 162 through 166), which displays an appropriate diagnostic message. The diagnostic message states that the transaction record has no corresponding match in the current master file. Following a return from M430.Display.Error.Message, the PC reads the next transaction record.

B100.Process.Files maintains control of the PC until end-of-file is sensed on either the current master file or the transaction file. Here again the switches Master.Eof$ and Transaction.Eof$, not the EOF function, are used to control the Do-While loops. If the EOF function is used to control the looping, it is possible that the last record in either input file will not be processed.

Once the end-of-file mark is sensed on either input file, the appropriate end-of-file switch is set equal to the value ON, and control passes back to the Main Program. C100.Wrap.Up then flushes either file that may have records remaining. If records remain in the current master file, then they are written to the new master file. If records remain in the transaction file, then they have no match and are considered to be in error.

Figure 10.8 shows the display due to the execution of Program 10.2.

FIGURE 10.8

The display due to the execution of Program 10.2.

```
Deleting Records and Changing Fields in Inventory File
--------------------------------------------------------

** ERROR ** Transaction record with stock number C402 has no match.

Total Number of Records Deleted ==========> 2
Total Number of Records Changed ==========> 2
Total Number of Records in New Master =====> 13

INV-2.DAT Update Complete
```

In the results displayed by Program 10.2, one of the five records in the transaction file, stock number C402, does not have a corresponding match in the current master file. Of the other four transaction records, two call for deleting records, and two for modifying the current master records. The new master file INV-2.DAT contains 13 records as shown in Figure 10.9.

FIGURE 10.9

A list of the records in the sequential file INV-2.DAT following execution of Program 10.2.

```
"C101","1","Roadhandler",97.56,125.11,25
"C103","2","Saw-Blades",5.06,6.04,15
"C206","1","Square",4.56,5.42,34
"C502","2","Tripod",32.5,38.99,10
"S209","1","Maxidrill",88.76,109.99,6
"S210","3","Microscope",31.5,41.99,8
"S416","2","Normalsaw",152.55,179.4,1
"S812","2","ROUTER-II",48.47,61.15,12
"S941","2","Hip-Boot",26.95,32.5,12
"S942","4","Radialsaw",376.04,419.89,3
"T713","2","Moc-Boot",24.99,29.99,30
"T731","1","Sandals",6.5,9.45,52
"T814","2","Work-Boot",22.99,27.99,56
```

10.3 RANDOM FILE PROCESSING

As you learned in Section 10.1, the sequence of processing a randomly organized file has no relationship to the sequence in which the records are stored in the file. Random files have several advantages over sequential files, even though fewer program steps are required to create and access records within sequential files than for the same procedure within random files. For example, random files require less space in auxiliary storage because numbers are stored in a compressed format and no commas are required between data items.

The main advantage of random files over sequential files is that their records may be processed randomly. In other words, processing a record in the middle of the file does not require all the records prior to that one to be read. This is true because each record within a random file has a key associated with it. The key indicates the position of the record from the beginning of the random file.

This section presents the file handling statements, functions, and programming techniques necessary to create and process files that can be accessed randomly.

Opening and Closing Random Files

As with sequential files, random files must be opened before they are read from or written to. When a program is finished with a random file, it must close the file. The general form of the OPEN statement for random files is shown in Table 10.4. The general form of the CLOSE statement is the same as for sequential files and is shown in Table 7.2 on page 225.

TABLE 10.4   The OPEN Statement for Random Files

General Form:	OPEN filespec FOR RANDOM AS #filenumber LEN = recl
	where **filespec** is the name of the random file;
	filenumber is a numeric expression whose value is between 1 and 255; and
	recl is a value equal to the length of the record.
Purpose:	Allows a program to read from or write records to a random file.
Examples:	1. OPEN "ACCOUNT.DAT" FOR RANDOM AS #2 LEN = 59
	2. OPEN "WHSEDATA.DAT" FOR RANDOM AS #1 LEN = LEN(Warehouse)
	3. OPEN "EX101PAY.DAT" FOR RANDOM AS #1
	4. OPEN Filename AS #1
Note:	QuickBASIC provides a second general form for the OPEN statement: OPEN "R", #filenumber, filespec, recl
	This second general form is less contemporary than the general form specified at the top of this table, and therefore is not used in this book.

In Example 1 of Table 10.4, ACCOUNT.DAT is opened as a random file. Filenumber 2 is assigned to ACCOUNT.DAT. Recall from Chapter 7, that the filenumber is used in file handling statements to reference the associated file. The length parameter LEN specifies that each record in ACCOUNT.DAT is exactly 59 bytes. If ACCOUNT.DAT does not exist in auxiliary storage, then it is created. If ACCOUNT.DAT already exists as a random file, records may be added, read, and rewritten.

In Example 2 of Table 10.4, the LEN function is used to assign the random file WHSEDATA.DAT a **record length** equal to the length of the variable Warehouse. As we see in the next section, this technique for specifying the record length is commonly used.

Example 3 does not include a record length. In this case, QuickBASIC assigns a default length of 128 bytes. Finally, Example 4 shows that the keywords FOR RANDOM are optional. That is, if a mode is not specified in an OPEN statement, then QuickBASIC opens the file as a random file.

Creating the Record Structure for a Random File — The TYPE Statement

You define the fields, that is, data items, that make up the record to be read from or written to a random file with a TYPE statement. Each field is assigned a **field name** using the same rules as for variable names, except that the period (.) and trailing special characters (%, &, !, #, and $) are not allowed. Collectively, the fields are called the **record layout** or **record structure**, or **structure**. These field names are then used to access the data in the record. The TYPE statement is used to collectively assign the fields to a **label name** and to identify the fields with respect to their name, size, type, and location within the record. The label name follows the same rules as for field names.

Let us assume that the random file WHSEDATA.DAT contains a record for each warehouse that our company owns. Each record includes four fields:

Field	Type	Number of Characters
Warehouse Name	String	18
Street Address	String	17
City, State, Zip Code	String	20
Total Square Feet	Numeric	4

The following TYPE statement may be used to describe each field within the record:

```
TYPE WarehouseStructure
    Title AS STRING * 18
    Address1 AS STRING * 17
    Address2 AS STRING * 20
    Area AS SINGLE
END TYPE
```

The TYPE statement allocates the first 18 bytes (positions) in the record to the field Title (warehouse name); the next 17 bytes to Address1 (street address); the next 20 bytes to Address2 (city, state, zip code), and the last 4 bytes to Area (total square feet). A field name assigned a type SINGLE is allocated 4 bytes for a numeric value.

To use the field names in WarehouseStructure, the DIM statement must be used to declare a **record variable** as the same type as WarehouseStructure. The following statement

```
DIM Warehouse AS WarehouseStructure
```

declares the record variable Warehouse as the same type as WarehouseStructure. The TYPE statement allows you to identify fields with respect to their name, size, and location within the record, but it is the DIM statement that actually reserves main storage for the record to move through on its way to and from auxiliary storge. The rules regarding the creation of record variable names is the same as for field and label names. (See page 63.)

After data is read into the record variable Warehouse, the data items may be referenced by the names Warehouse.Title, Warehouse.Address1, Warehouse.Address2, and Warehouse.Area. Note that the record variable name in the DIM statement is *joined* to the field names in the TYPE statement by a period (.) to form the variable name. Also, these same variable names may be used to assign data items to the record before writing it to auxiliary storage.

The general form of the TYPE statement is shown in Table 10.5. Valid field types in a TYPE statement include INTEGER (short integer, 2 byte length); LONG (long integer, 4 byte length); SINGLE (single precision, 4 byte length); DOUBLE (double precision, 8 byte length); STRING (character); or another user-defined data type. Table 3.4 on page 61 lists the range and precision characteristics of these field types.

The field type STRING defines the field name as string. You must follow the keyword STRING by an asterisk and a factor equal to the number of bytes you want to allocate. For example, Title AS STRING * 20 allocates 20 bytes to the field name Title.

TABLE 10.5   The TYPE Statement

General Form:	TYPE label name field name₁ AS as field type

.
.
.

field nameₙ AS as field type
END TYPE

where **label name** is the name of the user-defined data type that identifies the group of field names;

field nameₙ names each field; and

field type is the field name's type: INTEGER, LONG, SINGLE, DOUBLE, STRING, or another user-defined data type.

Purpose: To create user-defined data types. The TYPE statement is often used for identifying the group of fields in a record layout (structure) for a random file.

Example:
```
TYPE TownshipStructure
   Number AS INTEGER
   Title AS STRING * 20
   Size AS SINGLE
   Value AS DOUBLE
END TYPE
```

Note: Use the DIM statement to declare a record variable as the same type as the label name. For example, DIM Township AS TownshipStructure allocates storage for the record variable Township and assigns it the user-defined data type TownshipStructure. To access the field names in the structure, use the variable name *record variable.field name*.

The following rules summarize the use and proper placement of the TYPE statement in a program:

TYPE RULE 1   *Label names and field names in a TYPE statement follow the same rules as for variable names, except they may not include a period (.) or trailing special characters (%, &, !, #, and $).*

TYPE RULE 2   *Following the TYPE statement, the label name that identifies the structure must be assigned to a record variable name through the use of the DIM statement. Record variable names must abide by the same rules as field and label names.*

TYPE RULE 3   *To reference the field names in a TYPE statement, use the record variable name followed by a period (.) and the field name — record variable.field name.*

TYPE RULE 4   *The TYPE and DIM statements that define and declare the structure must precede the OPEN statement for the random file.*

TYPE RULE 5   *TYPE statements can be placed only in the Main Program. They cannot be placed in subprograms.*

The GET and PUT Statements

The GET statement reads and transfers a record from a random file. The PUT statement writes a record to a random file.

The general forms of the GET and PUT statements are shown in Tables 10.6 and 10.7.

	TABLE 10.6 The GET Statement

General Form: GET #filenumber, record number, record variable

where **filenumber** is the number assigned to the random file in the OPEN statement;

record number is the number of the record to read from the random file; and

record variable is the variable assigned the user-defined structure.

Purpose: To read a record from the random file assigned to filenumber and assign it to record variable.

Examples:
```
GET #1, Record.Number, Warehouse
GET #2, , Department
GET #FILE, Rec, Account
GET #3, 15, Part
```

Note: If the record number is not included in the GET statement, then the next record in the random file is read into the record variable.

The partial program in Figure 10.10 illustrates the steps involved in accessing a random file and the relationships between the TYPE, DIM, OPEN, and GET statements.

FIGURE 10.10

The steps in accessing a random file and the relationships between the TYPE, DIM, OPEN, *and* GET *statements.*

Step 1: Use a TYPE statement to define the structure.

```
TYPE WarehouseStructure
    Title AS STRING * 18
    Address1 AS STRING * 17
    Address2 AS STRING * 20
    Area AS SINGLE
END TYPE
```

Step 2: Use a DIM statement to declare *Warehouse* as having the same data type as *WarehouseStructure*.

```
DIM Warehouse AS WarehouseStructure
```

Step 3: Use an OPEN statement to open the random file WHSEDATA.DAT as filenumber 1 with a length of *Warehouse*.

```
OPEN "WHSEDATA.DAT" FOR RANDOM AS #1 LEN = LEN(Warehouse)
```

reference to record variable Warehouse

Step 4: Use a GET statement to read a record from filenumber 1 (record 34 in this example) into *Warehouse*.

```
GET #1, 34, Warehouse
```

Step 5: To display the field names defined in the TYPE statement, use the prefix of the record variable *Warehouse*, separated by a period.

```
PRINT Warehouse.Title, Warehouse.Address1
PRINT Warehouse.Address2, Warehouse.Area
```

If Record.Number has a value of 29 when the statement

```
GET #1, Record.Number, Warehouse
```

is executed, then the twenty-ninth record in the random file assigned to filenumber 1 is read into the record variable Warehouse.

Records from a random file may be read sequentially, beginning at any record in the file. For example, if in the following partial program,

```
Record.Number = 26
GET #2, Record.Number, Warehouse
       .
       .
       .
GET #2, , Warehouse
       .
       .
       .
GET #2, , Warehouse
```

then the first GET reads the twenty-sixth; the next GET reads the twenty-seventh record, and the third one, the twenty-eighth record. If the first GET following an OPEN statement has no record number, then the first record in the random file is read and assigned to the record variable.

TABLE 10.7 The PUT Statement	
General Form:	PUT #filenumber, record number, record variable
Purpose:	To write the value of record variable to the random file assigned to filenumber.
Examples:	PUT #1, Record.Number, Warehouse PUT #2, 567, Order PUT #Filenum, , Count

As indicated in Table 10.7, the PUT statement writes the value of record variable to a random file. Thus the statement

```
PUT #2, 62, Hospital
```

writes the value of Hospital to filenumber 2 as record 62.

The LOC and LOF Functions

The LOC(n) function returns the record number of the last record read or written to the random file assigned to filenumber n. For example, in the following partial program,

```
GET #3, Record.Number, Model
Last.Record = LOC(3)
```

the variable Last.Record is assigned the value of Record.Number, since Record.Number is the record number of the last record read from the random file assigned to filenumber 3.

The LOF(n) function returns information regarding the character size of the random file assigned to filenumber n. This value may then be used to determine the number of records in a random file by dividing the record variable length into whatever the LOF function returns.

For example, assume you want to append records to an existing random file, but you do not know the last record number; then, the following partial program will accomplish the task:

```
Record.Number = LOF(2) \ LEN(Warehouse)
    .
    .
    .
PUT #2, Record.Number + 1, Warehouse
```

The first statement assigns Record.Number the number of records in the random file assigned to filenumber 2. The PUT statement then writes the next record to the random file after the last record, thereby not destroying any records in the random file.

Programming Case Study 20 | Creating a Random File

In earlier programming case studies, each record in INVNTORY.DAT included a number to indicate the warehouse in which the stock item was located. The warehouse numbers (location) varied between 1 and 4. The following problem creates a random file in which each record includes a warehouse name, an address, and a total number of square feet for warehouse 1, 2, 3, and 4.

Problem: The PUC Company requests a program that creates a random file in which each record represents one of its warehouses. Each record includes the following data items:

Data Item	Type	Number of Characters
Warehouse Name	String	18
Street Address	String	17
City State Zip Code	String	20
Total Square Feet	Numeric, single precision	4

The actual data for each record is shown below:

Warehouse Location	Warehouse Name	Street Address	City, State, Zip Code	Total Square Feet
1	PUC Gyte Whse	1498 Baring Ave.	Whitley, IN 46325	80,000
2	PUC Anderson Whse	612 45th St.	Calcity, IL 60618	220,000
3	PUC Potter Whse	1329 Olcot St.	Pointe, IN 46367	85,900
4	PUC Porter Whse	15 E 63rd St.	Polk, IN 45323	92,500

The user enters the warehouse number (location) to indicate the record that is to be created. The warehouse number is not to be part of the record.

Following are the program tasks in outline form, a program solution, and a discussion of the program solution.

Program Tasks

1. Main Program

    a. Use the TYPE statement to define the record structure.
    b. Use the DIM SHARED statement to assign a record variable (Warehouse) the same data type as the label name in the TYPE statement.
    c. Call the subprograms A100.Initialization, B100.Create.Random.File, and C100.Wrap.Up.

2. A100.Initialization — Open the file WHSEDATA.DAT for random access as filenumber 1 with a record length of Warehouse.

3. B100.Create.Random.File — Establish a Do-Until loop that executes until Control$ equals an N or n. Within the loop, do the following:

    a. Call B200.Accept.Warehouse.Record. In this subprogram, use INPUT statements to accept the warehouse number (Record.Number); warehouse name (Warehouse.Title); warehouse street address (Warehouse.Address1); warehouse city, state, zip code (Warehouse.Address2); and warehouse square feet (Warehouse.Area).
    b. Call B210.Write.Warehouse.Record. In this subprogram, use the PUT statement with the key Record.Number to write the record variable Warehouse to WHSEDATA.DAT.
    c. Use an INPUT statement to assign Control$ the value Y or y if the user wants to enter another record.

4. C100.Wrap.Up

    a. Close the random file WHSEDATA.DAT.
    b. Display an end-of-job message.

Program Solution

The following program corresponds to the preceding tasks:

PROGRAM 10.3

```
1     ' Program 10.3
2     ' Creating a Random File
3     ' Random File Created = WHSEDATA.DAT
4     ' **********************************
5     ' *            Main Program        *
6     ' **********************************
7     COMMON SHARED Record.Number
8     ' ***** Define Record Structure *****
9     TYPE WarehouseStructure
10       Title AS STRING * 18
11       Address1 AS STRING * 17
12       Address2 AS STRING * 20
13       Area AS SINGLE
14    END TYPE
15    ' ***** Declare Record Variable *****
16    DIM SHARED Warehouse AS WarehouseStructure
17    CALL A100.Initialization
18    CALL B100.Create.Random.File
19    CALL C100.Wrap.Up
20    END
21
```

TYPE must be in Main Program

DIM SHARED makes structure available to all subprograms

```
22    ' ***********************************
23    ' *           Initialization        *
24    ' ***********************************
25    SUB A100.Initialization
26       ' ****** Open Warehouse File *****
27       OPEN "WHSEDATA.DAT" FOR RANDOM AS #1 LEN = LEN(Warehouse)
28    END SUB
29
30    ' ***********************************
31    ' *         Create Random File      *
32    ' ***********************************
33    SUB B100.Create.Random.File
34       DO
35          CALL B200.Accept.Warehouse.Record
36          CALL B210.Write.Warehouse.Record
37          LOCATE 14, 10
38          INPUT "Enter Y to add another record, else N... ", Control$
39       LOOP UNTIL UCASE$(Control$) = "N"
40    END SUB
41
42    ' ***********************************
43    ' *    Accept a Warehouse Record    *
44    ' ***********************************
45    SUB B200.Accept.Warehouse.Record
46       CLS      ' Clear Screen
47       LOCATE 2, 10
48       PRINT "Warehouse Location Random File Create"
49       LOCATE 4, 10
50       INPUT "Warehouse Number =============> ", Record.Number
51       LOCATE 6, 10
52       INPUT "Warehouse Name ===============> ", Warehouse.Title
53       LOCATE 8, 10
54       INPUT "Warehouse Street =============> ", Warehouse.Address1
55       LOCATE 10, 10
56       INPUT "Warehouse City, State, Zip ===> ", Warehouse.Address2
57       LOCATE 12, 10
58       INPUT "Warehouse Total Square Feet ==> ", Warehouse.Area
59    END SUB
60
61    ' ***********************************
62    ' *     Write a Warehouse Record    *
63    ' ***********************************
64    SUB B210.Write.Warehouse.Record
65       PUT #1, Record.Number, Warehouse
66    END SUB
67
68    ' ***********************************
69    ' *             Wrap-Up             *
70    ' ***********************************
71    SUB C100.Wrap.Up
72       CLOSE #1
73       LOCATE 16, 10: PRINT "Random file WHSEDATA.DAT created"
74       LOCATE 18, 10: PRINT "Job Complete"
75    END SUB

      [run]
```

Discussion of the Program Solution

When Program 10.3 is executed, lines 9 through 14 define the record structure; line 16 declares the record variable Warehouse to be the same data type as WarehouseStructure, and line 27 opens the random file WHSEDATA.DAT as filenumber 1. As shown in Figure 10.11, B200.Accept.Warehouse.Record (lines 45 through 59) accepts the user's responses. The PUT statement in line 65 writes the record that corresponds to the warehouse number (Record.Number). Finally, line 38 in B100.Create.Random.File accepts a user response that determines whether the program should continue.

FIGURE 10.11

Display from the execution of Program 10.3 for warehouse location 2.

```
Warehouse Location Random File Create

Warehouse Number =============> 2

Warehouse Name ===============> PUC Anderson Whse

Warehouse Street =============> 612 45th St.

Warehouse City, State, Zip ===> Calcity IL 60618

Warehouse Total Square Feet ==> 220000

Enter Y to add another record, else N... Y
```

Program 10.3 can be rewritten without the user being required to enter the warehouse number (Record.Number). In the rewritten version, line 65 is modified to

```
PUT #1, , Warehouse.
```

A PUT statement without a record number writes the record as the next record. However, the user would then be required to enter the records in sequence. As it stands now, Program 10.3 will properly create the random file regardless of the order in which the records are entered. For example, warehouse location number 4 can be entered before warehouse number 1.

Because it requests a warehouse number, Program 10.3 can later be used to add new warehouse records or to modify existing warehouse records. For example, if a fifth warehouse is added by the PUC Company, Program 10.3 can be used to add this new record. Unlike sequential files, whose original contents are automatically deleted when opened for output, random files exist until they are physically deleted by a system command.

In the creation of random files, it is not necessary for a record to be entered for every record number. It is valid to number warehouses 1, 3, 6, and 10. When a random file like that is created without contiguous record numbers, the PC reserves areas for records 2, 4, 5, 7, 8, and 9. These areas are often called **empty cells**.

| Programming Case Study 21 | Accessing Records in a Random File |

The following problem includes a program that accesses records in the random file WHSEDATA.DAT, which was created in Programming Case Study 20.

Problem: The PUC Company has requested a program to be written to access and display records from the random file WHSEDATA.DAT. Following are the program tasks in outline form, a program solution, and a discussion of the program solution.

Program Tasks

1. Main Program

   a. Use the TYPE statement to define the record structure.
   b. Use the DIM SHARED statement to assign a record variable (Warehouse) the same data type as the label name in the TYPE statement.
   c. Call A100.Initialization, B100.Process.Request, and C100.Wrap.Up.

2. A100.Initialization — Open the file WHSEDATA.DAT for random access as filenumber 1 with a record length of Warehouse.

3. B100.Process.Request — establish a Do-Until loop that executes until Control\$ equals the value N or n. Within the loop, do the following:

   a. Call B200.Accept.Request. Within the subprogram, display a program title, and use the INPUT statement to accept the warehouse number (Record.Number).
   b. Call B210.Get.And.Display.Record. Within this subprogram, use the GET statement to access the requested record (Record.Number). Next, display the variables listed in the record structure.
   c. Use an INPUT statement to assign Control\$ the value Y or y if the user wants to display another record.

4. C100.Wrap.Up

   a. Close the random file WHSEDATA.DAT.
   b. Display an end-of-job message.

Program Solution

The following program corresponds to the preceding tasks:

PROGRAM 10.4

```
1    ' Program 10.4
2    ' Accessing Records in a Random File
3    ' Random File = WHSEDATA.DAT
4    ' **********************************
5    ' *            Main Program        *
6    ' **********************************
7    COMMON SHARED Record.Number
8    ' ***** Define Record Structure *****
9    TYPE WarehouseStructure
10      Title AS STRING * 18
11      Address1 AS STRING * 17
12      Address2 AS STRING * 20
13      Area AS SINGLE
14   END TYPE
15   ' ***** Declare Record Variable *****
16   DIM SHARED Warehouse AS WarehouseStructure
17   CALL A100.Initialization
18   CALL B100.Process.Request
19   CALL C100.Wrap.Up
20   END
21
22   ' **********************************
23   ' *         Initialization         *
24   ' **********************************
25   SUB A100.Initialization
26      ' ****** Open Warehouse File *****
27      OPEN "WHSEDATA.DAT" FOR RANDOM AS #1 LEN = LEN(Warehouse)
28   END SUB
29
30   ' **********************************
31   ' *         Process a Request       *
32   ' **********************************
33   SUB B100.Process.Request
34      DO
35         CALL B200.Accept.Request
36         CALL B210.Get.And.Display.Record
37         LOCATE 14, 10
38         INPUT "Enter Y to access another record, else N... ", Control$
39      LOOP UNTIL UCASE$(Control$) = "N"
40   END SUB
41
42   ' **********************************
43   ' *         Accept a Request        *
44   ' **********************************
45   SUB B200.Accept.Request
46      CLS  ' Clear Screen
47      LOCATE 2, 10
48      PRINT "Warehouse Location Random File Access"
49      LOCATE 4, 10
50      INPUT "Warehouse Number ============> ", Record.Number
51   END SUB
52
```

```
53    ' ********************************
54    ' *      Get and Display Record       *
55    ' ********************************
56    SUB B210.Get.And.Display.Record
57       GET #1, Record.Number, Warehouse
58       LOCATE 6, 10
59       PRINT "Warehouse Name ===============> "; Warehouse.Title
60       LOCATE 8, 10
61       PRINT "Warehouse Street =============> "; Warehouse.Address1
62       LOCATE 10, 10
63       PRINT "Warehouse City, State, Zip ===> "; Warehouse.Address2
64       LOCATE 12, 10
65       PRINT USING "Warehouse Total Square Feet ==> ###,###"; Warehouse.Area
66    END SUB
67
68    ' ********************************
69    ' *              Wrap-Up              *
70    ' ********************************
71    SUB C100.Wrap.Up
72       CLOSE #1
73       LOCATE 16, 10: PRINT "Job Complete"
74    END SUB

      [run]
```

Discussion of the Program Solution

Figure 10.12 shows the results displayed when warehouse number 2 is entered for Program 10.4. Line 57 in B210.Get.And.Display.Record reads the record that corresponds to the number entered by the user and assigned to Record.Number in line 50. Lines 59 through 65 show that the values found in a record can be displayed by using the field names preceded by the record variable name and a period.

It is important to note that records in WHSEDATA.DAT may be accessed in any desired order. After displaying warehouse location number 2, you may request 1, 3, 4, or 2 again, and the PC can respond immediately without rewinding the file or reading records between the previously accessed record and the next record.

FIGURE 10.12

Results displayed due to entering warehouse location number 2 for Program 10.4.

```
Warehouse Location Random File Access

Warehouse Number =============> 2

Warehouse Name ===============> PUC Anderson Whse

Warehouse Street =============> 612 45th St.

Warehouse City, State, Zip ===> Calcity IL 60618

Warehouse Total Square Feet ==> 220,000

Enter Y to access another record, else N... Y
```

10.4   SIMULATED-INDEXED FILES

Provided the record number is known, any record can be accessed in a random file. Unfortunately, few applications use integers, such as 1, 2, and 3, to represent the employee numbers, customer numbers, or stock numbers that commonly identify the record to be accessed in a file. More often, these keys are made up of several digits and letters that have no relationship to the location of the record in a random file. However, many applications require random access on the basis of these types of keys.

In many programming languages, such as COBOL and PL/I, indexed files—a third type of file organization—allow a relationship between a key and the record location to be automatically established. With QuickBASIC, indexed files are not available, and therefore, the relationship between the key and the record location must be handled by the programmer.

| Programming Case Study 22 | Using a Simulated-Indexed File for Inventory Retrieval and Update |

Problem: The Stores department of the PUC Company has requested computerized access to inventory records by stock number. Their request involves the creation of a simulated-indexed file as illustrated in Figure 10.13.

Two programs are required. The first program should create an index for up to 100 keys and a corresponding random file from the sequential file INV-2.DAT created earlier by Program 10.2 and shown in Figure 10.9 on page 399. Each record of INV-2.DAT contains the following fields:

Field	Type	Field Size
Stock Number	String	4
Warehouse Location	String	1
Description	String	15
Unit Cost	Single	4
Selling Price	Single	4
Quantity on Hand	Single	4

FIGURE 10.13

A system flow-chart representing Programs 10.5 and 10.6.

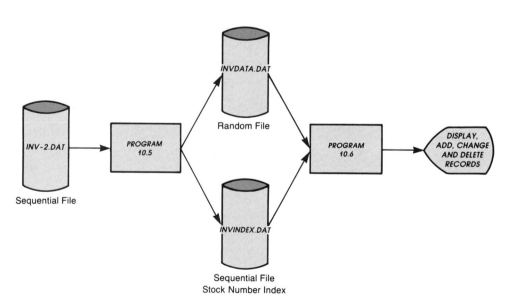

The second program should permit the user to display, add, change, and delete records in the file, provided the stock number is known.

Following are the program tasks for Part 1 of the problem, the Program 1 solution, and a discussion of the Program 1 solution.

Program 1 Tasks: Build Index File

1. Main Program

 a. Declare global variables.
 b. Use the following TYPE statement to define the record structure:

```
TYPE InventoryStructure
    Stock AS STRING * 4
    Location AS STRING * 1
    Desc AS STRING * 15
    Cost AS SINGLE
    Price AS SINGLE
    Quantity AS SINGLE
END TYPE
```

 c. Use the following DIM SHARED statement to declare the record variable:

```
DIM SHARED Inventory AS InventoryStructure
```

 d. Call the subprograms A100.Initialization, B100.Build.Data.Portion.Of.Index.File, and C100.Wrap.Up.

2. A100.Initialization

 a. Declare the array Index$ to 100 elements.
 b. Use a For loop to set each element in the array Index$ equal to the string value Empty.
 c. Set Record.Number% to zero.
 d. Open INV-2.DAT and INVDATA.DAT. Records will be read from the sequential file INV-2.DAT and written to the random file INVDATA.DAT.

3. B100.Build.Data.Portion.Of.Index.File — establish a Do-While loop that executes until end-of-file on INV-2.DAT. Within the loop, do the following:

 a. Read a record from INV-2.DAT.
 b. Call B200.Assign.Stock.Number.To.Index$(Record.Number%). In this subprogram, increment Record.Number% by 1 and set Index$(Record.Number%) equal to the stock number (M.Stock$).
 c. Call B210.Write.Record.To.Random.File. In this subprogram, do the following:
   (1) Set the field names in the record variable equal to the corresponding values from the record read from INV-2.DAT.
   (2) Use the PUT statement to write the record to the random file INVDATA.DAT with the value of Record.Number%.

4. C100.Wrap.Up

 a. Close the random file INVDATA.DAT.
 b. Display the number of records (Record.Number%) written to INVDATA.DAT.
 c. Call C200.Create.File.Of.Keys. In this subprogram, open the sequential file INVINDEX.DAT. Use a For loop to write the elements of the array Index$ to INVINDEX.DAT.
 d. Close INVINDEX.DAT and display the message Job Complete.

PROGRAM 10.5

```
1     ' Program 10.5
2     ' Create Initial Sequential Index File and Random File
3     '
4     ' This program reads the sequential file INV-2.DAT and creates
5     ' the random file INVDATA.DAT.  The stock number (Stock$) is
6     ' assigned to the element in array Index$ that corresponds to
7     ' the record number.  As part of the end-of-file routine, array
8     ' Index$ is written to the sequential file INVINDEX.DAT.  The
9     ' maximum no. of records that INVINDEX.DAT can contain is 100.
10    '
11    ' ******************************************************************
12    ' *                         Main Program                          *
13    ' ******************************************************************
14    COMMON SHARED Record.number%, Index$()
15    COMMON SHARED M.Stock$, M.Location$, M.Desc$, M.Cost, M.Price, M.Quantity
16    ' ***** Define Record Structure *****
17    TYPE InventoryStructure
18       Stock AS STRING * 4
19       Location AS STRING * 1
20       Desc AS STRING * 15
21       Cost AS SINGLE
22       Price AS SINGLE
23       Quantity AS SINGLE
24    END TYPE
25    DIM SHARED Inventory AS InventoryStructure   ' Declare Record Variable
26    CALL A100.Initialization
27    CALL B100.Build.Data.Portion.Of.Index.File
28    CALL C100.Wrap.Up
29    END
30
31    ' ******************************************************************
32    ' *                        Initialization                         *
33    ' ******************************************************************
34    SUB A100.Initialization
35       CLS   ' Clear Screen
36       DIM Index$(1 TO 100)
37       FOR Record.number% = 1 TO 100
38          Index$(Record.number%) = "Empty"
39       NEXT Record.number%
40       Record.number% = 0
41       ' ********** Open Files **********
42       OPEN "INV-2.DAT" FOR INPUT AS #1
43       OPEN "INVDATA.DAT" FOR RANDOM AS #2 LEN = LEN(Inventory)
44    END SUB
45
46    ' ******************************************************************
47    ' *            Build Data Portion of Index File                   *
48    ' ******************************************************************
49    SUB B100.Build.Data.Portion.Of.Index.File
50       DO WHILE NOT EOF(1)
51          INPUT #1, M.Stock$, M.Location$, M.Desc$, M.Cost, M.Price, M.Quantity
52          B200.Assign.Stock.Number.To.Index
53          B210.Write.Record.To.Random.File
54       LOOP
55    END SUB
56
57    ' ******************************************************************
58    ' *          Assign Key to Index$(Record.Number%)                 *
59    ' ******************************************************************
60    SUB B200.Assign.Stock.Number.To.Index
61       Record.number% = Record.number% + 1
62       Index$(Record.number%) = M.Stock$
63    END SUB
64
```

```
65    ' ****************************************************************
66    ' *                 Write Record to INVINDEX.DAT                 *
67    ' ****************************************************************
68    SUB B210.Write.Record.To.Random.File
69        Inventory.Stock = M.Stock$
70        Inventory.Location = M.Location$
71        Inventory.Desc = M.Desc$
72        Inventory.Cost = M.Cost
73        Inventory.Price = M.Price
74        Inventory.Quantity = M.Quantity
75        PUT #2, Record.number%, Inventory
76    END SUB
77
78    ' ****************************************************************
79    ' *                          Wrap-Up                            *
80    ' ****************************************************************
81    SUB C100.Wrap.Up
82        CLOSE
83        PRINT "The number of records in the file is"; Record.number%
84        CALL C200.Create.File.Of.Keys
85        PRINT : PRINT "Job Complete"
86    END SUB
87
88    ' ****************************************************************
89    ' *                      Create File of Keys                    *
90    ' ****************************************************************
91    SUB C200.Create.File.Of.Keys
92        OPEN "INVINDEX.DAT" FOR OUTPUT AS #1
93        FOR Record.number% = 1 TO 100
94           WRITE #1, Index$(Record.number%)
95        NEXT Record.number%
96        CLOSE
97    END SUB

[run]

The number of records in the file is 13

Job Complete
```

Discussion of the Program 1 Solution

When Program 10.5 is executed, the TYPE statement (lines 17 through 24) defines the record structure InventoryStructure, and the DIM SHARED statement (line 25) declares the record variable Inventory as the same type as InventoryStructure. Next, line 26 calls A100.Initialization. After the screen is cleared and the array Index$ is declared, lines 37 through 39 initialize all elements of the array Index$ to the string value Empty. Following the For loop, the record counter (Record.Number%) is set equal to zero. Finally, the two files are opened in lines 42 and 43.

B100.Build.Data.Portion.Of.Index.File maintains control of the program until the end-of-file mark is sensed on the master file INV-2.DAT. Within the loop, a record from INV-2.DAT is read, the stock number (M.Stock$) is assigned to the next element in Index$, and the data portion of the master record is written to INVDATA.DAT. Note the relationship established between the Record.Number% element of the array Index$ and the Record.Number% record in the random file INVDATA.DAT.

As part of C100.Wrap.Up, the array Index$ is written to the sequential file INVINDEX.DAT. This file contains 100 data items, some of which are equal to stock numbers and others of which are equal to the string value Empty. In part 2 of this programming case study, the array Index$ is used to determine the locations of records with corresponding stock numbers. The fact that unused elements of the array Index$ are equal to the string value Empty will be helpful both for adding and for deleting records.

Program 2

This second program displays and updates records in the simulated-indexed file created by Program 10.5. This is shown in Figure 10.13. A top-down chart (Figure 10.14), a list of the corresponding Program 2 tasks, the Program 2 solution, and a discussion of the Program 2 solution follow.

After reading this section, you are encouraged to load Program 10.6 (PRG10-6) from the Student Diskette and execute it. (See Exercise 13 in the Test Your BASIC Skills section at the end of this chapter.)

FIGURE 10.14

A top-down chart for Program 10.6.

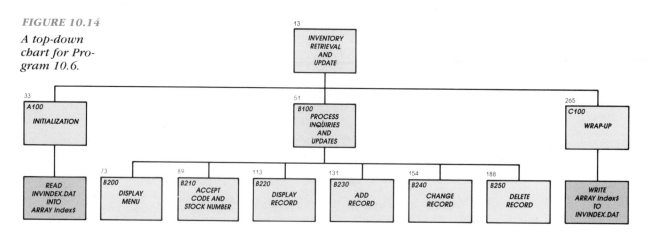

Program 2 Tasks: Display and Update Records in a Simulated-Indexed File

The following tasks correspond to the top-down chart in Figure 10.14.

1. Main Program

   a. Declare global variables
   b. Use the same TYPE statement and DIM SHARED statement that were used in Program 10.5 to define the record structure and declare the record variable.
   c. Call the subprograms A100.Initialization, B100.Process.Inquiries.And.Updates, and C100.Wrap.Up.

2. A100.Initialization

   a. Open the sequential file INVINDEX.DAT and random file INVDATA.DAT. INVINDEX.DAT contains the stock numbers; INVDATA.DAT contains the data that corresponds to the stock numbers.
   b. Use a DIM statement to declare the array Index$ to 100 elements.
   c. Use a For loop to read the 100 stock numbers in INVINDEX.DAT into the array Index$.
   d. Close INVINDEX.DAT.

3. B100.Process.Inquiries.And.Updates

a. Call B200.Display.Menu. In this subprogram, display a menu with the following valid codes:

Code	Function
1	Display Record
2	Add Record
3	Change Record
4	Delete Record
5	End Program

b. Call B210.Accept.Code.And.Stock.Number. In this subprogram, accept a function code (Code%) and stock number (Stock.Number$). Both Code% and Stock.Number$ must be validated. Code% must equal one of the valid function codes displayed by the menu.

The stock number Stock.Number$ is validated by comparing it to the elements of the array Index$. If the function code Code% equals 1, 3, or 4, then Stock.Number$ must equal the value of one of the elements of Index$. Assign Record.Number% the value of the subscript of the element of the array Index$ that is equal to the stock number. Use Record.Number% in B220.Display.Record, B240.Change.Record, and B260.Delete.Record to access the corresponding record in the random file INVDATA.DAT.

If the function code equals 2 (add record), then the stock number must not equal the value of an element in the array Index$.

Control remains in this subprogram until a valid function code and a valid stock number are entered by the user.

c. On the basis of the value of the function code accepted in B210, use a SELECT CASE statement to call the subprograms B220.Display.Record, B230.Add.Record, B240.Change.Record, or B250.Delete.Record. Following return of control from one of these subprograms, B200.Display.Menu is called to initiate the next user request.

(1) The function of B220.Display.Record is to display the record that corresponds to the stock number entered by the user in B200.Display.Menu. In this subprogram, do the following:

(a) Read the Record.Number% record in the random file INVDATA.DAT.

(b) Display the record read from INVDATA.DAT.

(c) Use the INPUT$ function to suspend execution so the user may view the record before the menu is displayed again.

(2) The function of B230.Add.Record is to add a record to INVDATA.DAT and a corresponding stock number to the array INDEX$. In this subprogram, do the following:

(a) Redisplay the stock number entered by the user.

(b) Determine the first element of Index$ that is equal to the string value Empty.

(c) If no element of Index$ is equal to the string value Empty, then the array is full, an appropriate diagnostic message is displayed, and control is returned to the menu.

(d) If an element of Index$ equals the value Empty, then assign the stock number (Stock.Number$) to the Record.Number% element of Index$ and request the remaining items that belong to this new record.

(e) Use the PUT statement to write the record to INVDATA.DAT that corresponds to Record.Number%. The record is written to INVDATA.DAT only after the user is given the opportunity to terminate the addition.

(3) The function of B240.Change.Record is to allow the user to change any item in the record except the stock number. In this subprogram, do the following:

(a) Use the GET statement to read the record in the random file INVDATA.DAT which corresponds to Record.Number%.

(b) Request the user to enter changes. If an item is to remain the same in the record, then the user responds by entering a -1 for the item in question.

(c) Check each response. If a response is not equal to -1, assign the response to the corresponding field name.

(d) Write the modified record to INVDATA.DAT only after the user has been given the opportunity to terminate the record change.

(4) The function of B250.Delete.Record is to delete an unwanted record. To delete a record, assign Index$(Record.Number%) the string value Empty only after giving the user the opportunity to terminate the record deletion. Note that nothing is done to the corresponding record in INVDATA.DAT. However, because Index$(Record.Number%) is assigned the string value Empty, this element may be used for a record addition at a later date; at this time, the record in the random file is changed.

4. C100.Wrap.Up

a. Close the random file INVDATA.DAT.

b. Open the sequential file INVINDEX.DAT for output.

c. Use a For loop to write the 100 elements of the array Index$ to INVINDEX.DAT.

d. Close the sequential file INVINDEX.DAT.

PROGRAM 10.6

e. Display an end-of-job message.

```
1   ' Program 10.6
2   ' Inventory and Retrieval and Update
3   '
4   ' This program displays or updates records in a simulated-indexed file.
5   ' The data for the simulated-indexed file is located in the random file
6   ' INVDATA.DAT.  The records in the random file are accessed by a key
7   ' (stock number) that is entered by the user.  Records may be displayed,
8   ' added to the file, deleted from the file, or changed.
9   '
10  ' *********************************************************************
11  ' *                         Main Program                            *
12  ' *********************************************************************
13  COMMON SHARED Record.Number%, Index$(), Code%, Stock.Number$, Switch$
14  ' ******** Define Record Structure ********
15  TYPE InventoryStructure
16      Stock AS STRING * 4
17      Location AS STRING * 1
18      Desc AS STRING * 15
19      Cost AS SINGLE
20      Price AS SINGLE
21      Quantity AS SINGLE
22  END TYPE
23  ' ******** Declare Record Variable ********
24  DIM SHARED Inventory AS InventoryStructure
25  CALL A100.Initialization
26  CALL B100.Process.Inquiries.And.Updates
27  CALL C100.Wrap.Up
28  END
29
```

```
30    ' **********************************************************************
31    ' *                         Initialization                            *
32    ' **********************************************************************
33    SUB A100.Initialization
34       CLS   ' Clear Screen
35
36       ' ************ Open Files ****************
37       OPEN "INVINDEX.DAT" FOR INPUT AS #1
38       OPEN "INVDATA.DAT" FOR RANDOM AS #2 LEN = LEN(Inventory)
39
40       ' ***** Declare and Load Array Index$ *****
41       DIM Index$(1 TO 100)
42       FOR Record.Number% = 1 TO 100
43          INPUT #1, Index$(Record.Number%)   ' Read Stock Numbers into Array
44       NEXT Record.Number%
45       CLOSE #1
46    END SUB
47
48    ' **********************************************************************
49    ' *                 Process Inquiries and Updates                     *
50    ' **********************************************************************
51    SUB B100.Process.Inquiries.And.Updates
52       CALL B200.Display.Menu
53       CALL B210.Accept.Code.And.Stock.Number
54       DO WHILE Code% <> 5
55          SELECT CASE Code%
56             CASE 1
57                CALL B220.Display.Record
58             CASE 2
59                CALL B230.Add.Record
60             CASE 3
61                CALL B240.Change.Record
62             CASE 4
63                CALL B250.Delete.Record
64          END SELECT
65          CALL B200.Display.Menu
66          CALL B210.Accept.Code.And.Stock.Number
67       LOOP
68    END SUB
69
70    ' **********************************************************************
71    ' *                         Display Menu                              *
72    ' **********************************************************************
73    SUB B200.Display.Menu
74       CLS
75       LOCATE 2, 19: PRINT "Menu for Inventory Retrieval And Update"
76       LOCATE 3, 19: PRINT "---------------------------------------"
77       LOCATE 5, 19: PRINT "   Code            Function"
78       LOCATE 6, 19: PRINT "   ----            --------"
79       LOCATE 7, 19: PRINT "    1             Display Record"
80       LOCATE 9, 19: PRINT "    2             Add Record"
81       LOCATE 11, 19: PRINT "   3             Change Record"
82       LOCATE 13, 19: PRINT "   4             Delete Record"
83       LOCATE 15, 19: PRINT "   5             End Program"
84    END SUB
85
```

(continued)

```
86      ' ********************************************************************
87      ' *                  Accept Code and Stock Number                  *
88      ' ********************************************************************
89      SUB B210.Accept.Code.And.Stock.Number
90         DO
91            Switch$ = "ON"
92            LOCATE 17, 52: PRINT SPC(10);
93            LOCATE 17, 19: INPUT "Enter a Code 1 through 5 ======> ", Code%
94            DO WHILE Code% < 1 OR Code% > 5
95               BEEP: BEEP: BEEP: BEEP
96               LOCATE 18, 19: PRINT "Code out of range, please reenter"
97               LOCATE 17, 52: PRINT SPC(10);
98               LOCATE 17, 52: INPUT "", Code%
99               LOCATE 18, 19: PRINT SPC(40);
100           LOOP
101           IF Code% <> 5 THEN
102              LOCATE 19, 19
103              INPUT "Stock Number ==================> ", Stock.Number$
104              CALL B300.Validate.Stock.Number
105           END IF
106        LOOP UNTIL Switch$ = "ON"
107        CLS
108     END SUB
109
110     ' ********************************************************************
111     ' *                       Display Record                           *
112     ' ********************************************************************
113     SUB B220.Display.Record
114        GET #2, Record.Number%, Inventory
115        PRINT : PRINT "Stock Number =============> "; Stock.Number$
116        PRINT : PRINT "Warehouse Location =======> "; Inventory.Location
117        PRINT : PRINT "Description ==============> "; Inventory.Desc
118        PRINT
119        PRINT USING "Unit Cost ================>#,###.##"; Inventory.Cost
120        PRINT
121        PRINT USING "Selling Price ============>#,###.##"; Inventory.Price
122        PRINT
123        PRINT USING "Quantity on Hand =========>#,###"; Inventory.Quantity
124        PRINT : PRINT "Press any key to continue..."
125        A$ = INPUT$(1)
126     END SUB
127
128     ' ********************************************************************
129     ' *                         Add Record                             *
130     ' ********************************************************************
131     SUB B230.Add.Record
132        PRINT : PRINT "Stock Number =============> "; Stock.Number$
133        Record.Number% = 0
134        FOR I% = 1 TO 100    ' Search for "Empty" element in array Index$
135           IF Index$(I%) = "Empty" THEN
136              Record.Number% = I%
137              EXIT FOR
138           END IF
139        NEXT I%
140        IF Record.Number% <> 0 THEN
141           Inventory.Stock = Stock.Number$
142           CALL B310.Request.Remaining.Data.Items
143        ELSE
144           PRINT
145           PRINT "** ERROR ** Index is full"
146           PRINT : PRINT "Press any key to continue..."
147           A$ = INPUT$(1)
148        END IF
149     END SUB
150
```

```
151   ' ***********************************************************************
152   ' *                          Change Record                            *
153   ' ***********************************************************************
154   SUB B240.Change.Record
155      GET #2, Record.Number%, Inventory
156      PRINT : PRINT "Stock Number =============> "; Stock.Number$
157      PRINT
158      PRINT "**** Enter a -1 if you do not want to change a data item ****"
159      PRINT : INPUT "Warehouse Location =======> ", T.Location$
160      IF T.Location$ <> "-1" THEN
161         Inventory.Location = T.Location$
162      END IF
163      PRINT : INPUT "Description =============> ", T.Desc$
164      IF T.Desc$ <> "-1" THEN
165         Inventory.Desc = T.Desc$
166      END IF
167      PRINT : INPUT "Unit Cost ================> ", T.Cost
168      IF T.Cost <> -1 THEN
169         Inventory.Cost = T.Cost
170      END IF
171      PRINT : INPUT "Selling Price ============> ", T.Price
172      IF T.Price <> -1 THEN
173         Inventory.Price = T.Price
174      END IF
175      PRINT : INPUT "Quantity on Hand =========> ", T.Quantity
176      IF T.Quantity <> -1 THEN
177         Inventory.Quantity = T.Quantity
178      END IF
179      PRINT : INPUT "Enter Y to update record, else N... ", Control$
180      IF UCASE$(Control$) = "Y" THEN
181         PUT #2, Record.Number%, Inventory
182      END IF
183   END SUB
184
185   ' ***********************************************************************
186   ' *                          Delete Record                            *
187   ' ***********************************************************************
188   SUB B250.Delete.Record
189      PRINT
190      PRINT "Are you sure you want to delete stock number "; Stock.Number$
191      PRINT : INPUT "Enter Y to delete record, else N... ", Control$
192      IF UCASE$(Control$) = "Y" THEN
193         Index$(Record.Number%) = "Empty"
194      END IF
195   END SUB
196
197   ' ***********************************************************************
198   ' *                 Determine If Stock Number Is Valid                *
199   ' ***********************************************************************
200   SUB B300.Validate.Stock.Number
201      Record.Number% = 0
202      FOR I% = 1 TO 100
203         IF Stock.Number$ = Index$(I%) THEN
204            IF Code% = 2 THEN
205               CALL B400.Stock.Number.Error.Routine
206            ELSE
207               Record.Number% = I%
208               EXIT FOR
209            END IF
210         END IF
211      NEXT I%
212      IF Record.Number% = 0 AND Code% <> 2 THEN
213         CALL B400.Stock.Number.Error.Routine
214      END IF
215   END SUB
216
```

(continued)

```
217     ' **********************************************************************
218     ' *                    Request Remaining Data Items                    *
219     ' **********************************************************************
220     SUB B310.Request.Remaining.Data.Items
221        PRINT : INPUT "Warehouse Location =======> ", Inventory.Location
222        PRINT : INPUT "Description ============> ", Inventory.Desc
223        PRINT : INPUT "Unit Cost ================> ", Inventory.Cost
224        PRINT : INPUT "Selling Price ============> ", Inventory.Price
225        PRINT : INPUT "Quantity on Hand ========> ", Inventory.Quantity
226        PRINT : INPUT "Enter Y to add record, else N... ", Control$
227        Inventory.Stock = Stock.Number$
228        IF UCASE$(Control$) = "Y" THEN
229           CALL B410.Set.Index.And.Write.Record
230        END IF
231     END SUB
232
233     ' **********************************************************************
234     ' *                    Stock Number Error Routine                      *
235     ' **********************************************************************
236     SUB B400.Stock.Number.Error.Routine
237        BEEP: BEEP: BEEP: BEEP
238        IF Code% = 2 THEN
239           LOCATE 20, 19
240           PRINT "Stock Number Already Exists"
241        ELSE
242           LOCATE 20, 19: PRINT "Stock Number Is Invalid"
243        END IF
244        LOCATE 22, 19
245        PRINT "Press any key to re-enter Code and Stock Number..."
246        A$ = INPUT$(1)
247        LOCATE 17, 52: PRINT SPC(10);
248        LOCATE 19, 52: PRINT SPC(10);
249        LOCATE 20, 19: PRINT SPC(50);
250        LOCATE 22, 19: PRINT SPC(50);
251        Switch$ = "OFF"
252     END SUB
253
254     ' **********************************************************************
255     ' *                    Set Index Array and Write Record                *
256     ' **********************************************************************
257     SUB B410.Set.Index.And.Write.Record
258        Index$(Record.Number%) = Stock.Number$
259        PUT #2, Record.Number%, Inventory
260     END SUB
261
262     ' **********************************************************************
263     ' *                              Wrap-Up                               *
264     ' **********************************************************************
265     SUB C100.Wrap.Up
266        CLOSE
267        OPEN "INVINDEX.DAT" FOR OUTPUT AS #1
268        FOR Record.Number% = 1 TO 100   ' Write New Index to INVINDEX.DAT
269           WRITE #1, Index$(Record.Number%)
270        NEXT Record.Number%
271        CLOSE
272        PRINT "Inventory Retrieval and Update Program Terminated"
273        PRINT : PRINT "Job Complete"
274     END SUB

        [run]
```

Discussion of the Program 2 Solution

When Program 10.6 is executed, the menu shown in Figure 10.15 displays.

FIGURE 10.15
Menu displayed for Program 10.6.

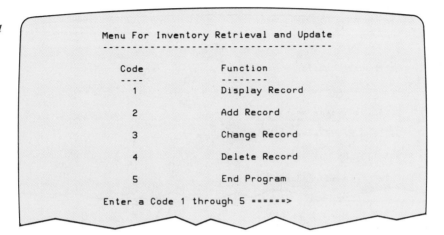

```
        Menu For Inventory Retrieval and Update
        ----------------------------------------

           Code              Function
           ----              --------
            1             Display Record

            2             Add Record

            3             Change Record

            4             Delete Record

            5             End Program

        Enter a Code 1 through 5 ======>
```

If a function code of 1 through 4 is entered, then line 103 requests the user to enter a stock number by displaying the following message:

```
Stock Number ==================>
```

B300.Validate.Stock.Number (lines 200 through 215) verifies the stock number. If a function code of 2 is entered, then the stock number Stock.Number$ must not equal the value of any of the elements of the array Index$. If a function code of 1, 3, or 4 is entered, then the stock number Stock.Number$ must be equal to one of the elements of the array Index$. An additional function of this validation process, when the function code is 1, 3, or 4, is to establish the record number (Record.Number%) of the corresponding record to be displayed, changed, or deleted.

If a function code of 1 and the stock number S941 are entered by the user, then B220.Display.Record (lines 113 through 126) displays the information shown in Figure 10.16.

FIGURE 10.16

The display from entering a function code of 1 (Display Record) and the stock number S941.

```
    Stock Number =============> S941

    Warehouse Location =======> 2

    Description ==============> Hip-Boot

    Unit Cost ================>    26.95

    Selling Price ============>    32.50

    Quantity On Hand =========>    12

    Press any key to continue...
```

If a function code of 2 and the stock number S429 are entered by the user, then B230.Add.Record (lines 131 through 149) requests the remaining items that make up this new record. This is shown in Figure 10.17.

FIGURE 10.17

The display from entering a funtion code of 2 (Add Record) and the data items for stock number S429.

```
Stock Number ==============> S429

Warehouse Location ========> 2

Description ==============> Pliers

Unit Cost ================> 3.45

Selling Price ============> 4.55

Quantity On Hand =========> 13

Enter Y to add record, else N... Y
```

Lines 134 through 139 determine the first element of Index$ that is equal to the string Empty. The subscript of this element is then used to indicate the record number in the PUT statement in line 259. Just before line 259, line 258 assigns the stock number Stock.Number$ to Index$(Record.Number%).

If a function code of 3 and the stock number T814 are entered, then B240.Change.Record (lines 154 through 183) reads the record that corresponds to Record.Number%, requests changes, and rewrites the record. Figure 10.18 shows the display for changing the selling price to 29.95 and the quantity on hand to 32 for record T814.

FIGURE 10.18

The display from entering a function code of 3 (Change Record) and the stock number T814.

```
Stock Number ==============> T814

**** Enter a -1 if you do not want to change a data item ****

Warehouse Location ========> -1

Description ==============> -1

Unit Cost ================> -1

Selling Price ============> 29.95

Quantity on Hand =========> 32

Enter Y to update record, else N... Y
```

If a function code of 4 and the stock number of C206 are entered, then the subprogram B250.Delete.Record (lines 188 through 195) assigns the string Empty to the element of Index$ that corresponds to Record.Number%. Note that the data record in INVDATA.DAT is not changed in any way. Later, when a new record is added, the record deleted in INVDATA.DAT is changed to the new record. Figure 10.19 shows the display due to entering a function code of 4 and the stock number C206.

FIGURE 10.19

The display from entering a function code of 4 and the stock number C206.

```
Are you sure you want to delete stock number C206

Enter Y to delete record, else N... Y
```

If a function code of 5 is entered in response to B200.Display.Menu, then the subprogram C100.Wrap.Up writes the array Index$ to the sequential file INVINDEX.DAT, closes the files, and displays the messages shown in Figure 10.20.

FIGURE 10.20

The display from entering a function code of 5.

```
Inventory Retrieval and Update Program Terminated

Job Complete
```

10.5 WHAT YOU SHOULD KNOW

1. QuickBASIC allows for two types of file organization — sequential and random. A file that is organized sequentially is limited to sequential processing. A file that is organized randomly can be processed either sequentially or in a random fashion. The sequence in which a random file is processed bears no relationship to the sequence in which the records are stored in it.
2. Indexed file organization is widely used in data processing. Although it is not directly available in QuickBASIC, indexed files may be simulated by using both a sequential file and a random file.
3. File maintenance is the process of updating files, by one or more of the following ways:
   a. Adding new records
   b. Deleting unwanted records
   c. Changing data within records
4. A transaction file contains data of a temporary nature.
5. A master file contains data that is, for the most part, permanent.
6. A file maintenance program that updates a sequential file must deal with at least three files: a transaction file, the current master file, and a new master file.
7. A system flowchart shows in graphic form the files, the flow of data, the equipment, and the programs involved in a particular application.
8. Merging is the process of combining two or more files that are in the same sequence into a single file that maintains that same sequence for a given data item in each record.
9. Matching records involves two or more related files that are in the same sequence according to a common data item. If a record in the transaction file matches a record in the current master file, then the current master record may be updated. If there is no match, appropriate action must be taken, depending on the application.

10. Like sequential files, random files must be opened before they are read from or written to. When a program finishes with a random file, it must close the file. The OPEN statement for a random file must include a record length. Never write a record that is longer than the assigned record length. You can, however, write records that are shorter than the length that is specified in the OPEN statement.

11. The TYPE statement is used to define fields with respect to their name, size, type, and location within the record. Collectively, the field names are assigned to a label name and are called the record layout, record structure, or structure. The label name is also referred to as a user-defined data type. The TYPE statement must be placed in the Main Program.

12. Following the TYPE statement, the label name that identifies the structure must be assigned to a record variable name through the use of the DIM statement.

13. Follow the same rules for label names, field names, and record variables that you follow for variable names, except that the period (.) and trailing special characters (%, &, !, #, and $) are not allowed.

14. To reference the field names in a TYPE statement, use the record variable name followed by a period (.) and the field name — record variable.field name.

15. The TYPE and DIM statements that define and declare the structure must precede the OPEN statement for the random file.

16. In the OPEN statement for the random file, use the LEN function to assign the length of record variable to the LEN parameter.

17. The GET #n, r, v statement reads the rth record from the random file assigned to filenumber n into record variable v.

18. The PUT #n, r, v statement writes the rth record to the random file assigned to filenumber n from record variable v.

19. If the second parameter in a GET or PUT statement is not included, then the PC reads or writes the next record in sequence in the random file.

20. The LOC(n) function returns the record number of the last record read or written to the random file assigned to filenumber n.

21. The LOF(n) function returns information regarding the character size of the random file assigned to filenumber n.

10.6   TEST YOUR BASIC SKILLS (Even-numbered answers are in Appendix E)

1. If the last record accessed in a program was record 10 of a random file assigned previously to filenumber 1, which record is accessed next by the following GET statements? (Assume that each GET statement is affected by the previous one.)

   a. GET #1, , RecVar   b. GET #1, 22, RecVar   c. GET #1, , RecVar
   d. GET #1, 96, Recvar   e. GET #1, , RecVar

2. Fill in the following:

   a. The GET statement reads a record into the _____ defined by the _____ statement.

   b. The _____ statement is used to define the field names for the record structure for a random file, and the _____ statement is used to declare the record variable.

   c. Assign the length of the corresponding _____ to the length parameter in the OPEN statement for a random file.

   d. The _____ function returns the record number of the last record read or written to the random file assigned as the argument.

3. Use a TYPE statement to construct a structure using the following field names and corresponding types and sizes. Call the structure Person.

Variable	Type	Size
Soc	String	9
Code	String	1
Value1	Numeric	Double Precision
Value2	Numeric	Single Precision
Value3	Numeric	Integer

4. Explain the difference between the label name in a TYPE statement and the record variable in the corresponding DIM statement.

5. The number of active records in the random file TABLE.DAT varies between 0 and 100 each day. Active records begin with 1 and continue by 1 until the last active record is reached. The number of the last active record in TABLE.DAT is always located in the first field of record 101. The active records each contain three data items defined in the TYPE statement by the names It1, It2, and It3 and assigned the type SINGLE. Use the label name DailyStructure and the variable name Daily.

   Write a partial program that first reads record 101 in TABLE.DAT, then dynamically dimensions the parallel arrays Item1, Item2, and Item3 to the number of active records. Finally, read the active records in TABLE.DAT and assign the three values in each record to the elements of the arrays Item1, Item2, and Item3 in the order in which the values are located in the record. Use filenumber 1.

6. Which of the following are invalid file handling statements? Why?
   a. `OPEN "SALES.DAT" FOR RANDOM AS #1 LEN = Sales`
   b. `GET #2, , Inventory`
   c. `GET #1, Recno`
   d. `GET #2, Recno$, Sales`
   e. `PUT #3, , Inventory`
   f. `DIM Inventory AS Inventory.Structure`
   g. `GET #1, LOC(1)`
   h. `GET FileNo, RecNo, RecVar`

7. Write a statement that assigns the random file PURCHASE.DAT to filenumber 1. The record variable name is Account.

8. Describe how a sequential data file, a random data file, and an array are used to simulate an indexed file.

9. **PC Hands-On Exercise:** Load Program 10.1 (PRG10-1) from the Student Diskette. Use the NAME statement in the immediate window to rename CURINV.DAT as CURINVSA.DAT and INVNTORY.DAT as CURINV.DAT. Execute the program and note the diagnostic messages. Don't forget to rename the files with their original names when you're finished.

10. **PC Hands-On Exercise:** Load Program 10.2 (PRG10-2) from the Student Diskette. In line 25, assign the variable Master.Eof$ the value ON. Execute the program and see what happens. Do you understand the importance of the switches defined in lines 25 and 26?

11. **PC Hands-On Exercise:** Load Program 10.3 (PRG10-3) from the Student Diskette. Execute the program and add warehouse number (record number) 6. Use your first name as the name of the warehouse, your address, and a square-foot area of 100,000.

12. **PC Hands-On Exercise:** Load Program 10.4 (PRG10-4) from the Student Diskette. Execute the program and request record number 6 — the one you added in question 11. After record number 6 displays, request record number 5 and see what happens. Can you explain the display?

13. **PC Hands-On Exercise:** Load Program 10.6 (PRG10-6) from the Student Diskette. Add the following line between lines 33 and 34:

```
COLOR 15, 1, 4
```

(The COLOR statement is discussed in detail in Chapter 11.) Execute the program and see what happens. Display, change, delete, and add several records to the file. Refer to Figure 10.9 on page 399 for a list of the records in the original file.

10.7   BASIC PROGRAMMING PROBLEMS

1. Adding, Changing, and Deleting Records in the Master File

Purpose: To become familiar with the maintenance of a sequential file.

Problem: Write a top-down program to match and merge the current payroll master file EX71PAY.DAT built in BASIC Programming Problem 1 in Chapter 7 with the transaction file EX101TRA.DAT described below under Input Data. Call the new master file EX101PAY.DAT. Include the following diagnostic messages:

```
**ERROR** Addition Invalid    - Employee XXX already in master file.
**ERROR** Transaction Invalid - Employee XXX not in master file.
```

Display as part of the end-of-job routine the total number of additions, changes, deletions, errors, and transactions and the number of records in the new master file.

FIGURE 10.21

Contents of the transaction file EX101PAY.DAT.

Input Data: The master file EX71PAY.DAT and the transaction file EX101TRA.DAT are on the Student Diskette. The contents of the transaction file EX101TRA.DAT are shown in Figure 10.21. The transaction code A represents an addition, C a record change, and D a record delete. "Null" represents the null character.

Transaction Code	Employee No.	Name	Dependents	Marital Status	Rate of Pay	Year-to-Date Gross Pay	Federal With. Tax	Social Security Tax
C	124	Null	4	Null	−1	$6,345.20	−1	−1
A	126	Fish, Joe	1	M	$6.00	0	0	0
D	134	Null	−1	Null	−1	−1	−1	−1
A	143	Byrd, Ed	3	S	9.00	0	0	0
C	167	Null	0	Null	−1	−1	−1	−1
C	225	Null	−1	S	−1	−1	−1	−1
D	250	Null	−1	Null	−1	−1	−1	−1

Output Results: The new master file EX101PAY.DAT is created. The following results are displayed:

```
Payroll File Maintenance
------------------------

**ERROR** Addition Invalid    - Employee 126 already in master file.

**ERROR** Transaction Invalid - Employee 225 not in master file.

**ERROR** Transaction Invalid - Employee 250 not in master file.

Total Number of Records Added ============> 1
Total Number of Records Changed ==========> 2
Total Number of Records Deleted ==========> 1
Total Number of Transaction Errors ======> 3
Total Number of Transactions ============> 7
Total Number of Records in New Master ===> 8

New master file EX101PAY.DAT build complete
```

2. Creating a Random File for Quarterly Payroll Totals

Purpose: To become familiar with creating a random file.

Problem: Write a top-down program that creates a random file with four records. Each record contains payroll information with respect to the following time periods:

Record Number	Time Period	Record Number	Time Period
1	January – March	3	July – September
2	April – June	4	October – December

Each record is made up of the following quarterly employee totals: gross pay, withholding tax, and social security tax. To ensure accuracy, use double-precision variables. Define the field names in the TYPE statement. Use the label name QuarterlyStructure and the record variable Quarterly. Call the random file EX102DAT.DAT.

Give the user the opportunity to cancel the record addition after the data is entered and displayed on the screen.

Input Data: Use the following sample data:

Quarter	Gross Pay	Withholding Tax	Social Security
1	$11,231.12	$3,998.34	$1,121.45
2	8,345.23	2,456.23	913.75
3	13,891.75	2,554.64	1,585.11
4	0.00	0.00	0.00

Output Results: The random file EX102DAT.DAT is created in auxiliary storage. The following partial results are displayed for the first record entered:

```
Quarterly Payroll Random File Create

Quarter ================> 1

Gross Pay ================> 11231.12

Withholding Tax =========> 3998.34

Social Security Tax =====> 1121.45
```

3. Random Access of Quarterly Payroll Totals

Purpose: To become familiar with accessing records in a random file.

Problem: Write a program that will randomly access any record in the random file EX102DAT.DAT created in the previous exercise. If the user enters 2, then the program should display the payroll totals for the second quarter. If the user enters 1, then the program should display the payroll totals for the first quarter.

Input Data: Use the random file EX102DAT.DAT created in BASIC Programming Problem 2.

Output Results: The following results are displayed for quarter 2:

```
Quarterly Payroll Random File Access

Quarter =================> 2

Gross Pay ================>    8,345.23

Withholding Tax =========>    2,456.23

Social Security Tax =====>      913.75
```

4. Employee Record Retrieval and Update — A Simulated-Indexed File

Purpose: To become familiar with the use of indexed files.

Problem: Construct two programs. The first program takes the file EX71PAY.DAT created in BASIC Programming Problem 1 of Chapter 7 and builds an index in a sequential file made up of the employee numbers. The programs also should build a corresponding random file made up of the data in EX71PAY.DAT. Declare 200 elements for the array written to the sequential file. (**Hint:** See Program 10.5 on page 414.)

Call the sequential file EX104IND.DAT and the random file EX104DAT.DAT. Use the following TYPE statement and corresponding DIM statement for the random file:

```
TYPE EmployeeStructure
   Number AS STRING * 3
   FullName AS STRING * 20
   Dep AS INTEGER
   Status AS STRING * 1
   Rate AS SINGLE
   YTDGross AS DOUBLE
   YTDFedTax AS DOUBLE
   YTDSocSec AS DOUBLE
END TYPE
DIM SHARED Employee AS EmployeeStructure
```

NOTE: Ask your instructor whether the first program is required. Copies of EX104IND.DAT and EX104DAT.DAT are on the Student Diskette.

The second program is to be a menu-driven program that allows the user to display, add, change, and delete records on a random basis. The user informs the PC of the record to access by entering the employee number. (See Program 10.6 on page 418.)

The menu-driven program should accept the following function codes:

Code	Function	Code	Function
1	Display record	4	Delete record
2	Add record	5	End program
3	Change record		

Input Data: Update the payroll file with the sample data given in BASIC Programming Problem 1 of this chapter.

Output Results: The program should generate results similar to those generated by Program 10.6 and shown in Figures 10.15 through 10.20 on pages 423 through 425.

5. Payroll Problem X: Matching Records

Purpose: To become familiar with matching records.

Problem: Modify Payroll Problem VII (Problem 8) in Chapter 7 to display diagnostic messages when there is no match between the record in the master file and the record in the transaction file. If a record in the master file has no corresponding match in the transaction file, write the current master record to the new master file and display the message

```
** NOTE ** Employee XXX has no timecard
```

If a record in the transaction file has no corresponding match in the master file, display the message

```
** ERROR ** Employee XXX has no master record
```

(**Hint:** The logic regarding matching records is similar to the logic in Program 10.2 on page 395.)

Page the report and print 21 lines per page.

Input Data: Use EX71PAY.DAT as the current master file. This is the same file that was used in Payroll Problem VII. The transaction file EX105TR.DAT is on the Student Diskette. The transaction file contains the following records:

Employee Number	Hours Worked	Employee Number	Hours Worked
123	88	167	70.5
125	72	168	68
126	80	210	80
134	80	234	32

Output Results: A new master payroll file is created as EX105PY.DAT. The following results are printed on the printer. Depending on your system, you may end up with 87.97 for employee 123's social security tax.

```
                         Preliminary
                    Biweekly Payroll Report              Page:   1

     Employee
     Number        Gross Pay       Fed. Tax      Soc. Sec.    Net Pay
     --------      ---------       --------      ---------    -------
       123         1,150.00         214.62          87.98     847.40

     ** ERROR ** Employee 124 has no timecard

       125           936.00         179.51           0.00     756.49

       126           360.00           2.77          27 54     329.69

       134           700.00         140.00          53.55     506.45

       167           733.20         123.56          56.09     553.55

     ** ERROR ** Employee 168 has no master record
```

```
                         Preliminary
                    Biweekly Payroll Report              Page:   2

     Employee
     Number        Gross Pay       Fed. Tax      Soc. Sec.    Net Pay
     --------      ---------       --------      ---------    -------
       210           704.00          94.65          53.86     555.49

       234           216.00          27.82          16.52     171.66

     Total Gross Pay ========>    4,799.20
     Total Withholding Tax ==>      782.93
     Total Social Security ==>      295.53
     Total Net Pay ==========>    3,720.74

     End of Payroll Report
```

Chapter

11

Computer Graphics and Sound

11.1 INTRODUCTION

The value of the computer for displaying information in the form of charts, figures, and graphs as opposed to printed characters, has long been recognized. For many years, however, the cost of equipment kept most users from incorporating **computer graphics** into their programs. With the advent of the PC, more and more users are displaying the results from their programs pictorially.

As you will see in this chapter, QuickBASIC has statements with considerable graphics capabilities. Figures 11.1 through 11.4 show a variety of different business-type charts, figures, and graphs that can be displayed on your PC. Business-type graphics are commonly used to summarize data. They are an effective way to show amounts or trends. Figure 11.5 shows nonbusiness-type graphics that may also be displayed on your PC. Although no attempt is made here to present sophisticated graphics, at the conclusion of this chapter you will have enough knowledge of the graphics features of Quick-BASIC to start using them in the programs you write.

This chapter also explores the QuickBASIC statements that allow you to play music and create sound and animation effects.

FIGURE 11.1

Line graphs (used to show business trends).

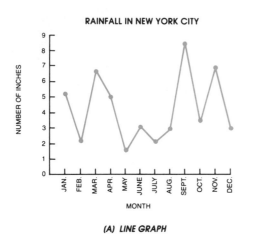

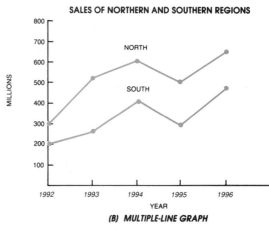

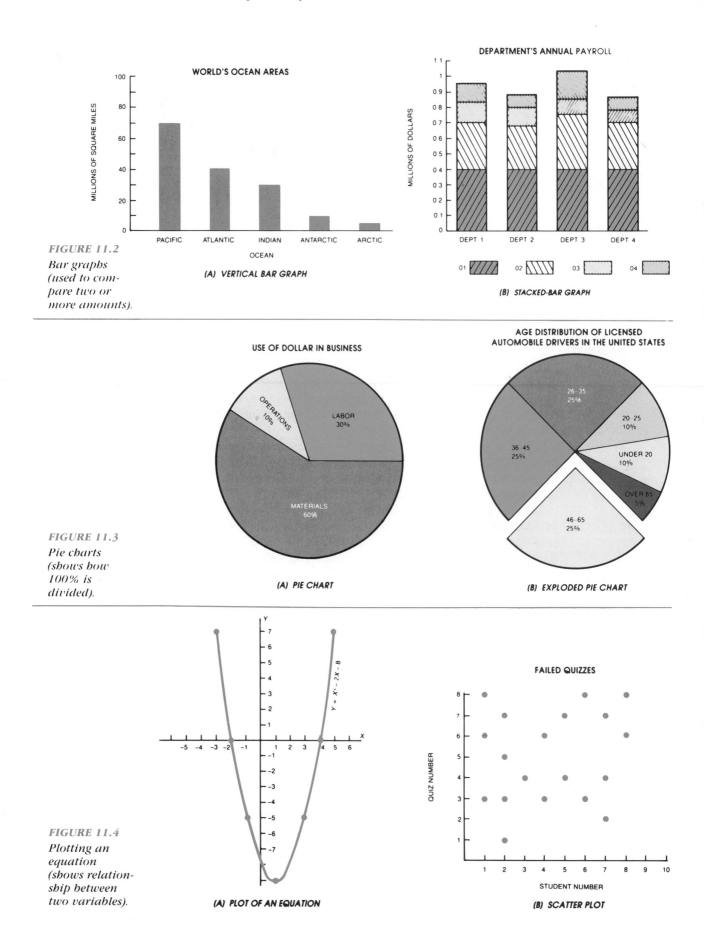

FIGURE 11.2
Bar graphs (used to compare two or more amounts).

WORLD'S OCEAN AREAS

(A) VERTICAL BAR GRAPH

DEPARTMENT'S ANNUAL PAYROLL

(B) STACKED-BAR GRAPH

FIGURE 11.3
Pie charts (shows how 100% is divided).

USE OF DOLLAR IN BUSINESS

(A) PIE CHART

AGE DISTRIBUTION OF LICENSED
AUTOMOBILE DRIVERS IN THE UNITED STATES

(B) EXPLODED PIE CHART

FIGURE 11.4
Plotting an equation (shows relationship between two variables).

$Y = X^2 - 2X - 8$

(A) PLOT OF AN EQUATION

FAILED QUIZZES

(B) SCATTER PLOT

PURDUE
UNIVERSITY

PC

CALUMET

FIGURE 11.5
*Logo and
animation.*

(A) LOGO   **(B) ANIMATION**

PC Graphics Modes

Depending on the display device (monitor) and display adaptor (graphics board), the PC can provide up to five different graphics modes: **text**, **medium resolution**, **high resolution**, **enhanced resolution**, and **very-high resolution**. As described in Table 11.1, the text mode is available on all PCs. Medium-resolution and high-resolution graphics are available on all the configurations, except the first one in Table 11.1.

TABLE 11.1	Graphics Capabilities with Different Hardware Configurations		
DISPLAY DEVICE	**DISPLAY ADAPTOR**	**GRAPHICS CAPABILITIES**	**SCREEN MODE**
1. IBM Compatible Monochrome (Black and White) Display	IBM Compatible Monochrome Display Adaptor (MDA)	Only text mode with a width of 40 or 80 characters. Black and white character graphics.	0
2. IBM Compatible Monochrome (Black and White) Display	Color/Graphics Adaptor (CGA)	Shades of black and white in text, medium resolution, and high resolution.	0,1,2
3. Standard Color Monitor	Color/Graphics Adaptor (CGA)	Color graphics in text and medium resolution. Black and white graphics in high resolution.	0,1,2
4. Monochrome (Black and White) Display	Enhanced Color Adaptor (EGA)	Shades of black and white in text, medium, and high resolution.	0,10
5. Standard Color Monitor	Enhanced Color Adaptor (EGA)	Color graphics in text, medium, high resolution, and enhanced resolution.	0,1,2 7,8
6. Enhanced Color Monitor	Enhanced Color Adaptor (EGA)	Color graphics in text, medium, high resolution, and enhanced resolution.	0,1,2 7,8,9
7. Video Graphics Array (VGA) Monitor	Video Graphics Array Adaptor (VGA)	Color graphics in text, medium, high resolution, enhanced resolution, and very-high resolution.	0,1,2 7,8,9 10,11 12,13
8. Multicolor Graphics Array (MCGA) Monitor	Multicolor Graphics Array Adaptor (MCGA)	Color graphics in text, medium, high resolution, and very-high resolution.	0,1,2 11,13

Enhanced resolution and very-high resolution are available with the more expensive graphics hardware (EGA, VGA, and MCGA). Many PCs sold today have at least a Color/Graphics Adaptor (CGA). Because the more advanced graphics hardware can also operate in the CGA mode, this chapter concentrates on CGA hardware graphics capabilities — text graphics, medium-resolution graphics, and high-resolution graphics.

The last column in Table 11.1 indicates the **screen mode** associated with each graphics mode. As you will see later, you tell QuickBASIC which graphics mode to work in by the screen mode you specify in the SCREEN statement.

FIGURE 11.6

Layout of the screen and color availability for the text mode, medium-resolution graphics mode, and high-resolution graphics mode.

The text mode is the one used in earlier chapters. In this mode, the screen is divided into either 25 rows and 80 columns, or 25 rows and 40 columns, as illustrated in Figures 11.6A and 11.6B. At the intersection of each row and column, the PC can display any one of the 256 characters shown in Table D.2 in Appendix D. Each intersection of a row and column is called a **character position**. In this mode, the PRINT statement and the ASCII character set are used to display figures and graphs as well as nongraphical information such as words and sentences. If you have the proper hardware, you can also display the characters in 16 different colors. You often use the text mode to create logos and simple animated designs.

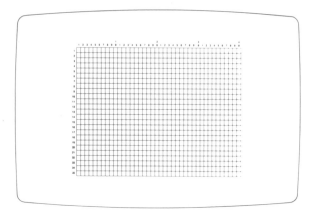

(A) SCREEN 0 : WIDTH 40

Mode:	Text
Rows:	25
Columns:	40
Colors:	16 Foreground
	8 Background
	16 Border

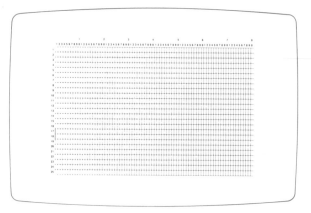

(B) SCREEN 0 : WIDTH 80

Mode:	Text
Rows:	25
Columns:	80
Colors:	16 Foreground
	8 Background
	16 Border

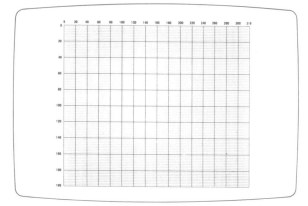

(C) SCREEN 1

Mode:	Medium Resolution
Rows:	200
Columns:	320
Characters per line:	40
Colors:	8 Foreground
	16 Background

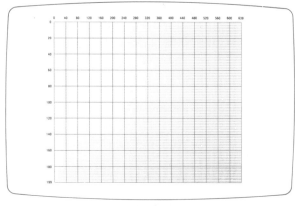

(D) SCREEN 2

Mode:	High Resolution
Rows:	200
Columns:	640
Characters per line:	80
Colors:	Black and White

With medium-resolution graphics, the screen is divided into 200 rows and 320 columns (Figure 11.6C). Each intersection of a row and column represents a small dot which can be turned on or off by QuickBASIC statements. The dots on the screen are called **pixels** (picture elements). The total number of pixels is 64,000 (200 × 320). Forty characters per line are displayed in this mode. If you have a color monitor, each pixel can be assigned any one of 16 colors (256 colors if you have VGA and MCGA hardware). In this mode you can plot points, draw figures, and create high-quality animated designs.

The high-resolution graphics mode divides the screen into 200 rows and 640 columns, as shown in Figure 11.6D. The total number of pixels is 128,000 (200 × 640). Eighty characters per line are displayed in this mode. With CGA hardware, only monochrome colors are available in this mode — black and white or amber or green. EGA hardware allows for 16 colors. With VGA or MCGA hardware, 256 colors are available.

If your PC allows for enhanced-resolution graphics and you select this mode, then the screen is divided into 350 rows and 640 columns, for a total of 320,000 pixels. The very high-resolution graphics mode divides the screen into 480 rows and 640 columns, for a total of 639,480 pixels. The greater number of pixels across the screen allows you to draw figures that require finer detail than is available with other graphics modes.

The SCREEN and WIDTH Statements

When QuickBASIC is started, the PC is in the text mode. The SCREEN statement may then be used to select between the modes as described in Table 11.2. If you select a mode that is not available on your PC (Table 11.1), then a dialog box with the diagnostic message Illegal function call displays when the SCREEN statement executes.

TABLE 11.2   SCREEN Value Descriptions*

STATEMENT	COLUMNS	ROWS	CHARACTERS PER LINE
SCREEN 0	40	25	40
	or		
	80	25	80
SCREEN 1	320	200	80
SCREEN 2	640	200	40
SCREEN 7	320	200	40
SCREEN 8	640	200	80
SCREEN 9	640	350	80
SCREEN 10	640	350	80
SCREEN 11	640	480	80
SCREEN 12	640	480	80
SCREEN 13	320	200	40

* With SCREEN 0, use the WIDTH statement to set the characters per line to 40 or 80. SCREEN statements that result in the same number of columns, rows and characters per line have different color capabilities.

The SCREEN statement may be entered in the immediate mode or as part of a program. Each time the SCREEN statement is executed, the screen is erased, and the color is set to white on black. However, nothing is changed on the screen if the mode in the SCREEN statement is the same as the current one. If there is a QuickBASIC program in main storage, it is not erased when you switch from one mode to another.

The general form of the SCREEN statement is shown in Table 11.3 on the next page.

TABLE 11.3   The SCREEN Statement

General Form:	SCREEN mode, color switch, active page, visual page
	where **mode** is one of the the following: 0, 1, 2, 7, 8, 9, 10, 11, 12, 13;
	color switch is 0 (disables color) or any other number (enables color) in the text mode. With medium resolution, 0 enables color, and any other number disables color;
	active page is an integer expression (in the range 0 to 7 for width 40 characters, and 0 to 3 for width 80) which specifies the page to be written to by output statements; and
	visual page is an integer expression in the same range as active page that selects the page to be displayed.
Purpose:	Selects the screen attributes to be used by subsequent output statements.
Examples:	1. SCREEN 1
	2. SCREEN ,,2, 3
	3. SCREEN 0, 1, 1, 0
	4. SCREEN 0,, 0, 1
	5. SCREEN 1, 1
	6. SCREEN 2
Note:	The parameters active page and visual page are valid only in the text mode, that is, mode = 0.

Example 1 in Table 11.3 clears the screen and switches to the medium-resolution mode. If any parameter is omitted in the SCREEN statement, the PC maintains the current status for each parameter.

In Example 2, the mode remains the same, and all future output statements are directed to page 2. Page 3 is immediately displayed. Here, the term *page* refers to a 2K (width = 40) or 4K (width = 80) byte area of the 16K display buffer. Note that in this example we are preparing to have the PC build one page (page 2) while displaying another (page 3). This form of flip-flopping the screens may be used in the text mode to create animations.

In Example 3 of Table 11.3, the mode is switched to text; color is enabled; all future output statements are directed to page 1, and page 0 is displayed. In Example 4, the mode is switched to text; color maintains its status; future output statements are directed to page 0, and page 1 is displayed. Example 5 switches the PC to medium resolution, and the color is disabled. Finally, line 6 switches the PC to high resolution.

Figure 11.6 illustrates how the screen is subdivided for the modes 0, 1, 2.

The WIDTH Statement

The PC automatically sets the maximum characters per line to 40 or 80, depending on the selected screen mode. (See Table 11.2.) It also sets the maximum number of lines on the screen to 25. You can change the maximum characters per line to 40 or 80 through the use of the WIDTH statement. In the 40-column display mode, the characters are displayed in a larger form and, therefore, are easier to read. However, the PC can display only half as many characters.

Depending on your display adaptor and selected screen mode, you can use the WIDTH statement to change the maximum number of lines to 25, 30, 43, 50, or 60.

The WIDTH statement can also be used to change the maximum number of columns on the printer. The general form of the WIDTH statement is given in Table 11.4.

TABLE 11.4   The WIDTH Statement

General Form: WIDTH columns, lines

or

WIDTH LPRINT columns

Purpose: The first general form clears the screen and sets the maximum number of columns (40 or 80) and the number of lines (25, 30, 43, 50, or 60). The second general form sets the number of columns for the printer.

Examples:
```
WIDTH 40
WIDTH 80
WIDTH 40, 50
WIDTH LPRINT 132
```

Notes:
1. When the statement WIDTH 40 is executed in high resolution, the PC switches to medium resolution. When the statement WIDTH 80 is executed in medium resolution, the PC switches to high resolution.
2. The WIDTH statement may also be used to set the maximum number of columns in a file. This form of the statement will not be used in this book.

11.2   TEXT-MODE GRAPHICS

You can produce interesting and useful graphics on any PC with the PRINT and PRINT USING statements, the CHR$ function, and the ASCII character set. Some elementary text-mode graphics using the typewriter keys (letters, numbers, and punctuation marks) were presented in Chapter 5, Exercises 11 and 12, on page 158.

The following program shows how you can access additional graphics characters (ASCII codes 128 through 255, also called the **USA character set** or **extended ASCII character set**) through the use of the CHR$ function. Recall from Chapter 9 that the CHR$ function returns a character that is equivalent in ASCII code to the numeric argument.

FIGURE 11.7

```
1    ' Displaying the Last Half of the ASCII Character Set
2    ' *****************************************************
3    CLS  ' Clear Screen
4    FOR CODE% = 128 TO 255
5       PRINT USING "###  !"; CODE%, CHR$(CODE%)
6    NEXT CODE%

[run]
```

When the partial program in Figure 11.7 is executed, the For loop (lines 4 through 6) causes the PC to display the last half of the ASCII character set, as shown in Table D.3 in Appendix D. Through the use of the CHR$ function, these characters may be used in the text mode to draw various figures. Besides characters made up of curved lines, you can choose characters that range from a solid dark color (codes 219 through 223) to a lighter shade (codes 176, 177, and 178) for drawing bar graphs.

Another way to print the extended ASCII characters is to create them as characters in a PRINT statement by holding down the Alt key and entering the decimal value of the desired character via the numeric keypad. For example, to create the character ▌, enter the following:

PRINT " (hold down Alt and enter 219)"

The above statement will appear on the screen as follows:

PRINT "▌"

Do not forget the quotation marks in the PRINT statement.

The cursor control keys also have ASCII values. You can use the INKEY$ function to return the proper ASCII value of the cursor control keys. For example, if a user presses one of the cursor control keys, the INKEY$ function returns a character string of length two. The first character is set to zero, and the second character is set to the ASCII value as follows:

Cursor Control Key	ASCII Value of Second Character
Up Arrow ↑	72
Down Arrow ↓	80
Left Arrow ←	75
Right Arrow →	77
Page Up	73
Page Down	81
Home	71
End	79

If a key corresponding to a standard ASCII character is pressed, then the INKEY$ function returns a character string of length one with the proper ASCII value.

Programming Case Study 23   Logo for the Bow-Wow Dog Food Company

The following programming case study pertains to the display of a logo that uses some of the graphics characters that make up the last half of the ASCII character set.

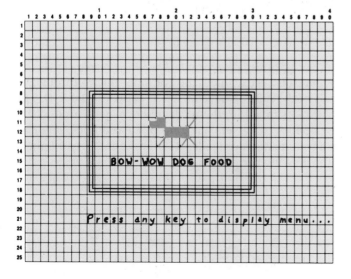

Problem: On a recent tour through the main office, Mr. Beagle, president of the Bow-Wow Dog Food Company, noticed the large number of PCs in use. To brighten the office area, he has requested the Computer Information Systems Department to display the company logo, shown in Figure 11.8, on all idle PCs.

FIGURE 11.8

The Bow-Wow Dog Food Company logo designed on a screen layout form with a width of 40 characters.

The program that displays the logo must chain to (call) a menu-driven program called MAINMENU when the user presses any key. (For a discussion of how a program chains to another program, see Section C.3 in Appendix C.)

Following are a top-down chart (Figure 11.9), a list of the program tasks in outline form, a program solution, and a discussion of the program solution.

FIGURE 11.9

A top-down chart for Program 11.1.

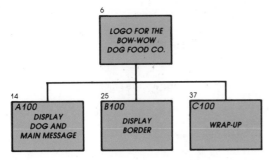

Program Tasks

The following program tasks correspond to the top-down chart in Figure 11.9:

1. A100.Display.Dog.And.Main.Message

   a. Use the WIDTH statement to set the display mode of the screen to 40 characters per line.

   b. Use the LOCATE and PRINT statements to position the dog and main message on the screen. Use the CHR$ function and the following ASCII character codes for the dog's body parts:

Body Part	ASCII Code	Body Part	ASCII Code
Nose	220	Tail	47
Head	219	Legs pointing left	47
Body	219 (three)	Leg pointing right	92

2. B100.Display.Border

   Use the LOCATE and PRINT statements to display the border surrounding the dog and the main message. Use the CHR$ function and the following ASCII character codes for the border:

Border Part	ASCII Code	Border Part	ASCII Code
Upper left corner	201	Lower right corner	188
Lower left corner	200	Vertical border	186
Upper right corner	187	Horizontal border	205

3. C100.Wrap.Up

   a. Display the message "Press any key to display menu..."

   b. Use the INPUT$ function to suspend execution until a key is pressed by the user.

   c. Set the display mode of the screen to 80 characters per line.

4. Use the following statement in place of the END statement in the Main Program to chain to MAINMENU:

```
CHAIN "MAINMENU"
```

Program Solution

Program 11.1 corresponds to the top-down chart in Figure 11.9 and to the preceding program tasks.

PROGRAM 11.1

```
1    ' Program 11.1
2    ' Logo for Bow-Wow Dog Food Company
3    ' *********************************
4    ' *         Main Program          *
5    ' *********************************
6    CALL A100.Display.Dog.And.Main.Message
7    CALL B100.Display.Border
8    CALL C100.Wrap.Up
9    CHAIN "MAINMENU"      ' Call Program Mainmenu
10
11   ' *********************************
12   ' *   Display Dog and Main Message  *
13   ' *********************************
14   SUB A100.Display.Dog.And.Main.Message
15      WIDTH 40        ' Switch to 40-Column Display
16      LOCATE 11, 17: PRINT CHR$(220); CHR$(219); SPC(3); CHR$(47)
17      LOCATE 12, 19: PRINT STRING$(3, 219)
18      LOCATE 13, 18: PRINT CHR$(47); SPC(2); CHR$(47); CHR$(92)
19      LOCATE 15, 12: PRINT "BOW-WOW DOG FOOD"
20   END SUB
21
22   ' *********************************
23   ' *          Display Border         *
24   ' *********************************
25   SUB B100.Display.Border
26      LOCATE 8, 9: PRINT CHR$(201); STRING$(20, 205); CHR$(187)
27      FOR I% = 9 TO 17
28         LOCATE I%, 9: PRINT CHR$(186)
29         LOCATE I%, 30: PRINT CHR$(186)
30      NEXT I%
31      LOCATE 18, 9: PRINT CHR$(200); STRING$(20, 205); CHR$(188)
32   END SUB
33
34   ' *********************************
35   ' *            Wrap-Up              *
36   ' *********************************
37   SUB C100.Wrap.Up
38      LOCATE 21, 9: PRINT "Press any key to display menu...";
39      Halt$ = INPUT$(1)
40      WIDTH 80   ' Switch to 80-Column Display
41   END SUB
```

[run]

Discussion of the Program Solution

When Program 11.1 is executed, line 15 clears the screen and switches the screen to the 40-column display mode. Lines 16 and 18 use the CHR$ function to display the various graphics characters. Note in line 17, the STRING$ function causes three solid dark characters to display.

Lines 25 through 32 in B100.Display.Border use a For loop to display the vertical lines. In C100.Wrap.Up, the INPUT$ function is used to suspend execution until the user wants to display the main menu. Line 9 of the Main Program chains to MAINMENU before Program 11.1 terminates execution.

The logo displayed by Program 11.1 is shown in Figure 11.10.

FIGURE 11.10
The logo dis-played through the execution of Program 11.1.

Programming Case Study 24 | Horizontal Bar Graph of Monthly Sales

The program solution to the following problem illustrates the capability of QuickBASIC to display information in the form of a horizontal bar graph.

Problem: The Sales Analysis Department of the ISCP Company wants to display a horizontal bar graph to illustrate the monthly sales trends of the previous year. Each month name and its sales are stored in the sequential data file MONSALES.DAT. The contents of MONSALES.DAT are as follows:

Month	Sales	Month	Sales
January	$41,000	July	$30,000
February	33,000	August	25,000
March	21,000	September	33,000
April	11,000	October	38,000
May	17,000	November	46,000
June	23,000	December	53,000

The desired bar graph is shown in Figure 11.11.

FIGURE 11.11

Output for Program 11.2 designed on a screen layout form.

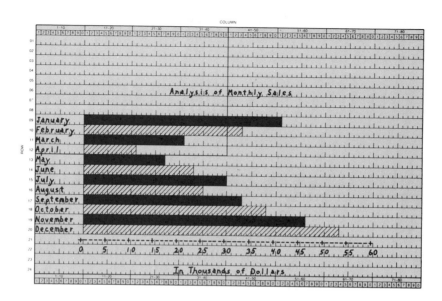

Following are a top-down chart, a list of the program tasks in outline form, a program solution, and a discussion of the program solution.

FIGURE 11.12

A top-down chart for Program 11.2.

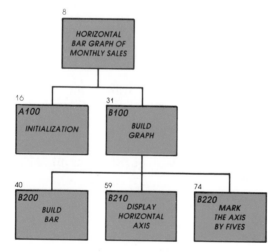

Program Tasks

The following program tasks correspond to the top-down chart in Figure 11.12:

1. Main Program
   a. Dimension the parallel arrays Month$ and Sales to 12.
   b. Call A100.Initialization and B200.Build.Graph

2. A100.Initialization

   a. Open MONSALES.DAT for input.
   b. Use a For loop to read the month names and corresponding sales into the parallel arrays Month$ and Sales.
   c. Close MONSALES.DAT.
   d. Clear the screen and display the bar graph title.

3. B200.Build.Graph

   a. Call B200.Build.Horizontal.Bars. Within this subprogram, use a For loop with a loop variable of Mon% to display the 12 monthly names and corresponding bars. Use alternate shadings for each bar. Use the ASCII code 219 to shade the first bar (January). Use the ASCII code 177 to shade the next bar (February). Set the variable Char$ to CHR$(219) prior to the loop. Within the For loop, do the following:

      (1) Display the month name and tab to column 11. Hold the cursor at column 11.

      (2) Use a For loop to display the bar for the month being processed. In the For loop, use the control variable Num%, an initial value of 1, and a limit value of Sales(Mon%) / 1000. Within the loop, print Char$ and keep the cursor on the same line.

      (3) Following the inner For loop, use an IF statement to switch the value of Char$. This causes the next bar to be a different shade. If Char$ is equal to CHR$(219), then assign Char$ the value CHR$(177); otherwise, assign Char$ the value CHR$(219).

   b. Call B210.Display.Horizontal.Axis. Tab to column 10. Use a For loop with a control variable of Ticks%, an initial value of 0, and a limit value of 60. Within the For loop, use an IF statement to display a minus sign if Ticks% is not a multiple of 5. If Ticks% is a multiple of 5, then display a plus sign. In either case, the PRINT statement should end with a semicolon so the cursor remains on the same line. The plus sign marks off the horizontal line in multiples of 5. These marks are called **ticks**.

   c. Call B220.Mark.Axis.By.Fives. Use a For loop with a loop variable of Mark%, an initial value of 0, a limit value of 60 and a step of 5. Within the loop, use a PRINT statement and TAB function to display multiples of 5, beginning with 0. At the conclusion of the For loop, label the horizontal axis as described in Figure 11.11.

Program Solution

Program 11.2 corresponds to the top-down chart in Figure 11.12 and to the preceding program tasks.

PROGRAM 11.2

```
1    ' Program 11.2
2    ' Horizontal Bar Graph of Monthly Sales
3    ' Input File Name = MONSALES.DAT
4    ' ********************************************************
5    ' *                   Main Program                      *
6    ' ********************************************************
7    ' **** Declare month names and month sales arrays ****
8    DIM SHARED Month$(1 TO 12), Sales(1 TO 12)
9    CALL A100.Initialization
10   CALL B100.Build.Graph
11   END
12
13   ' ********************************************************
14   ' *                   Initialization                    *
15   ' ********************************************************
16   SUB A100.Initialization
17      OPEN "MONSALES.DAT" FOR INPUT AS #1
18      ' ********* Read Names and Sales into Arrays *********
19      FOR Mon% = 1 TO 12
20         INPUT #1, Month$(Mon%), Sales(Mon%)
21      NEXT Mon%
22      CLOSE #1
23      CLS  ' Clear Screen
24      LOCATE 6, 29: PRINT "Analysis of Monthly Sales"
25      LOCATE 9
26   END SUB
27
28   ' ********************************************************
29   ' *                   Build Graph                       *
30   ' ********************************************************
31   SUB B100.Build.Graph
32      CALL B200.Build.Horizontal.Bars
33      CALL B210.Display.Horizontal.Axis
34      CALL B220.Mark.Axis.By.Fives
35   END SUB
36
37   ' ********************************************************
38   ' *                Build Horizontal Bars                *
39   ' ********************************************************
40   SUB B200.Build.Horizontal.Bars
41      Char$ = CHR$(219)
42      FOR Mon% = 1 TO 12
43         PRINT Month$(Mon%); TAB(11);
44         FOR Num% = 1 TO Sales(Mon%) / 1000
45            PRINT Char$;
46         NEXT Num%
47         PRINT
48         IF Char$ = CHR$(219) THEN
49            Char$ = CHR$(177)
50         ELSE
51            Char$ = CHR$(219)
52         END IF
53      NEXT Mon%
54   END SUB
55
```

```
56    ' ********************************************************
57    ' *                Display Horizontal Axis               *
58    ' ********************************************************
59    SUB B210.Display.Horizontal.Axis
60       PRINT TAB(10);
61       FOR Ticks% = 0 TO 60
62          IF Ticks% / 5 = INT(Ticks% / 5) THEN
63             PRINT "+";
64          ELSE
65             PRINT "-";
66          END IF
67       NEXT Ticks%
68       PRINT
69    END SUB
70
71    ' ********************************************************
72    ' *                Mark the Axis by Fives                *
73    ' ********************************************************
74    SUB B220.Mark.Axis.By.Fives
75       FOR Mark% = 0 TO 60 STEP 5
76          PRINT TAB(Mark% + 9); Mark%;
77       NEXT Mark%
78       PRINT
79       PRINT : PRINT TAB(30); "In Thousands of Dollars"
80    END SUB

   [run]
```

Discussion of the Program Solution

When Program 11.2 is executed, A100.Initialization fills the parallel arrays Month$ and Sales with the 12 month names and corresponding monthly sales.

In B200.Build.Horizontal.Bars, line 41 assigns Char$ the dark-shaded graphics character with an ASCII code 219. The outer For loop (lines 42 through 53) builds a bar on each pass. The inner For loop (lines 44 through 46) builds each individual bar. After each bar is displayed, lines 48 through 52 switch the shade of the character assigned to Char$. The new shade is used to build the next bar.

B210.Display.Horizontal.Axis (lines 59 through 69) displays the horizontal axis. Finally, B220.Mark.Axis.By.Fives (lines 74 through 80) assigns a multiple of 5, beginning with 0, to each tick.

The horizontal bar graph displayed by Program 11.2 is shown in Figure 11.13.

FIGURE 11.13

The horizontal bar graph displayed due to the execution of Program 11.2.

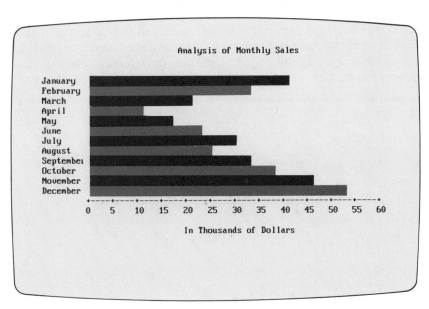

The COLOR Statement for the Text Mode

If your PC has a color monitor and a color/graphics adaptor, you can enhance your screen displays with color. There are four general forms for the COLOR statements: one for the text mode (SCREEN 0); one for medium-resolution graphics mode (SCREEN 1); one for screen modes 7 through 10, and, one for screen modes 12 and 13. In this section, we discuss the COLOR statement for the text mode. In the next section we cover color in the medium-resolution graphics mode.

FIGURE 11.14

The back-ground, fore-ground, and border of the screen.

The COLOR statement allows you to select colors for the foreground, background, and border of the screen. As illustrated in Figure 11.14, the **background** is that part of the screen against which the characters are displayed. Displayed characters are the **foreground**. The **border** is the edge of the screen. EGA, VGA, and MCGA do not support a border color.

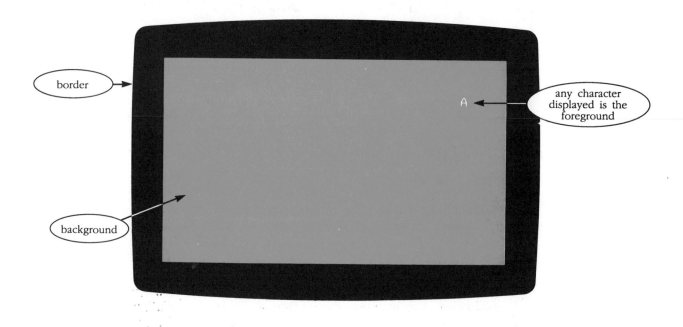

When you first enter QuickBASIC, the color of the output screen is set to white on black; that is, the foreground is set to white, and the background and border are set to black. The COLOR statement may then be used in the immediate mode or as a statement in a program to change the colors of the output screen as often as desired. The general form of the COLOR statement for the text mode is shown in Table 11.5.

TABLE 11.5   The COLOR Statement for the Text Mode

General Form:	COLOR foreground, background, border
	where **foreground** is a numeric expression in the range 0 to 31;
	       background is a numeric expression in the range 0 to 7; and
	       border is a numeric expression in the range 0 to 15.

Purpose:	Sets the color for the foreground, background, and border of the screen. The foreground and border may be set equal to any of the 16 colors described in Table 11.6. Adding the number 16 to the foreground value causes the characters to blink in that color. Only the colors with numbers 0 through 7 may be selected for the background.
Examples:	1. COLOR 14, 2, 6 ' Yellow on Green with a Brown Border 2. COLOR 12 ' Light Red Foreground 3. COLOR ,, 14 ' Yellow Border 4. COLOR 7, 0, 0 ' White on Black 5. COLOR 0, 7 ' Black on White 6. COLOR 0, 0, 0 ' Black on Black
Note:	EGA, VGA, and MCGA do not support a border color.

Example 1 in Table 11.5 sets a yellow foreground, a green background, and a brown border screen. Example 2 changes the foreground to light red; the background and border colors remain as they were. Example 3 changes only the border color to yellow. Example 4 resets the colors to the normal white on black. In this case, the background and border are the same. Example 5 reverses the colors; that is, it changes them to black on white. With Example 6, the foreground, background, and border are the same color; and, therefore, character images sent to the screen will not display. This method may be used to prevent the display of sensitive and confidential information, such as passwords, as they are entered via the keyboard.

When the COLOR statement is executed, all previously displayed characters remain in the original color. The new colors are used for future displays. For this reason, the COLOR statement is often followed by the CLS statement. The CLS statement causes the entire background and border to immediately display in the newly assigned colors. For example,

```
COLOR 14, 7, 2 : CLS
```

instructs the PC to change the screen immediately to a white background and green border. All characters displayed as a result of listing or executing a program will display in the color yellow.

If you have a monochrome display (black and white or green or amber color) and a color/graphics adaptor, the color settings in Table 11.6 are still useful, but the different colors will appear in various patterns of shading on your screen.

TABLE 11.6	The 16 Colors Available with a Color Monitor and Color/Graphics Adaptor				
COLOR	**NUMBER**	**COLOR**	**NUMBER**	**COLOR**	**NUMBER**
Black	0	Brown	6	Light Red	12
Blue	1	White	7	Light Magenta	13
Green	2	Grey	8	Yellow	14
Cyan (greenish blue)	3	Light Blue	9	Bright White	15
Red	4	Light Green	10		
Magenta (purplish)	5	Light Cyan	11		

The COLOR statement improves substantially the quality of the results displayed by a program. For example, if the following statement

```
COLOR 15, 1, 4
```

is added before the CLS statement in A100.Initialization of any of the previous menu-driven programs, then the main menu displays in bright white on a blue background with a red border. Other color combinations can be considered for submenus and the results displayed by a program.

Color monitors, sometimes called RGB monitors, create colors. The colors are determined by three independent bits representing the additive primary colors of red, green, and blue (hence, the term RGB), and a fourth bit representing the intensity (I). Collectively, these bits are called the IRGB color bits, and the color composition is referred to as the IRGB color. These bits form the 16 colors (2^4) in Table 11.6 by being on (1) or off (0) as shown in Table 11.7.

TABLE 11.7			IRGB Colors			
NUMBER	**I**	**R**	**G**	**B**	**COLOR**	**COMPOSITION**
0	0	0	0	0	Black	
1	0	0	0	1	Blue	Blue
2	0	0	1	0	Green	Green
3	0	0	1	1	Cyan	Green + Blue
4	0	1	0	0	Red	Red
5	0	1	0	1	Magenta	Red + Blue
6	0	1	1	0	Brown	Red + Green
7	0	1	1	1	White	Red + Green + Blue
8	1	0	0	0	Grey	Intensity
9	1	0	0	1	Light Blue	Intensity + Blue
10	1	0	1	0	Light Green	Intensity + Green
11	1	0	1	1	Light Cyan	Intensity + Green + Blue
12	1	1	0	0	Light Red	Intensity + Red
13	1	1	0	1	Light Magenta	Intensity + Red + Blue
14	1	1	1	0	Yellow	Intensity + Red + Green
15	1	1	1	1	Bright White	Intensity + Red + Green + Blue

The three additive primary colors can be mixed or added in various combinations to form the first eight colors in Table 11.7. The intensity control yields an additional eight colors, each a brighter version of its nonintensified counterpart.

You may instruct the PC to blink characters by adding the number 16 to the foreground color: For example,

```
COLOR 31, 4 : CLS
```

causes the PC to blink bright white characters on a red background. All of these colors are summarized in Table 11.8 for the foreground, background, and border.

TABLE 11.8 QuickBASIC Color Codes in the Text Mode

NUMBER	COLOR FOREGROUND	COLOR BACKGROUND	COLOR BORDER
0	Black	Black	Black
1	Blue	Blue	Blue
2	Green	Green	Green
3	Cyan (greenish blue)	Cyan	Cyan
4	Red	Red	Red
5	Magenta (purplish)	Magenta	Magenta
6	Brown	Brown	Brown
7	White	White	White
8	Grey		Grey
9	Light Blue		Light Blue
10	Light Green		Light Green
11	Light Cyan		Light Cyan
12	Light Red		Light Red
13	Light Magenta		Light Magenta
14	Yellow		Yellow
15	Bright White		Bright White
16	Black		
17	Blinking Blue		
18	Blinking Green		
19	Blinking Cyan		
20	Blinking Red		
21	Blinking Magenta		
22	Blinking Brown		
23	Blinking White		
24	Blinking Grey		
25	Blinking Light Blue		
26	Blinking Light Green		
27	Blinking Light Cyan		
28	Blinking Light Red		
29	Blinking Light Magenta		
30	Blinking Yellow		
31	Blinking Bright White		

| Programming Case Study 25 | Animating an Inchworm Creeping Across the Screen |

We can use the SCREEN statement in the text mode to build different pages and display them one after another. As illustrated in the following programming case study, this page switching allows us to instruct the PC to animate objects formed with characters.

Problem: Use the SCREEN statement to animate an inchworm creeping across the screen in a left-to-right direction. The five positions of the inchworm are shown by the filled-in squares in Figure 11.15.

FIGURE 11.15

The five positions of the creeping inchworm.

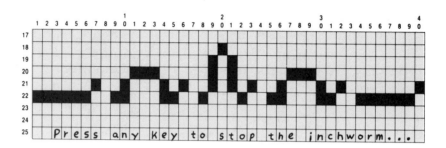

Use the 40-column display and build each position of the inchworm on a different page. Once all the pages have been built, display the pages in sequence until the user intervenes.

Following are a top-down chart, a list of the program tasks in outline form, a program solution, and a discussion of the program solution.

FIGURE 11.16

Top-down chart for Program 11.3.

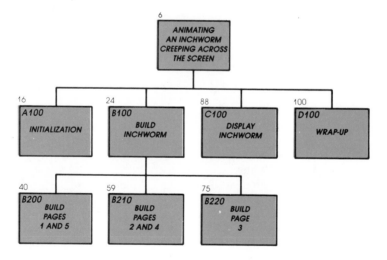

Program Tasks

The following program tasks correspond to the top-down chart in Figure 11.16.

1. A100.Initialization

   a. Use the SCREEN statement to select the text mode.
   b. Set the width of a line to 40 characters.

2. B100.Build.Inchworm — Build each position of the inchworm on a separate page. Note the identicalness of positions 1 and 5 and positions 2 and 4 of the inchworm in Figure 11.15. By adjusting the columns and the page number, the same code may be used to build the identical positions of the inchworm.

   a. Call B200.Build.Pages.1.5 — Use the SCREEN statement to write to page 1 or 5 while displaying page 0. (Page 0 is blank.) For page 1, set the column to 1. For page 5, set the column to 34. Use the LOCATE and PRINT statements and the shaded rectangle (ASCII code = 219) to build the inchworm. Color the body green (COLOR 2) and the head red (COLOR 4). The message that is located on line 25 of Figure 11.15 is then written to page 5.
   b. Call B210.Build.Pages.2.4 — Use the SCREEN statement to write to pages 2 and 4 while displaying page 0. For page 2, set the column to 9. For page 4, set the column to 25. Use the same statements and color described in 2a to build the inchworm.
   c. Call B220.Build.Page.3 — Use the SCREEN statement to write to page 3 while displaying page 0. Use the same statements and color described in 2a to build the inchworm.

3. C100.Display.Inchworm — Establish a Do-While loop that executes until the user presses a key. Use the statement DO WHILE INKEY$ = "" to control the loop. Within the loop, use a nested For loop like the one below to display pages 1 through 5:

```
FOR Page% = 1 TO 5
    SCREEN , , , Page%
    FOR Time.Delay% = 1 TO 32000: NEXT Time.Delay%
NEXT Page%
```

The SCREEN statement displays pages 1 through 5. The inner For loop delays the display of the next page for one-half of one second. The display of the pages in sequence at a set time interval animates the inchworm creeping across the screen in a left-to-right direction.

4. D100.Wrap.Up

   a. Use the SCREEN statement to write to page 0 and display page 0.
   b. Set the width of a line to 80 characters.
   c. Set the color to white on black.
   d. Clear the screen.

Program Solution

Program 11.3 corresponds to the top-down chart in Figure 11.16 and to the preceding tasks.

PROGRAM 11.3

```
 1   ' Program 11.3
 2   ' Animating an Inchworm Creeping Across the Screen
 3   ' **************************************************
 4   ' *                    Main Program                *
 5   ' **************************************************
 6   COMMON SHARED Page%
 7   CALL A100.Initialization
 8   CALL B100.Build.Inchworm
 9   CALL C100.Display.Inchworm
10   CALL D100.Wrap.Up
11   END
12
13   ' **************************************************
14   ' *                  Initialization                *
15   ' **************************************************
16   SUB A100.Initialization
17      SCREEN 0
18      WIDTH 40
19   END SUB
20
21   ' **************************************************
22   ' *                  Build Inchworm                *
23   ' **************************************************
24   SUB B100.Build.Inchworm
25      Page% = 1
26      CALL B200.Build.Pages.1.5
27      Page% = 2
28      CALL B210.Build.Pages.2.4
29      Page% = 3
30      CALL B220.Build.Page.3
31      Page% = 4
32      CALL B210.Build.Pages.2.4
33      Page% = 5
34      CALL B200.Build.Pages.1.5
35   END SUB
36
37   ' **************************************************
38   ' *              Build Pages 1 and 5               *
39   ' **************************************************
40   SUB B200.Build.Pages.1.5
41      SCREEN , , Page%, 0
42      IF Page% = 1 THEN
43         Col = 1
44      ELSE
45         Col = 34
46      END IF
47      LOCATE 22, Col: COLOR 2: PRINT STRING$(6, 219);
48      LOCATE 21, Col + 6: COLOR 4: PRINT CHR$(219)
49      IF Page% = 5 THEN
50         LOCATE 24, 3
51         COLOR 15
52         PRINT "Press any key to stop the inchworm..."
53      END IF
54   END SUB
55
```

```
56      ' ***************************************************
57      ' *                Build Pages 2 and 4              *
58      ' ***************************************************
59      SUB B210.Build.Pages.2.4
60         SCREEN , , Page%, 0
61         IF Page% = 2 THEN
62            Col = 9
63         ELSE
64            Col = 25
65         END IF
66         LOCATE 22, Col: COLOR 2: PRINT STRING$(2, 219); SPC(3); STRING$(2, 219)
67         LOCATE 21, Col + 1: PRINT CHR$(219); SPC(3); CHR$(219)
68         LOCATE 20, Col + 2: PRINT STRING$(3, 219)
69         LOCATE 21, Col + 7: COLOR 4: PRINT CHR$(219)
70      END SUB
71
72      ' ***************************************************
73      ' *                 Build Page 3                    *
74      ' ***************************************************
75      SUB B220.Build.Page.3
76         SCREEN , , Page%, 0
77         LOCATE 22, 18: COLOR 2: PRINT CHR$(219); SPC(3); CHR$(219)
78         LOCATE 21, 19: PRINT CHR$(219); SPC(1); CHR$(219)
79         LOCATE 20, 19: PRINT CHR$(219); SPC(1); CHR$(219)
80         LOCATE 19, 19: PRINT CHR$(219); SPC(1); CHR$(219)
81         LOCATE 18, 20: PRINT CHR$(219)
82         LOCATE 21, 23: COLOR 4: PRINT CHR$(219)
83      END SUB
84
85      ' ***************************************************
86      ' *                Display Inchworm                 *
87      ' ***************************************************
88      SUB C100.Display.Inchworm
89         DO WHILE INKEY$ = ""
90            FOR Page% = 1 TO 5
91               SCREEN , , , Page%
92               FOR Time.Delay% = 1 TO 32000: NEXT Time.Delay%
93            NEXT Page%
94         LOOP
95      END SUB
96
97      ' ***************************************************
98      ' *                    Wrap-Up                      *
99      ' ***************************************************
100     SUB D100.Wrap.Up
101        SCREEN , , 0, 0: WIDTH 80: COLOR 7  ' Reset Screen
102        CLS  ' Clear Screen
103     END SUB

        [run]
```

When Program 11.3 is executed, the five positions of the inchworm shown in Figure 11.17 are displayed from left to right, one after the other.

FIGURE 11.17

The five positions of the inchworm creeping across the screen, superimposed on one screen.

Discussion of the Program Solution

The five positions of the inchworm are each built on a separate page because of the calls made in the subprogram B100.Build.Inchworm. Each subprogram called from B100.Build.Inchworm begins with a SCREEN statement that establishes the page to write to and the page to display. It is important to include the parameter 0 for the visual page because the visual page defaults to the active page if no value is specified.

In C100.Display.Inchworm, the Do-While loop causes the inchworm to creep across the screen from left to right, over and over again, until the user presses a key on the keyboard. Within the loop, the five pages are displayed one after the other. The For loop in line 90 delays the display of the next page for about one-half of one second.

In the solution to Programming Case Study 25, we were able to build all the required positions on separate pages before displaying the animation. This is not always possible because most animations require more pages than are available (eight pages for 40-column display and four pages for 80-column display). When the number of required positions exceeds the number of available pages, the program must build one page while displaying another page.

11.3   MEDIUM-RESOLUTION AND HIGH-RESOLUTION GRAPHICS

To change to the medium-resolution graphics mode, enter the statement SCREEN 1. In this mode, the screen is divided into 200 rows and 320 columns. (See Figure 11.6C on page 436.) To change to the high-resolution graphics mode, enter the statement SCREEN 2. In the high-resolution graphics mode, the screen is divided into 200 rows and 640 columns. (See Figure 11.6D on page 436.)

Consider these important points regarding the medium-resolution and high-resolution graphics modes:

1. These two graphics modes are available only if your PC has a Color/Graphics Adaptor.
2. To send graphical designs to the printer, you must have one that emulates the IBM graphics printer. Also, you must enter the MS-DOS command GRAPHICS before you enter QuickBASIC.
3. With a color monitor, medium-resolution graphics allows you to color objects on the screen. High-resolution graphics allows displays in only black and white, but with much greater detail.
4. In either of the two graphics modes, the intersection of a row and column is a point, or pixel. You plot points and draw lines and curves by instructing the PC to turn on selected pixels.
5. The PC is given information about the points, lines, and curves to draw in the form of coordinates, such as (x, y), where x is the column (horizontal axis) and y is the row (vertical axis).

6. Coordinates are specified with the column first, then the row. This is different from the LOCATE statement in the text mode, which requires the row first, then the column.
7. Rows and columns are numbered beginning with 0, rather than 1.
8. There are two ways to indicate the coordinates of a point on the screen: absolute form and relative form. Coordinates of the form (x, y) are absolute in relation to the origin (0, 0). Coordinates of the form STEP(x, y) are relative to the last point referenced by the last graphics statement executed.
9. If you enter WIDTH 80 in the medium-resolution graphics mode, the PC will switch to the high-resolution graphics mode. If you enter WIDTH 40 in the high-resolution graphics mode, the PC will switch to the medium-resolution graphics mode.

In the sections that follow, several graphics statements and examples are presented.

The COLOR Statement for the Medium-Resolution Graphics Mode

The general form of the COLOR statement for the medium-resolution graphics mode is given in Table 11.9.

In Table 11.9, Example 1 sets the background color to light blue and selects palette 1 for the foreground. Graphics statements that follow the COLOR statement in Example 1 may select cyan (color number 1 in Table 11.9), magenta (2), white (3), or the background color (0) for the foreground. Selecting the background color turns off the referenced pixel(s).

Example 2 leaves the background color the same, and palette 0 is selected for the foreground. Graphics statements that follow this COLOR statement may select the foreground color from green (1), red (2), brown (3), or the background color (0). Finally, Example 3 in Table 11.9 selects the background color on the basis of the value of Back and a palette on the basis of whether Pal is odd (palette 1) or even (palette 0).

TABLE 11.9 The COLOR Statement for the Medium-Resolution Graphics Mode

General Form: COLOR background, palette
where **background** is a numeric expression in the range 0 to 15, and
palette is a numeric expression. If the expression is an even number, then palette 0 is selected for the foreground; otherwise, palette 1 is selected.

Purpose: Sets the background color of the screen and selects one of two palettes of color for the foreground. The background may be set equal to any of the 16 colors described in Table 11.6 on page 450. The choice of palettes for the foreground is as follows:

Palette 0	Palette 1	Number
Background Color	Background Color	0
Green	Cyan	1
Red	Magenta	2
Brown	White	3

Examples:
1. COLOR 9, 1
2. COLOR , 0
3. COLOR Back, Pal

Note: The COLOR statement selects the palette (0 or 1) for the foreground. Graphics statements that follow the COLOR statement select the color number from the palette. If no color number is selected, then the default color number 3 is used for medium resolution, and the color number 1 is used for high resolution. In medium resolution the border is always the same color as the background.

The PSET and PRESET Statements

The PSET (point set) and PRESET (point reset) statements can be used to set a point on the screen to one of the four colors in the active palette. The general forms of the PSET and PRESET statements are given in Table 11.10.

TABLE 11.10   The PSET and PRESET Statements

General Form:	PSET (x, y), color and PRESET (x, y), color where **(x, y)** are the coordinates of the point to be plotted (turned on), and **color** is an integer expression in the range 0 to 3. The color number selects the color from the active palette. (See Table 11.9.)
Purpose:	To plot a point on the screen.
Examples:	1. PSET (34, 72), 2 2. PSET (Col, Row) 3. PSET STEP (X, 5), 0 4. PRESET STEP (40, 90), Kolor 5. PRESET (34, 72)
Notes:	1. The coordinates (x, y) may be absolute, without STEP and from the origin, or relative, with STEP and from the current coordinates. 2. The PC ignores points referenced outside the range of the screen. 3. PSET and PRESET are identical statements except for the default color number when the color parameter is not included. With the PSET statement, the color number defaults to 3. With the PRESET statement, the color number defaults to 0, the background color. Thus, PSET (X, Y), 0 is identical to PRESET (X, Y).

Example 1 in Table 11.10 plots the point at the intersection of column 34 and row 72. Depending on which palette is active, the point is colored red or magenta. Example 2 plots the point (Col, Row) using the default color number 3 of the active palette. Examples 3 and 5 in Table 11.10 erase the point defined by the specified coordinates. Recall that a color number of 0 or a lack of the color parameter in the PRESET statement instructs the PC to use the background color. (That is, the pixel is turned off.) Example 4 plots the point that is 40 columns and 90 rows from the last point referenced. The color of the point is based upon the value of Kolor and the active palette.

Consider the partial program in Figure 11.18 and the results due to its execution in Figure 11.18. Line 4 switches the PC to the medium-resolution graphics mode and clears the screen. Line 5 sets the background color to yellow and selects palette 0. The For loop (lines 6 through 8) draws a green vertical line. The color number in line 7 selects the color green from palette 0. Lines 9 and 10 plot two points using the color red on the left and right sides of the green, vertical line. Finally, the second For loop (lines 11 through 13) erases part of the line drawn by the first For loop.

As we see in the next section, QuickBASIC has a LINE statement that simplifies drawing lines such as the one drawn by the partial program in Figure 11.18.

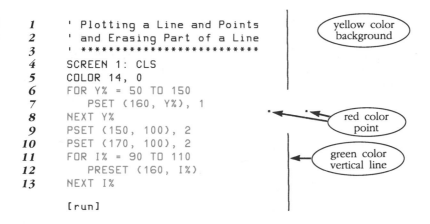

FIGURE 11.18

Plotting a line and points.

```
1    ' Plotting a Line and Points
2    ' and Erasing Part of a Line
3    ' *************************
4    SCREEN 1: CLS
5    COLOR 14, 0
6    FOR Y% = 50 TO 150
7       PSET (160, Y%), 1
8    NEXT Y%
9    PSET (150, 100), 2
10   PSET (170, 100), 2
11   FOR I% = 90 TO 110
12      PRESET (160, I%)
13   NEXT I%

[run]
```

The LINE Statement

The LINE statement can be used to draw a line or a box on the screen. The general form of the LINE statement is given in Table 11.11.

In Table 11.11, Example 1 draws a line from the point defined by the intersection of column 50 and row 70 to the point defined by the intersection of column 90 and row 100. The color of the line is either red (palette 0) or magenta (palette 1). Example 2 draws a line from the last point referenced to the point (65, 90) in the default color on the active palette.

Example 3 in Table 11.11 draws a diagonal line from the upper left-hand corner to the lower right-hand corner of the screen. If palette 0 is active, the color of the line is brown. Example 4 draws a box around the outer edge of the screen. If palette 0 is active, the lines making up the box are colored green. Otherwise, the lines of the box are colored cyan. Example 5 also draws a box. The location of the box on the screen is dependent on the values assigned to Col1, Row1, Col2, and Row2. The parameter BF instructs the PC to fill the box with the default color for the active palette. Example 6 draws a dotted box. If palette 0 is active, the dots forming the box are colored green; otherwise, the dots are colored cyan.

TABLE 11.11   The LINE Statement

General Form:	LINE $(x_1, y_1) - (x_2, y_2)$, color, box, style
	where (x_1, y_1) is the starting point;
	  (x_2, y_2) is the ending point;
	  color selects the color for the line from the active palette;
	  box is B or BF,
	    where **B** instructs the PC to draw a box, rather than a line with (x_1, y_1) and (x_2, y_2) as opposite coordinates; and
	    BF is similar to B, except that the box is filled with color; and
	    style is a 16-bit integer used to determine the type of line, dotted, dashed, or solid, to be drawn.

Purpose:	Connects two points with a line or draws a box, filled or unfilled, on the screen.
Examples:	1. LINE (50, 70)-(90, 100), 2 2. LINE -(65, 90) 3. LINE (0, 0)-(319, 199), 3 4. LINE (0, 199)-(319, 0), 1, B 5. LINE (Col1, Row1)-(Col2, Row2),, BF 6. LINE (10, 10)-(50, 50), 1, B, &H1111
Notes:	1. Lines that extend beyond the range of the screen are **clipped**; that is, the PC determines the intersection of the line with the edge of the screen and draws the line up to the edge. 2. The style parameter cannot be used with filled boxes (BF).

Consider the partial program in Figure 11.19 and the right triangle displayed as a result of its execution. In the partial program, line 3 switches the PC to the medium-resolution graphics mode and clears the screen. Line 4 changes the background of the screen to blue and selects palette 1. Line 5 draws the base of the triangle. Line 6 draws the altitude, and line 7 draws the hypotenuse. Because none of the LINE statements include a color number, the default color number 3 (white for palette 1) is used. Note also that lines 6 and 7 both draw lines from the last point referenced.

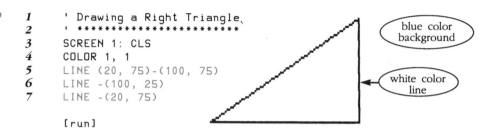

FIGURE 11.19

Drawing a right triangle.

```
1    ' Drawing a Right Triangle
2    ' ************************
3    SCREEN 1: CLS
4    COLOR 1, 1
5    LINE (20, 75)-(100, 75)
6    LINE -(100, 25)
7    LINE -(20, 75)

[run]
```

As two more examples of the use of the LINE statement, consider the partial programs in Figure 11.20. Partial program (A) instructs the PC to draw five boxes, one of which is inside another. Line 3 switches the PC to the medium-resolution graphics mode and clears the screen. Line 4 selects a black background and palette 0.

FIGURE 11.20

Drawing boxes.

(A)

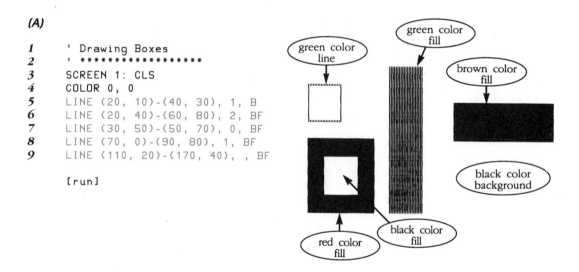

```
1    ' Drawing Boxes
2    ' *****************
3    SCREEN 1: CLS
4    COLOR 0, 0
5    LINE (20, 10)-(40, 30), 1, B
6    LINE (20, 40)-(60, 80), 2, BF
7    LINE (30, 50)-(50, 70), 0, BF
8    LINE (70, 0)-(90, 80), 1, BF
9    LINE (110, 20)-(170, 40), , BF

[run]
```

(B)

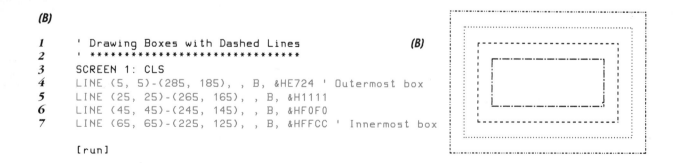

```
1    ' Drawing Boxes with Dashed Lines
2    ' *********************************
3    SCREEN 1: CLS
4    LINE (5, 5)-(285, 185), , B, &HE724 ' Outermost box
5    LINE (25, 25)-(265, 165), , B, &H1111
6    LINE (45, 45)-(245, 145), , B, &HF0F0
7    LINE (65, 65)-(225, 125), , B, &HFFCC ' Innermost box

[run]
```

The first LINE statement in Part (A) of Figure 11.20 draws the small, unfilled square box with opposite coordinates of (20, 10) and (40, 30) using the color green. Line 6 draws the large square box, using the color red. Next, line 7 draws a filled square within the square drawn by line 6. Because the background color is used in line 7, the red pixels are turned off to leave an unfilled square within the large red square.

Line 8 in Part (A) of Figure 11.20 draws the filled vertical box, using the color green. Finally, line 9 draws the filled horizontal box using the default color brown on palette 0.

The style of a line consists of a series of pixels that are on (1) or off (0). In the LINE statement, the style consists of a 16-bit integer mask representing 16 consecutive pixels, and this pattern is used to construct the style of the line, which can be a dotted or dashed line or a box.

The 16-bit pattern repeats as necessary for the entire length of the line or the entire perimeter of a box. The style is specified by a 4-digit hexadecimal number that represents the desired pattern. The four steps involved in representing a pattern are as follows:

1. Create the 16-bit pattern on paper. Assume that the following dashed-line pattern is desired:

   where the solid dot represents an on-pixel and the open dot represents an off-pixel.

2. Substitute a zero for each open dot and a one for each solid dot:

   1111000011110000

3. Divide the 16-bit pattern into four sets of 4-bit patterns where each of the four bits becomes a hexadecimal digit according to the conversion:

4-Bit Pattern	ASCII Value of Hexadecimal Digit	4-Bit Pattern	ASCII Value of Hexadecimal Digit
0000	0	1000	8
0001	1	1001	9
0010	2	1010	A
0011	3	1011	B
0100	4	1100	C
0101	5	1101	D
0110	6	1110	E
0111	7	1111	F

   Hence, the 4-bit patterns become:

   1111   0000   1111   0000
    F   0   F   0

4. Place an &H in front of the first hexadecimal number as shown:

   &HF0F0

   This now becomes a valid style for a LINE statement such as line 6 in Part (B) of Figure 11.20.

The partial program in Part (B) of Figure 11.20 instructs the PC to draw four dotted- or dashed-line boxes, each inside of one another. Line 3 switches the PC to medium-resolution graphics mode and clears the screen. Lines 4 through 7 draw the boxes with dotted or dashed lines by adding a style to the LINE statement.

The CIRCLE Statement

The `CIRCLE` statement draws circles, ellipses, arcs, and wedges. The general form of the `CIRCLE` statement is given in Table 11.12.

TABLE 11.12   The CIRCLE Statement

General Form: CIRCLE (x, y), radius, color, start, end, shape

where **(x, y)** is the center of the curved figure;

radius is the distance from the center to the outer edge of the curved figure, as measured in points (pixels);

color selects the color for the curved figure from the active palette;

start and **end** are the two ends of the arc to be drawn (The measures are angles in radians and can range between –2 * 3.141593 and 2 * 3.141593. Negative values [–0 is not allowed] cause a wedge or pie slice to be drawn. If these two parameters are omitted, the PC draws the entire curved figure.); and

shape is the ratio of the radius in the y direction to the radius in the x direction (height/width). This parameter is used to draw ellipses. If this parameter is omitted, the PC draws a partial or complete circle, depending on the start and end parameters.

Purpose: To draw circles, ellipses, arcs, and wedges.

Examples:
1. CIRCLE (160, 100), 20
2. CIRCLE (60, 40), 30, 1
3. CIRCLE (20, 20), 50
4. CIRCLE (Col, Row), Rad, Kolor
5. CIRCLE (120, 120), 35,, 0, 1.5708
6. CIRCLE (160, 100), 50, 1, -3.141593, -4.7124
7. CIRCLE (100, 100), 40,,,,5/18

Notes:
1. The last point referenced after the `CIRCLE` statement is executed is the center point (x, y).
2. If you want to draw a radius to angle 0 (a horizontal line), then use a small nonzero value, such as –0.0001, rather than –0 or –2 * 3.141593.

In Table 11.12, Example 1 instructs the PC to draw a circle with a center at column 160 and row 100 and with a radius of 20 points. The default color number 3 on the active palette is used to draw the circle. In Example 2, a circle with a center at (60, 40) with a radius of 30 points is drawn in green or cyan.

Example 3 in Table 11.12 draws a circle that is clipped because part of the circle goes beyond the screen. Example 4 causes a circle to be drawn, using the color number Kolor, with center at (Col, Row) and radius of Rad points.

FIGURE 11.21

A circle is composed of 2π or 6.28 radians, or 360°. (Note that the decimal fraction values are rounded to the nearest hundredths place.)

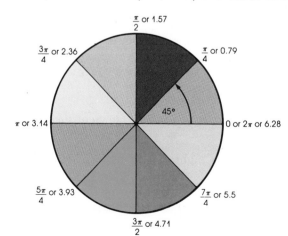

Example 5 draws an arc from 0° to 90° with a center at (120, 120) and a radius of 35 points. The default color on the active palette is used to color the curved figure. Example 6 draws a wedge. The negative start and end parameters instruct the PC to connect the center to the ends of the arc to form a wedge. The wedge extends from 180° to 270°. Figure 11.21 shows the relationship between radians and slices of a circle.

Example 7 in Table 11.12 draws a horizontal, flatter ellipse. The center of the ellipse is at (100, 100). Because the shape is less than 1, the radius parameter is the x radius. The product of the shape (5/18) and the radius parameter is the y radius.

In mathematics, when the shape is equal to 1, a circle is defined. A shape that is less than 1 causes the ellipse to be horizontal, flatter. A shape greater than 1 causes the ellipse to be vertical, taller.

Because the pixel length for the PC screen is not the same in both the x and y direction (320 × 200 for medium resolution), the default value of the shape that draws a circle is 5/6 (5 rows for every 6 columns) in medium resolution and 5/12 (5 rows for every 12 columns) in high resolution. With this in mind, you must adjust slightly the mathematical definition of the term *shape*. For example, the following statement

```
CIRCLE (160, 100), 50,,,, 1
```

does not result in a circle even though the shape is 1. The CIRCLE statement draws an ellipse that is slightly taller than it is wide. The following statement draws a circle because the PC uses a default value of 5/6 for the shape:

```
CIRCLE (160, 100), 50
```

(See the partial program in Figure 11.22 on the next page for additional examples of CIRCLE statements that draw ellipses.)

The PAINT Statement

Another color statement available with QuickBASIC is the PAINT statement. This statement paints (fills) an area on the screen with the selected color. The general form of the PAINT statement is given in Table 11.13.

TABLE 11.13 The PAINT Statement

General Form: PAINT (x, y), paint, boundary

where **(x, y)** are the coordinates of a point within the area to be filled with color;

paint is a numeric expression or a string expression (If paint is a numeric expression, then it must be within the range 0 to 3 for medium resolution and 0 or 1 for high resolution. The numeric expression determines the color the PC uses to paint the area on the screen. The default for medium resolution is 3 and for high resolution 1. If paint is a string expression, then it describes a tiling pattern for the area.); and

boundary is a numeric expression that defines the color of the edges of the area to be filled.

Purpose: Paints an area defined by the boundary color on the screen with the selected color.

Examples:
1. PAINT (50, 25), 2, 1
2. PAINT (Col, Row), Kolor, Edge
3. PAINT (200, 100)
4. PAINT (100, 150), Tile$

Notes:
1. The area defined by the boundary color must be completely enclosed, or the entire screen is painted.
2. In high resolution, the paint parameter should not be different from the boundary parameter.

Assuming that in medium resolution palette 0 is active, Example 1 in Table 11.13 paints the area with the color red that is bounded by the color green in which the point with coordinates (50, 25) is located. If there is no green boundary surrounding (50, 25), the entire screen is painted red. Example 1 is invalid in high resolution because the paint parameter is not 0 or 1.

In either medium resolution or high resolution, Example 2 paints the area encompassing the point with coordinates (Col, Row) and bounded by the color number Edge with the color associated with Kolor. Example 3 colors the area that includes the point with coordinates (200, 100) with the default color (3 in medium resolution and 1 in high resolution). If the edge of the area is not equal to the default color, the entire screen is painted.

Consider the partial program in Figure 11.22 and the results due to its execution, which are shown in Figure 11.22.

FIGURE 11.22

Examples of the COLOR *and* PAINT *statements.*

```
1     ' Drawing Circles, Arcs,
2     ' Wedges, and Ellipses
3     ' *********************
4     Pi = 3.141593
5     SCREEN 1: CLS
6     COLOR 1, 0
7     ' **** Draw Circle ****
8     CIRCLE (40, 40), 20, 1
9     PAINT (40, 40), 3, 1
10    ' ****** Draw Arc *****
11    CIRCLE (80, 40), 20, 1, 0, Pi / 2
12    ' **** Draw Wedge *****
13    CIRCLE (120, 40), 20, 3, -.0001, -Pi / 2
14    PAINT (125, 35), 1, 3
15    ' ** Draw Horizontal Ellipse **
16    CIRCLE (40, 100), 30, 3, , , 7 / 18
17    PAINT (40, 100), 2, 3
18    ' ** Draw Vertical Ellipse **
19    CIRCLE (90, 100), 30, 3, , , 18 / 7
20    PAINT (95, 95), 1, 3
21    ' ** Draw Circle Within Box **
22    LINE (120, 70)-(180, 130), 3, B
23    CIRCLE (150, 100), 20, 3
24    PAINT (125, 75), 2, 3

[run]
```

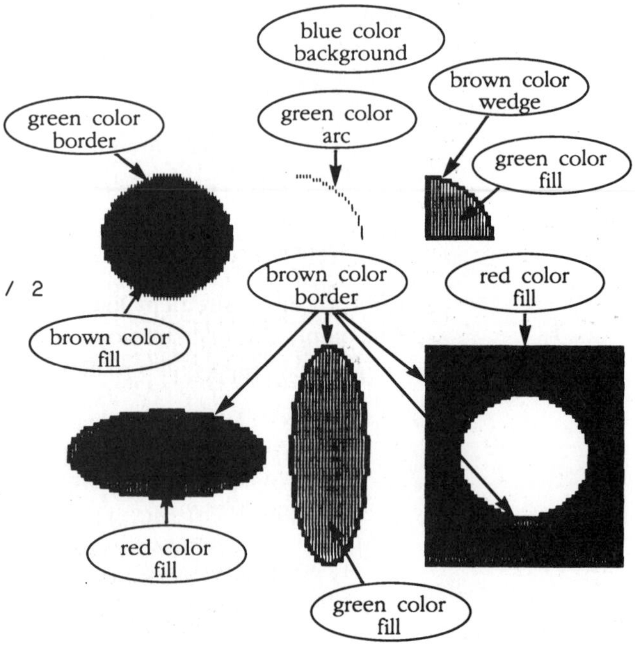

In the partial program in Figure 11.22, line 5 switches the PC to the medium-resolution graphics mode. The COLOR statement in line 6 selects a blue background and activates palette 0. Line 8 draws the circle in the upper left corner of the output results. Line 9 paints the circle brown. Note that the boundary parameter in line 9 is equal to the color number used to draw the circle in line 8.

Line 11 in the partial program draws an arc from $0°$ to $90°$ with a center at (80, 40). Line 13 draws the wedge illustrated in Figure 11.22. Line 14 paints the wedge green. Rather than using $-2 * Pi$ as the value for the start parameter in line 13, -0.0001 is used. Recall from Table 11.12 that the negative start and end parameters instruct the PC to draw lines from the center point to the end points of the arc to form a wedge. A start parameter of $-2 * Pi$, which is the same as $0°$, is represented in line 13 by the decimal fraction value −0.0001. Assigning the start parameter of −2 * Pi, or −0, causes a dialog box to display with the diagnostic message Illegal function call. Here a value (−0.0001) was selected that is very close to −2 * Pi, or −0.

Line 16 draws a horizontal ellipse. Line 19 draws a vertical ellipse. Both ellipses are shown in the output results in Figure 11.22. Each of the two CIRCLE statements is followed by a PAINT statement that paints the ellipses. Line 17 paints the horizontal ellipse the color red, and line 20 paints the vertical ellipse the color green.

The lower, right figure in Figure 11.22 is displayed because of lines 22 through 24. Line 22 draws the box. Line 23 draws the circle within the box. Both figures are drawn using the color brown (palette 0, color 3). Line 24 uses the color red to paint the area within the box and outside the circle. Painting continues in all directions until the brown border is reached.

Tiling

Example 4 in Table 11.13 causes the area to be tiled instead of painted. **Tiling** involves covering a specified area on the screen with a pattern. The pattern is uniformly repeated over the entire area.

The pattern of the tile is based on a series of binary digits assigned to the paint parameter in the form of a string expression. The string expression may contain from 1 to 64 bytes. Each byte, called a **tile mask**, contains 8 binary digits. A single tile mask is formed in a QuickBASIC program by means of the CHR$ function as follows:

CHR$(Decimal Number Representing the Tile Mask)

A series of tile masks is assigned to a string variable used as the paint parameter. An example of a tile pattern is shown in Figure 11.23. Each tile represents a single row of pixels.

FIGURE 11.23

An example of a tile pattern and the corresponding string expression assigned to the paint parameter Tile$.

	Bit Pattern								**CHR$ Argument**
	7	6	5	4	3	2	1	0	
Tile 0	1	0	1	0	1	0	1	0	170
Tile 1	1	1	1	1	1	1	1	1	255
Tile 3	0	1	0	0	0	1	0	0	68

Tile$ = CHR$(170) + CHR$(255) + CHR$(68)

With high resolution, every bit represents a pixel. If the bit is on (1), then the corresponding pixel is turned on; otherwise, the bit is assigned the background color (turned off). By scanning the bit pattern in Figure 11.23, you can get a feel for what each row in the pattern looks like in high resolution.

With medium resolution, every 2 bits represent a pixel, for a total of 4 pixels across per tile byte. Table 11.14 shows the binary color numbers for the foreground colors found on the two palettes and the equivalent CHR$ decimal representation for drawing solid lines. A solid line is defined as a single row of pixels.

Consider the partial programs (A) and (B) and their corresponding output results in Figure 11.24.

FIGURE 11.24

Partial programs (A) and (B) and their corresponding output results.

(A)

```
1    ' Tiling a Box in Medium Resolution
2    ' ********************************
3    Tile$ = CHR$(170) + CHR$(255) + CHR$(68)
4    SCREEN 1: CLS
5    COLOR 1, 1
6    LINE (40, 70)-(120, 120), 3, B
7    PAINT (117, 80), Tile$, 3

     [run]
```

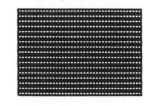

(B)

```
1    ' Tiling a Wedge in High Resolution
2    ' ********************************
3    Pi = 3.141593
4    Tile$ = CHR$(170) + CHR$(170) + CHR$(255) + CHR$(68) + CHR$(68)
5    SCREEN 2: CLS
6    CIRCLE (320, 100), 150, , -3 * Pi / 4, -Pi
7    PAINT (300, 95), Tile$

     [run]
```

In Part (A) of Figure 11.24, line 7 tiles the box defined by line 6. The pattern of the tile is assigned to the string variable Tile$ in line 3 and corresponds to the one described earlier in Figure 11.23. Tile$ describes a pattern of three lines. The first two are solid lines, and the third is of alternating colors. The first line is in the color magenta. The second line is in the color white. The third line is alternating between cyan and the background color blue.

In Part (B) of Figure 11.24, line 4 defines the pattern of the tile. Line 5 switches the PC to high resolution. Line 6 instructs the PC to draw a wedge. Finally, line 7 tiles the wedge by turning on the pixels described by the series of binary digits described in line 4.

Developing reasonable patterns for either graphics mode becomes easier with practice. We suggest that you enter the partial programs in Figure 11.24 into your PC and experiment with changing the patterns in the two partial programs.

TABLE 11.14   The Binary Color Numbers for Tiling and Equivalent CHR$ Decimal Values for Solid Lines

PALETTE 0	PALETTE 1	BINARY COLOR NUMBER	SOLID LINE PATTERN	CHR$ DECIMAL REPRESENTATION FOR SOLID LINE
Background	Background	00	00000000	0
Green	Cyan	01	01010101	85
Red	Magenta	10	10101010	170
Brown	White	11	11111111	255

The DRAW Statement

The DRAW statement instructs the PC to draw an object defined by a string expression. The string expression is made up of a series of easy-to-code commands. (See Table 11.16.) You can use the commands to draw lines, plot points, set colors, and perform other special operations — all within one statement. For example, DRAW "L75 U100" draws a horizontal line 75 columns (pixels) long in a left direction of the last point referenced. It then draws a line 100 points long upward toward the top of the screen, beginning at the leftmost point of the first line. The last point referenced is based on the most recently executed graphics statement, or it is at the center of the screen following the execution of the program or a CLS statement. Recall that the center of the screen is at (160, 100) for medium resolution and (320, 100) for high resolution.

The general form for the DRAW statement is shown in Table 11.15. The list of DRAW commands that can be assigned to the string expression in the DRAW statement is given in Table 11.16 on the next page.

TABLE 11.15   The DRAW Statement

General Form:	DRAW string expression where **string expression** is a command or series of commands as described in Table 11.16.
Purpose:	To draw an object as specified in the string expression.
Examples:	1. DRAW "BM75,120 M200,50 M100,150 M75,120" 2. DRAW "U100 R100 D100 L100" 3. DRAW "E=" + VARPTR$(S1) + "U25" 4. DRAW DESIGN$
Note:	A DRAW command, such as U or R, may be followed by a constant or variable. If a variable is used, then surround the command (and equal sign, if required) with quotation marks and add to the command the function VARPTR$ with the variable as the argument. (See the first command in Example 3.)

TABLE 11.16 DRAW Commands		
COMMAND	**FUNCTION**	**EXAMPLES**
M x,y	Moves and draws to (x,y).	M20,50
M ±x,±y	Moves and draws to (X + x, Y + y), where (X,Y) is the last referenced point.	M+30,+50
Un	Moves and draws up n rows.	U70
Dn	Moves and draws down n rows.	D35
Rn	Moves and draws right n columns.	R45
Ln	Moves and draws left n columns.	L27
En	Moves and draws diagonally up and right, where n = diagonal distance.	E40
Fn	Moves and draws diagonally down and right, where n = diagonal distance.	F90
Gn	Moves and draws diagonally down and left, where n = diagonal distance.	G10
Hn	Moves and draws diagonally up and left, where n = diagonal distance.	H36
B	Causes the next move command to move without drawing.	BM20,50
N	Instructs the PC to return to the current point after the next move command.	NR75
An	Sets angle n, where n ranges from 0 to 3. 0 = 0 degrees, 1 = 90 degrees, 2 = 180 degrees, and 3 = 270 degrees. Rotates next object drawn through the specified angle.	A2
Tn	Turns angle n for subsequent drawings, where n is in the range −360 to 360; n > 0 turns angle counterclockwise, n < 0 turns angle clockwise.	T30
Sn	Scales subsequent drawings, where n varies between 1 and 255. (All line lengths are multiplied by n/4.)	S24
Cn	Selects color from active palette.	C2
Pp,b	Fills area, using color number p to boundary b.	P1,2
"X" + v	Executes a subcommand, where v is equal to the VARPTR$ function with a string variable containing additional commands as the argument.*	"X" + VARPTR$ (Design2$)

* A command may be followed by a constant or variable. If a variable is used, then surround the command (and equal sign, if required) with quotation marks and add to the command the function VARPTR$ with the variable as the argument.

Partial programs (A), (B), and (C) in Figure 11.25 illustrate the use of the DRAW statement to instruct the PC to draw three simple figures — a bicycle wheel, a sailboat, and a flower.

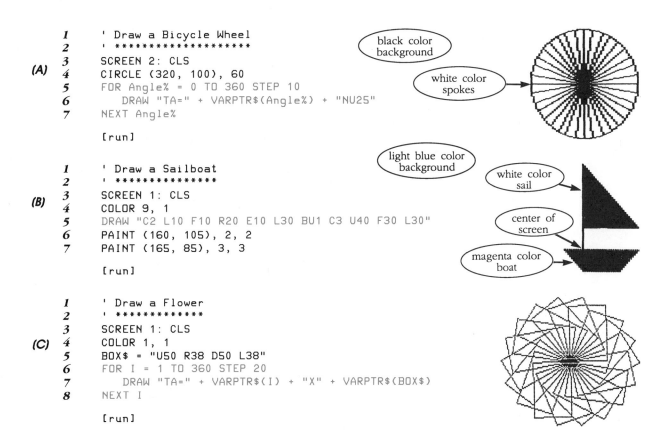

```
     1    ' Draw a Bicycle Wheel
     2    ' *******************
(A)  3    SCREEN 2: CLS
     4    CIRCLE (320, 100), 60
     5    FOR Angle% = 0 TO 360 STEP 10
     6       DRAW "TA=" + VARPTR$(Angle%) + "NU25"
     7    NEXT Angle%

          [run]
```

```
     1    ' Draw a Sailboat
     2    ' **************
(B)  3    SCREEN 1: CLS
     4    COLOR 9, 1
     5    DRAW "C2 L10 F10 R20 E10 L30 BU1 C3 U40 F30 L30"
     6    PAINT (160, 105), 2, 2
     7    PAINT (165, 85), 3, 3

          [run]
```

```
     1    ' Draw a Flower
     2    ' *************
(C)  3    SCREEN 1: CLS
     4    COLOR 1, 1
     5    BOX$ = "U50 R38 D50 L38"
     6    FOR I = 1 TO 360 STEP 20
     7       DRAW "TA=" + VARPTR$(I) + "X" + VARPTR$(BOX$)
     8    NEXT I

          [run]
```

FIGURE 11.25

Examples of the DRAW *statement.*

Partial program (A) in Figure 11.25 uses the DRAW statement in the high-resolution graphics mode to draw the bicycle wheel shown to the right of the program. Line 4 draws the rim with a center at (320, 100) and a radius of 60 points. The For loop (lines 5 through 7) draws the spokes. The loop variable Angle% starts at 0 and steps by 10 until it reaches 360. Each time through the loop, the TA command in line 6 causes the PC to rotate counterclockwise the direction of the next line drawn. Because we want to use the variable Angle%, rather than a constant, with the TA command, it is required that we use the VARPTR$ function. Note that the ratio of the length of a spoke to the radius of the circle is equal to 5/12. This ratio is required because the screen does not have the same number of rows (200) as columns (640).

Partial program (B) in Figure 11.25 uses the DRAW statement in medium resolution to draw a sailboat on a light blue background. The boat is drawn first, then the sail. The color of the boat is magenta, and the sail is white. The 11 commands in the string expression of the DRAW statement in line 5 do this: (1) C2 — select the color magenta for the boat; (2) L10 — move and draw to the left 10; (3) F10 — move and draw down and to the right 10; (4) R20 — move and draw right 20; (5) E10 — move and draw up and to the right 10; (6) L30 — move and draw left 30; (7) BU1 — move up one row; (8) C3 — select the color white for the sail; (9) U40 — draw and move up 40; (10) F30 — draw and move down and to the right 30; (11) L30 — move and draw to the left 30.

Two important points to remember about partial program (B): First, prior to the DRAW statement, the last point referenced is the center of the screen. Hence, the second command moves and draws a line 10 columns to the left of the center. Second, command 7 (BU1) is required so the sail does not intersect the boat. If the sail intersects the boat, the color magenta used in line 7 to paint the boat would leak out and would cover the entire screen except for the sail.

Partial program (C) in Figure 11.25 uses the DRAW statement in medium resolution to draw the flower shown to the right of the program. This program rotates a box about a central point, thereby producing the flower.

The WINDOW Statement

The WINDOW statement redefines the coordinates of the screen. In both medium resolution and high resolution, the physical coordinates are such that the upper left corner is the origin (0, 0) and the coordinate system extends down and to the right. This is called the **physical coordinate system**.

The WINDOW statement allows you to draw graphs and other objects in a different coordinate space called the **world coordinate system**. Once the WINDOW statement modifies the coordinate system, subsequent figures are scaled to the new system. Quick-BASIC automatically converts the world coordinates into the normal physical coordinates so the figure can be displayed on the screen.

The general form of the WINDOW statement is given in Table 11.17.

TABLE 11.17   The WINDOW Statement

General Form: WINDOW $(x_1, y_1) - (x_2, y_2)$

or

WINDOW SCREEN $(x_1, y_1) - (x_2, y_2)$

where **(x_1, y_1)** are the upper left coordinates and **(x_2, y_2)** are the lower right coordinates of the screen, as described below.

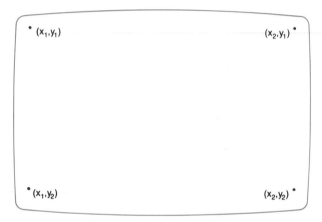

Active window coordinates are mapped onto any viewports subsequently opened by the VIEW statement.

If the SCREEN parameter is not included in the WINDOW statement, then the screen is the normal Cartesian coordinate system, with x increasing to the right and y increasing upward. Furthermore, if the x and y values have the same magnitude, then the origin (0, 0) of the newly defined coordinate system is at the center of the screen. If the SCREEN parameter is included, then the coordinates are not inverted, and y values increase downward from the origin.

Purpose: Redefines the coordinates of the viewport. Allows one to ''zoom'' and ''pan'' a figure. Subsequent PSET, PRESET, LINE, and CIRCLE statements reference the new coordinate system.

Examples: WINDOW (-1, 1)-(1, - 1)
WINDOW (-4, 4)-(4, -4)
WINDOW (0, 9)-(10, 0)
WINDOW SCREEN (0, 0)-(10, 9)

Notes: 1. All possible pairs of x and y are valid. The only restriction is that x_1 cannot equal x_2 and y_1 cannot equal y_2. The SCREEN or WINDOW statements, with no parameters, return the screen to its normal physical coordinates with the origin (0, 0) at the upper left corner.

2. The DRAW statement always references the physical coordinates of the screen.

Figure 11.26 illustrates the view of the graph of the function y = x² through the various WINDOW statements in Table 11.17. Study Figure 11.26 closely. Larger value coordinates tend to miniaturize the figure, as in (B), while smaller value coordinates force clipping and only a portion of the figure to be displayed and magnified as in (C) and (D).

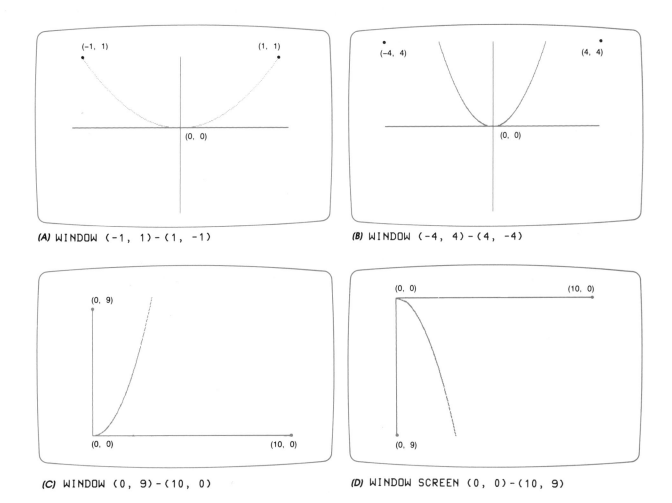

(A) WINDOW (-1, 1)-(1, -1)

(B) WINDOW (-4, 4)-(4, -4)

(C) WINDOW (0, 9)-(10, 0)

(D) WINDOW SCREEN (0, 0)-(10, 9)

FIGURE 11.26

Viewing the graph of the function y = x² through different window coordinates

See the partial program in Figure 11.27 on page 473 for an example of how to graph a function, such as y = x² using a For loop and the PSET statement. To display the screens in Figure 11.26, modify Figure 11.27 by deleting line 7, increasing the non-zero coordinates in lines 8 and 9 by a factor of 10, and increasing the limit parameter in line 10 by a factor of 10. Finally, execute the program with the different WINDOW statements shown in Figure 11.26.

The PMAP and POINT Functions

The PMAP and POINT functions are useful for determining screen characteristics when the WINDOW statement is used to change the coordinate system of the screen.

The PMAP function maps the specified physical coordinate to a world coordinate, or a specified world coordinate to a physical coordinate. That is, you can determine the physical coordinate that corresponds to a world coordinate, and vice versa.

The general form of the PMAP function is

numeric variable = PMAP(c, n)

where c is the x or y coordinate of the point that is to be mapped from one coordinate system to the other, and n is in the range 0 to 3. The descriptions of the permissible values of n are given in Table 11.18.

TABLE 11.18   Descriptions of the Permissible Values for n for the PMAP Function

VALUE OF n	DESCRIPTION
0	Returns the physical coordinate that corresponds to the world coordinate x.
1	Returns the physical coordinate that corresponds to the world coordinate y.
2	Returns the world coordinate that corresponds to the physical coordinate x.
3	Returns the world coordinate that corresponds to the physical coordinate y.

The POINT function has two general forms, as follows:

numeric variable = POINT(x, y)

or

numeric variable = POINT(n)

For the first general form, the PC returns the foreground color attribute of the point (x, y). If a WINDOW statement is active, then the point refers to the world coordinates.

The second general form returns the x or y coordinate of the last point referenced. The descriptions of the permissible values of n are given in Table 11.19.

TABLE 11.19   Descriptions of the Permissible Values for n for the POINT Function

VALUE OF n	DESCRIPTION
0	Returns the physical x coordinate of the last point referenced.
1	Returns the physical y coordinate of the last point referenced.
2	Returns the world x coordinate that corresponds to the last point referenced (physical x coordinate if no WINDOW statement is active).
3	Returns the world y coordinate that corresponds to the last point referenced (physical y coordinate if no WINDOW statement is active).

The VIEW Statement

The VIEW statement defines a viewport, or rectangular subset of the screen, onto which figures can be displayed. The active window coordinates are mapped onto the viewport. Subsequent figures drawn in the viewport are scaled to the window coordinates. The general form of the VIEW statement is given in Table 11.20.

TABLE 11.20	The VIEW Statement

General Form: VIEW $(x_1, y_1) - (x_2, y_2)$, color, boundary

or

VIEW SCREEN $(x_1, y_1) - (x_2, y_2)$, color, boundary

where (x_1, y_1) are the upper left and (x_2, y_2) are the lower right coordinates of the viewport; (the coordinates must be defined in terms of the actual physical coordinates of the screen;)

color is a number (0 to 3 for medium resolution and 0 or 1 for high resolution) which corresponds to a color used to paint the viewport; and

boundary is a number (0 to 3 for medium resolution and 0 or 1 for high resolution) which corresponds to a color used to draw a boundary around the viewport. If the SCREEN parameter is omitted, all points are relative to the viewport; otherwise, they are absolute.

Purpose: Defines a viewport, or rectangular subset of the screen, onto which figures can be displayed. The VIEW statement causes subsequent figures to be scaled to fit the viewport.

Examples:
```
VIEW (75, 75) - (200, 100), 2, 3
VIEW (100, 100) - (150, 150)
VIEW SCREEN (25, 50) - (100, 150)
```

Notes:
1. Only one viewport is active at a time. The CLS statement only clears the active viewport. Initial execution or the execution of a SCREEN statement disable the viewports. VIEW with no parameters defines the entire screen as the viewport.
2. A viewport is scaled according to the most recently executed WINDOW statement.

FIGURE 11.27
Multiple viewports.

Consider the partial program in Figure 11.27 and the results displayed from its execution. Line 4 selects the medium-resolution graphics mode and clears the output screen. Line 5 colors the screen background light blue and selects palette 0.

```
1    ' The Graph of y = x ^ 2 Between x = -1
2    ' and x = 1 Drawn in a Secondary Viewport
3    ' ******************************************
4    SCREEN 1: CLS
5    COLOR 9, 0
6    WINDOW (-1, 1)-(1, -1)
7    VIEW (100, 50)-(250, 150), 1, 3
8    LINE (-1, 0)-(1, 0), 2
9    LINE (0, 1)-(0, -1), 2
10   FOR X = -1 TO 1 STEP .01
11       PSET (X, X * X)
12   NEXT X

[run]
```

The WINDOW statement in line 6 redefines the coordinates of the screen. The new coordinate system has its origin (0, 0) exactly in the middle of the screen, with both the x axis and y axis extending from −1 to 1. The screen represents the Cartesian coordinate system magnified near the origin.

Line 7 of the partial program in Figure 11.27 defines and activates a second viewport with upper left coordinates of (100, 50) and lower right coordinates of (250, 150). These coordinates are not based on the coordinate system established by the WINDOW statement in line 6. Instead they relate to the original coordinate system, where the origin is at the upper left corner. However, except for its being scaled down, the coordinate system in the viewport is identical to the one defined by the WINDOW statement in line 6. The viewport has a blue background.

Because only one viewport is active at a time, lines 8 and 9 draw red lines representing the x and y axes within the second viewport defined by line 7. The For loop (lines 10 through 12) graphs the equation $y = x^2$ between $x = -1$ and $x = 1$, with a point plotted every one-hundredth of one unit. The points making up the graph are colored red.

The GET and PUT Statements for Graphics

The GET and PUT statements are used for high-speed object motion. With these two statements, you can save and recall the contents of any rectangle on the screen. The activity of saving and recalling images in medium or high resolution can be very useful for producing high-quality computer animation.

The GET statement reads the colors of the points in the specified area of the screen into an array. The PUT statement writes the colors of the points in the array onto an area of the screen. The idea behind these two statements is that you can instruct the PC to draw a figure on the screen, use the GET statement to store the figure in a numeric array, then move the figure from one location to another with the PUT statement. The general forms of the GET and PUT statements are given in Tables 11.21 and 11.22.

TABLE 11.21 The GET Statement for Graphics

General Form:	GET $(x_1, y_1) - (x_2, y_2)$, array name
	where (x_1, y_1) and (x_2, y_2) are the opposite coordinates of a rectangle on the screen (the coordinates may be absolute or relative;) and
	array name is the name of a numeric array into which the GET statement reads the information about the points in the specified area.
Purpose:	Reads the colors of the points in the specified area on the screen into an array.
Examples:	GET (250, 50) - (300, 100), Animation1
	GET (0, 0) - (319, 199), Screen1%
	GET (0, 100) - (160, 199), Animation2
Note:	The required size of the array in bytes is as follows:
	4 + H * INT((W * bits + 7) / 8)
	where **H** is the height (number of rows) of the rectangle;
	W is the width (number of columns) of the rectangle; and
	bits is 2 in medium resolution and 1 in high resolution. Recall that there are 2 bytes per element in an integer array; 4 bytes per element in a single-precision array; and 8 bytes per element in a double-precision array.

TABLE 11.22   The PUT Statement for Graphics

General Form: PUT (x, y), array name, action

where **(x, y)** are the coordinates of the top left corner of the rectangular area on the screen, where the pixel pattern in **array name** is displayed; and **action** specifies the manner in which the pixel pattern is displayed on the existing screen background. The action parameter may be one of the following:

PSET   – Puts the pixel pattern on the screen exactly as defined in array name.

PRESET – Puts the inverse pixel pattern in array name (negative image) on the screen.

AND   – Turns "on" those pixels that are both "on" in array name and "on" on the screen.

OR   – Superimposes the pixel pattern in array name onto the existing pattern on the screen.

XOR   – Turns "on" those pixels that are "on" in array name and "off" on the screen or "off" in array name and "on" on the screen. (If the action parameter is not used, then XOR is the default value.)

Purpose: Writes the colors of the points in the array onto an area of the screen.

Examples:
```
PUT (25, 50) - (75, 100), Animation1
PUT (0, 0) - (220, 99), Screen1%, XOR
PUT (0, 50) - (60, 199), Animation2, OR
PUT (160, 100) - (319, 199), Array1, PSET
```

With the PUT statement, the action parameter XOR is the most interesting because if you use it twice in succession, the original scene within the specified area will reappear. This is critical to computer animation when you are required to move an object across the screen. Before you can move an image to a new location on the screen, you must return the current location to its old scene. Two successive PUTs with the XOR action parameter and a slight time delay in between gives us the desired action.

Here is a step-by-step algorithm for moving an object across the screen:

1. Draw the desired image on the screen.
2. Use the GET statement to store the image into an array.
3. Clear the screen.
4. Draw background figures that will remain constant during the animation.
5. Establish a For loop that determines the coordinates at which the image is to appear. Within the loop, do the following:
   a. Use the PUT statement with the action parameter XOR to put the image at the desired location.
   b. Use a For loop to delay execution of the next statement so that the figure may be seen.
   c. Use the PUT statement with the action parameter XOR to erase the image at the current location.

Consider the animation of a bus traveling on a highway, right to left, produced in the medium-resolution graphics mode by the partial program in Figure 11.28. Lines 7 through 13 plot the bus in the upper left corner of the screen. Line 15 stores the points within the rectangle defined by the coordinates (26, 40) and (71, 53) into the integer array Bus%.

The formula given in Table 11.21 is used to determine the size of BUS%. For example, from lines 7 through 11 it can be determined that the minimum size rectangle that includes the bus (plus the wheels) is $71 - 26 + 1 = 46$ points wide and $53 - 40 + 1 = 14$ points high. Furthermore, we are working in medium resolution, which requires 2 bits per point. Hence, the formula after substitution looks like this:

$$4 + 14 * INT((46 * 2 + 7) / 8) = 172$$

With an integer array, divide the byte requirement by 2. The result is that 86 elements are required in Bus%.

Lines 17 through 23 of the partial program in Figure 11.28 clear the screen, display a message, and then draw the highway and telephone poles. Finally, lines 25 through 31 animate the bus driving on the highway over and over again until the user presses any key on the keyboard.

The first PUT statement (line 27) in the For loop plots the bus to the far right and just above the highway. Line 28 delays the next PUT statement (line 29) for a fraction of a second. This second PUT statement erases the bus plotted by line 27. The next time line 27 is executed, it plots the bus 50 points to the left. This plotting and erasing continues until the bus is near the left side of the screen. At this point, the Do-While loop starts the bus back at the right side of the screen. This animation continues until the user intervenes.

FIGURE 11.28

Computer animation in the medium-resolution graphics mode of a bus traveling down a highway, right to left.

```
1    ' Animating a Moving Bus
2    '************************
3    DIM Bus%(1 TO 86)
4    CLS : SCREEN 1
5    COLOR 0, 0
6    '******** Draw Bus Body ********
7    LINE (31, 40)-(71, 50), 2, BF
8    LINE (26, 45)-(31, 50), 2, BF
9    '******* Draw Bus Wheels *******
10   CIRCLE (29, 50), 3, 3
11   CIRCLE (66, 50), 3, 3
12   PAINT (29, 50), 3, 3
13   PAINT (66, 50), 3, 3
14   '******* Store Bus Image *******
15   GET (26, 40)-(71, 53), Bus%
16   '*** Draw Highway with Telephone Poles ***
17   CLS
18   LOCATE 15, 7: PRINT "Press any key to stop bus..."
19   LINE (0, 100)-(319, 100), 2
20   FOR Col% = 5 TO 319 STEP 40
21      LINE (Col%, 100)-(Col%, 85)
22      LINE (Col% - 3, 88)-(Col% + 2, 88)
23   NEXT Col%
24   ' ********* Animate Bus *********
25   DO WHILE INKEY$ = ""
26      FOR Animation% = 250 TO 0 STEP -50
27         PUT (Animation%, 87), Bus%, XOR
28            FOR Time.Delay = 1 TO 500: NEXT Time.Delay
29         PUT (Animation%, 87), Bus%, XOR
30      NEXT Animation%
31   LOOP

[run]
```

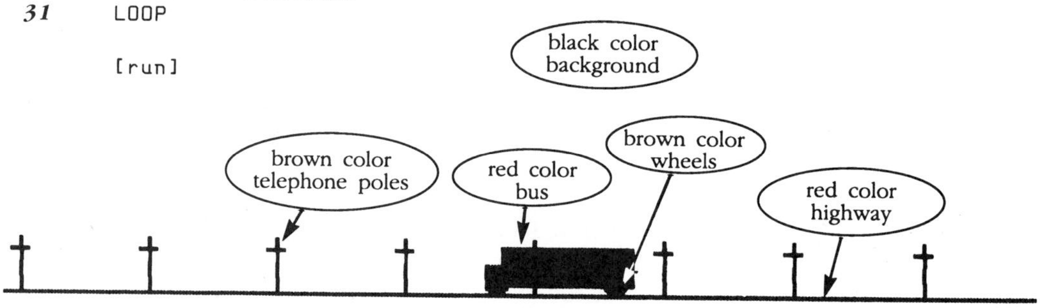

Press any key to stop bus...

11.4   SOUND AND MUSIC

A speaker is located toward the front of the system unit of the PC. Though this speaker is small, it is capable of producing a variety of sounds. For example, in Chapter 6 we used the BEEP statement to produce a high-pitched sound and draw the user's attention to data-entry errors. In this section, we explore two additional statements that can activate the speaker under program control. They are the SOUND and PLAY statements.

The SOUND Statement

The SOUND statement is used to create a sound of variable frequency and duration. The general form of the SOUND statement is given in Table 11.23.

TABLE 11.23   The SOUND Statement

General Form:	SOUND frequency, duration
	where **frequency** is a numeric expression between 37 and 32767; and **duration** is a numeric expression in the range 0 to 65535. The expression represents the duration in clock ticks, and there are 18.2 clock ticks per second. A duration of zero turns off the current sound.
Purpose:	To generate sound through the speaker.
Examples:	SOUND 1000, 85 SOUND 32767, 0 SOUND Freq, Dur
Note:	The frequency is measured in hertz (cycles per second).

The partial program in Figure 11.29 illustrates the use of the SOUND statement to generate a siren sound. Line 3 changes the width to 40 characters and clears the output screen. Line 4 selects a blinking, red foreground on a black background. Lines 5 and 6 display messages. The Do-While loop (lines 7 through 11) executes until the user presses a key on the keyboard.

The For loop (lines 8 through 10) in the partial program in Figure 11.29 generates a siren-like sound, using the PC's speaker. Each time through the For loop, the frequency increases until it reaches 1,100 hertz (cycles per second).

FIGURE 11.29

Generating a siren sound.

```
1    ' Using the Speaker as a Siren
2    ' ****************************
3    WIDTH 40
4    COLOR 20, 0
5    LOCATE 13, 8: PRINT "EMERGENCY!!  EMERGENCY!!"
6    LOCATE 24, 4: PRINT "Press any key to stop the siren...";
7    DO WHILE INKEY$ = ""
8       FOR Freq% = 500 TO 1100 STEP 20
9          SOUND Freq%, .05
10      NEXT Freq%
11   LOOP
12   WIDTH 80: COLOR 7, 0

[run]
```

The PLAY Statement

The PLAY statement converts your PC into a piano. Like the DRAW statement, the PLAY statement instructs the PC to play music that is defined by a string expression. The string is made up of a series of easy-to-code commands. (See Table 11.25.) The music you compose may be as simple as a single note or as complex as the counterpoint in Bach or a symphony by Beethoven. The general form of the PLAY statement is shown in Table 11.24.

Example 1 in Table 11.24 plays the C scale. The greater than sign (>) causes the PC to climb to the next octave. The less than sign (<) has the opposite effect. Example 2 plays the song "Stepping Up Stepping Down." The L command establishes the length of all subsequent notes played. The command E2 changes the length only for that note.

Example 3 in Table 11.24 plays the tune definition assigned to Music$. Example 4 illustrates how you can instruct the PC to execute a series of subcommands. This can be useful when you want to play a chorus after each bridge.

TABLE 11.24   The PLAY Statement

General Form: PLAY string expression

where **string expression** is a command or series of commands, as described in Table 11.25.

Purpose: Plays music as specified in the string expression.

Examples:
1. PLAY "C D E F G A B >C C< B A G F E D C"
2. PLAY "L4 C D E2 L4 E D L2 C D E C"
3. PLAY Music$
4. PLAY "L =" + VARPTR$(Length) + "X" + VARPTR$(Chorus$)
   PLAY "X" + VARPTR$(Bridge$) + "X" + VARPTR$(Chorus$)

Note: A PLAY command, such as L or E, may be followed by a constant or variable. If a variable is used, then surround the command (and equal sign, if required) with quotation marks and add to the command the function VARPTR$ with the variable as the argument. (See Example 4.)

As a sample program that uses the PLAY statement, consider the partial program in Figure 11.30. This program plays the tune "Twinkle Twinkle Little Star" over and over again until the user presses a key on the keyboard. Both the chorus and the bridge are defined prior to the PLAY statement in lines 6 and 8. In lines 11 through 13, the PLAY statement uses the X command to reference the subcommands assigned to Chorus$ and Bridge$.

FIGURE 11.30

Playing a tune with the PC.

```
 1    ' Twinkle Twinkle Little Star
 2    ' ***************************
 3    CLS
 4    LOCATE 13, 25: PRINT "Press any key to stop the song..."
 5    ' ****** Define Chorus ******
 6    Chorus$ = "L4 C C G G A A L2 G L4 F F E E D D L2 C"
 7    ' ****** Define Bridge ******
 8    Bridge$ = "L4 G G F F E E L2 D L4 G G F F E E L2 D"
 9    ' ******** Play Song ********
10    DO WHILE INKEY$ = ""
11        PLAY "X" + VARPTR$(Chorus$)
12        PLAY "X" + VARPTR$(Bridge$)
13        PLAY "X" + VARPTR$(Chorus$)
14    LOOP

      [run]
```

TABLE 11.25 PLAY Commands

COMMAND	FUNCTION	EXAMPLES
A to G with optional #, +, or –	Plays the specified note in the current octave. A number sign (#) or plus sign (+) appended to the letter indicates a sharp; a minus sign (–) indicates a flat.	C A+ D-
On	Sets the octave for the notes that follow. There are 7 octaves, numbered 0 to 6. Octave 4 is the default. Each octave goes from C to B, and octave 3 starts with middle C.	O2
>n or <n	The greater than sign (>) instructs the PC to climb to the next octave and play note n. The less than sign (<) lowers the octave by 1. Either sign affects all notes that follow.	>C <D-
Nn	Plays note n, where n ranges from 0 to 84. This serves as an alternative to using the O command followed by the note name. N0 is a "rest."	N27 N0
Ln	Sets the length of the notes that follow. The parameter n can range from 1 to 64. The PC interprets n as 1/n. The length of a note may also follow the note. For example, C4 is the same as L4C.	L4 L=S;
Pn	Pause. The parameter n can range from 1 to 64. As with the L command, the PC interprets n as 1/n.	P16 P=R;
.	Dot. Placed after a note, the dot causes the note to be played as a dotted note. Multiple dots are valid.	A. C+..
Tn	Tempo. Defines the number of quarter notes per minute. The parameter n can range from 32 to 255. The default is 120.	T110 T=NU;
MF	Music foreground. The music created by the SOUND or PLAY statement runs in the foreground. The program is put into a wait state until the music statement is finished. A note does not start until the previous note is finished. MF is the default.	MF
MB	Music background. The music created by the SOUND or PLAY statement runs in the background. That is, the BASIC program continues to execute while the music plays in the background.	MB
ML	Music legato. Each note that follows plays the full period set by L.	ML
MN	Music normal. Each note that follows plays 7/8 of the time specified by L. Default between MN, ML, and MS.	MN
MS	Music staccato. Each note that follows plays 3/4 of the time specified by L.	MS
"X" + v	Executes a subcommand, where v is equal to the VARPTR$ function with a string variable that contains additional commands as the argument.	"X" + VARPTR$ (Music$)

11.5   WHAT YOU SHOULD KNOW

1. The PC provides five graphics modes — text, medium resolution, high resolution, enhanced resolution, and very high resolution.

2. When you enter QuickBASIC, the PC is in the text mode. In this mode, the output screen has 25 lines (rows) of 80 columns each. You can switch to the 40-column display by using the WIDTH statement.

3. The SCREEN statement can be used to switch between the different graphics modes. The SCREEN statement can also be used in the text mode to do simple animation through the use of the active and visual pages.

4. In the medium-resolution graphics mode, the screen is divided into 200 rows and 320 columns. In the high-resolution graphics mode, the screen is divided into 200 rows and 640 columns. Each intersection of a column and row defines a point (pixel), which can be turned on or off.

5. The text mode is often used to create logos and simple animations. The medium-resolution graphics mode is used to plot points, draw figures, and create sophisticated animated designs. The high-resolution graphics mode allows you to draw very detailed designs.

6. In the text mode, you can produce interesting and useful graphics with the PRINT and PRINT USING statements, the CHR$ function, and the ASCII character set.

7. If you have a color monitor and a color/graphics adaptor, you can enhance your displays in the text and medium-resolution graphics modes with a variety of colors. With high resolution, figures can be displayed only in black and white or green or amber.

8. In the text mode, the COLOR statement sets the color for the foreground, background, and border. The foreground and border can be set to 16 different colors and the background to eight colors. By adding the number 16 to the foreground color number, all characters displayed will blink.

9. In the text mode, a CLS statement should follow the COLOR statement to ensure the color takes effect immediately over the entire screen.

10. To send graphics designs to the printer, you must have one that emulates the IBM graphics printer. You must also enter the system command GRAPHICS before you enter QuickBASIC.

11. In both medium resolution and high resolution, you plot points and draw lines by instructing the PC to turn on pixels. Lines and curves are defined in the form of coordinates, such as (x, y), where x is the column and y is the row. Each pixel has a unique set of coordinates.

12. There are two ways to indicate the coordinates of a point: absolute form and relative form.

13. The COLOR statement for medium resolution allows you to select from 16 different background colors and 1 of 2 palettes of colors for the foreground. Each palette carries four colors, numbered 0 through 3.

14. The PSET and PRESET statements are used to turn individual points (pixels) on or off. The PC turns off a point by assigning it the background color.

15. The LINE statement is used to draw lines and boxes in a color selected off the active palette. When the LINE statement is used to draw a box, you can instruct the PC to fill the box with the color selected off the active palette. In high resolution, the active palette has no meaning.

16. The CIRCLE statement is used to draw circles, ellipses, arcs, and wedges.

17. The PAINT statement can be used to paint an enclosed area. In medium resolution, the colors on the active palette are available. In high resolution, only black and white are available.
18. The PAINT statement can also be used to tile an enclosed area on the screen. The tile pattern is based on the binary value of the tile mask. The CHR$ function is used to establish the tile mask in a program.
19. The DRAW statement is used to draw complicated objects on the basis of commands assigned to a string expression.
20. The normal coordinates of the screen are called physical coordinates. The WINDOW statement can be used to redefine the coordinates into what are called world coordinates. Any viewport subsequently opened by the VIEW statement is defined in terms of the world coordinates.
21. Depending on the argument, the PMAP and POINT functions return either physical or world coordinates.
22. The GET and PUT statements are used for high-speed object motion. These statements can be very useful in producing high-quality computer animation.
23. The SOUND statement generates sound through the speaker.
24. The PLAY statement converts your PC into a piano. The music you compose in the form of a string expression may be as simple as a single note or as complex as the counterpoint in Bach or a symphony by Beethoven.

11.6 TEST YOUR BASIC SKILLS (Even-numbered answers are in Appendix E)

1. Consider the four valid programs below. What is displayed if each is executed?

a.
```
' Exercise 11.1a
SCREEN 2: CLS
WINDOW (-100, 100)-(100, -100)
LINE (-100, 0)-(100, 0)
LINE (0, 100)-(0, -100)
FOR X% = -50 TO 50 STEP 1
    Y% = X% + 8
    PSET (X%, Y%)
NEXT X%
END
```

b.
```
' Exercise 11.1b
SCREEN 1: CLS
COLOR 1, 0
WINDOW (-10, 10)-(10, -10)
LINE (-10, 0)-(10, 0)
LINE (0, 10)-(0, -10)
FOR X% = 1 TO 7
    CIRCLE (0, 0), X%, 2
NEXT X%
END
```

c.
```
' Exercise 11.1c
CLS
WIDTH 40
COL = 2
FOR COUNT = 1 TO 21 STEP 2
    PRINT TAB(COL);
    FOR STARS = 1 TO COUNT
        PRINT "*";
    NEXT STARS
    PRINT
    COL = COL + 1
NEXT COUNT
END
```

```
d. ' Exercise 11.1d
   CLS
   WIDTH 80
   INPUT "ENTER THE ROW & COLUMN FOR UPPER LEFT CORNER "; ROW, COL
   INPUT "ENTER THE WIDTH AND HEIGHT OF THE BOX "; BWIDTH, HEIGHT
   CLS
   LOCATE ROW, COL
   PRINT "/";
   FOR COUNT = 1 TO (BWIDTH - 2)
      PRINT "*";
   NEXT COUNT
   PRINT "\"
   FOR COUNT = 1 TO HEIGHT
      PRINT TAB(COL); "¦"; TAB(COL + BWIDTH - 1); "¦"
   NEXT COUNT
   PRINT TAB(COL); "\";
   FOR COUNT = 1 TO (BWIDTH - 2)
      PRINT "*";
   NEXT COUNT
   PRINT "/"
   END
```

2. Use PSET, LINE, and CIRCLE statements to draw the following figures. Assume that the PC is in the medium-resolution graphics mode.

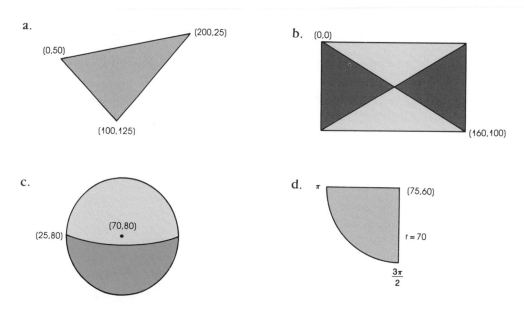

3. Use the DRAW statement to draw the figures in 2a and 2b. Use the scale factor to double the size of each figure.

4. Assume you are working with a PC that has a color/graphics adaptor and color monitor. Describe the appearance of the screen after each of the following is executed:

a. SCREEN 0 : COLOR 4, 1, 0 : CLS

b. SCREEN 1 : COLOR 0, 0 : CLS

5. Describe the display of characters following the execution of a COLOR statement with a foreground color number of 20 in the text mode.

6. Fill in the following:

   a. In the medium- and high-resolution graphics modes, the intersection of a row and column is called a _____ or _____.

   b. If you plan to print a graphics display, you must enter the system command _____ before entering QuickBASIC.

   c. If you enter WIDTH _____ in the medium-resolution graphics mode, the PC will switch to the high-resolution graphics mode.

   d. Use the _____ function to describe a tile pattern for the PAINT statement.

   e. To draw a wedge with the CIRCLE statement, add a _____ before the start and end parameters.

   f. The _____ and _____ statements are used in the medium- and high-resolution graphics modes to produce high-quality computer animation.

   g. There are _____ bytes per element in an integer array; _____ bytes per element in a single-precision array; and _____ bytes per element in a double-precision array.

7. Consider the following valid program below and answer these three questions:

   a. What is displayed if this program is executed?

   b. What are the foreground, background, and border colors that are due to line 3?

   c. What is the purpose of the second to the last line?

```
' Exercise 11.7
INPUT "Density (0 to 1) ===> ", Density
COLOR 4, 0, 0: CLS
WIDTH 40
RANDOMIZE TIMER
FOR Row% = 1 TO 24
   FOR Col% = 1 TO 40
      IF RND <= Density THEN
         LOCATE Row%, Col%
         PRINT CHR$(219);
      END IF
   NEXT Col%
NEXT Row%
LOCATE 25, 1
INPUT "Press the Enter key to quit...", Control$
COLOR 7, 0, 0: WIDTH 80
END
```

8. Write a program that draws the following three-dimensional box in the medium-resolution graphics mode, using the color brown. Color the background blue and activate palette 0. Paint the face of the figure red, the side brown, and the top green.

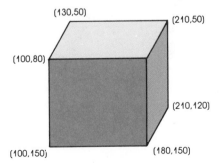

(130,50)   (210,50)

(100,80)

(210,120)

(100,150)   (180,150)

9. Evaluate each of the following. Assume that the statements are executed in the high-resolution graphics mode.

    a. PSET (320, 100)
    b. GET (23, 46) - (75, 80), A%
    c. PUT (72, 96) - (125, 130), A%
    d. CIRCLE (50, 50), 15,, -3, -4
    e. CIRCLE (320, 160), 30,,,, 5/8
    f. LINE - (40, 30)
    g. LINE (0, 0) - (160, 100)
    h. DRAW "BM320,160 NR45 D45"
    i. SOUND 200, .03
    j. PLAY "XMUSIC$;"

10. Use the PRINT statement, the CHR$ function, and ASCII code 219 to draw a box with the following characteristics in the text mode. Assume that the screen is set to the 40-column display mode.

    a. Horizontal lines at rows 4 and 22.
    b. Vertical lines at columns 9 and 32.

11. Write a program that uses the WINDOW statement with coordinates $(-25, 25) - (25, -25)$ in the high-resolution graphics mode to establish the Cartesian coordinate system. Draw the x and y axes and the graph of the equation $y = 3x + 2$ between $x = 20$ and $x = -20$. Plot points, using the PSET statement every 0.01 units.

12. Identify each of the following PLAY commands:

    a. A-   b. L8   c. >C   d. "X" + VARPTR$(M$)   e. NO
    f. T100   g. P8   h. MS   i. ML   j. O3

13. Identify each of the following DRAW commands:

    a. BM 10, 20   b. M+3, +5   c. C1   d. F5   e. E20
    f. A3   g. U75   h. H5   i. L20   j. NL20

14. With respect to the PUT statement, define the action parameters PSET, AND, and XOR.

15. Write a program that constructs the following international logo of a child using a collection of simple overlapping primitives, such as circles and rectangles. For extra credit, also write programs to draw the international logos of a man and a woman.

Man Logo   Child Logo   Woman Logo

16. Determine the required size for the integer array Animation% in the following GET statement. Assume that the statement is executed in the high-resolution graphics mode.

    GET (20, 30) - (80, 100), Animation%

17. Write a program that displays the following Olympic flag with the five interlocking rings on a white background. The rings are blue, black, red, yellow, and green, respectively, in color. As an option, have the program play a few bars of the Olympic theme song.

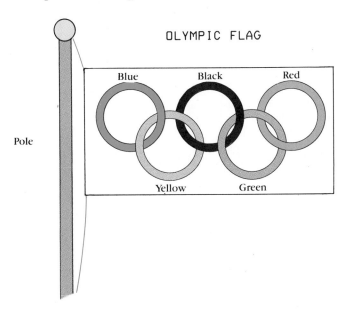

18. Sketch the actions of the following partial program. Also specify the colors displayed.

a.
```
KEY OFF
SCREEN 1, 0
COLOR 1, 0
CLS
PSET (0, 0)
FOR K = 0 to 199
    PSET STEP(K, K)
NEXT K
```

b.
```
RANDOMIZE TIMER
KEY OFF
SCREEN 1, 0
COLOR 1, 0
FOR K = 1 TO 100
    X = 319 * RND
    Y = 199 * RND
    Z = 3 * RND
    IF Z < 1 THEN
        Z = 1
    END IF
    PSET (X, Y), Z
NEXT K
```

19. Write a program that illustrates the additive effects of the primary colors of red (R), green (G), and blue (B). Initially, three circles are filled respectively with the three aforementioned colors. Via animation, move and superimpose the three circles in such a manner as to blend and display the colors of white (W), magenta (M), cyan (C), and yellow (Y) (or brown on some PC monitors).

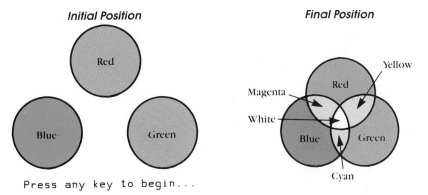

20. Sketch the display of following partial programs.

    a.
    ```
    SCREEN 1: CLS
    WINDOW (0, 0)-(60, 60)
    CIRCLE (15, 50), 5
    ' **************************
    VIEW (180, 60)-(250, 130), , 3
    CIRCLE (15, 50), 5
    ```

    b.
    ```
    SCREEN 1: CLS
    COLOR 1, 0
    WINDOW (60, 60)-(350, 200)
    LINE (60, 70)-(350, 200), , B
    CALL DRAW.CIRCLE
    VIEW (30, 30)-(150, 100), 1, 3
    CALL DRAW.CIRCLE
    VIEW (180, 130)-280, 175), 1, 2
    CALL DRAW.CIRCLE

    SUB DRAW.CIRCLE
        CIRCLE (250, 150), 40, 2, , , 5 / 18
        CIRCLE (250, 150), 40, 2, , , 1
    END SUB
    ```

21. **PC Hands-On Exercise:** Enter the partial program in Figure 11.7 on page 439. Display and execute the program. Change the `PRINT USING` statement in line 5 to a `LPRINT USING` statement. (See the printer user's manual regarding the proper switch settings for displaying the USA character set.) When the printer is ready, execute the modified version of the program.

22. **PC Hands-On Exercise:** Load Program 11.3 (PRG11-3) from the Student Diskette. Change the limit value in the `FOR` statement in line 90 to 6000. Execute the program and see what happens. Try other values for the limit. Can you explain the function of this statement?

23. **PC Hands-On Exercise:** Enter the partial program in Figure 11.18 on page 459. Delete lines 9 through 13. In line 6, change the initial value to 1 and the limit value to 1000. Replace line 7 with the following:

    ```
    PSET(INT(319 * RND + 1), INT(199 * RND + 1))
    ```

    Execute the program and see what happens.

24. **PC Hands-On Exercise:** Enter the partial program in Figure 11.19 on page 460. Change the background color to 0 and the palette to 0. Add the following line after line 7:

    ```
    LINE -(100, 125) : LINE -(100, 75)
    ```

    Execute the program and see what happens.

25. **PC Hands-On Exercise:** Enter the partial program in Figure 11.20(A) on page 460. Change the background color to blue and the active palette to 1. Delete the color parameters in lines 5 through 9. Execute the program and see what happens.

26. **PC Hands-On Exercise:** Enter the partial program in Figure 11.29 on page 477. Execute the program. Now modify the initial, terminal, and step values in line 8 and the duration parameter in line 9. See if you can get the program to cause the speaker to sound more like a police-car siren.

27. **PC Hands-On Exercise:** Enter the partial program in Figure 11.30 on page 478. Execute the program and listen to it play "Twinkle Twinkle Little Star." Double the parameter following each `L` command in lines 6 and 8. Execute the program and listen to the sound. Now triple the original values and execute the program again.

11.7 BASIC PROGRAMMING PROBLEMS

1. Horizontal Bar Graph of Annual Sales for the Past Ten Years

Purpose: To become familiar with graphing in the text mode.

Problem: A graph gives the user of a report a pictorial view of the information. Consider the following problem, which has as its defined output a horizontal bar graph. The Sales Analysis Department of the PUC Company requests from the Data Processing Department a report in the form of a horizontal bar graph representing the company's annual sales trend for the ten-year period 1987 through 1996. The annual sales are as follows:

Year	Sales (in millions)	Year	Sales (in millions)
1987	$22	1992	$43
1988	26	1993	40
1989	28	1994	45
1990	35	1995	50
1991	40	1996	48

Include the following characteristics in the graph:

1. Display the bar graph horizontally in the 80-column display mode.
2. Display vertically the column that represents the years.
3. Use a series of asterisks to represent the sales for each year.
4. Mark off the horizontal axis in increments of 5, beginning with 0 and ending with 55. Each unit represents a million dollars.

(**Hint:** See Program 11.2 on page 446.)

Input Data: Use the ten-year PUC Company data shown above. The data (year and sales) for each year is in the sequential data file EX111SAL.DAT on the Student Diskette.

Output Results: The following results are displayed:

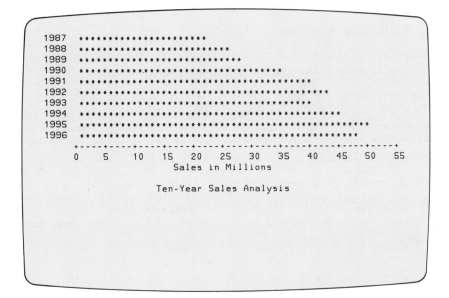

2. Graphing a Function

Purpose: To become familiar with using the PSET statement to graph a function on a world coordinate system in the high-resolution graphics mode.

Problem: Graph the function $y = 2x^3 + 6x^2 - 18x + 6$. Use a WINDOW statement with coordinates (–6, 70) – (6, –70) to define the Cartesian coordinate system with its origin at the center of the screen. Graph the function between x = –5 and x = 3. Plot points every 1/100th of one unit. Label the axes as shown in the Output Results.

(**Hint:** See the partial program in Figure 11.27 on page 473 and choose your own colors for the axes, graph, border, and background.)

Input Data: None.

Output Results: The following results are displayed:

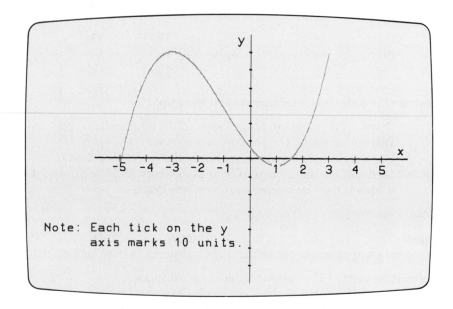

3. Animating Push-ups

Purpose: To become familiar with simple animation through the use of the GET and PUT statements in the medium-resolution graphics mode.

Problem: Draw an animation of the Mechanical Man doing push-ups. Phase 1 and Phase 2 of the animation are illustrated in Figure 11.31. Draw Phase 1 and use the GET statement to store it in an array. Do the same with Phase 2. Have the Mechanical Man do 50 push-ups by switching from one figure to another. Color the Mechanical Man's torso red and his head brown.

(**Hint:** See the partial program in Figure 11.28 on page 476).

Extra Credit: Every time the Mechanical Man completes a push-up, display this value in a counter. As the Mechanical Man approaches 50 push-ups, make him slow down and "grunt".

FIGURE 11.31

Positions of the Mechanical Man doing push-ups.

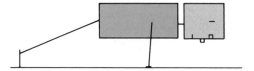

Phase 1: The Mechanical Man in position 1.

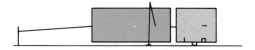

Phase 2: The Mechanical Man in position 2.

Input Data: None.

Output Results: The display of the Mechanical Man will switch between Phase 1 and Phase 2 fifty times as shown in Figure 11.31. Also, when the user presses a key, halt the display and *freeze* the screen.

4. Drawing a Design

Purpose: To become familiar with the LINE, CIRCLE, and PAINT statements.

Problem: Construct a top-down program that draws the design shown in the Output Results. Draw the design in the medium-resolution graphics mode. Use the PAINT statement to color and tile the various sections of the design.

Input Data: None.

Output Results: The following results are displayed:

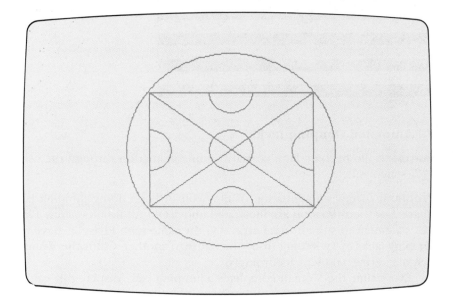

5. Playing the Musical Score "Yankee Doodle" on the PC

Purpose: To become familiar with the PLAY statement.

Problem: Obtain a song sheet of "Yankee Doodle." Use a For loop to play the song seven times, starting at octave 0 and ending at octave 6.

Input Data: None.

Output Results: The PC plays the song "Yankee Doodle" seven times, each time at a higher octave.

6. The U.S.A. Flag and the National Anthem

Purpose: To illustrate graphical concepts with music.

Problem: Display the red-white-blue U.S.A. flag with the 50 stars. The flag is to be rigid and a few bars of the National Anthem — "The Star Spangled Banner" should play in background mode. In addition, display the title: UNITED STATES OF AMERICA above the flag. As an option, display the words of the National Anthem as the music is played.

Extra Credit: Wave the flag gently (not flap).

Input Data: None.

Output Results: The following results are displayed:

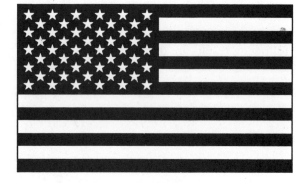

7. Animated Jumping Jacks

Purpose: To become familiar with simple animation through the use of the GET and PUT statements.

Problem: Draw an animation of the Woman Logo doing jumping jacks. Phase 1 and Phase 2 of the animation are illustrated under Output Results. Draw Phase 1 and use the GET statement to store it in an array. Do the same with Phase 2. Have the Woman do 50 jumping jacks by switching from one figure to another. Color the Woman's dress red and her face, arms, and legs accordingly.

Every time the Woman completes a jumping jack, display this value in a counter. As the Woman approaches 50 jumping jacks, make her slow down and "grunt" in a female tone.

Extra Credit: Add features to the Woman's face, such as eyes, nose, mouth, smile, frown, and so on. Also, add the following self-explanatory options: (1) Pause: halt and freeze the display on the screen, (2) Continue: the animation and display, and (3) Abort: the animation and display.

Input Data: None.

Output Results: The display of the Woman will switch between Phase 1 and Phase 2 fifty times.

Phase 1: The Woman in Position 1   *Phase 2: The Woman in Position 2*

8. RGB Color Cube

Purpose: To display colors in a three-dimensional model.

Problem: Display the RGB color cube model and the text description for each of the points in their respective colors. Assume this: x-axis represents the color blue, y-axis represents the color red, and z-axis represents the color green. The point (0,0,0) corresponds to the color black, and the point (1,1,1) corresponds to the color white.

All definable colors should lie on the cube and should be derived from the primary colors of red, green, and blue in either an additive process or from the subdivision of the large cube into smaller units and the generation of colors in a definable spectrum. Also, display the words such as Green, White, Cyan and so forth. The word Black will not be displayed for obvious reasons. (**Hint:** Use a PC with a VGA monitor. Insert the statement `Screen 9` in your program.

Extra Credit: Rotate the cube around the y-axis so the colors from the other faces are visible; or, remove the top, side, and front face of the cube to see the colors on the remaining faces.

Input Data: None.

Output Results: The results to the right are displayed preceded by the title:
`RGB COLOR CUBE`

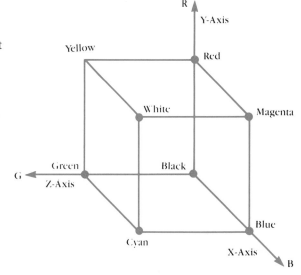

9. Pouring a Liquid

Purpose: To illustrate two- and three-dimensional transformations.

Problem: An opaque container is partially filled with some kind of liquid as shown in Phase 1 of the Output Results. The container is lifted and rotated in order to pour the liquid into another container, which is transparent, as shown in Phase 2 of the Output Results.

Input Data: None

Extra Credit: As the liquid is poured, the liquid will be seen rising in the receiving container. Use a menu to select the following variables.

1. The display of the liquid splashing in the receiving container vs. no splashing.
2. The position from where the liquid is poured; for example, if the liquid is poured by the edge of the container, a vortex occurs; if the liquid is poured by the center of the container, splashing occurs.
3. Viscosity of the liquid; for example, water vs. thick molasses vs. a cryogenic liquid vs. a molten metal.
4. Shrinkage or expansion of the receiving container due to the temperature of the liquid.
5. Type of logo appearing on the opaque container.
6. Shape of the container; for example, cylindrical shape vs. bottle shape vs. carton shape.
7. Type of sounds made when liquid is poured; for example, splashing vs. fizzing vs. bubbling.

Output Results: The following results are displayed for a variation of the problem:

Phase 1
Opaque Container

Phase 2
Transparent Container

Appendix A

Program Design Tools—Flowcharts, Pseudocode, Nassi-Schneiderman Charts, and Warnier-Orr Diagrams

The purpose of this appendix is to concentrate on preparing, using, and reading program flowcharts, pseudocode, Nassi-Schneiderman charts, and Warnier-Orr diagrams.

A.1 PROGRAM FLOWCHARTING

A **program flowchart** shows in graphic form the algorithm, the method of solution, used in a program. By depicting a procedure for arriving at a solution, a program flowchart also shows how the application or job is to be accomplished. The term *flowchart* is used throughout this appendix to mean program flowchart.

Purpose of Flowcharting

A flowchart is used by programmers and analysts for the following purposes:

1. An aid in developing the logic of a program
2. An aid in breaking the program into smaller units when the top-down or modular approach is used
3. A verification that all possible conditions have been considered in a program
4. A means of communicating with others about the program
5. A guide in coding the program
6. Documentation for the program

Flowchart Notation

Eight basic symbols are commonly used in flowcharting a program. They are given in Chapter 1, Table 1.5 on page 14, with their names and meanings and with some of the QuickBASIC statements represented by them. In a flowchart, the process, input/output, decision, terminal, connector, and predefined process symbols are connected by solid lines. These solid lines, called flowline symbols, show the direction of flow. The annotation symbol, on the other hand, is connected by a broken line to any one of the other flowchart symbols, including any of the flowline symbols.

A fundamental rule to all flowcharts concerns direction. In constructing a flowchart, start at the top (or at the left-hand corner) of a page. The flow should be top to bottom or left to right. If the flow takes any other course, arrowheads must be used. No curved or diagonal flowline symbols are ever drawn. Although arrowheads are shown in Figure A.1 and in other flowcharts throughout this book, they need not be used in these cases, because their usage is optional when flow is both left to right and top to bottom.

Inside each of the symbols, except the flowline symbols, write either English-sentence-type notation, mathematical notation or program language statements. These notations are arbitrary, and their use depends on the kind of program being flowcharted, on the experience of the person constructing the flowchart and on the standards that are used in the computer installation. One symbol or abbreviated description may represent more than one QuickBASIC statement. The annotation symbol, with comments written inside it, is optional and is used whenever additional information is desired for the sake of clarity.

The first symbol in a flowchart is usually a terminal symbol with Start written inside it. This corresponds to no QuickBASIC *statement* but is used solely to provide aid in finding the beginning point to a person who is unfamiliar with the flowchart.

Figure A.1 illustrates the logic of Program A.1, which calculates the state income tax. Two versions of the flowchart are given to show that the choice of the written contents inside each symbol is an arbitrary matter. Both versions have the same logic because the number, type, and arrangement of flowchart symbols are identical. The flowchart in Figure A.1(A) is more like English, and it would be used to communicate with a nonprogrammer, while the flowchart in Figure A.1(B) is more like QuickBASIC and would be used to communicate with a programmer who is familiar with QuickBASIC. A slight disadvantage in using English-sentence-type notation is that ordinary English can become wordy and, at times, even unclear.

PROGRAM A.1

```
' Program A.1
' Computation of State Tax
' ************************
CLS : KEY OFF  ' Clear Screen
INPUT "Please enter the salary =================> ", Salary
INPUT "Please enter the number of dependents ==> ", Dep
Tax = 0.02 * (Salary - 500 * Dep)
PRINT
PRINT "The state tax is ========================> $"; Tax
END

[run]

Please enter the salary =================> 19500
Please enter the number of dependents ==> 5

The state tax is ========================> $ 340
```

FIGURE A.1

Flowcharts for Program A.1 (A), English-like, and A.1 (B), QuickBASIC-like.

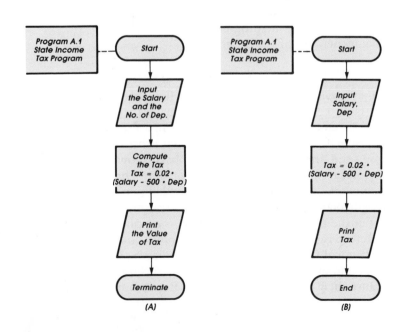

(A)   (B)

The advantage of using QuickBASIC-like notation rather than English-like notation is that it permits the description of the operation to be presented in a compact and precise form. Table A.1 lists common notations, including mathematical ones, used in flowcharts.

TABLE A.1 Common Notations Used in Flowcharts			
SYMBOL OR NOTATION	**EXPLANATION**	**SYMBOL OR NOTATION**	**EXPLANATION**
$+$	Addition or Positive Value	$\leq$	Is Less Than or Equal To
$-$	Subtraction or Negative Value	| |	Absolute Value
$*$ or $\times$	Multiplication	⌐ or !	Negation
$/$	Division	EOF	End-of-File
$\setminus$	Integer Division	HI	High
$\wedge$	Exponentiation	LO	Low
$\leftarrow$	Is Replaced By or Is Assigned To	EQ	Equal
$=$	Is Equal To	MOD	Modulo
$\neq$ or ⌐$=$ or $!=$	Is Not Equal To	Yes or Y	
$:$	Comparison	No or N	
$>$	Is Greater Than	On	Self-Explanatory
$\geq$	Is Greater Than or Equal To	Off	
$<$	Is Less Than	True or T	
		False or F	

The advantage of using program-language statements in a flowchart is that this type of flowchart can improve communication among programmers who are familiar with the given language. This book, which favors a combination of English-sentence-type, mathematical, and QuickBASIC–type notation, will use whichever notation renders a given operation clear and unambiguous.

A.2 GUIDELINES FOR PREPARATION OF FLOWCHARTS

Before the flowchart can be drawn, a thorough analysis of the problem, the data, and the desired output results must be performed. The logic required to solve the problem also must be determined. On the basis of this analysis, a **general flowchart** of the main path of the logic can be sketched. This can then be refined until the overall logic is fully determined. This general flowchart is used to make one or more **detailed flowcharts** of the various parts and levels in and exceptions to the main path of logic. After each detailed flowchart has been freed of logical errors and other undesirable features such as unnecessary steps, the actual coding of the program in a computer language can be undertaken.

Straight-Line Flowcharts

Figure A.2 illustrates a general flowchart, that is straight-line. A **straight-line flowchart** is one in which the symbols are arranged sequentially, without any deviations or looping, until the terminal symbol that represents the end of the flowchart is reached. Once the operation indicated in any one symbol has been performed, that operation is never repeated.

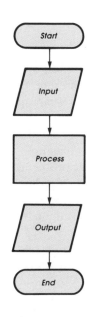

FIGURE A.2

Basic pattern of a straight-line general flowchart.

Flowcharts with Looping

A general flowchart that illustrates an iterative, or repeating, process known as looping is shown in Figure A.3. The logic illustrated by this flowchart is in three major parts: initialization, process, and wrap-up. A flowline exits from the bottom symbol in Figure A.3 and enters above the diamond-shaped decision symbol that determines whether the loop is to be executed again. This flowline forms part of a loop inside which some operations are repeatedly executed until specified conditions are satisfied. This flowchart shows the input, process, and output pattern; it also uses a decision symbol that shows where the decision is made to continue or stop the looping process.

FIGURE A.3

Basic pattern of a general flowchart with looping.

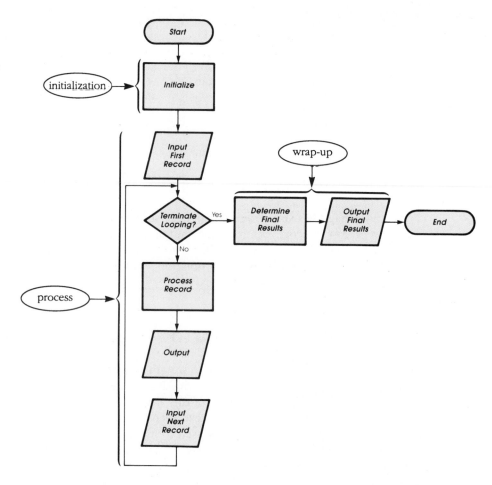

The flowchart in Figure A.3 also contains two braces that show initialization and wrap-up operations. For example, setting the program counters to 0 may represent an initialization operation, and displaying the values of counters may represent a wrap-up operation.

Like the straight-line flowchart, a flowchart with looping need not have all the symbols shown in Figure A.3, or a flowchart can have many more symbols. For example, the process symbol within the loop in Figure A.3, when applied to a particular problem, may expand to include branching forward to bypass a process or backward to redo a process. It is also possible that through the use of decision symbols, the process symbol in Figure A.3 could be shown expanded to several loops, some of which might be independent from each other and some of which might be within other loops.

The main point to remember is that the flowchart shows a process that is carried out. Flowcharts are flexible; they can show any process no matter how complex it may be, and they can show it in whatever detail is needed.

The two flowcharts illustrated in Figure A.4 represent the same program; that is, the program simply reads and then prints a record. Then the program loops back to the reading operation and repeats the sequence, reading and printing for any number of records.

FIGURE A.4
Two methods of representing a loop in a flowchart.

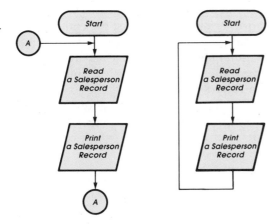

Although the flowcharts in Figure A.4 illustrate two ways a loop can be represented, the particular loop that is shown is an **endless**, or **infinite**, loop. This type of loop should be avoided in constructing programs. In order to make a program such as the one shown in Figure A.4 finite, you must define it so it will terminate when specified conditions are satisfied. For example, if 15 aging accounts are to be processed, the program can be instructed to process no more than 15 accounts and then stop. Figure A.5 illustrates the use of a counter in terminating the looping process. Note that the counter is first set to 0 in the initialization step. After an account is read and a message of action is printed, the counter is incremented by 1 and tested to find whether it is now equal to 15. If the value of the counter is not 15, the looping process continues. If the value of the counter is 15, the looping process terminates.

FIGURE A.5
Termination of a loop by use of a counter.

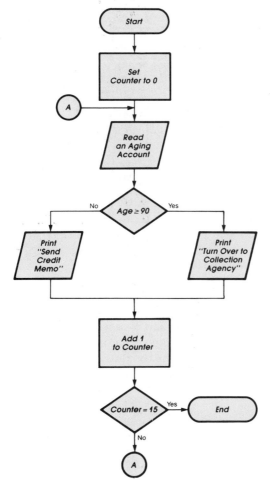

For the flowchart used in Figure A.5, the exact number of accounts to be processed must be known beforehand. In practice, this will not always be the case since the number of accounts may vary from one run to the next.

A way to solve this type of problem is shown in Figure A.6, which illustrates the use of an end-of-file test to terminate the looping process. The value –999999 has been chosen to be the last account number. This kind of value is sometimes known as the **sentinel value** because it *guards* against reading past the end-of-file. Also, the numeric item chosen for the last value cannot possibly be confused with a valid item because it is outside the range of the account numbers. Programs using an end-of-file test such as the one shown in Figure A.6 are far more flexible and far less limited than programs that do not such as those illustrated in Figures A.4 and A.5.

Two more flowcharts with loops are shown in Figures A.7 and 1.12 on page 15. Figure A.7 illustrates the concept of counting, and Figure 1.12 illustrates the computations required to compute the average commission paid a company's sales personnel. Both flowcharts incorporate the end-of-file test.

FIGURE A.6

Termination of a loop by testing for the end-of-file.

FIGURE A.7

Flowchart with looping, illustrating the concept of counting the number of records in an inventory file.

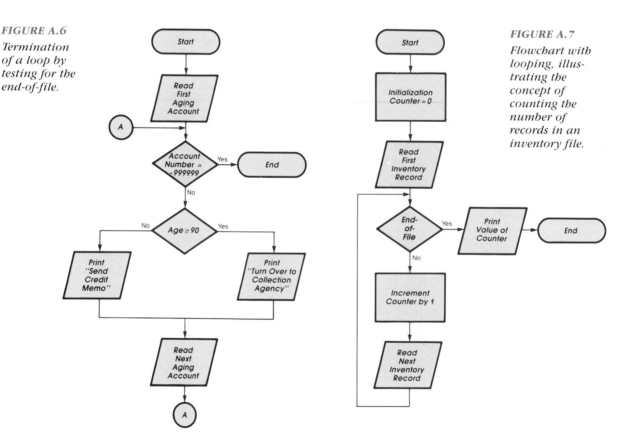

The technique of flowcharting may not be very useful in simple computer programs such as Program A.1 on page 494. However, as programs become more complex with many different paths of execution, a flowchart is not only useful but sometimes is a prerequisite for successful analysis and coding of the program. Indeed, developing the problem solution by arranging and rearranging the flowchart symbols can lead to a more efficient computer program.

A.3 CONTROL STRUCTURES

Computer professionals agree that high-quality programs can be constructed from the following three basic logic structures:

1. Sequence
2. If-Then-Else or Selection
3. Do-While or Repetition

The following are two common extensions to these logic structures:

Do-Until or Repeat-Until
Case (an extension of the If-Then-Else logic structure)

The **Sequence structure** is used to show one action or one action followed by another, as illustrated in Figure A.8. Every flowchart in this text includes this control structure.

FIGURE A.8

Sequence structure: (A) one action; (B) one action followed by another.

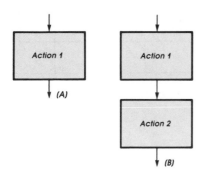

The **If-Then-Else** structure represents a two-way decision with action specified for each of the two alternatives. This logic structure is shown in Figure A.9. The flowcharts presented earlier in Figures A.5 and A.6 include this logic structure. The action can be null for one alternative, as shown in Figure A.9(B).

The **Do-While structure** is the logic structure most commonly used to create a process that will repeat as long as the condition is true. The Do-While structure is illustrated in Figure A.10 and has been used earlier in Figures A.3, A.6, and A.7. Because the decision to perform the action within the structure is at the top of the loop, the action may not occur.

FIGURE A.9

If-Then-Else structure: (A) action specified for each of the two alternatives (true or false); (B) additional action taken for one alternative.

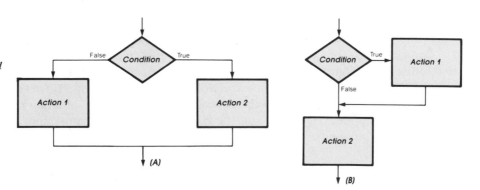

FIGURE A.10

Do-While structure.

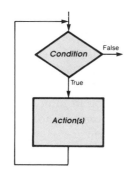

The **Do-Until structure** (Figure A.11 on the next page) is also used for creating a process that will be repeated. The major differences between the Do-Until and the Do-While structures are that (1) the action within the structure of a Do-Until will always be executed at least once, (2) the decision to perform the action within the structure is at the bottom of the loop, and (3) the Do-Until loop exits when the condition is true.

Figure A.11 illustrates the Do-Until structure, and the flowchart presented in **Figure A.5** included a Do-Until structure.

The **Case structure** is similar to the If-Then-Else structure except that it provides more than two alternatives. Figure A.12 illustrates the Case structure.

A high-quality program can be developed through the use of just these five logic structures. The program will be easy to read, easy to modify, and reliable; most important of all, the program will do what it is intended to do!

FIGURE A.11
Do-Until structure.

FIGURE A.12
Case structure.

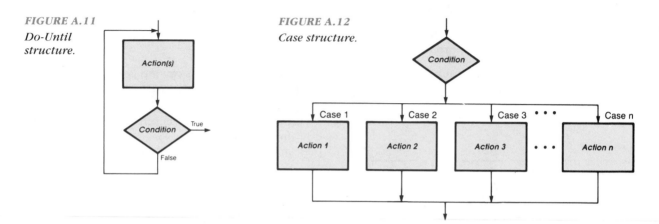

A.4   PROPER PROGRAMS

A **proper program** is one that has the following characteristics:

1. One entry point
2. One exit point
3. No unreachable code
4. No infinite loops

A program constructed with just the five logic structures will form the basis for a proper program. Figure A.13 illustrates the breaking up — the decomposition — of a program into some of the control structures presented in the previous section. On the other hand, Figure A.14 illustrates a program that will result in an **improper program**.

This book stresses the construction of proper programs. However, you should be aware that in the real world the characteristics of a proper program may be relaxed or even intentionally violated, and these types of real-world programs are referred to as improper programs.

A.5   FLOWCHARTING TIPS

Shown below and on page 501 are some flowchart suggestions. These suggestions assume that the input, processing, and output of the problem are defined properly.

1. Sketch a general flowchart and the necessary detail flowcharts before coding the problem. Repeat this step until you are satisfied with your flowcharts.
2. Use the control structures described in section A.3.
3. Put yourself in the position of the reader, keeping in mind that the purpose of the flowchart is to improve communications between one person and another concerning the method of solution for the problem.
4. Show the flow of processing from top to bottom and from left to right. When in doubt, use arrowheads, as required, to indicate the direction of flow.

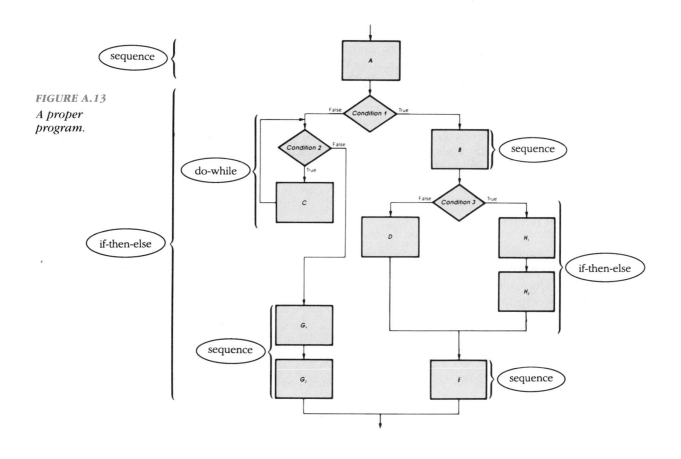

FIGURE A.13
A proper program.

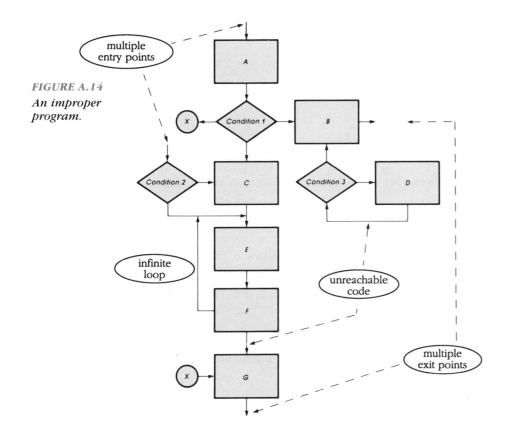

FIGURE A.14
An improper program.

5. Draw the flowchart so that it is neat and clear. Use the connector symbols to avoid excessively long flowlines.

6. Choose notation and wording that explain the function of each symbol in a clear and precise manner.

7. Do your best to avoid endless loops; construct loops so they will be terminated when specific conditions are satisfied.

The reason that flowcharts are so important is simple: the difficulties in programming lie mostly in the realm of logic, not in the syntax and semantics of the computer language. In other words, most computer-use errors are mistakes in logic, and a flowchart aids in detecting logic mistakes!

A.6   PSEUDOCODE

Pseudocode is a program design technique that uses natural English and resembles QuickBASIC code. It is an intermediate notation that allows the logic of a program to be formulated without diagrams or charts. Pseudocode resembles QuickBASIC in that specific operations can be expressed, as the following three examples demonstrate:

Read employee record
Add 1 to male counter
Display employee record

What makes pseudocode appealing to many programmers is that it has no formal syntactical rules, which allows him or her to concentrate on the design of the program rather than on the peculiarities of the logic tool itself.

Although pseudocode has no formal rules, the following are commonly accepted:

1. Begin the pseudocode with a program title statement.

   Program: Monthly Sales Analysis Report

2. End the pseudocode with a terminal program statement.

   End: Monthly Sales Analysis Report

3. Begin each statement on a new line. Use simple and short imperative sentences that contain a single transitive verb and a single object.

   Open employee file

   Subtract 10 from quantity

4. Express assignment as a formula or as an English-like statement.

   Withholding tax = 0.20 × (gross pay – 38.46 × dependents)

   or

   Compute withholding tax

5. To implement the design, try to avoid using logic structures not available in the programming language being used.

6. For the If-Then-Else structure, use the following conventions:

   a. Indent the true and false tasks.
   b. Use "End If" as the structure terminator.

These conventions for the If-Then-Else structure are illustrated in Figures A.15 and A.16.

FIGURE A.15	If balance < 500 Then
	   Display credit ok
	Else
	   Display credit not ok
	End If

FIGURE A.16	If sex code = male Then
	   Add 1 to male count
	   If age > 21 Then
	     Add 1 to male adult count
	   Else
	     Add 1 to male minor count
	   End If
	Else
	   Add 1 to female count
	   If age > 21 Then
	     Add 1 to female adult count
	   Else
	     Add 1 to female minor count
	   End If
	End if

7. For the Do-While structure, use the following conventions:
   a. If the structure represents a counter-controlled loop, begin the structure with "Do."
   b. If the structure does not represent a counter-controlled loop, begin the structure with "Do While."
   c. Specify the condition on the Do While or Do line.
   d. Use "End Do" as the last statement of the structure.
   e. Align the Do While or Do and the End Do vertically.
   f. Indent the statements within the loop.

The conventions for the Do-While structure are illustrated in Figures A.17 and A.18

FIGURE A.17	Program: Employee File List
	Display report and column headings
	Set employee count to 0
	Read first employee record
	Do While not end-of-file
	   Add 1 to employee count
	   Display employee record
	   Read next employee record
	End Do
	Display employee count
	Display end-of-job message
	End: Employee File List

FIGURE A.18	Program: Sum first 100 Integers Set sum to 0 Do integer = 1 to 100 Add integer to sum End Do Display sum Display end-of-job message End: Sum first 100 Integers

8. For the Do-Until structure, use the following conventions:
   a. Begin the structure with "Do Until."
   b. Specify the condition on the Do Until line.
   c. Use "End Do" as the last statement of the structure.
   d. Align the Do Until and the End Do vertically.
   e. Indent the statements within the loop.

The conventions for the Do-Until structure are illustrated in Figure A.19.

FIGURE A.19	Program: Sum first 100 Integers
	Set sum to 0
	Set integer to 1
	Do Until integer > 100
	   Add integer to sum
	   Add 1 to integer
	End Do
	Display sum
	Display end-of-job message
	End: Sum first 100 Integers

9. For the Case structure, use the following conventions:
   a. Begin the structure with "Start Case," followed by the variable to be tested.
   b. Use "End Case" as the structure terminator.
   c. Align "Start Case" and "End Case" vertically.
   d. Indent each alternative.
   e. Begin each alternative with "Case," followed by the value of the variable that equates to the alternative.
   f. Indent the action of each alternative.

These conventions are illustrated in Figure A.20.

FIGURE A.20

```
Start Case customer code
    Case 100
        Add 1 to high-risk customer count
    Case 200
        Add 1 to risk customer count
    Case 300
        Add 1 to regular customer count
    Case 400
        Add 1 to special customer count
End Case
```

For an additional example on using pseudocode, see Figure 1.13 in Chapter 1 on page 15 and Figure 1.14 on page 16.

A.7 NASSI-SCHNEIDERMAN CHARTS

Nassi-Schneiderman charts, also called **N-S charts**, are often referred to as structured flowcharts. Unlike program flowcharts, they contain no flowlines or flowchart symbols and thus have no provision to include a GOTO statement.

N-S charts are made up of a series of rectangles. The flow of control always runs top-to-bottom. The sequence structure in an N-S chart is illustrated in Figure A.21.

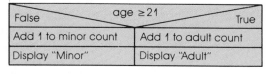

FIGURE A.21   **FIGURE A.22**

The If-Then-Else structure is shown by three triangles within a rectangle and a vertical line separating the true and false tasks, as shown in Figure A.22. The N-S chart indicates a decision (age ≥ 21) and the actions to be taken for an adult and minor. If a person's age is greater than or equal to 21, then the actions specified for the true case are processed. If a person's age is less than 21, then the actions specified for the false case are processed. It is not possible for both the true and false tasks to be processed for the same person.

The Do-While structure (test at the top of the loop) is referred to by a rectangle within a rectangle, as shown in Figure A.23.

FIGURE A.23

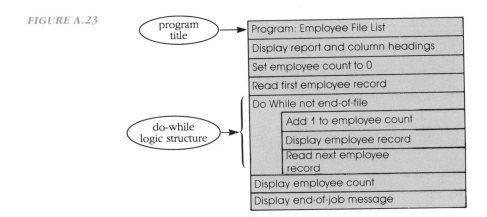

The diagram indicates that the statements within the inner rectangle are to be processed in sequence as long as it is not end-of-file. When the end-of-file is sensed, control passes to the statement below the Do-While structure.

The Do-Until structure (test at the bottom of the loop) is similarly referred to by a rectangle within a rectangle, as shown in Figure A.24.

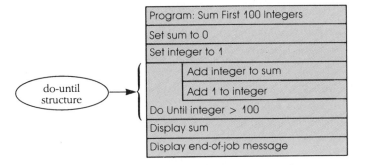

FIGURE A.24

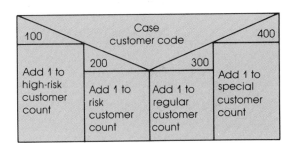

FIGURE A.25

The Case structure is represented as shown in Figure A.25. As with the If-Then-Else structure, only one of the actions specified will be processed for each customer.

Those professionals who advocate the use of N-S charts claim they are effective in all phases of the program development cycle, especially for system and program documentation. Nassi and Schneiderman go even further. They write:

Programmers who first learn to design programs with these symbols never develop the bad habits which other flowchart notation systems permit. . . . Since no more than fifteen or twenty symbols can be drawn on a single sheet of paper, the programmer must modularize his program into meaningful sections. The temptation to use off-page connectors, which lead only to confusion, is eliminated. Finally, the ease with which a structured flowchart can be translated into a structured program is pleasantly surprising.*

Other professionals argue that N-S charts are nothing more than pseudocode with lines and rectangles around it.

---

*I. Nassi and B. Schneiderman, "Flowchart Techniques for Structured Programming," SIGPLAN, Notices of the ACM, v.8, n. 8, August 1973: 12-16.

A.8   WARNIER-ORR DIAGRAMS

In some respects, a **Warnier-Orr diagram** is similar to a top-down chart laid on its side. Both place a heavy emphasis on the idea of hierarchies. Warnier-Orr diagrams, however, go one step further and place an equal emphasis on flow of control.

Recall from Chapter 4 that a top-down chart is used primarily to show functionality or *what* must be done to solve a problem. Once a top-down chart is complete, an intermediate tool, such as a program flowchart, an N-S chart, or pseudocode must be used to show the flow of control, or *how* and *when* things are to be done in the framework of a solution. With Warnier-Orr diagrams, no such intermediate step is required.

As with N-S charts, solutions are constructed by means of the three basic logic structures: sequence, selection (If-Then-Else or Case); and repetition (Do While or Do Until).

A Warnier-Orr diagram is made up of a series of left braces, pseudocode-like statements, and a few special symbols, as shown in Table A.2.

TABLE A.2	Warnier-Orr Symbols and Their Meanings
SYMBOL	**MEANING**
{	The brace is used to enclose logically related events.
(0, 1)	An event is done zero or one time. Notation for selection structure.
(0, n) or (n)	An event is done n times. Notation for Do-While structure.
(1, n)	An event is done one to n times. Notation for Do-Until structure.
blank or (1)	An event is done one time.
⊕	Exclusive OR. Used together with the notation (0, 1) to show a Selection structure.

The Sequence structure is illustrated in a Warnier-Orr diagram by listing the sequence of events from top to bottom within a brace, as shown in Figure A.26.

FIGURE A.26

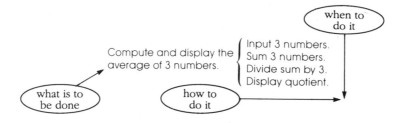

The left brace points to what is to be done. Within the brace is the list of events that show how to do it and, from top to bottom, when each event is to take place.

The If-Then-Else structure is shown by the use of the notation (0, 1) and the exclusive OR symbol. (See Figure A.27.) The Case structure is shown in a similar fashion. (See Figure A.28.)

FIGURE A.27

Increment male and female counters. {
  Male (0, 1) { Add 1 to male count.
  ⊕
  Not Male (0, 1) { Add 1 to female count.

FIGURE A.28

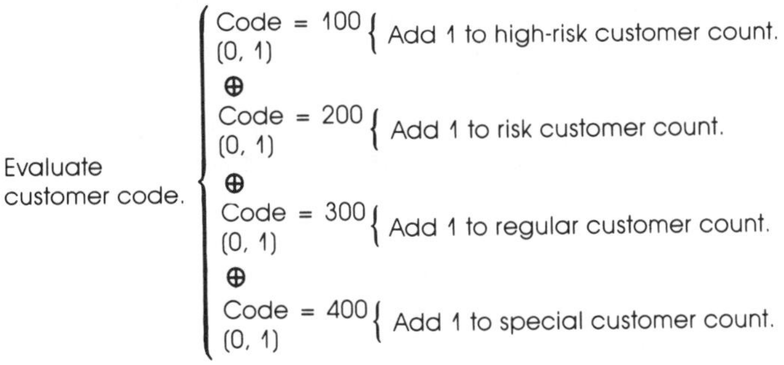

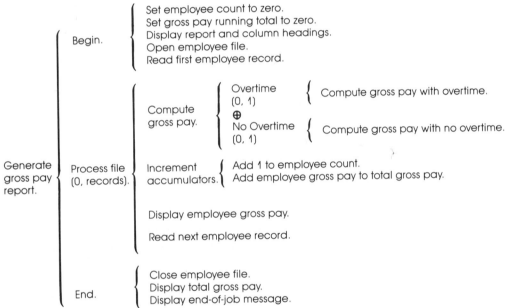

The Warnier-Orr diagram in Figure A.29 shows a solution for reading an employee file and computing the gross pay for each employee. The solution includes a Do-While structure.

FIGURE A.29

The event "Process file (0, records)" illustrates a Do-While structure. The "0" within parentheses means that the loop can be executed zero times if, for example, the employee file is empty. The term *records* within parentheses indicates the number of times the loop is to be executed. It is also valid to write the notation for the Do-While structure as (*records*), rather than (*0, records*).

The notation used to represent a Do-Until structure is similar to that of the Do-While structure except the notation below the event is written as (1, n) rather than (0, n), because the Do-Until structure is executed at least one time.

A.9   TEST YOUR BASIC SKILLS (Even-numbered answers are in Appendix E)

1. What is the first step in solving a problem that uses a computer?
2. Which of the flowchart symbols given in Chapter 1, Table 1.5 on page 14 are not required, in that any program may be flowcharted without using them?
3. Can one flowchart symbol be used to simultaneously represent two or more Quick-BASIC statements?

4. In the flowchart in Figure A.30, what are the value of I and the value of J at the instant just after the statement J = J + 1 is executed for the fifth time? The value of I and J after the statement I = I + 2 is executed the tenth time? (A statement such as J = J + 1 is valid and is read as "the new value of J equals the old value of J plus one" or, equivalently, "the value of J is to be replaced by the value of J plus one.")

5. Consider the flowchart portion in Figure A.31. It assumes that a relatively intelligent person is going to work. This individual usually has the car keys but occasionally forgets them. Does the flowchart portion in Figure A.31 incorporate the most efficient method of representing the actions to be taken? If not, redraw the flowchart portion given in Figure A.31.

FIGURE A.30   *FIGURE A.31*

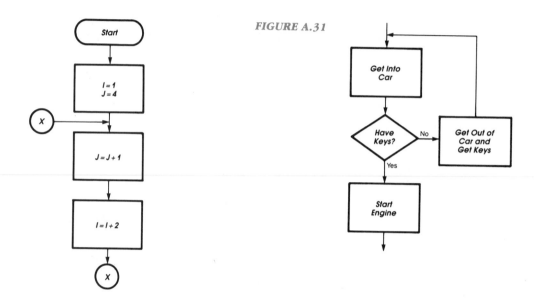

6. In the flowchart in Figure A.32, of a valid though trivial program, what values of I and of J are printed when the output symbol is executed for the fiftieth time?

FIGURE A.32   *FIGURE A.33*

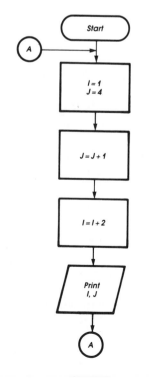

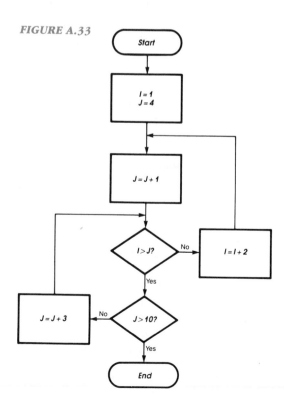

7. Two numbers U and V located in the main storage, are to be interchanged. Construct the flowchart (or N-S chart, or psuedocode or Warnier-Orr diagram) to represent this interchange.

8. Construct an efficient flowchart to solve for the roots of the following equation:

$$ax^2 + bx + c = 0 \text{ using the following formula: } x = \frac{-b \pm \sqrt{b^2 - 4ac}}{2a}$$

Input three values containing the coefficients *a*, *b*, and *c*, respectively. Print the values of the two real roots. If complex roots exist ($b^2 - 4ac < 0$), print a message to that effect. If the roots are equal, print one root. (Assume that the coefficient *a* does not have a value of zero so that an attempted division by zero will not occur.)

Problems 9–12.   An employee file contains the following data on each employee:

- Name
- Sex — M for male or F for female
- Age — A two-digit number between 18 and 65 inclusive
- Education — 1 for 11th grade education or less, 2 for high school diploma, 3 for bachelor's degree, or 4 for master's degree
- Race — 1 for Black, 2 for Caucasian, 3 for Hispanic, or 4 for Other.
- Seniority — A two-digit number between 0 and 46.

9. Construct the flowchart (or N-S chart, or pseudocode, or Warnier-Orr Diagram) to read the records in the employee file, print the number of males, the number of females, the total number of employees, and the percent that are male and percent female.

10. Construct the flowchart (or N-S chart, or pseudocode, or Warnier-Orr Diagram) to print the number of employees who are female Blacks or female Hispanics that have a college or masters degree.

11. Construct the flowchart (or N-S chart, or pseudocode, or Warnier-Orr Diagram) to print the name and age of all male employees greater than or equal to the age of 64.

12. Construct the flowchart (or N-S chart, or pseudocode, or Warnier-Orr Diagram) to print the Name, Sex, Education, Race, and Seniority of those employees who are female, Hispanic or Other, have a high school diploma or less, and have more than 20 years seniority. Also print the number of employees that meets these requirements.

13. An opaque urn contains three diamonds, four rubies, and two pearls. Construct a flowchart that describes the following events: Draw a gem from the urn. If it is a diamond, lay it aside. If it is not a diamond, return it to the urn. Continue in this fashion until all the diamonds have been removed. After all the diamonds have been removed, repeat the same procedure until all the rubies have been removed. After all the rubies have been removed, continue in the same fashion until all the pearls have been removed.

14. In the flowchart represented by Figure A.33, what is the value of I and the value of J at the instant the terminal symbol with the word End is reached?

15. Part I: Draw one flowchart, and only one, that will cause the "mechanical mouse" to go through any of the four mazes shown in Figure A.34. At the beginning, a user will place the mouse on the entry side of the maze, in front of the entry point, facing "up" toward the maze. The instruction "Move to next cell" will put the mouse inside the maze. Each maze has four cells. After that, the job is to move from cell to cell until the mouse emerges on the exit side. If the mouse is instructed to "Move to next cell" when there is a wall in front of it, it will hit the wall and blow up. Obviously, the mouse must be instructed to test whether it is "Facing a wall" before any "Move." The mechanical mouse's instruction set is listed below Figure A.34 on the next page.

FIGURE A.34

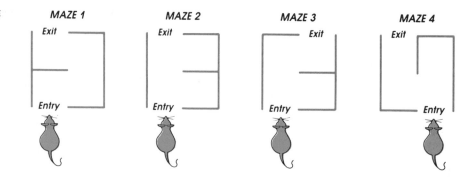

A. Physical movement:
    1. Move to next cell. (The mouse will move in the direction it is facing.)
    2. Turn right.
    3. Turn left.
    4. Turn around. (All turns are made in place, without moving to another cell.)
    5. Halt.

B. Logic:
    1. Facing a wall? (Through this test, the mouse determines whether there is a wall immediately in front of it, that is, on the border of the cell it is occupying and in the direction it is facing.)
    2. Outside the maze?
    3. On the entry side?
    4. On the exit side?

Part II (Extra Credit):   If your flowchart can cause the mechanical mouse to go through all of the mazes in part I without blowing up, then try your flowchart for mazes 5, 6, and 7 in Figure A.35. See whether you can produce one flowchart that will work for mazes 1 through 7.

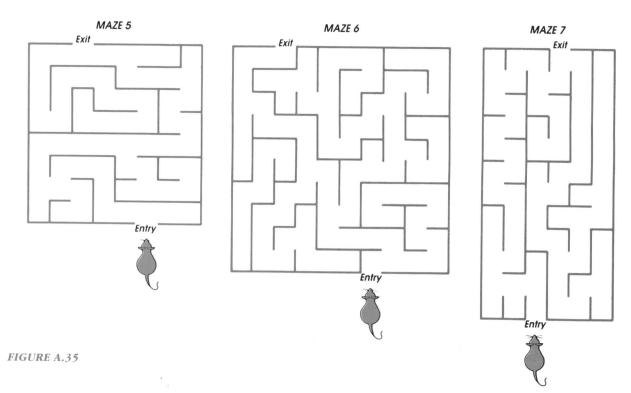

FIGURE A.35

Menu Commands and Windows

This appendix describes the functions of the QuickBASIC commands that are accessible through the menu bar at the top of the screen. The first section describes how to activate the menu bar and select a command. The next section covers the menu bar for MS-DOS QBasic. The third section of this appendix covers the menu bar for the commercial version of QuickBASIC with Full Menus toggled on. The commercial version includes commands that are not available with the MS-DOS QBasic version. Finally, the appendix describes how to manipulate the windows on the screen to your advantage.

B.1 SELECTING COMMANDS

To select a QuickBASIC command, you must first activate the menu bar at the top of the screen (Figure B.1). To activate the menu bar, press the Alt key. Next, open a menu in one of two ways: (1) type the first letter of the menu name; or (2) use the Left or Right Arrow key to move the cursor to the menu name, then press the Enter key. For example, to open the File menu (Figure B.2 on the next page), type the letter F or use the Left or Right Arrow key to highlight the word File, then press the Enter key.

FIGURE B.1
The menu bar for MS-DOS QBasic.

511

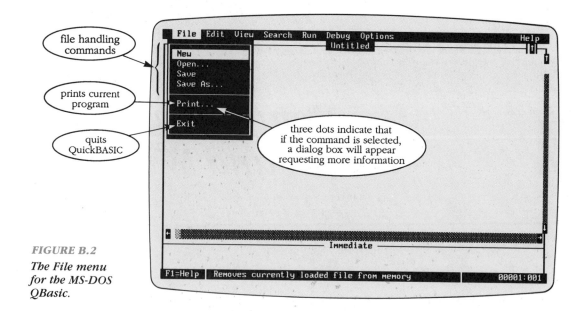

file handling
commands

prints current
program

quits
QuickBASIC

three dots indicate that
if the command is selected,
a dialog box will appear
requesting more information

FIGURE B.2

*The File menu
for the MS-DOS
QBasic.*

To execute a command in an opened menu, type the letter highlighted in the command. You can also use the Up and Down Arrow keys to highlight a command and then press the Enter key to execute it.

If you choose the wrong menu, use the Left or Right Arrow key to open the correct menu. To close an opened menu and activate the view window, press the Escape key (Esc).

Certain menu commands can be executed directly from the view window by pressing the corresponding shortcut key. **Shortcut keys** reduce the number of keystrokes required to execute a command, and thus save time. The shortcut keys and the commands they execute are described in the appropriate tables of this appendix.

If you have a mouse, open a menu by clicking the menu name. Once the menu is open, click the desired command. To close the opened menu, click the view window or click another menu name in the menu bar. The term "click" means move the mouse pointer to the command or area and press the left button.

Obtaining Help from the QB Advisor

Instant help is available for any QuickBASIC command. To obtain help, activate the menu that lists the command. Next, use the arrow keys to highlight the command and then press F1. The QB Advisor immediately displays helpful information about the command.

B.2   THE MS-DOS QBASIC MENU BAR

The menu bar for MS-DOS QBasic is shown in Figure B.2. The following sections describe the commands available in each menu of MS-DOS QBasic.

The File Menu

The File menu (Figure B.2) is used more than any other menu. It includes the commands that allow you to create a new program, load a program from disk, save the current program to disk, print the current program, and quit QuickBASIC. (See Sections

2.7 and 2.8 in Chapter 2 for examples of the use of the commands in the File menu.) Table B.1 summarizes the functions of the commands in the File menu. Note that any command that ends with three dots means additional information will be requested via a dialog box.

TABLE B.1   The File Menu

COMMAND	FUNCTION
New...	Causes the current program to be erased and indicates the beginning of a new program.
Open...	Loads a previously stored program on disk into main storage.
Save...	Saves the current program to disk under its previously assigned name.
Save As...	Saves the current program to disk under a specified name.
Print...	Prints all or part of the current program to the printer.
Exit	Causes the PC to permanently exit QuickBASIC and returns control to DOS.

The Edit Menu

The Edit menu (Figure B.3) is primarily used to delete, copy, and move blocks of code in the current program. (See Section 2.6 in Chapter 2 for additional editing techniques.)

FIGURE B.3

The Edit menu for MS-DOS QBasic.

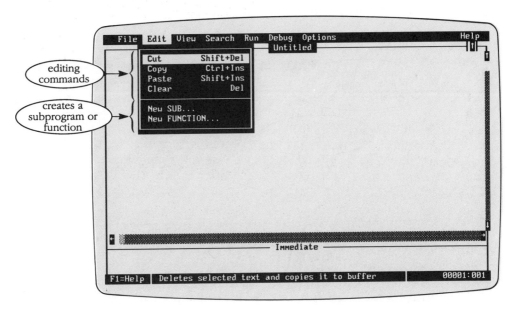

Some of the Edit commands require you to first select the block of code in the current program. Hold down the Shift key and use the arrow keys to highlight a block of code.

If you have a mouse, move the mouse pointer from the first character of the block to the last. Moving the pointer highlights the block of code. You move the pointer by dragging the mouse in the proper direction with the left button held down.

Table B.2 describes the functions of the Edit commands and the shortcut keys. For example, the shortcut key Shift + Delete means hold down the Alt key and press the Delete key to delete the selected text and place it on the clipboard.

TABLE B.2	The Edit Menu	
COMMAND	**SHORTCUT KEYS**	**FUNCTION**
Cut	Shift + Delete	Cuts (deletes) the selected block of code from the current program and places it on the clipboard.
Copy	Ctrl + Insert	Copies the selected block of code in the current program on the clipboard.
Clear	Delete	Cuts (deletes) the selected block of code from the current program.
Paste	Shift + Insert	Pastes (inserts) at the cursor location of the current program the block of code on the clipboard.
New SUB...		Opens a window for a new Subprogram.
New FUNCTION...		Opens a window for a new Function.

The View Menu

The View menu (Figure B.4) includes commands that allow you to modify what is displayed on the screen. Table B.3 summarizes the View menu commands.

FIGURE B.4
The View menu for MS-DOS QBasic.

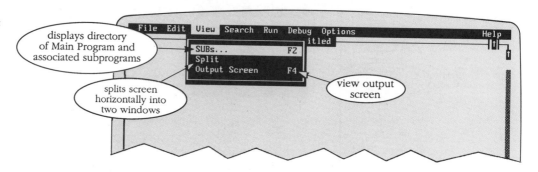

TABLE B.3	The View Menu	
COMMAND	**SHORTCUT KEYS**	**FUNCTION**
SUBs...	F2	Displays a list of the names of the Main Program and associated subprograms and functions. (For additional information, see Section 4.4 in Chapter 4.)
Split		Toggles between a split-view window and a single-view window.
Output Screen	F4	Switches the display from the view window to the output screen.

The Search Menu

The Search menu (Figure B.5) is used to find strings as well as replace strings in the current program. Table B.4 describes the functions of the Search commands.

FIGURE B.5
The Search
menu for MS-
DOS QBasic.

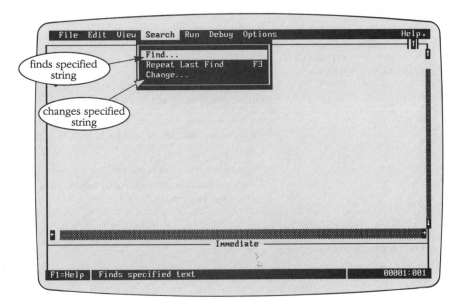

TABLE B.4   The Search Menu

COMMAND	SHORTCUT KEYS	FUNCTION
Find...		Finds specified string.
Repeat Last Find	F3	Finds next specified string.
Change...		Changes specified string to another string.

The Run Menu

The Run menu (Figure B.6) includes commands that are primarily used to execute the current program. Table B.5 describes the functions of the Run commands.

FIGURE B.6
The Run menu
for MS-DOS
QBasic.

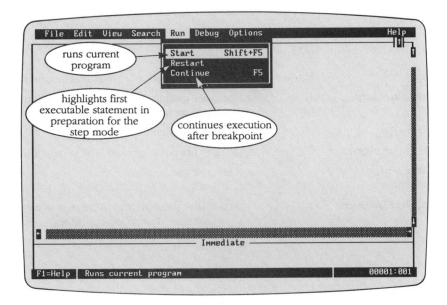

TABLE B.5 The Run Menu		
COMMAND	**SHORTCUT KEYS**	**FUNCTION**
Start	Shift + F5	Runs current program in view window.
Restart		Restarts current program from beginning. Halts on line with first executable statement and highlights it in preparation for the step mode.
Continue	F5	Continues execution from the last statement executed if the current program was suspended, or executes the current program from the beginning.

The Debug Menu

The Debug menu (Figure B.7) includes commands used to debug the current program. Table B.6 describes the functions of the Debug commands. (For additional information and examples on the use of the commands in the Debug menu, see Section C.1 in Appendix C.)

FIGURE B.7

The Debug menu for MS-DOS QBasic.

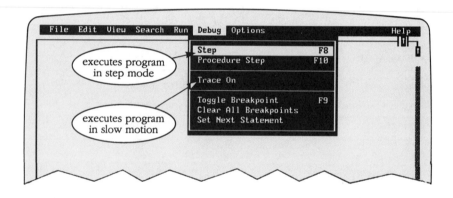

TABLE B.6 The Debug Menu		
COMMAND	**SHORTCUT KEYS**	**FUNCTION**
Step	F8	Executes program one statement at a time.
Procedure Step	F10	Executes program one statement at a time and bypasses any subprogram or function calls.
Trace On		Executes program in slow motion.
Toggle Breakpoint	F9	Toggles breakpoint on and off at cursor location.
Clear All Breakpoints		Clears all breakpoints.
Set Next Statement		Establishes the next line to execute in a program that has been halted. Execution continues at the line to which the cursor was moved.

The Options Menu

The Options menu (Figure B.8) contains commands that control some of the special features of QuickBASIC. Table B.7 describes the functions of the Options commands.

FIGURE B.8

The Options menu for MS-DOS QBasic

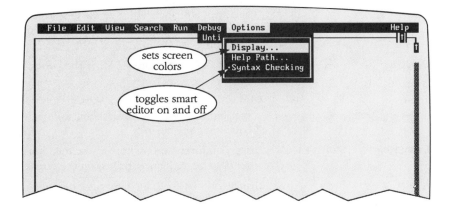

TABLE B.7	The Options Menu

COMMAND	FUNCTION
Display...	Sets the display attributes (colors, scroll bars, tab stops).
Help Path...	Sets the search paths for help files.
Syntax Checking	Turns QuickBASIC's smart editor on and off. The **smart editor** checks for **syntax errors**, formats lines, and translates the line to executable form if the syntax is correct.

The Help Menu

The Help menu (Figure B.9) offers on-line help through the QB Advisor. Table B.8 on the next page summarizes the five Help commands found in the Help menu. (For additional information on the QB Advisor, see Section 2.9 in Chapter 2.)

FIGURE B.9

The Help menu for MS-DOS QBasic.

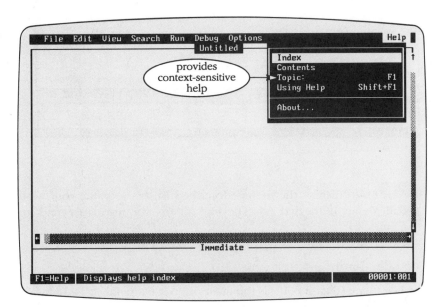

COMMAND	SHORTCUT KEYS	FUNCTION
		TABLE B.8 The Help Menu
Index		Displays an alphabetical list of the QuickBASIC keywords. Move the cursor to any keyword and press F1 for information on the keyword.
Contents		Displays a table of contents. Move the cursor to any subject and press F1.
Topic:	F1	Displays information on the syntax and usage of the QuickBASIC variable, symbol, keyword, menu, command, dialog box at or containing the cursor.
Using Help	Shift + F1	Displays information on how to use the mouse or keyboard to get help on an item displayed on the screen.
About...		Displays MS-DOS QBasic copyright message.

B.3   THE QuickBASIC COMMERCIAL VERSION MENU BAR (FULL MENUS ONLY)

The menu bar for the commercial version of QuickBASIC is shown in Figure B.10. The commercial version includes additional commands not found in MS-DOS QBasic that can be useful in a production environment. The following sections describe the commands available in each menu of the commercial version.

FIGURE B.10
The menu bar for the commercial version of QuickBASIC.

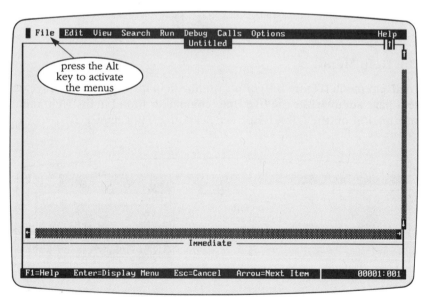

NOTE: To display the menus described in this section, you must be sure that Full Menus is toggled on. The Full Menus command is found in the Options menu.

The File Menu

The File menu (Figure B.11) is the most often used menu. It includes the commands that allow you to create a new program, load a program from disk, save the current program to disk, print the current program, and quit QuickBASIC. (See Sections 2.7 and 2.8 in Chapter 2 for examples of the use of the commands in the File menu.) Table B.9 summarizes the functions of the commands in the File menu. Note that any command that ends with three dots means that additional information will be requested via a dialog box.

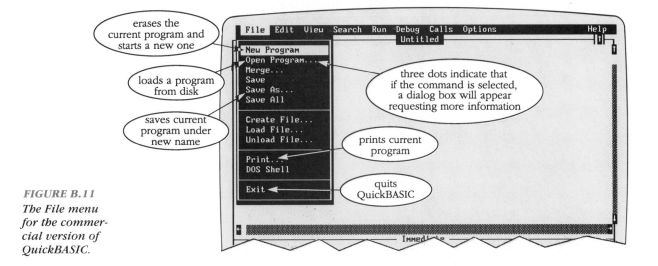

FIGURE B.11
The File menu for the commercial version of QuickBASIC.

TABLE B.9   The File Menu

COMMAND	FUNCTION
New Program	Causes the current program to be erased and indicates the beginning of a new program.
Open Program...	Loads a previously stored program on disk into main storage.
Merge...	Inserts a program from disk into the current program at the cursor location.
Save	Saves the current program to disk under its previously assigned name.
Save As...	Saves the current program to disk under a specified name.
Save All	Saves all loaded programs to disk.
Create File...	Creates an include file or document.
Load File...	Loads from disk an include file or document.
Unload File...	Removes an include file or document from main storage.
Print...	Prints all or part of the current program to the printer.
DOS Shell	Causes the PC to temporarily exit QuickBASIC and return control to DOS. To return to QuickBASIC, enter the DOS command EXIT.
Exit	Causes the PC to permanently exit QuickBASIC and returns control to DOS.

The Edit Menu

The Edit menu (Figure B.12 on the next page) is used to delete, copy, and move blocks of code in the current program. (See Section 2.6 in Chapter 2 for additional editing techniques.)

Some of the Edit commands require you to first select the block of code in the current program. Hold down the Shift key and use the arrow keys to highlight a block of code.

If you have a mouse, move the mouse pointer from the first character of the block to the last. Moving the pointer highlights the block of code. You move the pointer by dragging the mouse in the proper direction with the left button held down.

FIGURE B.12

*The Edit menu
for the commer-
cial version of
QuickBASIC.*

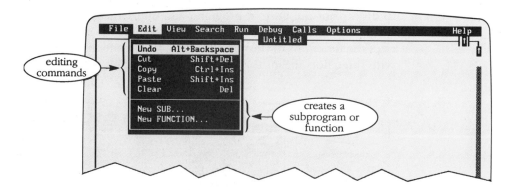

Table B.10 describes the functions of the Edit commands and the shortcut keys. For example, the shortcut key Shift + Delete means hold down the Alt key and press the Delete key to undo changes to the current line.

TABLE B.10   The Edit Menu

COMMAND	SHORTCUT KEYS	FUNCTION
Undo	Alt + Backspace	Reverses the last edit in the current line.
Cut	Shift + Delete	Cuts (deletes) the selected block of code from the current program and places it on the clipboard.
Copy	Ctrl + Insert	Copies the selected block of code in the current program on the clipboard.
Paste	Shift + Insert	Pastes (inserts) at the cursor location of the current program the block of code on the clipboard.
Clear	Delete	Cuts the selected block of code from the current program.
New SUB...		Opens a window for a new Subprogram.
New FUNCTION...		Opens a window for a new Function.

The View Menu

The View menu (Figure B.13) includes commands that allow you to modify what is displayed on the screen. Table B.11 summarizes the View menu commands.

FIGURE B.13

*The View menu
for the commer-
cial version of
QuickBASIC.*

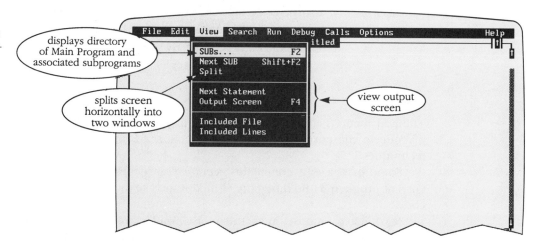

TABLE B.11   The View Menu

COMMAND	SHORTCUT KEYS	FUNCTION
SUBs...	F2	Displays a list of names of the Main Program and associated subprograms and functions. (For additional information, see Section 4.4 in Chapter 4).
Next SUB	Shift + F2	Displays next subprogram.
Split		Toggles between a split-view window and a single-view window.
Next Statement		Moves the cursor to the next statement to be executed. Used together with the Continue command to debug programs.
Output Screen	F4	Switches the display from the view window to the output screen.
Included File		Displays lines from an include file for editing.
Included Lines		Displays lines from an include file.

The Search Menu

The Search menu (Figure B.14) is used to find strings as well as replace strings in the current program. Table B.12 describes the functions of the Search commands.

FIGURE B.14

The Search menu for the commercial version of QuickBASIC.

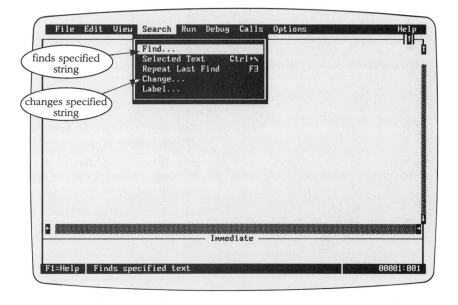

TABLE B.12   The Search Menu

COMMAND	SHORTCUT KEYS	FUNCTION
Find...		Finds specified string.
Selected Text	Ctrl + \	Finds specified string highlighted in the active window.
Repeat Last Find	F3	Finds next specified string.
Change...		Changes specified string to another string.
Label...		Finds specified line label.

The Run Menu

The Run menu (Figure B.15) includes commands primarily used to execute the current program. Table B.13 describes the functions of the Run commands.

FIGURE B.15

The Run menu for the commercial version of QuickBASIC.

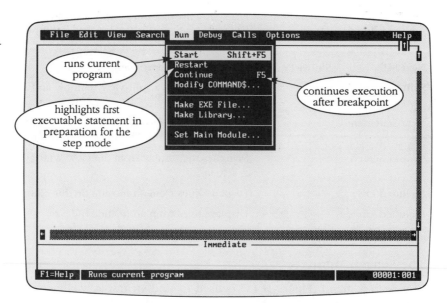

COMMAND	SHORTCUT KEYS	FUNCTION
Start	Shift + F5	Runs current program in view window.
Restart		Restarts current program from beginning. Serves as an alternative to the Continue command when debugging the current program.
Continue	F5	Continues execution from the last statement executed if the current program was suspended, or executes the current program from the beginning.
Modify COMMAND$...		Sets string returned by COMMAND$ function.
Make EXE File...		Compiles current program thereby creating an executable file on disk.
Make Library...		Creates QuickBASIC library of procedures on disk that can be linked with programs.
Set Main Module...		Changes main module.

TABLE B.13   The Run Menu

The Debug Menu

The Debug menu (Figure B.16) includes commands that are used to debug the current program. Table B.14 describes the functions of the Debug commands. (For additional information and examples on the use of the commands in the Debug menu, see Section C.1 in Appendix C.)

FIGURE B.16

*The Debug
menu for the
commercial
version of
QuickBASIC.*

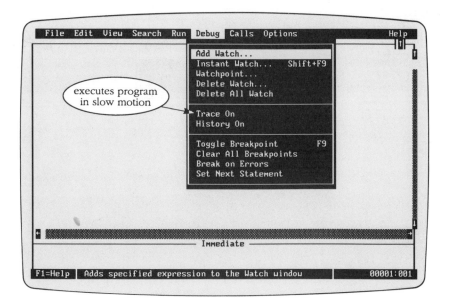

```
    File  Edit  View  Search  Run  Debug  Calls  Options                    Help
                                    ┌──────────────────────────┐
                                    │ Add Watch...             │
                                    │ Instant Watch...  Shift+F9│
                                    │ Watchpoint...            │
                                    │ Delete Watch...          │
                                    │ Delete All Watch         │
 ╭──────────────╮                   ├──────────────────────────┤
 │executes program│ ───────────────▶│ Trace On                 │
 │ in slow motion │                  │ History On               │
 ╰──────────────╯                   ├──────────────────────────┤
                                    │ Toggle Breakpoint     F9 │
                                    │ Clear All Breakpoints    │
                                    │ Break on Errors          │
                                    │ Set Next Statement       │
                                    └──────────────────────────┘




 ←████████████████████████████████████████████████████████████████████→
 ────────────────────────────── Immediate ──────────────────────────────

  F1=Help │ Adds specified expression to the Watch window        00001:001
```

TABLE B.14	The Debug Menu	

COMMAND	SHORTCUT KEYS	FUNCTION
Add Watch...		Sets watch expression.
Instant Watch...	Shift + F9	Displays the value of an expression or condition in a suspended or stopped program.
Watchpoint...		Sets watchpoint.
Delete Watch...		Deletes watch-window entry.
Delete All Watch		Deletes all watch-window entries.
Trace On		Executes program in slow motion and records the last 20 statements executed.
History On		Records the last 20 statements executed.
Toggle Breakpoint	F9	Toggles breakpoint on and off at cursor location.
Clear All Breakpoints		Clears all breakpoints.
Break on Errors		Traces an error-causing statement in a program that uses the ON ERROR GOTO statement. (See Section C.2 in Appendix C for a discussion of the ON ERROR GOTO statement.)
Set Next Statement		Sets the statement that the cursor is in as the next statement to be executed. Used together with a breakpoint to debug a program.

The Calls Menu

The Calls menu does not contain commands. If your program invokes subprograms from within other subprograms through the use of the CALL statement, the Calls menu shows the stack of called procedures. In Figure B.17 on the next page, the subprogram Tax is called from Compute, which is called from Process, which is called from MAIN.BAS. The procedure at the top of the stack (Tax) is the current one in which execution halted for one reason or another. See Chapter 4 for additional information on the CALL statement.

FIGURE B.17

The Calls menu for the commercial version of QuickBASIC.

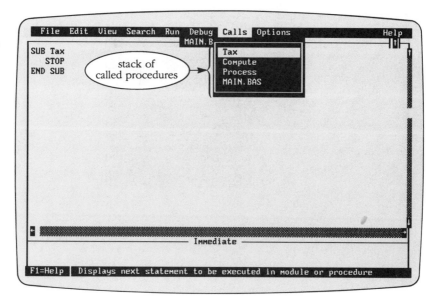

The Options Menu

The Options menu (Figure B.18) controls some of the special features of QuickBASIC. Table B.15 describes the functions of the Options commands.

FIGURE B.18

The Options menu for the commercial version of QuickBASIC.

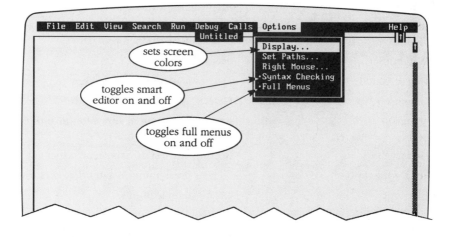

TABLE B.15 The Options Menu

COMMAND	FUNCTION
Display...	Sets the display attributes (colors, scroll bars, tab stops).
Set Paths...	Sets the search paths depending on file type.
Right Mouse...	Establishes the effect of clicking the right mouse button. The two choices are context-sensitive help, and execution of the program up to the location of the mouse pointer on the screen.
Syntax Checking	Turns QuickBASIC's smart editor on and off. The **smart editor** checks for **syntax errors**, formats lines, and translates the line to executable form if the syntax is correct.
Full Menus	Turns full menus on and off.

The Help Menu

The Help menu (Figure B.19) offers on-line help through the QB Advisor. Table B.16 summarizes the four Help commands found in the Help menu. (For additional information on the QB Advisor, see Section 2.9 in Chapter 2.)

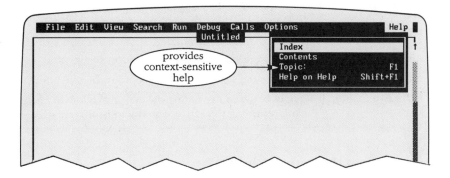

FIGURE B.19

The Help menu for the commercial version of QuickBASIC.

TABLE B.16   The Help Menu

COMMAND	SHORTCUT KEYS	FUNCTION
Index		Displays an alphabetical list of the QuickBASIC keywords. Move the cursor to any keyword and press F1 for information on the keyword.
Contents		Displays a table of contents. Move the cursor to any subject and press F1.
Topic:	F1	Displays information on the syntax and usage of the QuickBASIC variable, symbol, keyword, menu, command, dialog box at or containing the cursor.
Help on Help	Shift + F1	Displays information on how to use the mouse or keyboard to get help on an item displayed on the screen.

B.4   USING WINDOWS TO YOUR ADVANTAGE

When you start QuickBASIC, there are two windows on the screen — the view window and the immediate window as shown in Figure 2.4 on page 33. There are also two other windows that open up when certain commands are used. The help window opens at the top of the screen when you request context-sensitive help. With the commercial version of QuickBASIC, the **watch window** opens at the top of the screen when you set a watchpoint or a watch expression in your program. (See Appendix C.) In this section we describe how you can change the active window, change the window size, and scroll in the window.

Changing the Active Window

The window that contains the cursor is the **active window**. To make another window active, press F6 or Shift + F6. F6 cycles the cursor down through the windows. Shift + F6 cycles the cursor up through the windows.

If you have a mouse, move the mouse pointer to the window you want to activate and press the left button.

Changing the Window Size

You can increase or decrease the size of a window, or expand a window to encompass the entire screen. The keys used to change the window size are summarized in Table B.17.

TABLE B.17 Changing the Window Size	
KEYS	**FUNCTION**
Alt + Plus key (+)	Increases the size of the active window by one line.
Alt + Minus key (–)	Decreases the size of the active window by one line.
Ctrl + F10	Toggles between expanding the active window to encompass the screen and returning the active window to its former size.

Scrolling in the Active Window

If the program is too wide or too long to fit in the view window, you can move the window up, down, right, or left one character at a time by using the arrow keys. Table B.18 summarizes the keys for moving the window more than one character at a time. Moving the window to view parts of the program that do not fit on the screen is called **scrolling**.

TABLE B.18 Scrolling More Than One Character at a Time	
KEYS	**FUNCTION**
Home	Beginning of line.
End	End of line.
Page Up	Page up one full window.
Page Down	Page down one full window.
Ctrl + Page Up	Left one full window.
Ctrl + Page Down	Right one full window.
Ctrl + Home	Move window so beginning of program shows.
Ctrl + End	Move window so end of program shows.

If you have a mouse, you can move the window up, down, right, or left by moving the mouse pointer along the scroll bar located at the bottom right side of the view window. The scroll bars are shown in Figure 2.4 on page 33.

QuickBASIC Debugging Techniques, CHAIN Statement, and Programming Tips

C.1 DEBUGGING TECHNIQUES

Although the top-down approach and structured programming techniques help minimize errors, they by no means guarantee error-free programs. Owing to carelessness or insufficient thought, program portions can be constructed which do not work as anticipated and give erroneous results. When such problems occur, techniques are needed to isolate the errors and correct the erroneous program statements.

QuickBASIC can detect many different **grammatical errors** and display appropriate diagnostic messages. However, there is no BASIC system that can detect all errors. Some of these errors can go undetected by QuickBASIC until either an abnormal end occurs during execution or the program terminates with the results in error.

There are several techniques for attempting to discover the portion of the program that is in error. These methods are **debugging techniques**. The errors themselves are **bugs**, and the activity involved in their detection is **debugging**. QuickBASIC has a fully integrated debugger which pinpoints errors by tracing, or highlighting through the QuickBASIC source code. The QuickBASIC debugging features include the following:

1. Examining values through the immediate window
2. Executing one statement at a time
3. Setting breakpoints
4. Tracing
5. Set next statement
6. Recording
7. Watch variables and watchpoints
8. Break on errors

This appendix covers the first seven debugging features. *Break on errors* is used with the ON ERROR GOTO statement and is available only with the commercial version of QuickBASIC. For more information on this advanced debugging feature, load Quick-BASIC, toggle on Full Menus in the Options menu, activate the Debug menu, move the cursor to Break on Errors, and press Shift + F1.

Examining Values Through the Immediate Window

Following the termination of execution of a program, the program's variables remain equal to the latest values assigned. Through the immediate window, you can examine their values. This is an easy-to-use, and yet, powerful debugging tool.

To activate the immediate window, press F6. You may then display the value of any variables in the program by using the PRINT statement and the names of the variables. Recall that when a statement is entered in the immediate window, it is executed immediately. After viewing the values, press F6 to deactivate the immediate window and activate the view window.

If you have a mouse, move the pointer to the inactive window and click the mouse button.

Executing One Statement At a Time

Another debugging tool is the step mode. In the **step mode**, the PC executes the program one statement at a time. To activate the step mode, press F8. The first time you press F8, the PC displays and highlights the first executable statement in reverse video. Thereafter, each time you press the F8 key, the PC executes the statement in reverse video and displays the next executable statement in reverse video. Hence, the PC steps through the program one statement at a time as you press F8.

While the PC is in the step mode and before you press the F8 key again, you can do any of the following to better understand what the program is doing:

1. Activate the immediate window and use the PRINT statement to display the values of variables.
2. Use the F4 key to toggle between displaying the program and the output screen.
3. Modify any statement in the program. If you modify the statement in reverse video, the reverse video disappears. However, it reappears as soon as you move the cursor off the line.

To exit the step mode, press F5. The F5 key continues normal execution of the program. If you want to halt the program again, press Ctrl + Break. To continue execution after pressing Ctrl + Break, you can do one of the following:

1. Press F5 to continue normal execution.
2. Press Shift + F5 to start execution from the beginning of the program.
3. Press F8 to activate the step mode.

Setting Breakpoints

A **breakpoint** is a line in the program where you want execution to halt. Breakpoints are established by moving the cursor to the line in question, followed by pressing F9 or selecting the Toggle Breakpoint command in the Debug menu. When you execute the program after setting one or more breakpoints, the PC halts execution at the next breakpoint and displays and highlights it in reverse video. Once the program halts at a breakpoint, you can do one of the following:

1. Press F8 to enter the step mode and execute from the one statement at a time to the next breakpoint.
2. Display the values of variables in the immediate window.
3. Edit the program.
4. Delete or add new breakpoints.
5. Press F5 to continue execution of the program.

To toggle off a breakpoint, move the cursor to the breakpoint and press F9. An alternative method for clearing breakpoints is to select the command Clear All Breakpoints in the Debug menu. This latter method can be useful, especially when you have set a number of breakpoints and can't remember where they are located in the program. A breakpoint displays only in reverse video when it halts execution of the program.

To save time, you should carefully select breakpoints. Commonly used breakpoints include lines immediately following input, calculations, and decision statements.

Tracing

The Trace On command in the Debug menu (Figure B.7 on page 516) causes the PC to trace the program. **Tracing** means that the program will execute in slow motion. As the program executes in slow motion, the PC highlights each statement as it executes it. With the Trace On command you can quickly get an idea of the flow of control in your program. This activity must be observed to be appreciated.

The Trace On command works like a toggle switch. Select it once and the PC will trace the flow of control. Select it again, and you turn tracing off. You know that tracing is on when there is a bullet in front of the command in the Debug menu. Note that if you are using the commercial version of QuickBASIC, then you must toggle on Full Menus in the Option menu for the Trace On command to display in the Debug menu.

Two QuickBASIC statements that carry out the same function as the Trace On command are TRON and TROFF. The TRON statement turns on tracing for all future statements executed. The TROFF statement turns tracing off. Although most QuickBASIC programmers use the Trace On command to trace a program, some find the TRON and TROFF statements useful for tracing small sections of a program.

Set Next Statement

The Set Next Statement command in the Debug menu allows you to establish with the cursor where execution will continue following a program halt. For example, assume that you have set a breakpoint in a program. When the PC halts execution at the statement, you can move the cursor to any line in the program and select the Set Next Statement command. When execution resumes, it will begin at the line where the cursor resides rather than at the statement in reverse video. The Set Next Statement command works much like the infamous GOTO statement. Use caution when evaluating the program results following the use of this command because skipping over code can produce unexpected results. Note that if you are using the commercial version of QuickBASIC, then you must toggle on Full Menus in the Option menu for the Trace On command to display in the Debug menu.

Recording — Available Only with the Commercial Version of QuickBASIC

The History On command in the Debug menu (Figure B.16 on page 523) is often used together with breakpoints. When you select the History On command, the PC records the last 20 lines executed by the program. When the program halts at a breakpoint, you can use Shift + F8 to go back through the last 20 lines executed. You can use Shift + F10 to go forward through the last 20 lines executed.

Stepping through the last 20 lines can also be useful when your program halts due to a logic error. If you select History On prior to execution, you can step through the last 20 lines executed before the program's premature termination.

To stop recording the last 20 lines, select History On. This command acts like a toggle switch. Select it once and it's on. Select it again and it's off. You know that the History On command is active when there is a bullet in front of the command in the Debug menu. (Note that Full Menus in the Option menu must be active for the History On command to display in the Debug menu.)

Watch Variables and Watchpoints — Available Only with the Commercial Version of QuickBASIC

The Add Watch command in the Debug menu allows you to enter the names of variables or expressions you want displayed in the watch window. The **watch window** (Figure C.1 on the next page) displays above the view window whenever watch variables are active. Watching a variable is often combined with the step mode (F8) or breakpoints to track its value, thus avoiding repeated use of the PRINT statement in the immediate window.

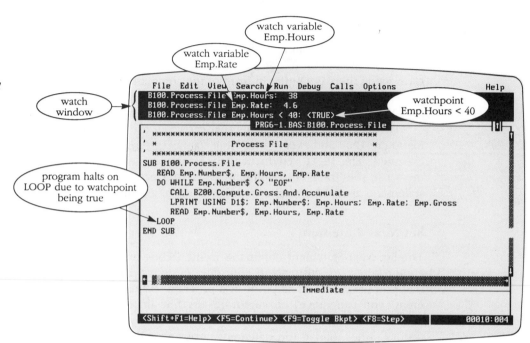

FIGURE C.1

The watch window displays above the view window. Program halted on LOOP statement when Emp.Hours: is less than 40. Value of Emp.Hours is 38. Value of Emp.Rate is 4.6.

With the commercial version of QuickBASIC, you can add watch variables or conditions to the watch window by pressing Shift + F9 or selecting the Instant Watch command. The main difference between the Instant Watch and Add Watch commands is that with Instant Watch you do not have to type the variable name or condition. You simply select a watch variable by moving the cursor within the variable name in the program. To select a condition, you must use the Shift and arrow keys to highlight it before pressing Shift + F9.

The Watchpoint command in the Debug menu allows you to enter a watchpoint in the watch window. A **watchpoint** (Figure C.1) is a condition that halts program execution when it becomes true.

To delete individual watch variables or watchpoints, select the Delete Watch command in the Debug menu. To delete all watch variables and watch points, select the Delete All Watch command.

C.2 TRAPPING USER ERRORS (ON ERROR GOTO AND RESUME)

A thoroughly tested program cannot be guaranteed to be reliable once it is turned over to a user. Most abnormal terminations in a production environment are due to user errors and not programmer errors. This is especially true for programs that interact with the user. Good programmers will attempt to trap as many user errors as possible. User errors fall into two basic categories:

1. Erroneous data entered in response to INPUT statements
2. Failure to follow the instructions given in the user's manual

Errors that fall into the first category can be trapped by validating incoming data to ensure it is reasonable or within limits as shown in Chapter 5. The second category of user errors includes both soft errors and hard errors. A **soft error** is any error that causes the PC to display a diagnostic message followed by continued execution of the program. Entering string data in response to an INPUT statement with a numeric variable is an example of a soft error. The PC will display an error message and request the data be reentered.

A **hard error** is any error that causes the PC to display a dialog box with a diagnostic message followed by termination of execution of the program. Examples of hard errors include the following:

1. Not placing a diskette in the disk drive
2. Not closing the door on the disk drive
3. A defective diskette
4. A diskette that has not been formatted

In some situations, it is preferable to handle both hard and soft errors within the program through the use of the ON ERROR GOTO and RESUME statements. The ON ERROR GOTO provides a common branch point for any error that occurs following its execution in a program. The branch point and the statements that follow it are an **error-handling routine**. In an error-handling routine, it is often desirable to resume execution of the program at a specified point. The RESUME statement is used for this purpose. The general forms of the ON ERROR GOTO and RESUME statements are shown in Tables C.1 and C.2.

TABLE C.1   The ON ERROR GOTO Statement

General Form:	ON ERROR GOTO label where **label** is equal to a line label or line number.
Purpose:	Activates error trapping and specifies the line label or line number of an error-handling routine to transfer control to when an error occurs. When label = 0, error trapping is deactivated, and a diagnostic message is displayed followed by termination of the program.
Examples:	ON ERROR GOTO X100.Special.Handler ON ERROR GOTO X200.Error.Routine ON ERROR GOTO 0
Note:	In the error-trapping routine, the special variables ERR and ERL may be tested where ERR represents the error code of the last error and ERL represents the line number of the statement that caused the error. ERL returns 0 if no line numbers are used in the program.

TABLE C.2   The RESUME Statement

General Form:	RESUME n where **n** is null, zero, label, or the keyword NEXT.
Purpose:	Continues execution of the program after an error-handling routine has been performed. RESUME or RESUME 0 resumes execution at the statement that caused the error. RESUME NEXT resumes execution at the statement immediately following the one that caused the error. RESUME label resumes execution at the specified line label or line number.
Examples:	RESUME RESUME 0 RESUME NEXT RESUME Around
Note:	This statement should not be executed unless the ON ERROR GOTO statement has been previously executed.

Once the ON ERROR GOTO statement is inserted in a program, any error that normally terminates execution now causes the PC to transfer control to the error-handling routine. QuickBASIC provides two functions ERL and ERR that return values before the ON ERROR GOTO statement transfers control to the error-handling routine. ERL is assigned the line number of the statement that caused the error. If line numbers are not used, then ERL returns a zero. ERR is assigned an error code as shown in Table C.3.

TABLE C.3   Error Descriptions and Their Corresponding Error Codes

ERROR DESCRIPTION	ERROR CODE	ERROR DESCRIPTION	ERROR CODE	ERROR DESCRIPTION	ERROR CODE
Advanced feature	73	Permission Denied	70	Out of string space	14
Bad file mode	54	Division by zero	11	Overflow	6
Bad file name	64	Duplicate definition	10	Path/file access error	75
Bad file number	52	Field overflow	50	Path not found	76
Bad record number	63	FIELD statement		Rename across disks	74
Bad record length	59	active	56	RESUME without	
CASE ELSE expected	39	File already exists	58	error	20
Communication		File already open	55	RETURN without	
buffer overflow	69	File not found	53	GOSUB	3
Device fault	25	Illegal function call	5	String formula too	
Device I/O error	57	Input past end	62	complex	16
Device timeout	24	Internal error	51	Subscript out of range	9
Device unavailable	68	No RESUME	19	Syntax error	2
Disk full	61	Out of data	4	Too many files	67
Disk media error	72	Out of memory	7	Type mismatch	13
Disk not ready	71	Out of paper	27	Variable required	40

Table C.3 lists the error description and corresponding error code the ON ERROR GOTO statement traps. The table entries are alphabetized by error description. (For an in-depth discussion of the error descriptions, see the QuickBASIC user's manual.)

Through the use of IF statements, a decision can be made in the error-handling routine to terminate execution or resume execution at some point in the program. The ON ERROR GOTO 0 statement directs the PC to disable error trapping, display a diagnostic message, and terminate execution. On the other hand, the RESUME statement may be used to transfer control to any point in the program to continue execution. If execution is to resume following an error, an error recovery procedure, such as displaying a message or assigning a value to a variable, is performed before resuming execution outside the error-handling routine. The ON ERROR GOTO statement must be placed in a program in such a way that it is executed before the lines in which errors are to be trapped.

Program C.1 uses the ON ERROR GOTO statement to trap user errors. In the error-handling routine, the ERR function is compared to selected error codes. If ERR is equal to 25 (Device fault, such as printer not ready) or 27 (Out of paper), a recovery procedure is executed. If ERR equals any other code, then a message is displayed informing the user to write the program name and the error code, and transmit this information to someone in charge of resolving the error.

Notice that the error handling routine is part of the Main Program. Following the DATA statements, the first END statement, line 18, terminates after normal execution of the Main Program. The second END statement, line 33, is the physical end of the Main Program.

Use the letter X to identify error-catching subprograms. The letter X will cause these subprograms to reside at the very bottom of the program listing.

PROGRAM C.1

```
1   ' Program C.1
2   ' Illustrating the Use of
3   ' the ON ERROR GOTO Statement
4   ' **************************
5   ON ERROR GOTO Handler
6   LPRINT "Number", "Amount"
7   LPRINT
8   READ Number$, Amount
9   DO WHILE Number$ <> "EOF"
10     LPRINT Number$, Amount
11     READ Number$, Amount
12  LOOP
13  LPRINT "Job Complete"
14  ' *******Data Follows********
15  DATA 123, 124.89, 126, 145.91, 134, 234.78
16  DATA 210, 567.34, 235, 435.12, 345, 192.45
17  DATA EOF, 0
18  END
19
20  ' **************************
21  ' *   Error-Handling Routine *
22  ' **************************
23  Handler:
24     CLS  ' Clear Screen
25     SELECT CASE ERR
26        CASE 25, 27
27           CALL X100.Printer.Error
28           RESUME
29        CASE ELSE
30           CALL X110.Irrecoverable.Error
31           STOP
32     END SELECT
33  END
34
35  ' **************************
36  ' *       Printer Error        *
37  ' **************************
38  SUB X100.Printer.Error
39     PRINT "Please check the printer."
40     PRINT "It may be turned off, out of"
41     PRINT "paper or it is not properly"
42     PRINT "connected."
43     PRINT
44     INPUT "Press the Enter key when the printer is ready....", Control$
45  END SUB
46
47  ' **************************
48  ' *   Irrecoverable Error    *
49  ' **************************
50  SUB X110.Irrecoverable.Error
51     BEEP: BEEP: BEEP: BEEP
52     PRINT "An Irrecoverable error has occurred"
53     PRINT "Please copy down the following:"
54     PRINT "error code.  Transmit the error code"
55     PRINT "and the program name to the Data"
56     PRINT "Processing department."
57     PRINT
58     PRINT "Error code ========> "; ERR
59     PRINT : PRINT "Thank You"
60     END SUB
```

In Program C.1, line 5 activates QuickBASIC's error-trapping feature. If an error occurs following line 5, then control transfers to line 23. In the SELECT CASE (lines 25 through 32), if the error code is equal to 25 or 27, then control passes to the subprogram X100.Printer.Error (lines 38 through 45), and an appropriate message is displayed. If the error code is not 25 or 27, then control transfers to the X110.Irrecoverable.Error subprogram (lines 50 through 60), and a message is displayed requesting the user to transmit the error code and the program name to someone in charge of resolving the error.

An END statement is used in line 18 of the Main Program instead of a STOP statement or ON ERROR GOTO 0, so the output screen remains on the monitor to give the user the opportunity to write the message. Both STOP and ON ERROR GOTO 0 cause the PC to immediately display the view window rather than the output screen.

C.3   CHAINING

Another technique that may be used to implement the top-down approach, especially when the programs are very large, involves writing external programs that are linked together by the CHAIN statement. The CHAIN statement may be used within a QuickBASIC program to instruct your PC to stop executing the current program, load into main storage another program from auxiliary storage, and start executing the new program.

The COMMON statement is used together with the CHAIN statement to pass selected variables from the current program, also called the **chaining program**, to the new program, also called the **chained-to program**.

The general form of the CHAIN statement is shown in Table C.4.

TABLE C.4 The CHAIN Statement	
General Form:	CHAIN "filespec" where **filespec** is the name of the program loaded from auxiliary storage and executed.
Purpose:	Instructs the PC to stop executing the current program, load into main storage another program from auxiliary storage, and start executing the new program.
Examples:	1. CHAIN "B:PROG2" 2. CHAIN "PROG3"
Note:	Don't use the *named* COMMON *block* form of the COMMON statement because *named* COMMON *blocks* are not preserved when chaining. Use a *blank* COMMON statement as shown in Programs C.2 and C.3.

In the first example in Table C.4, the CHAIN statement terminates execution of the current program (the chaining program); loads PROG2 from the B drive; and begins execution of PROG2. PROG2 is the chained-to program.

Unless otherwise specified in a COMMON statement, none of the variables defined in the chaining program are available to PROG2, the chained-to program.

In the second example in Table C.4, the CHAIN statement loads PROG3 from the default drive.

Care must be taken when using the READ and DATA statements in a chained-to program that may be called a number of times. Each time a chained-to program is executed, the pointer is moved back to the beginning of the data-sequence holding area. However, files that are opened in a chaining program remain opened, with the pointer at the same position in the file.

Assume that Program C.2 is in main storage. Assume also that Program C.3 is stored on the default drive.

PROGRAM C.2

```
1     ' Program C.2
2     ' The Chaining Program
3     ' *******************
4     COMMON A, B, C
5     A = 3
6     B = 5
7     C = 10
8     CHAIN "PRGC-3"
9     END

      [run]
```

PROGRAM C.3

```
10    ' Program C.3
11    ' The Chained-To Program
12    ' *********************
13    COMMON D, E, F
14    Total = D + E + F
15    CLS
16    PRINT "Value of D ====================>"; D
17    PRINT: PRINT "Value of E ===================>"; E
18    PRINT: PRINT "Value of F ===================>"; F
19    PRINT: PRINT "Value of Total ================>"; Total
20    END
```

When Program C.2 is executed, the COMMON statement in line 4 establishes A, B, and C as common variables available to any program chained to a similar COMMON statement. Lines 5 through 7 assign the values 3, 5, and 10 to A, B, and C. Line 8 instructs the PC to stop executing the Program C.2, load Program C.3 from auxiliary storage, and start executing it.

The COMMON statement in line 13 instructs the PC to assign the values of A, B, and C to D, E, and F. Line 14 assigns Total the sum of D, E, and F. Lines 16 through 19 display the values of D, E, F, and Total as shown in Figure C.2. Note that the values of D, E, and F are identical to the values assigned to A, B, and C in Program C.2.

FIGURE C.2

The display due to Program C.2 chaining to Program C.3.

```
Value of D ====================> 3

Value of E ====================> 5

Value of F ====================> 10

Value of Total ================> 18
```

In most beginning programming classes, programs seldom reach the size that would require the use of the CHAIN statements and the chaining concept. However, in the real world of programming, programs that use the techniques described in Programs C.2 and C.3 are the rule rather than the exception.

C.4   PROGRAMMING TIPS

With QuickBASIC there are many different ways you can code a program and still obtain the same results. This section presents some tips for coding a program to improve its performance, efficiency, structure, and clarity. Each tip is explained and applied accordingly. You are encouraged to add to the tips in this section.

Tip 1: Use Simple Arithmetic

Addition is performed faster than multiplication, which in turn is faster than division or exponentiation. For example, use the code on the left rather than on the right below:

```
Area = Base * Height * .5        instead of:    Area = Base * Height / 2
Length = Side1 + Side1                           Length = 2 * Side1
Vol = Length * Length * Length                   Vol = Length ^ 3
```

Tip 2: Avoid Repetitive Evaluations of Expressions

If identical computations are performed in several statements, evaluate the common expression once and save the result in a variable for use in later statements. For example, use the code on the left rather than on the right below:

```
Disc = SQR(B * B - 4 * A * C)    instead of:    Root1 = -B + SQR(B * B - 4 * A * C)
Root1 = -B + Disc                                Root2 = -B - SQR(B * B - 4 * A * C)
Root2 = -B - Disc
```

Tip 3: Avoid Recomputation of Constants within a Loop

Do not make unnecessary computations. Remove the unnecessary code from a loop including expressions and statements which do not affect the loop. Place such code outside and before the range of the loop. For example, use the code on the left rather than on the right below:

```
Pi = 3.141598              instead of:    Pi = 3.141598
K = 4 * Pi                                FOR Rad = 1 TO 500
X = Y + 2                                     PRINT 4 * Pi * Rad * Rad
FOR Rad = 1 TO 500                            X = Y + 2
    PRINT K * Rad * Rad                   NEXT Rad
NEXT Rad
```

Regardless of the value of Rad, 4π is always constant. Instead of calculating 4π five hundred times, remove this expression from the loop and compute it once. It is also not necessary to compute the value of X each time through the loop, since the loop never changes the value of X.

Tip 4: Use Integer Variables for Counters and Whole Number Running Totals

Integer arithmetic is many times faster than single-precision arithmetic. Hence, use integer variables for counters and whole number running totals in a program. For example, use the code at the top of the next page.

```
Count% = Count% + 1
Enrollment% = Enrollment% + Division%
```

instead of:

```
Count = Count + 1
Enrollment = Enrollment + Division
```

If you wish to avoid writing the percent sign (%) after each variable name and still use the latter two statements as they are, you may precede these statements with:

```
DEFINE C-E
```

which declares all variables whose names begin with C through E as integer type.

Tip 5: Use Integer Variables As the Control Variables in For Loops

For the same reason indicated in Tip 4, use integer variables rather than single-precision variables for the loop variable in a FOR statement as shown by the partial programs in Figures 9.6 and 9.7 on page 354. For example, use the following code:

```
FOR Loop.Variable% = 1 TO 1000
```

instead of:

```
FOR Loop.Variable = 1 TO 1000
```

(Note that the code in Tip 3 can further be improved by applying Tip 5 to the variable named RAD.)

Tip 6: Use For Loops Instead of Do Loops for Counter-Controlled Loops

For loops execute faster than Do loops. Thus, when the loop is controlled by a counter, use a For loop rather than a Do loop. For example, use the code on the left rather than on the right below:

```
FOR I% = 1 TO 10                       I% = 1
       .                               DO WHILE I% <= 10
       .                                      .
       .                                      .
NEXT I%                                        .
                                       I% = I% + 1
                                       LOOP
```
instead of:

Tip 7: Use QuickBASIC Functions

Use the QuickBASIC functions wherever possible because in many cases they conserve main storage and always execute faster than the same capability written in QuickBASIC. For example, use the code on the left rather than on the right below:

```
Disc = SQR(B * B - 4 * A * C)
```
instead of:
```
Disc = (B * B - 4 * A * C) ^ (0.5)
```

Tip 8: Write Clearly and Avoid Clever or Tricky Code

Resist the temptation to write clever or tricky code that is difficult to understand. Later modification by someone else may take additional time and may be costly in the long run. For example, do the following:

```
FOR Row% = 1 TO 10
   FOR Column% = 1 TO 10
      IF Row% = Column% THEN
         Array(Row%, Column%) = 1
      ELSE
         Array(Row%, Column%) = 0
      END IF
   NEXT Column%
NEXT Row%
```

instead of:

```
FOR Row = 1 TO 10
   FOR Column = 1 TO 10
      Array(Row, Column) = INT(Row / Column) * INT(Column / Row)
   NEXT Column
NEXT Row
```

This section of code generates an array called Array where ones are placed on the main diagonal and zeros everywhere else.

Tip 9: Avoid Needless IF Statements Whenever Possible

You can avoid the need for more IF statements and additional code if you use compound conditions in IF statements. For example, do the following:

```
IF I = J AND K = L THEN
   A = 99
END IF
```

instead of:

```
IF I = J THEN
   IF K = L THEN
      A = 99
   END IF
END IF
```

Tip 10: Use the SELECT CASE Rather Than IF Statements When More than Two Paths are Involved

The SELECT CASE statement is easier for maintenance programmers to read and interpret than a series of nested IF statements. For an example, see page 192 in Chapter 6.

To make a SELECT CASE statement efficient, place the CASE statements with the most frequently occurring conditions first.

C.5 PROGRAM STYLE TIPS

Throughout this book we have offered tips on how to style your program. The following list summarizes these tips:

Tip 1: A program should be easy for a person to read and understand.

Tip 2: Use blank spaces to improve readability.

Tip 3: Use one statement per line unless multiple statements improve readability. .

Tip 4: At the beginning of the program, include comments to identify the author, date written, program name, and to describe what the program does. (See Chapter 2, page 53.) Depending on the complexity of the program, you may want to include comments pertaining to usage, I/O requirements, execution time, and special operating requirements.

Tip 5: Use a boxed-in comment at the beginning of each subprogram to identify it and clarify any ambiguities.

Tip 6: Begin a subprogram name with a letter. The letter should identify the leg to which the subprogram belongs in the top-down chart. Begin with the letter A in the leftmost leg, followed by the letter B for the next leg and so on.

Tip 7: Develop a method for naming special-type subprograms, such as those that have multiple superiors or are error-catching subprograms. For example, begin subprogram names that have multiple superiors with the letter M. Begin error-catching subprograms with the letter X.

Tip 8: Follow the letter in a subprogram name with a level number (for example, 100, 200, 310, etc.). The level number should correspond to the level of the corresponding module in the top-down chart.

Tip 9: Follow the letter and level number with a period (.) and a self-explanatory subprogram name.

Tip 10: Do not comment for the sake of commenting. Comments should add to the understanding of a section of code.

Tip 11: Be sure all variable names and label names are meaningful and self-explanatory.

Tip 12: Capitalize only the first letter in a variable name or label name. If two or more words make up the name, then separate the two words with a period and capitalize the first letter of each word. Capitalize all the letters in a FUNCTION name.

Tip 13: Use parentheses in complex expressions with arithmetic, relational, or logical operators to prevent errors and improve readability.

Tip 14: Use at most one variable per INPUT statement.

Tip 15: Place the DATA statements near the end of the Main Program.

Tip 16: Include in each DATA statement the number of data items read each time the READ statement is executed.

Tip 17: Indent the statements within a subprogram by three spaces.

Tip 18: Indent the statements within any loop by three spaces.

Tip 19: Indent the statements in the true task and false task of an IF statement by three spaces.

Tip 20: Indent the statements in a CASE statement by three spaces.

Formatting a Diskette, DOS Commands, ASCII Character Set, and Personal Computer Literature

This appendix presents a series of topics that relate specifically to the personal computer. Included are the operating instructions to format a diskette; MS-DOS commands (also called DOS commands); and a list of popular magazines, newspapers, and manuals for the personal computer.

D.1 FORMATTING A DISKETTE

You must format a diskette before the IBM PC can use it for the first time. Formatting is the process of marking off a diskette into sections in which programs or data can be stored. Later, these numbered sections are used by the PC to recall information. For example, when you save a program, the name of the program and its location are recorded by the PC in the diskette's directory. Then when you instruct the PC to load the program back into main storage, it searches the directory for the name and corresponding location.

A diskette has to be formatted only once. If you format a diskette that contains programs or data, they will be lost; the formatting process erases any information that is on the diskette.

To format a diskette, ask your instructor for a system diskette. The system diskette contains the operating system, MS-DOS or PC-DOS, and a number of utilities (programs supplied by the computer manufacturer). One of the utilities is called FORMAT, and it is used to format a diskette. With the system diskette and the diskette to be formatted in hand, do the following:

1. Boot the PC following the direction of your instructor.
2. Enter the following command to the right of the DOS prompt:

   FORMAT A: (Press the Enter key.)

   If you are formatting a low-density 3-1/2 inch diskette in a high-density disk drive, use the following command:

   FORMAT A:/N:9   (Press the Enter key.)

3. Insert the diskette to be formatted in the A drive.
4. Press any key.
5. After a short time, the PC displays the number of bytes available on the newly formatted diskette and responds with the following question:

   Format another (Y/N)?

   Enter N to quit the FORMAT utility or Y to format another diskette.

D.2   DOS COMMANDS

There are two categories of DOS commands — **internal** and **external**. Internal commands, such as COPY and DIR, are part of the operating system program COMMAND.COM. External commands, such as FORMAT and DISKCOPY, are separate from COMMAND.COM; they are utilities that normally reside on the **system diskette**. For example, when you list the files on the system diskette, FORMAT.COM and DISKCOPY.COM will list along with COMMAND.COM. If these utilities do not show up in a listing of the files on the system diskette, then the commands are not available to you.

Two important DOS commands are COPY and DIR. A discussion of these two DOS commands follows, and a summary of additional commands is given in Table D.1.

COPY

The COPY command is used to copy files from one diskette to another. It may also be used to copy files to the same diskette, provided a different file name is used for the duplicate. The general form for the COPY command is:

```
COPY source-file Target-file
```

Following are some examples.

1. COPY B:LAB2-1.BAS   A:

    LAB2-1.BAS on the diskette in the B drive is copied to the diskette in the A.

2. COPY B:*.BAS   A:

    All the files on the diskette in the B drive which have an extension of .BAS are copied to the diskette in the A drive. The asterisk (*) and question mark (?) are global characters (**wild card characters**). The **asterisk** indicates that any character can occupy that position and all the remaining positions in the file name or extension. The **question mark** indicates that any character can occupy that position only.

3. COPY A:*.*   B:

    Copies all files on the diskette in the A drive to the diskette in the B drive.

4. COPY LAB2-?.* A:

    Copies all files with six-character file names beginning with LAB2- from the diskette in the default drive to the diskette in the A drive. If the A drive is the default drive, an error message will display, because you cannot copy files to the same diskette unless you specify new names for the duplicate files.

5. COPY B:LAB2-3.BAS   B:LAB2-4.BAS

    Copies LAB2-3.BAS on the diskette in the B drive under the file name LAB2-4.BAS.

DIR

The DIR (DIRectory) command is used to list information about a diskette in the specified drive. Depending on how the command is entered, the information displayed may include a list of the file names; the size of each file (in bytes); the date and time each file was created; the number of files listed; and the amount of free area left on the diskette (in bytes). Here are some examples.

1. DIR

    Lists, one to a line, the names of the files on the diskette in the default drive and all relevant information concerning the files and the diskette.

2. `DIR B:.BAS`

   Lists, one to a line, the names of the files that have an extension of .BAS on the diskette in the B drive and all relevant information concerning the listed files and the diskette.

3. `DIR /P`

   Lists one full screen at a time, one to a line, the names of the files on the diskette in the default drive and all relevant information concerning the files and the diskette. Press any key to continue with the directory listing.

4. `DIR B:/W`

   The `/W` parameter lists the file names five to a line (wide display). Additional information about each file (size, time, and date) is not included in the display.

5. `DIR /O`

   Lists in alphabetical order, the names of the files on the diskette in the default drive (MS-DOS 5.0 and higher).

6. `DIR >PRN`

   The `PRN` parameter prints on the attached printer, one to a line, the names of the files on the diskette in the default drive.

Summary of Important DOS Commands

Table D.1 summarizes the important DOS commands. (For examples of how to use these commands, see the appropriate Disk Operating System User's manual.)

TABLE D.1   Summary of Important DOS Commands

DOS COMMAND	FUNCTION
`CD or CHDIR`	Changes the current directory of the specified or default drive. `CD\CHAP78` changes the current directory to CHAP78. `CD\` changes the current directory to the root directory on the default drive.
`CLS`	Clears the screen and places the cursor in the upper left corner.
`COPY`	Copies one or more files from the diskette in the source disk drive to the diskette in the target disk drive.
`DATE`	Displays the current system date and allows you to enter a new date.
`DEL`	Deletes one or more files from the diskette in the specified disk drive; same as the `ERASE` command.
`DIR`	Lists all files which meet a criterion in a directory on the specified disk drive.
`DISKCOPY`	Duplicates the diskette in the source disk drive to the diskette in the target disk drive. `DISKCOPY` is a utility; it is not part of `COMMAND.COM`. Therefore, this command will work only if the system diskette contains `DISKCOPY.COM`.
`ERASE`	Deletes one or more files from the diskette in the specified disk drive, same as the `DEL` command.
`FORMAT`	Prepares a diskette so the PC can read and write data and information to the diskette. `FORMAT` is a utility; it is not part of `COMMAND.COM`. Therefore, this command will work only if the system diskette contains `FORMAT.COM`.
`MD or MKDIR`	Creates a new directory.
`MODE`	MODE 40 sets the display mode of the screen to 40 characters per line. `MODE 80` sets the display mode to 80 characters per line.

(continued)

TABLE D.1 Summary of Important DOS Commands (continued)	
DOS COMMAND	**FUNCTION**
PRINT	Prints the specified ASCII file on the attached printer. PRINT is a utility; it is not part of COMMAND.COM. Therefore, this command will work only if the system diskette contains PRINT.COM.
RENAME	Changes the name of the specified file.
RD or RMDIR	Removes a directory from a multilevel directory structure. Before you remove a directory, you must delete its files and subdirectories.
TIME	Displays the current system time and allows you to enter a new time.
TYPE	Displays the specified ASCII file on the screen.

D.3   QuickBASIC DOS-LIKE STATEMENTS

QuickBASIC includes statements that function the same as many of the DOS commands. Additional QuickBASIC statements allow you to temporarily or permanently return control to DOS. These statements are summarized in Table D.2 They may be included in a program or executed in the immediate window.

TABLE D.2 QuickBASIC DOS-Like Statements	
STATEMENT	**FUNCTION**
CHDIR pathspecification	Changes the current directory for the specified drive.
DATE$	Returns the current date. (See Chapter 9, page 338.)
DATE$ = mm/dd/yy	Sets the system date. (See Chapter 9, page 342.)
FILES filespecification	Lists the names of all programs and data files in auxiliary storage on the default drive or as specified by file specification.
KILL filespecification	Deletes a file from disk.
MKDIR pathname	Creates a new directory.
NAME oldfilespec AS newfilespec	Renames a file on disk.
RMDIR pathname	Removes a directory from disk.
SHELL commandstring	Places the current QB session in a temporary wait state and returns control to DOS. Can also execute another program or DOS command as specified in commandstring. Type EXIT to return control to QuickBASIC.
SYSTEM	Closes all open files and returns control to DOS.
TIME$	Returns the current time. (See Chapter 9, page 338.)
TIME$ = hh:m:ss	Sets the system time. (See Chapter 9, page 342.)

D.4   ASCII CHARACTER CODES

Table D.3 lists all 256 ASCII decimal codes and their corresponding characters. Each time you press a key, the associated *decimal code* is transmitted to main storage and the *character* is displayed on the screen. Special characters may be displayed on the screen by using PRINT CHR$(n), where n is the corresponding decimal code. (See Figure 11.7 on page 439.)

ASCII decimal codes 126 to 255 represent the USA character set. However, foreign character sets may also be represented by these decimal codes. Note also the appearance of some of the mathematical and graphical characters by these decimal codes.

TABLE D.3   ASCII Character Set

DECIMAL CODE	CHARACTER	DECIMAL CODE	CHARACTER	DECIMAL CODE	CHARACTER	DECIMAL CODE	CHARACTER	DECIMAL CODE	CHARACTER
000	(null)	052	4	104	h	156	£	208	⊥⊥
001	☺	053	5	105	i	157	¥	209	╤
002	☻	054	6	106	j	158	Pt	210	╥
003	♥	055	7	107	k	159	ƒ	211	╙
004	♦	056	8	108	l	160	á	212	╘
005	♣	057	9	109	m	161	í	213	╒
006	♠	058	:	110	n	162	ó	214	╓
007	(beep)	059	;	111	o	163	ú	215	╫
008	◘	060	<	112	p	164	ñ	216	╪
009	(tab)	061	=	113	q	165	Ñ	217	┘
010	(line feed)	062	>	114	r	166	ª	218	┌
011	(home)	063	?	115	s	167	º	219	█
012	(form feed)	064	@	116	t	168	¿	220	▄
013	(carriage return)	065	A	117	u	169	⌐	221	▌
014	♫	066	B	118	v	170	¬	222	▐
015	☼	067	C	119	w	171	½	223	▀
016	►	068	D	120	x	172	¼	224	α
017	◄	069	E	121	y	173	¡	225	β
018	↕	070	F	122	z	174	«	226	Γ
019	‼	071	G	123	{	175	»	227	π
020	¶	072	H	124			176	░	228	Σ
021	§	073	I	125	}	177	▒	229	σ
022	▬	074	J	126	~	178	▓	230	µ
023	↨	075	K	127	⌂	179	│	231	τ
024	↑	076	L	128	Ç	180	┤	232	Φ
025	↓	077	M	129	ü	181	╡	233	Θ
026	←	078	N	130	é	182	╢	234	Ω
027	→	079	O	131	â	183	╖	235	δ
028	(cursor right)	080	P	132	ä	184	╕	236	∞
029	(cursor left)	081	Q	133	à	185	╣	237	Ø
030	(cursor up)	082	R	134	å	186	║	238	∈
031	(cursor down)	083	S	135	ç	187	╗	239	∩
032	(space)	084	T	136	ê	188	╝	240	≡
033	!	085	U	137	ë	189	╜	241	±
034	"	086	V	138	è	190	╛	242	≥
035	#	087	W	139	ï	191	┐	243	≤
036	$	088	X	140	î	192	└	244	⌠
037	%	089	Y	141	ì	193	┴	245	⌡
038	&	090	Z	142	Ä	194	┬	246	÷
039	'	091	[	143	Å	195	├	247	≈
040	(	092	\	144	É	196	─	248	°
041	)	093	]	145	ae	197	┼	249	●
042	*	094	^	146	Æ	198	╞	250	·
043	+	095	_	147	ô	199	╟	251	√
044	,	096	`	148	ö	200	╚	252	ⁿ
045	-	097	a	149	ò	201	╔	253	²
046	.	098	b	150	û	202	╩	254	■
047	/	099	c	151	ù	203	╦	255	(blank)
048	0	100	d	152	ÿ	204	╠		
049	1	101	e	153	Ö	205	═		
050	2	102	f	154	Ü	206	╬		
051	3	103	g	155	¢	207	╧		

D.5   PERSONAL COMPUTER MAGAZINES, NEWSPAPERS, AND MANUALS

This section contains a selected list of some of the popular magazines, newspapers, and manuals for personal computers. Many libraries have copies of these materials, and you are encouraged to look them over.

You can subscribe to the following magazines by contacting the publisher at the addresses listed below.

Personal Computer Magazines

1. *Byte*, Subscription Department, P.O. Box 555, Hightstown, New Jersey 08520
2. *LOTUS*, P.O. Box 5289, Boulder, Colorado 80321
3. *LAN*, 12 West 21st St., New York, New York 10010
4. *PC Computing*, P.O. Box 50253, Boulder, Colorado 80321
5. *PC Magazine*, P.O. Box 51524, Boulder, Colorado 80321
6. *PC Tech Journal*, P.O. Box 2966, Boulder, Colorado 80321
7. *PC World*, P.O. Box 51833, Boulder, Colorado 80321
8. *Personal Computing*, P.O. Box 420110, Palm Coa, Florida 32142
9. *Publish*, Subscriber Services, P.O. Box 55400, Boulder, Colorado 80322
10. *SIGSMALL/PC Notes*, 11 West 42nd St., New York, New York 10036
11. *WordPerfect Magazine*, Circulation Dept., 270 W. Center, Orem, Utah 84057.
12. *Home Office Computing*, P.O. Box 51344, Boulder, Colorado 80321.

Personal Computer Newspapers

There are a number of newspapers that cover a variety of topics concerning personal computers. As with PC magazines, you can subscribe to these newspapers by contacting the publisher.

1. *Computerworld*, P.O. Box 1016, Southeastern, Pennsylvania 19398
2. *Info World*, P.O. Box 1018, Southeastern, Pennsylvania 19398
3. *MIS Week*, P.O. Box 2036, Mahopac, New York 10541
4. *Network World*, 161 Worchester Road, Framingham, Massachusetts 01701
5. *PC Week*, One Park Avenue, 4th Floor, New York, New York 10016

Manuals

Microsoft Corporation publishes manuals that cover QuickBASIC and other programming languages. These manuals may be purchased from your local personal computer dealer or by contacting:

Microsoft Press
One Microsoft Way
Redmond, WA 98073–0399
1–800–426–9400

1. *Microsoft QuickBASIC: BASIC Language Reference*
2. *Microsoft QuickBASIC: Learning and Using Microsoft QuickBASIC*
3. *Microsoft QuickBASIC: Programming in BASIC—Selected Topics*
4. *Microsoft QuickBASIC: Programmer's Toolbox*
5. *Microsoft QuickBASIC: Programmer's Quick Reference*
6. *Microsoft QuickBASIC: Primer Plus*
7. *Microsoft QuickBASIC: Bible*
8. *Beginning MS-DOS QBasic*
9. *MS-DOS QBasic*

Answers to the Even-Numbered Test Your Basic Skills Exercises

CHAPTER 1

2. The basic subsystems of a computer are input, main storage, central processing unit, auxiliary storage, and output.

   Input — a device that allows programs and data to enter into the computer system.

   Main Storage — a subsystem that allows for the storage of programs and data for the central processing unit to process at a given time.

   Central Processing Unit (CPU) — the unit that controls and supervises the entire computer system and performs the arithmetic and logical operations on data that is specified by the stored program.

   Auxiliary Storage — a subsystem that is used to store programs and data for immediate recall.

   Output — a device that allows the computer system to communicate the results of a program to the user.

4. A diskette unit and a hard disk unit both serve as input and output devices.

6. Hardware is the physical equipment of a computer system. The subsystems as described in number 2 above are hardware. Software refers to the programs, languages, written procedures, and documentation concerned with the operation of a computer system.

8. The different sized diskettes and storage capacities are as follows:

   5 1/4'' low density — 360K; 5 1/4'' high density — 1.2M; 3 1/2'' low density — 720K; 3 1/2'' high density — 1.44M; 3 1/2'' very high density — 2.88M; and 2'' low density — 360K.

10. a. Male.Cnt = 1, Female.Cnt = 2, Sale.Cnt = 3, Commission Average = 700
    b. Male.Cnt = 1, Female.Cnt = 0, Sale.Cnt = 1, Commission Average = 300
    c. Male.Cnt = 0, Female.Cnt = 0, a diagnostic message displays when an attempt is made to compute Commission Average because the value of Sale.Cnt is zero and division by zero is not permitted.

12. **Word processing** — A program used to write, revise, and edit letters, reports, and manuscripts with efficiency and economy (Microsoft Word).

    Spreadsheets — A program used to organize data that can be defined in terms of rows and columns (Lotus 1-2-3).

    Database — A program used to organize data into files and easily generate reports and access the data (dBASE IV).

    Graphics — A program used to create line graphs, bar graphs, pie charts, and 3-D graphic images (Harvard Presentation Graphics).

    Desktop Publishing — A program used to integrate words and pictures and generate typeset-quality documents quickly and economically (Ventura).

    Windows — A program interface between the user and the PC. This graphical user interface (GUI) allows for the direct manipulation of objects on the screen and has a consistent appearance across applications (Microsoft Windows).

14. Answer will vary depending on your system.

CHAPTER 2

2.

Line	W	X	Y	Displayed
1	4	0	0	
2	4	2	0	
3	4	2	6	
4	4	2	6	6
5	5	2	6	
6	5	30	6	
7	5	30	6	30
8	5	9	6	
9	5	9	4	
10	5	9	4	4
11	5	0	4	
12	5	0	4	0
13	5	0	4	

4. a. T = 3
    b. X = T - 2
    c. P = T * X
    d. T = 3 * T
    e. A = P / X
    f. X = X + 1
    g. R = R ^ 3 or R = R * R * R

6. (1) Insert the data as constants in the LET statement used to calculate a result.
    (2) Assign each data item to a variable. Use these variables in the LET statement to calculate a result.
    (3) Use the INPUT statement to assign the data items to variables. Use these variables in the LET statement to calculate a result.

8. **Exit** — Causes the PC to permanently exit QuickBASIC and returns control to DOS.

    New Program — Causes the current program to be erased and indicates the beginning of a new program.

    Open Program — Loads a previously stored program on disk into main storage.

    Print — Prints all or part of the current program to the printer.

    Save As — Saves the current program to disk under a specified name.

    Start — Runs the current program.

10. No. Although the PRINT statement displays the correct result (270), it does not display the value of Pay. If the rate of pay (Rate) or the hours (Hours) are assigned different values, the program will still display the following: The gross pay is 270

12. a. **Alt** — Activates the menu bar.
　　b. **Shift + Delete** — Cuts (deletes) highlighted text and places it into the clipboard.
　　c. **Enter** — Inserts a new or blank line.
　　d. **Home** — Moves the cursor left to the beginning position on the same line.
　　e. **End** — Moves the cursor right to the last position on the same line.
　　f. **Ctrl + Home** — Moves the cursor to the first position in the first line of the program.
　　g. **Ctrl + Q, X** — Moves the cursor to the bottom of the screen.
　　h. **Shift + F5** — Executes the current program.
　　i. **F4** — Views the output screen.
　　j. **F6** — Cycles the cursor down through the windows (immediate, view, or help).
　　k. **Backspace** — Deletes the character to the left of the cursor.
　　l. **Delete** — Deletes the character under the cursor or the highlighted text.
　　m. **Insert** — Switches QuickBASIC between insert and overtype modes.
　　n. **Shift + Insert** — Pastes (inserts) at the location of the cursor text from the clipboard.
　　o. **Page Up** — Moves the view window up one full screen (page) of lines.

CHAPTER 3

2. 568962500000
　 The error is 17,824.

4. a. −6.333334　　　b. 23　　　c. 8

6. c — Int is a reserved word (keyword).
　 e — First character is not a letter.
　 f — Print is a reserved word.
　 g — First character is not a letter.
　 h — For is a reserved word.

8. The formulation of a numeric expression concerns the proper placement of constants, variables, function references, parentheses, and arithmetic operators in a numeric expression. The evaluation of a numeric expression is concerned with the manner in which a validly formed numeric expression is to be evaluated by the computer.

10. a. 11　　b. 1　　c. −.6666667　　d. 262144　　e. 17　　f. 2320

12. a. Q = (D + E) ^ (1 / 3)
　　b. D = (A ^ 2) ^ 3.2
　　c. B = 20 / (6 − S)
　　d. Y = A1 * X + A2 * X ^ 2 + A3 * X ^ 3 + A4 * X ^ 4
　　e. H = X ^ (1/2) + X / (X − Y)
　　f. S = (19.2 * X ^ 3) ^ (1/2)
　　g. V = 100 − (2 / 3) ^ (100 − B)
　　h. T = (76234 / (2.37 + D)) ^ (1 / 2)
　　i. V = 1234.0005D-4 * M − (.123458 ^ 3 / (M − N))
　　j. Q = ((F − M * 1000) ^ (2 * B)) / (4 * M) − 1 / E

14. a, b, c, d, e, f, g, i

16. a. −1
　　b. −3.8

18. a. Net Pay
```
          Net Pay
     N e t   P a y
```

b. Hours   Gross   FICA   FIT
   HoursGrossFICAFIT

```
     10                  20             30            20
     10   20   30   20
                  Hours
     Hours                                      Gross
```

20. a. 3
    b. −4
    c. 20
    d. Illegal function call

CHAPTER 4

2. The value of C = 320

4. Principal ===> 100
   Rate in % ===> 15
   Amount ======> 115

6. Any variable listed in the SHARED statement is available to the Main Program and subprogram. The variables in the SHARED statement can be defined in the Main Program or subprogram. The SHARED statement is placed in the subprogram.

8.
```
' Exercise 4.8
' Computing Ounces from Gallons, Quarts and Pints
' ****************************************************
' *                   Main Program                  *
' ****************************************************
CALL A100.Accept.Input(Gallons, Quarts, Pints)
CALL B100.Compute.Ounces(Gallons, Quarts, Pints, Ounces)
CALL C100.Display.Ounces(Ounces)
END


' ****************************************************
' *               Accept Input                      *
' *        Returns Gallons, Quarts, Pints           *
' ****************************************************
SUB A100.Accept.Input (Gallons, Quarts, Pints)
  CLS
  INPUT "Gallons ===> ", Gallons
  INPUT "Quarts ====> ", Quarts
  INPUT "Pints =====> ", Pints
END SUB


' ****************************************************
' *               Compute Ounces                    *
' * Receives Gallons, Quarts, Pints; Returns Ounces *
' ****************************************************
SUB B100.Compute.Ounces (Gallons, Quarts, Pints, Ounces)
   Ounces = 128 * Gallons + 32 * Quarts + 16 * Pints
END SUB
```

```
' *****************************************************
' *                  Display Ounces                   *
' *                  Receives Ounces                  *
' *****************************************************
SUB C100.Display.Ounces (Ounces)
    PRINT
    PRINT "Ounces ====>"; Ounces
END SUB
```

CHAPTER 5

2. a. ```
' Exercise 5.2a
READ S, B
D = S - B
LOCATE 16, 14, 1: PRINT SPC(5); D
DATA 4, 6 ' Data for READ
END
```

    b.  ```
' Exercise 5.2b
DATA 1, 2, 5, 6, 8, 7, 1, 3, 2, 0, 0, 0
READ X, Y, Z
DO WHILE X > 0
    X1 = X * Y
    X1 = X1 * Z
    READ X, Y, Z
LOOP
PRINT X1
END
```

4.  ```
LOCATE 1, 7: PRINT A
LOCATE 4, 45: PRINT B
```

6.  ```
PRINT USING "The amount is **$####.##+"; Amount
```

8.  ```
CLS
LOCATE 6, 6: PRINT 6
```

10. The cursor is located in column 1 of line 14.

12. ```
' Exercise 5.12
CLS
LOCATE 8, 33:  PRINT "*************"
LOCATE 9, 33:  PRINT "* B A S I C *"
LOCATE 10, 33: PRINT "B L       N B"
LOCATE 11, 33: PRINT "A   E   R   A"
LOCATE 12, 33: PRINT "S     A     S"
LOCATE 13, 33: PRINT "I   E   R   I"
LOCATE 14, 33: PRINT "C L       N C"
LOCATE 15, 33: PRINT "* B A S I C *"
LOCATE 16, 33: PRINT "*************"
END
```

14. ' Exercise 5.14

```
CLS
Row = 9
Column = 20
LOCATE Row, Column, 0: PRINT "*"
Factor = 1
Row = Row + 1
DO WHILE Factor <= 3
    LOCATE Row, Column - 2 * Factor
    PRINT "*"
    LOCATE Row, Column + 2 * Factor
    PRINT "*"
    Factor = Factor + 1
    Row = Row + 1
LOOP
LOCATE Row, Column - 2 * Factor
Print "* * * * * * * *"
```

CHAPTER 6

2. X = 0
    T = 10

    a. X = X + 1
        T = T + 1
    b. X = X + 7
        T = T + 7
    c. X = X + 2
        T = T + 2
    d. X = 2 * X
        T = 2 * T
    e. X = X - 1
        T = T - 1

4. a. Q value greater than 8 or Q value equal to 3.
    b. Q value greater than or equal to 0.
    c. Q value less than 27.
    d. Q may be equal to any value that is within the limits of the PC.

6. a. ```
        IF Age >= 21 THEN
            C = C + 1
        END IF
        S = S + 1
        ```

    b.  ```
        IF Sex.Code$ = "M" THEN
            M = M + 1
        ELSE
            F = F + 1
        END IF
        ```

8. a.

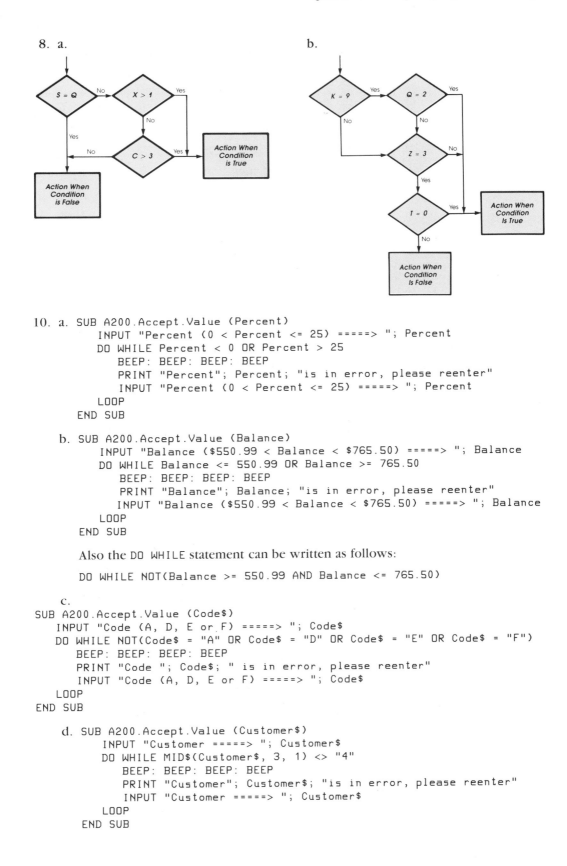

b.

10. a.
```
SUB A200.Accept.Value (Percent)
      INPUT "Percent (0 < Percent <= 25) =====> "; Percent
      DO WHILE Percent < 0 OR Percent > 25
         BEEP: BEEP: BEEP: BEEP
         PRINT "Percent"; Percent; "is in error, please reenter"
         INPUT "Percent (0 < Percent <= 25) =====> "; Percent
      LOOP
   END SUB
```

b.
```
SUB A200.Accept.Value (Balance)
      INPUT "Balance ($550.99 < Balance < $765.50) =====> "; Balance
      DO WHILE Balance <= 550.99 OR Balance >= 765.50
         BEEP: BEEP: BEEP: BEEP
         PRINT "Balance"; Balance; "is in error, please reenter"
         INPUT "Balance ($550.99 < Balance < $765.50) =====> "; Balance
      LOOP
   END SUB
```

Also the DO WHILE statement can be written as follows:

```
DO WHILE NOT(Balance >= 550.99 AND Balance <= 765.50)
```

c.
```
SUB A200.Accept.Value (Code$)
   INPUT "Code (A, D, E or F) =====> "; Code$
   DO WHILE NOT(Code$ = "A" OR Code$ = "D" OR Code$ = "E" OR Code$ = "F")
      BEEP: BEEP: BEEP: BEEP
      PRINT "Code "; Code$; " is in error, please reenter"
      INPUT "Code (A, D, E or F) =====> "; Code$
   LOOP
END SUB
```

d.
```
SUB A200.Accept.Value (Customer$)
      INPUT "Customer =====> "; Customer$
      DO WHILE MID$(Customer$, 3, 1) <> "4"
         BEEP: BEEP: BEEP: BEEP
         PRINT "Customer"; Customer$; "is in error, please reenter"
         INPUT "Customer =====> "; Customer$
      LOOP
      END SUB
```

```
12. '  Exercise 6.12 Solution
    SUB B300.Count.Numbers (Negative, Zero, Positive)
       Negative = 0
       Zero = 0
       Positive = 0
       READ Number
       DO WHILE Number <> -1E37
          IF Number < 0 THEN
             Negative = Negative + 1
          ELSE
             IF Number = 0 THEN
                Zero = Zero + 1
             ELSE
                Positive = Positive + 1
             END IF
          ENDIF
          READ Number
       LOOP
       PRINT Negative, Zero, Positive
    END SUB
```

The nested IF can also be written as follows:

```
IF Number < 0 THEN Negative = Negative + 1
IF Number = 0 THEN Zero = Zero + 1
IF Number > 0 THEN Positive = Positive + 1
```

```
14. '  Exercise 6.14 Solution
    CLS   ' Clear Screen
    INPUT "Number of Fibonacci Numbers (0 < X < 186) ===> ", X%
    DO WHILE X% < 0 OR X% > 185
       PRINT "The number"; X%; "is out of range, please reenter"
       INPUT "Number of Fibonacci Numbers ===> ", X%
    LOOP
    Fib1 = 1
    Fib2 = 1
    PRINT
    PRINT Fib1;
    PRINT Fib2;
    Number% = 3
    DO WHILE Number% <= X%
       Fib3 = Fib2 + Fib1
       PRINT Fib3;
       Fib1 = Fib2
       Fib2 = Fib3
       Number% = Number% + 1
    LOOP
    PRINT : PRINT : PRINT "Job Complete"
```

16.
```
' Exercise 6.16 Solution
IF U < V THEN
    IF U < W THEN
        Small = U
    ELSE
        Small = W
    END IF
ELSE
    IF V < W THEN
        Small = V
    ELSE
        Small = W
    END IF
END IF
```

18. a. X
    b. Count = 0; Sum = 68
    c. 4
    d. 68
    e. −2

20.
```
' Exercise 6.20 Solution
IF C = 0 AND D = 0 THEN
    A = -1
ELSE
    IF C <> 0 AND D <> 0 THEN
        A = -2
    ELSE
        A = -3
    END IF
END IF
```

CHAPTER 7

2. a. OPEN, OUTPUT, APPEND
   b. OPEN, INPUT
   c. closed
   d. EOF(n)
   e. APPEND

4.
```
OPEN "B:SALES1.DAT" FOR INPUT AS #1
OPEN "B:SALES2.DAT" FOR INPUT AS #2
OPEN "B:SALES3.DAT" FOR INPUT AS #3
```

6. a — Filespec must precede the mode.
   e — Comma must immediately follow filenumber.
   g — Filenumber must not be preceded by a number sign (#).
   h — Comma at the end of the list is invalid.

8. a. `Line.Count = Line.Count + 1`
   b. `Line.Count = Line.Count + 2`
   c. `Line.Count = Line.Count + 3`

CHAPTER 8

2. a. L(2, 2)   b. L(3, 3) or L(2, 4)   c. L(3, 2)   d. L(5, 2)
   e. L(3, 4)   f. L(2, 1)   g. L(1, 3)   h. L(5, 1)

4. The partial program assigns the value of each element of the array A to the corresponding element in the array B and then displays the lower bound of the first dimension of the array A, the upper bound of the first dimension of the array A, the lower bound of the second dimension of the array B, and the upper bound of the second dimension of the array B.

6. a. c   b. c   c. e   d. a

8.
```
' Exercise 8.8 Solution
SUB B400.Count.Element (Number())
    Low  = 0
    Mid  = 0
    High = 0
    FOR I = 1 TO 50
        IF Number(I) >=  0 AND Number(I) <= 18 THEN
            Low  = Low + 1
        END IF
        IF Number(I) >= 26 AND Number(I) <= 29 THEN
            Mid  = Mid + 1
        END IF
        IF Number(I) >  42 AND Number(I) <  47 THEN
            High = High + 1
        END IF
    NEXT I
END SUB
```

10.
```
' Exercise 8.10 Solution
SUB B300.Move.Up (A(), B(), C())
    FOR I = 1 TO 50
        IF A(I) < B(I) THEN
            C(I) = -1
        ELSE
            IF A(I) = B(I) THEN
                C(I) = 0
            ELSE
                C(I) = 1
            END IF
        END IF
    NEXT I
END SUB
```

The nested IF statement may also be written as follows:

```
IF A(I) < B(I) THEN C(I)) = -1
IF A(I) = B(I) THEN C(I) =  0
IF A(I) > B(I) THEN C(I) =  1
```

12.
```
' Exercise 8.12 Solution
OPTION BASE 1
SUB A200.SUM (Sum, R(), S())
  Sum = 0
  FOR J = 1 TO 10
    FOR K = 1 TO 10
      Sum = Sum + R(J, K) * S(J, K)
    NEXT K
  NEXT J
END SUB
```

14. 1600

16.
```
' Exercise 8.16 Solution
DIM A(1 TO 50)
  .

  .

  .

Positive = 0
Zero = 0
Negative = 0
FOR I = 1 TO 50
    IF A(I) > 0 THEN
        Positive = Positive + 1
    ELSE
        IF A(I) = 0 THEN
            Zero = Zero + 1
        ELSE
            Negative = Negative + 1
        END IF
    END IF
NEXT I
```

You may also write the nested IF statement as follows:

```
IF A(I) > 0 THEN Positive = Positive + 1
IF A(I) = 0 THEN Zero = Zero + 1
IF A(I) < 0 THEN Negative = Negative + 1
```

18.
```
' Exercise 8.18 Solution
SUB B300.LEAST
    Greatest.Sales = Sales(1)
    Sales.Person.Name$ = Person$(1)
    FOR I = 2 TO 50
        IF Sales(I) < Greatest.Sales THEN
            Sales.Person.Name$ = Person$(I)
            Greatest.Sales = Sales(I)
        END IF
    NEXT I
    PRINT Sales.Person.Name$, Greatest.Sales
END SUB
```

20. ' Exercise 8.20 Solution
    DIM Item$(1 TO 200), Sales(1 TO 200)
        .
        .
        .

    FOR I = 1 TO 200
       IF Sales(I) > 3000 THEN
           PRINT Item$(I), Sales(I)
       END IF
    NEXT I

CHAPTER 9

2. a. 69
    b. The entire string
    c. Ifɓ1ɓ (where ɓ indicates a blank character)
    d. seen
    e. 36.8
    f. 73
    g. G
    h. AAAAAAAAAAAAAA
    i. "−13.691"
    j. 24
    k. The word giants is replaced by the word midgets in the string assigned to Phr$.
    l. ɓɓɓɓ (where ɓ indicates a blank character)

4. a. 99   b. 43   c. ?   d. "48.9"   e. 1
    f. ABC   g. %   h. 58   i. 15   j. 69

6. ' Exercise 9.6 Solution
    Number$ = "1698"
    Number = VAL(Number$)
    D4   = INT(Number / 1000)
    D3   = INT((Number - D4 * 1000) / 100)
    D2   = INT((Number - D4 * 1000 - D3 * 100) / 10)
    D1   = INT(Number - D4 * 1000 - D3 * 100 - D2 * 10)
    Sum   = D4 + D3 + D2 + D1
    PRINT "The sum of the digits is"; Sum

    Also, lines 3 to 7 may be written as follows:

    D1 = VAL(MID$(Number$, 1, 1))
    D2 = VAL(MID$(Number$, 2, 1))
    D3 = VAL(MID$(Number$, 3, 1))
    D4 = VAL(MID$(Number$, 4, 1))

8. The program displays the prime numbers between 1 and 100. Any whole number greater than 1 that has no factors other than 1 and itself is called a **prime number**. In number theory, it can be proven that if a number has no factors between 2 and the square root of the number, then the number is prime. The program uses this method for finding the prime numbers between 1 and 100.

10. a. `P = SQR(A * A + B * B)`
    b. `B = SQR(ABS(TAN(X) - .51))`
    c. `Q = 8 * (COS(X)) ^ 2 + 4 * SIN(X)`
    d. `Y = EXP(X) + LOG(1 + X)`

12. a. `Sign = SGN(2 * X ^ 3 + 3 * X + 5)`
    b. `Inte = INT(4 * X + 5)`
    c. `Rounded.2 = INT(( X + .005) * 100) / 100`
       `Rounded.1 = INT(( X + .05) * 10) / 10`

14. `POS` — returns the current column position of the cursor relative to the left edge of the display screen.

    `SCREEN` — returns the ASCII code for the character found at the specified location.

    `CSRLIN` — equal to the current row position of the cursor relative to the top of the display screen.

16.
```
' Exercise 9.16 Solution
RANDOMIZE TIMER
FOR R% = 1 TO 100
    PRINT INT(52 * RND + 1)
NEXT R%
END
```

18. `DEF FNDISCOUNT(Purchase) = .10 * (Purchase - 200)`

20. The program is invalid because a user-defined function must be defined before it can be invoked. The correct order of statements for Exercise 9.20 is shown below.

```
' Exercise 9.20 Corrected
DEF FNW (B) = B ^ 4
DEF FNA (B) = FNW(B) * 7
DEF FNX (B) = FNA(B) + 5
PRINT FNX(5)
END
```

22.
```
FUNCTION SWITCH (W)
    SELECT CASE W
        CASE IS < 10
            SWITCH = 1
        CASE 10 TO 100
            SWITCH = 2
        CASE IS > 100
            SWITCH = 3
    END SELECT
END FUNCTION
```

CHAPTER 10

2. a. record variable, `DIM`   b. `TYPE`, `DIM`
   c. record variable   d. `LOC(n)`

4. The label name is used in the `TYPE` statement to identify the group of fields in the random record. The record variable is assigned the same type as the label name in the `DIM` statement and reserves main storage for the random record.

6. a — The parameter LEN must be assigned the length of the record variable (LEN(Sales)) rather than the value of the record variable.

d — A string variable as the second parameter in a GET statement is invalid.

f — Period (.) is invalid in a label name.

g — The GET requires a record variable to indicate where the record is to be placed in main storage.

8. The sequential data file contains the keys that are read into an array by the Initialization subprogram. The random data file contains the data records that are accessed by using the subscript of the element in the array that has the key as its value.

CHAPTER 11

2. a.
```
' Exercise 11.2a Solution
SCREEN 1: CLS
PSET (0, 50)
LINE -(200, 25)
LINE -(100, 125)
LINE -(0, 50)
END
```

b.
```
' Exercise 11.2b Solution
SCREEN 1: CLS
LINE (0, 0) - (160, 100),, B
LINE -(0, 0)
LINE (160, 0) - (0, 100)
END
```

c.
```
' Exercise 11.2c Solution
SCREEN 1: CLS
Pi = 3.141593
CIRCLE (70, 80), 45
PSET (70, 80)
CIRCLE (70, 80), 45,, Pi, 1/6
END
```

d.
```
' Exercise 11.2d Solution
SCREEN 1: CLS
Pi = 3.141593
CIRCLE (75, 60), 70,, -Pi, -3 * Pi/2
END
```

4. a. The screen has a blue background, a black border, and a red foreground.

b. The screen has a black background and border and a brown foreground, the default color on palette 0.

6. a. point, pixel   b. GRAPHICS   c. 80

d. CHR$ e. minus sign

f. GET, PUT   g. 2, 4, 8

8. ' Exercise 11.8 Solution
```
SCREEN 1: CLS
COLOR 1, 0
LINE (100, 80) - (180, 150), 3, B
PAINT(140, 135), 2, 3
LINE (100, 80) - (130, 50), 3
LINE -(210, 50), 3
LINE -(180, 80), 3
PAINT (140, 65), 1, 3
LINE (210, 50) - (210, 120), 3
LINE -(180, 150), 3
PAINT (185, 135), 3, 3
END
```

10. ' Exercise 11.10 Solution
```
CLS: WIDTH 40
LOCATE 4, 9
FOR I% = 9 TO 32
    PRINT CHR$(219);
NEXT I%
LOCATE 22, 9
FOR I% = 9 TO 32
    PRINT CHR$(219);
NEXT I%
FOR I% = 4 TO 22
    LOCATE I%, 9: PRINT CHR$(219)
NEXT I%
FOR I% = 4 TO 22
    LOCATE I%, 32: PRINT CHR$(219)
NEXT I%
END
```

12. a. Causes the note A flat to be played.
    b. Sets all notes that follow to lengths of 1/8.
    c. Sets all notes that follow to the next octave and causes the C note to be played.
    d. Executes the subcommand M$, which contains additional commands.
    e. Rest.
    f. Sets the tempo to 100 quarter notes per minute.
    g. Pauses a length of 1/8.
    h. Music staccato—each note that follows plays 3/4 of the time specified by L.
    i. Music legato—each note that follows plays the full period set by L.
    j. Sets the octave to 3.

14. PSET — Puts the pixel array on the screen exactly as defined in the array named in the PUT statement.

    AND — Within the specified area on the screen, turns ''on'' those pixels that are ''on'' in the array named in the PUT statement and ''on'' on the screen.

    XOR — Within the specified area, turns ''on'' those pixels that are ''on'' in the array named in the PUT statement and ''off'' on the screen or ''off'' in the array named in the PUT statement and ''on'' on the screen.

16. (4 + 60 * INT ((70 + 7) / 8)) /2 = 272 bytes

18. a. The background will be blue with red dots as shown below:

b. The background will be blue with a random pattern 100 colored dots.

20. a.

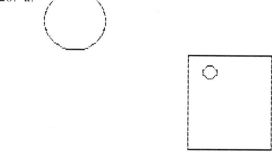

b.

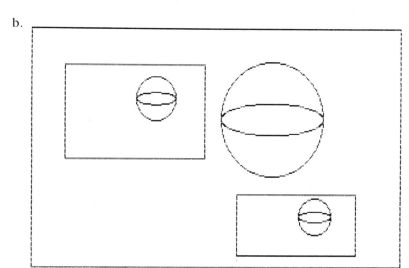

APPENDIX A

2. The annotation, terminal, and connector symbols.

4. Part I: I = 9, J = 9
   Part II: I = 21, J = 14

6. I = 3, J = 5

8.

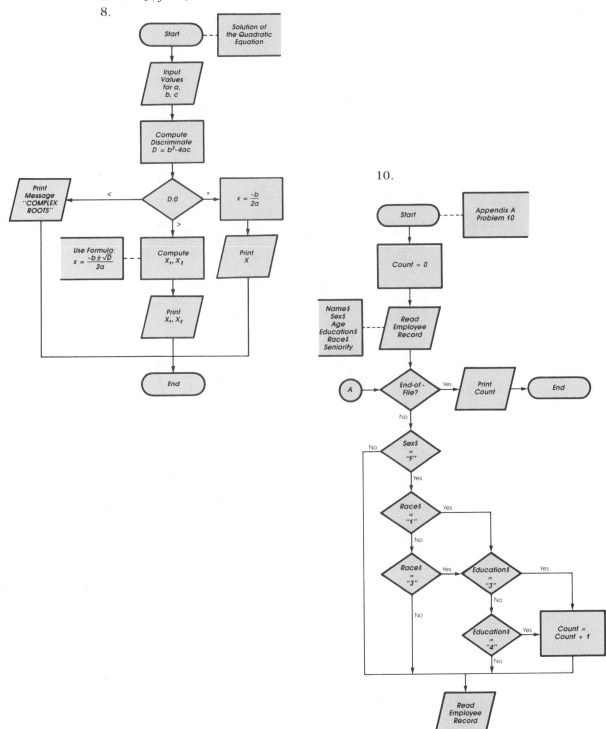

10.

12.

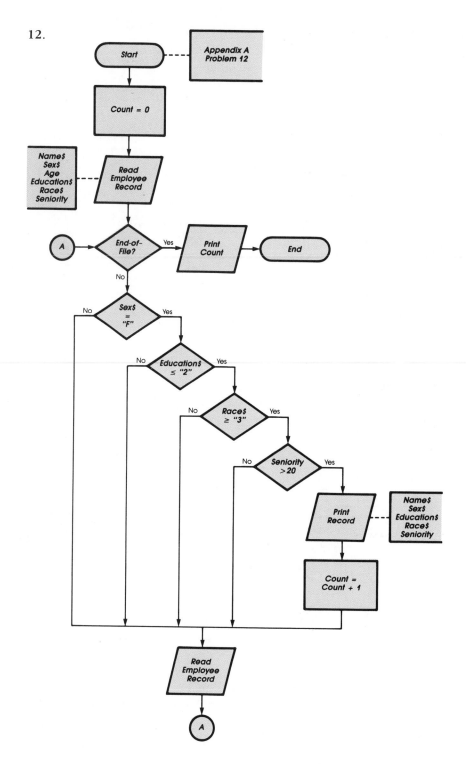

14. I = 17 and J = 16

Index

MICROSOFT QuickBASIC REFERENCE CARD

Legend: Uppercase letters are required keywords. You must supply items within < >s. You must select one of the entries within { }'s. Items within [ ]'s are optional. Three ellipsis points (...) indicate that an item may be repeated as many times as you wish. The symbol **b** represents a blank character.

A page number of QBA means that the seldom-used statement or function is not covered in the text, but additional information is available through the QB Advisor On-Line Help System. (See page 44.)

Summary of BASIC Statements

STATEMENT	PAGE
BEEP Causes the speaker on the PC to beep for a fraction of a second.	188
CALL <name> [(argumentlist)] Transfers control to a subprogram.	96
CHAIN <"filespec"> Instructs the PC to stop executing the current program, load another program from auxiliary storage and start executing it.	534
CHDIR <pathspecification> Changes the current directory for the specified drive.	544
CIRCLE <(x, y), radius> [,color [,start,end [,shape]]] Causes the PC to draw an ellipse, circle, arc, or wedge with center at (x, y).	462
CLEAR [,,stack] Reinitializes all program variables, closes files, and sets the stack size.	QBA
CLOSE [#] [filenumber] [,[#] [filenumber]]... Closes specified files.	225
CLS Erases the information on the screen and places the cursor in the upper left corner of the screen.	28
COLOR [background] [,palette] In medium-resolution graphics mode, sets the color for the background and palette of colors.	449
COLOR [foreground] [,background] [,border] In the text mode, defines the color of the foreground characters, background, and border around the screen.	449
COM(n) {ON/OFF/STOP} Enables or disables trapping of communications activity on adaptor n.	370
COMMON [SHARED] <variable> [,variable]... Passes specified variables to a subprogram or chained program.	106
CONST <constantname> = <expression> [, constantname = expression]... Declares symbolic constants that can be used in place of numeric or string expressions.	QBA

STATEMENT	PAGE
DATA <data item> [,data item]... Provides for the creation of a sequence of data items for use by the READ statement.	129
DATE$ = mm{/-}dd{/-}yy[yy] Sets the system date, where mm = month, dd = day, yy = 2-digit year, yyyy = 4-digit year.	342
DECLARE {FUNCTION/SUB} name [(parameterlist)] Declares references to QuickBASIC procedures and invokes argument-type checking.	101
DEF FN<name> [(variable, [, variable,...])] = <expression> Defines and names a function that can be referenced in a program as often as needed. Multiline functions end with an END DEF statement.	360
DEFtype <letterrange> [,letterrange]... Sets the data type for variables and functions.	65
DIM [SHARED] <arrayname(size)> [AS type] [,arrayname(size) [AS type]]... Reserves storage locations for arrays and declares the array type.	278
DO Causes the statements between DO and LOOP to be executed repeatedly. The loop is controlled by a condition in the corresponding LOOP statement.	126
DO UNTIL <condition> Causes the statements between DO UNTIL and LOOP to be executed repeatedly until the condition is true.	126
DO WHILE <condition> Causes the statements between DO WHILE and LOOP to be executed repeatedly while the condition is true.	126
DRAW <string expression> Causes the PC to draw the object that is defined by the value of the string expression.	126
END {DEF/FUNCTION/IF/SELECT/SUB/TYPE} Ends a QuickBASIC program, procedure, or block of code.	467
ERASE <arrayname> [,arrayname]... Eliminates previously defined arrays.	168
ERROR <integerexpression> Simulates the occurrence of a QuickBASIC error or allows the user to define error codes.	QBA
EXIT <statement> Exits statement, where statement is equal to FOR, DO, DEF, FUNCTION, or SUB.	272

STATEMENT	PAGE
FIELD [#filenumber, width AS string variable> [,width AS string variable]... Allocates space for variables in a random file buffer.	QBA
FILES [filespecification] Lists the names of all programs and data files in auxiliary storage on the default drive or the drive specified by file specification.	544
FOR <loopvariable> = <initial> TO <limit> [STEP increment] Causes the statements between the FOR and NEXT statements to be executed until the value of loopvariable exceeds the value of the limit.	267
FUNCTION <name> [(parameterlist)] [STATIC] Declares the name, the parameters, and initiates a function procedure that ends with an END FUNCTION.	366
GET <(x_1, y_1) - (x_2, y_2), arrayname> Reads the colors of the points in the specified area on the screen into an array.	474
GET [#[filenumber> [,record number] Reads the specified record from a random file and transfers it to the buffer that is defined by the corresponding FIELD statement.	403
GOSUB {linelabel/linenumber} Causes control to transfer to a subroutine beginning at the specified line. Also retains the location of the next statement following the GOSUB statement.	370
GOTO {linelabel/linenumber} Transfers control to the specified line.	QBA
IF <condition> THEN [clause] [ELSE [clause]] The single line IF statement causes execution of the THEN clause if the condition is true. If the ELSE clause is included, it causes execution of the ELSE clause if the condition is false.	168
IF <condition> THEN [$statementblock_1$] [ELSE [$statementblock_2$]] END IF The block IF statement allows for multiple lines in the THEN and ELSE clauses. Causes execution of the THEN clause if the condition is true. Causes execution of the ELSE clause if the condition is false. The ELSE IF <condition> THEN clause may be used in place of the ELSE clause.	168
INPUT [;][;"prompt message"{;/,}] <variable> [,variable]... Provides for the assignment of values to variables from a source external to the program such as the keyboard.	QBA
INPUT <#filenumber, variable> [,variable]... Provides for the assignment of values to variables from a sequential file in auxiliary storage.	235

(BASIC Statements continued on page R.2 in left column)

MICROSOFT QuickBASIC REFERENCE CARD

Summary of BASIC Statements (continued)

STATEMENT	PAGE	Description
KEY { n, string value / ON / OFF / LIST }	QBA	Assigns a string value to a function key. Also used to display the values and enable or disable the function key display line.
KEY(n) { ON / OFF / STOP }	370	Activates or deactivates trapping of the specified key n.
KILL <filespecification>	544	Deletes a file from disk.
[LET] <variable> = <expression>	65	Causes the evaluation of the expression, followed by the assignment of the resulting value to the variable to the left of the equal sign.
LINE [(x₁,y₁)] -(x₂,y₂)] [,color] [,B[F]][,Style]	459	Draws a line or a box on the screen.
LINE INPUT [;]["prompt message";] <string variable> or LINE INPUT [#<filenumber>,] <string variable>	344	Provides for the assignment of a line of up to 255 characters from a source external to the program, such as the keyboard or a sequential file
LOCATE [row] [,column] [,cursor] [,start] [,stop]	149	Positions the cursor on the screen. Can also be used to make the cursor visible or invisible, and to control the size of the cursor.
LOCK [#]filenumber>, { record / [start] TO end }	QBA	Locks all or some of the records in a file.
LOOP { WHILE: / UNTIL: } [condition]	126	Identifies the end of a loop.
LPRINT [item]...	81	Provides for the generation of output to the printer.
LPRINT USING <string expression;> <item>...	143	Provides for the generation of formatted output to the printer.
LSET <string variable> = <string expression>	QBA	Moves string data left-justified into an area of a random file buffer that is defined by the string variable.
MID$ <string var, start position [,number]> = <substring>	331	Replaces a substring within a string.
MKDIR <pathname>	544	Creates a new directory.
NAME <oldfile-specification> AS <newfilespecification>	544	Renames a file on disk.

STATEMENT	PAGE	Description
NEXT [numeric variable] [,numeric variable]...	267	Identifies the end of the For loop(s).
ON COM(n) GOSUB { linelabel / linenumber }	370	Causes control to transfer to the specified line when data is filling the communications buffer (n).
ON ERROR GOTO { linelabel / linenumber }	531	Enables error trapping and specifies the first line of an error-handling routine that the PC is to branch to in the event of an error. If linenumber is zero, error trapping is disabled.
ON <numeric expression> GOSUB { linelabel-list / linenumber-list }	QBA	Causes control to transfer to the subroutine represented by the selected line. Also retains the location of the next statement following the ON-GOSUB statement.
ON <numeric expression> GOTO { linelabel-list / linenumber-list }	QBA	Causes control to transfer to one of several lines according to the value of the numeric expression.
ON KEY(n) GOSUB { linelabel / linenumber }	371	Causes control to transfer to the specified line when the function key or cursor control key (n) is pressed.
ON PEN GOSUB { linelabel / linenumber }	370	Causes control to transfer to the specified line when the light pen is activated.
ON PLAY(n) GOSUB { linelabel / linenumber }	370	Plays continuous background music. Transfers control to the specified line when a note (n) is sensed.
ON STRIG(n) GOSUB { linelabel / linenumber }	370	Causes control to transfer to the specified line when one of the joystick buttons (n) is pressed.
ON TIMER(n) GOSUB { linelabel / linenumber }	370	Causes control to transfer to the specified line when the specified period of time (n) in seconds has elapsed.
ON UEVENT GOSUB { linelabel / linenumber }	QBA	Defines the event-handler for a user-defined event.
OPEN <filespec> FOR <mode> AS <[#]filenumber> [LEN = record length]	224 and 400	Allows a program to read or write records to a file. If record length is specified, then the file is opened as a random file. If the record length is not specified, then the file is opened as a sequential file.

STATEMENT	PAGE	Description
OPTION BASE {0/1}	279	Assigns a lower bound of 0 or 1 to all arrays declared with only an upper-bound value.
OUT <port>, <data>	QBA	Sends a byte to a machine I/O port.
PAINT <(x, y)> [[,paint] [,boundary]]	463	Paints an area on the screen with the selected color.
PALETTE [attribute, color] or PALETTE USING <arrayname> [(array.index)]	QBA	Changes one or more of the colors in the palette
PCOPY <sourcepage> , <destinationpage>	QBA	Copies one screen page to another.
PEN(n) { ON / OFF / STOP }	370	Enables or disables the PEN read function used to analyze light pen activity.
PLAY <string expression>	479	Causes the PC to play music according to the value of the string expression.
PLAY(n) { ON / OFF / STOP }	370	Enables, disables, or suspends play event trapping.
POKE <address>, <byte>	QBA	Writes a byte into a storage location.
PRESET <(x, y)> [,color]	458	Draws a point in the color specified at (x, y). If no color is specified, it erases the point.
PRINT { ? } [item] [	;	item]...	77	Provides for the generation of output to the screen.
PRINT { ? } <#filenumber,> [item] [	;	item]...	226	Provides for the generation of output to a sequential file.
PRINT USING <string expression;> <item> [	;	item]...	134	Provides for the generation of formatted output to the screen.
PRINT <#filenumber,> USING <string expression;> <item> [	;	item]...	227	Provides for the generation of formatted output to a sequential file.

(*BASIC Statements* continued on page R.3 in left column)

MICROSOFT QuickBASIC REFERENCE CARD

Summary of BASIC Statements (continued)

STATEMENT — **PAGE**

PSET <(x, y)> [,color] — 458
Draws a point in the color specified at (x, y).

PUT <(x1, y1), arrayname> [,action] — 475
Writes the colors of the points in the array onto an area of the screen.

PUT <[#]filenumber> [,record number] — 404
Writes a record to a random file from a buffer defined by the corresponding FIELD statement.

RANDOMIZE [numeric expression] — 356
Reseeds the random number generator.

READ <variable> [,variable]... — 131
Provides for the assignment of values to variables from a sequence of data items created from DATA statements.

REDIM [SHARED] <arrayname(size)> [AS type] [,arrayname(size) [AS type]]... — 544
Changes the space allocated to an array declared $DYNAMIC.

{REM}{comment} / **{ ' }** — QBA
Provides for the insertion of comments in a program.

RESET — QBA
Closes all disk files.

RESTORE {linelabel / linenumber} — 132
Allows the data items in DATA statements to be reread.

RESUME {linelabel / NEXT / 0 / b} — 531
Continues program execution at the linelabel, or the line following that which caused the error, after an error-recovery procedure.

RETURN {linelabel / linenumber} — 370
Causes control to transfer from a subroutine back to the statement that follows the corresponding GOSUB or ON-GOSUB statement.

RMDIR <pathname> — 544
Removes a directory from disk after all files and subdirectories have been removed.

RSET <string variable> = <string expression> — QBA
Moves string data right-justified into an area of a random file buffer that is defined by string variable.

RUN {linenumber / linelabel / b} — QBA
Restarts the program in main storage.

SCREEN [mode] [,color switch] [,active page] [,visual page] — 438
Sets the screen attributes for text mode, medium-resolution graphics, or high-resolution graphics.

SEEK <[#]filenumber>, <position> — QBA
Sets the position in a file for the next read or write.

STATEMENT — **PAGE**

SELECT CASE <testexpression>
  CASE <matchexpression1>
    [range of statements1]
  [CASE <matchexpression2>
    [range of statements2]
    .
    .
  [CASE ELSE
    [range of statementsn]
END SELECT — 193
Causes execution of one of several ranges of statements depending on the value of testexpression.

SHARED <variable> [AS type] [,variable [AS type]]... — 112
Gives a SUB or FUNCTION procedure access to variables declared at the subprogram level without passing them as parameters.

SHELL [commandstring] — 31
Places the current QB session in a temporary wait state and returns control to MS-DOS. Can also execute another program or MS-DOS command as specified in commandstring.

SLEEP [seconds] — QBA
Suspends execution of the calling program.

SOUND <frequency>, <duration> — 477
Causes the generation of sound through the PC speaker.

STATIC <variablelist> — QBA
Causes variables and arrays to be local to either a DEF FN, a FUNCTION, or a SUB, and maintains values between calls.

STOP — QBA
Stops execution of a program. Unlike the END statement, files are left open.

STRIG(n) {ON / OFF / STOP} — 370
Enables or disables trapping of the joystick buttons.

SUB <globalname> [(parameterlist)] [STATIC] — 95
Establishes the beginning of a subprogram. The end of the subprogram is identified by the END SUB statement.

SWAP <variable1>, <variable2> — 293
Exchanges the values of two variables or two elements of an array.

SYSTEM — 544
Closes all open files and returns control to MS-DOS.

TIME$ = hh[:mm[:ss]] — 343
Sets the system time, where hh = hours, mm = minutes, and ss = seconds.

TIMER {ON / OFF / STOP} — 370
Enables or disables trapping of timed events.

STATEMENT — **PAGE**

TROFF — 529
Disables statement tracing.

TRON — 529
Causes the PC to trace execution of program statements.

TYPE <labelname>
  <fieldname1> AS <fieldtype>
  .
  .
  <fieldnamen> AS <fieldtype>
END TYPE — 402
Creates user-defined data types containing one or more elements.

UEVENT {ON / OFF / STOP} — QBA
Enables, disables, or suspends user-defined event trapping.

UNLOCK <[#]filenumber> [, {record / [start] TO end}] — QBA
Unlocks records in a file.

VIEW [[SCREEN] (x1, y1) - (x2, y2)] [,color] [,boundary] — QBA
Defines a viewport.

VIEW PRINT [topline TO bottomline] — 473
Establishes boundaries for the screen text viewport.

WEND — QBA
Identifies the end of a While loop.

WHILE <condition> — 178
Identifies the beginning of a While loop. Causes the statements between WHILE and WEND to be executed repeatedly while the condition is true.

WIDTH {40 / 80} — 178
Erases the information on the screen, sets the width of the line on the screen to 40 or 80 characters, and places the cursor in the upper, left corner of the screen.

WIDTH LPRINT <width> — 439
Sets the printer column width.

WINDOW <[SCREEN] (x1, y1) - (x2, y2)> — 439
Redefines the coordinates of the viewport. Allows you to draw objects in space and not be bounded by the limits of the screen.

WRITE [expression list] — 470
Writes data to the screen.

WRITE <[#]filenumber,> [item] [{, / ;} item]... — 231
Writes data to a sequential file. Causes the PC to insert commas between the items written to the sequential file.

MICROSOFT QuickBASIC REFERENCE CARD

Summary of BASIC Functions

FUNCTION	PAGE	
ABS(N)	346	Returns the absolute value of the argument N.
ASC(X$)	332	Returns a two-digit numeric value that is equivalent in ASCII code to the first character of the string argument X$.
ATN(N)	352	Returns the angle in radians whose tangent is the value of the argument N.
CDBL(N)	QBA	Returns N converted to a double-precision value.
CHR$(N)	332	Returns a single string character that is equivalent in ASCII code to the numeric argument N.
CINT(N)	343	Returns N converted to an integer after rounding the fractional part of N.
CLNG(N)	QBA	Returns N converted to a long integer after rounding the fractional part of N.
COMMAND$	QBA	Returns the command line used to start the program.
COS(N)	351	Returns the cosine of the argument N where N is in radians.
CSNG(N)	QBA	Returns N converted to a single-precision value.
CSRLIN	352	Returns the vertical (row) coordinate of the cursor.
CVI(X$), CVL(X$), CVS(X$), CVD(X$)	QBA	Returns the integer, long integer, single-precision, or double-precision numeric value equivalent to the string X$. Used with random files.
DATE$	337	Returns the current date (mm-dd-yyyy).
EOF(filenumber)	236	Returns -1 (true) if the end-of-file has been sensed on the sequential file associated with filenumber. Returns 0 (false) if the end-of-file has not been sensed.
ERDEV	QBA	Returns an error code from the last device that caused an error.
ERDEV$	QBA	Returns a string expression containing the name of the device that generated a vital error.
ERL	346	Returns the line number preceding the line that caused the error. If no line numbers are used, then ERL returns a zero.
ERR	332	Returns the error code for the last error that occurred.
EXP(N)	352	Returns e(2.71828...) raised to the argument N.
FILEATTR	348	Returns the file mode for an open file.
FIX(N)	346	Returns value of N truncated to an integer.
FRE(N)	QBA	Returns the amount of available stack space (N = -2), string space (N not equal to -1 or -2), or size in bytes of the largest array you can create (N = -1).
FREEFILE	QBA	Returns the next free QuickBASIC file number.
HEX$(N)	QBA	Returns the hexadecimal equivalent of N.
INKEY$	344	Returns the last character entered from the keyboard.
INP(N)	351	Returns the byte read from an I/O port N.
INPUT$(N)	QBA	Suspends execution of the program until a string of N characters is received from the keyboard.
INPUT$(N, [#filenumber])	345	Returns a string of characters from the specified file.
INSTR([P,]X$, S$)	QBA	Returns the beginning position of the substring S$ in string X$. P indicates the position at which the search begins in the string X$.
INT(N)	330	Returns the largest integer that is less than or equal to the argument N.
LBOUND(arrayname[,dimension])	290	Returns the lower-bound value for the specified dimension of arrayname.
LCASE$(X$)	333	Returns X$ in all lowercase letters.
LEFT$(X$, N)	327	Returns the left-most N characters of the string argument X$.
LEN(X$)	327	Returns the length of the string argument X$.
LOC(#filenumber)	404	With a random file, it returns the number of the last record read or written. With a sequential file, it returns the number of records read from or written to the file.
LOF(#filenumber)	404	Returns the number of bytes allocated to a file.
LOG(N)	348	Returns the natural log of the argument N where N is greater than 0.
LPOS(N)	352	Returns the current position of the line printer's print head within the printer buffer where N is equal to 1 for LPT1, 2 for LPT2, and so on.
LTRIM$(X$)	337	Returns the string argument X$ with leading spaces removed.
MID$(X$, P, N)	328	Returns N characters of the string argument X$ beginning at position P.
MKI$(N), MKL$(N), MKS$(N), MKD$(N)	QBA	Returns the string equivalent of an integer, long integer, single-precision, or double-precision value. Used with random files.
OCT$(N)	QBA	Returns the octal equivalent of N.
PEEK(N)	QBA	Returns the value of the byte stored at the specified storage location N.
PEN(N)	365	Returns light pen coordinate information. The information is dependent on the value assigned to N.
PLAY(n)	343	Returns the number of notes currently in the music background buffer.
PMAP (c, n)	472	Returns the world coordinate of the physical coordinate c or vice versa. The parameter n varies between 0 and 3, and determines whether c is an x or y coordinate, and whether the coordinate is to be mapped from the physical to the world coordinate or vice versa.

(BASIC Functions continued on page R.5 in left column)

MICROSOFT QuickBASIC REFERENCE CARD

Summary of BASIC Functions (continued)

FUNCTION	PAGE	
POINT { (x, y) / (n) }	472	With the argument (x, y), the PC returns the foreground color attribute of the point (x, y). With the argument n, the PC returns the physical or world x or y coordinate of the last point referenced. The parameter n varies in the range 0 to 3.
POS(O)	352	Returns the current position of the cursor on the screen.
RIGHT$(X$, N)	328	Returns the right-most N characters of the string argument X$.
RND(N)	354	Returns a random number between 0 (inclusive) and 1 (exclusive). If N is positive or not included, the next random number is returned. If N is 0 (zero), the previous random number is returned. If N is negative, the random number generator is reseeded before a random number is returned.
RTRIM$(X$)	337	Returns X$ with trailing spaces removed.
SCREEN(row, column)	353	Returns the ASCII code for the character at the specified row (line) and column on the screen.
SEEK(filenumber)	QBA	Returns the current file position.
SGN(N)	347	Returns the sign of the argument N: −1 if the argument N is less than 0; 0 if the argument N is equal to 0; or +1 if the argument N is greater than 0.
SIN(N)	351	Returns the sine of the argument N where N is in radians.
SPACE$(N)	336	Returns a string of N spaces.
SPC(N)	108	Displays N spaces. Can be used only in an output statement such as PRINT or LPRINT.
SQR(N)	348	Returns the square root of the positive argument N.
STICK(N)	QBA	Returns the x and y coordinates of joystick N.
STR$(N)	335	Returns the string equivalent of the numeric argument N.
STRIG(n)	QBA	Returns the status of the joystick buttons.
STRING$(N, X$)	336	Returns N times the first character of X$.

FUNCTION	PAGE	
TAB(N)	79	Causes the PC to tab over to position N on the output device. Can be used only in an output statement such as PRINT or LPRINT.
TAN(N)	351	Returns the tangent of the argument N where N is in radians.
TIMER	353	Returns a value that is equal to the number of seconds elapsed since midnight.
TIME$	337	Returns the current time (hh:mm:ss).
UBOUND(arrayname[,dimension])	354	Returns the upper-bound value for the specified dimension of arrayname.
UCASE$(X$)	337	Returns X$ in all uppercase letters.
VAL(X$)	353	Returns the numeric equivalent of the string argument X$.
VARPTR(variablename)	QBA	Returns the storage address of variablename.
VARPTR$(variablename)	467	Returns a string representation of the storage address of variablename for use in DRAW and PLAY statements.

Summary of All Operators

ORDER OF PRECEDENCE	OPERATOR	SYMBOL	PAGE
Highest	Arithmetic	^	351
		+ or − (Unary + or − sign)	336
		* or /	108
		MOD	348
		+ or − (Binary + or − sign)	128
	Concatenation	+	75
	Relational	=, >, >=, <, <=, or <>	335
Lowest	Logical	NOT / AND / OR or XOR / EQV / IMP	182–186

Summary of Command Line Options

For the desired effect, append one or more of the following to the QB or QBI command when you enter QuickBASIC:

OPTION	FUNCTION
/ah	Permits arrays to exceed 64 KB.
/b	Designates monochrome display.
/c:size	Sets the size of the communications port buffer.
/cmd str	Passes the string str to the COMMAND$ function.
file	Loads and displays the QuickBASIC program file.
/g	Designates faster video output.
/h	Designates maximum resolution for the video device.
/l[lib]	Loads the specified library or QB QLB if lib is omitted
/mbf	Causes conversion to treat IEEE-format numbers as Microsoft binary format numbers.
/nohi	Allows monitor that does not support high intensity.
/run file	Loads and executes the QuickBASIC program file before displaying it.

Limits to QuickBASIC

	MAXIMUM	MINIMUM
Variable name	40 characters	1 character
String length	32,767 characters	0 characters
Array dimensions	60	1
Array subscript value	32,767	−32,768
Integers	32,767	−32,768
Long integers	2,147,483,647	−2,147,483,648
Single precision (+)	3.402823E+38	1.401298E−45
Single precision (−)	−1.401298E−45	−3.402823E+38
Double precision (+)	1.797693134862315D+308	4.940656458412465D−324
Double precision (−)	−4.940656458412465D−324	−1.797693134862315D+308

Variable Type Definition

APPEND CHARACTER	DECLARATION
%	Integer variable
&	Long integer variable
!	Single-precision variable
#	Double-precision variable
$	String variable

QuickBASIC Character Set

The QuickBASIC character set consists of numeric characters, alphabetic characters, and special characters as described in Table D.3 of Appendix D on page 545.

MICROSOFT QuickBASIC REFERENCE CARD

Cursor Movement Keys

KEYS	FUNCTION
←	Character left
→	Character right
↓	Down one line
↑	Up one line
Ctrl + ←	Word left
Ctrl + →	Word right
Ctrl + End	End of program
Ctrl + Enter	Beginning of next line
Ctrl + Home	Beginning of program
Ctrl + Q + E	Top of window
Ctrl + Q + S	Beginning of current line
Ctrl + Q + X	Bottom of window
End	End of line
Home	First indent of current line
Tab	Tab to next tab setting

Scroll Keys

KEYS	FUNCTION	KEYS	FUNCTION
Ctrl + ↓	Line down	Page Up	Page up
Ctrl + ↑	Line up	Ctrl + Page Down	Left one full screen
Page Down	Page down	Ctrl + Page Up	Right one full screen

Execution and Debugging Keys

KEYS	FUNCTION
F5	Continues execution from current statement.
Shift + F5	Starts execution from beginning.
F7	Executes program to cursor.
F8	Executes next program statement.
Shift + F8	Traces execution history backward.
F9	Toggles the Debug menu Breakpoint command.
Shift + F9	Instant watch.
F10	Single step, tracing around a procedure call.
Shift + F10	Traces execution history forward.

View Keys

KEYS	FUNCTION
F2	Displays list of SUBs, modules, and files.
Shift + F2	Displays the next procedure.
Ctrl + F2	Displays previous procedure.
F4	Toggles between view window and output screen.
F6	Makes next window the active one.
Shift + F6	Makes previous window the active one.
Alt + Minus	Decreases size of window.
Alt + Plus	Increases size of window.

Help Keys

KEYS	FUNCTION
F1	Displays help on the item in which the cursor is located.
Shift + F1	Displays help on help.
Alt + F1	Displays previously requested help topic. (Repeat up to 20 times.)
Ctrl + F1	Displays next help topic in Help file.
Shift + Ctrl + F1	Displays previous help topic in Help file.
Alt + H	Displays help through Help menu commands.
Esc	Clears help from the screen.
Letter	Moves cursor to help-topic title beginning with letter entered.
Shift + letter	Moves cursor to previous help-topic title beginning with letter entered.
Tab	Moves cursor to next help-topic title in help screen.
Shift + Tab	Moves cursor to previous help-topic title in help screen.

Insert and Copy Keys

KEYS	FUNCTION
Insert	Toggles insert or overtype.
Ctrl + Insert	Copies selection to clipboard and keeps.
Shift + Insert	Inserts contents of clipboard.
Shift + Delete	Copies selection to clipboard and deletes.
Ctrl + Y	Copies current line to clipboard and deletes.
Ctrl + Q + Y	Copies from cursor to end of line to clipboard and deletes.

Search Keys

KEYS	FUNCTION
F3	Repeats the last find.
Ctrl + \	Searches for selected (highlighted) text.

Selection (Highlight) Keys

KEYS	FUNCTION
Shift + ←	Character left
Shift + →	Character right
Shift + Ctrl + →	Word right
Shift + Ctrl + ←	Word left
Shift + ↓	Current line
Shift + ↑	Line above
Shift + PgDn	Screen down
Shift + PgUp	Screen up
Shift + Ctrl + Home	To beginning of program
Shift + Ctrl + End	To end of program

Delete Keys

KEYS	FUNCTION
Backspace	Deletes character to left.
Ctrl + T	Deletes rest of word.
Delete	Deletes character at cursor or selected text.
Shift + Tab	Deletes leading spaces from selected lines.

Reserved Words

ABS	ELSEIF	LOOP	SCREEN
ACCESS	END	LPOS	SEEK
ALIAS	ENDIF	LPRINT	SGN
AND	ENVIRON	LSET	SELECT
ANY	ENVIRON$	LTRIM$	SETMEM
APPEND	EOF	MID$	SGN
AS	EQV	MKD$	SHARED
ASC	ERASE	MKDIR	SHELL
ATN	ERDEV	MKDMBF$	SIGNAL
BASE	ERDEV$	MKI$	SIN
BEEP	ERL	MKL$	SINGLE
BINARY	ERR	MKS$	SLEEP
BLOAD	ERROR	MKSMBF$	SOUND
BSAVE	EXIT	MOD	SPACE$
CALL	EXP	NAME	SPC
CALLS	FIELD	NEXT	SQR
CASE	FILEATTR	NOT	STATIC
CDBL	FILES	OCT$	STEP
CDECL	FIX	OFF	STICK
CHAIN	FOR	ON	STOP
CHDIR	FRE	OPEN	STR$
CHR$	FREEFILE	OPTION	STRIG
CINT	FUNCTION	OR	STRING
CIRCLE	GET	OUT	STRING$
CLEAR	GOSUB	OUTPUT	SUB
CLOSE	GOTO	PAINT	SWAP
CLS	HEX$	PALETTE	SYSTEM
COLOR	IF	PCOPY	TAB
COM	IMP	PEEK	TAN
COMMAND$	INKEY$	PEN	THEN
COMMON	INP	PLAY	TIME$
CONST	INPUT	PMAP	TIMER
COS	INPUT$	POINT	TO
CSNG	INSTR	POKE	TROFF
CSRLIN	INT	POS	TRON
CVD	INTEGER	PRESET	TYPE
CVDMBF	IOCTL	PRINT	UBOUND
CVI	IOCTL$	PRINT#	UCASE$
CVS	IS	PSET	UNLOCK
CVSMBF	KEY	PUT	UNTIL
DATA	KILL	RANDOM	VAL
DATE$	LBOUND	RANDOMIZE	VARPTR
DECLARE	LCASE$	READ	VARPTR$
DEF	LEFT$	REDIM	VARSEG
DEFDBL	LEN	REM	VIEW
DEFINT	LET	RESET	WAIT
DEFLNG	LINE	RESTORE	WEND
DEFSNG	LIST	RESUME	WHILE
DEFSTR	LOC	RETURN	WIDTH
DIM	LOCAL	RIGHT$	WINDOW
DO	LOCATE	RMDIR	WRITE
DOUBLE	LOCK	RND	WRITE#
DRAW	LOF	RSET	XOR
ELSE	LOG	RUN	
	LONG	SADD	